CLYMER®
SUZUKI
BANDIT 600 • 1995-2000

The world's finest publisher of mechanical how-to manuals

PRIMEDIA
Business Directories & Books

P.O. Box 12901, Overland Park, Kansas 66282-2901

Copyright © 2001 PRIMEDIA Business Magazines & Media Inc.

FIRST EDITION
First Printing September, 2001

Printed in U.S.A.

CLYMER and colophon are registered trademarks of PRIMEDIA Business Magazines & Media Inc.

ISBN: 0-89287-782-0

Library of Congress: 2001094190

Technical illustrations by Mitzi McCarthy and Robert Caldwell.

Technical photography and motorcycle teardown by Ron Wright.

Technical assistance by Bradley Wright.

Special thanks to Robert J. Lewallen Jr. for his assistance with this book

COVER: Photographed by Mark Clifford, Mark Clifford Photography, Los Angeles, California.

PRODUCTION: Darin Watson.

All rights reserved. Reproduction or use, without express permission, of editorial or pictorial content, in any manner, is prohibited. No patent liability is assumed with respect to the use of the information contained herein. While every precaution has been taken in the preparation of this book, the publisher assumes no responsibility for errors or omissions. Neither is any liability assumed for damages resulting from use of the information contained herein. Publication of the servicing information in this manual does not imply approval of the manufacturers of the products covered.

All instructions and diagrams have been checked for accuracy and ease of application; however, success and safety in working with tools depend to a great extent upon individual accuracy, skill and caution. For this reason, the publishers are not able to guarantee the result of any procedure contained herein. Nor can they assume responsibility for any damage to property or injury to persons occasioned from the procedures. Persons engaging in the procedure do so entirely at their own risk.

Chapter One
General Information

Chapter Two
Troubleshooting

Chapter Three
Lubrication, Maintenance and Tune-up

Chapter Four
Engine Upper End

Chapter Five
Engine Lower End

Chapter Six
Clutch

Chapter Seven
Transmission and Gearshift Mechanisms

Chapter Eight
Fuel, Emission Control and Exhaust Systems

Chapter Nine
Electrical System

Chapter Ten
Wheels, Tires and Drive Chain

Chapter Eleven
Front Suspension and Steering

Chapter Twelve
Rear Suspension

Chapter Thirteen
Brakes

Chapter Fourteen
Body and Frame

Index

Wiring Diagrams

CLYMER PUBLICATIONS
PRIMEDIA Business Magazines & Media
Chief Executive Officer Timothy M. Andrews
President Ron Wall
Vice President, PRIMEDIA Business Directories & Books Rich Hathaway

EDITORIAL

Editorial Director
Mark Jacobs

Editor
Mike Hall

Associate Editors
James Grooms
Dustin Uthe

Technical Writers
Ron Wright
Ed Scott
George Parise
Mark Rolling
Michael Morlan
Jay Bogart
Sherwood Lee
Kevin Maher
Rodney J. Rom

Production Supervisor
Dylan Goodwin

Lead Editorial Production Coordinator
Shirley Renicker

Editorial Production Coordinators
Greg Araujo
Dennis Conrow
Shara Pierceall

Editorial Production Assistants
Susan Hartington
Holly Messinger
Darin Watson

Technical Illustrators
Steve Amos
Robert Caldwell
Mitzi McCarthy
Bob Meyer
Michael St. Clair
Mike Rose

MARKETING/SALES AND ADMINISTRATION

Publisher
Randy Stephens

Marketing Manager
Elda Starke

Advertising & Promotions Coordinator
Melissa Abbott

Associate Art Directors
Chris Paxton
Tony Barmann

Sales Manager/Marine
Dutch Sadler

Sales Manager/Motorcycles
Matt Tusken

Sales Manager/Manuals
Ted Metzger

Customer Service Manager
Terri Cannon

Fulfillment Coordinator
Susan Kohlmeyer

Customer Service Representatives
April LeBlond
Courtney Hollars

Warehouse & Inventory Manager
Leah Hicks

The following books and guides are published by PRIMEDIA Business Directories & Books.

CLYMER® **I&T SHOP SERVICE** **AC-U-KWIK** **EC&M Books**

EQUIPMENT WATCH™ www.equipmentwatch.com
The Electronics Source Book
BLUE BOOK Values National Market Reports™...Since 1911
WATERWAY GUIDE®

More information available at *primediabusiness.com*

CONTENTS

QUICK REFERENCE DATA IX

CHAPTER ONE
GENERAL INFORMATION 1

Manual organization
Warnings, cautions and notes
Safety
Serial numbers
Fasteners
Shop supplies
Basic tools
Precision measuring tools
Electrical system fundamentals
Special tools
Basic service methods
Storage

CHAPTER TWO
TROUBLESHOOTING 36

Operating requirements
Starting the engine
Starting difficulties
Engine performance
Engine noises
Engine lubrication
Cylinder leakdown test
Clutch
Transmission
Fuel system
Drivetrain noise
Electrical troubleshooting
Test equipment
Basic test procedures
Charging system
Ignition system
Starting system
Handling
Brakes
Frame noise

CHAPTER THREE
LUBRICATION, MAINTENANCE AND TUNE-UP 61

- Pre-ride check list
- Maintenance schedule
- Tires and wheels
- Battery
- Periodic lubrication
- Periodic maintenance
- Non-scheduled maintenance
- Engine tune-up
- Spark plugs
- Storage

CHAPTER FOUR
ENGINE TOP END 101

- Engine service notes
- Engine principles
- Cylinder head cover
- Camshafts
- Cam chain tensioner
- Cam chain
- Rocker arms
- Cylinder head
- Valves and valve components
- Cylinder block
- Piston and piston rings

CHAPTER FIVE
ENGINE LOWER END 146

- Servicing the engine in frame
- Engine
- Oil pump
- Oil cooler
- Oil pan, oil strainer and oil pressure regulator
- Starter clutch and gears
- Crankcase
- Crankshaft
- Connecting rods
- Break-in

CHAPTER SIX
CLUTCH 185

- Clutch
- Clutch release mechanism
- Clutch cable replacement

CHAPTER SEVEN
TRANSMISSION AND GEARSHIFT MECHANISMS 195

- Engine drive sprocket cover
- Engine drive sprocket
- External gearshift mechanism
- Transmission
- Internal gearshift mechanism

CHAPTER EIGHT
FUEL, EMISSION CONTROL AND EXHAUST SYSTEMS 218

Carburetor operation
Carburetor service
Carburetor assembly
Carburetor
Pilot screw
Throttle position sensor (2000 models)
Carburetor heater (UK models)
Carburetor separation
Float height adjustment
Throttle cable replacement
Starter cable replacement
Air filter housing
Fuel tank
Fuel valve
Fuel filter
Crankcase breather system
Evaporative emission control system
  (California models only)
Purge control valves and charcoal canister
PAIR system (1995-1999 California and
  Switzerland, 2000 models)
Exhaust system

CHAPTER NINE
ELECTRICAL SYSTEM 259

Preliminary information
Negative battery terminal
Charging system
Alternator
Ignition system
Starting system
Starter motor
Starter relay
Lighting system
Switches
Relays
Combination meter
Fuses
Main fuse
Wiring diagrams

CHAPTER TEN
WHEELS, TIRES AND DRIVE CHAIN 309

Motorcycle stand
Front wheel
Rear wheel
Rear coupling and rear sprocket
Front and rear hubs
Wheels
Tires
Tire repairs
Drive chain

CHAPTER ELEVEN
FRONT SUSPENSION AND STEERING 333

Handlebar
Left handlebar grip replacement
Steering head and stem
Steering head bearing race replacement
Steering stem bearing replacement
Front fork

CHAPTER TWELVE
REAR SUSPENSION 353

    Shock absorber
    Shock lever assembly
    Swing arm
    Bearing replacement

CHAPTER THIRTEEN
BRAKES 366

    Brake service
    Front brake pad replacement
    Front caliper
    Rear brake pad replacement
    Rear brake caliper
    Front master cylinder
    Rear master cylinder
    Brake hose replacement
    Brake disc
    Bleeding the brakes
    Rear brake pedal

CHAPTER FOURTEEN
BODY AND FRAME 400

    Seat
    Front fender and brace (1995-1999 models)
    Front fender (2000 models)
    Fairing (1995-1999 GSF600S models)
    Fairing (2000 GSF600S models)
    Fairing inspection
    Rear frame cover
    Side cover (2000 models)
    Sidestand
    Centerstand (GSF600S models)

INDEX 409

WIRING DIAGRAMS 415

QUICK REFERENCE DATA

VEHICLE DATA

MODEL:_____ YEAR:_____
VIN NUMBER:_____
ENGINE SERIAL NUMBER:_____
CARBURETOR SERIAL NUMBER OR I.D. MARK:_____

TUNE-UP SPECIFICATIONS

Battery	
Type	YTX9-BS Maintenance free (sealed)
Capacity	12 volt 8 amp hour
Spark plug	
Standard	NGK: CR9EK, ND: U27ETR
Hot type	NGK: CR8EK, ND: U24ETR
Cold type	NGK: CR10EK, ND: UT31ETR
Spark plug gap	0.6-0.7 mm (0.024-0.028 in.)
Idle speed	
1995 models	
All models except Switzerland	1100-1300 rpm
Switzerland models	1150-1300 rpm
1996 models	
All models except Switzerland	1100-1300 rpm
Switzerland models	
GSF600	1100-1300 rpm
GSF600S	1150-1300 rpm
1997-1999 models	
All models except Switzerland	1100-1300 rpm
Switzerland models	1150-1300 rpm
2000 models	1100-1300 rpm
Firing order	1-2-4-3
Valve clearance (cold)	
Intake	0.10-0.15 mm (0.004-0.006 in.)
Exhaust	0.18-0.23 mm (0.007-0.090 in.)
Compression pressure (at sea level)	
Standard	1000-1500 kPa (142-213 psi)
Service limit	800 kPa (114 psi)
Maximum difference between cylinders	200 kPa (28 psi)
Engine oil pressure (@ 60° C /140° F)	300-600 kPa (43-85 psi) @ 3000 rpm

FREE PLAY SPECIFICATIONS

Brake pedal height	
1995-1999 models	45 mm (1.8 in.)
2000 models	50 mm (2.0 in.)
Throttle cable free play	
1995-1999 models	
Return (push) cable	0 mm
Pull cable	0.5-1.0 mm (0.02-0.04 in.)
2000 models	2.0-4.0 mm (0.08-0.16 in.)
Clutch lever free play	10-15 mm (0.4-0.6 in.)
Drive chain free play	25-35 mm (0.9-1.4 in.)

TIRE SPECIFICATIONS

Item	Front	Rear
Tire type	Tubeless	Tubeless
Size		
1995-1999 GSF600 models	110/70-17 54H	150/70-17 69H
1996-1999 GSF600S models		
U.S.A., California and Canada models	110/70-17 54H	150/70-17 69H
All models except U.S.A., California and Canada	110/70 ZR17	150/70 ZR17
2000 models	120/60 ZR17 (55W)	160/60 ZR17 (69W)
Minimum tread depth	1.6 mm (0.06 in.)	2.0 mm (0.08 in.)
Inflation pressure (cold)*		
Solo	225 kPa (33 psi)	250 kPa (36 psi)
Rider and passenger	225 kPa (33 psi)	250 kPa (36 psi)

*Tire inflation pressure is for original equipment tires. Aftermarket tires may require different inflation pressure. The use of tires other than those specified by Suzuki may cause instability.

FLUIDS AND CAPACITIES

Fuel	Unleaded
Octane	87 [(R + M)/2 method] or research octane of 91 or higher
Fuel tank capacity	
1995-1999	19.0 L (5.0 U.S. gal., 4.2 Imp. gal.)
2000	
California models	19.0 L (5.0 U.S. gal., 4.2 Imp. gal.)
U.S.A., Australia, Canada and European models	20.0 L (5.3 U.S. gal., 4.4 Imp. gal.)
Fuel tank reserve capacity	4.5 L (1.2 U.S. gal., 1.0 Imp. gal.)
Engine oil	
Grade	API SF or SG
Viscosity	SAE 10W40
Capacity	
Oil change only	3.3 L (3.5 U.S. qt., 2.9 Imp. qt.)
Oil and filter change	3.5 L (3.7 U.S. qt., 3.1 Imp. qt.)
Engine completely dry	4.6 L (4.9 U.S. qt., 4.0 Imp. qt.)
Brake fluid	DOT 4
Fork oil	
Viscosity	Suzuki #10 fork oil or equivalent
Capacity per leg	
1995-1999 GSF600 models	521 ml (17.6 U.S. oz., 18.3 Imp. oz.)
1996-1999 GSF600S models	
U.S.A., California and Canada models	522 ml (17.7 U.S. oz., 18.4 Imp. oz.)
All models except U.S.A., California and Canada models	521 ml (17.6 U.S. oz., 18.3 Imp. oz.)
2000 GSF600 models	508 ml (17.18 U.S. oz., 17.9 Imp. oz.)
2000 GSF600S models	
U.S.A., California and Canada models	506 ml (17.11 U.S. oz., 17.8 Imp. oz.)
All models except U.S.A., California and Canada	510 ml (17.24 U.S. oz., 18.0 Imp. oz.)

CHAPTER ONE

GENERAL INFORMATION

This detailed and comprehensive manual covers the Suzuki Bandit (GSF600 and GSF600S models) from 1995-2000. The text provides complete information on maintenance, tune-up, repair and overhaul. Hundreds of photos and drawings guide the reader through every job.

A shop manual is a reference tool and, as in all Clymer manuals, the chapters are thumb-tabbed for easy reference. Important items are indexed at the end of the book. All procedures, tables and figures are designed for the reader who may be working on the Bandit for the first time. Frequently used specifications and capacities from each individual chapter are summarized in the *Quick Reference Data* at the front of the book.

Tables 1-8 are at the end of this chapter.
Table 1 lists models and serial numbers.
Table 2 lists vehicle dimensions.
Table 3 lists vehicle weight.
Table 4 lists decimal and metric equivalents.
Table 5 lists conversion tables.
Table 6 lists general torque specifications.
Table 7 lists technical abbreviations.
Table 8 lists metric tap and drill sizes.

MANUAL ORGANIZATION

All dimensions and capacities are expressed in metric and U.S. standard units of measurement.

This chapter provides general information on shop safety, tool use, service fundamentals and shop supplies. The tables at the end of the chapter include general vehicle information.

Chapter Two provides methods for quick and accurate diagnosis of problems. Troubleshooting procedures present typical symptoms and logical methods to pinpoint and repair the problem.

Chapter Three explains all routine maintenance necessary to keep the vehicle running well. Chapter Three also includes recommended tune-up procedures, eliminating the need to constantly consult the chapters on the various assemblies.

Subsequent chapters describe specific systems such as engine, transmission, clutch, drive system, fuel and exhaust systems, suspension and brakes. Each disassembly, repair and assembly procedure is discussed in step-by-step form.

Some of the procedures in this manual specify special tools. In most cases, the tool is illustrated in use. Well-equipped mechanics may be able to substitute similar tools or fabricate a suitable replacement. However, in some cases, the specialized equipment or expertise may make it impractical for the home mechanic to attempt the procedure. When necessary, such operations are identified in the text with the recommendation to have a dealership or specialist perform the task. It may be less expensive to have a professional perform these jobs, especially when considering the cost of the equipment.

WARNINGS, CAUTIONS AND NOTES

The terms, WARNING, CAUTION and NOTE have specific meanings in this manual.

A WARNING emphasizes areas where injury or even death could result from negligence. Mechanical damage may also occur. WARNINGS *should be taken seriously.*

A CAUTION emphasizes areas where equipment damage could result. Disregarding a CAUTION could cause permanent mechanical damage, though injury is unlikely.

A NOTE provides additional information to make a step or procedure easier or clearer. Disregarding a NOTE could cause inconvenience but would not cause equipment damage or personal injury.

SAFETY

Professional mechanics can work for years and never sustain a serious injury or mishap. Follow these guidelines and practice common sense to safely service the vehicle.

1. Do not operate the vehicle in an enclosed area. The exhaust gases contain carbon monoxide, an odorless, colorless, and tasteless poisonous gas. Carbon monoxide levels build quickly in enclosed areas and can cause unconsciousness and death in a short time. Make sure the work area is properly ventilated or operate the vehicle outside.

2. *Never* use gasoline or any extremely flammable liquid to clean parts. Refer to *Cleaning Parts* and *Handling Gasoline Safely* in this chapter.

3. *Never* smoke or use a torch in the vicinity of flammable liquids, such as gasoline or cleaning solvent.

4. If welding or brazing on the vehicle, remove the fuel tank, carburetor and shocks to a safe distance at least 50 ft. (15 m) away.

5. Use the correct type and size of tools to avoid damaging fasteners.

6. Keep tools clean and in good condition. Replace or repair worn or damaged equipment.

7. When loosening a tight fastener, be guided by what would happen if the tool slips.

8. When replacing fasteners, make sure the new fasteners are of the same size and strength as the original ones.

9. Keep the work area clean and organized.

10. Wear eye protection *anytime* the safety of your eyes is in question. This includes procedures involving drilling, grinding, hammering, compressed air and chemicals.

11. Wear the correct clothing for the job. Tie up or cover long hair so it does not get caught in moving equipment.

12. Do not carry sharp tools in clothing pockets.

13. Always have an approved fire extinguisher available. Make sure it is rated for gasoline (Class B) and electrical (Class C) fires.

14. Do not use compressed air to clean clothes, the motorcycle or the work area. Debris may be blown into your eyes or skin. *Never* direct compressed air at yourself or someone else. Do not allow children to use or play with any compressed air equipment.

15. When using compressed air to dry rotating parts, hold the part so it can not rotate. Do not allow the force of the air to spin the part. The air jet is capable of rotating parts at extreme speed. The part may be damaged or disintegrate, causing serious injury.

16. Do not inhale the dust created by brake pad and clutch wear. In most cases these particles contain asbestos. In addition, some types of insulating ma-

GENERAL INFORMATION

terials and gaskets may contain asbestos. Inhaling asbestos particles is hazardous.

17. Never work on the vehicle while someone is working under it.

18. When placing the vehicle on a stand, make sure it is secure before walking away.

Handling Gasoline Safely

Gasoline is a volatile, flammable liquid and is one of the most dangerous items in the shop.

Because gasoline is used so often, many people forget that it is hazardous. Only use gasoline as fuel for gasoline internal combustion engines. Keep in mind when working on a vehicle that gasoline is always present in the fuel tank, fuel line and carburetor. To avoid a disastrous accident when working around the fuel system, carefully observe the following precautions:

1. *Never* use gasoline to clean parts. See *Cleaning Parts* in this chapter.
2. When working on the fuel system, work outside or in a well-ventilated area.
3. Do not add fuel to the fuel tank or service the fuel system while the vehicle is near open flames, sparks or where someone is smoking. Gasoline vapor is heavier than air, it collects in low areas and is more easily ignited than liquid gasoline.
4. Allow the engine to cool completely before working on any fuel system component.
5. When draining the carburetor, catch the fuel in a plastic container and then pour it into an approved gasoline storage device.
6. Do not store gasoline in glass containers. If the glass breaks, a serious explosion or fire may occur.
7. Immediately wipe up spilled gasoline with rags. Store the rags in a metal container with a lid until they can be properly disposed of, or place them outside in a safe place for the fuel to evaporate.
8. Do not pour water onto a gasoline fire. Water spreads the fire and makes it more difficult to put out. Use a class B, BC or ABC fire extinguisher to extinguish a gasoline fire.
9. Always turn off the engine before refueling. Do not spill fuel onto the engine or exhaust system. Do not overfill the fuel tank. Leave an air space at the top of the tank to allow room for the fuel to expand due to temperature fluctuations.

Cleaning Parts

Cleaning parts is one of the more tedious and difficult service jobs performed in the home garage. There are many types of chemical cleaners and solvents available for shop use. Most are poisonous and extremely flammable. To prevent chemical exposure, vapor buildup, fire and serious injury, observe each product warning label and note the following:

1. Read and observe the entire product label before using any chemical. Always know what type of chemical is being used and whether it is poisonous and/or flammable.
2. Do not use more than one type of cleaning solvent at a time. If mixing chemicals is called for, measure the proper amounts according to the manufacturer's instructions.
3. Work in a well-ventilated area.
4. Wear chemical-resistant gloves.
5. Wear safety glasses.
6. Wear a vapor respirator if the instructions call for it.
7. Wash hands and arms thoroughly after cleaning parts.
8. Keep chemical products away from children and pets.
9. Thoroughly clean all oil, grease and cleaner residue from any part that must be heated.
10. Use a nylon brush when cleaning parts. Metal brushes may cause a spark.
11. When using a parts washer, only use the solvent recommended by the manufacturer. Make sure the parts washer is equipped with a metal lid that will lower in case of fire.

Warning Labels

Most manufacturers attach information and warning labels to the vehicle. These labels contain instructions that are important to personal safety when operating, servicing, transporting and storing the vehicle. Refer to the owner's manual for the description and location of labels. Order replacement labels from the manufacturer if they are missing or damaged.

SERIAL NUMBERS

Serial numbers are stamped onto the frame and engine. Record these numbers in the *Quick Reference Data* section at the front of the book. Have these numbers available when ordering parts.

The frame number (**Figure 1**) or vehicle identification number (VIN) is stamped on the right side of the steering head.

The engine number (**Figure 2**) is stamped on a pad on the right side of the crankcase just above the clutch cover.

Table 1 list model years and numbers.

FASTENERS

Proper fastener selection and installation is important to ensure that the motorcycle operates as designed, and can be serviced efficiently. The choice of original equipment fasteners is not arrived at by chance. Make sure that replacement fasteners meet all the same requirements as the originals.

Threaded Fasteners

Threaded fasteners secure most of the components on the vehicle. Most are tightened by turning them clockwise (right-hand threads). If the normal rotation of the component would loosen the fastener, it may have left-hand threads. If a left-hand threaded fastener is used, it is noted in the text.

Two dimensions are required to match the size of the fastener: the number of threads in a given distance and the outside diameter of the threads.

Two systems are currently used to specify threaded fastener dimensions: the U.S. Standard system and the metric system (**Figure 3**). Pay particular attention when working with unidentified fasteners. Mismatching thread types can damage threads.

NOTE
To ensure that the fastener threads are not mismatched or cross-threaded, start all fasteners by hand. If a fastener is hard to start or turn, determine the cause before tightening it with a wrench.

The length (L, **Figure 4**), diameter (D) and distance between thread crests (pitch) (T) classify metric screws and bolts. A typical bolt may be identified by the numbers, 8—1.25 × 130. This indicates the bolt has diameter of 8 mm, the distance between thread crests is 1.25 mm and the length is 130 mm. Always measure bolt length as shown in **Figure 4** to avoid purchasing replacements of the wrong length.

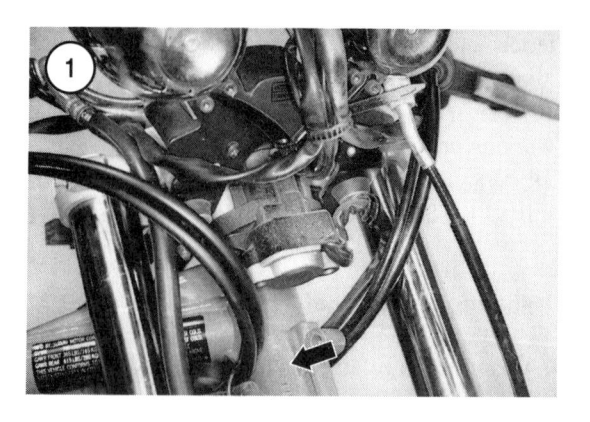

The numbers located on the top of the fastener (**Figure 4**) indicate the strength of metric screws and bolts. The higher the number, the stronger the fastener. Unnumbered fasteners are the weakest.

Many bolts and studs are combined with nuts to secure particular components. To indicate the size of a nut, manufacturers specify the internal diameter and the thread pitch.

The measurement across two parallel flats on a nut or bolt head indicates the wrench size that fits the fastener.

WARNING
Do not install fasteners with a strength classification lower than what was originally installed by the manufacturer. Doing so may cause equipment failure and/or damage.

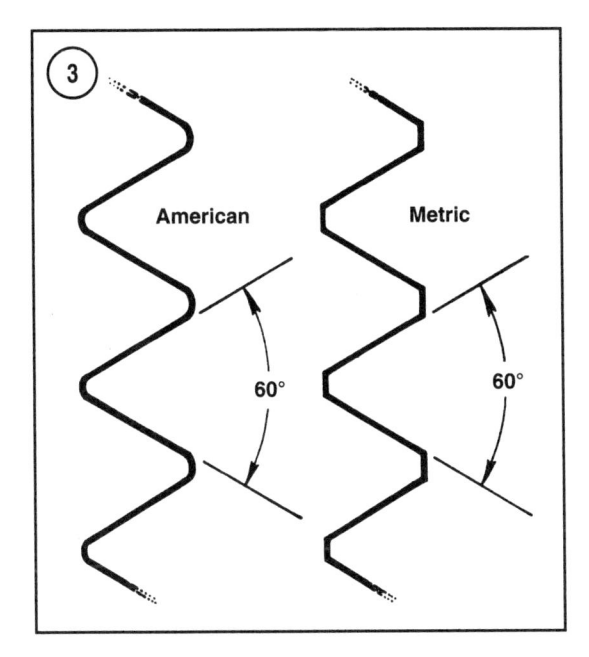

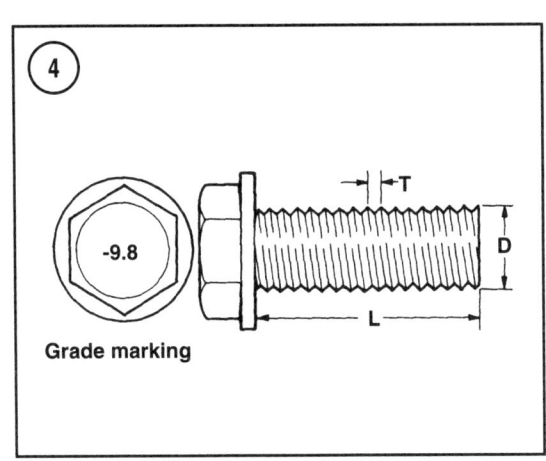

GENERAL INFORMATION

tors and to **Table 6** for general torque specifications. To use **Table 6**, first determine the size of the fastener as described in *Fasteners* in this chapter. Locate that size of fastener in **Table 6**, and tighten the fastener to the indicated torque. Torque wrenches are described in the *Basic Tools* section of this chapter.

Self-Locking Fasteners

Several types of bolts, screws and nuts incorporate a system that creates interference between the two fasteners. Interference is achieved in various ways. The most common are the nylon-insert nut and a dry adhesive coating on the threads of a bolt.

Self-locking fasteners offer greater holding strength than standard fasteners, which improve their resistance to vibration. Most self-locking fasteners cannot be reused. The materials used to form the lock become distorted after the initial installation and removal. It is a good practice to discard and replace self-locking fasteners after their removal. Do not replace self-locking fasteners with standard fasteners.

Washers

There are two basic types of washers: flat washers and lockwashers. Flat washers are simple discs with a hole to fit a screw or bolt. Lockwashers are used to prevent a fastener from working loose. Washers can be used as spacers and seals, to help distribute fastener load and to prevent the fastener from damaging the component.

As with fasteners, when replacing washers make sure the replacement washers are of the same design and quality.

Cotter Pins

A cotter pin is a split metal pin inserted into a hole or slot to prevent a fastener from working loose. In certain applications, such as the rear axle on an ATV or motorcycle, the fastener must be secured in this way. For these applications, a cotter pin and castellated (slotted) nut is used.

To use a cotter pin, first make sure the pin's diameter is correct for the hole in the fastener. After correctly tightening the fastener and aligning the holes, insert the cotter pin through the hole and bend the

Torque Specifications

The materials used in the manufacture of the motorcycle may be subjected to uneven stresses if the fasteners of the various subassemblies are not installed and tightened correctly. Fasteners that are improperly installed or that work loose can cause extensive damage. Use an accurate torque wrench when tightening fasteners, and tighten each fastener to its specified torque.

Torque specifications for specific components are at the end of the appropriate chapters. Specifications for torque are provided in Newton-meters (N•m), foot-pounds (ft.-lb.) and inch-pounds (in.-lb.). Refer to **Table 5** for torque conversion fac-

ends over the fastener (**Figure 5**). Unless instructed to do so, never loosen a torqued fastener to align the holes. If the holes do not align, tighten the fastener just enough to achieve alignment.

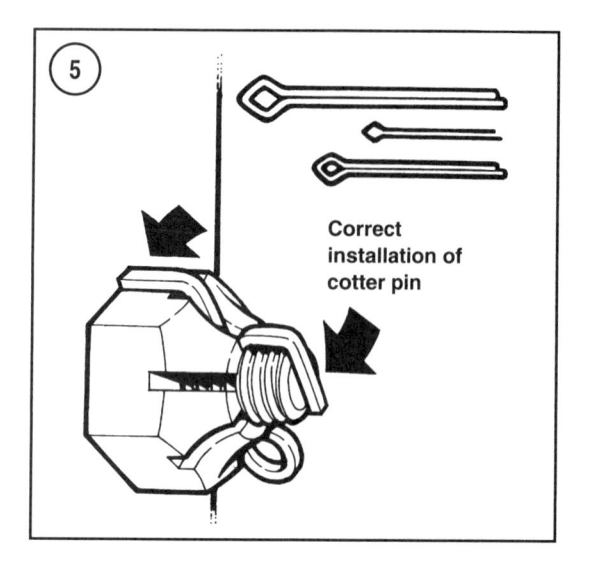

Cotter pins are available in various diameters and lengths. Measure length from the bottom of the head to the tip of the shortest pin.

Snap rings and E-clips

Snap rings (**Figure 6**) are circular-shaped metal retaining clips. They are required to secure parts and gears onto shafts, pins or rods. External type snap rings are used to retain items on shafts. Internal type snap rings secure parts within housing bores. In some applications, in addition to securing the component(s), snap rings of varying thickness also determine endplay. These are usually called selective snap rings.

Two basic types of snap rings are used: machined and stamped snap rings. Machined snap rings (**Figure 7**) can be installed in either direction, since both faces have sharp edges. Stamped snap rings (**Figure 8**) are manufactured with a sharp edge and a round edge. When installing a stamped circlip in a thrust application, install the sharp edge facing away from the part producing the thrust.

E-clips and circlips are used when it is not practical to use a snap ring. Remove these clips with a flat blade screwdriver by prying between the shaft and the clip. To install an E-clip, center it over the shaft groove and push or tap it into place.

Observe the following when installing snap rings:

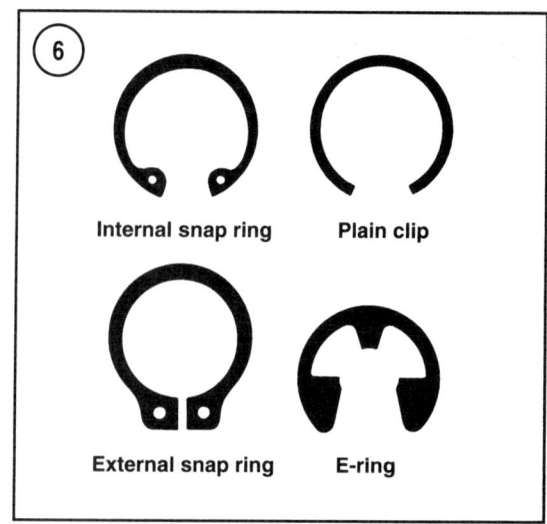

1. Remove and install snap rings with snap ring pliers. See *Snap Ring Pliers* in this chapter.
2. In some applications, it may be necessary to replace snap rings after removing them.
3. Compress or expand snap rings only enough to install them. If overly expanded, they lose their retaining ability.
4. After installing a snap ring, make sure it seats completely.
5. Wear eye protection when removing and installing snap rings.

SHOP SUPPLIES

Lubricants and Fluids

Periodic lubrication helps ensure a long service life for any type of equipment. Using the correct type of lubricant is as important as performing the lubrication service, although in an emergency the wrong type of lubricant is better than none. The following section describes the types of lubricants most often required. Make sure to follow the manufacturer's recommendations for lubricant types.

Engine oils

Generally all liquid lubricants are called oil. They may be mineral-based (including petroleum bases), natural-based (vegetable and animal bases), synthetic-based or emulsions (mixtures).

GENERAL INFORMATION

Always use an oil with a classification recommended by the manufacturer. Using an oil with a classification different than that recommended can cause engine damage.

Viscosity is an indication of the oil's thickness. Thin oils have a lower number while thick oils have a higher number. A "W" after the number indicates that the viscosity testing was done at low temperature to simulate cold-weather operation. Engine oils fall into the 5- to 50-weight range for single-grade oils.

Most manufacturers recommend multigrade oil. Multi-grade oils (for example 10W-40) are less viscous (thinner) at low temperatures and more viscous (thicker) at high temperatures. This allows the oil to perform efficiently across a wide range of engine operating conditions. The lower the number, the better the engine will start in cold climates. Higher numbers are usually recommended when operating an engine in hot weather. When selecting engine oil, follow the manufacturer's recommendation for type, classification and viscosity.

Greases

Grease is an oil to which a thickening base has been added so the end product is semi-solid. Grease is often classified by the type of thickener added, such as lithium soap. The National Lubricating Grease Institute (NLGI) grades grease. Grades range from No. 000 to No. 6, with No. 6 being the thickest. Typical multipurpose grease is NLGI No. 2. For specific applications, manufacturers may recommend water-resistant type grease or one with an additive such as molybdenum disulfide (MoS_2).

Use Suzuki Super Grease A or an equivalent waterproof grease when grease is called for.

Brake fluid

Brake fluid is the hydraulic fluid used to transmit hydraulic pressure (force) to the wheel brakes. Brake fluid is classified by the Department of Transportation (DOT). Current designations for brake fluid are DOT 3, DOT 4 and DOT 5. This classification appears on the fluid container.

Each type of brake fluid has its own definite characteristics. Do not intermix different types of brake fluid. DOT 5 fluid is silicone-based. DOT 5 is not compatible with other fluids or systems for which it

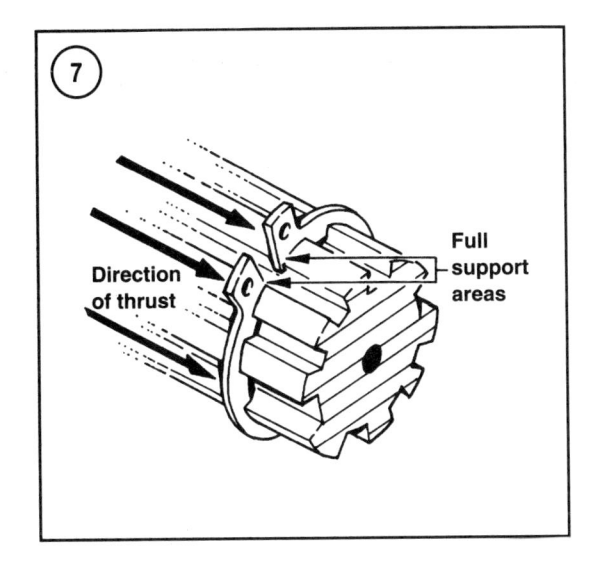

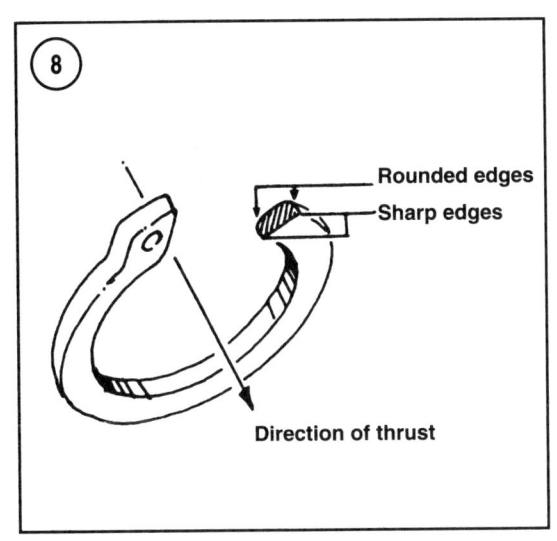

Engine oil is classified by two standards: the American Petroleum Institute (API) service classification and the Society of Automotive Engineers (SAE) viscosity rating. This information is on the oil container label. Two letters indicate the API service classification. The number or sequence of numbers and letter (10W-40 for example) is the oil's viscosity rating (SF, SG, etc.). The API service classification and the SAE viscosity index are not indications of oil quality.

The service classification indicates that the oil meets specific lubrication standards. The first letter in the classification (*S*) indicates that the oil is for gasoline engines. The second letter indicates the standard the oil satisfies. The classification started with the letter *A* and is currently at the letter *J*.

was not designed. Mixing DOT 5 fluid with other fluids may cause brake system failure. When adding brake fluid, *only* use the fluid recommended by the vehicle manufacturer.

Brake fluid will damage plastic, painted or plated surfaces. Use extreme care when working with brake fluid. Immediately wash any spills with soap and water. Rinse the area with plenty of clean water.

Hydraulic brake systems require clean and moisture-free brake fluid. Never reuse brake fluid. Keep containers and reservoirs properly sealed.

Brake fluid absorbs moisture, which greatly reduces its ability to perform correctly. Purchase brake fluid in small containers, and discard any small left-over quantities properly. Do not store a container of brake fluid with less than 1/4 of the fluid remaining. This small amount absorbs moisture very rapidly.

WARNING
Never put a mineral-based (petroleum) oil into the brake system. Mineral oil will cause rubber parts in the system to swell and break apart, resulting in complete brake failure.

Cleaners, Degreasers and Solvents

Many chemicals are available to remove oil, grease and other residue from the vehicle.

Before using cleaning solvents, consider how they will be used and disposed of, particularly if they are not water-soluble. Local ordinances may require special procedures for the disposal of various cleaning chemicals. Refer to *Safety and Cleaning Parts* in this chapter for more information on their use.

Use brake parts cleaner to clean brake system components when contact with petroleum-based products will damage seals. Brake parts cleaner leaves no residue. Use electrical contact cleaner to clean electrical connections and components without leaving any residue. Carburetor cleaner is a powerful solvent used to remove fuel deposits and varnish from fuel system components. Use this cleaner carefully, as it may damage finishes.

Generally, degreasers are strong cleaners used to remove heavy accumulations of grease from engine and frame components.

Most solvents are designed to be used in a parts washing cabinet for individual component cleaning.

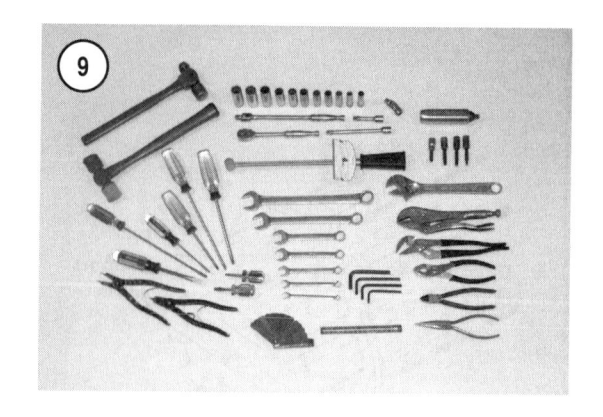

For safety, use only nonflammable or high flash point solvents.

Gasket Sealant

Sealants are used in combination with a gasket or seal or are occasionally used alone. Follow the manufacturer's recommendation when using sealants. Use extreme care when choosing a sealant different from the type originally recommended. Choose sealants based on their resistance to heat and various fluids and their sealing capabilities.

One of the most common sealants is RTV, or room temperature vulcanizing sealant. This sealant cures at room temperature over a specific time period. It allows the repositioning of components without damaging gaskets.

Moisture in the air causes the RTV sealant to cure. Always install the tube cap as soon as possible after applying RTV sealant. RTV sealant has a limited shelf life and will not cure properly if the shelf life has expired. Keep partial tubes sealed, and discard them if they have passed the expiration date.

Applying RTV sealant

Clean all old gasket residue from the mating surfaces. Remove all gasket material from blind threaded holes; it can cause inaccurate bolt torque. Spray the mating surfaces with aerosol parts cleaner, and then wipe them with a lint-free cloth. The area must be clean for the sealant to adhere.

Apply RTV sealant in a continuous bead 2-3 mm (0.08-0.12 in.) thick. Circle all the fastener holes unless otherwise specified. Do not allow any sealant to enter these holes. Assemble and tighten the fasteners to the specified torque within the time

GENERAL INFORMATION

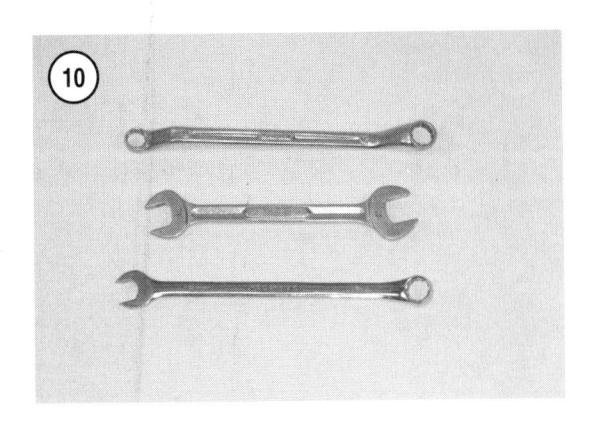

frame recommended by the RTV sealant manufacturer.

Gasket Remover

Aerosol gasket remover can help remove stubborn gaskets. This product can speed up the removal process and prevent damage to the mating surface that may be caused by using a scraping tool. Most of these types of products are very caustic. Follow the gasket remover manufacturer's instructions for use.

Threadlocking Compound

A threadlocking compound is a fluid applied to the threads of fasteners. After tightening the fastener, the fluid dries and becomes a solid filler between the threads. This makes it difficult for the fastener to work loose from vibration, or heat expansion and contraction. Some threadlocking compounds also provide a seal against fluid leakage.

Before applying threadlocking compound, remove any old compound from both thread areas and clean them with acrosol parts cleaner. Use the compound sparingly. Excess fluid can run into adjoining parts.

Threadlocking compounds are available in different strengths. Follow the particular manufacturer's recommendations regarding compound selection. Two manufacturers of threadlocking compound are ThreeBond and Loctite. They both offer a wide range of compounds for various strength, temperature and repair applications.

BASIC TOOLS

Most of the procedures in this manual can be carried out with simple hand tools and test equipment familiar to the home mechanic. Always use the correct tools for the job at hand. Keep tools organized and clean. Store them in a tool chest with related tools organized together.

Quality tools are essential. The best are constructed of high-strength alloy steel. These tools are light, easy to use and resistant to wear. Their working surface is smooth, and the tool is carefully polished. They have an easy-to-clean finish and are comfortable to use. Quality tools are a good investment.

When building a new tool kit, consider purchasing a basic tool set (**Figure 9**) from a large tool supplier. These sets contain a variety of commonly used tools, and they provide substantial savings when compared to individually purchased tools. As one becomes more experienced and tasks become more complicated, specialized tools can be added.

Screwdrivers

Screwdrivers of various lengths and types are mandatory for the simplest tool kit. The two basic types are the slotted tip (flat blade) and the Phillips tip. These are available in sets that often include an assortment of tip sizes and shaft lengths.

As with all tools, use a screwdriver designed for the job. Make sure the size of the tip conforms to the size and shape of the fastener. Use them only for driving screws. Never use a screwdriver for prying or chiseling metal. Repair or replace worn or damaged screwdrivers. A worn tip may damage the fastener, making it difficult to remove.

Wrenches

Box-end, open-end and combination wrenches (**Figure 10**) are available in a variety of types and sizes.

The number stamped on the wrench refers to the distance between the work areas. This must match the distance across two parallel flats on the bolt head or nut.

The box-end wrench is an excellent tool because it grips the fastener on all sides. This reduces the chance of the tool slipping. The box-end wrench is designed with either a 6- or 12-point opening. For stubborn or damaged fasteners, the 6-point provides superior holding ability by contacting the fastener across a wider area at all six edges. For general use, the 12-point works well. It allows the wrench to be removed and reinstalled without moving the handle over a wide arc.

An open-end wrench is fast and works best in areas with limited overhead access. Because it contacts the fastener at only two points, an open-end wrench is subject to slipping under heavy force or if the tool or fastener is worn. A box-end wrench is preferred in most instances, especially when applying considerable force to a fastener.

The combination wrench has a box-end on one end and an open-end on the other. This combination makes it a very convenient tool.

Adjustable Wrenches

An adjustable wrench or crescent wrench (**Figure 11**) fits nearly any nut or bolt head that has clear access around its entire perimeter. An adjustable wrench is best used as a backup wrench to hold a large nut or bolt while the other end is being loosened or tightened with a box-end or socket wrench.

Adjustable wrenches contact the fastener at only two points, making them more subject to slipping off the fastener. The fact that one jaw is adjustable and may loosen only aggravates this shortcoming. These wrenches are directional. Make certain the solid jaw is the one transmitting the force.

Socket Wrenches, Ratchets and Handles

Sockets that attach to a ratchet handle (**Figure 12**) are available with 6-point (A, **Figure 13**) or 12-point (B) openings and different drive sizes. The drive size indicates the size of the square hole that accepts the ratchet handle. The number stamped on the socket is the size of the work area and must match the fastener head.

As with wrenches, a 6-point socket provides superior holding ability, while a 12-point socket needs to be moved only half as far to reposition it on the fastener.

Sockets are designated for either hand or impact use. Impact sockets are made of thicker material for more durability. Compare the size and wall thickness of a 19-mm hand socket (A, **Figure 14**) and the

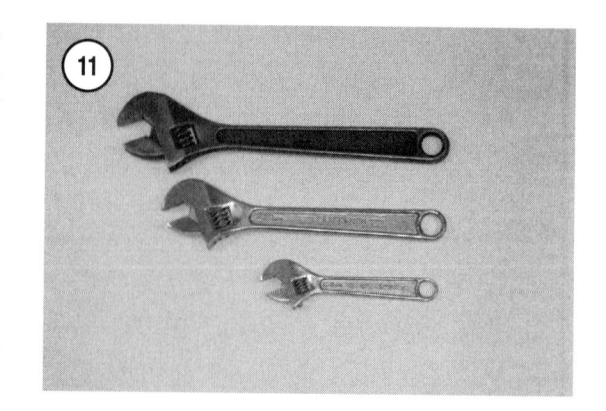

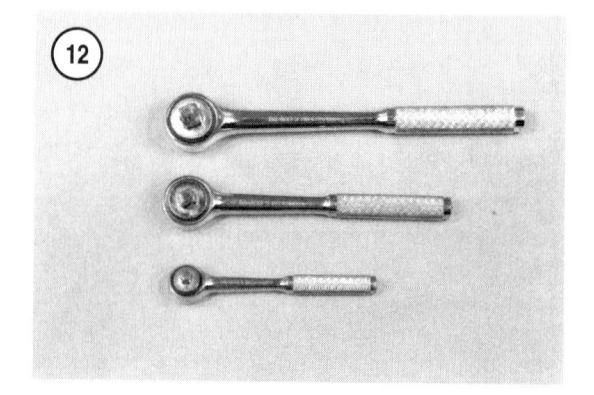

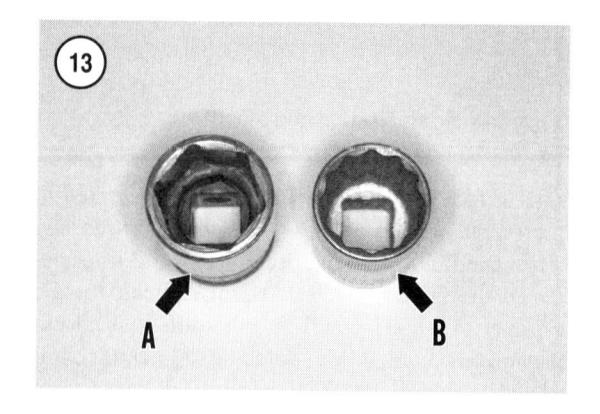

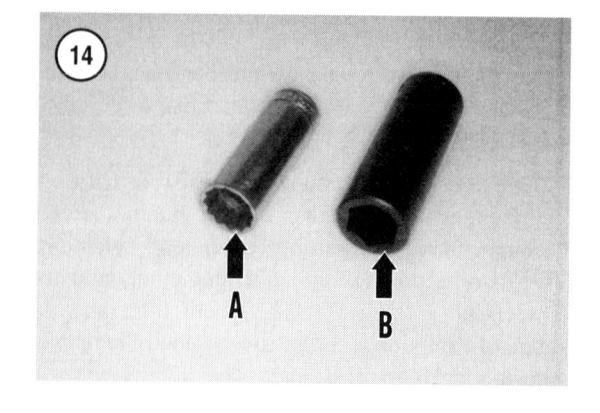

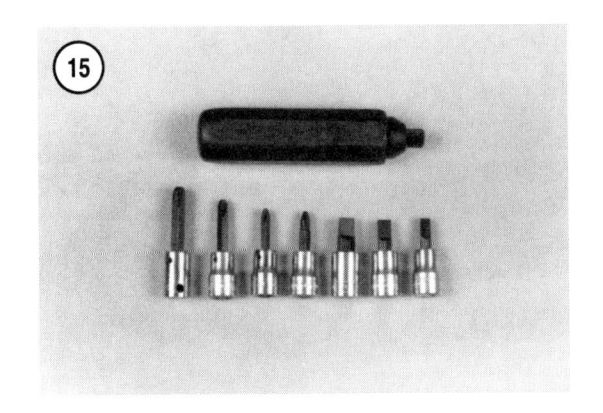

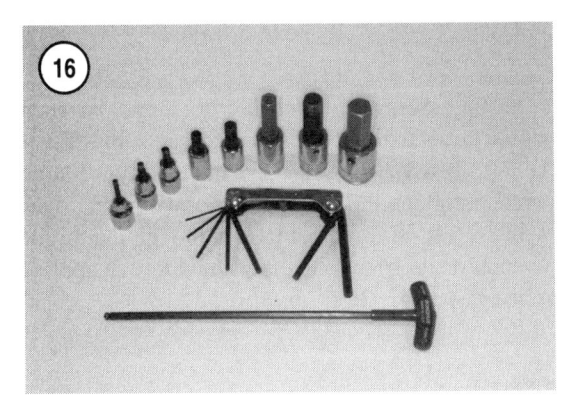

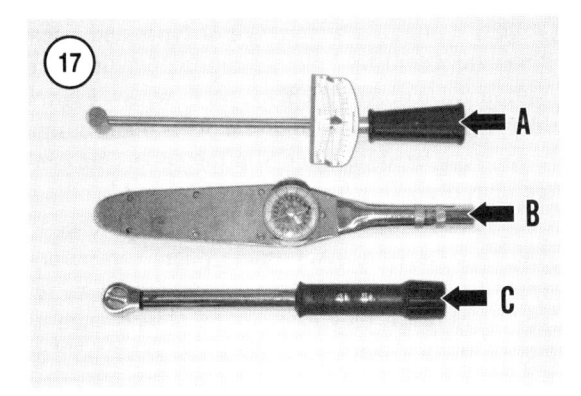

GENERAL INFORMATION

ratchet heads in varying lengths allow the socket to be turned with varying force, and at odd angles. Extension bars allow the socket setup to reach difficult areas. The ratchet is the most versatile wrench. It allows the user to install or remove the nut without removing the socket.

Sockets combined with any number of drivers make them undoubtedly the fastest, safest and most convenient tool for fastener removal and installation.

Impact Driver

An impact driver provides extra force for removing fasteners by converting the impact of a hammer into a turning motion. This makes it possible to remove stubborn fasteners without damaging them. Impact drivers and interchangeable bits (**Figure 15**) are available from most tool suppliers. When using a socket with an impact driver, make sure the socket is designed for impact use. Refer to *Socket Wrenches, Ratchets and Handles* in this section.

WARNING
Do not use hand sockets with air or impact tools, They may shatter and cause injury. Always wear eye protection when using impact or air tools.

Allen Wrenches

Allen or setscrew wrenches (**Figure 16**) are used on fasteners with hexagonal recesses in the fastener head. These wrenches are available in L-shaped bar, socket and T-handle types. A metric set is required when working on most vehicles made by Japanese and European manufacturers. Allen bolts are sometimes called socket bolts.

Torque Wrenches

A torque wrench is used with a socket, torque adapter or similar extension to tighten a fastener to a measured torque. Torque wrenches come in several drive sizes (1/4, 3/8, 1/2 and 3/4) and have various methods of reading the torque value. The drive size indicates the size of the square drive that accepts the socket, adapter or extension. Common methods of reading the torque value are the deflecting beam (A, **Figure 17**), the dial indicator (B) and the audible click (C).

19-mm impact socket (B). Use impact sockets when using an impact driver or air tools. Use hand sockets with hand-driven attachments.

WARNING
Do not use hand sockets with air or impact tools. They may shatter and cause injury. Always wear eye protection when using impact or air tools.

Various handles are available for sockets. The speed handle is used for fast operation. Flexible

When choosing a torque wrench, consider the torque range, drive size and accuracy. The torque specifications in this manual provide an indication of the range required.

A torque wrench is a precision tool that must be properly cared for to remain accurate. Store torque wrenches in cases or separate padded drawers within a toolbox. Follow the manufacturer's instructions for their care and calibration.

Torque Adapters

Torque adapters extend or reduce the reach of a torque wrench. The torque adapter shown in **Figure 18** is used to tighten a fastener that cannot be reached due to the size of the torque wrench head, drive, and socket. If a torque adapter changes the effective lever length (**Figure 19**) of a torque wrench, the torque reading on the wrench does not equal the actual torque applied to the fastener. It is necessary to calculate the adjusted torque reading on the wrench to compensate for the change of lever length. When a torque adapter is used at a right angle to the drive head, calibration is not required, since the effective length has not changed.

To calculate the adjusted torque reading when using a torque adapter, use the following formula:

$$TW = \frac{TA \times L}{L + A}$$

TW is the torque setting or dial reading on the wrench.

TA is the torque specification and the actual amount of torque that will be applied to the fastener.

A is the amount that the adapter increases (or in some cases reduces) the effective lever length as measured along the centerline of the torque wrench from the center of the drive to the center of adapter box end (**Figure 19**).

L is the lever length of the wrench as measured from the center of the drive to the center of the grip.

The effective length of the torque wrench is the sum of L and A.

For example:

To apply 20 ft.-lb. to a fastener using an adapter as shown in the top example in **Figure 19**,

TA = 20 ft.-lb.

A = 3 in.

L = 14 in.

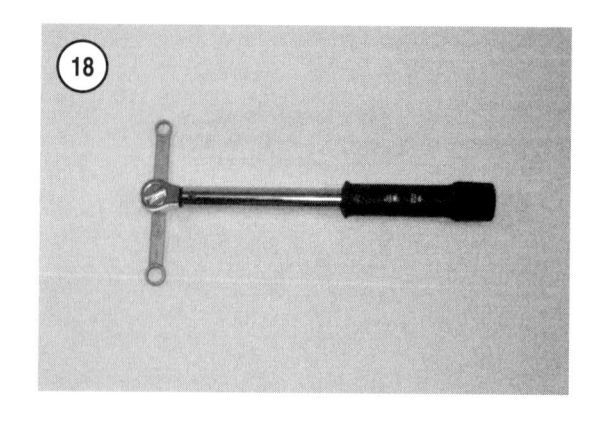

$$TW = \frac{20 \times 14}{14 + 3} = \frac{280}{17} = 16.5 \text{ ft.-lb.}$$

In this example, a click-type torque wrench would be set to the recalculated torque value (TW = 16.5 ft.-lb.). When using a dial or beam-type torque wrench, tighten the fastener until the pointer aligns with 16.5 ft.-lb. In either case, although the torque wrench reads 16.5 ft.-lb., the actual torque applied to the fastener is 20 ft.-lb.

Pliers

Pliers come in a wide range of types and sizes. Pliers are useful for holding, cutting, bending, and crimping. Do not use them to turn fasteners. **Figure 20** shows several types of useful pliers. Each design has a specialized function. Slip-joint pliers are general purpose pliers used for gripping and bending. Diagonal cutting pliers cut wire and can be used to remove cotter pins. Adjustable pliers can be adjusted to hold different size objects. The jaws remain parallel so they grip around objects such as pipe or tubing. Needlenose pliers are used to hold or bend small objects. Locking pliers (**Figure 21**), sometimes called vise-grips, are used to hold objects very tightly. They have many uses, ranging from holding two parts together to gripping the end of a broken stud. Use caution when using locking pliers, as the sharp jaws will damage the objects they hold.

Snap Ring Pliers

Snap ring pliers (**Figure 22**) are specialized pliers with tips that fit into the ends of snap rings to remove and install them.

GENERAL INFORMATION

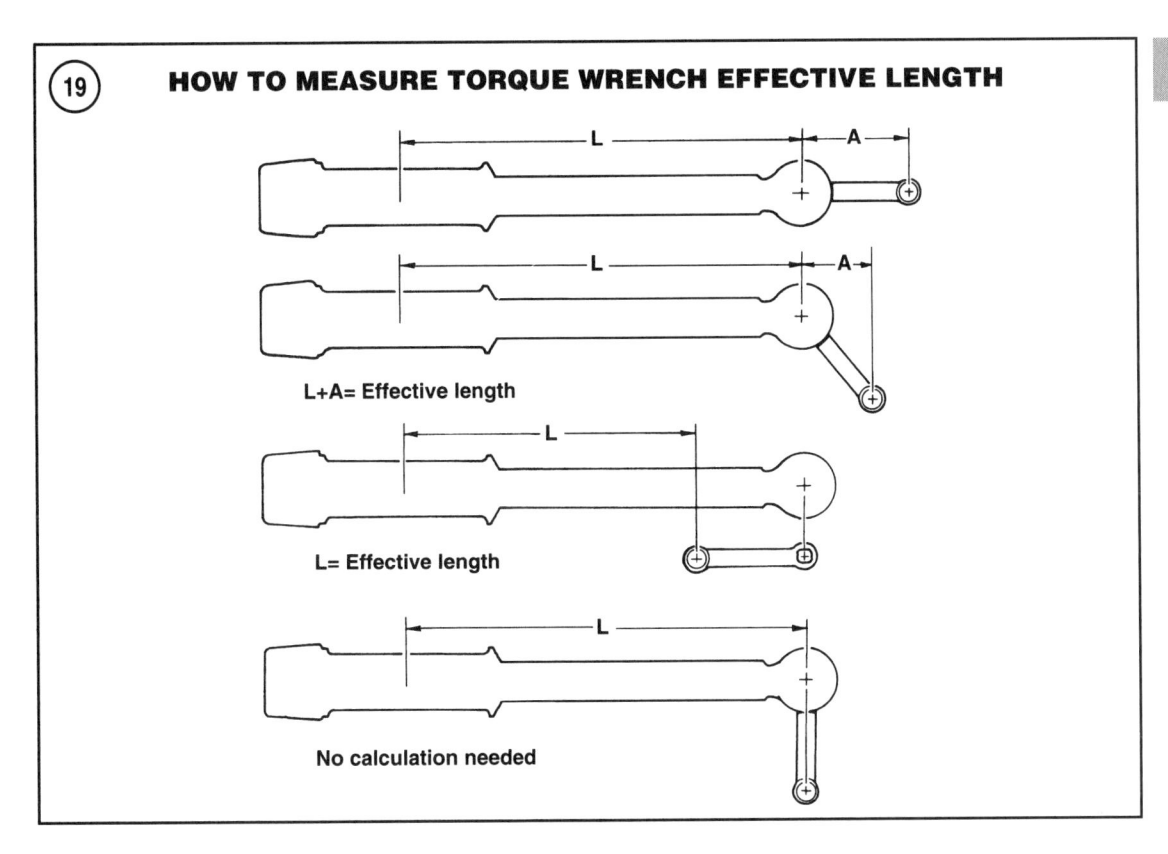

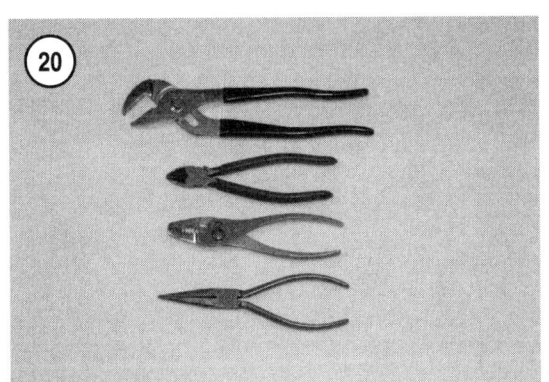

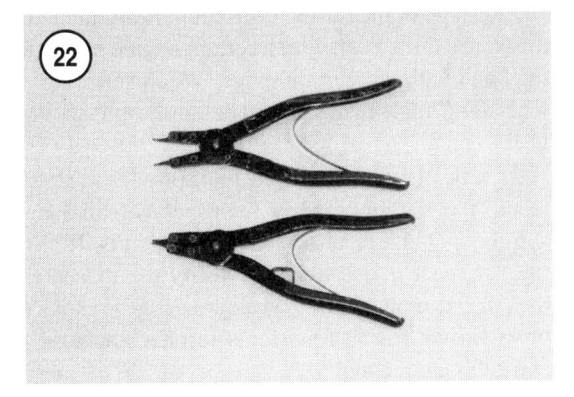

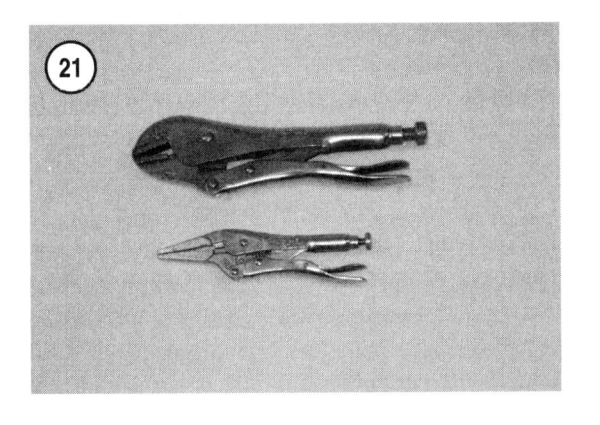

HOW TO MEASURE TORQUE WRENCH EFFECTIVE LENGTH

L+A= Effective length

L= Effective length

No calculation needed

Snap ring pliers are available with a fixed action (either internal or external) or convertible (one tool works on both internal and external snap rings). They may have fixed tips or interchangeable ones of various sizes and angles. For general use, select a convertible type plier with interchangeable tips.

WARNING
Snap rings can slip and fly off when removing and installing them. Also, the plier tips may break. Always wear eye protection when using snap ring pliers.

Hammers

Various types of hammers (**Figure 23**) are available to fit a number of applications. A ball-peen hammer is used to strike another tool, such as a punch or chisel. Soft-faced hammers are required when a metal object must be struck without damaging it. *Never* use a metal-faced hammer on engine and suspension components. Damage will occur in most cases.

Always wear eye protection when using hammers. Make sure the hammer face is in good condition and the handle is not cracked. Select the correct hammer for the job and make sure to strike the object squarely. Do not use the handle or the side of the hammer to strike an object.

PRECISION MEASURING TOOLS

The ability to accurately measure components is essential to successfully rebuild an engine. Equipment is manufactured to close tolerances, and obtaining consistently accurate measurements is essential to determining which components require replacement or further service.

Each type of measuring instrument is designed to measure a dimension with a certain degree of accuracy and within a certain range. When selecting a measuring tool, make sure it is applicable to the task.

As with all tools, measuring tools provide the best results if cared for properly. Improper use can damage the tool and result in inaccurate results. If any measurement is questionable, verify the measurement using another tool. A standard gauge is usually provided with measuring tools to check accuracy and calibrate the tool.

Precision measurements can vary according to the experience of the person taking the measurement. Accurate results are possible only if the mechanic possesses a feel for using the tool. Heavy-handed use of measuring tools produces less accurate results than if the tool is handled properly. Grasp precision measuring tools gently with your fingertips so the point at which the tool contacts the object is easily felt. This feel for the equipment produces consistently accurate measurements and reduces the risk of damaging the tool or component. Refer to the following sections for a description of various measuring tools.

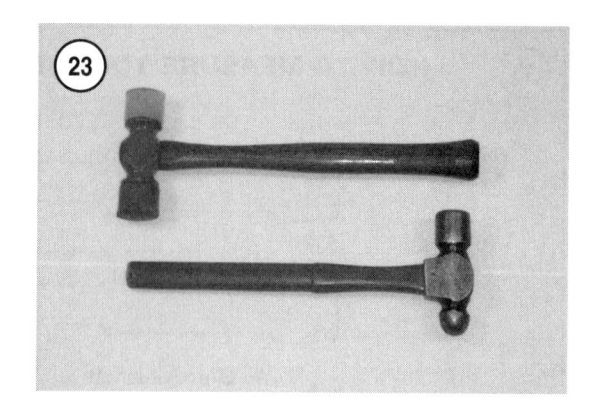

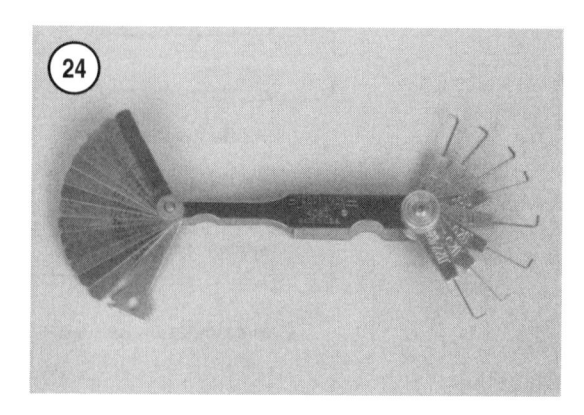

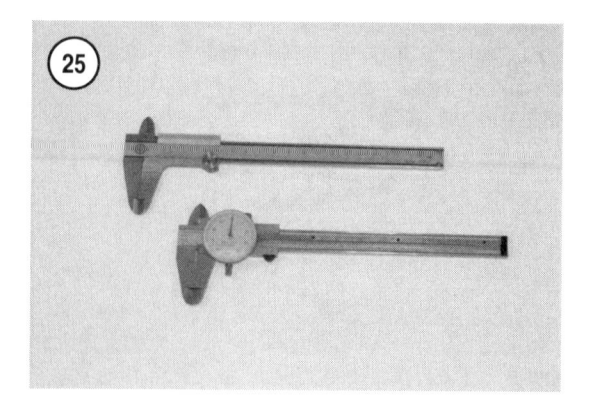

Feeler Gauge

The feeler or thickness gauge (**Figure 24**) is used for measuring the distance between two surfaces.

A feeler gauge set consists of an assortment of steel strips of graduated thicknesses. Each blade is marked with its thickness. Blades can be of various lengths and angles for different procedures.

A common use for a feeler gauge is to measure valve clearance. Wire (round) type gauges are used to measure spark plug gap.

GENERAL INFORMATION

METRIC VERNIER CALIPER

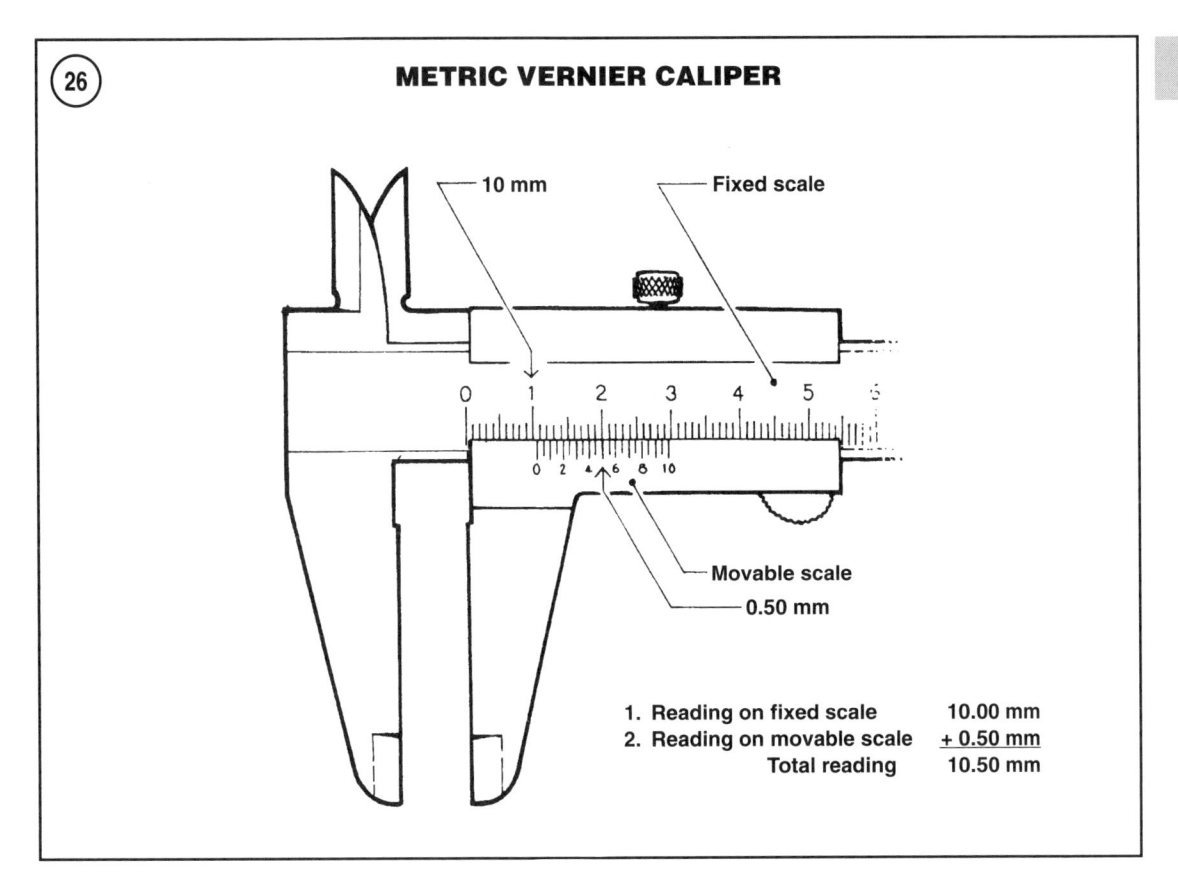

- 10 mm
- Fixed scale
- Movable scale
- 0.50 mm

1. Reading on fixed scale   10.00 mm
2. Reading on movable scale   + 0.50 mm
                      Total reading   10.50 mm

Calipers

Calipers (**Figure 25**) are excellent tools for obtaining inside, outside and depth measurements. Although not as precise as a micrometer, they allow reasonable precision, typically to within 0.05 mm (0.001 in.). Most calipers have a range up to 150 mm (6 in.).

Calipers are available in dial, vernier or digital versions. Dial calipers have a dial readout that provides convenient reading. Vernier calipers have marked scales that must be compared to determine the measurement. The digital caliper uses an LCD display to show the measurement.

Properly maintain the measuring surfaces of the caliper. There must not be any dirt or burrs between the tool and the object being measured. Never force the caliper closed around an object. Close the caliper around the highest point so it can be removed with a slight drag. Some calipers require calibration. Always refer to the manufacturer's instructions when using a new or unfamiliar caliper.

Figure 26 shows a measurement taken with a metric vernier caliper. To read the measurement, note that the fixed scale is graduated in centimeters, which is indicated by the whole numbers 1, 2, 3 and so on. Each centimeter is then divided into millimeters, which are indicated by the small line between the whole numbers. (1 centimeter equals 10 millimeters). The movable scale is marked in increments of 0.05 (hundredths) mm. The value of a measurement equals the reading on the fixed scale plus the reading on the movable scale.

To determine the reading on the fixed scale, look for the line on the fixed scale immediately to the left of the 0-line on the movable scale. In **Figure 26**, the fixed scale reading is 1 centimeter (or 10 millimeters).

To determine the reading on the movable scale, note the one line on the movable scale that precisely aligns with a line on the fixed scale. Look closely. A number of lines will seem close, but only one aligns precisely with a line on the fixed scale. In **Figure 26**, the movable scale reading is 0.50 mm.

To calculate the measurement, add the fixed scale reading (10 mm) to the movable scale reading (0.50 mm) for a value of 10.50 mm.

(27)

DECIMAL PLACE VALUES*

0.1	Indicates 1/10 (one tenth of an inch or millimeter)
0.010	Indicates 1/100 (one one-hundreth of an inch or millimeter)
0.001	Indicates 1/1,000 (one one-thousandth of an inch or millimeter)

*This chart represents the values of figures placed to the right of the decimal point. Use it when reading decimals from one-tenth to one one-thousandth of an inch or millimeter. It is not a conversion chart (for example: 0.001 in. is not equal to 0.001 mm).

Micrometers

A micrometer is an instrument designed for linear measurement using the decimal divisions of the inch or meter (**Figure 27**). While there are many types and styles of micrometers, most of the procedures in this manual call for an outside micrometer. The outside micrometer is used to measure the outside diameter of cylindrical forms and the thickness of materials.

A micrometer's size indicates the minimum and maximum size of a part that it can measure. The usual sizes (**Figure 28**) are 0-1 in. (0-25 mm), 1-2 in. (25-50 mm), 2-3 in. (50-75 mm) and 3-4 in. (75-100 mm).

Micrometers that cover a wider range of measurement are available. These use a large frame with interchangeable anvils of various lengths. This type of micrometer offers a cost savings; however, its overall size may make it less convenient.

Reading a Micrometer

When reading a micrometer, numbers are taken from different scales and added together. The following sections describe how to read the measurements of various types of outside micrometers.

For accurate results, properly maintain the measuring surfaces of the micrometer. There cannot be any dirt or burrs between the tool and the measured object. Never force the micrometer closed around an object. Close the micrometer around the highest point so it can be removed with a slight drag. **Figure 29** shows the markings and parts of a standard inch

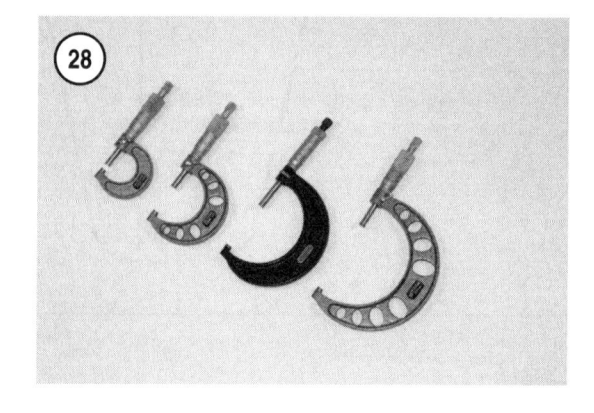

(28)

micrometer. Be familiar with these terms before using a micrometer in the following sections.

Standard inch micrometer

The standard inch micrometer is accurate to one-thousandth of an inch or 0.001. The sleeve is marked in 0.025 in. increments. Every fourth sleeve mark is numbered 1, 2, 3, 4, 5, 6, 7, 8, 9. These numbers indicate 0.100, 0.200, 0.300, and so on.

The tapered end of the thimble has twenty-five lines marked around it. Each mark equals 0.001 in. One complete turn of the thimble will align its zero mark with the first mark on the sleeve or 0.025 in.

When reading a standard inch micrometer, perform the following steps while referring to **Figure 30**.

1. Read the sleeve and find the largest number visible. Each sleeve number equals 0.100 in.

GENERAL INFORMATION

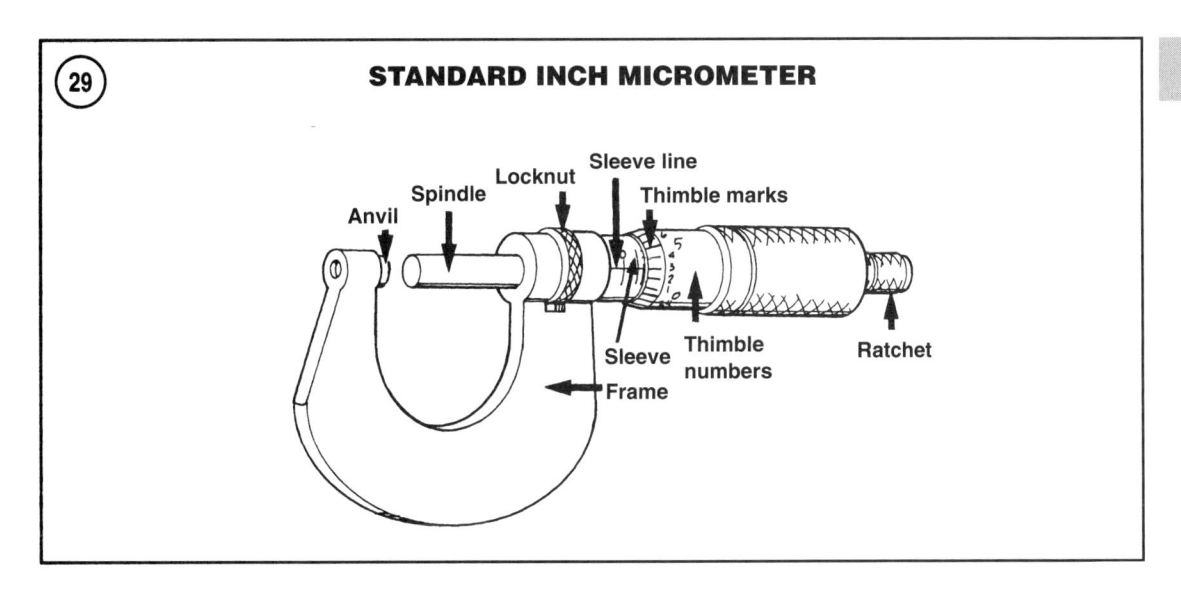

STANDARD INCH MICROMETER

Figure 29: Standard inch micrometer components: Anvil, Spindle, Locknut, Sleeve line, Thimble marks, Sleeve, Thimble numbers, Ratchet, Frame.

Figure 30: Sleeve and Thimble reading example.

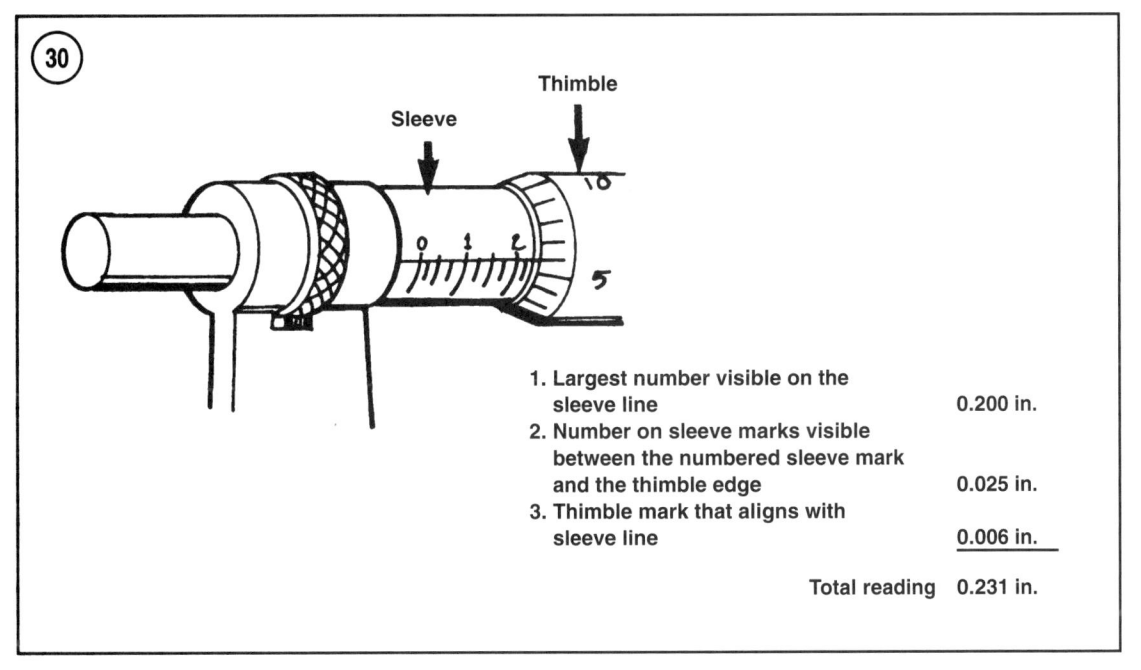

1. Largest number visible on the sleeve line	0.200 in.
2. Number on sleeve marks visible between the numbered sleeve mark and the thimble edge	0.025 in.
3. Thimble mark that aligns with sleeve line	0.006 in.
Total reading	0.231 in.

2. Count the number of lines between the numbered sleeve mark and the edge of the thimble. Each sleeve mark equals 0.025 in.

3. Read the thimble mark that aligns with the sleeve line. Each thimble mark equals 0.001 in.

NOTE
If a thimble mark does not align exactly with the sleeve line, estimate the amount between the lines. For accurate readings in ten-thousandths of an inch (0.0001 in.), use a vernier inch micrometer.

4. Add the readings from Steps 1-3.

Vernier inch micrometer

A vernier inch micrometer is accurate to one ten-thousandth of an inch or 0.0001 in. It has the same markings as a standard inch micrometer with

31

Vernier scale

1. Largest number visible on sleeve line	0.100 in.
2. Number of sleeve marks visible between the numbered sleeve mark and the thimble edge	0.050 in.
3. Thimble is between 0.018 and 0.019 in. on the sleeve line	0.018 in.
4. Vernier line coinciding with thimble line	0.0003 in.
Total reading	0.1683 in.

32

STANDARD METRIC MICROMETER

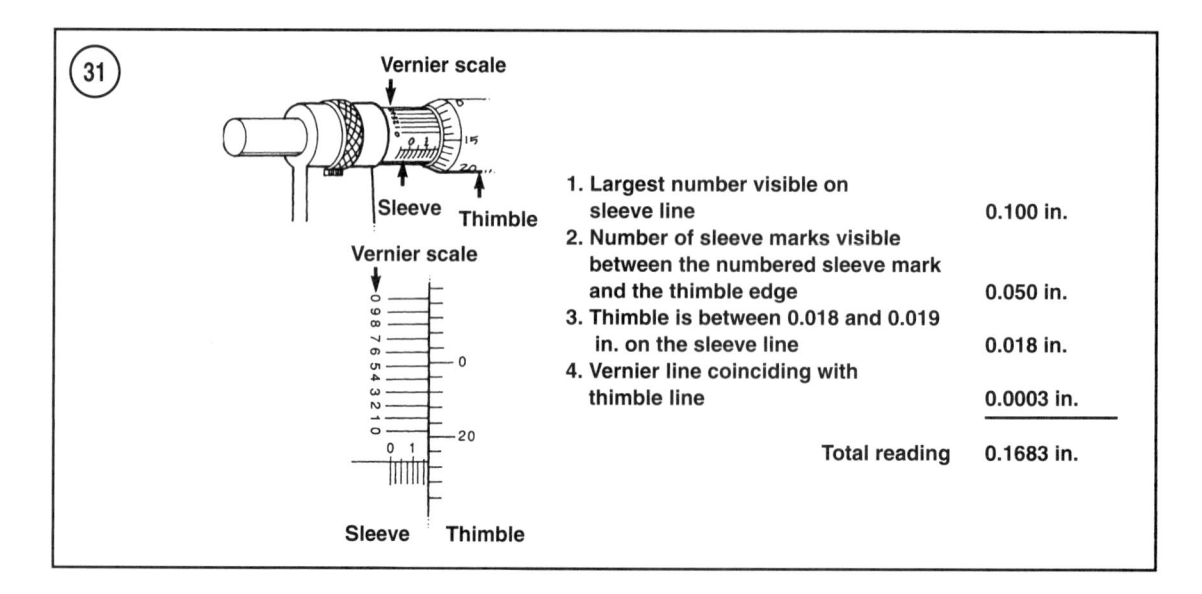

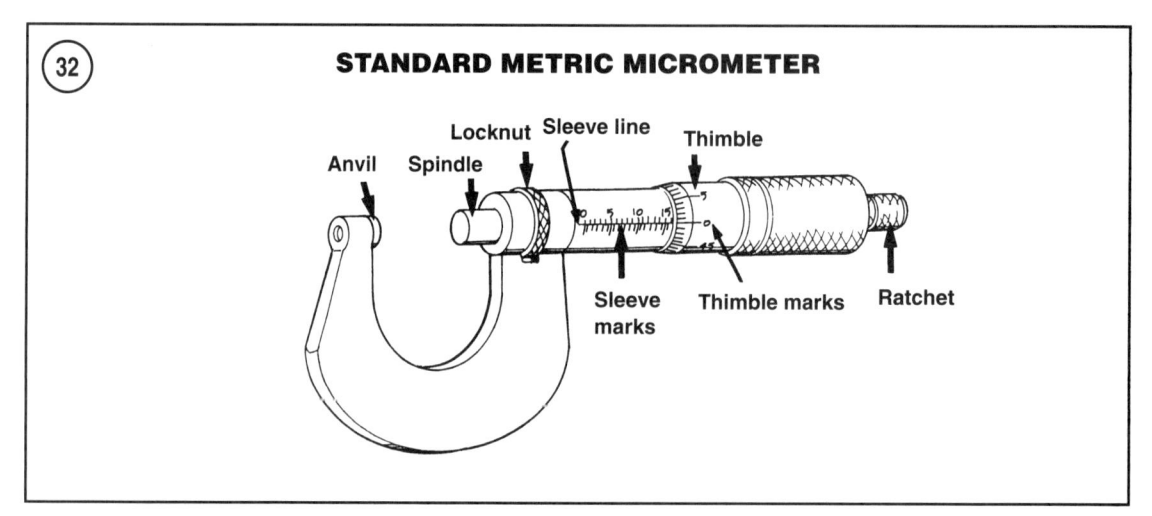

Anvil, Spindle, Locknut, Sleeve line, Thimble, Sleeve marks, Thimble marks, Ratchet

an additional vernier scale on the sleeve (**Figure 31**).

The vernier scale consists of 11 lines marked 1-9 with a 0 on each end. These lines run parallel to the thimble lines and represent 0.0001 in. increments.

When reading a vernier inch micrometer, perform the following steps while referring to **Figure 31**.

1. Read the micrometer in the same way as a standard micrometer. This is the initial reading.
2. If a thimble mark aligns exactly with the sleeve line, reading the vernier scale is not necessary. If they do not align, read the vernier scale in Step 3.
3. Determine which vernier scale mark aligns with one thimble mark. The vernier scale number is the amount in ten-thousandths of an inch to add to the initial reading from Step 1.

Metric micrometer

The standard metric micrometer (**Figure 32**) is accurate to one one-hundredth of a millimeter (0.01-mm). The sleeve line is graduated in millimeter and half-millimeter increments. The marks on the upper half of the sleeve line equal 1.00 mm. Every fifth mark above the sleeve line is identified with a number. The number sequence depends on the size of the micrometer. A 0-25 mm micrometer, for example, will have sleeve marks numbered 0 through 25 in 5 mm increments. This numbering se-

GENERAL INFORMATION

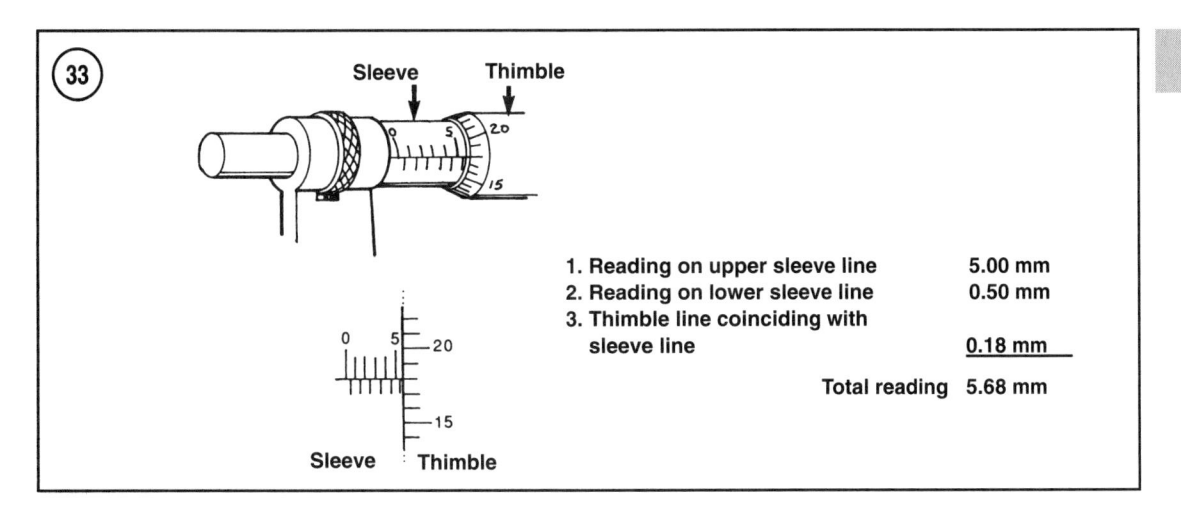

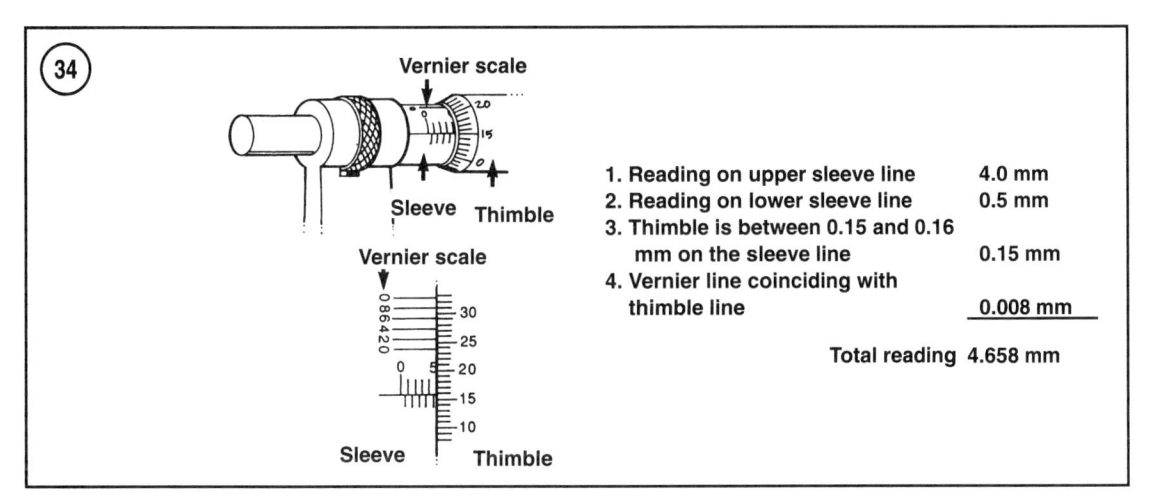

Figure 33

1. Reading on upper sleeve line — 5.00 mm
2. Reading on lower sleeve line — 0.50 mm
3. Thimble line coinciding with sleeve line — 0.18 mm

Total reading — 5.68 mm

Figure 34

1. Reading on upper sleeve line — 4.0 mm
2. Reading on lower sleeve line — 0.5 mm
3. Thimble is between 0.15 and 0.16 mm on the sleeve line — 0.15 mm
4. Vernier line coinciding with thimble line — 0.008 mm

Total reading — 4.658 mm

quence continues with larger micrometers. On all metric micrometers, each mark on the lower half of the sleeve equals 0.50 mm.

The tapered end of the thimble has 50 lines marked around it. Each mark equals 0.01 mm.

One complete turn of the thimble aligns its 0 mark with the first line on the lower half of the sleeve line or 0.50 mm.

When reading a metric micrometer, add the number of millimeters and half-millimeters on the sleeve line to the hundredths of a millimeter shown on the thimble. Perform the following steps while referring to **Figure 33**.

1. Read the upper half of the sleeve line and count the number of lines visible. Each upper line equals 1 mm.
2. If the half-millimeter line is visible on the lower sleeve line, add 0.50 to the reading in Step 1.
3. Read the thimble mark that aligns with the sleeve line. Each thimble mark equals 0.01 mm.

NOTE
If a thimble mark does not align exactly with the sleeve line, estimate the amount between the lines. For accurate readings to two-thousandths of a millimeter (0.002 mm), use a metric vernier micrometer.

4. Add the readings from Steps 1-3.

Metric vernier micrometer

A metric vernier micrometer is accurate to two-thousandths of a millimeter (0.002-mm). It has the same markings as a standard metric micrometer with the addition of a vernier scale on the sleeve (**Figure 34**). The vernier scale consists of five lines marked 0, 2, 4, 6, and 8. These lines run parallel to the thimble lines and represent 0.002-mm increments.

When reading a metric vernier micrometer, perform the following steps and refer to **Figure 34**.

1. Read the micrometer in the same way as a standard metric micrometer. This is the initial reading.
2. If a thimble mark aligns exactly with the sleeve line, reading the vernier scale is not necessary. If they do not align, read the vernier scale in Step 3.
3. Determine which vernier scale mark aligns exactly with one thimble mark. The vernier scale number is the amount in two-thousandths of a millimeter to add to the initial reading from Step 1.

Micrometer Adjustment

Before using a micrometer, check its adjustment as follows.
1. Clean the anvil and spindle faces.
2A. To check a 0-1 in. or 0-25 mm micrometer:
   a. Turn the thimble until the spindle contacts the anvil. If the micrometer has a ratchet stop, use it to ensure that the proper amount of pressure is applied.
   b. If the adjustment is correct, the 0 mark on the thimble will align exactly with the 0 mark on the sleeve line. If the marks do not align, the micrometer is out of adjustment.
   c. Follow the manufacturer's instructions to adjust the micrometer.
2B. To check a micrometer larger than 1 in. or 25 mm, use the standard gauge supplied by the manufacturer. A standard gauge is a steel block, disc or rod that is machined to an exact size.
   a. Place the standard gauge between the spindle and anvil, and measure its outside diameter or length. If the micrometer has a ratchet stop, use it to ensure that the proper amount of pressure is applied.
   b. If the adjustment is correct, the 0 mark on the thimble will align exactly with the 0 mark on the sleeve line. If the marks do not align, the micrometer is out of adjustment.
   c. Follow the manufacturer's instructions to adjust the micrometer.

Micrometer Care

Micrometers are precision instruments. They must be used and maintained with great care.

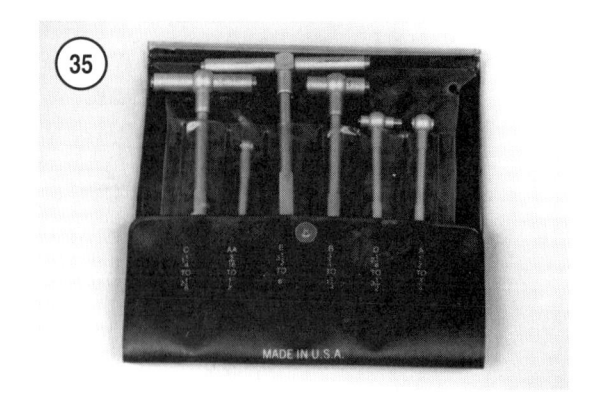

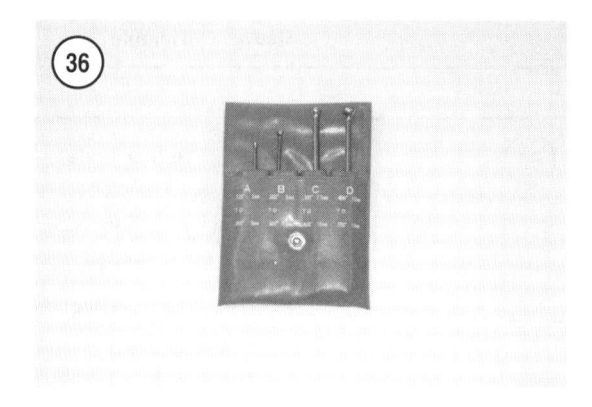

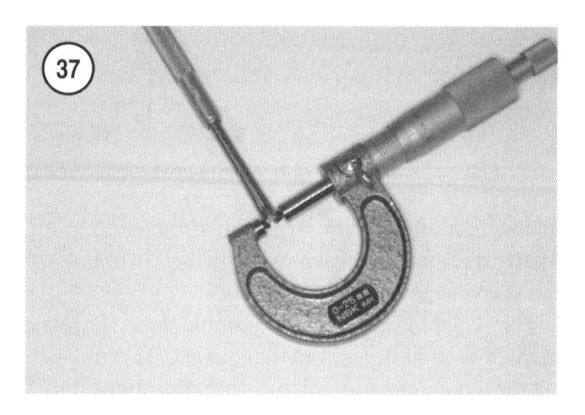

Note the following:

1. Store micrometers in protective cases or separate padded drawers in a toolbox.

2. When in storage, make sure the spindle and anvil faces do not contact each other or another object. If they do, temperature changes and corrosion may damage the contact faces.

3. Do not clean a micrometer with compressed air. Dirt forced into the tool will cause wear.

4. Lubricate micrometers with WD-40 to prevent corrosion.

GENERAL INFORMATION

and measure the length of the posts. Telescoping gauges are typically used to measure cylinder bores.

To use a small bore gauge, select the correct size gauge for the bore. Carefully insert the gauge into the bore. Tighten the knurled end of the gauge to carefully expand the gauge fingers to the limit within the bore. Do not overtighten the gauge, as there is no built-in release. Excessive tightening can damage the bore surface and damage the tool. Remove the gauge and measure the outside dimension (**Figure 37**). Small hole gauges are typically used to measure valve guides.

Dial Indicator

A dial indicator (A, **Figure 38**) is a gauge with a dial face and needle used to measure variations in dimensions and movements. Measuring brake rotor runout is a typical use for a dial indicator.

Dial indicators are available in various ranges and graduations and with three basic types of mounting bases: magnetic, clamp, or screw-in stud. When purchasing a dial indicator, select the magnetic stand type (B, **Figure 38**) with a continuous dial.

Cylinder Bore Gauge

A cylinder bore gauge is similar to a dial indicator. The gauge set shown in **Figure 39** consists of a dial indicator, handle, and different length adapters (anvils) to fit the gauge to various bore sizes. The bore gauge is used to measure bore size, taper and out-of-round. When using a bore gauge, follow the manufacturer's instructions.

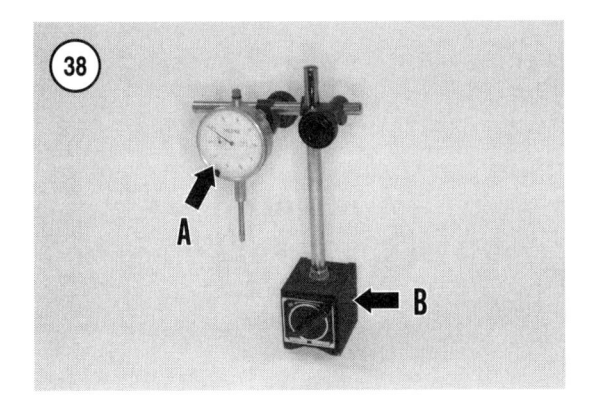

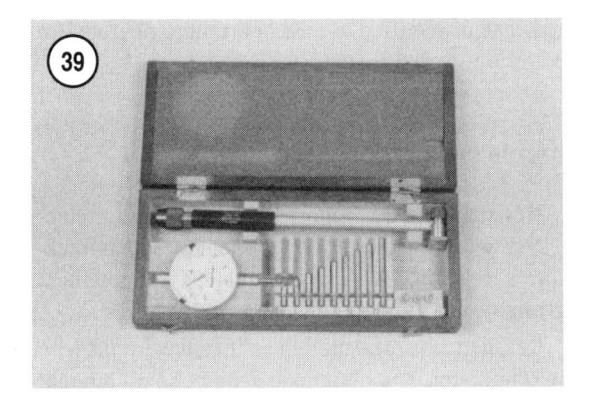

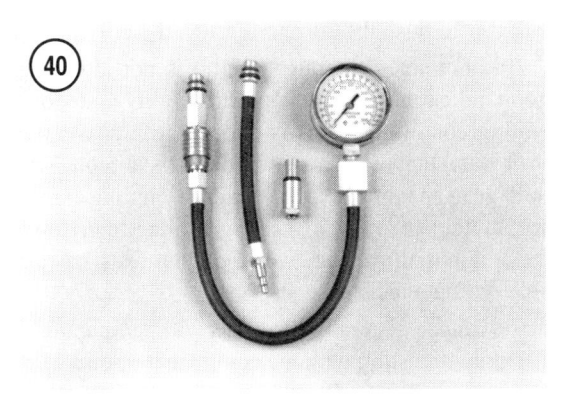

Telescoping and Small Bore Gauges

Use telescoping gauges (**Figure 35**) and small bore gauges (**Figure 36**) to measure bores. Neither gauge has a scale for direct readings. An outside micrometer must be used to determine the reading.

To use a telescoping gauge, select the correct size gauge for the bore. Compress the movable post and carefully insert the gauge into the bore. Carefully move the gauge in the bore to make sure it is centered. Tighten the knurled end of the gauge to hold the movable post in position. Remove the gauge,

Compression Gauge

A compression gauge (**Figure 40**) measures combustion chamber (cylinder) pressure, usually in psi or kg/cm^2. The gauge adapter is either inserted or screwed into the spark plug hole to obtain the reading. Disable the engine so it will not start and hold the throttle in the wide-open position when performing a compression test. An engine that does not have adequate compression cannot be properly tuned. See Chapter Three.

Multimeter

A multimeter (**Figure 41**) is an essential tool for electrical system diagnosis. The voltage function indicates the voltage applied or available to various electrical components. The ohmmeter function tests circuits for continuity and measures the resistance of a circuit.

Some manufacturers' specifications for electrical components are based on results using a specific test meter. Results may vary if using a meter not recommend by the manufacturer. Such requirements are noted when applicable.

Ohmmeter (analog) calibration

Each time an analog ohmmeter is used or if the scale is changed, the ohmmeter must be calibrated. Digital ohmmeters do not require calibration.
1. Make sure the meter battery is in good condition.
2. Make sure the meter probes are in good condition.
3. Touch the two probes together and watch the needle. It must align with the 0 mark on the scale.
4. If necessary, rotate the set-adjust knob until the needle points directly to the 0 mark.

ELECTRICAL SYSTEM FUNDAMENTALS

A thorough study of the many types of electrical systems used in today's vehicles is beyond the scope of this manual. However, an understanding of electrical basics is necessary to perform simple diagnostic tests.

Voltage

Voltage is the electrical potential or pressure in an electrical circuit and is expressed in volts. The more pressure (voltage) in a circuit, the more work that can be performed.

Direct current (DC) voltage means the electricity flows in one direction. All circuits powered by a battery are DC circuits.

Alternating current (AC) means that the electricity flows in one direction momentarily, then switches to the opposite direction. Alternator output is an example of AC voltage. This voltage must be changed or rectified to direct current to operate in a battery-powered system.

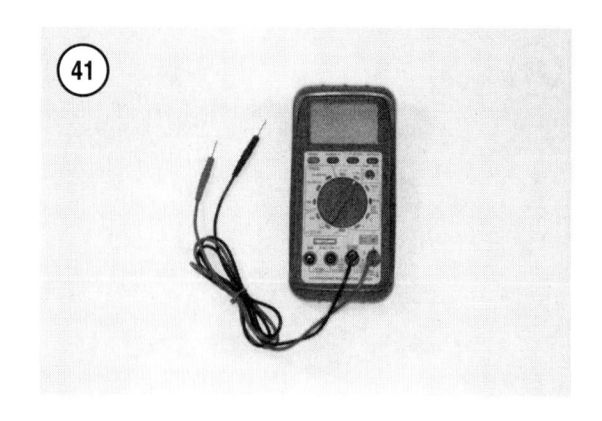

Resistance

Resistance is the opposition to the flow of electricity within a circuit or component and is measured in ohms. Resistance causes a reduction in available current and voltage.

Resistance is measured in an inactive circuit with an ohmmeter. The ohmmeter sends a small amount of current into the circuit and measures how difficult it is to push the current through the circuit.

An ohmmeter, although useful, is not always a good indicator of a circuit's actual ability under operating conditions. This is due to the low voltage (6-9 volts) that the meter uses to test the circuit. The voltage in an ignition coil secondary winding can be several thousand volts. Such high voltage can cause the coil to malfunction, even though it tests acceptable during a resistance test.

Resistance generally increases with temperature. Perform all testing with the component or circuit at room temperature. Resistance tests performed at high temperatures may indicate high resistance readings and result in the unnecessary replacement of a component.

Amperage

Amperage is the unit of measure for the amount of current within a circuit. Current is the actual flow of electricity. The higher the current, the more work that can be performed. However, if the current flow exceeds the circuit or component capacity, the system will be damaged.

GENERAL INFORMATION

Electrical Tests

Refer to Chapter Two for a description of various electrical tests.

SPECIAL TOOLS

Some of the procedures in this manual require special tools. These are described in the appropriate chapter and are available from either the manufacturer or a tool supplier.

In many cases, an acceptable substitute may be found in an existing tool kit. Another alternative is to make the tool or have one made. Many schools with a machine shop curriculum welcome outside work that can be used as practical shop applications for students.

BASIC SERVICE METHODS

Most of the procedures in this manual are straightforward and can be performed by anyone reasonably competent with tools. However, consider personal capabilities carefully before attempting any operation involving major disassembly of the motorcycle.

1. Front, in this manual, refers to the front of the motorcycle. The front of any component is the end closest to the front of the motorcycle. The left and right sides refer to the position of the parts as viewed by the rider sitting on the seat facing forward.
2. Whenever servicing an engine or suspension component, secure the motorcycle in a safe manner.
3. Tag all similar parts for location and mark all mating parts for position. Record the number and thickness of any shims as they are removed. Identify parts by placing them in sealed and labled plastic bags.
4. Tag disconnected wires and connectors with masking tape and a marking pen. Do not rely on memory alone.
5. Protect finished surfaces from physical damage or corrosion. Keep gasoline and other chemicals off painted surfaces.
6. Use penetrating oil on frozen or tight bolts. Avoid using heat where possible. Heat can warp, melt or affect the temper of parts. Heat also damages the finish of paint and plastics.
7. When a part is a press fit or requires a special tool for removal, the information or type of tool is identified in the text. Otherwise, if a part is difficult to remove or install, determine the cause before proceeding.
8. To prevent objects or debris from falling into the engine, cover all openings.
9. Read each procedure thoroughly and compare the illustrations to the actual components before starting the procedure. Perform the procedure in sequence.
10. Recommendations are occasionally made to refer service to a dealership or specialist. In these cases, the work can be performed more economically by the specialist than by the home mechanic.
11. The term *replace* means to discard a defective part and install a new part. *Overhaul* means to remove, disassemble, inspect, measure, repair and/or replace parts as required to recondition an assembly.
12. Some operations require the use of a hydraulic press. If a press is not available, have these operations performed by a shop equipped with the necessary equipment. Do not use makeshift equipment that may damage the motorcycle.
13. Repairs are much faster and easier if the motorcycle is clean before starting work. Degrease the motorcycle with a commercial degreaser; follow the directions on the container for the best results. Clean all parts with cleaning solvent as they are removed.

CAUTION
Do not apply a chemical degreaser to an O-ring drive chain. These chemicals will damage the O-rings. Use kerosene to clean O-ring type chains.

CAUTION
Do not direct high-pressure water at steering bearings, carburetor hoses, wheel bearings, suspension and electrical components, or O-ring drive chains. The water will force the grease out of the bearings and possibly damage the seals.

14. If special tools are required, have them available before starting the procedure. When special tools are required, they will be described at the beginning of the procedure.
15. Make diagrams of similar-appearing parts. For instance, crankcase bolts are often not the same lengths. Do not rely on memory alone. It is possible that carefully laid out parts will become disturbed,

making it difficult to reassemble the components correctly without a diagram.

16. Make sure all shims and washers are reinstalled in the same location and position.

17. Whenever a rotating part contacts a stationary part, look for a shim or washer.

18. Use new gaskets if there is any doubt about the condition of old ones.

19. If self-locking fasteners are used, replace them with new ones. Do not reuse a self-locking fastener. Also, do not install standard fasteners in place of self-locking ones.

20. Use grease to hold small parts in place if they tend to fall out during assembly. Do not apply grease to electrical or brake components.

Removing Frozen Fasteners

If a fastener cannot be removed, several methods may be used to loosen it. First, apply penetrating oil such as Liquid Wrench or WD-40. Apply it liberally, and let it penetrate for 10-15 minutes. Rap the fastener several times with a small hammer. Do not hit it hard enough to cause damage. Reapply the penetrating oil if necessary.

For frozen screws, apply penetrating oil as described. Insert a screwdriver in the slot, and rap the top of the screwdriver with a hammer. This loosens the rust so the screw can be removed in the normal way. If the screw head is too damaged to use this method, grip the head with locking pliers and twist the screw out.

Avoid applying heat unless specifically instructed, as it may melt, warp or remove the temper from parts.

Removing Broken Fasteners

If the head breaks off a screw or bolt, several methods are available for removing the remaining portion. If a large portion of the remainder projects out, try gripping it with locking pliers. If the projecting portion is too small, file it to fit a wrench or cut a slot in it to fit a screwdriver (**Figure 42**).

If the head breaks off flush, use a screw extractor. To do this, centerpunch the exact center of the remaining portion of the screw or bolt. Drill a small hole in the screw and tap the extractor into the hole. Back the screw out with a wrench on the extractor (**Figure 43**).

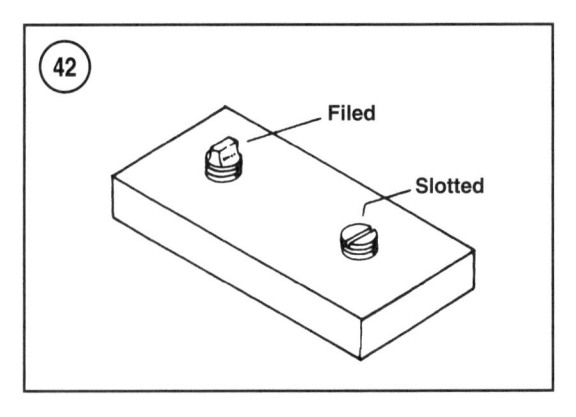

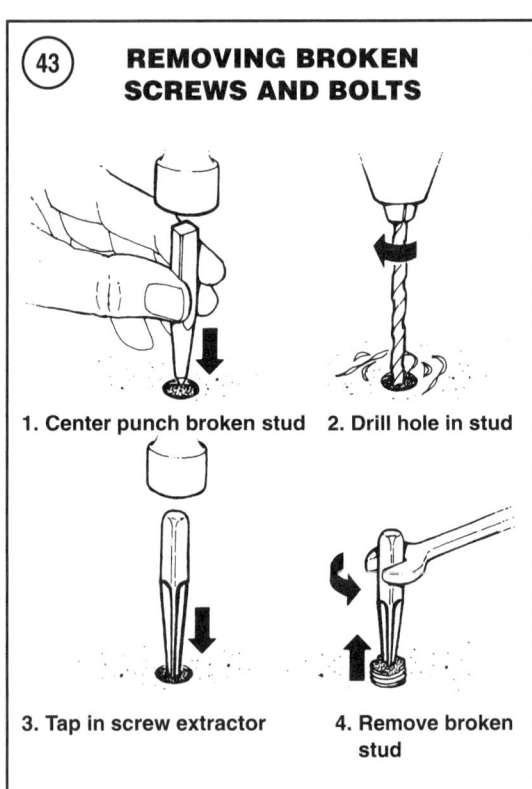

Repairing Damaged Threads

Occasionally, threads are stripped through carelessness or impact damage. Often the threads can be repaired by running a tap (for internal threads on nuts) or die (for external threads on bolts) through the threads (**Figure 44**). To clean or repair spark plug threads, use a spark plug tap.

If an internal thread is damaged, it may be necessary to install a Helicoil or some other type of thread insert. Follow the manufacturer's instructions when installing their insert.

GENERAL INFORMATION

1. Measure the height of the stud above the surface.
2. Thread the stud removal tool onto the stud and tighten it, or thread two nuts onto the stud.
3. Remove the stud by turning the stud remover or the lower nut.
4. Remove any threadlocking compound from the threaded hole. Clean the threads with an aerosol parts cleaner.
5. Install the stud removal tool onto the new stud or thread two nuts onto the stud.
6. Apply threadlocking compound to the threads of the stud.
7. Install the stud and tighten with the stud removal tool or the top nut.
8. Install the stud to the height noted in Step 1 or its torque specification.
9. Remove the stud removal tool or the two nuts.

Removing Hoses

When removing stubborn hoses, do not exert excessive force on the hose or fitting. Remove the hose clamp and carefully insert a small screwdriver or pick tool between the fitting and hose. Apply a spray lubricant under the hose and carefully twist the hose off the fitting. Clean the fitting of any corrosion or rubber hose material with a wire brush. Clean the inside of the hose thoroughly. Do not use any lubricant when installing the hose (new or old). The lubricant may allow the hose to come off the fitting, even with the clamp secure.

Bearings

Bearings are used in the engine and transmission assembly to reduce power loss, heat and noise resulting from friction. Because bearings are precision parts, they must be maintained by proper lubrication and maintenance. If a bearing is damaged, replace it immediately. When installing a new bearing, take care to prevent damaging it. Bearing replacement procedures are included in the individual chapters where applicable; however, use the following sections as a guideline.

NOTE
Unless otherwise specified, install bearings with the manufacturer's mark or number facing outward.

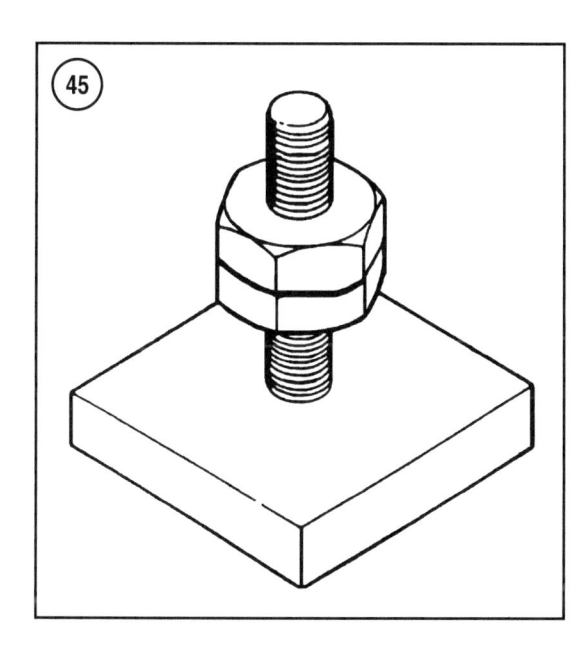

If it is necessary to drill and tap a hole, refer to **Table 8** for metric tap and drill sizes.

Stud Removal/Installation

A stud removal tool is available from most tool suppliers. This tool makes the removal and installation of studs easier. If one is not available, thread two nuts onto the stud and tighten them against each other. Remove the stud by turning the lower nut (**Figure 45**).

26   CHAPTER ONE

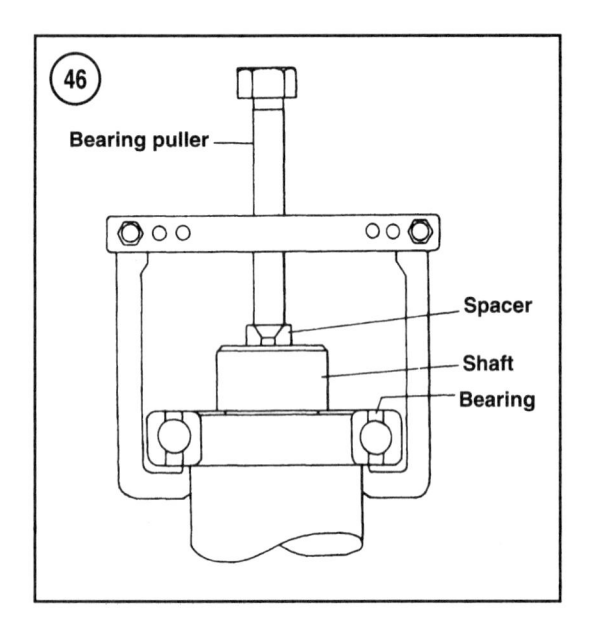

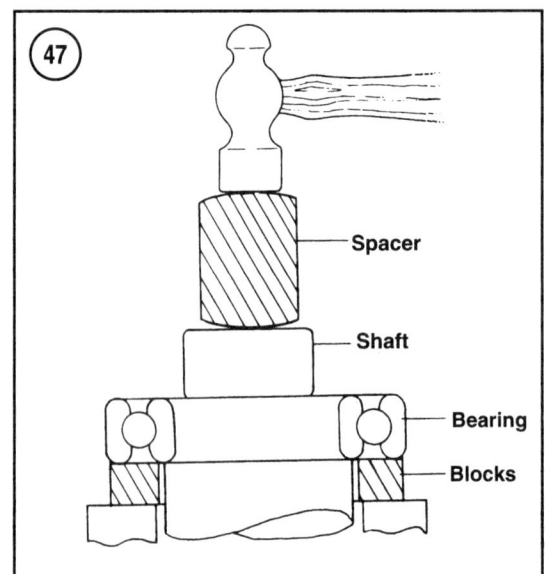

Removal

While bearings are normally removed only when damaged, there may be times when it is necessary to remove a bearing that is in good condition. However, improper bearing removal will damage the bearing and possibly the shaft or case half. Note the following when removing bearings.

1. When using a puller to remove a bearing from a shaft, take care that the shaft is not damaged. Always place a piece of metal between the end of the shaft and the puller screw. In addition, place the puller arms next to the inner bearing race. See **Figure 46**.

2. When using a hammer to remove a bearing from a shaft, do not strike the hammer directly against the shaft. Instead, use a brass or aluminum spacer between the hammer and shaft (**Figure 47**) and make sure to support both bearing races with wooden blocks as shown.

3. A hydraulic press is the ideal tool for bearing removal. Note the following when using a press:

    a. Always support the inner and outer bearing races with a correctly-sized wooden or aluminum ring (**Figure 48**). If only the outer race is supported, pressure applied against the balls and/or the inner race will damage them.

    b. Always make sure the press ram (**Figure 48**) aligns with the center of the shaft. If the ram is not centered, it may damage the bearing and/or shaft.

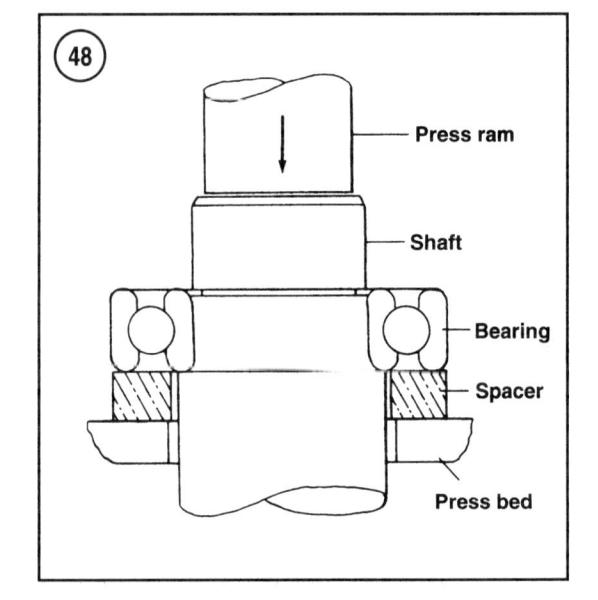

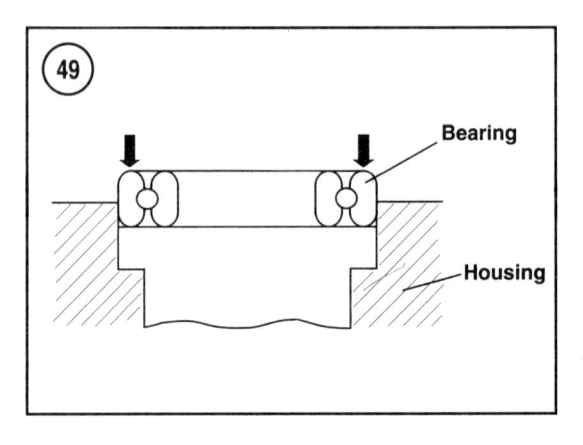

GENERAL INFORMATION

Figure 50 — Bearing, Shaft

Figure 51 — Socket, Bearing, Shaft

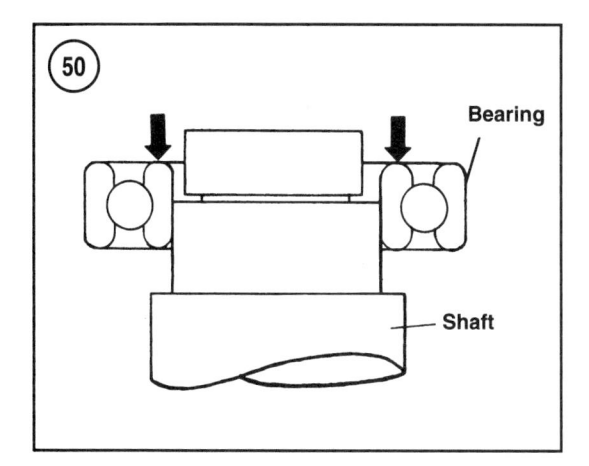

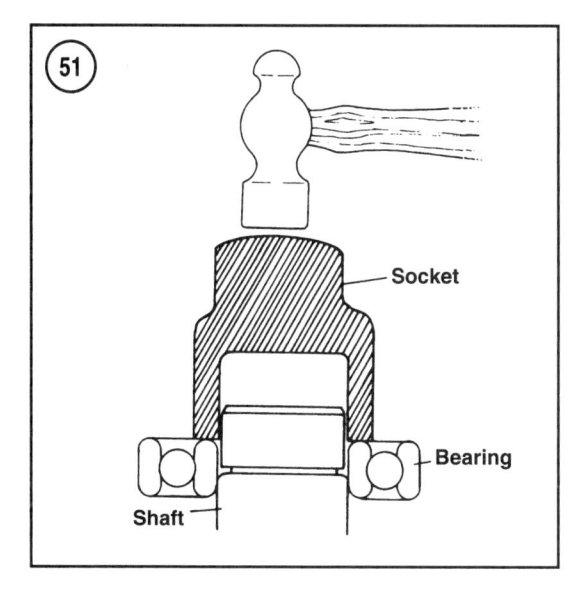

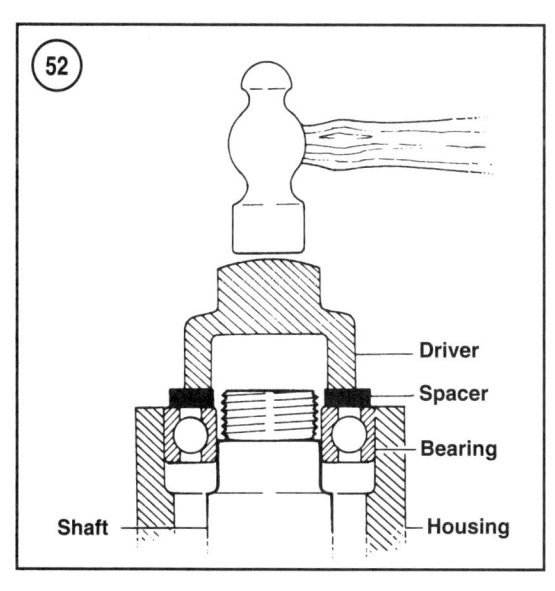

Figure 52 — Driver, Spacer, Bearing, Shaft, Housing

c. The moment the shaft is free of the bearing, it will drop to the floor. Secure or hold the shaft to prevent it from falling.

Installation

1. When installing a bearing in a housing, apply pressure to the *outer* bearing race (**Figure 49**). When installing a bearing on a shaft, apply pressure to the *inner* bearing race (**Figure 50**).
2. When installing a bearing as described in Step 1, some type of driver is required. Never strike the bearing directly with a hammer or the bearing will be damaged. When installing a bearing, use a piece of pipe or a driver with a diameter that matches the bearing race. **Figure 51** shows the correct way to use a driver and hammer to install a bearing.
3. Step 1 describes how to install a bearing in a case half and over a shaft. However, when installing a bearing over a shaft and into a housing at the same time, a tight fit will be required for both outer and inner bearing races. In this situation, install a spacer underneath the driver tool so that pressure is applied evenly across both races. See **Figure 52**. If the outer race is not supported as shown in **Figure 52**, the balls will push against the outer bearing race and damage it.

Interference Fit

1. Follow this procedure when installing a bearing over a shaft. When a tight fit is required, the bearing inside diameter will be smaller than the shaft. In this case, driving the bearing onto the shaft using normal methods may cause bearing damage. Instead, heat the bearing before installation. Note the following:
   a. Secure the shaft so it is ready for bearing installation.
   b. Clean all residue from the bearing surface of the shaft. Remove burrs with a file or sandpaper.
   c. Fill a suitable pot or beaker with clean mineral oil. Place a thermometer rated above 120° C (248° F) in the oil. Support the thermometer so that it does not rest on the bottom or side of the pot.
   d. Remove the bearing from its wrapper and secure it with a piece of heavy wire bent to hold

it in the pot. Hang the bearing in the pot so it does not touch the bottom or sides of the pot.

e. Turn the heat on and monitor the thermometer. When the oil temperature rises to approximately 120° C (248° F), remove the bearing from the pot and quickly install it. If necessary, place a socket on the inner bearing race and tap the bearing into place. As the bearing chills, it will tighten on the shaft, so installation must be done quickly. Make sure the bearing is installed completely.

2. Follow this step when installing a bearing in a housing. Bearings are generally installed in a housing with a slight interference fit. Driving the bearing into the housing using normal methods may damage the housing or cause bearing damage. Instead, heat the housing before the bearing is installed. Note the following:

CAUTION
Before heating the housing, wash the housing thoroughly with detergent and water. Rinse and rewash the cases as required to remove all traces of oil and other chemical deposits.

a. Heat the housing to approximately 212° F (100° C) in an oven or on a hot plate. An easy way to check that it is at the proper temperature is to place tiny drops of water on the housing; if they sizzle and evaporate immediately, the temperature is correct. Heat only one housing at a time.

CAUTION
Do not heat the housing with a propane or acetylene torch. Never bring a flame into contact with the bearing or housing. The direct heat will destroy the case hardening of the bearing and will likely warp the housing.

b. Remove the housing from the oven or hot plate, and hold onto the housing with a kitchen potholder, heavy gloves or heavy shop cloth. It is hot!

NOTE
Remove and install the bearings with a correctly-sized socket and extension.

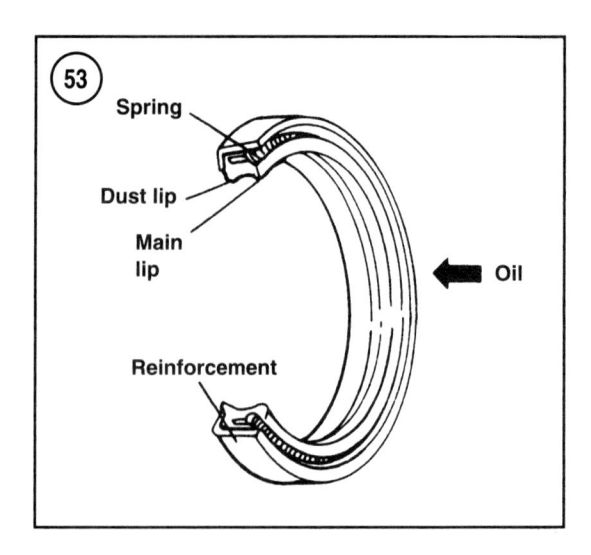

c. Hold the housing with the bearing side down and tap the bearing out. Repeat for all bearings in the housing.

d. Before heating the bearing housing, place the new bearing in a freezer if possible. Chilling a bearing slightly reduces its outside diameter while the heated bearing housing assembly is slightly larger due to heat expansion. This will make bearing installation easier.

NOTE
Always install bearings with the manufacturer's mark or number facing outward.

e. While the housing is still hot, install the new bearing(s) into the housing. Install the bearings by hand, if possible. If necessary, lightly tap the bearing(s) into the housing with a socket placed on the outer bearing race (**Figure 49**). Do not install new bearings by driving on the inner-bearing race. Install the bearing(s) until it seats completely.

Seal Replacement

Seals (**Figure 53**) are used to contain oil, water, grease or combustion gasses in a housing or shaft. Improper removal of a seal can damage the housing or shaft. Improper installation of the seal can damage the seal. Note the following:

1. Prying is generally the easiest and most effective method of removing a seal from a housing. However, always place a rag underneath the pry

GENERAL INFORMATION

tool (**Figure 54**) to prevent damage to the housing.
2. Pack waterproof grease in the seal lips before the seal is installed.
3. Install seals with the manufacturer's numbers or marks facing out.
4. Install seals with a socket placed on the outside of the seal as shown in **Figure 55**. Drive the seal squarely into the housing. Never install a seal by hitting against the top of the seal with a hammer.

STORAGE

Several months of non-use can cause a general deterioration of the vehicle. This is especially true in areas of extreme temperature variations. This deterioration can be minimized with careful preparation for storage. A properly stored vehicle will be much easier to return to service.

Storage Area Selection

When selecting a storage area, consider the following:

1. The storage area must be dry. A heated area is best, but not necessary. It should be insulated to minimize extreme temperature variations.
2. If the building has large window areas, mask them to keep sunlight off the vehicle.
3. Avoid buildings in industrial areas where corrosive emissions may be present. Avoid areas close to saltwater.
4. Consider the area's risk of fire, theft or vandalism. Check with an insurer regarding vehicle coverage while in storage.

Preparing the Vehicle for Storage

The amount of preparation a vehicle should undergo before storage depends upon the expected length of non-use, storage area conditions and personal preference. Consider the following list the minimum requirement:

1. Wash the vehicle thoroughly. Make sure all dirt, mud and road debris are removed.
2. Start the engine and allow it to reach operating temperature. Drain the engine oil regardless of the riding time since the last service. Fill the engine with the recommended type of oil.
3. Drain all fuel from the fuel tank, and run the engine until all the fuel is consumed from the lines and carburetor(s).
4. Remove the spark plug(s) and pour a teaspoon of engine oil into the cylinder(s). Place a rag over the opening(s) and slowly turn the engine over to distribute the oil. Reinstall the spark plug(s).
5. Remove the battery. Store the battery in a cool, dry location.
6. Cover the exhaust and intake openings.
7. Reduce the normal tire pressure by 20 percent.
8. Apply a protective substance to the plastic and rubber components, including the tires. Make sure to follow the manufacturer's instructions for each type of product being used.
9. Place the vehicle on a stand or wooden blocks, so the wheels are off the ground. If this is not possible, place a piece of plywood between the tires and the ground. Inflate the tires to the recommended pressure if the vehicle can not be elevated.
10. Cover the vehicle with old bed sheets or something similar. Do not cover it with any plastic material that will trap moisture.

Returning the Vehicle to Service

The amount of service required when returning a vehicle to service after storage depends on the length of non-use and storage conditions. In addition to performing the reverse of the above procedure, make sure the brakes, clutch, throttle and engine stop switch work properly before operating the vehicle. Refer to Chapter Three and evaluate the service intervals to determine which areas require service.

Table 1 FRAME SERIAL NUMBERS

Model	Frame number
1995 models	
GSF600	
U.K., France, Switzerland, Austria	
and Netherlands	GN77A-100001-on
Italy, Belgium and Spain	JS1GN77A000500001-on
GSF600U/600SU	
Germany	GN77B-100001-on
1996 models	
GSF600S	
U.S.A., California and Canada	JS1GN77A T2100001-on
Australia	JS1GN77A000502065-on
GSF600/600S	
U.K., France, Switzerland, Austria	
and Netherlands	GN77A-103184-on
Finland, Norway and Sweden	GN77B-105788-on
Italy, Belgium and Spain	JS1GN77A000501371-on
Brazil	NA
GSF600/600U/600S/600SU	
Germany	GN77B-104385-on
1997 models	
GSF600S	
U.S.A., California and Canada	JS1GN77A V2100001-on
Australia	JS1GN77A000504247-on
GSF600/600S	
U.K., France, Switzerland, Austria	
and Netherlands	GN77A-111124-on
Finland, Norway and Sweden	JS1GN77B000500001-on
Italy, Belgium and Spain	JS1GN77A000504141-on
Brazil	NA
GSF600/600U/600S/600SU	
Germany	GN77B-111684-on
1998 models	
GSF600S	
U.S.A., California and Canada	JS1GN77A W2100001-on
Australia	JS1GN77A000506011-on
GSF600/600S	
U.K., France, Switzerland, Austria	
and Netherlands	GN77A-120060-on
Finland, Norway and Sweden	JS1GN77B000500389-on
Italy, Belgium and Spain	JS1GN77A000506011-on
Brazil	NA
GSF600/600U/600S/600SU	
Germany	GN77B-117365-on
(continued)	

GENERAL INFORMATION

Table 1 FRAME SERIAL NUMBERS (continued)

Model	Frame number
1999 models	
GSF600S	
U.S.A., California and Canada	JS1GN77A X2100001-on
Australia	JS1GN77A000507256-on
GSF600/600S	
U.K., France, Switzerland, Austria and Netherlands	GN77A-134002-on
Finland, Norway and Sweden	JS1GN77B000500703-on
Italy, Belgium and Spain	JS1GN77A000508157-on
Brazil	NA
GSF600/600U/600S/600SU	
Germany	GN77B-123519-on
2000 models	
GSF600	
U.K.	JS1A8112200100001-on
European markets	JS1A8112100100001-on
GSF600S	
U.S.A., California and Canada	JS1GN77A Y2100001-on
Australia	JS1A8111300100001-on
U.K. models	JS1A8111200100001-on
European markets	JS1A8111100100001-on
GSF600U	
European markets	JS1A8212100100001-on
GSF600SU	
European markets	JS1A8211100100001-on

Table 2 VEHICLE DIMENSIONS

1995-1999 models	
Overall length	
Finland, Norway, Sweden and Germany models; 1997-on Switzerland models	2155 mm (84.8 in.)
All models except Finland, Norway, Sweden, Germany and 1997-on Switzerland	2085 mm (82.0 in.)
Overall width	745 mm (29.3 in.)
Overall height	
1995-1999 GSF600	1100 mm (43.3 in.)
1996-1999 GSF600S	1205 mm (47.4 in.)
Seat height	805 mm (31.6 in.)
Wheelbase	1430 mm (56.2 in.)
Ground clearance	125 mm (4.9 in.)
2000 models	
Overall length	
GSF600	2130 mm (83.9 in.)
GSF600S	2060 mm (81.1 in.)
Overall width	770 mm (30.3 in.)
Overall height	
GSF600	1095 mm (43.1)
GSF600S	1220 mm (48.0 in.)
Seat height	790 mm (31.1 in.)
Wheelbase	1440 mm (56.7 in.)
Ground clearance	130 mm (5.1 in.)

Table 3 VEHICLE WEIGHT

Dry	
1995-1997 GSF600	196 kg (432 lb.)
1998-1999 GSF600	196 kg (432 lb.)
2000 GSF600	198 kg (436 lb.)
1996-1999 GSF600S	204 kg (449 lb.)
California models	205 kg (451 lb.)
All models except California	202 kg (445 lb.)
2000 GSF600S	
California models	209 kg (460 lb.)
All models except California	208 kg (458 lb.)

Table 4 DECIMAL AND METRIC EQUIVALENTS

Fractions	Decimal in.	Metric mm	Fractions	Decimal in.	Metric mm
1/64	0.015625	0.39688	33/64	0.515625	13.09687
1/32	0.03125	0.79375	17/32	0.53125	13.49375
3/64	0.046875	1.19062	35/64	0.546875	13.89062
1/16	0.0625	1.58750	9/16	0.5625	14.28750
5/64	0.078125	1.98437	37/64	0.578125	14.68437
3/32	0.09375	2.38125	19/32	0.59375	15.08125
7/64	0.109375	2.77812	39/64	0.609375	15.47812
1/8	0.125	3.1750	5/8	0.625	15.87500
9/64	0.140625	3.57187	41/64	0.640625	16.27187
5/32	0.15625	3.96875	21/32	0.65625	16.66875
11/64	0.171875	4.36562	43/64	0.671875	17.06562
3/16	0.1875	4.76250	11/16	0.6875	17.46250
13/64	0.203125	5.15937	45/64	0.703125	17.85937
7/32	0.21875	5.55625	23/32	0.71875	18.25625
15/64	0.234375	5.95312	47/64	0.734375	18.65312
1/4	0.250	6.35000	3/4	0.750	19.05000
17/64	0.265625	6.74687	49/64	0.765625	19.44687
9/32	0.28125	7.14375	25/32	0.78125	19.84375
19/64	0.296875	7.54062	51/64	0.796875	20.24062
5/16	0.3125	7.93750	13/16	0.8125	20.63750
21/64	0.328125	8.33437	53/64	0.828125	21.03437
11/32	0.34375	8.73125	27/32	0.84375	21.43125
23/64	0.359375	9.12812	55/64	0.859375	22.82812
3/8	0.375	9.52500	7/8	0.875	22.22500
25/64	0.390625	9.92187	57/64	0.890625	22.62187
13/32	0.40625	10.31875	29/32	0.90625	23.01875
27/64	0.421875	10.71562	59/64	0.921875	23.41562
7/16	0.4375	11.11250	15/16	0.9375	23.81250
29/64	0.453125	11.50937	61/64	0.953125	24.20937
15/32	0.46875	11.90625	31/32	0.96875	24.60625
31/64	0.484375	12.30312	63/64	0.984375	25.00312
1/2	0.500	12.70000	1	1.00	25.40000

Table 5 CONVERSION TABLES

Multiply:	By:	To get the equivalent of:
Length		
Inches	25.4	Millimeter
Inches	2.54	Centimeter
Miles	1.609	Kilometer
Feet	0.3048	Meter
	(continued)	

GENERAL INFORMATION

Table 5 CONVERSION TABLES (continued)

Multiply:	By:	To get the equivalent of:
Millimeter	0.03937	Inches
Centimeter	0.3937	Inches
Kilometer	0.6214	Mile
Meter	3.281	Mile
Fluid volume		
U.S. quarts	0.9463	Liters
U.S. gallons	3.785	Liters
U.S. ounces	29.573529	Milliliters
Imperial gallons	4.54609	Liters
Imperial quarts	1.1365	Liters
Liters	0.2641721	U.S. gallons
Liters	1.0566882	U.S. quarts
Liters	33.814023	U.S. ounces
Liters	0.22	Imperial gallons
Liters	0.8799	Imperial quarts
Milliliters	0.033814	U.S. ounces
Milliliters	1.0	Cubic centimeters
Milliliters	0.001	Liters
Torque		
Foot-pounds	1.3558	Newton-meters
Foot-pounds	0.138255	Meters-kilograms
Inch-pounds	0.11299	Newton-meters
Newton-meters	0.7375622	Foot-pounds
Newton-meters	8.8507	Inch-pounds
Meters-kilograms	7.2330139	Foot-pounds
Volume		
Cubic inches	16.387064	Cubic centimeters
Cubic centimeters	0.0610237	Cubic inches
Temperature		
Fahrenheit	(F − 32°) × 0.556	Centigrade
Centigrade	(C × 1.8) + 32	Fahrenheit
Weight		
Ounces	28.3495	Grams
Pounds	0.4535924	Kilograms
Grams	0.035274	Ounces
Kilograms	2.2046224	Pounds
Pressure		
Pounds per square inch	0.070307	Kilograms per square centimeter
Kilograms per square centimeter	14.223343	Pounds per square inch
Kilopascals	0.1450	Pounds per square inch
Pounds per square inch	6.895	Kilopascals
Speed		
Miles per hour	1.609344	Kilometers per hour
Kilometers per hour	0.6213712	Miles per hour

TABLE 6 GENERAL TORQUE SPECIFICATIONS

Fastener size or type	N•m	in.-lb.	ft.-lb.
5 mm screw	4	35	–
5 mm bolt and nut	5	44	–
6 mm screw	9	80	–
	(continued)		

TABLE 6 GENERAL TORQUE SPECIFICATIONS (continued)

Fastener size or type	N•m	in.-lb.	ft.-lb.
6 mm bolt and nut	10	88	–
6 mm flange bolt (8 mm head, small flange)	9	80	–
6 mm flange bolt (10 mm head) and nut	12	106	–
8 mm bolt and nut	22	–	16
8 mm flange bolt and nut	27	–	20
10 mm bolt and nut	35	–	25
10 mm flange bolt and nut	40	–	29
12 mm bolt and nut	55	–	40

Table 7 TECHNICAL ABBREVIATIONS

ABDC	After bottom dead center
ATDC	After top dead center
BBDC	Before bottom dead center
BDC	Bottom dead center
BTDC	Before top dead center
C	Celsius (Centigrade)
cc	Cubic centimeters
cid	Cubic inch displacement
CDI	Capacitor discharge ignition
cu. in.	Cubic inches
DOHC	Dual overhead cam
F	Fahrenheit
ft.	Feet
ft.-lb.	Foot-pounds
gal.	Gallons
H/A	High altitude
hp	Horsepower
in.	Inches
in.-lb.	Inch-pounds
I.D.	Inside diameter
kg	Kilograms
kgm	Kilogram meters
km	Kilometer
kPa	Kilopascals
L	Liter
m	Meter
MAG	Magneto
ml	Milliliter
mm	Millimeter
N•m	Newton-meters
O.D.	Outside diameter
oz.	Ounces
psi	Pounds per square inch
PTO	Power take off
pt.	Pint
qt.	Quart
rpm	Revolutions per minute
TSCC	Twin Swirl Combustion Chambers

GENERAL INFORMATION

Table 8 METRIC TAP AND DRILL SIZES

Metric size	Drill equivalent	Decimal fraction	Nearest fraction
3 × 0.50	No. 39	0.0995	3/32
3 × 0.60	3/32	0.0937	3/32
4 × 0.70	No. 30	0.1285	1/8
4 × 0.75	1/8	0.125	1/8
5 × 0.80	No. 19	0.166	11/64
5 × 0.90	No. 20	0.161	5/32
6 × 1.00	No. 9	0.196	13/64
7 × 1.00	16/64	0.234	15/64
8 × 1.00	J	0.277	9/32
8 × 1.25	17/64	0.265	17/64
9 × 1.00	5/16	0.3125	5/16
9 × 1.25	5/16	0.3125	5/16
10 × 1.25	11/32	0.3437	11/32
10 × 1.50	R	0.339	11/32
11 × 1.50	3/8	0.375	3/8
12 × 1.50	13/32	0.406	13/32
12 × 1.75	13/32	0.406	13/32

CHAPTER TWO

TROUBLESHOOTING

The troubleshooting procedures described in this chapter provide typical symptoms and logical methods for isolating the cause(s). There may be several ways to diagnose a problem, but only a systematic approach can successfully avoid wasted time and possibly unnecessary parts replacement.

Gather as much information as possible to aid in diagnosis. Never assume anything and do not overlook the obvious. Make sure there is fuel in the tank and the spark plug wires are securely attached to the spark plugs.

Learning to recognize symptoms will make troubleshooting easier. In most cases, expensive and complicated test equipment is not needed to determine whether repairs can be performed at home. On the other hand, be realistic and do not start procedures that are beyond your experience and equipment on hand. Many service departments will not take work that involves the reassembly of damaged or abused equipment. If they do, expect the cost to be high. If the motorcycle does require the attention of a professional, describe symptoms and conditions accurately and fully. The more information a technician has, the easier it will be to diagnose the problem.

Proper lubrication, maintenance and periodic tune-ups reduce the chance that problems will occur. However, even with the best of care the motorcycle may require troubleshooting.

OPERATING REQUIREMENTS

An engine needs three basic requirements to run properly: correct air/fuel mixture, compression and

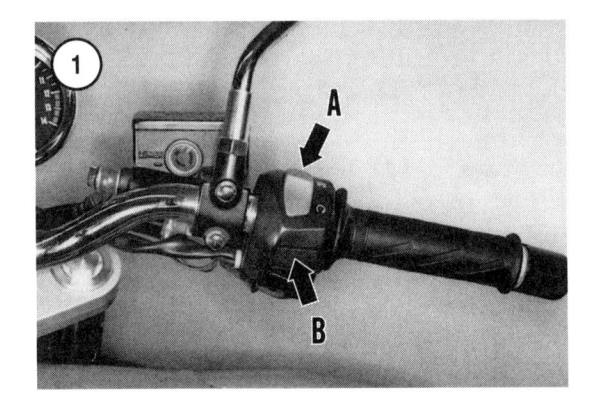

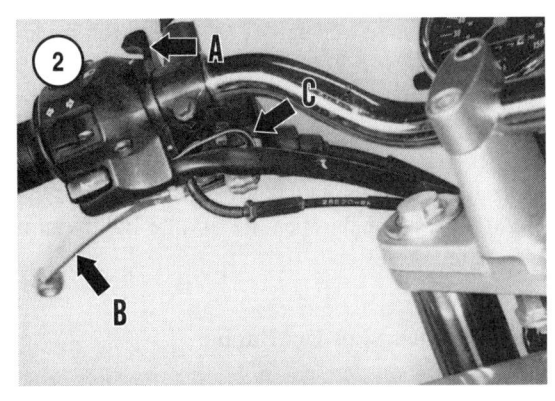

TROUBLESHOOTING

a spark at the proper time. If any one element is missing, the engine will not run. Four-stroke engine operating principles are described in Chapter Four.

If the machine has been sitting for any length of time and refuses to start, check and clean the spark plugs and inspect the fuel delivery system. This includes the fuel tank, fuel valve, fuel pump and fuel lines to the carburetors. Gasoline deposits may have gummed up the carburetor jets and air passages. Gasoline tends to lose potency after standing for long periods. Condensation may contaminate the fuel with water. Drain the old fuel (fuel tank, fuel lines and carburetor) and start with a tank of fresh gasoline.

STARTING THE ENGINE

If the engine refuses to start, refer to the following procedure that best describes the symptom. In all cases, make sure that there is an adequate supply of fuel in the tank.

Starting Notes

1. The ignition and starting system circuits are protected with a switch interlock system. The position of the sidestand and clutch lever (on models with a clutch switch) as well as transmission gear selection affect starting. The engine can only be started if the following conditions are met:
    a. The transmission is in neutral and the clutch is disengaged.
    b. The transmission is in gear, the sidestand is up and the clutch is disengaged.
    c. The engine cannot start when the sidestand is down and the transmission is in gear. It also will not start if the clutch is engaged.
2. Before starting the engine, shift the transmission into NEUTRAL and confirm that the engine stop switch is in the RUN position.
3. Turn the main (ignition) switch to the ON position and confirm the following:
    a. The neutral indicator light is ON (when the transmission is in NEUTRAL).
    b. The engine oil pressure warning light is ON.
4. The engine is now ready to start. Refer to the starting procedure in the section that best meets engine conditions.

CAUTION
*The oil pressure warning light should go out a few seconds after the engine starts. If not, stop the engine **immediately**. Check the oil level as described in Chapter Three. If the oil level is correct, determine whether insufficient oil pressure (Chapter Three) or an electrical problem (Chapter Nine) is the cause.*

Starting a Cold Engine

1. Shift the transmission into NEUTRAL.
2. Move the engine stop switch (A, **Figure 1**) to the RUN position.
3. Turn the ignition switch ON.
4. Pull the choke lever (A, **Figure 2**) all the way rearward to the ON position.
5. Pull the clutch lever (B, **Figure 2**) all the way to the handlebar grip and disengage the clutch.
6. With the throttle completely closed, push the START button (B, **Figure 1**).

7. Once the engine is running, operate the choke lever as required to keep the engine idling at 2000 rpm.
8. Idle the engine for approximately 30 seconds (longer in cold weather), and then push the choke lever all the way forward to the OFF position. If the engine idle is rough, open the throttle lightly until the engine warms up.

Starting a Warm or Hot Engine

1. Shift the transmission into NEUTRAL.
2. Move the engine stop switch (A, **Figure 1**) to the RUN position.
3. Turn the ignition switch to the ON position.
4. Make sure the choke lever (A, **Figure 2**) is all the way forward to the OFF position.
5. Pull the clutch lever (B, **Figure 2**) all the way to the handlebar grip and disengage the clutch.
6. Open the throttle slightly and operate the START button (B, **Figure 1**).

Starting a Flooded Engine

If the engine will not start after a few attempts, it may be flooded. If a gasoline smell is present, the engine may be flooded. To start a flooded engine:
1. Turn the engine stop switch to the RUN position (A, **Figure 1**).
2. Push the choke lever (A, **Figure 2**) forward to the fully OFF position.
3. Pull the clutch lever (B, **Figure 2**) all the way to the handlebar grip and disengage the clutch.
4. Turn the ignition switch ON.

NOTE
If the engine refuses to start, check the carburetor overflow hoses attached to the fittings at the bottom of the float bowls. If fuel runs out the end of a hose(s), a float is stuck open and allowing the carburetor to overfill. If this problem exists, remove the carburetors and correct the problem as described in Chapter Eight.

5. Open the throttle completely and depress the starter button (B, **Figure 1**). If the engine starts, close the throttle quickly. If necessary, operate the throttle to keep the engine running until it smooths out. If the engine does not start, wait 15 seconds and then try to restart the engine by following normal starting procedures. If the engine will not start, refer to *Starting Difficulties* in this chapter.

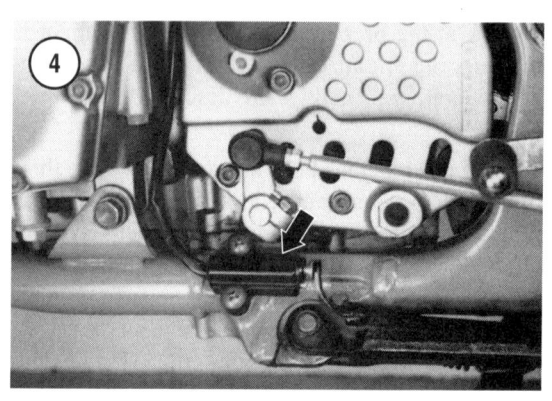

STARTING DIFFICULTIES

If the engine turns over but is difficult to start or will not start at all, perform the following procedure step-by-step. Do each one while remembering the engine operating requirements described in *Operating Requirements* earlier in this chapter. If the engine still will not start, refer to the appropriate troubleshooting procedures which follow in this section.

NOTE
1995-1996 non-U.S.A., California and Canada models are not equipped with a clutch switch.

1. Make sure the choke lever (A, **Figure 2**) is in the correct position. Open the choke for a cold engine, and close it for a warm or hot engine.

TROUBLESHOOTING

necessary, test the engine stop switch as described in Chapter Eight.

6. Make sure the clutch is disengaged and that the clutch switch (C, **Figure 2**) operates properly.

7. Make sure that the sidestand is up and that the sidestand switch (**Figure 4**) operates properly.

8. Make sure all four spark plug wires are secure. Push the spark plug caps and slightly rotate them to clean the electrical connection between the plug and the connector.

9. Perform a spark test as described in this chapter. If there is a strong spark, perform Step 10. If there is no spark or if the spark is very weak, test the ignition system as described in this chapter.

10. Check cylinder compression as described in Chapter Three.

Spark Test

Perform a spark test to determine if the ignition is producing adequate spark. This test can be performed with a spark plug or a spark tester. A spark tester (**Figure 5**) is used as a substitute for the spark plug and allows the spark to be more easily observed between the adjustable air gap. The tool shown is available from Motion Pro (part No. 08-0122).

CAUTION
Before removing the spark plugs, remove the spark plug caps and clean the area around each plug base with compressed air. Dirt that falls into the cylinder will cause rapid piston, piston ring and cylinder wear.

1. Remove the spark plugs from each cylinder as described in Chapter Three.

2. Connect a spark plug wire to a new spark plug (or tester) and touch each spark plug base (or tester) to a good engine ground (**Figure 6**). Position the spark plug so the electrodes can be seen. Position the spark tester so the terminals can be seen.

WARNING
Mount the spark plugs, or spark tester, away from the spark plug holes in the cylinder head so the spark plugs or tester cannot ignite the gasoline vapors in the cylinder. If the engine is flooded, do not perform this test. Fuel

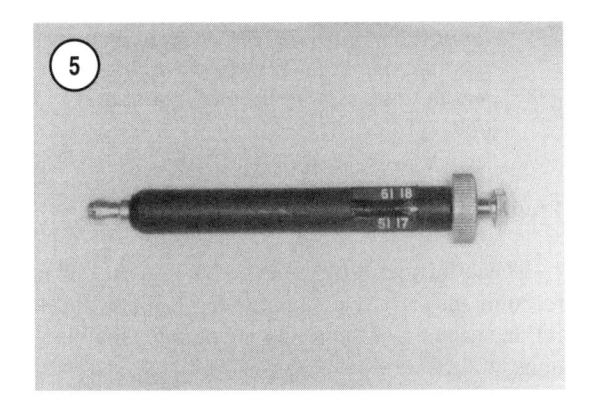

WARNING
Do not use an open flame to check fuel in the tank. A serious explosion is certain to result.

2. Make sure there is fuel in the tank. Open the fuel filler cap and rock the motorcycle. Listen for the fuel sloshing inside the tank. Fill the tank if necessary. Make sure the fuel is in good condition. If in doubt, drain the fuel from the tank, and fill with it with fresh fuel.

3. Make sure the fuel valve (**Figure 3**) is in the ON position. If it is, turn the valve to the RES position to ensure the remaining gas is used.

4. If the cylinders are flooded or if there is a strong smell of gasoline, open the throttle all the way and operate the START button. If the cylinders are severely flooded (fouled or wet spark plugs), remove the spark plugs and dry the base and electrode thoroughly with a soft cloth or with an aerosol electrical contact cleaner. Reinstall the plugs and attempt to start the engine.

5. Make sure the engine stop switch (A, **Figure 1**) is not stuck, working improperly or shorting out. If

that is ejected through the spark plug holes can be ignited by the firing of the spark plugs or spark tester.

3. With the transmission in neutral, turn the ignition switch ON, and move the engine stop switch to its RUN position.

*WARNING
Do not hold the spark plugs, tester, wire or connector. Serious electrical shock may result.*

4. Push the starter button to turn the engine over. A fat blue spark must be evident across the spark plug electrodes or between the tester terminals. Repeat this test for each cylinder.
5. If the spark is good at each spark plug, the ignition system is functioning properly. Check for one or more of the following possible malfunctions:
   a. Obstructed fuel line or fuel filter (models so equipped).
   b. Low engine compression or engine damage.
   c. Flooded engine.
6. If the spark was weak or if there was no spark at one or more plugs, note the following:
   a. If there is no spark at all of the plugs, there may be a problem in the input side of the ignition system: the igniter, signal generator, sidestand switch, clutch switch or neutral switch. Refer to *Ignition System* in this chapter.
   b. If there is no spark at only one spark plug, the spark plug is probably faulty or there is a problem with the spark plug wire or plug cap. Retest with a spark tester or use a new spark plug. If there is still no spark at that one plug, make sure the spark plug cap is installed correctly.
   c. If there is no spark with one ignition group (cylinders No. 1 & 4 or cylinders No. 2 & 3), switch the ignition coils and retest. If there is now spark (both spark plugs), the ignition coil is faulty.
   d. Troubleshoot the ignition system as described in this chapter.

*NOTE
If the engine backfires during starting attempts, the ignition timing may be incorrect. A signal generator rotor, loose signal generator or a defective ignition component will change the ignition timing. Refer to **Ignition System** in this chapter for more information.*

Engine is Difficult to Start

1. Check for fuel flow to the carburetors. If fuel is reaching the carburetors, go to Step 2. If not, check for one or more of the following possible malfunctions:
   a. Clogged fuel tank breather hose.
   b. Clogged or defective fuel valve.
   c. Defective carburetor needle valve.
   d. Clogged fuel hose or filter.
2. Perform the spark test as described in this chapter. Note the following:
   a. If the spark plugs are wet, go to Step 3.
   b. If the spark is weak or if there is no spark, go to Step 4.
   c. If the spark is good, go to Step 5.
3. If the plugs are wet, the engine may be flooded. Check the following:
   a. Flooded carburetors.
   b. Dirty air filter.
   c. Worn or damaged needle valve.
   d. Broken needle valve spring.
   e. Improperly working float.
4. If the spark is weak or if there is no spark, check the following:
   a. Fouled or wet spark plug(s).
   b. Damaged spark plug(s).
   c. Loose or damaged spark plug wire(s).
   d. Loose or damaged spark plug cap(s).
   e. Damaged ignition coil.
   f. Damaged igniter.
   g. Damaged signal generator.
   h. Damaged engine stop switch.
   i. Damaged ignition switch.
   j. Dirty or loose-fitting terminals.
5. If the spark is good, check the following:
   a. Try starting the engine by following normal starting procedures. If the engine does not fire, go to Step 6.
   b. If the engine starts but then stops, check for an inoperative choke, incorrect carburetor adjustment, leaking intake manifolds, or contaminated fuel.

TROUBLESHOOTING

6. If the engine turns over but does not fire, the engine compression is probably low. Check for the following possible malfunctions:
   a. Leaking cylinder head gasket.
   b. Improperly adjusted valve clearance.
   c. Bent or stuck valve.
   d. Worn valve guides or poor valve seating.
   e. Incorrect valve timing.
   f. Worn cylinders and/or pistons rings.
   g. Poor spark plug seating.

Engine Will Not Crank

If the engine will not turn over, check for one or more of the following possible malfunctions:
1. Blown fuse.
2. Discharged battery.
3. Defective starter motor, starter relay or starter switch.
4. Seized piston(s).
5. Seized crankshaft bearings.
6. Broken connecting rod.
7. Locked-up transmission or clutch assembly.
8. Defective starter clutch.

ENGINE PERFORMANCE

Engine Idles Poorly

1. Improperly adjusted valve clearance.
2. Poorly seating valves.
3. Defective valve guides.
4. Worn rocker arms or rocker arm shafts.
5. Excessive spark plug gap.
6. Defective ignition coil.
7. Defective signal generator.
8. Defective igniter.
9. Improper carburetor fuel level.
10. Clogged carburetor jets.
11. Unsynchronized carburetors.

Low or Poor Engine Power

1. Support the motorcycle with the rear wheel off the ground, and then spin the rear wheel by hand. If the wheel spins freely, perform Step 2. If the wheel does not spin freely, check for the following conditions:
   a. Dragging rear brake.
   b. Excessive rear axle tightening torque.
   c. Worn or damaged rear wheel bearings.
   d. Damaged drive chain (swollen O-rings).
2. Check the clutch adjustment and operation. If the clutch slips, refer to *Clutch* in this chapter.
3. If Steps 1 and 2 did not locate the problem, test ride the motorcycle and accelerate lightly. If the engine speed increased according to throttle position, perform Step 4. If the engine speed did not increase, check for one or more of the following problems:
   a. Clogged or damaged air filter.
   b. Restricted fuel flow.
   c. Pinched fuel tank breather hose.
   d. Incorrect choke operation.
   e. Clogged or damaged muffler.
   f. Partially plugged fuel valve vacuum hose.
4. Check for one or more of the following problems:
   a. Low engine compression.
   b. Worn spark plugs.
   c. Fouled spark plug(s).
   d. Incorrect spark plug heat range.
   e. Clogged carburetor jet(s).
   f. Incorrect oil level (too high or too low).
   g. Contaminated oil.
   h. Worn or damaged valve train assembly.
5. If the engine knocks when it is accelerated or when running at high speed, check for one or more of the following possible malfunctions:
   a. Incorrect type of fuel.
   b. Lean carburetor jetting.
   c. Excessive carbon build-up in combustion chamber.
   d. Worn pistons and/or cylinder bores.

Poor Idle or Low Speed Performance

If the engine starts but off-idle performance is poor (engine hesitation, cutting out, etc.), check the following:
1. Improperly adjusted valves.
2. Worn valve seats or valve guides.
3. Check for damaged intake manifolds or loose carburetor/air filter housing hose clamps.
4. Excessive spark plug gap.
5. Perform the spark test described in this chapter.
6. Clogged jets or unsynchronized carburetors.
7. Starter plunger stuck open.

Poor High Speed Performance

1. *Ignition system:*
   a. Spark plug gap too narrow.
   b. Defective igniter.
   c. Defective ignition coil.
   d. Defective signal generator.
2. *Carburetor:*
   a. Clogged air filter element or fuel filter (2000 models).
   b. Clogged fuel hose.
   c. Carburetor fuel level too low.
   d. Clogged main jet, needle jet or main air jet.
   e. Improperly operating throttle valve.
3. *Engine:*
   a. Weak valve springs.
   b. Worm camshafts.
   c. Improper valve timing.

Engine Overheating

1. Carbon deposits on piston crowns.
2. Low oil level.
3. Defective oil pump.
4. Oil not circulating properly.
5. Low carburetor fuel level.
6. Air leaking from intake manifolds.
7. Improper oil used in engine.
8. Dragging brakes.
9. Clutch slipping.

ENGINE NOISES

Often the first evidence of an internal engine problem is a strange noise. A new knocking, clicking or tapping sound may be warning of impending trouble. While engine noises can indicate problems, they are difficult to interpret correctly. Inexperienced mechanics can be seriously misled by them.

Professional mechanics often use a special stethoscope to isolate engine noise. The home mechanic can do nearly as well with an ordinary piece of doweling or a section of small hose. By placing one end in contact with the affected area and the other end to the front of the ear (not directly on the ear), sounds emanating from that area can be heard. At first, the sounds from the engine may be confusing. If possible, have an experienced mechanic help sort out the noises.

Consider the following when troubleshooting engine noises:

1. Knocking or pinging during acceleration may be caused by poor fuel or by the use of a lower-than-recommended octane fuel. Pinging can also be caused by a spark plug with the wrong heat range or carbon build-up in the combustion chamber. Refer to *Spark Plugs* and *Compression Test* in Chapter Three.

2. Slapping or rattling noises at low speed or during acceleration may be caused by excessive piston-to-cylinder clearance (piston slap).

NOTE
Piston slap is easier to detect when the engine is cold, before the pistons have expanded. Once the engine warms up, piston expansion reduces piston-to-cylinder clearance.

3. Knocking or rapping while decelerating is usually caused by excessive rod bearing clearance.

4. Persistent knocking and vibration occurring every crankshaft rotation is usually caused by worn rod or main bearing(s). It can also be caused by broken piston rings or damaged piston pins.

5. A rapid on-off squeal is usually caused by a compression leak around the cylinder head gasket or spark plug(s).

6. Valve train noise is usually caused by the following:
   a. Excessive valve clearance.
   b. Weak or damaged valve springs.
   c. Worn rocker arm or rocker arm shaft.
   d. Worn or burnt camshaft journal.
   e. Excessively worn or damaged camshaft.
   f. Damaged cam chain tensioner.
   g. Worn cam chain and/or cam chain sprockets.
   h. Clogged cylinder oil hole or oil passage.
   i. Excessively worn or damaged cam chain.
7. Clutch noise is usually caused by the following:
   a. Worn splines on the mainshaft or clutch hub.
   b. Worn clutch plate teeth.
   c. Distorted clutch and friction plates.
   d. Worn clutch release bearing.
   e. Weak clutch dampers.

TROUBLESHOOTING

8. Crankshaft noise is usually caused by the following:
   a. Worn crankpin bearings.
   b. Worn or burnt main bearings.
   c. Excessive thrust clearance.
9. Transmission noise is usually caused by the following:
   a. Worn gears.
   b. Worn splines.
   c. Worn primary gear.
   d. Excessively worn bearings.

ENGINE LUBRICATION

An improperly operating engine lubrication system will quickly lead to engine seizure. Check the engine oil level before each ride. If necessary, add oil as described in Chapter Three. Oil pump service is described in Chapter Five.

Oil Consumption High or Engine Smokes Excessively

1. Worn valve guides.
2. Worn or damaged piston rings.

Excessive Engine Oil Leaks

1. Clogged air filter breather hose.
2. Loose engine parts.
3. Damaged gasket sealing surfaces.

Black Smoke

1. Clogged air filter.
2. Incorrect carburetor fuel level (too high).
3. Choke stuck open.
4. Incorrect main jet (too large).

White Smoke

1. Worn valve guide.
2. Worn valve oil seal.
3. Worn piston oil ring.
4. Excessive cylinder and/or piston wear.

Oil Pressure Too High

1. Clogged oil filter.

2. Clogged oil gallery or metering jets.
3. Incorrect type engine oil being used.

Low Oil Pressure

1. Low oil level.
2. Damaged oil pump.
3. Clogged oil strainer screen.
4. Clogged oil filter.
5. Internal oil leakage.
6. Incorrect engine oil being used.

High Oil Pressure

1. Incorrect type engine oil being used.
2. Plugged oil filter, oil gallery or metering jets.

No Oil Pressure

1. Damaged oil pump.
2. Excessively low oil level.
3. Damaged oil pump drive shaft.
4. Damaged oil pump drive sprocket.
5. Incorrect oil pump installation.

Oil Pressure Warning Light Stays On

1. Low oil pressure.
2. No oil pressure.
3. Damaged oil pressure switch.
4. Short circuit in warning light circuit.

Oil Level Too Low

1. Oil level not maintained at correct level.
2. Worn piston rings.
3. Worn cylinder.
4. Worn valve guides.
5. Worn valve stem seals.
6. Piston rings incorrectly installed during engine overhaul.
7. External oil leakage.
8. Oil leaking into the cooling system.

CYLINDER LEAKDOWN TEST

An engine leakdown test locates engine problems from leaking valves; blown head gaskets; or broken, worn or stuck piston rings. A cylinder leakdown test is performed by applying compressed air to a cylinder and then measuring the percent of leakage. A cylinder leakdown tester (**Figure 7**) and an air compressor are required for this test.

Follow the manufacturer's directions along with the following information when performing a cylinder leakdown test.

1. Start and run the engine until it reaches normal operating temperature. Then turn off the engine.
2. Remove the air filter housing. Open and secure the throttle so that it remains in the wide open position.
3. Set the piston for the cylinder being tested to TDC on its compression stroke. See *Valve Clearance Measurement* in Chapter Three.
4. Remove the spark plug as described in Chapter Three.
5. Install the leakdown tester into the cylinder spark plug hole. Connect an air compressor to the tester fitting.

NOTE
The engine may turn over when air pressure is applied to the cylinder. To prevent this from happening, shift the transmission into fifth gear and apply the rear brake.

6. Apply compressed air to the leakdown tester and perform a cylinder leakdown test following the manufacturer's instructions. Read the rate of leakage on the gauge. Record the leakage rate for that cylinder.
7. After recording the leakage rate of the cylinder, listen for air escaping from the engine.
    a. Air leaking through the exhaust pipe points to a leaking exhaust valve.
    b. Air leaking through the carburetor points to a leaking intake valve.
    c. Air leaking through the crankcase breather tube indicates worn piston rings.
8. Repeat Steps 3-7 for the remaining cylinders.
9. Use the following to interpret the results.
    a. For a new or rebuilt engine, a leakage rate of 0 to 5 percent per cylinder is desirable. A leakage rate of 6 to 14 percent is acceptable and means the engine is in good condition.
    b. If testing a used engine, the critical parameter is not each cylinder's actual leakage rate but the difference in the leakage rates between the various cylinders. On a used engine, a difference of 10 percent or less between cylinders is acceptable.
    c. If the leakage rate of any two cylinders differs by more than 10 percent, the engine is in poor condition and further testing is required.

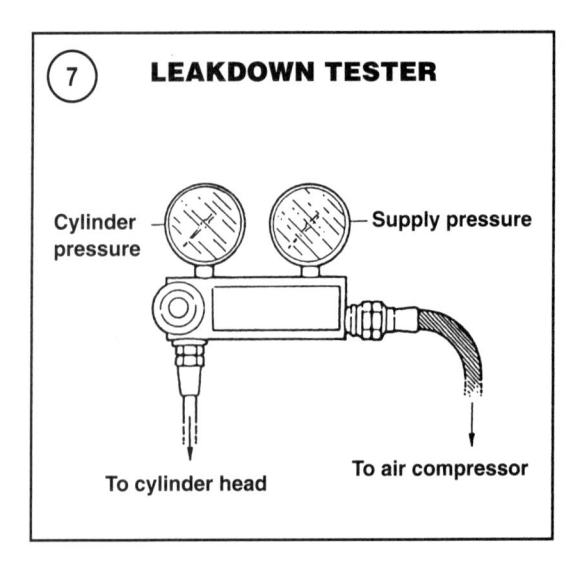

CLUTCH

The two basic clutch troubles are slipping and dragging.

All clutch troubles require partial engine disassembly to identify and cure the problem. Refer to Chapter Six for disassembly/assembly procedures.

Clutch Slipping

If the engine speed increases without an increase in motorcycle speed, the clutch is probably slipping. Some main causes of clutch slipping are:
1. Loose, weak or damaged clutch springs.
2. Worn clutch and friction plates.
3. Incorrectly adjusted clutch.
4. Severely worn clutch hub and/or clutch housing.
5. Incorrectly assembled clutch.
6. Engine oil additives used.

Clutch Drag

If the clutch will not disengage or if the motorcycle creeps with the transmission in gear and the

TROUBLESHOOTING

clutch disengaged, the clutch is dragging. Some main causes of clutch drag are:
1. Excessive clutch lever free play.
2. Warped clutch plates.
3. Damaged clutch lifter assembly.
4. Weak or damaged clutch springs.
5. Engine oil level too high.
6. Incorrect oil viscosity.
7. Engine oil additive being used.
8. Damaged clutch hub and clutch housing splines.

TRANSMISSION

Transmission symptoms are sometimes hard to distinguish from clutch symptoms. Common transmission troubles and their causes are listed below. Refer to Chapter Seven for transmission service procedures. Prior to working on the transmission, make sure the clutch and gearshift linkage assembly are not causing the trouble.

Difficult Shifting

1. Incorrect clutch adjustment.
2. Incorrect clutch operation.
3. Damaged shift cam.
4. Bent shift fork(s).
5. Damaged shift fork guide pin(s).
6. Bent shift fork shaft(s).
7. Bent shift spindle.
8. Damaged shift drum grooves.
9. Worn gearshift pawl.

Jumps Out Of Gear

1. Loose or damaged shift drum stopper arm.
2. Bent or damaged shift fork(s).
3. Bent shift fork shaft(s).
4. Damaged shift drum grooves.
5. Worn gear dogs or slots.
6. Broken shift shaft return springs or stopper spring.
7. Worn gearshift pawl.

Incorrect Shift Lever Operation

1. Bent shift pedal or linkage.
2. Stripped shift pedal splines.
3. Damaged shift pedal linkage.

Excessive Gear Noise

1. Worn or damaged transmission bearings.
2. Worn or damaged gears.
3. Excessive gear backlash.

FUEL SYSTEM

Many riders automatically assume that the carburetors are at fault when the engine does not run properly. While fuel system problems are not uncommon, carburetor adjustment is seldom the answer. In many cases, adjusting the carburetors only compounds the problem by making the engine run worse.

Start fuel system troubleshooting at the fuel tank and work through the system, reserving the carburetor assembly as the final point. Most fuel system problems result from an empty fuel tank, a plugged fuel filter or fuel valve, or sour fuel.

Fuel system troubleshooting is covered thoroughly in *Engine Is Difficult To Start, Poor Idle or Low Speed Performance* and *Poor High Speed Performance* earlier in this chapter.

The carburetor starter system can also present problems. A starter valve stuck closed will show up as a hard starting problem. One that sticks open will result in a flooding condition. Check starter valve operation by moving the choke lever back and forth by hand. The starter valve should move freely without binding or sticking in one position. If necessary, remove the starter valve as described in *Carburetor Disassembly* in Chapter Eight. Inspect its plunger and spring for severe wear or damage.

DRIVETRAIN NOISE

This section deals with noises in the drive chain, clutch and transmission. While some drivetrain noises have little meaning, abnormal noises indicate a developing problem. The difficulty is recognizing the difference between a normal and an abnormal noise. By maintaining the motorcycle and being attentive, one should become accustomed to the normal noises that occur during engine starting and when riding. Investigate any new noise, no matter how minor.

1. *Drive chain noise*—A low-pitched, continuous whining sound can be considered normal. The noise can vary, depending on the speed of the motorcycle and the terrain. The level of lubrication, wear (both chain and sprockets) and alignment also affect drive chain noise. When checking for an abnormal drive chain noise, consider the following:
   a. *Inadequate lubrication*—A dry chain gives off a loud whining sound. Clean and lubricate the drive chain at regular intervals; see Chapter Three.
   b. *Incorrect drive chain adjustment*—Check and adjust the drive chain as described in Chapter Three.
   c. *Worn drive chain*—Check the drive chain for wear at regular intervals. Replace a chain when its overall length reaches the wear limit specified in Chapter Three.
   d. *Worn or damaged sprockets*—Worn or damaged engine and rear sprockets accelerate drive chain wear. Inspect both sprockets carefully as described in Chapter Three.
   e. *Worn drive chain guide or swing arm slider*—A damaged or worn chain guide or slider allows the drive chain to contact the swing arm or frame. Drive chain wear will be rapid and damage to the frame or swing arm possibly severe. A new, regular clicking or grinding noise may point to a worn chain guide or slider. Inspect them regularly. Replace a worn guide or slider before the drive chain wears through and causes expensive secondary damage.

2. *Clutch noise*—Investigate any noise that develops in the clutch. First, drain the engine oil. Check the oil for bits of metal or clutch plate material. If the oil looks and smells normal, remove the clutch cover and the clutch (Chapter Six). Check for the following:
   a. Worn or damaged clutch housing gear teeth.
   b. Excessive clutch housing axial play.
   c. Excessive clutch housing-to-friction plate clearance.
   d. Excessive clutch housing gear-to-primary drive gear backlash.
   e. Worn splines on the mainshaft or hub.
   f. Distorted clutch or friction plates.
   g. Worn clutch release bearing.
   h. Weakened clutch dampers.

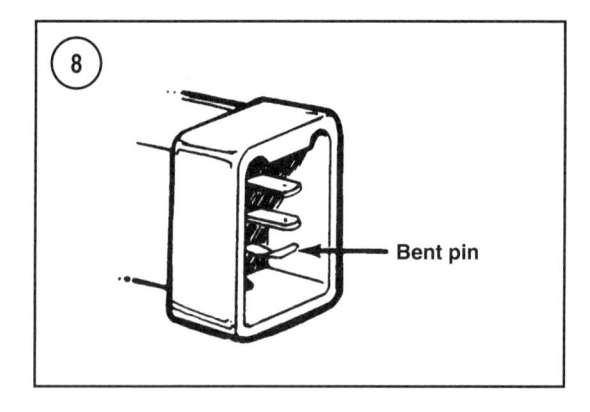

3. *Transmission noise check*—The transmission typically exhibits more normal noises than the clutch. However, investigate any new transmission noise. Drain the engine oil into a clean container. Wipe a small amount of oil on a finger and rub your finger and thumb together. Check for the presence of metallic particles. Inspect the drain container for signs of water separation from the oil. Transmission noises can be caused by:
   a. Insufficient engine oil level.
   b. Contaminated engine oil.
   c. Engine oil viscosity too thin. A thin oil raises the transmission operating temperature.
   d. Worn transmission gear(s).
   e. Chipped or broken transmission gear(s).
   f. Excessive transmission gear side play.
   g. Worn or damaged crankshaft-to-transmission bearing(s).

ELECTRICAL TROUBLESHOOTING

This section describes the basics of electrical troubleshooting, the use of test equipment and the basic test procedures when using the various pieces of test equipment.

Electrical troubleshooting can be very time-consuming and frustrating without proper knowledge and a suitable plan. Refer to the wiring diagrams at the end of the book for component and connector identification. Determine how a circuit should work by tracing the current path from the power source through the circuit components to ground. Also check any circuits that share the same fuse, ground or switch. If the other circuits work properly and the shared wiring is in good condition, the problem must be in the wiring used only by the suspect circuit. If all related circuits are faulty at the

TROUBLESHOOTING

Figure 9 Loose connector

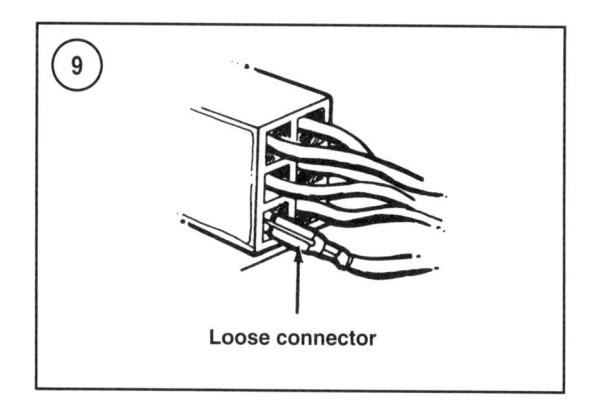

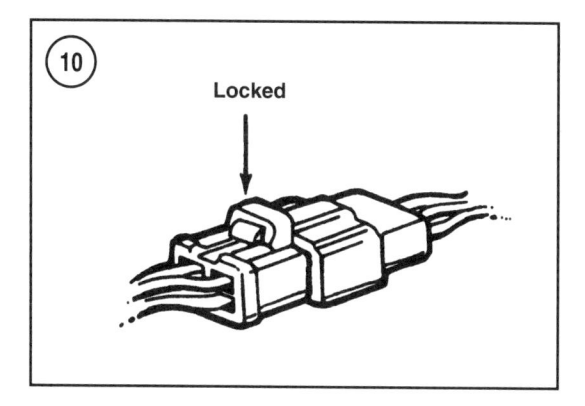

Figure 10 Locked

same time, the probable cause is a poor ground connection or a blown fuse(s).

As with all troubleshooting procedures, analyze typical symptoms in a systematic manner. Never assume anything and do not overlook the obvious like a blown fuse or an electrical connector that has separated. Test the simplest and most obvious items first, and try to test components at easily accessible points on the motorcycle.

Preliminary Checks and Precautions

Prior to starting any electrical troubleshooting procedure perform the following:

1. Check the main fuse (Chapter Nine). If the fuse is blown, replace it.

2. Check the individual fuses mounted in the fuse box (Chapter Nine). Remove the suspected fuse. Replace it if it is blown.

3. Inspect the battery. Make sure it is fully charged, and that the battery leads are clean and securely attached to the battery terminals. Refer to *Battery* in Chapter Three.

4. Disconnect each electrical connector in the suspect circuit. Check metal pins on the male side of the electrical connector. They should be clean and straight. A bent pin (**Figure 8**) will not connect to its mate in the female end of the connector, causing an open circuit.

5. Check each female end of the connector. Make sure the female terminal on the end of each wire (**Figure 9**) is pushed all the way into the plastic housing. If not, carefully push them in with a narrow blade screwdriver.

6. Check all electrical wires where they enter the individual metal terminals in both the male and female plastic housings.

7. Make sure all electrical terminals within the connector are clean and free of corrosion. Clean, if necessary, and pack the connectors with a dielectric grease.

NOTE
Dielectric grease is a special grease that can be used on electrical components such as connectors and battery connections. Dielectric grease can be purchased at automotive part stores.

8. After all fuses, connectors and wires are checked out, push the connector halves together. Make sure the connectors are fully engaged and locked together (**Figure 10**).

9. Never pull on the electrical wires when disconnecting an electrical connector. Pull only on the connector's plastic housing.

NOTE
Always consider electrical connectors the weak link in the electrical system. Dirty, loose-fitting and corroded connectors cause numerous electrical related problems. When troubleshooting an electrical problem, carefully inspect the connectors and wiring harness.

NOTE
If bulbs burn out frequently, the cause may be excessive vibration, loose connections that permit sudden current surges or the installation of the wrong type of bulb.

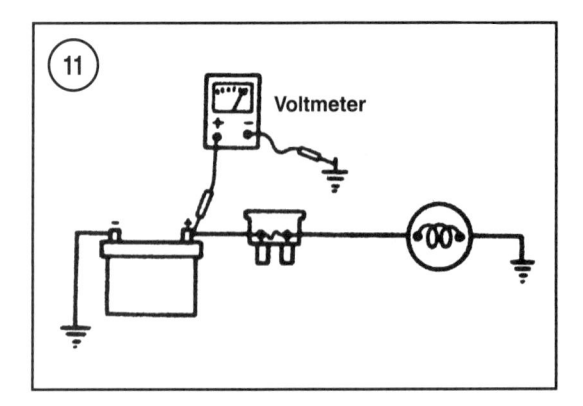

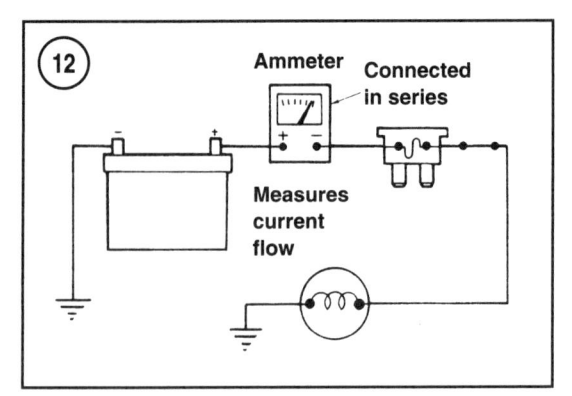

10. Most light and ignition problems are caused by loose or corroded ground connections. Check these before replacing a blown bulb or electrical component.

11. Never use a self-powered test light on circuits that contain solid-state devices. The solid-state devices may be damaged.

TEST EQUIPMENT

Test Light or Voltmeter

A test light can be constructed from a 12-volt light bulb with a pair of test leads carefully soldered to the bulb. To check for battery voltage (12 volts) in a circuit, attach one lead to ground and the other lead to various points along the circuit. Where battery voltage is present the light bulb will light.

A voltmeter is used in the same manner as the test light to find out if voltage is present in any given circuit. The voltmeter, unlike the test light, also indicates how much voltage is present at each test point. When using a voltmeter, attach the red lead to the component or wire to be checked and the negative lead to a good ground (**Figure 11**).

Ammeter

An ammeter measures the flow of current (amps) in a circuit (**Figure 12**). When connected in series in the circuit, the ammeter determines if current is flowing through the circuit and if that current flow is excessive because of a short in the circuit. Current flow is often referred to as current draw. Comparing actual current draw in the circuit or component to the manufacturer's specified current draw provides useful diagnostic information.

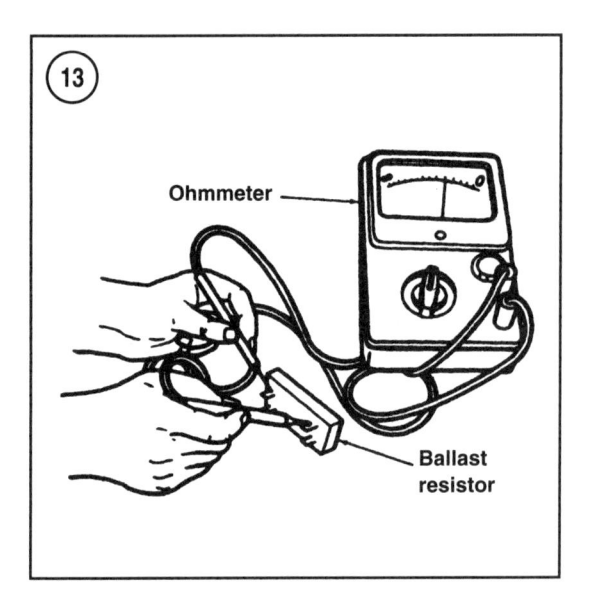

Self-powered Test Light

A self-powered test light can be constructed from a 12-volt light bulb, a pair of test leads and a 12-volt battery. When the test leads are touched together the light bulb should go on.

Use a self-powered test light as follows:
1. Touch the test leads together to make sure the light bulb goes on. If not, correct the problem prior to using it in a test procedure.
2. Disconnect the motorcycle's battery or remove the fuse(s) that protects the circuit to be tested.
3. Select two points within the circuit where there should be continuity.
4. Attach one lead of the self-powered test light to each point.

TROUBLESHOOTING

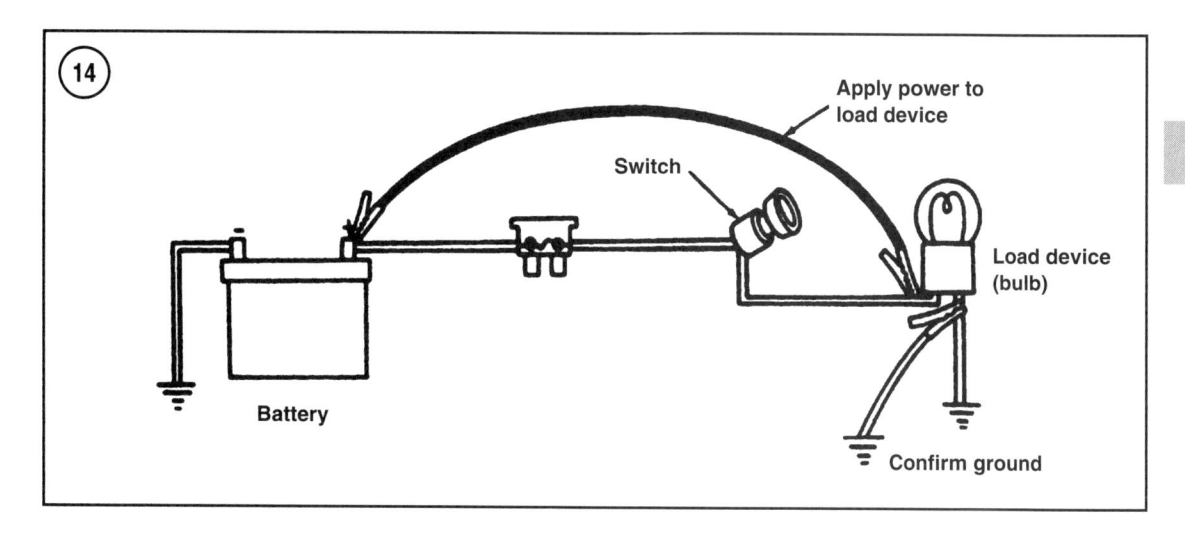

Figure 14

- Apply power to load device
- Switch
- Load device (bulb)
- Battery
- Confirm ground

5. If there is continuity, the self-powered test light bulb will come on.

6. If there is no continuity, the self-powered test light bulb will not come on, indicating an open circuit.

Ohmmeter

The ohmmeter measures the resistance (in ohms) to current flow in a circuit or component. Like the self-powered test light, an ohmmeter contains its own power source and should not be connected to a live circuit.

Ohmmeters may be analog type (needle scale) or digital type (LCD or LED readout). Both types of ohmmeters have a switch which allows the user to select different resistance ranges. The analog ohmmeter also has a set-adjust control which is used to zero or calibrate the meter (digital ohmmeters do not require calibration).

Use an ohmmeter by connecting its test leads to the terminals or leads of the circuit or component to be tested (**Figure 13**). An analog meter must be calibrated by touching the test leads together and turning the set-adjust knob until the meter needle reads zero. When the leads are uncrossed, the needle should move to the other end of the scale indicating infinite resistance.

During a continuity test, a reading of infinity indicates that there is an open in the circuit or component. A reading of zero indicates continuity or a closed circuit; that is, there is no measurable resistance in the circuit or component being tested. If the meter needle falls between these two ends of the scale, the reading indicates the actual resistance to current flow that is present. To determine the resistance, multiply the meter reading by the ohmmeter scale. For example, a meter reading of 5 multiplied by the R × 1000 scale is 5000 ohms of resistance.

CAUTION
Never connect an ohmmeter to a circuit which has power applied to it. Always disconnect the negative battery cable before using an ohmmeter.

Jumper Wire

A jumper wire is a simply way to bypass a potential problem and isolate it to a particular point in a circuit. If a faulty circuit works properly with a jumper wire installed, an open exists between the two jumper points in the circuit.

To troubleshoot with a jumper wire, first use the wire to determine if the problem is on the ground side or the load side of a device. In the example shown in **Figure 14**, test the ground by connecting a jumper between the lamp and a good ground. If the lamp comes on, the problem is the connection between the lamp and ground. If the lamp does not come on with the jumper installed, the lamp's connection to ground is good, so the problem is between the lamp and the power source.

To isolate the problem, connect the jumper between the battery and the lamp. If it comes on, the problem is between these two points. Next, connect the jumper between the battery and the fuse side of the switch. If the lamp comes on, the switch is good.

By successively moving the jumper from one point to another, the problem can be isolated to a particular place in the circuit.

When using a jumper wire always install an inline fuse/fuse holder (available at most auto supply stores or electronic supply stores) to the jumper wire. Never use a jumper wire across any load (a component that is connected and turned on). This would result in a direct short and will blow the fuse(s).

Pay attention to the following when using a jumper wire:

1. Make sure the jumper wire gauge (thickness) is the same as that used in the circuit being tested. Smaller gauge wire will rapidly overheat and could melt.
2. Install insulated boots over alligator clips. This prevents accidental grounding, sparks or possible shock when working in close quarters.
3. Jumper wires are temporary test measures only. Do not leave a jumper wire installed as a permanent solution. This creates a severe fire hazard that could easily lead to complete loss of the motorcycle.

BASIC TEST PROCEDURES

Voltage Testing

Unless otherwise specified, all voltage tests are made with the electrical connector still connected. Insert the test leads into the backside of the connector and make sure the test lead touches the electrical wire or metal terminal within the connector housing. If the test lead only touches the wire insulation, a false reading will result.

Always check both sides of the connector, as one side may be loose or corroded, thus preventing electrical flow through the connector. This type of test can be performed with a test light or a voltmeter. A voltmeter gives the best results.

NOTE
If using a test light, it does not make any difference which test lead is attached to ground.

1. Attach the voltmeter's negative test lead to a good ground (bare metal). Make sure the part used for ground is not insulated with a rubber gasket or rubber grommet.

2. Attach the voltmeter positive test lead to the point (an electrical connector, for example) being tested (**Figure 11**).
3. Turn the ignition switch ON. If using a test light, the test light will come on if voltage is present. If using a voltmeter, note the voltage reading. The reading should be within 1 volt of battery voltage (12 volts). If the voltage is 11 volts or less, there is a problem in the circuit.

Voltage Drop Test

Since resistance causes voltage to drop, resistance can be determined in an active circuit using a voltmeter. This is called a voltage drop test. A voltage drop test measures the difference between the voltage at the beginning of the circuit and the available voltage at the end of the circuit while the circuit is operating. If the circuit has no resistance, there is no voltage drop and the voltmeter indicates 0 volts. The greater the resistance in a circuit, the greater the voltage drop reading. A voltage drop of 1 or more volts indicates that a circuit has excessive resistance.

It is important to remember that a 0 reading on a voltage drop test is good. Battery voltage, on the other hand, indicates an open circuit. A voltage drop test is an excellent way to check the condition of solenoids, relays, battery cables and other high-current electrical components.

1. Connect the voltmeter positive test lead to the end of the wire or switch closest to the battery.
2. Connect the voltmeter negative test lead to the other end of the wire or switch (**Figure 15**).
3. Turn the components on in the circuit.
4. The voltmeter should indicate 0 volts. If there is a drop of 1 volt or more, there is a problem within the circuit. A voltage drop reading of 12 volts indicates an open in the circuit.

Peak Voltage Tests (2000 models)

Peak voltage tests check the voltage output of the ignition coils and signal generator at normal cranking speed. These tests make it possible to identify ignition system problems quickly and accurately.

Peak voltage test results are based on the use of the Suzuki multicircuit tester (part No. 09900-25008) with the peak voltage adapter. If

TROUBLESHOOTING

Voltage drop (15) — Battery

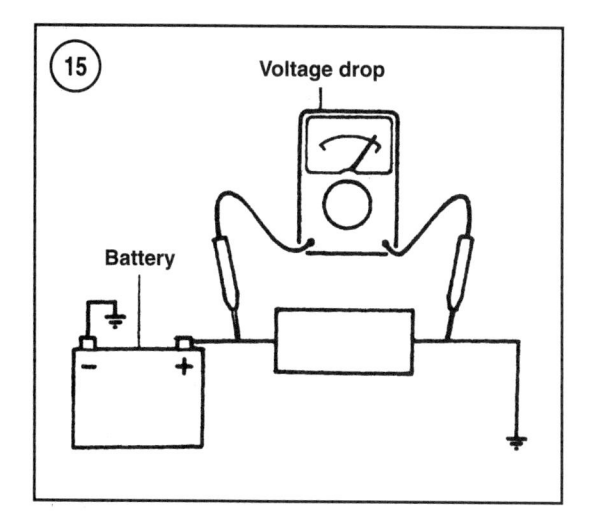

these tools are not available, refer testing to a Suzuki dealership.

WARNING
High voltage is present during ignition system operation. Do not touch ignition components, wires or test leads while cranking or running the engine.

NOTE
*All peak voltage specifications are **minimum** values. If the measured voltage meets or exceeds the specification, the test results are satisfactory. On some components, the voltage may greatly exceed the minimum specification.*

Continuity Test

A continuity test is used to determine the integrity of a circuit, wire or component. A circuit has continuity if it forms a complete circuit; that is, if there are no opens in either the electrical wires or components. An open circuit, on the other hand, has no continuity.

This type of test can be performed with a self-powered test light or an ohmmeter. An ohmmeter gives the best results. If using an analog ohmmeter, calibrate the meter by touching the leads together and turning the calibration knob until the meter reads zero.

1. Disconnect the negative battery cable.
2. Attach one test lead (test light or ohmmeter) to one end of the part of the circuit to be tested.
3. Attach the other test lead to the other end of the part of the circuit to be tested.
4. The self-powered test light comes on if there is continuity. An ohmmeter reads 0 or very low resistance if there is continuity. A reading of infinite resistance indicates no continuity; the circuit is open.

Testing for a Short with a Self-powered Test Light or Ohmmeter

1. Disconnect the negative battery cable.
2. Remove the blown fuse from the fuse panel.
3. Connect one test lead of the test light or ohmmeter to the load side (battery side) of the fuse terminal in the fuse panel.
4. Connect the other test lead to a good ground (bare metal). Make sure the part used for a ground is not insulated with a rubber gasket or rubber grommet.
5. With the self-powered test light or ohmmeter attached to the fuse terminal and ground, wiggle the wiring harness relating to the suspect circuit at 6 in. (15.2 cm) intervals. Start next to the fuse panel and work away from the fuse panel. Watch the self-powered test light or ohmmeter while progressing along the harness.
6. If the test light blinks or the needle on the ohmmeter moves, there is a short-to-ground at that point in the harness.

Testing For a Short with a Test Light or Voltmeter

1. Remove the blown fuse from the fuse panel.
2. Connect the test light or voltmeter across the fuse terminals in the fuse panel. Turn the ignition switch on and check for battery voltage (12 volts).
3. With the test light or voltmeter attached to the fuse terminals, wiggle the wiring harness relating to the suspect circuit at 6 in. (15.2 cm) intervals. Start next to the fuse panel and work away from the panel. Watch the test light or voltmeter while progressing along the harness.
4. If the test light blinks or if the needle on the voltmeter moves, there is a short-to-ground at that point in the harness.

CHAPTER TWO

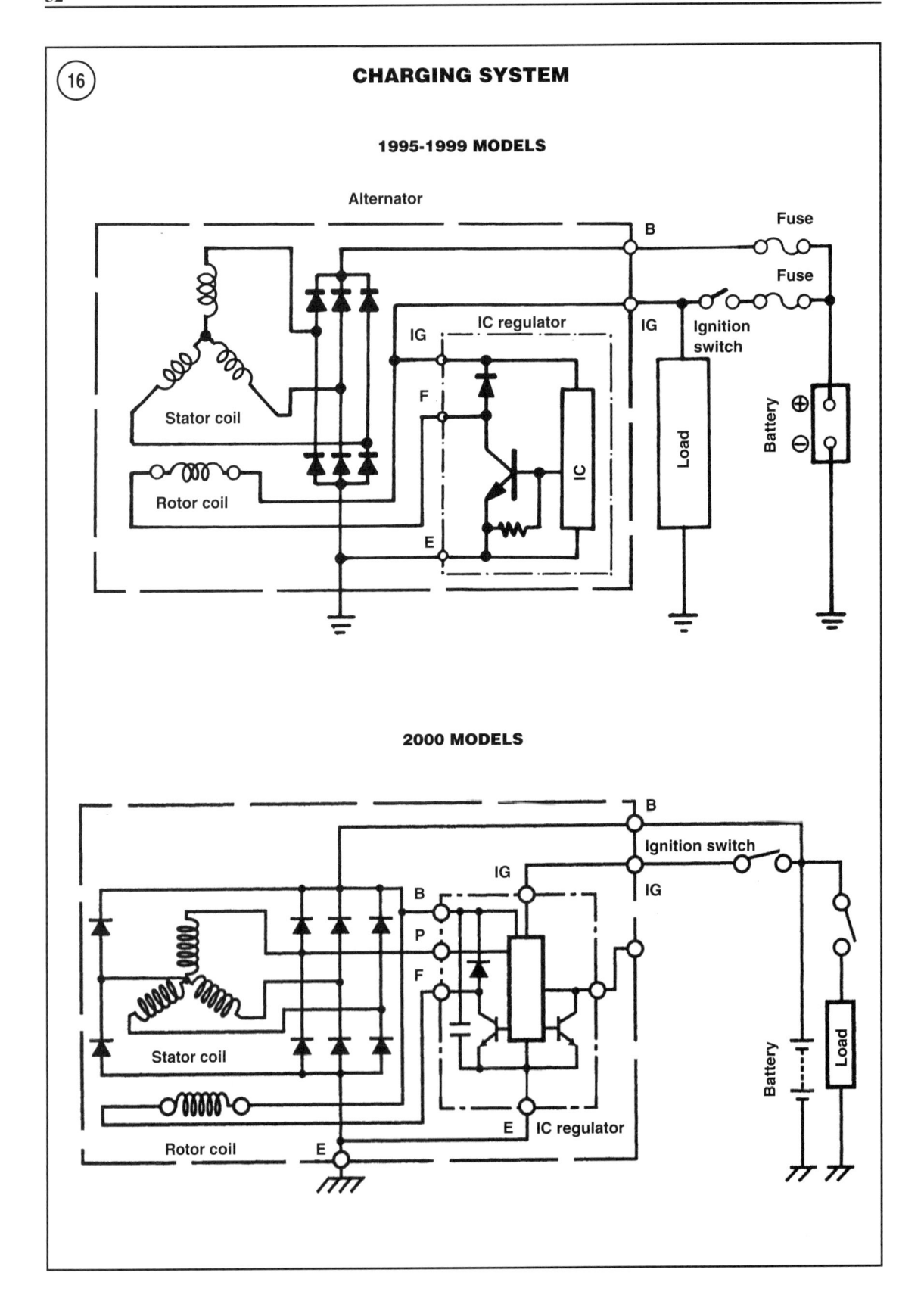

CHARGING SYSTEM

1995-1999 MODELS

2000 MODELS

TROUBLESHOOTING

CHARGING SYSTEM

The charging system consists of the battery, alternator, solid-state voltage regulator and rectifier (**Figure 16**). A 30-amp main fuse protects the circuit. Alternating current generated by the alternator is rectified to direct current. The voltage regulator maintains the voltage to the battery and electrical loads (for example, lights and ignition) at a constant voltage regardless of variations in engine speed and load.

The basic charging system complaints are:
1. Battery discharging.
2. Battery overcharging.

Battery Discharging

Before testing the charging system, make sure the battery is in good condition and fully charged. If necessary, inspect and charge the battery as described in Chapter Three.
1. Check all of the charging system connections. Make sure they are tight and free of corrosion.
2. Perform the *Current Draw Test* described in Chapter Nine. Current draw should be less than 1 mA. If it exceeds 1 mA, perform the following:
   a. Check for loose or disconnected connectors.
   b. Check for a short in the wiring harness as described in *Current Draw Test* in Chapter Nine.
   c. If neither of these conditions exists, the battery is faulty. Replace the battery and retest.
3. Perform the *Regulated Voltage Test* described in Chapter Nine.
   a. If the measurement is within specification, the battery is faulty. Replace the battery.
   b. If regulated voltage is outside the specified range, perform Step 4.

NOTE
Stator and rotor removal requires special tools and a press. If these components require replacement, have the procedures performed by a Suzuki dealership.

4. Check the continuity of the stator coil and rotor coil as described in *Alternator Testing* in Chapter Nine. If either unit does not have continuity, it must be replaced.
5. Measure the diameter of the alternator slip ring as described in *Alternator Testing* in Chapter Nine. Replace the rotor if the slip ring is worn to the wear limit.
6. Measure the length of the brushes as described in *Brush Inspection* in Chapter Nine. Replace the brush assembly if worn to the wear limit.
7. Inspect the alternator rectifier as described in *Alternator Testing* in Chapter Nine. Replace the rectifier if it is defective.
8. Inspect the IC regulator as described in Chapter Nine. Replace the IC regulator if it is defective.
9. Inspect the wiring for a short or for loose and/or dirty connectors.
10. If the charging system is not the problem, replace the battery.

Battery Overcharging

If the battery is overcharging, perform the following test. Make sure the battery is in good condition and fully charged. If necessary, inspect the battery as described in Chapter Three.
1. Test the IC regulator as described in Chapter Nine. Replace it if it is defective.
2. Inspect the battery as described in Chapter Three. Replace the battery if it is defective.
3. Check for a dirty or loose alternator connector.

IGNITION SYSTEM

All models are equipped with a transistorized ignition system (**Figure 17** and **Figure 18**). This solid state system uses no contact breaker points or other moving parts.

Refer to the wiring diagrams at the end of this book and the appropriate figure for specific model and year.

Because of the solid state design, problems with the system are rare. If a problem occurs, it generally causes a weak spark or no spark at all. An ignition system with a weak spark or no spark is relatively easy to troubleshoot. It is difficult, however, to troubleshoot an ignition system that only malfunctions when the engine is hot or under load.

Prior to troubleshooting the ignition system, perform the following:
1. Check the battery to make sure it is fully charged and in good condition. A weak battery will result in a slower engine cranking speed.
2. Perform the spark test as described in this chapter. Then refer to the appropriate ignition system complaint.

IGNITION SYSTEM (1995-1999 MODELS)

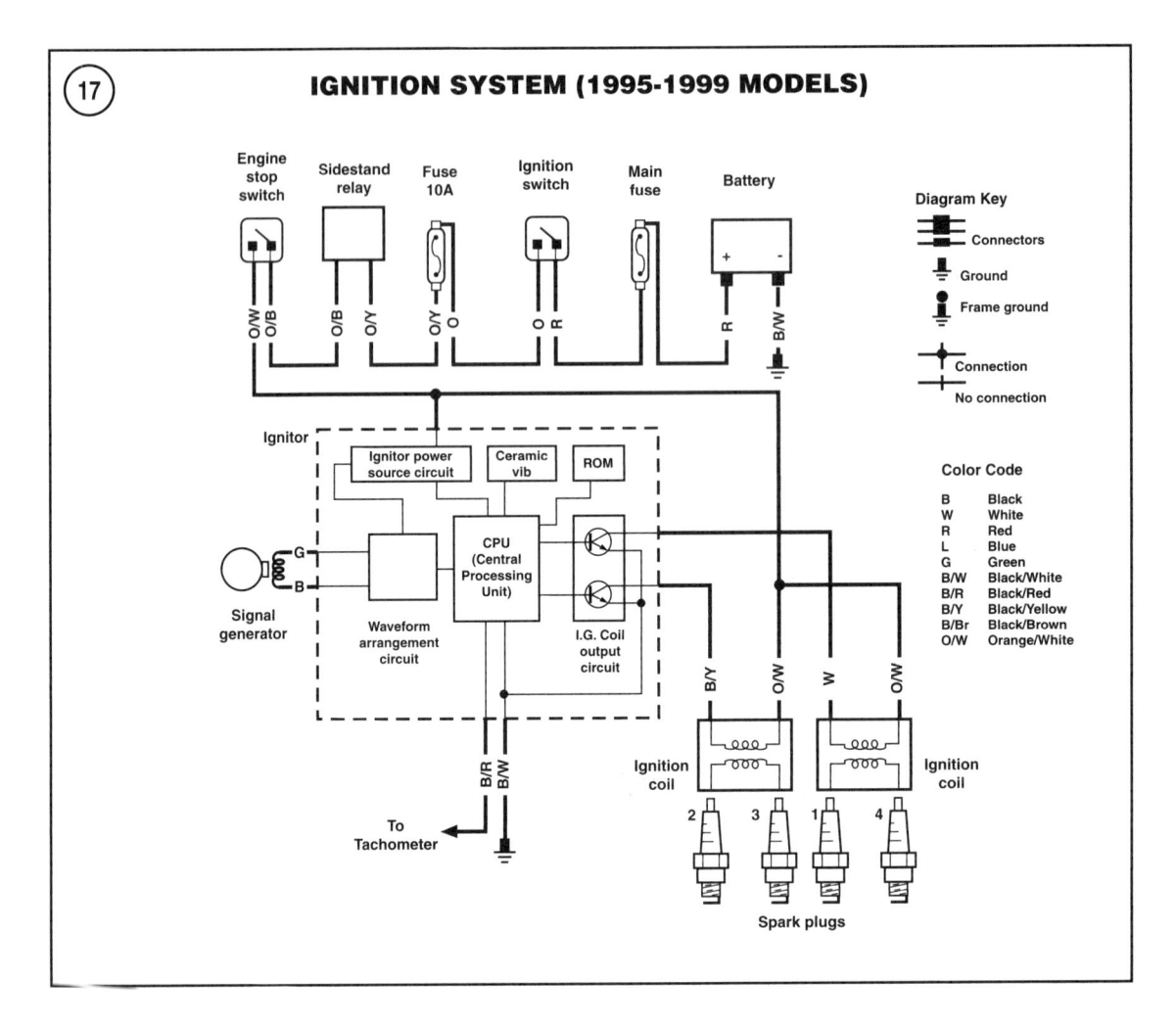

3. Because a loose or dirty electrical connector can prevent the ignition system from operating properly, check the connector terminals in the ignition circuit. For additional information, refer to *Electrical Troubleshooting* earlier in this chapter.

No Spark at All Four Spark Plugs (1995-1999 models)

1. Check for dirty or loose-fitting connector terminals as previously described. Clean and repair them as required.
2. Perform the *Input Voltage Test* described in Chapter Nine. If the input voltage is not within specification, check for the following:
   a. Faulty ignition switch.
   b. Faulty sidestand relay.
   c. Faulty engine stop switch.
   d. Broken wiring harness or faulty connector.

3. Measure the resistance of the signal generator as described in Chapter Nine. Replace the signal generator if the resistance is outside the specified range.
4. Check the primary and secondary resistance of each ignition coil. Replace them if necessary.
5. The igniter unit may be faulty. Have it tested by a Suzuki dealership.

No Spark at Two Cylinders (1995-1999 models)

The No. 1 and No. 4 cylinders share one ignition coil; the No. 2 and No. 3 cylinders share the other. If only one spark plug fails to fire, that spark plug or the spark plug wire is faulty.

1. If the spark test shows that there is spark at two cylinders that share the same ignition coil, switch the ignition coils and repeat the spark test. If the in-

TROUBLESHOOTING

IGNITION SYSTEM (2000 MODELS)

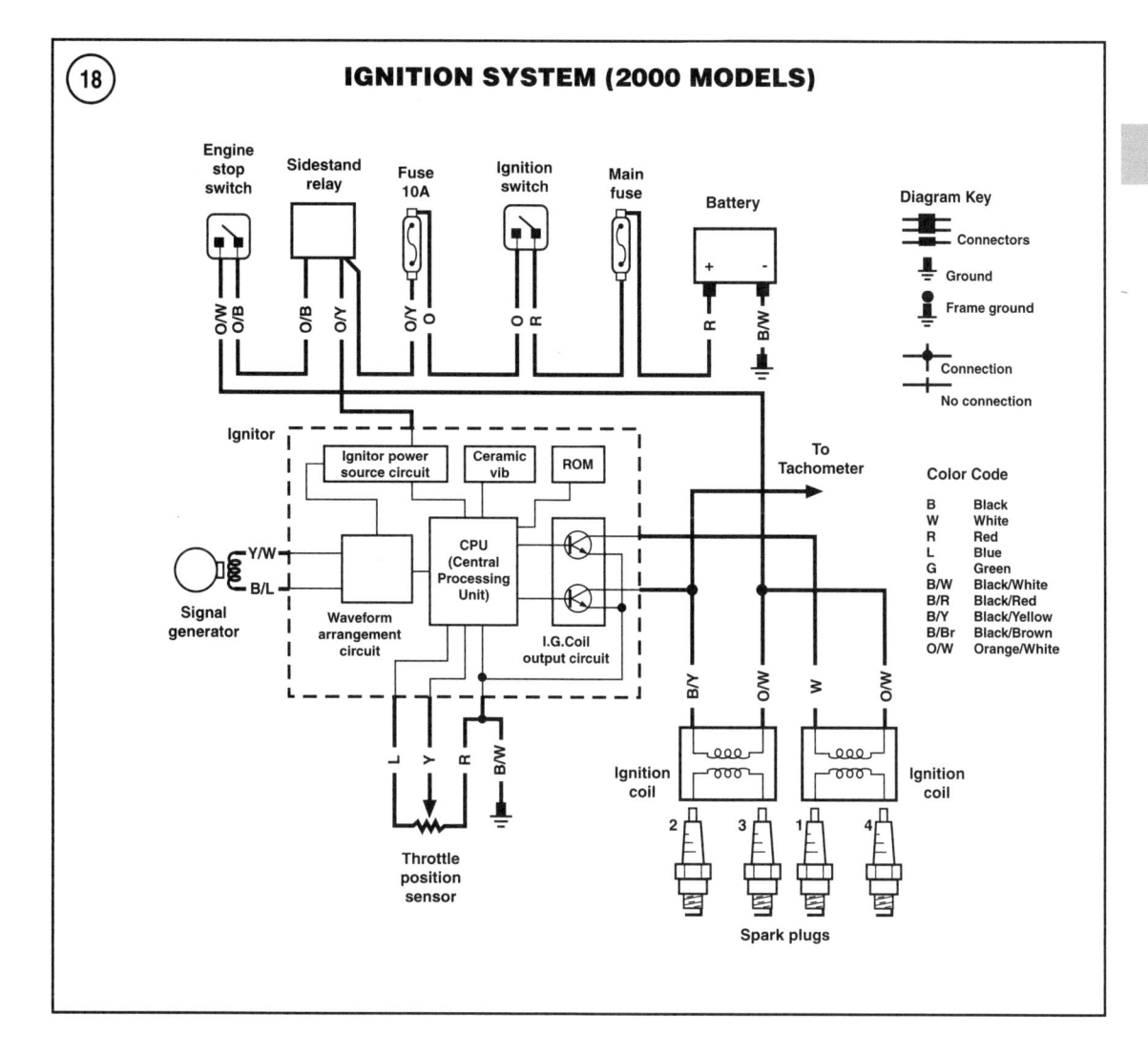

operative cylinders now have spark, replace the original ignition coil.

2. The igniter unit may be faulty. Have it tested by a Suzuki dealership.

No Spark or Weak Spark (2000 models)

1. Check for dirty or loose-fitting connector terminals as previously described. Clean and repair them as required.
2. Perform the *Input Voltage Test* described in Chapter Nine. If the input voltage is not within specification, check for the following:
    a. Faulty ignition switch.
    b. Faulty turn signal/sidestand relay.
    c. Faulty engine stop switch.
    d. Broken wiring harness or faulty connector.

3. Perform the *Ignition Coil Primary Peak Voltage* test described in Chapter Nine.
    a. If the primary peak voltage is within specification, inspect the spark plugs and spark plug wires.
    b. If the primary peak voltage is out if specification, proceed to Step 4.

4. Inspect the ignition coil by measuring the ignition coil resistance as described in Chapter Nine. Replace the ignition coil if it is out of specification.

5. Check the signal generator primary peak voltage and the signal generator resistance as described in Chapter Nine. Replace the signal generator if it is faulty.

6. The igniter unit may be faulty. Have it tested by a Suzuki dealership.

STARTING SYSTEM (1995-1996 NON-U.S.A, CALIFORNIA AND CANADA MODELS)

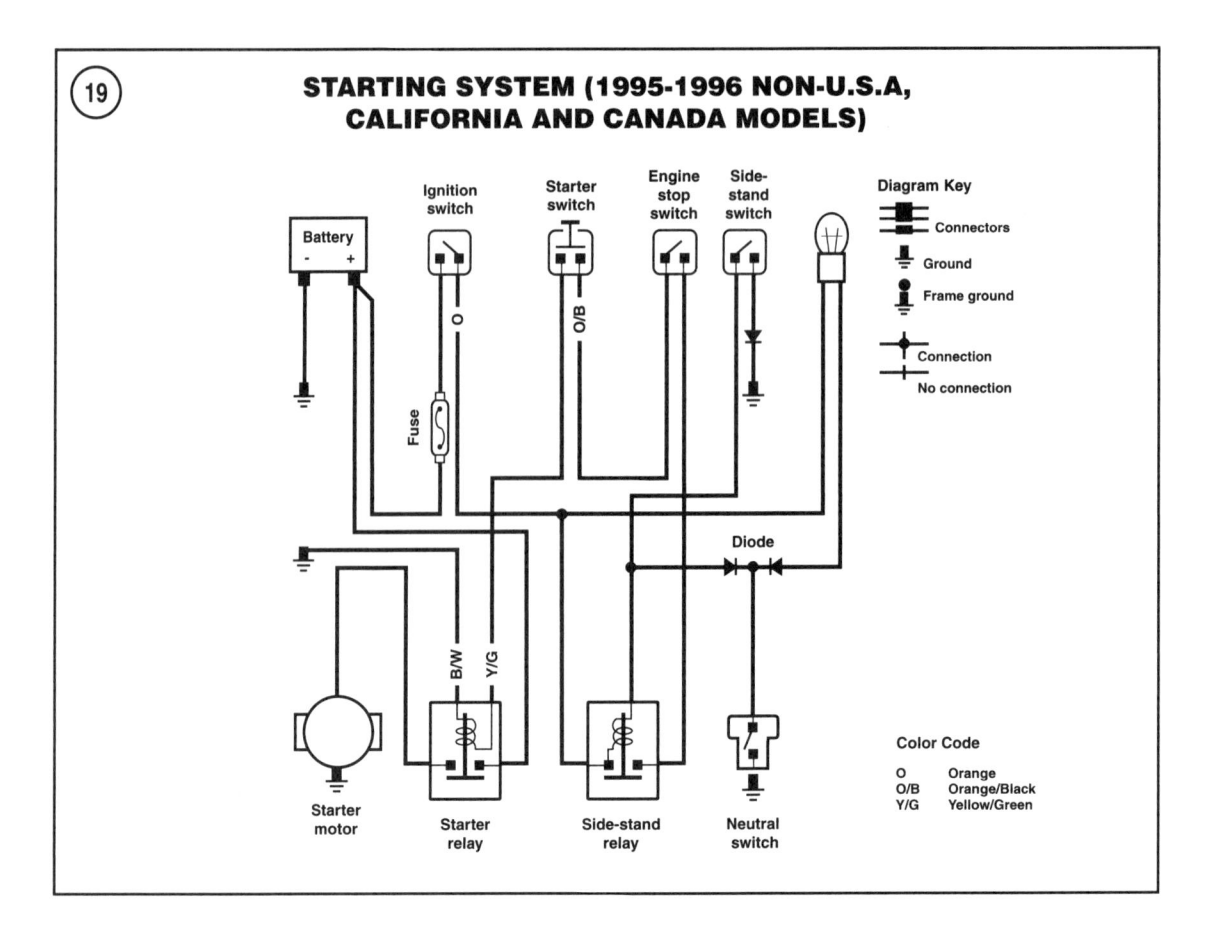

STARTING SYSTEM

The starting system (**Figures 19-21**) consists of the starter motor, starter relay, clutch switch, sidestand switch, sidestand relay (which is a combined turn signal/sidestand relay on 2000 models), neutral switch, engine stop switch and the starter button. When the starter button is pressed, it allows current flow through the starter relay coil. The coil contacts close, allowing electricity to flow from the battery to the starter motor.

Refer to the wiring diagrams at the end of the book and the appropriate figure for specific model and year.

CAUTION
Do not operate the starter motor for more than five seconds. Allow the starter motor to cool for 15 seconds between starting attempts.

The starter should turn whenever the starter button is pressed, the transmission is in neutral and the clutch disengaged. If the starter does not operate properly, follow the procedure that best describes the symptom.

Before troubleshooting the starting system, make sure that:

1. The battery is fully charged.
2. Battery cables are the proper size and length. Replace cables that are undersized or damaged.
3. All electrical connections are clean and tight, especially the battery terminals.
4. The wiring harness is in good condition with no worn or frayed insulation and no loose harness sockets.
5. The fuel tank is filled with an adequate supply of fresh gasoline.

Starter Motor Does Not Turn

1. Check for a blown fuse (Chapter Nine). If the fuses are good, continue with Step 2.
2. Check the starter motor cable for an open circuit and for dirty or loose-fitting terminals.

TROUBLESHOOTING

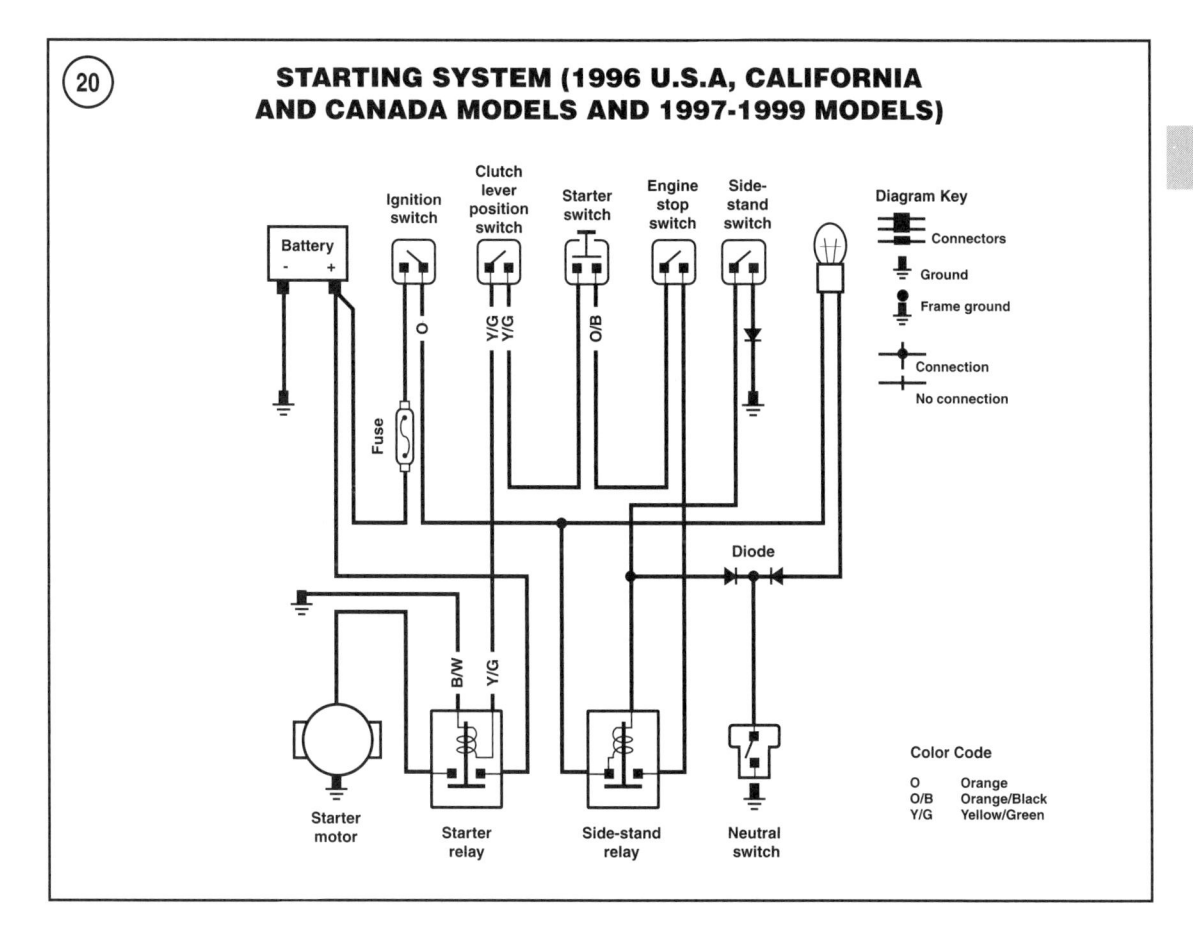

STARTING SYSTEM (1996 U.S.A, CALIFORNIA AND CANADA MODELS AND 1997-1999 MODELS)

3. Check the starter relay connector for dirty or loose-fitting terminals. Clean and repair the connector as required.
4. Check the starter relay as follows. Turn the ignition switch ON and depress the starter switch button. When the starter button is depressed, the starter relay switch should click once.
   a. If the relay clicks, continue with Step 5.
   b. If the relay does not click, go on to Step 6.

CAUTION
Because of the large amount of current that flows from the battery to the starter, use a large diameter cable when performing Step 5.

5. Remove the starter from the motorcycle as described in Chapter Nine. Using an auxiliary battery, apply battery voltage directly to the starter. The starter should turn when battery voltage is directly applied. Note the following:
   a. If the starter motor did not turn, disassemble and inspect the starter motor as described in Chapter Nine. Replace worn or damaged parts as required.
   b. If the starter motor turned, check for loose or damaged starter motor cables. If the cables are good, perform Step 6.
6. Perform the *Starter Relay Voltage Test* as described in Chapter Nine. If the voltage equals or exceeds battery voltage, proceed to Step 7. If the voltage is less than battery voltage, refer to Chapter Nine and check the following items:
   a. Check the ignition switch.
   b. Check the engine stop switch.
   c. Check the neutral switch.
   d. Check the diode.
   e. Check the sidestand relay.
   f. Check the clutch switch.
   g. Check for a poor contact in the starting system wiring.
   h. Check for an open in the starting system wiring.
7. Perform the *Starter Relay Continuity and Resistance Test* as described in Chapter Nine. Replace the

21 STARTING SYSTEM (2000 MODELS)

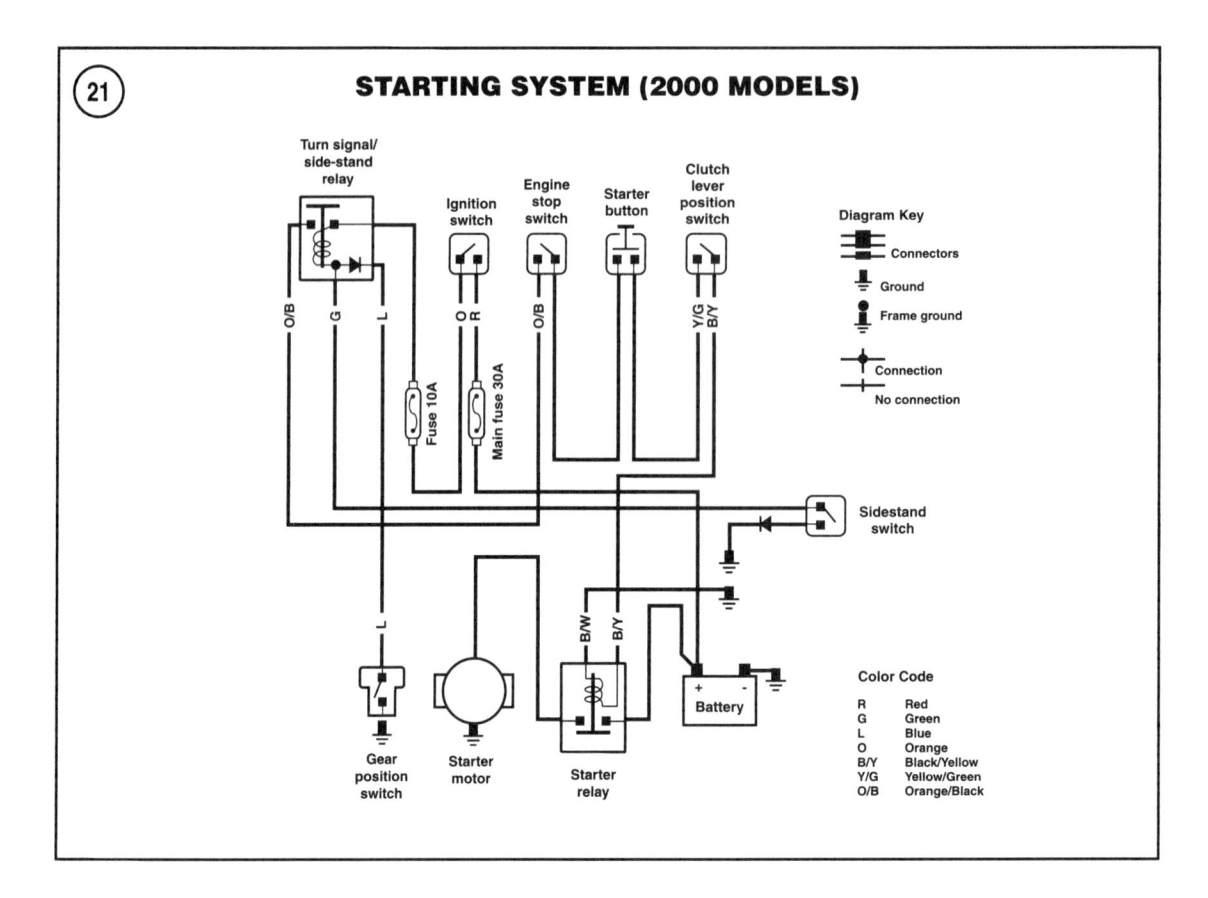

relay if it is faulty. Check for dirty or poor terminals in the starter relay.

Starter Motor Turns but the Engine Does Not

1. Check for a damaged starter clutch or starter clutch gears (Chapter Five).
2. If the starter motor is running backwards and the starter was just reassembled, or if the starter motor cables were disconnected and then reconnected to the starter:
   a. The starter motor was reassembled incorrectly.
   b. The starter motor cables were incorrectly installed.

Starter Motor Works Intermittently

If the starter operates with the transmission in neutral but does not operate when the transmission is in gear, the clutch lever pulled in and the sidestand up, check the following:

1. Test the sidestand switch as described in Chapter Nine.
2. Check for an open circuit in the wiring harness. Check for loose or damaged electrical connectors.

WARNING
Before riding the motorcycle, make sure the sidestand switch works properly. Riding a motorcycle with the sidestand down can cause a crash.

HANDLING

Poor handling may be caused by improper tire pressure, a damaged or bent frame or front steering components, a worn front fork assembly, worn wheel bearings or dragging brakes.

Steering is Sluggish

1. Incorrect steering stem adjustment (too tight).
2. Damaged steering head bearings.
3. Distorted steering stem.
4. Low tire pressure.

TROUBLESHOOTING

Motorcycle Steers to One Side

1. Bent front or rear axle.
2. Bent frame.
3. Worn or damaged wheel bearings.
4. Worn or damaged swing-arm pivot bearings.
5. Damaged steering head bearings.
6. Bent swing arm.
7. Incorrectly installed wheels.
8. Front and rear wheels are not aligned.
9. Front fork legs positioned unevenly in steering stem.
10. Incorrect chain adjustment.

Wobbly Handlebars.

1. Imbalance between the fork legs.
2. Bent or damaged fork leg(s).
3. Bent or damaged front axle.

Front Suspension Noise

1. Loose mounting fasteners.
2. Damaged fork or rear shock absorber.
3. Low fork oil level.
4. Loose or damaged fairing mounts.

Front Wheel Wobble/Vibration

1. Loose front wheel axle.
2. Loose or damaged wheel bearing(s).
3. Damaged wheel rim(s).
4. Damaged or incorrect tire(s).
5. Loose swing arm pivot bolts.
6. Unbalanced tire and wheel assembly.
7. Incorrect fork oil level.

Front Suspension Too Soft

1. Insufficient tire pressure.
2. Insufficient fork oil level.
3. Incorrect oil viscosity.
4. Weak or damaged fork springs.

Front Suspension Too Hard

1. Excessive tire pressure.
2. Damaged steering head bearings.
3. Incorrect steering head bearing adjustment.

4. Bent fork tubes.
5. Binding slider.
6. Incorrect weight fork oil.
7. Fork oil level too low.
8. Plugged fork oil passage.

Rear Wheel Wobble/Vibration

1. Bent or damaged wheel rim.
2. Worn wheel bearings.
3. Damaged or incorrect tire.
4. Worn swing arm or shock linkage bearings.
5. Loosen rear suspension hardware.

Rear Suspension Too Soft

1. Insufficient rear tire pressure.
2. Weak or damaged shock absorber spring.
3. Damaged shock absorber.
4. Incorrect shock absorber adjustment.
5. Leaking damper unit.

Rear Suspension Too Hard

1. Excessive rear tire pressure.
2. Bent damper rod.
3. Incorrect shock adjustment.
4. Damaged shock absorber bushing(s).
5. Damaged shock linkage bearing.
6. Damaged swing arm pivot bearings.

BRAKES

The front and rear brake units are critical to riding performance and safety. Inspect the front and rear brakes frequently and repair any problem immediately. When replacing or refilling the disc brake fluid, use only DOT 4 brake fluid from a closed container. See Chapter Thirteen for additional information on brake fluid selection and disc brake service.

When checking brake pad wear, check that the brake pads in each caliper contact the disc squarely. If one of the brake pads is wearing unevenly, suspect a warped or bent brake disc or a damaged caliper.

Brake Drag

1. Clogged brake hydraulic system.

2. Sticking caliper pistons.
3. Sticking master cylinder piston.
4. Incorrectly installed brake caliper.
5. Warped brake disc.
6. Incorrect wheel alignment.
7. Contaminated brake pad and disc.

Brakes Grab

1. Contaminated brake pads and disc.
2. Incorrect wheel alignment.
3. Warped brake disc.
4. Rear caliper not sliding correctly.

Brake Squeal or Chatter

1. Contaminated brake pads and disc.
2. Incorrectly installed brake pad.
3. Severely worn brake pads.
4. Incorrectly installed brake caliper.
5. Warped brake disc.
6. Incorrect wheel alignment.
7. Contaminated brake fluid.
8. Clogged master cylinder return port.
9. Loose front or rear axle.

Soft or Spongy Brake Lever or Pedal

1. Low brake fluid level.
2. Air in brake hydraulic system.
3. Leaking brake hydraulic system.
4. Worn brake caliper seals.
5. Worn master cylinder seals.
6. Rear brake caliper not sliding correctly.
7. Sticking caliper piston.
8. Sticking master cylinder piston.
9. Damaged front brake lever.
10. Damaged rear brake pedal.

Hard Brake Lever or Pedal Operation

1. Clogged brake hydraulic system.
2. Sticking caliper piston.
3. Sticking master cylinder piston.
4. Glazed or worn brake pads.
5. Damaged front brake lever.
6. Damaged rear brake pedal.
7. Rear brake caliper not sliding correctly.

FRAME NOISE

Noises traced to the frame or suspension are usually caused by loose, worn or damaged parts. Various noises that are related to the frame are listed below.

Front Fork Noise

1. Contaminated fork oil.
2. Low fork oil level.
3. Broken fork spring.
4. Worn front fork bushings.
5. Loose suspension hardware.

Rear Suspension Noise

1. Loose shock absorber mounting hardware.
2. Cracked or broken shock spring.
3. Damage shock absorber.
4. Loose shock linkage mounting hardware.
5. Damage shock absorber linkage.
6. Worn swing arm or shock linkage bearings.

General Frame Noise

1. Cracked or broken frame.
2. Broken swing arm or shock linkage.
3. Loose engine mounting bolts.
4. Damaged steering bearings.
5. Loose mounting bracket(s).

CHAPTER THREE

LUBRICATION, MAINTENANCE AND TUNE-UP

This chapter covers lubrication, maintenance and tune-up procedures. A maintenance schedule, specifications, lubricants and capacities are listed in **Tables 1-6** at the end of this chapter.

Refer to *Shop Supplies* in Chapter One for the necessary supplies required to perform the maintenance described in this chapter.

To maximize the service life of the motorcycle and gain the utmost in safety and performance, it is necessary to perform periodic inspections and maintenance. Minor problems found during routine service can be corrected before they develop into major ones.

PRE-RIDE CHECK LIST

Perform the following checks, as described in this chapter, prior to the first ride of the day. If a component requires service, refer to the appropriate chapter.

At the end of each riding day, clean the motorcycle thoroughly and inspect it carefully. Then give it a good general lubrication and make any necessary adjustments.

1. Check the engine oil level in the oil inspection window (**Figure 1**) located on the clutch cover. The oil level must be between the upper and lower lines.
2. Turn the handlebar from side-to-side and check for steering play. Make sure the control cables are properly routed and do not interfere with the handlebar or the handlebar controls.
3. Check the throttle operation. Open the throttle all the way and release it. The throttle must close quickly with no binding or roughness. Repeat this step with the handlebar facing straight ahead and at both full lock positions.

4. Operate the clutch and the brake levers. Each should move properly with no binding. Replace any broken levers. Check the lever housings for damage.

WARNING
When checking the brake and clutch levers, check the ball on the end of the lever. If it is broken off, replace the lever immediately. The lever balls help to prevent the lever from puncturing hands or arms during a fall or crash.

5. Inspect the front and rear suspension. Make sure they have a good solid feel with no looseness.
6. Check both wheels and tires for damage.
7. Inspect the drive chain for wear, correct tension and proper lubrication.
8. Check the drive chain guide and chain slider for wear or damage; replace either if necessary.
9. Lubricate the drive chain.
10. Make sure the air filter element is clean and that the air box and carburetor boots are secured tightly.
11. Make sure the tires are inflated to the pressures listed in **Table 2**.
12. Check the exhaust system for damage or loose fasteners.
13. Check the tightness of all fasteners, especially engine, steering and suspension mounting hardware.
14. Check the rear sprocket bolts and nuts for tightness.
15. Make sure the fuel tank is full of fresh gasoline.
16. Inspect the fuel lines and fittings for wetness.
17. Check the brake fluid level in both front and rear brake master cylinder reservoirs. Add fluid if necessary.

MAINTENANCE SCHEDULE

Table 1 lists the recommended maintenance schedule. Strict adherence to these recommendations will ensure long service from the motorcycle. However, if the motorcycle is run in an area of high humidity, perform the lubrication and services more frequently to prevent possible rust damage.

For convenience when maintaining the motorcycle, most of the services shown in **Table 1** are described in this chapter. However, some procedures that require more than minor disassembly or adjustment are covered elsewhere in the appropriate chapter.

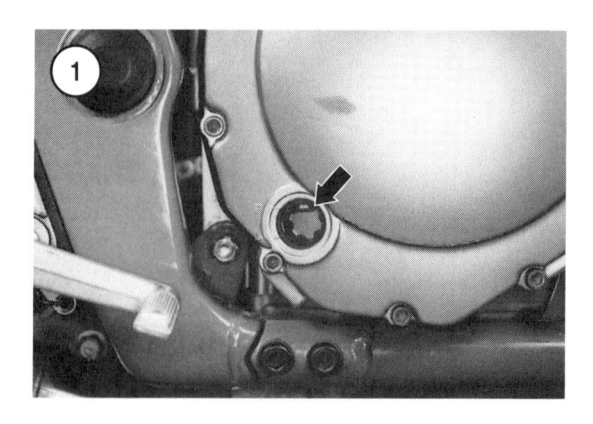

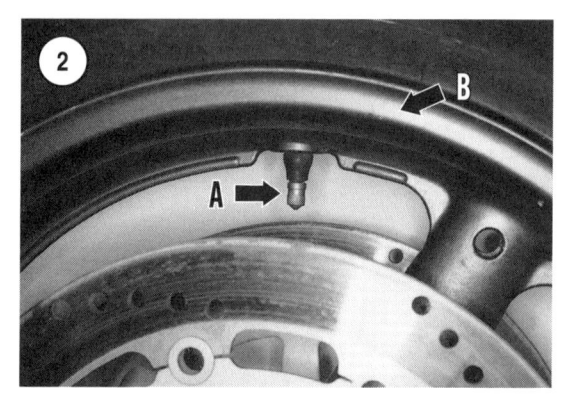

TIRES AND WHEELS

Tire Pressure

Check and adjust tire pressure to maintain good traction and handling and to prevent rim damage. A simple, accurate gauge can be purchased for a few dollars and should be carried in a tool kit. The recommended OEM tire pressures for the Bandit are listed in **Table 2**.

NOTE
After checking and adjusting the tire pressure, make sure to install the valve stem cap (A, Figure 2). The cap prevents small pebbles and dirt from collecting in the valve stem. This could allow air leakage or result in incorrect tire pressure readings.

Tire Inspection

The tires take a lot of punishment. Inspect them weekly for excessive wear, cuts or abrasions. If a nail or other object is found in the tire, mark its location with a light crayon prior to removing it. This

LUBRICATION, MAINTENANCE AND TUNE-UP

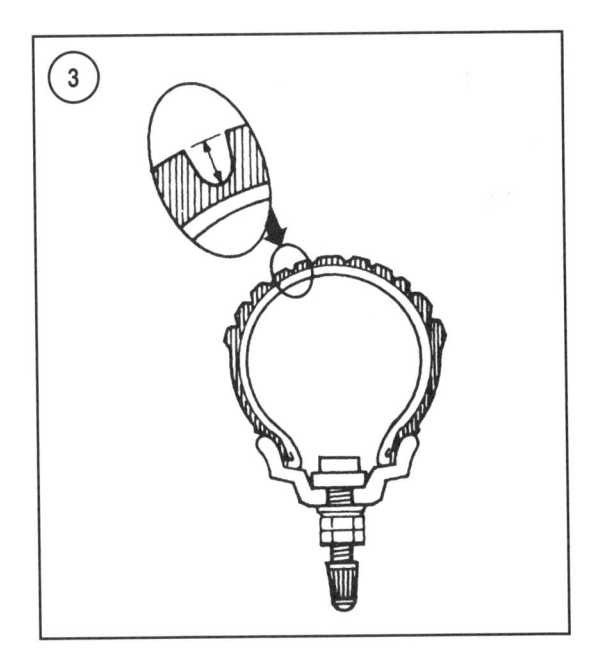

helps locate the hole for repairs. Refer to the tire changing procedure in Chapter Ten.

Measure the tread depth at the center of the tire and to the center of the tire thread (**Figure 3**) using a tread depth gauge or small ruler. Replace the original equipment tires when the tread has worn to the dimensions specified in **Table 2**.

Rim Inspection and Runout

Frequently inspect wheel rims (B, **Figure 2**) for cracks, warpage or dents. A damaged rim may cause an air leak or wheel imbalance. If the rim portion of an alloy wheel is damaged, the wheel must be replaced. It *cannot* be serviced or repaired.

Wheel rim runout is the amount of wobble a wheel shows as it rotates. It is possible to check runout with the wheels on the motorcycle by simply supporting the motorcycle with the wheel off the ground. Slowly turn the wheel while holding a pointer solidly against a fork leg or the swing arm with the other end against the wheel rim. If rim runout seems excessive, measure the runout by following the procedure described in Chapter Ten. If the runout is excessive, replace the wheel.

BATTERY

The battery is an important component in the motorcycle's electrical system, yet most electrical system troubles can be traced to battery neglect. Clean and inspect the battery at periodic intervals. All Bandits are equipped with a maintenance-free battery. This is a sealed battery, so the electrolyte level cannot be checked.

On all models covered in this manual, the negative side is grounded. When removing the battery, disconnect the negative (−) cable first, and then disconnect the positive (+) cable. This minimizes the chance of a tool shorting to ground when the positive battery cable is disconnected.

Battery

Removal/installation

1. Turn the ignition switch OFF.
2. Remove the seat as described in Chapter Fourteen. On 2000 models, remove the document tray.
3. Disconnect the negative battery cable from the battery terminal (A, **Figure 4**).
4. Move the negative cable out of the way so it will not accidentally contact the negative battery terminal.
5. Remove the red terminal cap from the positive battery terminal. Disconnect the positive battery cable from the positive battery terminal (B, **Figure 4**).
6. Remove the battery from the motorcycle.
7. To install the battery, set the battery into the battery compartment. Make sure the negative terminal (A, **Figure 4**) is on the left side of the motorcycle.

> *CAUTION*
> *Be sure the battery cables are connected to their proper terminals. The red battery cable must be connected to the positive battery terminal and the black or black/white battery cable*

must be connected to the negative battery terminal. Connecting the battery backwards reverses the polarity and damages the rectifier.

8. Install and tighten the positive battery cable (B, **Figure 4**).
9. Install and tighten the negative battery cable (A, **Figure 4**).
10. Coat the battery connections with dielectric grease to retard corrosion. Reinstall the red terminal cap over the positive battery terminal.
11. On 2000 models, install the document tray.
12. Install the seat as described in Chapter Fourteen.

Inspection and testing

The battery electrolyte level cannot be serviced. *Never* attempt to remove the sealing bar from the top of the battery. This bar was removed for the initial filling of electrolyte prior to delivery of the motorcycle or the installation of a new battery. It is not to be removed thereafter. The battery does not require periodic electrolyte inspection or water refilling.

Even though the battery is sealed, protect eyes, skin and clothing in the event that the battery is cracked and leaking electrolyte. Battery electrolyte is very corrosive and can cause severe chemical burns and permanent injury. If electrolyte spills onto clothing or skin, immediately neutralize the electrolyte with a solution of baking soda and water, and then flush the area with an abundance of clean water.

> **WARNING**
> *Electrolyte splashed into the eyes is extremely harmful. Safety glasses must always be worn while working with a battery. If electrolyte gets in one's eyes, call a physician immediately. Force the eyes open and flush them with cool, clean water for approximately 15 minutes or until medical help arrives.*

1. Remove the battery as described in this chapter. Do not clean the battery while it is mounted in the frame.
2. Inspect the battery pads in the battery compartment for contamination or damage. Clean the pads and compartment with a baking soda and water solution.
3. Set the battery on a stack of newspapers or shop cloths to protect the workbench surface.
4. Check the entire battery case (**Figure 5**) for cracks or other damage. If the battery case is warped, discolored or has a raised top, the battery has overheated from overcharging.
5. Check the battery terminals (**Figure 5**) and bolts for corrosion or damage. Clean parts thoroughly with a baking soda and water solution. Replace severely corroded or damaged parts.
6. If corroded, clean the top of the battery with a stiff bristle brush using the baking soda and water solution.
7. Check the battery cable clamps for corrosion and damage. If corrosion is minor, clean the battery cable clamps with a stiff wire brush. Replace severely worn or damaged cables.
8. Connect a digital voltmeter across the negative and positive battery terminals (**Figure 6**). Note the following:
   a. If the battery voltage is 12.6 volts (at 20° C, 68° F), or greater, the battery is fully charged.
   b. If the battery voltage is 12.0 to 12.5 volts (at 20° C, 68° F), or lower, the battery is undercharged. Recharge it as described in this chapter.
   c. Once the battery is fully charged, test the charging system as described in Chapter Nine.

Charging

Refer to *Battery Initialization* in this chapter if the battery is new.

If recharging is required on a maintenance-free battery, a digital voltmeter and a charger with an adjustable amperage output are required. If this equip-

LUBRICATION, MAINTENANCE AND TUNE-UP

⑥

Voltmeter

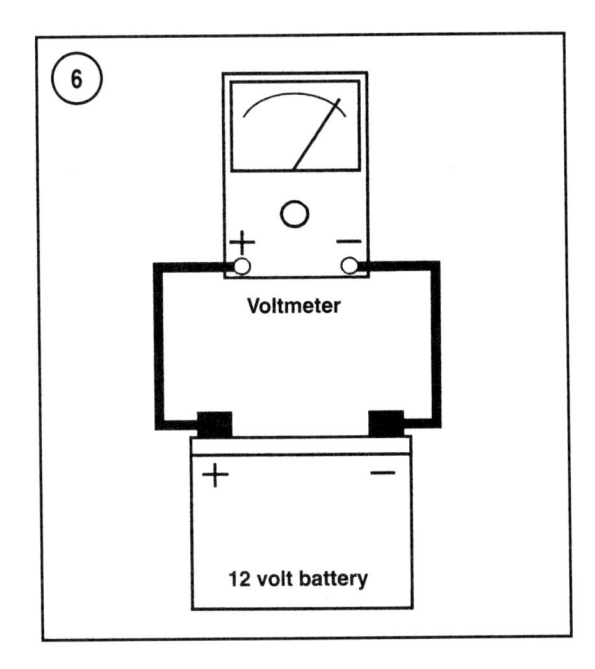

12 volt battery

ment is not available, entrust battery charging to a shop with the proper equipment. Excessive voltage and amperage from an unregulated charger can damage the battery and shorten service life.

The battery should only self-discharge approximately one percent each day. If a battery not in use, with no loads connected, loses it charge within a week after charging, the battery is defective.

If the motorcycle is not used for long periods of time, an automatic battery charger with variable voltage and amperage outputs is recommended for optimum battery service life.

WARNING
During charging, highly explosive hydrogen gas is released from the battery. Only charge the battery in a well-ventilated area away from open flames (including pilot lights on some gas home appliances). Do not allow any smoking in the area. Never check the charge of the battery by arcing across the terminals; the resulting spark can ignite the hydrogen gas.

CAUTION
Always disconnect the battery cables from the battery. If the cables are left connected during the charging procedure, the charger may destroy the diodes within the voltage regulator/rectifier.

1. Remove the battery from the motorcycle as described in this chapter.
2. Set the battery on a stack of newspapers or shop cloths to protect the surface of the workbench.
3. Make sure the battery charger is turned to the OFF position, prior to attaching the charger leads to the battery.
4. Connect the positive charger lead to the positive battery terminal and the negative charger lead to the negative battery terminal.
5. Set the charger at 12 volts. If the output of the charger is variable, select the low setting.

CAUTION
Never set the battery charger to more than 4 amps. The battery will be damaged if the charge rate exceeds 4 amps.

6. The charging time (B, **Figure 5**) depends on the discharged condition of the battery. Refer to **Table 6** for the suggested charging time. Normally, a battery should be charged at 1/10th its given capacity.
7. Turn the charger to the ON position.
8. After the battery has been charged for the pre-determined time, turn the charger to the OFF position and disconnect the leads. Wait 30 minutes and measure the battery voltage. Refer to the following:
   a. If the battery voltage is 12.6 volts (at 20° C [68° F]), or greater, the battery is fully charged
   b. If the battery voltage is 12.5 volts (at 20° C [68° F]), or lower, the battery is undercharged and requires additional charging time.
9. If the battery remains stable for one hour, the battery is charged.
10. Install the battery into the motorcycle as described in this chapter.

Battery Initialization

A new battery must be *fully* charged to a specific gravity of 1.260-1.280 before installation. To bring the battery to a full charge, give it an initial charge. Using a new battery without an initial charge will cause permanent battery damage. That is, the battery will never be able to hold more than an 80% charge. Charging a new battery after it has been used will not bring its charge to 100%.

When purchasing a new battery, verify its charge status.

> **NOTE**
> ***Recycle the old battery***. *When a new battery is purchased, turn in the old one for recycling. Most motorcycle dealerships will accept the old battery in trade when purchasing a new one. Never place an old battery in the household trash since it is illegal, in most states, to place any acid or lead (heavy metal) contents in landfills.*

PERIODIC LUBRICATION

Perform the services listed in this section at the maintenance intervals listed in **Table 1**. If the motorcycle is exposed to harder than normal use or constant exposure to water and high humidity, perform the services more frequently.

Engine Oil Level Check

Engine oil level is checked with the oil level gauge located on the clutch cover.

1. If the motorcycle has not been run, start the engine and let it warm up approximately 2-3 minutes.
2. Park the motorcycle on level ground.
3. Shut off the engine and let the oil settle for 2-3 minutes.

> **CAUTION**
> *Do not take this oil level reading with the motorcycle on the sidestand, as the oil will flow away from the gauge, giving a false reading.*

4. Have an assistant sit on the motorcycle to hold it vertically on level ground, or set the motorcycle on the centerstand, if so equipped.
5. Check the engine oil level in the oil inspection window (**Figure 1**) on the clutch cover. The oil level must be between the upper and lower lines.
6. If the oil level is low, unscrew the oil filler cap (**Figure 7**) from the clutch cover. Insert a small funnel into the hole. Correct the oil level by adding the recommended classification and viscosity oil listed in **Table 3**.
7. Inspect the O-ring seal on the oil filler cap. Replace the O-ring if it is starting to deteriorate or harden.
8. Install the oil filler cap, and tighten it securely.

> **NOTE**
> *Refer to* **Engine Oil and Filter Change** *in this chapter for additional information on oil selection.*

9. If the oil level is too high, remove the oil filler cap and draw out the excess oil with a syringe or suitable pump.
10. Recheck the oil level. Adjust it if necessary.

Engine Oil and Filter Change

Regular oil and filter changes contribute more to engine longevity than any other maintenance service. The recommended oil and filter change interval is listed in **Table 1**. This assumes that the motorcycle is operated in moderate climates. If it is operated under dusty conditions, the oil will get dirty more quickly and should be changed more frequently than recommended.

Use only a high-quality detergent motor oil with an API classification of SF or SG. The classification is printed on the container. Use SAE 10W/40 weight oil in all models. Use lighter viscosity oil in cold climates and heavier viscosity oil in hot cli-

LUBRICATION, MAINTENANCE AND TUNE-UP

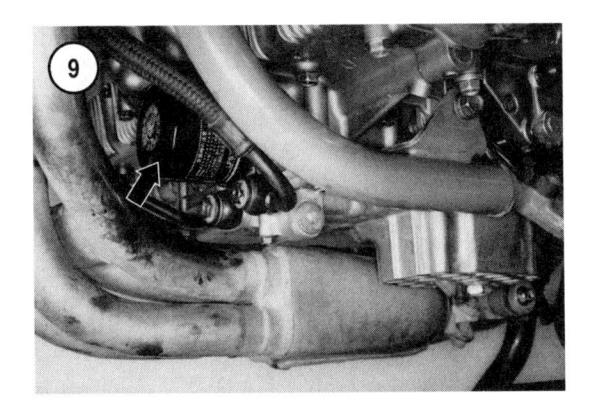

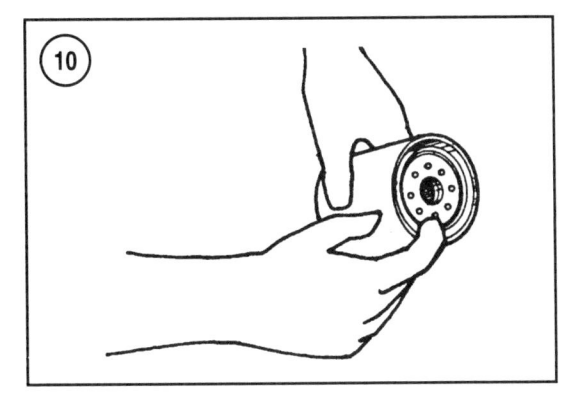

mates. If possible, use the same brand of oil at each oil change.

NOTE
A socket-type oil filter wrench (Suzuki part No. 09915-40610, Vector part No. 17070c or equivalent) is required to remove the oil filter because of the small working area between the oil filter, the exhaust system and the engine.

NOTE
Never dispose of motor oil in the trash, on the ground, or down the storm drain. Many service stations accept used motor oil and waste haulers provide curbside used motor oil collection. Do not combine other fluids with motor oil to be recycled. To locate a recycler, contact the American Petroleum Institute (API) at www.recycleoil.org.

NOTE
Warming up the engine heats the oil so it flows freely and carries out contamination and sludge.

1. Securely support the motorcycle on level ground.
2. Start the engine and let it warm up approximately 2-3 minutes. Shut the engine off.
3. Place a drain pan under the engine.
4. Remove the oil drain plug (**Figure 8**) and gasket from the bottom of the oil pan.
6. Loosen the oil filler cap (**Figure 7**). This speeds up the flow of oil.
7. Allow the oil to completely drain.
8. Inspect the condition of the drained oil for contamination. After it has cooled down, check for any metal particles or clutch friction disc particles. Remove the oil pan from the bottom of the engine. Clean the pan and the pickup screen as described in this chapter.

WARNING
The exhaust system must be completely cool before removing the oil filter. The oil cooler and exhaust system surround the oil filter, and the working area is very small. The oil filter is hot, so protect hands accordingly.

9. To replace the oil filter, perform the following:
    a. Move the drain pan under the oil filter (**Figure 9**) so it will catch residual oil that drains from the filter.
    b. Install a socket-type oil filter wrench onto the oil filter, and turn the filter *counterclockwise* until oil begins to run out. Wait until the oil stops, then loosen the filter until it is easy to turn.
    c. Due to limited space, remove the oil filter wrench from the end of the filter. Completely unscrew the filter by hand and remove it. Hold it with the open end facing up.
    d. Hold the filter over the drain pan, and pour out any remaining oil. Place the old filter in a heavy-duty, freezer-grade reclosable plastic bag and close the bag. Discard the old filter properly.
    e. Thoroughly clean the oil-filter sealing surface on the crankcase. This surface must be clean to achieve a good seal with the oil filter.
    f. Apply a light coat of clean engine oil to the rubber seal on the new filter (**Figure 10**).
    g. Install a new oil filter onto the threaded fitting.

h. Tighten the filter by hand until the rubber seal contacts the crankcase surface, and then tighten it an additional two full turns.

10. Inspect the drain plug gasket for damage. Replace the gasket if necessary.

11. Install the drain plug (**Figure 8**) and its gasket. Tighten the oil drain plug to the torque specification in **Table 5**.

12. Insert a funnel into the oil filler hole, and add the quantity of oil specified in **Table 3**.

13. Remove the funnel and screw in the oil filler cap securely.

14. If oil drips onto the exhaust pipes during this procedure, wipe off as much as possible with a shop rag. Then spray some aerosol parts cleaner onto the pipes to remove most of the oil residue. This will help eliminate the burned oil smoke and smell when first starting the motorcycle.

NOTE
If servicing a rebuilt engine, inspect the lubrication system. Check the engine oil pressure as described in this chapter.

15. Start the engine, and let it idle.

16. Check the oil filter and drain plug for leaks. Tighten either if necessary.

17. Turn off the engine, and check the engine oil level as described in this chapter. Adjust the oil level if necessary.

WARNING
Prolonged contact with oil may cause skin cancer. Wash hands thoroughly with soap and water as soon as possible after handling or coming in contact with motor oil.

Engine Oil Pan, Oil Strainer and Oil Pressure Regulator

The engine oil pan, oil sump strainer and oil pressure regulator can be removed, inspected and installed with the engine in the frame. Refer to the procedure in Chapter Five.

Engine Oil Pressure Test

Perform this procedure after reassembling the engine or when troubleshooting the lubrication system.

To check the oil pressure, a Suzuki oil pressure gauge (part No. 09915-74510), gauge attachment (09915-74540) and high-pressure meter (09915-77300) are required.

1. Check that the engine oil level is correct as described in this chapter. Add oil if necessary.

2. Start the engine and allow it to reach normal operating temperature. Turn off the engine.

3. Place a drain pan under the main oil gallery plug (**Figure 11**) to catch the oil that drains out during the test.

4. Unscrew and remove the main oil gallery plug from the crankcase.

5. Install the adapter, and then the gauge into the main oil gallery. Make sure the fitting is tight to avoid oil loss.

WARNING
Keep the gauge hose away from the exhaust pipe during this test. If the hose contacts the exhaust pipes, it will probably melt and spray hot oil onto the hot exhaust pipe, resulting in a dangerous fire.

6. Start the engine, and warm it up to a test temperature of 60° C (140° F) by running the engine at 2000 rpm for approximately 10 to 20 minutes.

7. Increase engine speed to 3000 rpm, and measure the oil pressure. The oil pressure should be within the range specified in **Table 4** when the oil temperature is 60° C (140° F).

8. If the oil pressure is lower than specified, check the following:
   a. Clogged oil filter.
   b. Oil leak from oil passageway.
   c. Damaged oil seal(s).
   d. Defective oil pump.
   e. Combination of the above.

LUBRICATION, MAINTENANCE AND TUNE-UP

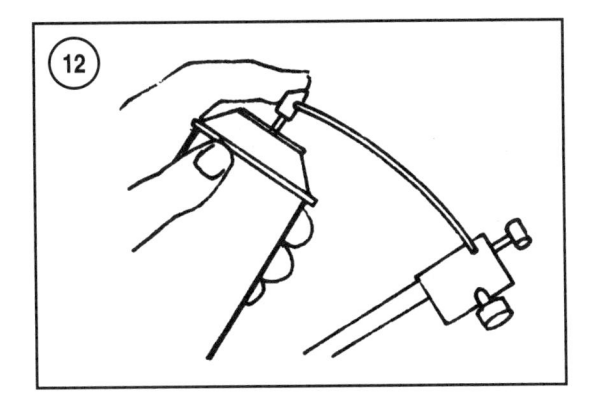

9. If the oil pressure is higher than specified check the following:
   a. Oil viscosity too heavy (drain oil and install lighter weight oil).
   b. Clogged oil passageway.
   c. Combination of the above.
10. Shut off the engine and remove the test equipment.
11. Apply a light coat of gasket sealer to the main oil gallery plug, and then install the plug (**Figure 11**) onto the crankcase. Tighten it to the torque specification listed in **Table 5**.
12. Check oil level and adjust if necessary.

General Lubrication

At the service intervals listed in **Table 1**, lubricate the drive chain with Suzuki chain lube, its equivalent or with SAE 20W/50 engine oil. Lubricate the brake pedal pivot, gearshift lever pivot, footpeg pivots, brake lever holder, clutch lever holder, and the sidestand/centerstand pivot and springs with waterproof grease.

Control Cable Lubrication

Clean and lubricate the throttle cables and clutch cable at the intervals indicated in **Table 1**. In addition, check the cables for kinks and signs of wear and damage or fraying that could cause the cables to fail or stick. Cables are expendable items that do not last forever, even under the best of conditions.

The most positive method of control cable lubrication involves the use of a cable lubricator like the one shown in **Figure 12**. A can of cable lube or an aerosol general lubricant is required. Do *not* use chain lube as a cable lubricant.

1. Remove the fuel tank as described in Chapter Eight. This is necessary to gain access to the lower end of the cables being lubricated.
2. Disconnect both throttle cables from the right handlebar switch. Refer to *Throttle Cable Replacement* in Chapter Eight.
3. Disconnect the clutch cable from the left handlebar switch. Refer to *Clutch Cable Replacement* in Chapter Six.
4. Attach a cable lubricator to the end of the cable following the manufacturer's instructions.

NOTE
Place a shop cloth at the end of the cables to catch the oil as it runs out.

5. Insert the lubricant can nozzle into the lubricator. Press and hold the button on the can until the lubricant begins to flow out of the other end of the cable. If the cable lube will not flow through the cable at one end, remove the lubricator from the cable end. Disconnect the cable from the carburetor assembly or the clutch, and try at the opposite end of the cable.
6. Disconnect the lubricator.
7. Apply a light coat of grease to the cable ends before reconnecting them. Reconnect the cable(s), and adjust them as described in this chapter.
8. After lubricating the throttle cables, operate the throttle at the handlebar. It should open and close smoothly with no binding.
9. After lubricating the clutch cable, operate the clutch lever at the handlebar. It should open and close smoothly with no binding.

Drive Chain Cleaning and Lubrication

Clean and lubricate the drive chain at the interval indicated in **Table 1** or whenever it becomes dry. If the drive chain tends to rust between cleanings, clean and lubricate the chain at more frequent intervals. A properly maintained drive chain will provide maximum service life and reliability.

NOTE
On O-ring type drive chains, the chain lubrication described in this procedure is used mainly to keep the

CHAPTER THREE

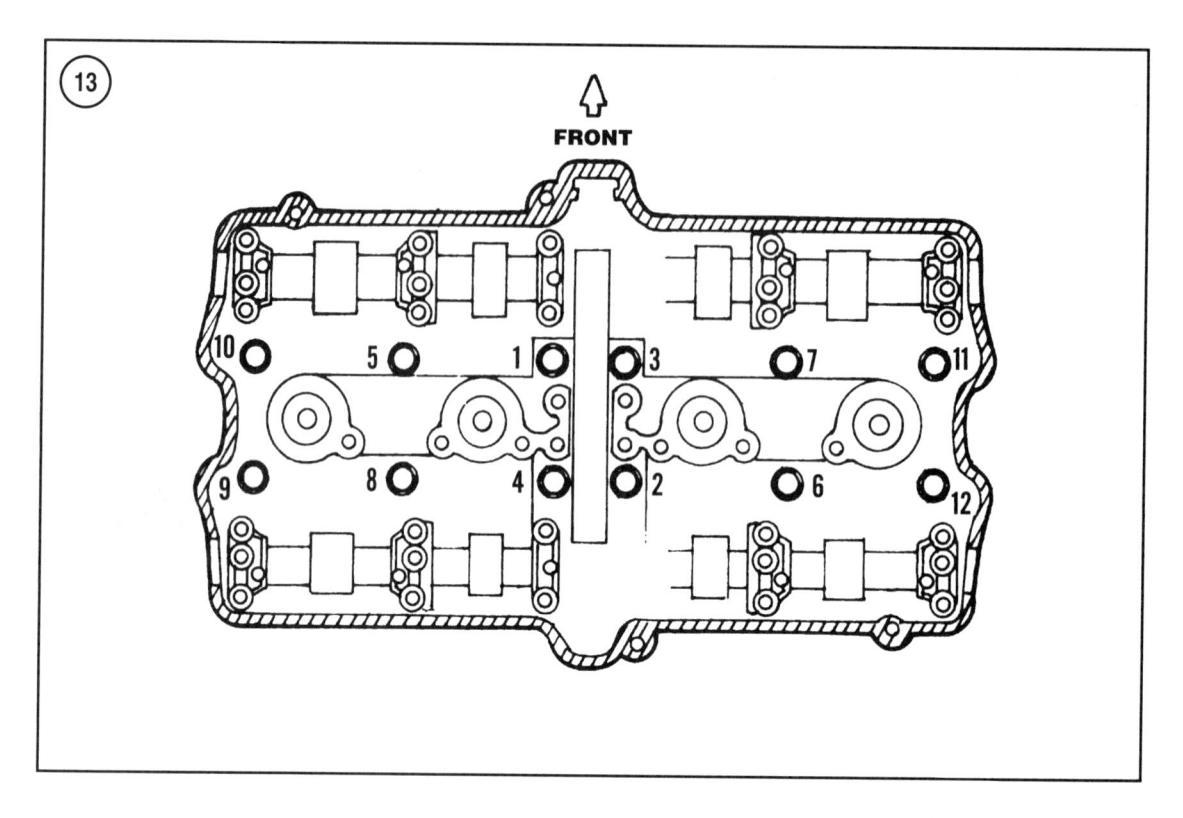

⑬

FRONT

side plates and rollers from rusting. The actual chain lubrication is trapped within each chain roller cavity by the O-rings.

1. Securely support the motorcycle on level ground.
2. Shift the transmission into NEUTRAL.
3. Place a suitable size jack or wooden blocks under the engine to securely support the motorcycle with the rear wheel off the ground.

CAUTION
Do not use gasoline or solvent to clean the chain. Only use kerosene. Other fluids can damage the O-rings in the chain.

4. Carefully and thoroughly clean the drive chain with kerosene and a brush. Dry with clean cloth and then with compressed air.

CAUTION
Lubricate the drive chain with Suzuki chain lube, its equivalent or with SAE 20W/50 engine oil. If using engine oil, do not use a lighter weight oil. It will not stay on the chain as long.

5. Apply the lubricant to the bottom chain run. Concentrate on getting the oil down between the side plates on both sides of the chain. Do not over-lubricate the chain. This will cause dirt to collect on the chain and sprockets.
6. Rotate the wheel and continue applying lubricant until the entire chain is lubricated.
7. Turn the wheel slowly, and wipe excess oil from the chain with a clean shop cloth. Also wipe off any oil that got onto the rear hub, wheel and tire.

Swing Arm Bearing Assembly Lubrication

Frequent lubrication of the swing arm bearings is vital to keep the rear suspension in peak condition. Lubricate the swing arm bearing assemblies whenever they are disassembled. Use a good grade waterproof grease.

The swing arm must be removed and partially disassembled to lubricate the needle bearings and collars. Remove the swing arm as described in Chapter Twelve. Clean, inspect and lubricate the bearings while they are still installed in the swing arm. Do *not* remove the bearings. They are damaged during removal.

LUBRICATION, MAINTENANCE AND TUNE-UP

Shock Lever Lubrication

The shock lever must be removed and partially disassembled to lubricate the needle bearings and collars.

To clean, examine and lubricate the shock lever bearings and collars, remove the shock lever as described in Chapter Twelve. Clean, inspect and lubricate the bearings while they are still installed in the shock lever. Do *not* remove the bearings during lubrication. The bearings will be damaged during removal.

PERIODIC MAINTENANCE

Periodic maintenance intervals are listed in **Table 1**.

Cylinder Head Tightening

The cylinder head (not the cylinder head cover) is held in place with twelve nuts (**Figure 13**), one cylinder head bolt (**Figure 14**) and one cylinder base nut (**Figure 15**).

Tighten the cylinder head after the first 600 miles (1,000 km) of operation, after the cylinder head has been removed for service or at the interval specified in **Table 1**.

> *NOTE*
> *This procedure is shown with the engine removed from the frame for clarity. Do not remove the engine for this procedure.*

> *NOTE*
> *This procedure must be performed with the engine cool, at room temperature (below 35° C [95° F]).*

1. Remove the cylinder head cover as described in Chapter Four.
2. Using the torque pattern shown in **Figure 13**, loosen all cylinder head nuts.
3. Torque the cylinder head nuts in sequence (**Figure 13**) to the torque specification listed in **Table 5**.
4. Tighten the cylinder head bolt (**Figure 14**) and the cylinder base nut (**Figure 15**) to the specified torque.
5. Check the valve adjustment as described in this chapter.

Air Filter Cleaning

Remove and clean the air filter at the interval indicated in **Table 1**. Replace the element at the specified interval or whenever it is damaged or starting to deteriorate.

Proper air filter servicing can ensure long service from the engine.

The air filter removes dust and abrasive particles from incoming air before it enters the carburetors and the engine. Without the air filter, very fine particles will enter the engine and cause rapid wear of the piston rings, cylinder bores and bearings. They also might clog small passages in the carburetors. Never run the motorcycle without the air filter element installed.

1. Securely support the motorcycle on level ground.
2. Remove the seat as described in Chapter Fourteen.
3. Remove the fuel tank as described in Chapter Eight.
4. On 2000 models, remove the fuel tank mounting bracket (A, **Figure 16**) from the frame.

5. Thoroughly clean any road dirt and debris from the area surrounding the air filter housing.

6. Remove the screws (B, **Figure 16**) securing the cover to the air filter housing, and remove the cover. On 2000 models, remove the air filter cover gasket.

7. Remove the air filter element (**Figure 17**) from the housing.

8. Cover the air filter housing with a heavy towel to prevent the entry of objects or debris.

NOTE
If the air filter element is extremely dirty or if it has any holes, wipe out the interior of the air filter housing with a shop rag dampened in cleaning solvent. Remove any debris that may have passed through a broken element.

9. Gently tap the air filter to loosen the trapped dirt and dust.

CAUTION
In the next step, do not apply compressed air toward the outside surface of the filter. Air directed at the outside surface will force the dirt and dust into the pores of the element thus restricting air flow.

10. Apply compressed air to the *inside surface* (**Figure 18**) of the air filter element, and remove all loosened dirt and dust.

11. Thoroughly and carefully inspect the filter element. If it is torn or broken in any area, replace it. Do not run the motorcycle with a damaged air filter element. It may allow dirt to enter the engine. If the element is not damaged, it can be used until the indicated time for replacement listed in **Table 1**.

12. Remove the plug (**Figure 19**) from the air filter drain hose, and drain out any water and debris. Securely reinstall the plug into the drain hose.

13. Install the air filter into the housing so the "S" on the filter frame sits at the top of the housing.

14. Install the air filter cover and screws. Tighten the screws securely.
   a. On 2000 models, install a *new* air filter cover gasket.
   b. Insert the legs on the bottom of the cover into the two square holes in the bottom of the air filter housing.

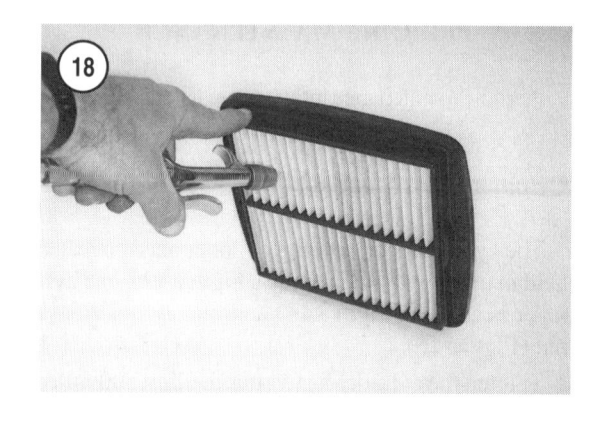

LUBRICATION, MAINTENANCE AND TUNE-UP

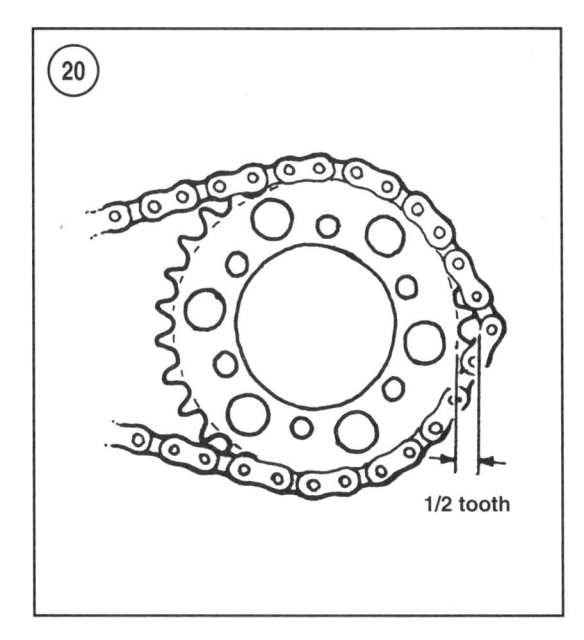

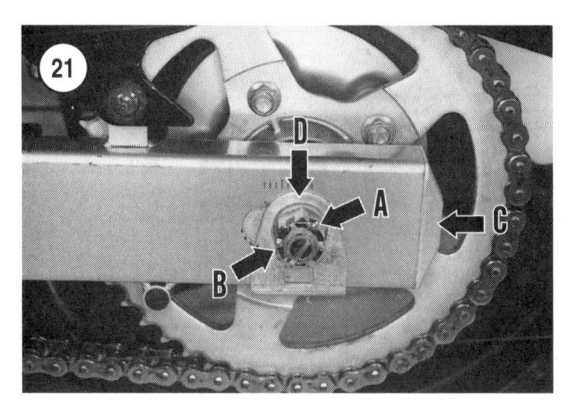

20

1/2 tooth

21

c. Fit the cover onto the housing. Make sure the wiring harness is not pinched by the cover.

d. Tighten the screws (B, **Figure 16**) securely.

15. On 2000 models, reinstall the fuel tank bracket (A, **Figure 16**).

16. Install the fuel tank and the seat.

Drive Chain and Sprocket Wear Inspection

Frequently check the drive chain and replace it when it is excessively worn or damaged. The following simple test quickly indicates the condition of the drive chain.

At the rear sprocket, pull one of the links away from the sprocket. If the link pulls away more than 1/2 the height of a sprocket tooth as shown in Fig-

ure 20, the chain is probably worn beyond the service limit. Confirm this by measuring drive chain length as described below.

Drive Chain Length

1. Securely support the motorcycle on level ground.
2. On U.S.A, California and Canada models, remove the cotter pin (A, **Figure 21**) from the rear axle nut. Discard the cotter pin. A new one must be installed during assembly.
3. Loosen the rear axle nut (B, **Figure 21**).
4. Tighten the chain adjuster (C, **Figure 21**) on the each side of the swing arm, and move the wheel rearward until the chain is tight with no slack.
5. Place a vernier caliper along the chain run and measure the distance between 21 pins (20 links) in the chain as shown in **Figure 22**. If the 21-pin length exceeds the specification in **Table 4**, install a new drive chain as described in Chapter Ten.
6. Inspect the faces of the inner chain plates (**Figure 23**). They should be lightly polished on both sides. If they show considerable uneven wear on one side, the engine and rear sprockets are not aligned properly. Severe wear requires replacement of not only the drive chain but also the engine and rear sprockets.

NOTE
The engine sprocket cover must be partially removed to visually inspect the engine drive sprocket.

7. If the drive chain is severely worn, remove the engine sprocket cover as described in Chapter Seven. Inspect both the engine sprocket and rear sprocket for the following defects:
   a. Undercutting or sharp teeth (**Figure 24**).
   b. Broken teeth.

CAUTION
On a new machine or after a new rear sprocket has been installed, check the torque on the rear sprocket nuts after ten minutes of riding and after each ten-minute riding period until the nuts have seated and remain tight. Failure to keep the sprocket nuts correctly tightened

74 CHAPTER THREE

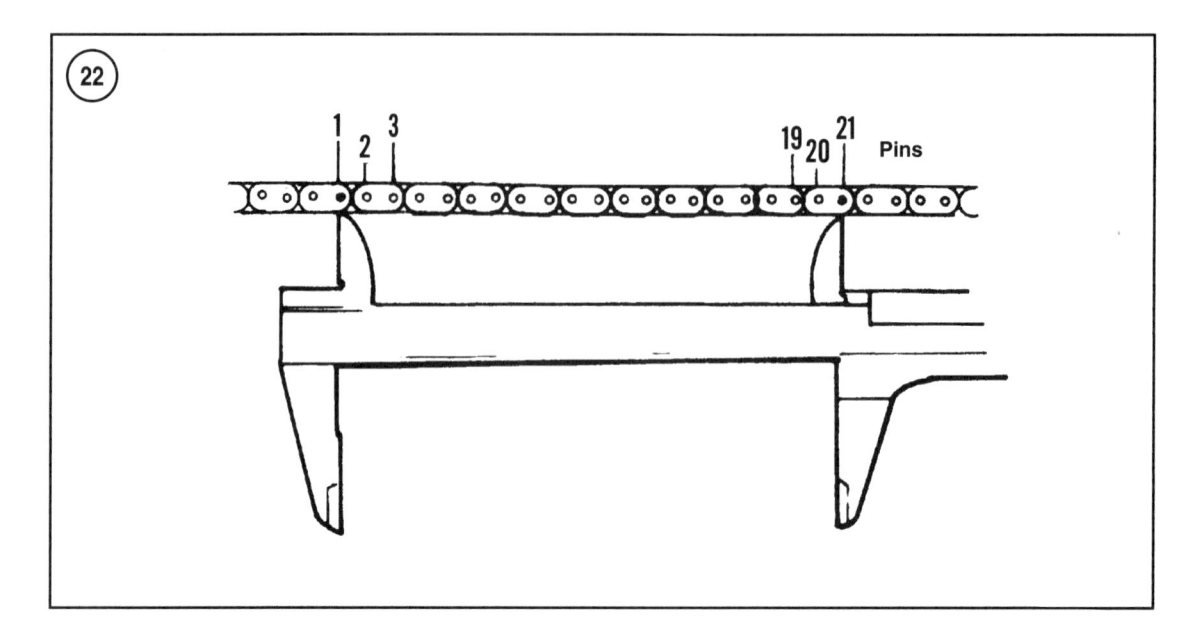

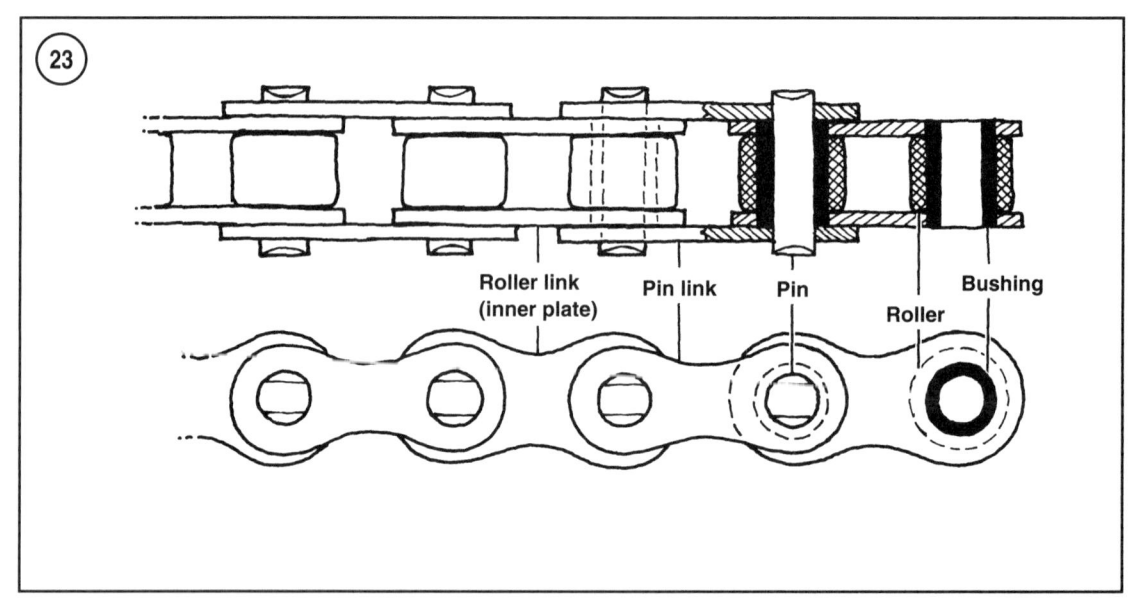

22

23

Roller link (inner plate) | Pin link | Pin | Roller | Bushing

will damage the rear hub. Refer to Chapter Ten.

8. If wear is evident, replace the drive chain, the engine sprocket and the rear sprocket as a complete set. If only the drive chain is replaced, the worn sprockets will quickly wear out the new chain. Refer to Chapter Seven for engine sprocket removal/installation. Refer to Chapter Ten for rear sprocket removal/installation.

9. Adjust the drive chain as described in this chapter.

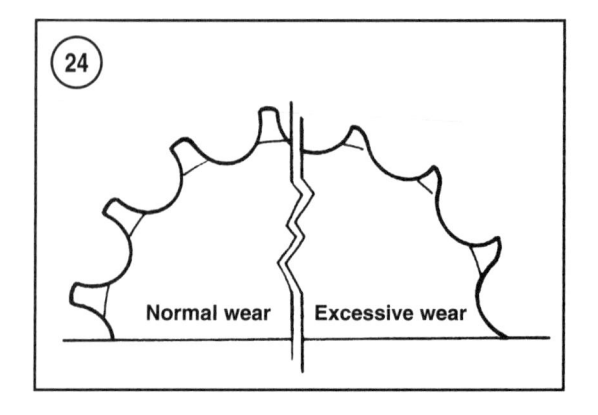

24

Normal wear | Excessive wear

LUBRICATION, MAINTENANCE AND TUNE-UP

25

Chain slack

Engine sprocket | Drive chain | Rear sprocket

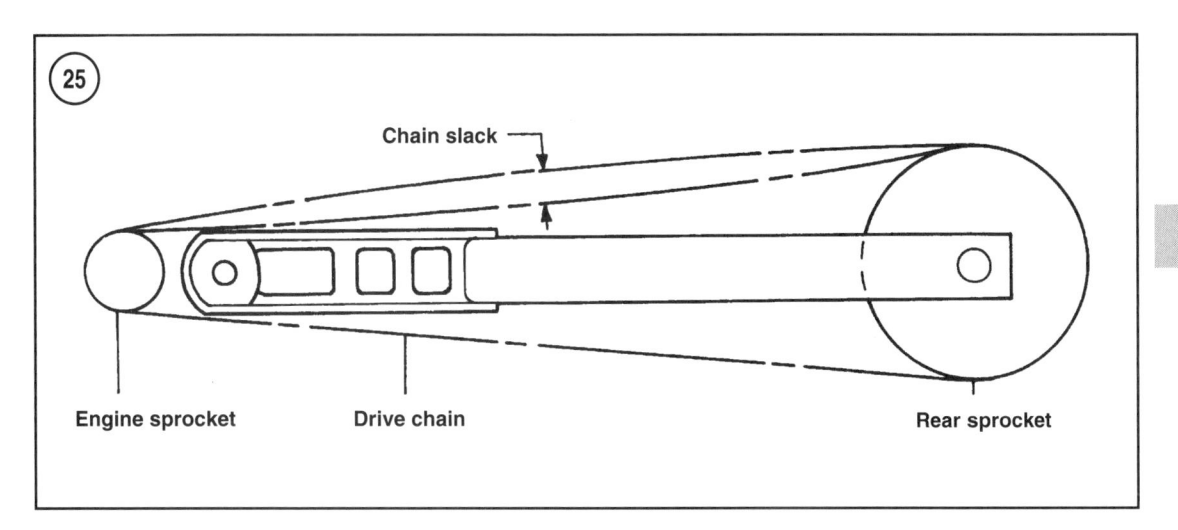

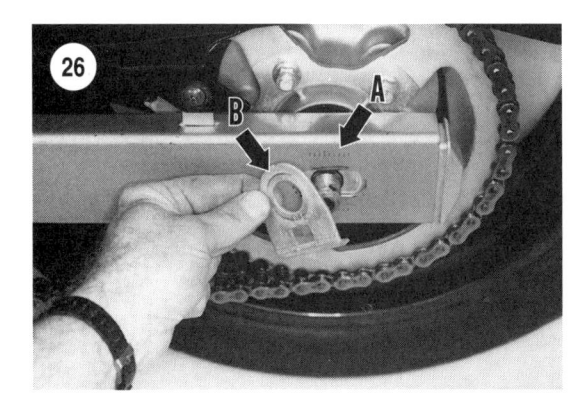

26

10. Install the engine sprocket cover as described in Chapter Seven.

Drive Chain Free Play Adjustment

The drive chain must have adequate play so that the chain is not strung tightly when the swing arm is horizontal. On the other hand, too much slack may cause the chain to jump off the sprockets with potentially dangerous consequences.

Check and adjust the drive chain at the interval listed in **Table 1**. A properly lubricated and adjusted drive chain provides maximum service life and reliability.

When adjusting the chain, check the free play at several places along its length by rotating the rear wheel. The chain rarely wears uniformly and as a result will be tighter at some places than at others. Measure the chain free play when the chain's tightest point is halfway between the sprockets.

1. Roll the motorcycle back and forth and check the chain for tightness at several points on the chain. Identify the tightest point, and mark this spot with a piece of chalk.
2. Turn the wheel until this mark is on the lower chain run, midway between the engine and rear sprockets.
3. Securely support the motorcycle on level ground.
4. With thumb and forefinger, grasp the chain at the center of the chain run, and move the chain up and down. Measure the distance the chain moves vertically (**Figure 25**). Compare the measurement to the drive chain free play specified in **Table 4**. If necessary, adjust the free play by performing the following.

NOTE
On 1995-1999 models, the rear axle nut is on the left side of the motorcycle. On 2000 models, it is on the right.

5. On U.S.A, California and Canada models, remove the cotter pin (A, **Figure 21**) from the rear axle nut. Discard the cotter pin. A new one must be installed during assembly.
6. Loosen the rear axle nut (B, **Figure 21**).

NOTE
*Always maintain rear wheel alignment when adjusting drive chain free play. A misaligned rear wheel can cause poor handling. For alignment purposes, all models are equipped with an alignment scale (A, **Figure 26**) and an adjuster plate (B, **Figure 26**) on each side of the swing arm.*

7. Tighten or loosen the adjuster bolt (C, **Figure 21**) on each side an equal amount until the chain free play is within the range specified in **Table 4**. Make sure the indexing mark on the left adjuster plate (D, **Figure 21**) aligns with the same point on its alignment scale as the indexing mark on the right side of the swing arm.

8. When drive chain free play is correct, check the wheel alignment by looking along the top of the drive chain from the rear sprocket. The chain should form a straight line as it leaves the rear sprocket and travels to the engine sprocket (A, **Figure 27**). If the chain veers to one side or the other (B and C, **Figure 27**), perform the following:

    a. Check that the indexing mark on the left (D, **Figure 21**) and right adjuster plates align with the same points on their respective alignment scales.

    b. If not, readjust the drive chain so the adjuster plates are at the same positions on their respective scales and the free play is within specification.

9. Tighten the rear axle nut to the torque specification listed in **Table 5**.

10. On U.S.A., California and Canada models, install a *new* cotter pin (A, **Figure 21**), and bend the ends over completely.

11. If the drive chain cannot be adjusted to the correct measurement, the drive chain is excessively worn and must be replaced as described in Chapter Ten. Replace both the engine and rear sprockets when replacing the drive chain. Never install a new drive chain over worn sprockets.

Drive Chain Slider

Inspect the drive chain slider (**Figure 28**) on the left side of the swing arm for wear. Replace the slider if it is excessively worn.

Routine inspection and replacement of the drive chain slider prevents the drive chain from damaging the swing arm. A chain with too much free play causes rapid wear of the slider.

To replace the drive chain slider, remove the swing arm as described in Chapter Twelve and remove the slider. Whenever the swing arm is removed for slider replacement, inspect and lubricate the swing arm bearings. Use a good grade of waterproof grease such as Suzuki Super Grease A or equivalent.

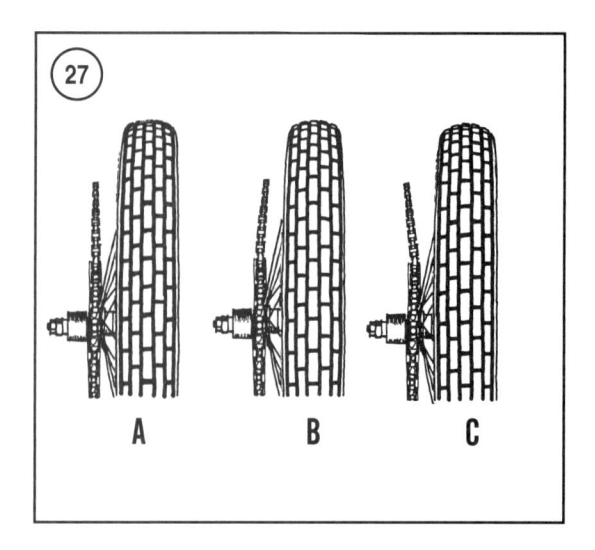

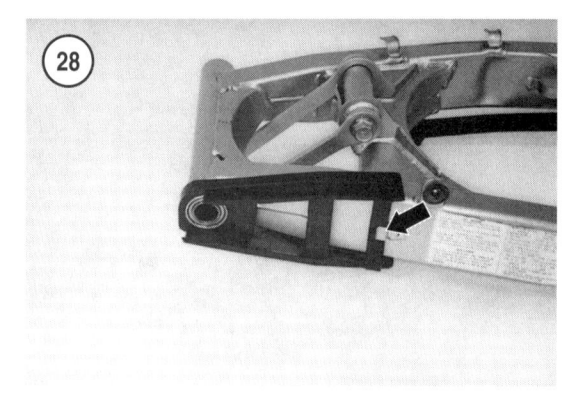

Throttle Operation

Check the throttle operation at the interval indicated in **Table 1**.

Operate the throttle grip. Check for smooth throttle operation from fully closed to fully open and then back to the fully closed position. The throttle should automatically return to the fully closed position without any hesitation.

Check the throttle cables for damage, wear or deterioration. Make sure the throttle cables are not kinked at any place.

If the throttle does not return to the fully closed position smoothly and if the exterior of the cable sheaths appears to be in good condition, lubricate the throttle cables as described in this chapter. Also apply a light coat of grease to the throttle cable spool at the hand grip.

If cable lubrication does not solve the problem, replace the throttle cables as described in Chapter Eight.

LUBRICATION, MAINTENANCE AND TUNE-UP

Figure 29 — Rotational free play

Figure 30

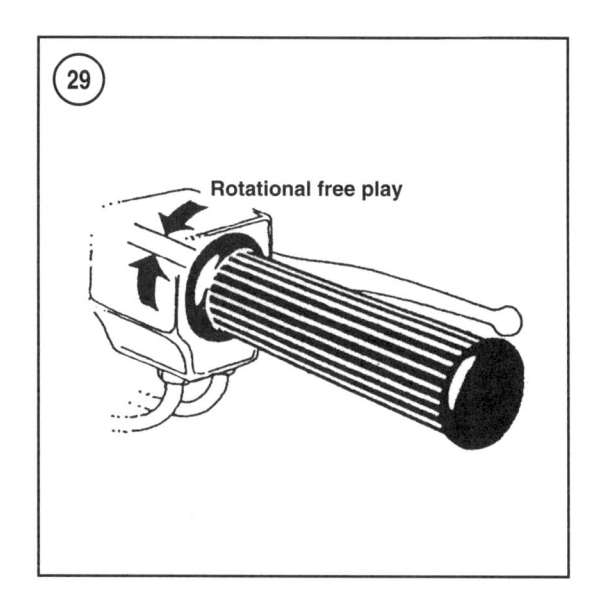

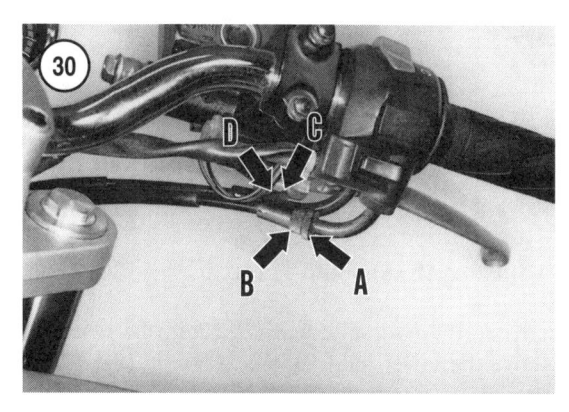

Throttle Cable Free Play

Check the throttle cable free play at the interval indicated in **Table 1**.

In time, the throttle cable free play becomes excessive from cable stretch. This delays throttle response and affects low speed operation. On the other hand, insufficient throttle cable free play can lead to an excessively high idle.

Minor adjustments can be made at the throttle grip end of the throttle cables. If proper adjustment cannot be achieved at this location, the cables must be adjusted at the throttle wheel on the carburetor assembly.

1. Shift the transmission into NEUTRAL.
2. Start the engine and allow it to idle.
3. With the engine at idle speed, slowly twist the throttle to raise engine speed. Note the amount of rotational movement (**Figure 29**) required to raise the idle. This amount of movement is the throttle cable free play.
4. If throttle cable free play is outside the range specified in **Table 4**, adjust it by performing the following procedure.
5. Shut off the engine.
6A. On 1995-1999 models, perform the following:
   a. Loosen the locknut on the return cable (A, **Figure 30**) and turn the adjuster (B, **Figure 30**) in either direction until free play in the return cable is zero.
   b. Hold onto the return cable adjuster and tighten the locknut.
   c. Loosen the locknut on the pull cable (C, **Figure 30**) and turn the adjuster (D, **Figure 30**) in either direction until the correct amount of free play is achieved.
   d. Hold onto the pull cable adjuster and tighten the locknut.

6B. On 2000 models, minor adjustments can be made to the throttle grip. Perform the following:
   a. Loosen the locknut (A, **Figure 30**) on the return cable and turn the adjuster (B, **Figure 30**) all the way in.
   b. Loosen the locknut (C, **Figure 30**) on the pull cable, and turn the adjuster (D, **Figure 30**) in either direction until the correct amount of free play is achieved. Hold the pull cable adjuster, and tighten the locknut securely.
   c. Hold the throttle grip in the fully closed position.
   d. Slowly turn the adjuster on the return cable (B, **Figure 30**) until resistance is felt and then stop. Hold onto the return cable adjuster (B) and tighten the locknut (A).

7. Restart the engine and repeat Steps 3-5 to make sure the adjustment is correct.

8A. On 1995-1999 models, if the throttle cable free play cannot be adjusted to specification at the throttle grip, the cable(s) is stretched beyond the wear limit and must be replaced. Refer to Chapter Eight for this service procedure.

8B. On 2000 models, if the throttle cable free play cannot be adjusted to specification at the throttle grip, major adjustment can be made at the carburetor. Perform the following:
   a. Remove the fuel tank as described in Chapter Eight.

b. Loosen the locknut (A, **Figure 31**) on the throttle return cable.

c. Turn the return cable adjuster (B, **Figure 31**) until free play is within specification.

d. Loosen the locknut (C, **Figure 31**) on the pull cable.

e. Turn the pull cable adjuster (D, **Figure 31**) until the rotational free play at the throttle grip is within specification.

f. Hold the pull cable adjuster (D, **Figure 31**) and tighten the locknut (C) securely.

g. While holding the throttle grip fully closed, check the slack at the carburetor end of the return cable by pushing the cable inner wire from side-to-side. Slowly turn the return cable adjuster (A, **Figure 31**) until the side-to-side free play equals 1.0 mm (0.04 in.)

h. Hold the return cable adjuster (A, **Figure 31**), and tighten the locknut (B) securely.

9. Check the operation of the throttle. Make sure it opens and closes smoothly.

10. Check the throttle cables from grip to carburetor. Make sure they are not kinked or chafed. Replace as necessary.

11. Install the fuel tank as described in Chapter Eight.

WARNING
*With the engine idling, move the handlebar from side to side. If the idle speed increases during this movement, the throttle cables may need adjusting or may be incorrectly routed through the frame. Correct this problem immediately. Do **not** ride the motorcycle in this unsafe condition.*

12. Test ride the motorcycle, slowly at first, and make sure the throttle cables are operating correctly. Readjust if necessary.

Disc Brakes

Check the hydraulic brake fluid in each disc brake master cylinder at the interval listed in **Table 1**. Check the brake pads for wear at the same time. Bleeding the system, servicing the brake system components and replacing the brake pads are covered in Chapter Thirteen.

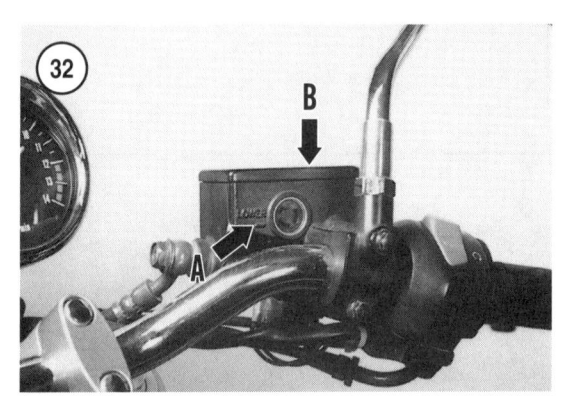

Adjusting Brake Fluid Level

Keep the hydraulic brake fluid in the reservoir above the lower mark on the reservoir. If the fluid level drops to the low level line on the front brake reservoir (A, **Figure 32**) or the rear brake reservoir (A, **Figure 33**), correct the level by adding fresh brake fluid.

CAUTION
Be careful when adding brake fluid. Do not spill it on plastic, painted or plated surfaces. Brake fluid damages these surfaces. Immediately wash off spilled brake fluid with soapy water. Thoroughly rinse the area with clean water.

1. Securely support the motorcycle on level ground.

2. On the front master cylinder, perform the following:

a. Position the handlebar so the front master cylinder is horizontal.

b. Clean all dirt and debris from the top of the master cylinder reservoir.

LUBRICATION, MAINTENANCE AND TUNE-UP

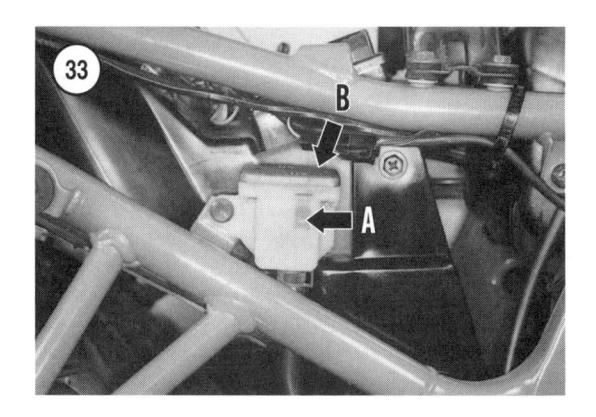

c. Remove the top cover screws, and remove the top cover (B, **Figure 32**), the diaphragm plate and diaphragm from the master cylinder reservoir.

3. On the rear master cylinder, perform the following:
   a. Remove the rear frame cover as described in Chapter Fourteen.
   b. Clean all dirt and debris from the top of the master cylinder reservoir.
   c. Remove the screws securing the top cover (B, **Figure 33**). Remove the top cover and diaphragm.

WARNING
Use brake fluid clearly marked DOT 4 from a sealed container. Other types may vaporize and cause brake failure. Always use the same brand of brake fluid. Do not intermix different brands. They may not be compatible. Do not use silicone based (DOT 5) brake fluid. It can cause brake component damage, leading to brake system failure.

NOTE
To control the small flow of hydraulic fluid, punch a small hole into the seal of a new container of brake fluid next to the edge of the pour spout. This will help eliminate fluid spillage while adding fluid to the very small reservoirs.

4. Refill the master cylinder reservoir, if necessary, to maintain the correct fluid level as indicated on the side of the reservoir.
5. On the front master cylinder, install the diaphragm, diaphragm plate and cover. Tighten the cover screws securely.
6. On the rear master cylinder, perform the following:
   a. Install the diaphragm and cover. Tighten the cover screws securely.
   b. Install the rear frame cover as described in Chapter Fourteen.

Disc Brake Hoses

Check the brake hoses between each master cylinder and each brake caliper assembly.

If there is any leakage, tighten the connections and bleed the brakes as described in Chapter Thirteen. If tightening the connection does not stop the leak or if the brake hose(s) is obviously damaged, cracked or chafed, replace the brake hose(s) and bleed the system as described in Chapter Thirteen.

Disc Brake Pad Wear

Inspect the brake pads for wear at the interval indicated in **Table 1**.

On the front brake caliper, look into the caliper assembly (**Figure 34**), and inspect the brake pads for excessive or uneven wear.

On the rear caliper, remove the dust cover (**Figure 35**) and inspect the brake pads for excessive wear.

If any pad is worn to the wear limit (**Figure 36**), the pads must be replaced. Follow the pad replacement procedure in Chapter Thirteen.

NOTE
Always replace both pads in each caliper at the same time to maintain even

pressure on the brake disc. On the front brakes, replace both brake pads in both calipers at the same time to maintain even braking.

Disc Brake Fluid Change

Every time the reservoir top cover and diaphragm are removed, a small amount of dirt and moisture enter the brake fluid system. The same thing happens if a leak occurs or if any part of the hydraulic brake system is loosened or disconnected. Dirt can clog the system and cause unnecessary wear. Water in the brake fluid vaporizes at high temperature, impairing the hydraulic action and reducing the brake's stopping ability.

To maintain peak braking efficiency, change the brake fluid at the interval listed in **Table 1**. To change brake fluid, follow the *Bleeding The Brakes* procedure in Chapter Thirteen. Continue adding new brake fluid to the master cylinder and bleed the fluid from the caliper bleeder valve until the brake fluid leaving the caliper is clean and free of contaminants.

> *WARNING*
> *Use brake fluid clearly marked DOT 4 from a sealed container. Other types may vaporize and cause brake failure. Always use the same brand of brake fluid. Do not intermix different brands. They may not be compatible. Do not use silicone based (DOT 5) brake fluid. It can cause brake component damage, leading to brake system failure.*

Rear Disc Brake Pedal Height Adjustment

The brake pedal height changes as the brake pads wear. The top of the brake pedal should be positioned below the top surface of the footpeg as shown in **Figure 37**. The distance between the top of the brake pedal and the top of the footpeg should equal the specification listed in **Table 4**. If the dimension is incorrect, adjust the brake pedal height by performing the following.

1. Securely support the motorcycle on level ground.
2. Make sure the brake pedal is in the at-rest position.

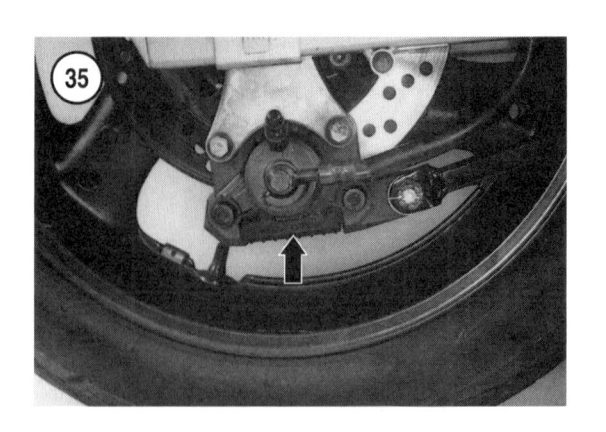

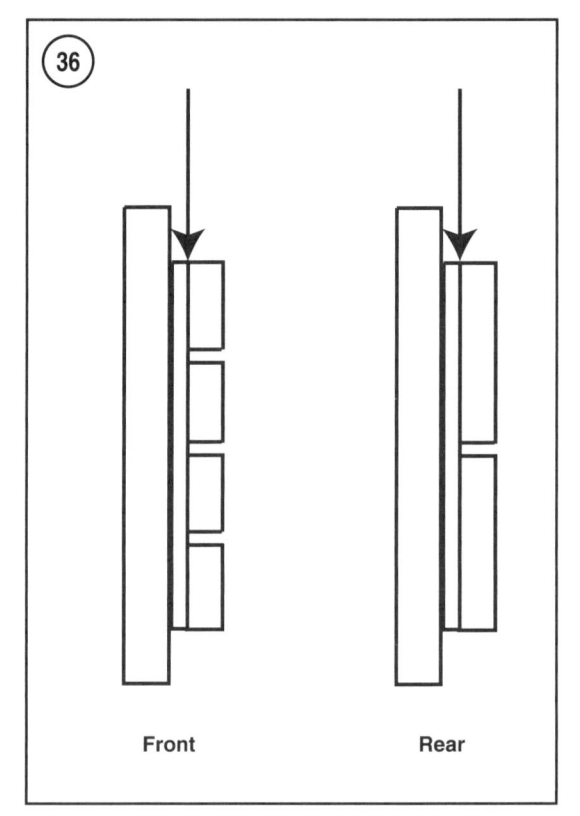

LUBRICATION, MAINTENANCE AND TUNE-UP

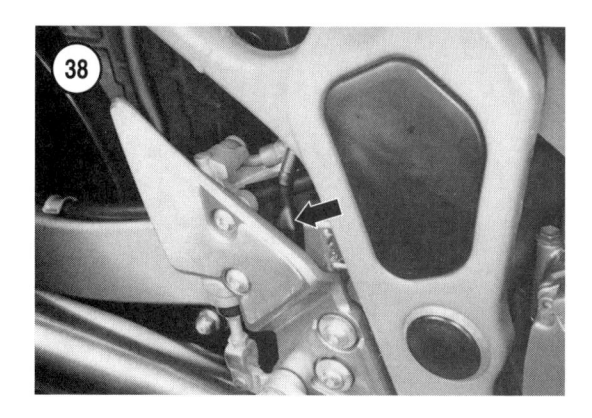

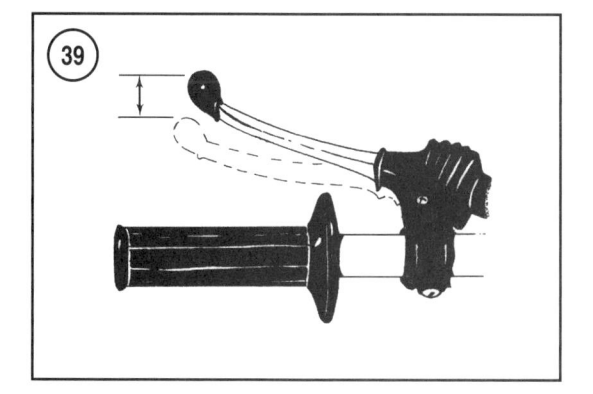

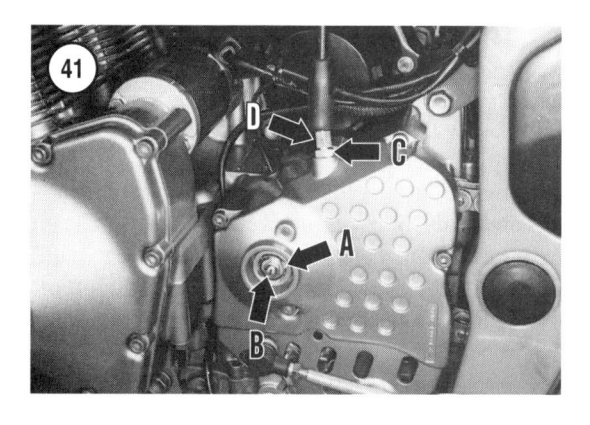

3. At the rear brake master cylinder, loosen the locknut (A, **Figure 37**) and turn the pushrod (B, **Figure 37**) in either direction until the brake pedal height equals specification.

4. Tighten the rear brake master cylinder locknut to the torque specification listed in **Table 5**.

Rear Brake Switch Adjustment

1. Turn the ignition switch to the ON position.
2. Depress the brake pedal. The brake light should come on just as the brake begins to work.

> *NOTE*
> *Some riders prefer that the brake light turns on a little early. This way, they can tap the pedal without braking to warn drivers who are following too closely.*

3. To make the brake light come on earlier, hold the brake light switch body (**Figure 38**) and turn the adjusting nut clockwise as viewed from the top. Turn the adjusting nut counterclockwise to delay the light from coming on.
4. Turn the ignition switch OFF.

Clutch Lever Free Play Adjustment

Adjust the clutch lever free play at the interval listed in **Table 1**. For the clutch to fully engage and disengage, there must be free play at the tip of the clutch lever (**Figure 39**). The clutch lever free play specification is listed in **Table 4**.

1. Pull back the boot (A, **Figure 40**) from the clutch lever.
2. Loosen the locknut (B, **Figure 40**), and turn the adjuster (C, **Figure 40**) all the way into the clutch lever.
3. Remove the clutch release cover from the engine sprocket cover.
4. Loosen the locknut (A, **Figure 41**) on the clutch release mechanism, and turn the adjusting screw (B, **Figure 41**) two or three turns out.
5. Slowly turn the clutch-release adjusting screw (B, **Figure 41**) in until resistance is felt.
6. Turn the adjusting screw (B, **Figure 41**) 1/4 turn out and tighten the locknut (A, **Figure 41**).
7. Lift the rubber boot from the clutch cable adjuster.
8. Loosen the clutch cable locknut (C, **Figure 41**).

9. Turn the clutch cable adjuster (D, **Figure 41**) until the free play at the clutch lever end is within the specification.

10. Tighten the clutch cable locknut (C, **Figure 41**) at the engine sprocket cover, and tighten the locknut (B, **Figure 40**) at the clutch lever.

11. Reposition the boots at both cable ends, and reinstall the clutch release cover.

Crankcase Breather

1. Remove the fuel tank as described in Chapter Eight.
2. Inspect the breather hose (**Figure 42**) from the cylinder head cover to the air filter housing. If it is cracked or deteriorated it must be replaced. Make sure the hose clamps are in place and secure.
3. Install the fuel tank.

Evaporative Emission Control System (California Models Only)

The evaporative emissions control system (**Figure 43**) captures fuel system vapors and stores them so they will not be released into the atmosphere. The fuel vapors are routed through the roll-over valve and stored in the charcoal canister located on the right side of the frame. When the engine is started, the stored vapors are drawn from the canister. They pass through the purge control valves, flow to the carburetors and then into the engine, where they are burned.

Make sure all evaporative emission control hoses are correctly routed and properly attached to their respective components. Inspect the hoses and replace any if necessary as described in Chapter Eight.

PAIR System (1995-1999 California and Switzerland Models, and 2000 Models)

The PAIR system introduces fresh air into the exhaust ports to reduce the exhaust emission level.

Refer to *PAIR System* in Chapter Eight for complete inspection and service procedures.

NON-SCHEDULED MAINTENANCE

Exhaust System

1. Inspect the exhaust system for cracks or dents that could alter performance.
2. Check all exhaust system fasteners and mounting points for loose or damaged parts.
3. Make sure all mounting bolts and nuts are tight. Tighten any loose fasteners to the torque specification in Table Five.

Fuel Line Inspection

Inspect the fuel lines from the fuel tank to the carburetor assembly and other remaining hoses. Replace any hose that is cracked or starting to deteriorate. Make sure the small hose clamps are in place and holding securely.

> *WARNING*
> *A damaged or deteriorated fuel line presents a very dangerous fire hazard to both the rider and the motorcycle. Fuel could spill onto the hot engine or exhaust pipe.*

Wheel Bearings

Routinely inspect the front and rear wheel bearings and seals for excessive wear or damage. Clean and repack non-sealed bearings once a year with Suzuki Super Grease A or an equivalent waterproof grease. Repack the bearings more often if the vehicle is operated in wet, muddy conditions. The service procedures are covered in Chapter Ten.

LUBRICATION, MAINTENANCE AND TUNE-UP

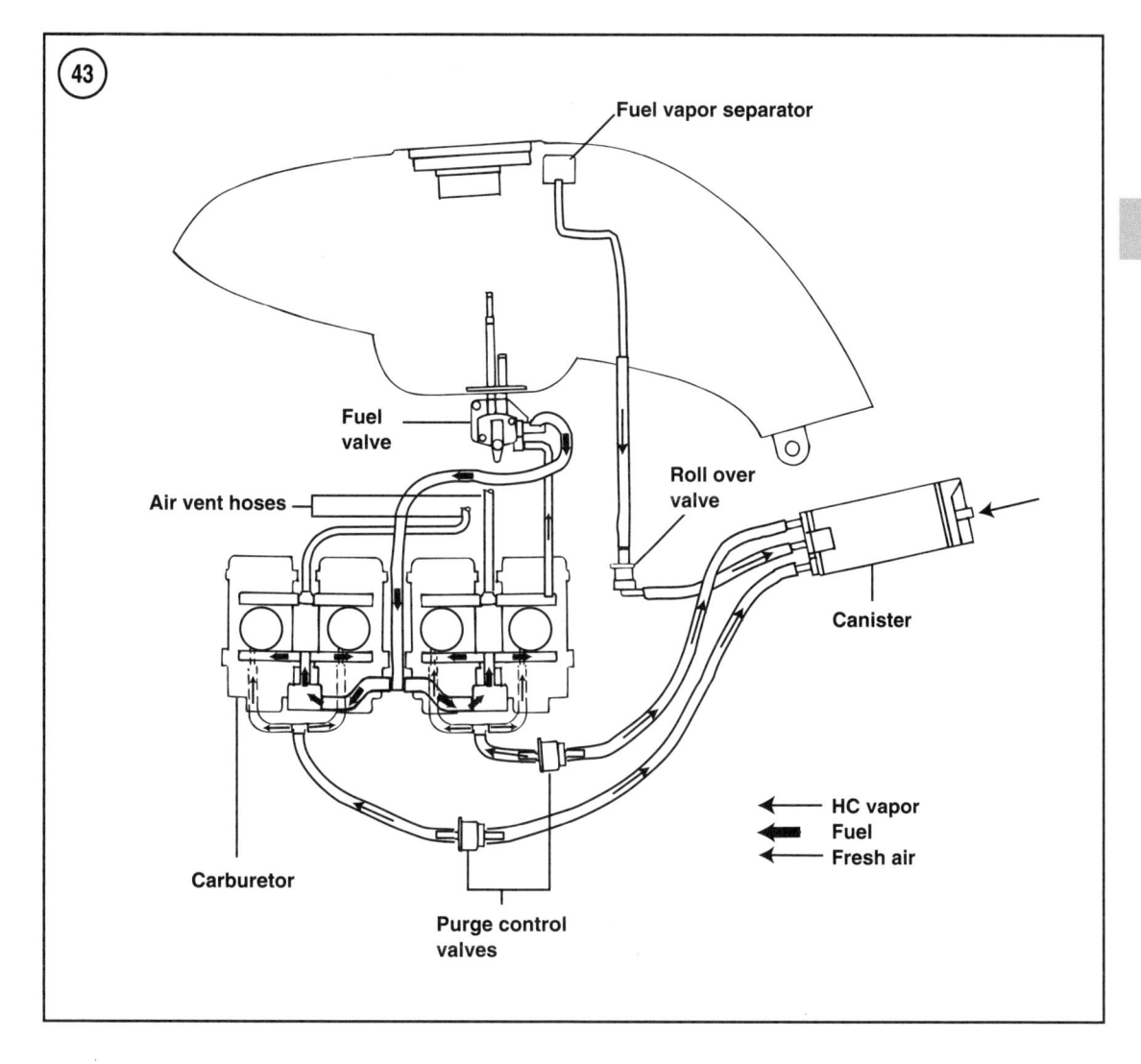

43

Fuel vapor separator
Fuel valve
Air vent hoses
Roll over valve
Canister
Carburetor
Purge control valves

← HC vapor
← Fuel
← Fresh air

Steering Head Adjustment Check

The steering head on all models consists of upper and lower caged ball bearings. A loose bearing adjustment will hamper steering. In severe conditions, a loose bearing adjustment can cause loss of control.

1. Securely support the motorcycle on level ground.

2. Place wooden blocks under the engine.

3. Have an assistant sit on the seat to raise the front wheel off the ground.

4. Hold onto the front fork tubes and gently rock the fork assembly back and forth. If it feels loose, adjust the steering head as described in *Steering Head Installation* in Chapter Eleven.

Handlebars

Inspect the handlebar weekly for any signs of damage. Replace a bent or damaged handlebar. Check the tightness of the clamping bolts.

Front Suspension Inspection

1. Wipe each front fork leg with a soft wet cloth. Remove any dirt, road tar or bugs from the fork legs. This debris will eventually work its way into the seals and cause an oil leak.

2. Check the fork tubes for signs of leaks or damage.

3. Apply the front brake and pump the front fork up and down vigorously. Check for smooth operation and for any oil leaks.

84 CHAPTER THREE

4. Make sure the upper (**Figure 44**) and lower fork bridge clamp bolts (**Figure 45**) are tight.
5. On the right side, make sure the front axle clamp bolts (A, **Figure 46**) are tight and check the tightness of the front axle nut (B, **Figure 46**).

Front Fork Oil

Each front fork leg must be partially disassembled for fork oil replacement and oil level adjustment. Refer to *Front Fork Disassembly and Assembly* in Chapter Eleven.

Rear Suspension Check

1. With both wheels on the ground, check the shock absorber by bouncing the seat several times.
2. Securely support the motorcycle on a stand with the rear wheel off the ground.
3. Have an assistant steady the motorcycle.
4. Push hard on the rear wheel (sideways) to check for side play in the rear swing arm bearings.
5. Check the shock absorber for oil leaks, loose mounting fasteners or other damage.
6. Check the rear suspension for loose or missing fasteners.
7. Make sure the rear axle nut is tight.
8. Check the chain guard for loose or missing fasteners.

> *CAUTION*
> *If any previously mentioned fastener is loose, refer to Chapter Twelve for correct tightening procedures and torque specifications.*

Rear Shock Absorber Adjustment

The rear shock can be adjusted to suit the load and ride preference. The spring preload can be adjusted by varying the spring installed length. The shock absorber rebound damping can also be adjusted on 1999-on GSF600S models.

Spring preload adjustment

> *CAUTION*
> *Never turn the upper spring seat beyond the maximum or minimum position.*

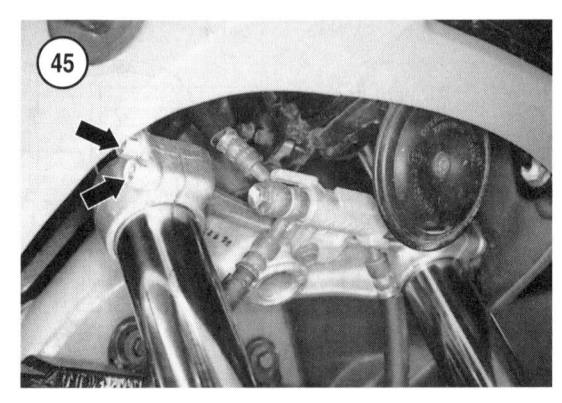

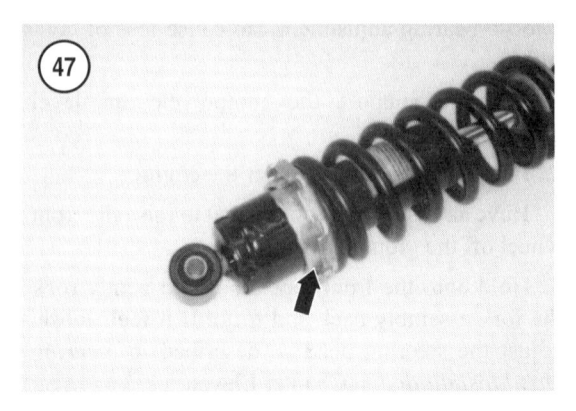

LUBRICATION, MAINTENANCE AND TUNE-UP

NOTE
The shock absorber is shown removed from the motorcycle for clarity. Adjust the preload while the shock is installed on the motorcycle.

Use the ring nut wrench to adjust the preload by rotating the upper spring seat (**Figure 47**) at the top of the shock absorber. Turning the spring seat clockwise to a higher-numbered setting increases the preload and provides a stiffer suspension. Turning the ring counterclockwise to a lower-numbered setting decreases preload and provides a softer suspension.

Rebound damping adjustment
1999-on GSF600S models

Rebound damping affects the rate at which the shock absorber returns to its extended position after compression. Rebound damping does not affect the action of the shock on compression.

The rebound damping adjuster (B, **Figure 48**) at the bottom of the shock absorber has four settings. Position 1 is the softest setting. It provides the least amount of rebound damping. Position 4 is the stiffest setting. It provides the greatest amount of rebound damping. Position 2 is the standard setting.

CAUTION
The rebound damping adjuster must click into one of the detent positions. The rebound damping is set to the stiffest setting when the adjuster sits between detent positions.

To adjust the rebound damping, turn the adjuster to the desired setting. Make sure the adjuster clicks into a detent. If the adjuster is not set to a detent, the rebound damping is set to the stiffest setting.

Frame Inspection

Inspect the frame for cracks or other damage. Check all areas where welded sections attached to the main frame spar. Check the tightness of the removable frame downtube mounting bolts (**Figure 49** and **Figure 50**), If necessary, torque the bolts to the specification in **Table 5**.

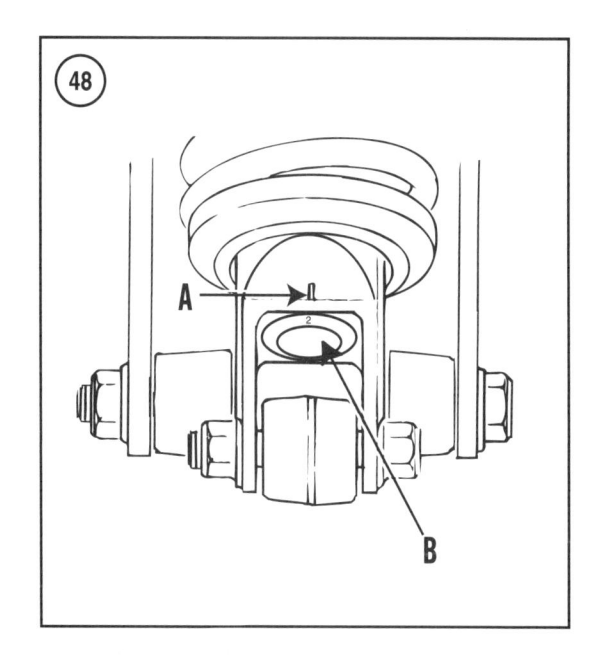

The spring preload can be adjusted to seven different positions to best suit riding, load and speed conditions. The third position is the standard setting on 1995-1999 models. On 2000 models, the fourth position is the standard setting.

Fasteners

Constant vibration can loosen many of the fasteners on a motorcycle. Check the tightness of all fasteners, especially those on:
1. Engine mounting hardware.
2. Engine crankcase covers.
3. Handlebar and front fork.
4. Gearshift lever.
5. Brake pedal and lever.
6. Exhaust system.
7. Removable frame downtube.

ENGINE TUNE-UP

The following section describes tune-up procedures. Perform these tasks in the following order:
1. Clean or replace the air filter element.
2. Check and adjust the valve clearances (engine must be cold).
3. Perform a compression test.
4. Check or replace the spark plugs.
5. Check and adjust the carburetor idle speed and synchronization.

Air Filter Element

Clean or replace the air filter element, as previously described in this chapter, prior to performing the following tune-up procedures.

Valve Clearance Measurement

The correct valve clearance for all models is listed in **Table 4**. The exhaust valves are located at the front of the engine and the intake valves are located at the rear.

The cylinders are numbered from left to right, 1-4. The left and right sides refer to the position of the parts as viewed by the rider sitting on the seat facing forward.

The figures in this procedure show the engine removed from the frame for clarity, it is not necessary to remove the engine to adjust the valves.

The engine *must* be cold (below 35° C [95° F]) to obtain accurate results.

NOTE
For this procedure the camshaft lobes must point away from the tappet as

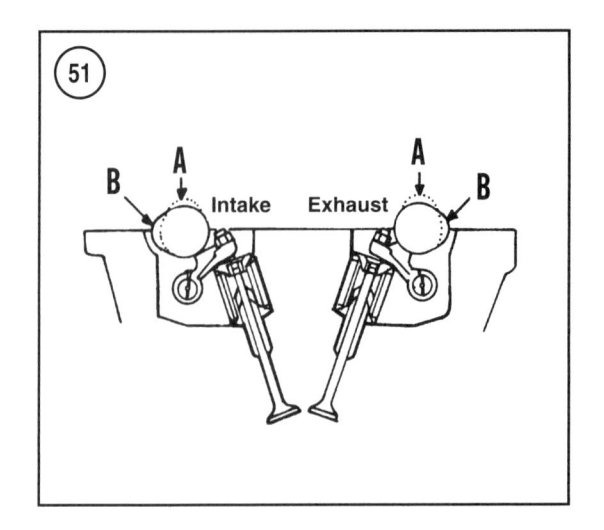

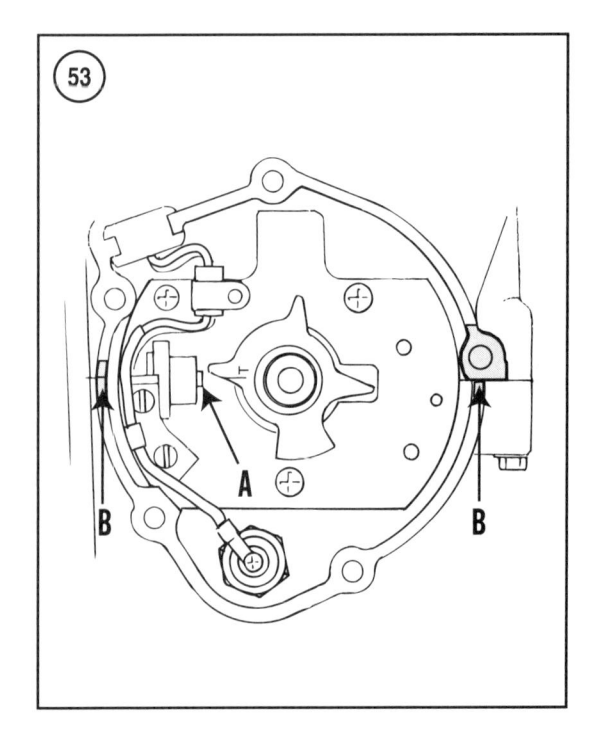

LUBRICATION, MAINTENANCE AND TUNE-UP

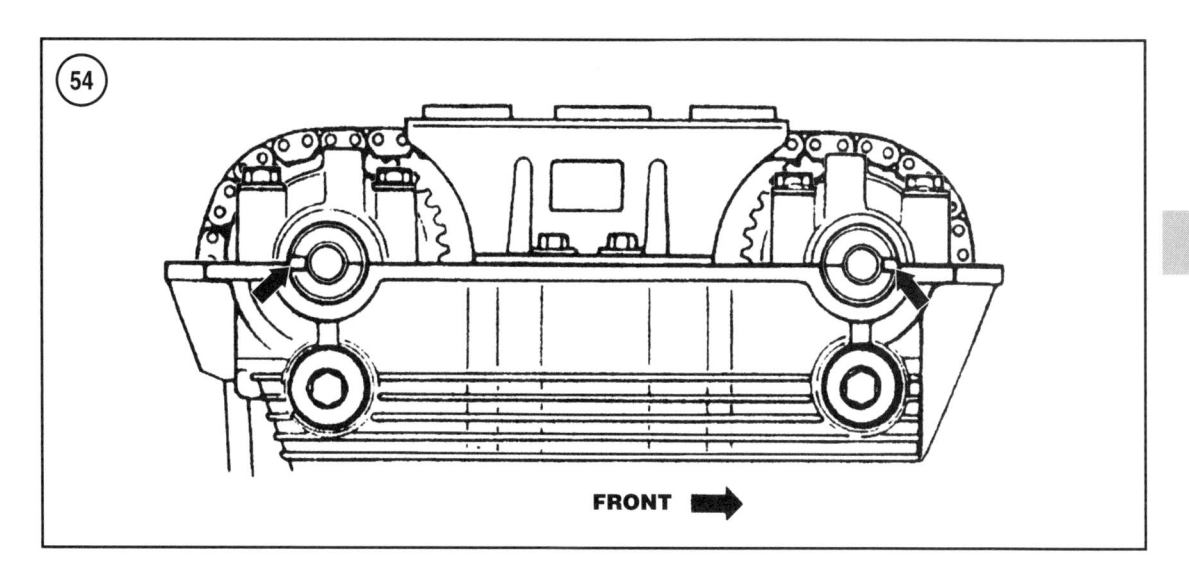

54

*shown in either position A or B, **Figure 51**. Clearance dimensions taken with the camshaft in any other position will give a false reading, leading to incorrect valve clearance adjustment and possible engine damage.*

1. Remove the seat as described in Chapter Fourteen.
2. Remove the fuel tank as described in Chapter Eight.
3. Remove all four spark plugs as described in this chapter. This will make it easier to turn the engine by hand.
4. Following a crisscross pattern, evenly loosen the cylinder head cover bolts, and remove the cylinder head cover as described in Chapter Four.
5. Remove the signal-generator-cover bolts, and remove the cover and its gasket. One bolt has a sealing washer installed beneath it. Note the position of this bolt. It will have to be reinstalled in the same location during assembly. See **Figure 52**.

CAUTION
Always use a 19 mm wrench on the flats of the signal generator rotor when rotating the engine. Do not use the Allen bolt that secures the rotor to turn the crankshaft. This bolt may shear off.

6. Correctly position the camshafts by performing the following:
    a. Place a 19 mm wrench on the flats of the signal generator rotor. Rotate the engine *clockwise* until the T-mark on the signal generator rotor aligns with the center of the pickup coil (A, **Figure 53**).
    b. At the same time, bring the camshaft notches, on the right side of each camshaft, to the positions shown in **Figure 54**.
    c. If the camshaft notches do not point out as shown, rotate the engine 360° (one full revolution) until the camshaft notches are positioned correctly and the signal generator T-mark aligns with the pickup coil.
7. With the engine in this position, check the valve clearance for each valve indicated by C, **Figure 55**. These are:
    a. No. 1 cylinder: Intake and exhaust valves.
    b. No. 2 cylinder: Exhaust valves.
    c. No. 3 cylinder: Intake valves.
8. Check the clearance by inserting a flat feeler gauge (**Figure 56**) between the adjusting screw and each valve stem. When the clearance is correct, there will be a slight drag on the feeler gauge when it is inserted and withdrawn.
9. To adjust the clearance, perform the following:
    a. Loosen the adjuster locknut.
    b. Screw the adjuster in or out so there is a slight resistance felt on the feeler gauge.
    c. Hold the adjuster to prevent it from turning further, and tighten the locknut securely.
    d. Recheck the clearance to make sure the adjuster did not turn after the correct clearance was achieved. Readjust if necessary.
    e. Repeat for the adjuster of the other valve controlled by the same rocker arm.

55

FRONT

Cylinder No. 1 2 3 4

Exhaust

Intake

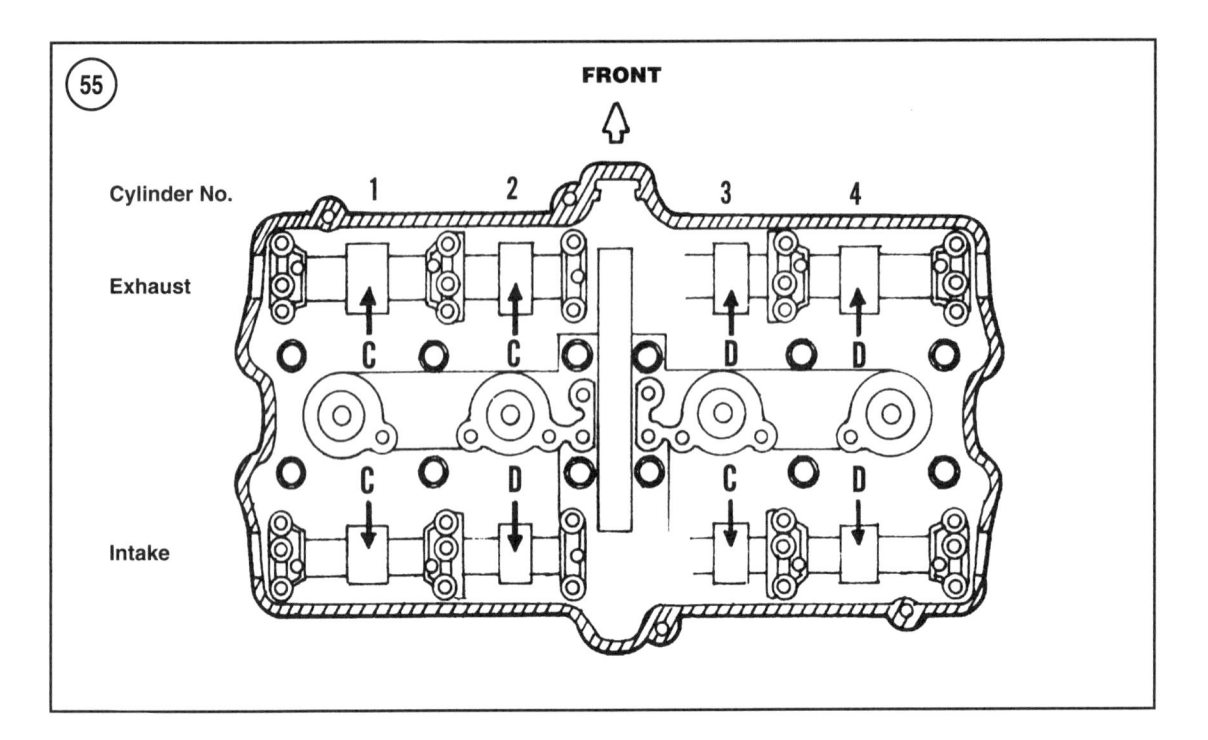

f. Repeat this checking/adjustment procedure for all the valves indicated at C, **Figure 55**.

10. Correctly reposition the camshafts by performing the following:
   a. Place a 19 mm wrench on the flats of the signal generator rotor. Rotate the engine one full turn (360°) *clockwise* until the T-mark on the signal generator rotor aligns with the center of the pickup coil (A, **Figure 53**).
   b. At the same time, bring the camshaft notches, on the right side of each camshaft, to the position shown in **Figure 57**.
   c. If the camshaft notches do not point inward as shown, rotate the engine 360° (one full revolution) until the camshaft notches are positioned correctly and the signal generator T-mark aligns with the pickup coil.

11. With the engine in this position, check the valve clearance for each valve indicated by D, **Figure 55**. These are:
   a. Cylinder No. 2: intake valves.
   b. Cylinder No. 3: exhaust valves.
   c. Cylinder No. 4: intake and exhaust valves.

12. Check the valve clearances as described in Step 8. If any valve indicated by D, **Figure 55** is out of specification, adjust it as described in Step 9.

13. Once all valves are within specification, install the cylinder head cover as described in Chapter Four.

56

14. Install the signal generator cover and a *new* gasket.
   a. Apply a light coat of gasket sealer to the groove in the rubber grommet (**Figure 58**).
   b. Also apply gasket sealer to the cover mating surfaces shown by A, **Figure 53**.
   c. Tighten the cover bolts securely. Be sure the bolt with the sealing washer is in the location noted during disassembly (**Figure 52**).

Cam Chain Adjustment

An automatic cam chain tensioner assembly is attached to the backside of the cylinder head. Adjustment is neither possible nor required.

LUBRICATION, MAINTENANCE AND TUNE-UP

57

58

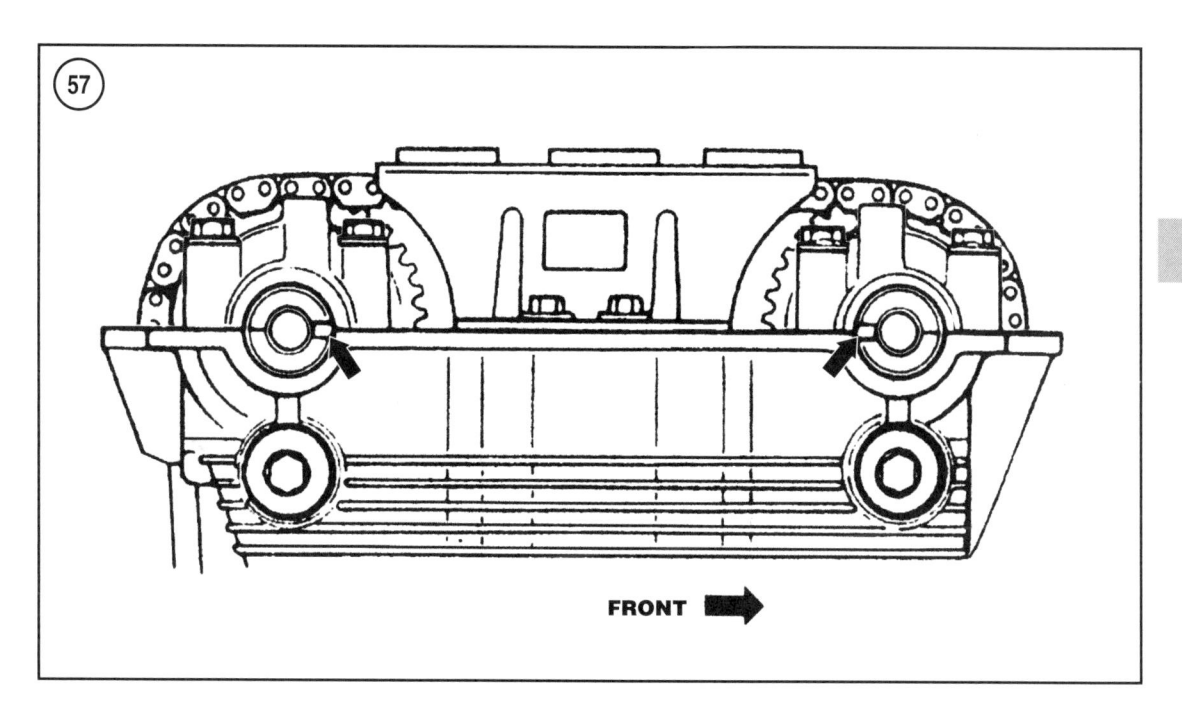

Compression Test

A cylinder cranking compression check is one of the quickest ways to check the internal condition of the engine, including the pistons, piston rings and head gasket. Check the compression at each tune-up, record the readings and compare them with the readings at the next tune-up. This may help reveal developing problems.

1. Prior to starting the compression test, make sure the following items are correct:
   a. The cylinder head bolts are tightened to the specified torque. Refer to Chapter Four.
   b. The valves are properly adjusted as described in this chapter.
   c. The battery is fully charged to ensure proper engine cranking speed.
2. Warm the engine to normal operating temperature. Turn the engine off.
3. Remove the fuel tank as described in Chapter Eight.
4. Remove all four spark plugs as described in this chapter.

NOTE
A screw-in type compression gauge with a flexible adapter is required for this procedure. Before using this gauge, check the condition of the rubber gasket on the end of the adapter. This gasket is very important. It seals the spark plug hole and cylinder to ensure accurate compression readings. Replace the seal if it is cracked or starting to deteriorate.

5. Lubricate the adapter with a light coat of antiseize compound to prevent damaging the spark plug hole threads in the cylinder head.
6. Thread the tip of a compression gauge into the No. 4 cylinder following the manufacturer's instructions.

CAUTION
Do not crank the engine more than absolutely necessary. When the spark

plug leads are disconnected, the electronic ignition will produce the highest voltage possible and the coils may overheat and be damaged.

7. *Open the throttle completely* and turn the engine over until there is no further rise in pressure. Maximum pressure is usually reached within 4-7 seconds. Record the pressure reading for that cylinder. The recommended cylinder compression and the maximum allowable difference between cylinders are listed in **Table 4**.

8. Remove the compression gauge from that cylinder.

9. Repeat Steps 5-8 for the remaining three cylinders and record the readings.

10. Compare the compression readings of the cylinders. Engine service is required if the readings are as follows:
  a. Compression in any cylinder is less than 800 kPa (114 psi).
  b. The compression in all four cylinders is less than 1000 kPa (142 psi).
  c. The difference in readings between any two cylinders exceeds 200 kPa (28 psi).

11. Low compression pressure indicates one or more of the following:
  a. Excessively worn cylinder walls.
  b. Worn piston or piston rings.
  c. Piston ring stuck in its groove.
  d. Poor valve seating.
  e. Defective cylinder head gasket.

12. To determine whether the problem is valve or ring related, pour a teaspoon of engine oil into the spark plug hole of the low-reading cylinder and repeat Step 6-7.
  a. If the compression increases significantly, the piston rings are probably worn.
  b. If the compression does not increase, the valves are leaking.

13. Install the spark plugs, plug caps, and the fuel tank.

SPARK PLUGS

Heat Range Selection

Spark plugs are available in various heat ranges, hotter or colder than the OEM plugs.

Select a plug with a heat range designed for the loads and conditions under which the motorcycle will be run. A plug with an incorrect heat range can foul, overheat and cause piston damage.

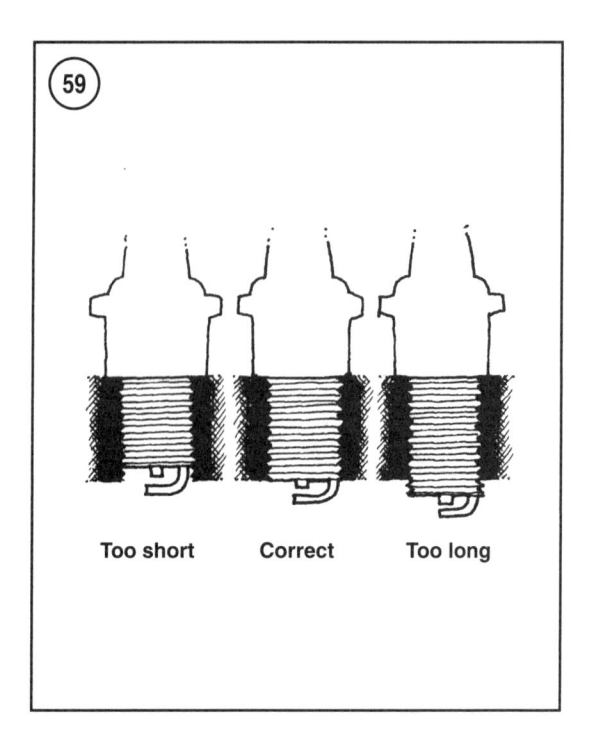

In general, use a hot plug for low speeds and low temperatures. Use a cold plug for high speeds, high engine loads and high temperatures. The plug should operate hot enough to burn off unwanted deposits, but not so hot that it is damaged or causes preignition. To determine if the plugs have a proper heat range, remove each spark plug and examine the portion of the insulator that sits inside the combustion chamber. Its color should be light tan.

Do not change the spark plug heat range to compensate for adverse engine or carburetion conditions.

LUBRICATION, MAINTENANCE AND TUNE-UP

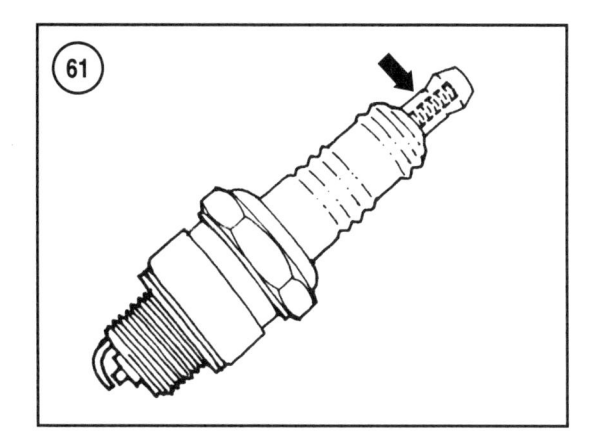

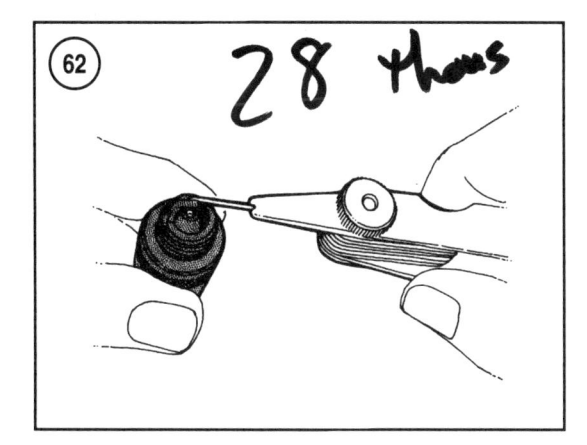

61

62 28 thous

The reach (length) of a plug is also important. A longer than normal plug could interfere with the piston, causing permanent and severe damage; refer to **Figure 59**.

Refer to **Table 4** for recommended spark plugs.

Spark Plugs Removal

A spark plug can be used to help determine the operating condition of its cylinder when properly read. As each spark plug is removed, label it with its cylinder number. If anything turns up during the inspection, knowing which cylinder a plug came from will be useful.

The cylinders are numbered from left to right, 1-4. The left and right sides refer to the position of the parts as viewed by the rider sitting on the seat facing forward.

1. Remove the seat as described in Chapter Fourteen.
2. Remove the fuel tank as described in Chapter Eight.

CAUTION
Whenever a spark plug is removed, dirt around it can fall into the plug hole. This can cause serious engine damage.

3. Blow away all loose dirt, and then wipe off the top surface of the cylinder head cover. Remove all loose debris that could fall into the cylinder head spark plug tunnels.
4. Carefully disconnect the spark plug cap from each spark plug. The plug caps form a tight seal on the cylinder head cover as well as the spark plugs. Grasp the plug cap (**Figure 60**), and twist it from side-to-side to break the seal loose. Carefully pull the plug cap up and off the spark plug. If it is stuck to the plug, twist it slightly to break it loose.

NOTE
If plugs are difficult to remove, apply penetrating oil around base of plugs and let it soak in about 10-20 minutes.

5. Remove the spark plugs with an 18 mm spark plug wrench. Label each spark plug by cylinder number.

NOTE
Do not clean the spark plugs with a sand-blasting type device. While this type of cleaning is thorough, the plug must be absolutely free of all abrasive cleaning material when done. Any cleaning material left on the plug will fall into the cylinder during operation and cause damage.

6. Inspect the spark plug carefully. Look for a plug with broken center porcelain, excessively eroded electrodes and excessive carbon or oil fouling. Replace such a plug. If deposits are light, the plug may be cleaned in solvent with a wire brush or in a special spark plug cleaner. Regap the plug as explained in this chapter.

Gapping and Installing the Plugs

Carefully gap the spark plugs to ensure a reliable, consistent spark with a special spark plug gapping tool and a wire feeler gauge.

1. Remove the new spark plugs from the boxes. If installed, unscrew the small adapter from the end of the plug (**Figure 61**). This adapter is *not* used.
2. Insert a wire feeler gauge between the center and side electrodes of the plug (**Figure 62**). The speci-

fied gap is listed in **Table 4**. If the gap is correct, a slight drag will be felt as the wire is pulled through. If there is no drag or if the gauge will not pass through, bend the side electrode with a gapping tool (**Figure 63**) and set the gap to specification.

3. Apply a light coat of antiseize compound onto the threads of the spark plug before installing it. Do not use engine oil on the plug threads.

CAUTION
The cylinder head is aluminum. The spark plug hole threads can be easily damaged by cross-threading of the spark plug.

4. Attach a length of vinyl or rubber hose to the top end of the spark plug. Screw the spark plug in by hand until it seats. Very little effort is required. If force is necessary, the plug is cross-threaded. Unscrew it and try again. Once screwed on several complete revolutions, remove the hose.

NOTE
Do not overtighten the spark plug. This will only squash the gasket and destroy its sealing ability.

5. Use the same tool set-up used during removal and hand tighten the plug until it seats on the spark plug hole in the cylinder head. Tighten the plug to the torque specification listed in **Table 5**.

CAUTION
Do not use a plastic hammer or any type of tool to tap the plug cap assembly onto the spark plug, as the assembly will be damaged. Use fingers only.

NOTE
Be sure to push the plug cap all the way down to make full contact with the spark plug post. If the cap does not completely contact the plug, the engine may start to falter and cut out at high engine speeds.

6. Refer to the marks made during removal and install each plug cap onto the correct spark plug. Press the cap (**Figure 60**) onto the spark plug, rotate the assembly slightly in both directions and make sure it is attached to the spark plug and to the sealing surface of the cylinder head cover.

7. Install the fuel tank as described in Chapter Eight.

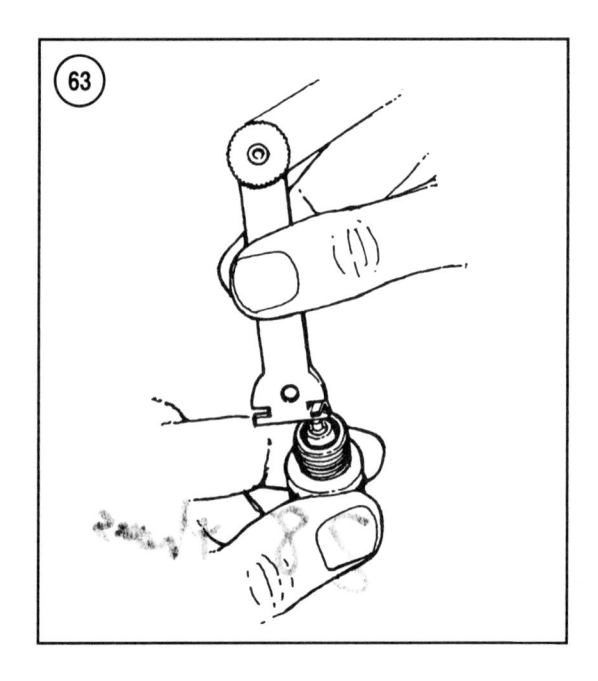

8. Install the seat as described in Chapter Fourteen.

Reading Spark Plugs

Reading the spark plugs can provide a significant amount of information regarding engine performance. Reading plugs that have been in use will give an indication of spark plug operation, air/fuel mixture composition and engine condition (oil consumption, pistons, etc.). Before checking the spark plugs, operate the motorcycle under a medium load for approximately 6 miles (10 km). Avoid prolonged idling before shutting off the engine. Remove the spark plugs as described in this chapter. Examine each plug and compare it to those in **Figure 64**.

If the plugs are being read to determine if carburetor jetting is correct, start with new plugs and operate the motorcycle at the load that corresponds to the jetting information desired. For example, if the main jet is in question, operate the motorcycle at full throttle and shut the engine off and coast to a stop.

Normal condition

A light tan- or gray-colored deposit on the firing tip and no abnormal gap wear or erosion indicate good engine, ignition and air/fuel mixture conditions. A plug with the proper heat range is being used. It may be serviced and returned to use.

LUBRICATION, MAINTENANCE AND TUNE-UP

SPARK PLUG CONDITIONS

NORMAL USE

OIL FOULED

CARBON FOULED

OVERHEATED

GAP BRIDGED

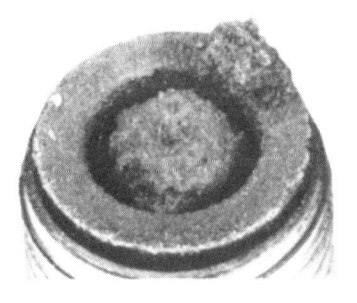

SUSTAINED PREIGNITION

WORN OUT

Carbon fouled

Soft, dry, sooty deposits covering the entire firing end of the plug are evidence of incomplete combustion. Even though the firing end of the plug is dry, the deposits decrease the plug's insulation. The carbon forms an electrical path that bypasses the electrodes resulting in a misfire condition. Carbon fouling can be caused by one or more of the following conditions:
1. Rich air/fuel mixture.
2. Cold spark plug heat range.
3. Clogged air filter.
4. Improperly operating ignition component.
5. Ignition component failure.
6. Low engine compression.
7. Prolonged idling.

Oil fouled

An oil-fouled plug has a black insulator tip, a damp oily film over the firing end and a carbon layer over the entire nose. The electrodes are not worn. Common causes for this condition are:
1. Incorrect air/fuel mixture.
2. Low idle speed or prolonged idling.
3. Ignition component failure.
4. Cold spark plug heat range.
5. Engine still being broken in.
6. Worn valve guides.
7. Worn or broken piston rings.

Oil-fouled spark plugs may be cleaned in an emergency, but it is better to replace them. It is important to correct the cause of fouling before the engine is returned to service.

Gap bridging

Plugs with this condition have deposits building up between the electrodes. The deposits reduce the gap and eventually close it entirely. If this condition is encountered, check for excessive carbon or oil in the combustion chamber. Be sure to locate and correct the cause of this condition.

Overheating

Badly worn electrodes and premature gap wear are signs of overheating, along with a gray or white blistered porcelain insulator surface. This condition is commonly caused by a spark plug with a heat range that is too hot. If the plug is overheated, consider the following causes:
1. Lean air/fuel mixture.
2. Improperly operating ignition component.
3. Engine lubrication system malfunction.
4. Cooling system malfunction.
5. Engine air leak.
6. Improper spark plug installation (for example, overtightening).
7. No spark plug gasket.

Worn out

Corrosive gases formed by combustion and high voltage sparks have eroded the electrodes. A spark plug in this condition requires more voltage to fire under hard acceleration. Install a new spark plug.

Preignition

If the electrodes are melted, preignition is almost certainly the cause. Check for carburetor mounting or intake manifold leaks and advanced ignition timing. The plug heat range may also be too hot. Find the cause of the preignition before returning the engine into service. For additional information on preignition, refer to Chapter Two.

Ignition Timing

The engine is equipped with fully transistorized ignition system. This solid-state system uses no breaker points or other moving parts, and there are no means of adjusting or checking ignition timing. Because of the solid-state design, problems with the transistorized system are rare. If there is an ignition-related problem, inspect the ignition components as described in Chapter Nine.

Incorrect ignition timing can cause a drastic loss of engine performance and efficiency. It may also cause overheating.

Idle Speed Adjustment

Before making this adjustment, clean the air filter element and check engine compression as described in this chapter. Idle speed cannot be properly set un-

LUBRICATION, MAINTENANCE AND TUNE-UP

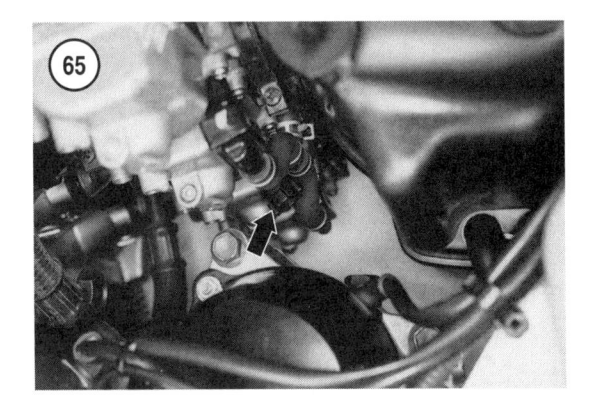

less the filter is clean and the engine has adequate compression.

1. Make sure the throttle cable free play is adjusted correctly. Adjust free play if necessary as described in this chapter.

2. Connect a tachometer following the manufacturer's instructions.

3. Start the engine and let it warm up approximately 2-3 minutes. Make sure the choke lever is all the way forward in the OFF position.

4. The idle speed knob (**Figure 65**) is under the carburetor assembly, between the second and third carburetors. Turn the idle speed knob in or out to adjust the idle speed to the specification in **Table 4**.

5. Open and close the throttle a couple of times. Check for variations in idle speed, and readjust if necessary.

WARNING
With the engine running at idle speed, move the handlebar from side to side. If idle speed increases during this movement, the throttle cable needs adjusting or may be incorrectly routed through the frame. Correct this problem immediately. Do not ride the vehicle in this unsafe condition.

6. Turn off the engine.
7. Disconnect the tachometer.

Carburetor Idle Mixture

The idle mixture (pilot screw) is pre-set by the manufacturer and is *not* to be reset. Do not adjust the pilot screws unless the carburetors have been overhauled. If so, refer to Chapter Eight.

Carburetor Synchronization

To ensure maximum engine performance, the carburetors must be synchronized. This procedure ensures that each carburetor is opening the same amount throughout the throttle range.

Synchronization tools are available in a number of different styles; some measure engine vacuum with a traditional vacuum gauge or by the movement of mercury within a glass tube, while some perform this function electronically. In addition to the synchronization tool, an auxiliary fuel tank and tachometer are required for this procedure. If this equipment is not available, have a Suzuki dealership or motorcycle specialist perform the operation. Do not attempt to synchronize the carburetors without the proper equipment. Doing so will result in misadjustment and poor engine performance.

NOTE
Prior to synchronizing the carburetors, clean the air filter element and adjust the valve clearance.

1. Start the engine and let it reach normal operating temperature.

2. Adjust the idle speed as described in this chapter, and then shut off the engine.

3. Install a portable tachometer following the manufacturer's instructions.

4. Remove the fuel tank as described in Chapter Eight.

WARNING
When using an auxiliary fuel tank, make sure the tank is secure and that all fuel lines are tight to prevent leaks.

NOTE
Fuel tanks from small displacement motorcycles, ATV's and lawn mowers make excellent auxiliary fuel tanks. Make sure the tank is mounted securely and positioned so that the connecting fuel hose is not kinked or obstructed.

5. Install an auxiliary fuel tank onto the motorcycle, and attach its fuel hose to the carburetor assembly.

6. Balance the vacuum gauge set, following the manufacturer's instructions.

7. Label and disconnect the vacuum hose or vacuum cap from the vacuum fitting on each carburetor.

   a. Disconnect the fuel-valve vacuum hose (**Figure 66**) from the fitting on the No. 4 carburetor.

   b. On models with a PAIR system, disconnect the PAIR vacuum hose from the vacuum fitting on the No. 3 carburetor. On models without a PAIR system, remove the vacuum plug from this fitting.

   c. Remove the vacuum plug from the vacuum fittings on the No 1 and No 2 carburetors.

8. Connect the vacuum gauge set to the vacuum fittings following the manufacturer's instructions.

9. Start the engine. Turn the idle adjust knob (**Figure 65**) until the engine idles at 1750 rpm.

10. If the carburetors are correctly balanced, the steel balls in the vacuum gauge set will all be at the same level.

NOTE
The No. 3 carburetor is the base carburetor. It has no synchronizing screw. The other carburetors must be synchronized to the No. 3 carburetor.

11. Turn the synchronizing screws (**Figure 67**), and adjust the No 1, 2 and 4 carburetors so they each have the same gauge reading as the No. 3 carburetor. Snap the throttle a few times and recheck the synchronization readings. Readjust synchronization if required.

12. Reset the idle speed to the specification in **Table 4**.

13. Shut off the engine.

14. Disconnect the auxiliary fuel tank and the vacuum gauge set from the carburetors.

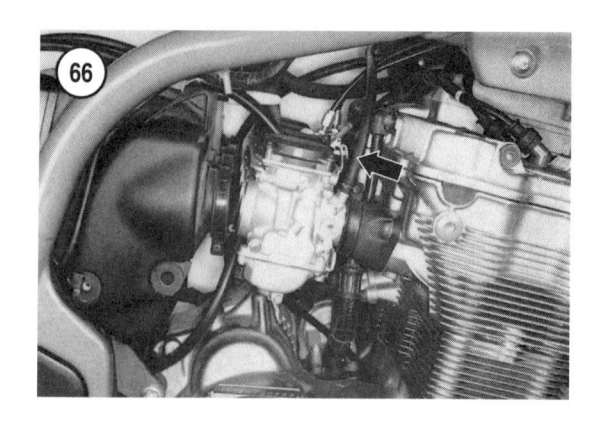

15. Install the vacuum hoses or plugs to the correct fittings. Make sure they are properly seated to avoid a vacuum leak.

16. Install the fuel tank as described in Chapter Eight.

17. Restart the engine and reset the engine idle speed to the value specified in **Table 4**, if necessary.

18. Shut off the engine.

STORAGE

Refer to Chapter One.

Table 1 MAINTENANCE SCHEDULE

Weekly/gas stop
Check tire pressure cold; adjust to suit load (Table 2)
Check condition of tires
Check brakes for a solid feel
Check throttle grip for smooth operation and return
Check for smooth but not loose steering
Check axles, suspension, controls, linkage nuts, bolts and fasteners; tighten if necessary
Check engine oil level; add oil if necessary
Check lights and horn operation, especially brake light
(continued)

LUBRICATION, MAINTENANCE AND TUNE-UP

Table 1 MAINTENANCE SCHEDULE (continued)

Weekly/gas stop (continued)
  Check for any abnormal engine noise and leaks
  Check kill switch operation

Every 600 miles (1,000 km) or 1 month
  Check the valve clearance; adjust if necessary
  Change engine oil and replace oil filter
  Check idle speed; adjust if necessary
  Check throttle cable free play; adjust if necessary
  Clean, lubricate and adjust the drive chain
  Check brake pads for wear
  Check brake discs thickness; replace if necessary
  Check brake discs for rust and corrosion; clean if necessary
  Check steering play; adjust if necessary
  Check and tighten all nuts, bolts and fasteners on the cylinder head and exhaust system
  Check tightness of all chassis bolts and nuts; tighten if necessary
  On California models, inspect the EVAP system and synchronize the carburetors

Every 4,000 miles (6,000 km) or 12 months
  Check the valve clearance; adjust if necessary
  Check air filter element for contamination; clean or replace if necessary
  Check spark plugs; replace if necessary
  Check all fuel system hoses for leakage; repair or replace if necessary
  Check the EVAP system on California models
  Replace the engine oil and filter
  Check idle speed; adjust if necessary
  Check throttle cable free play; adjust if necessary
  Check clutch lever free play; adjustment; adjust if necessary
  Check battery charge and condition of battery
  Clean and lubricate the drive chain
  Check drive chain and sprockets for wear or damage
  Check drive chain slack; adjust if necessary
  Check brake pads for wear
  Check brake discs thickness; replace if necessary
  Check brake discs for rust and corrosion; clean if necessary
  Check brake system for leakage; repair if necessary
  Check brake fluid level in both reservoirs; add fluid if necessary
  Check tire and wheel rim condition
  Lubricate all pivot points
  Check and tighten all nuts, bolts and fasteners on the cylinder head and exhaust system
  Check tightness of all chassis bolts and nuts; tighten if necessary

Every 7,500 miles (12,000 km) or 24 months
  All of the checks listed in 4,000 miles (6,000 km) or 12 months and the following
  Replace all four spark plugs
  Synchronize carburetors
  Check front fork operation and for leakage
  Check PAIR (air supply) system
  Check steering play; adjust if necessary
  Check the rear suspension
  Lubricate control cables

Every 11,000 miles (18,000 km) or 36 months
  All of the checks listed in 4,000 miles (6,000 km) or 12 months and the following
  Replace air filter element

Every 15,000 miles (24,000 km) or 48 months
  All of the checks listed in 7,500 miles (12,000 km) or 24 months
  Replace all four spark plugs

(continued)

CHAPTER THREE

Table 1 MAINTENANCE SCHEDULE (continued)

Every 2 years
  Replace brake fluid

Every 4 years
  Replace all brake hoses
  Replace EVAP hoses (California models)
  Replace all fuel lines

Table 2 TIRE SPECIFICATIONS

Item	Front	Rear
Tire type	Tubeless	Tubeless
Size		
1995-1999 GSF600 models	110/70-17 54H	150/70-17 69H
1996-1999 GSF600S models		
U.S.A., California and Canada models	110/70-17 54H	150/70-17 69H
All models except U.S.A., California and Canada	110/70 ZR17	150/70 ZR17
2000 models	120/60 ZR17 (55W)	160/60 ZR17 (69W)
Minimum tread depth	1.6 mm (0.06 in.)	2.0 mm (0.08 in.)
Inflation pressure (cold)*		
Solo	225 kPa (33 psi)	250 kPa (36 psi)
Rider and passenger	225 kPa (33 psi)	250 kPa (36 psi)

*Tire inflation pressure is for original equipment tires. Aftermarket tires may require different inflation pressure. The use of tires other than those specified by Suzuki may cause instability.

Table 3 RECOMMENDED LUBRICANTS AND FLUIDS

Fuel	Unleaded
Octane	87 [(R + M)/2 method] or research octane of 91 or higher
Fuel tank capacity, including reserve	
1995-1999	19.0 L (5.0 U.S. gal., 4.2 Imp. gal.)
2000	
California models	19.0 L (5.0 U.S. gal., 4.2 Imp. gal.)
U.S.A., Australia, Canada and European models	20.0 L (5.3 U.S. gal., 4.4 Imp. gal.)
Fuel tank reserve capacity	4.5 L (5.3 U.S. gal., 1.0 Imp. gal.)
Engine oil	
Grade	API SF or SG
Viscosity	SAE 10W40
Capacity	
Oil change only	3.3 L (3.5 U.S. qt., 2.9 Imp. qt.)
Oil and filter change	3.5 L (3.7 U.S. qt., 3.1 Imp. qt.)
When engine completely dry	4.6 L (4.9 U.S. qt., 4.0 Imp. qt.])
Brake fluid	DOT 4
Fork oil	
Viscosity	Suzuki #10 fork oil or equivalent
Capacity per leg	
1995-1999 GSF600 models	521 ml (17.6 U.S. oz., 18.3 Imp. oz.)
1996-1999 GSF600S models	
U.S.A., California and Canada models	522 ml (17.7 U.S. oz., 18.4 Imp. oz.)
All models except U.S.A., California and Canada models	521 ml (17.6 U.S. oz., 18.3 Imp. oz.)

(continued)

LUBRICATION, MAINTENANCE AND TUNE-UP

Table 3 RECOMMENDED LUBRICANTS AND FLUIDS (continued)

Fork oil (continued)	
Capacity per leg (continued)	
2000 GSF600 models	508 ml (17.18 U.S. oz., 17.9 Imp. oz.)
2000 GSF600S models	
U.S.A., California and Canada models	506 ml (17.11 U.S. oz., 17.8 Imp. oz.)
All models except U.S.A., California and Canada	510 ml (17.24 U.S. oz., 18.0 Imp. oz.)

Table 4 MAINTENANCE AND TUNE-UP SPECIFICATIONS

Battery	
Type	YTX9-BS Maintenance free (sealed)
Capacity	12 volt 8 amp hour
Spark plug	
Standard	NGK: CR9EK, ND: U27ETR
Hot type	NGK: CR8EK, ND: U24ETR
Cold type	NGK: CR10EK, ND: UT31ETR
Spark plug gap	0.6-0.7 mm (0.024-0.028 in.)
Idle speed	
1995 models	
All models except Switzerland	1100-1300 rpm
Switzerland models	1150-1300 rpm
1996 models	
All models except Switzerland	1100-1300 rpm
Switzerland models	
GSF600	1100-1300 rpm
GSF600S	1150-1300 rpm
1997-1999 models	
All models except Switzerland	1100-1300 rpm
Switzerland models	1150-1300 rpm
2000 models	1100-1300 rpm
Firing order	1-2-4-3
Valve clearance (cold)	
Intake	0.10-0.15 mm (0.004-0.006 in.)
Exhaust	0.18-0.23 mm (0.007-0.090 in.)
Compression pressure (at sea level)	
Standard	1000-1500 kPa (145-218 psi)
Service limit	800 kPa (116 psi)
Maximum difference between cylinders	200 kPa (29 psi)
Engine oil pressure @ 60° C (140° F)	300-600 kPa (43-87 psi) @ 3000 rpm
Brake pedal height	
1995-1999 models	45 mm (1.8 in.)
2000 models	50 mm (2.0 in.)
Throttle cable free play	
1995-1999 models	
Return (push) cable	0 mm
Pull cable	0.5-1.0 mm (0.02-0.04 in.)
2000 models	2.0-4.0 mm (0.08-0.16 in.)
Clutch lever free play	10-15 mm (0.4-0.6 in.)
Rim runout (front and rear)	
Axial	2.0 mm (0.08 in.)
Radial	2.0 mm (0.08 in.)
Drive chain 21-pin length	319.4 mm (12.6 in.)
Drive chain free play	25-35 mm (0.9-1.4 in.)

Table 5 MAINTENANCE AND TUNE UP TORQUE SPECIFICATIONS

Item	N•m	in.-lb.	ft.-lb.
Brake hose banjo bolt	23	–	17
Cylinder base nut	9	80	–
Cylinder head bolt, 6 mm	10	88	–
Cylinder-head-cover banjo bolt	16	–	11.5
Cylinder head cover bolt	14	–	10
Cylinder head nut, 10 mm	38	–	28
Engine sprocket nut	115	–	85
Exhaust pipe bolt	23	–	17
Front axle	65	–	48
Front axle pinch bolt	23	–	17
Handlebar clamp bolt	23	–	17
Main oil gallery plug	40	–	29
Muffler mounting bolt			
1995-1999 models	23	–	17
2000 models	29	–	21
Oil cooler hose banjo bolt			
1995-1999 models	28	–	21
2000 models	23	–	17
Oil drain plug	23	–	17
Oil pan bolt	14	–	10
Rear axle nut	100	–	74
Rear brake master cylinder locknut	18	–	13
Rear torque link nut	35	26	
Removable frame downtube mounting bolt	32	–	23
Spark plug	11	97	–
Valve adjuster locknut	10	88	–

Table 6 BATTERY STATE OF CHARGE

Specific gravity reading	Percentage of charge remaining
1.120-1.140	0
1.135-1.155	10
1.150-1.170	20
1.160-1.180	30
1.175-1.195	40
1.190-1.210	50
1.205-1.255	60
1.215-1.235	70
1.230-1.250	80
1.245-1.265	90
1.260-1.280	100

CHAPTER FOUR

ENGINE TOP END

This chapter provides complete service and overhaul procedures for the top end engine components: the camshafts, valves, cylinder head, pistons, piston rings and the cylinder block.

The Bandit is powered by an air/oil-cooled, in-line four-cylinder, DOHC, 16-valve engine. A single cam chain drives the dual overhead camshafts. Valve actuation is via rocker arms operating directly on the valves.

Cooling is provided by a unique oil system that helps dissipate the engine heat. In addition to the normal engine components that require lubrication, engine oil is also routed through the cylinder head, sprayed onto the lower portion of the pistons and piston pins and directed to any portion of the engine where there is normal heat build-up.

The oil is pumped from the engine and into a frame-mounted oil cooler in front of the engine. From here, the cooled oil returns to the engine. Lubrication system service is covered in Chapter Five.

The cylinder head cover, cylinder head and cylinder block have shallow cooling fins that also help dissipate engine heat.

Tables 1-3 appear at the end of the chapter.

ENGINE SERVICE NOTES

An important part of successful engine service is preparation. Before servicing the engine, note the following:

1. Review the information in Chapter One, especially the *Basic Service Methods* and *Precision*

FOUR-STROKE ENGINE PRINCIPLES

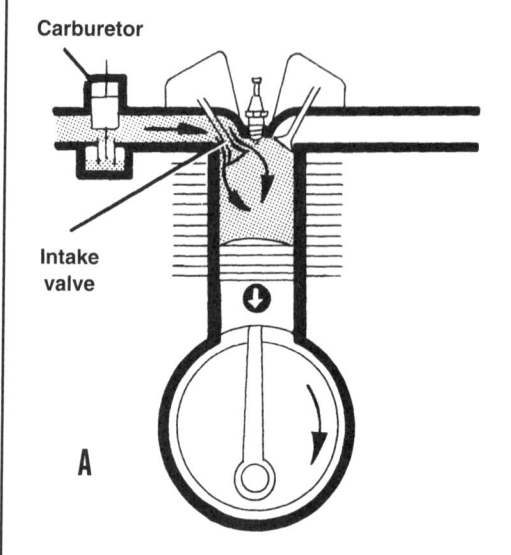

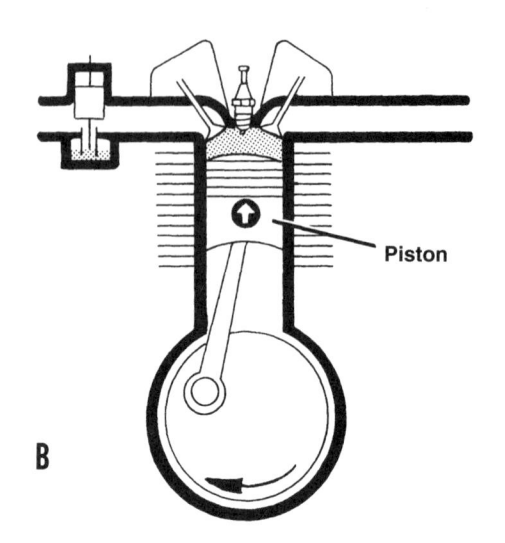

A. As the piston travels downward, the exhaust valve closes and the intake valve opens, drawing the new air-fuel mixture from the carburetor into the cylinder. When the piston reaches the bottom of its travel (BDC), the intake valve closes and remains closed for the next 1 1/2 revolutions of the crankshaft.

B. While the crankshaft continues to rotate, the piston moves upward, compressing the air-fuel mixture.

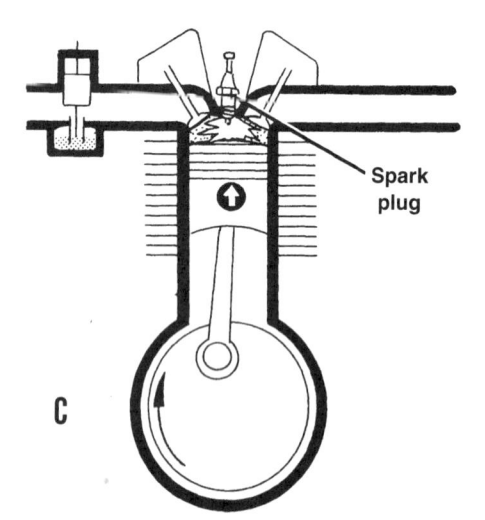

C. As the piston nears the top of its travel, the spark plug fires, igniting the compressed air-fuel mixture. This piston continues to top dead center (TDC) and is pushed downward by the expanding gasses.

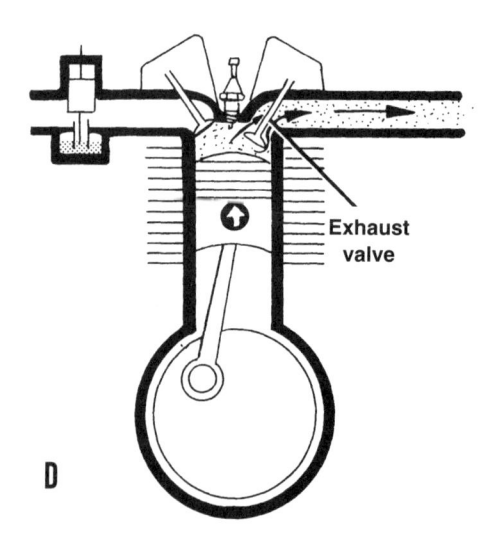

D. When the piston almost reaches BDC, the exhaust valve opens and remains open until the piston is near TDC. The upward travel of the piston forces the exhaust gases out of the cylinder. After the piston has reached TDC, the exhaust valve closes and the cycle repeats.

ENGINE TOP END

Measuring Tools sections. Accurate measurements are critical to a successful engine rebuild.

2. Clean the entire engine and frame with a commercial degreaser before removing engine components. A clean motorcycle is easier to work on and this will help prevent the possibility of dirt and debris falling into the open engine.

3. Have all the necessary tools and parts on hand before starting the procedure(s). Store parts in boxes, plastic bags and containers. Use masking tape and a permanent, waterproof marking pen to label parts. Record the location, position and thickness of all shims as they are removed.

4. Use a box of assorted size and color vacuum hose identifiers (Lisle part No. 74600) for identifying hoses and fittings during engine service.

5. Throughout the text there are references to the left and right side of the engine. This refers to the engine as it is mounted in the frame, not how it may sit on the workbench.

6. When inspecting components described in this chapter, compare the measurements to the service specifications listed in **Table 2**. Replace any part that is out of specification, worn to the service limit or damaged.

7. Always replace worn or damaged fasteners with those of the same size, type and torque requirements. If a specific torque value is not listed in **Table 3**, refer to the general torque specifications in Chapter One.

8. Use a vise with protective jaws to hold parts.

9. Use a press or special tools when force is required to remove and install parts. Do not try to pry, hammer or otherwise force them on or off.

10. Replace all O-rings and oil seals during reassembly. Set aside old seals and O-rings so they can be compared with the new ones if necessary. Apply a small amount of grease to the inner lips of each new seal to prevent damage during installation and when the engine is first started.

ENGINE PRINCIPLES

Figure 1 explains basic four-stroke engine operation. This will be helpful when troubleshooting or repairing the engine.

CYLINDER HEAD COVER

The cylinder head cover can be removed with the engine mounted in the frame.

Removal

1. Place the motorcycle on level ground on the centerstand.
2. Remove the fairing and fairing mounting brackets as described in Chapter Fourteen.
3. Disconnect the negative battery cable as described in Chapter Three.
4. Remove the fuel tank as described in Chapter Eight.
5. On models with a PAIR system, remove the PAIR valve assembly as described in Chapter Eight.
6. Disconnect the spark plug wires and caps.
7. Disconnect the crankcase breather hose (A, **Figure 2**) from the breather cover.
8. Remove the breather cover (B, **Figure 2**) and gasket from the top of the cylinder head cover.
9. Remove the mounting bolts securing the oil hose fittings (C, **Figure 2**) to the cylinder head cover, and move the hoses out of the way. Remove the O-rings from each hose fitting. Install *new* O-rings during installation to prevent oil leaks.
10. Using a crisscross pattern, loosen the cylinder head cover bolts and the cylinder head cover banjo bolts. Remove the bolts and their washers.
11. Pull the cover straight up and off the cylinder head, and remove the cover and the gasket (A, **Figure 3**). Do not lose the two locating dowels or the small rubber gasket (B, **Figure 3**) around each spark plug hole in the cover.

Installation

1. Install *new* gaskets onto the cylinder head by performing the following.

a. Remove the old gaskets and clean all gasket sealer residue from the gasket groove around the perimeter of the cover and from the groove around each spark plug hole.
b. Apply ThreeBond Liquid Gasket 1104 or equivalent to the grooves in the cylinder head cover. Follow the sealant manufacturer's instructions.
c. Install a *new* gasket around the perimeter of the cover (A, **Figure 3**) and around each spark plug hole (B, **Figure 3**). Be sure the holes in the spark plug gaskets align with the holes in the cylinder head cover.
d. Apply ThreeBond Liquid Gasket 1104 or equivalent to the half-round camshaft end caps (C, **Figure 3**) on the cylinder head gasket.

2. Fit the cylinder head cover in place on the cylinder head. Make sure the gaskets remain in place on the cover and that they properly mate with the cylinder head. Pay particular attention to the camshaft end caps. Oil will leak if the half-round sections are not properly mated with the cylinder head.

3. Install a new washer onto each cylinder head cover banjo bolt (A, **Figure 4**). Install the banjo bolts into the hole beside the spark plug holes (**Figure 5**), and finger-tighten the bolts.

4. Install the two shouldered cylinder head cover bolts (B, **Figure 4**) into the mounts on the front and rear of the cylinder head cover. See **Figure 6**.

5. Install *new* gaskets onto the eight remaining cylinder head cover bolts (C, **Figure 4**). Install and finger-tighten the bolts.

6. Torque the cylinder head cover banjo bolts to the specification in **Table 3**.

7. Using a crisscross pattern, torque the cylinder head cover bolts to the specification in **Table 3**.

8. Install a *new* O-ring (**Figure 7**) into each fitting on the oil hoses.

9. Move the fittings (C, **Figure 2**) into place on the cylinder head cover, and install the oil hose mounting bolts. Torque the bolts to the specification in **Table 3**.

10. Install the gasket onto the breather cover (**Figure 8**), and set the cover in place on the cylinder head cover (B, **Figure 2**).

11. Spray the breather cover bolts with a rust inhibitor. Install and tighten the bolts securely.

12. Connect the crankcase breather hose (A, **Figure 2**) to the port on the breather cover.

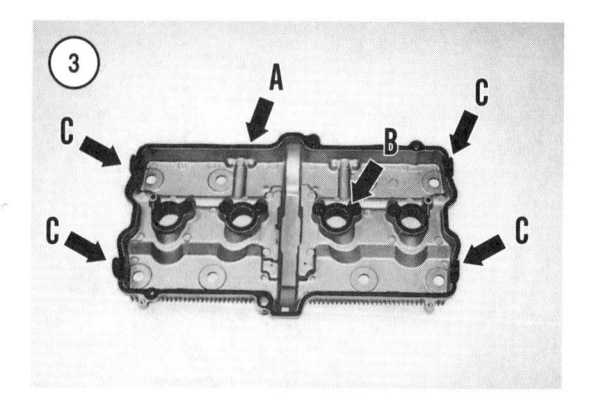

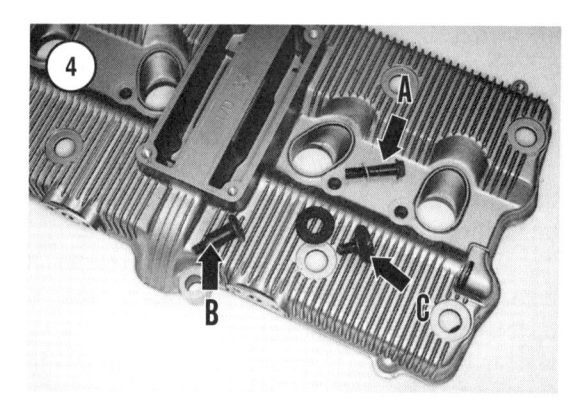

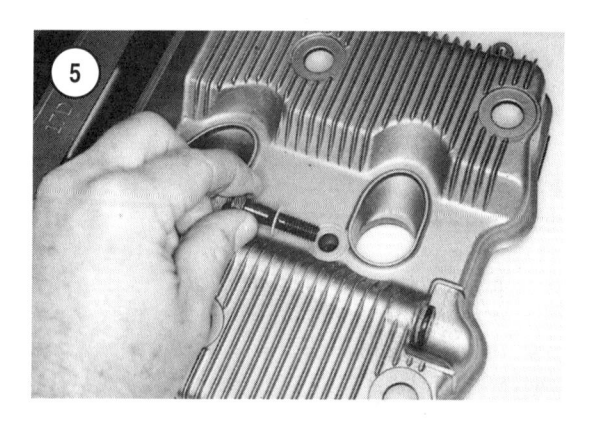

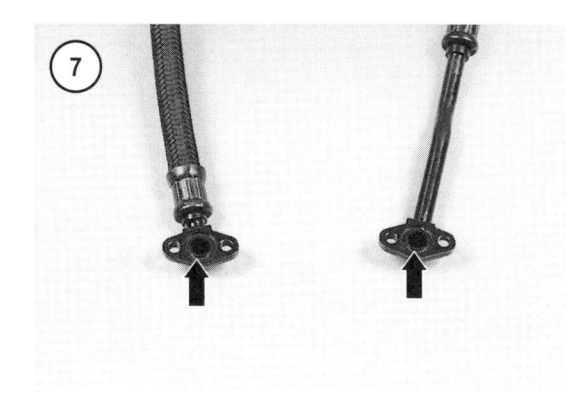

ENGINE TOP END

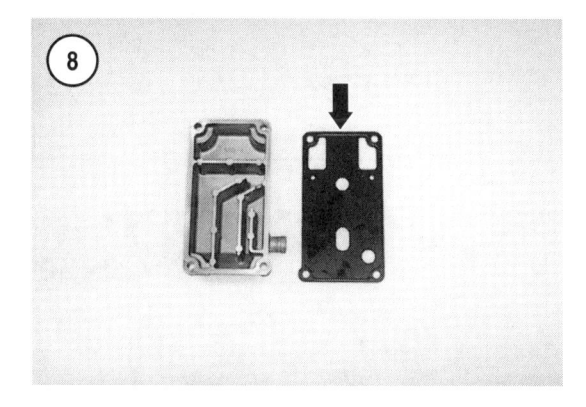

Inspection and Gasket Replacement

1. Make sure the gasket sealing surfaces in the cover are clean and free of any oil buildup from a previously leaking gasket. These surfaces must be clean and smooth to provide an oil-tight seal.
2. Remove the old gaskets from the cylinder head or cover.
3. Remove all old gasket sealer residue from the gasket sealing surface around the perimeter of the cylinder head and from the grooves around the spark plug holes. Be sure to clean off all old sealer from the crescent-shaped machined surfaces at each end of the cylinder head.
4. Check the cylinder head cover (see **Figure 3**) for warp, cracks or damage. Replace the cover if necessary.
5. Inspect the cover bolts for thread damage. Replace the bolts as necessary.

CAMSHAFTS

Removal

1. Remove the cylinder head cover as described in this chapter.
2. Remove all four spark plugs as described in Chapter Three. This makes it easier to turn the engine by hand.
3. Remove the cam chain tensioner as described in this chapter.
4. Remove the signal generator cover bolts, and remove the cover and its gasket. One bolt has a sealing washer installed beneath it (**Figure 9**). Note the position of this bolt. It must be reinstalled in the same location during assembly.

CAUTION
Always use a 19 mm wrench on the flats of the signal generator rotor when rotating the engine. Do not use the Allen bolt that secures the rotor to the crankshaft. This bolt may shear off.

5. Place a 19 mm wrench on the flats of the signal generator rotor. Rotate the engine *clockwise* until the T-mark on the signal generator rotor aligns with the center of the pickup coil (**Figure 10**).
6. Remove the upper cam chain guide mounting bolts (A, **Figure 11**) and remove the upper cam

13. Connect the spark plug wires to the plugs. Make sure each cap securely engages the cylinder head cover.
14. On models with a PAIR system, install the PAIR valve assembly as described in Chapter Eight.
15. Install the fuel tank as described in Chapter Eight.
16. Connect the negative battery cable to the battery terminal as described in Chapter Three.
17. Install the fairing brackets and fairing as described in Chapter Fourteen.

chain guide (B, **Figure 11**) from the cylinder head.

7. Using a crisscross pattern, evenly loosen the bolts securing the camshaft bearing caps (A, **Figure 12**) on the intake camshaft.

8. Using a crisscross pattern, loosen the bolts securing the camshaft bearing caps (B, **Figure 12**) on the exhaust camshaft.

> *NOTE*
> *Note the identification mark on each camshaft bearing cap (**Figure 13**). Each camshaft bearing cap must be reinstalled in its original location in the cylinder head.*

9. Remove all the bearing caps from both camshafts. Do not lose the locating dowel beneath each cap.

10. Disengage the cam chain from the camshaft sprockets, and remove both the intake and exhaust camshafts.

> *CAUTION*
> *If the crankshaft must be rotated while the camshafts are removed, pull the cam chain up so it properly engages the crankshaft timing sprocket. Hold the chain taut on the timing sprocket while rotating the crankshaft. If this is not done, the cam chain could become kinked, which could cause damage to the chain, timing sprocket and surrounding crankcase area.*

11. Tie a piece of wire to the cam chain (**Figure 14**), and secure the loose end of the wire to the frame.

12. Inspect the camshafts as described in this chapter.

Installation

1. Pull the cam chain taut, and make sure it properly engages the crankshaft timing sprocket.

> *CAUTION*
> *Always use a 19 mm wrench on the flats of the signal generator rotor when rotating the engine. Do not use the Allen bolt that secures the rotor to the crankshaft. This bolt may shear off.*

2. Place a 19 mm wrench on the flats of the signal generator rotor. Rotate the engine *clockwise* until the T-mark on the signal generator rotor aligns with the center of the pickup coil (**Figure 10**).

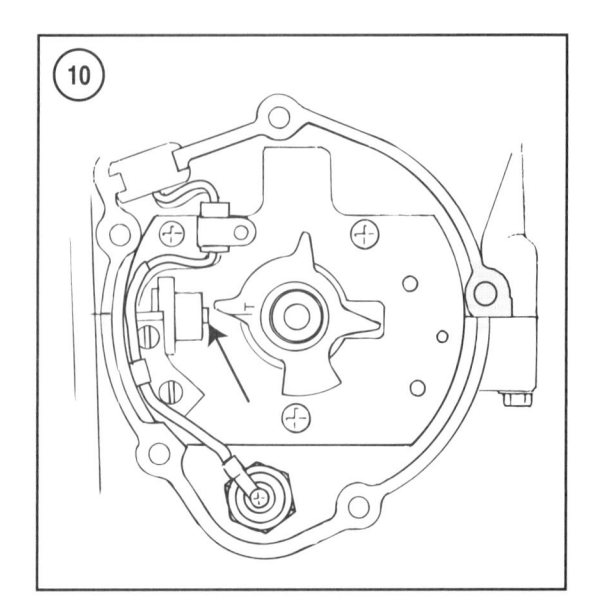

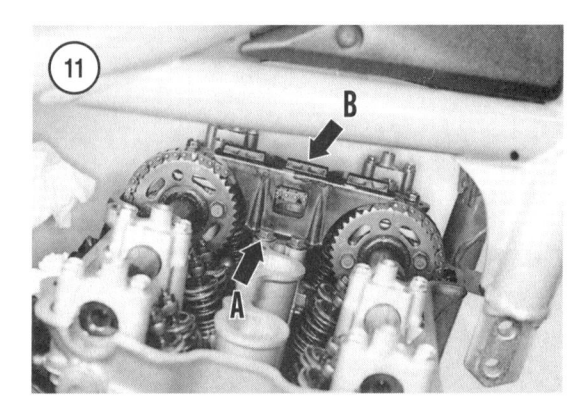

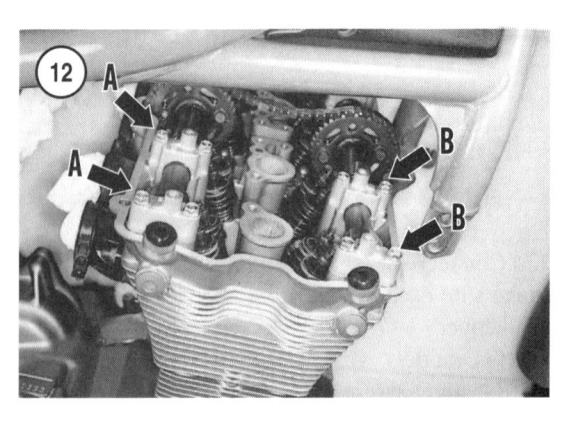

3. Check the camshaft sprocket bolts (**Figure 15**) on both camshafts. If either sprocket bolt is loose on a camshaft, remove and reinstall both bolts. Apply ThreeBond Threadlock No. 1303 to the threads of

ENGINE TOP END

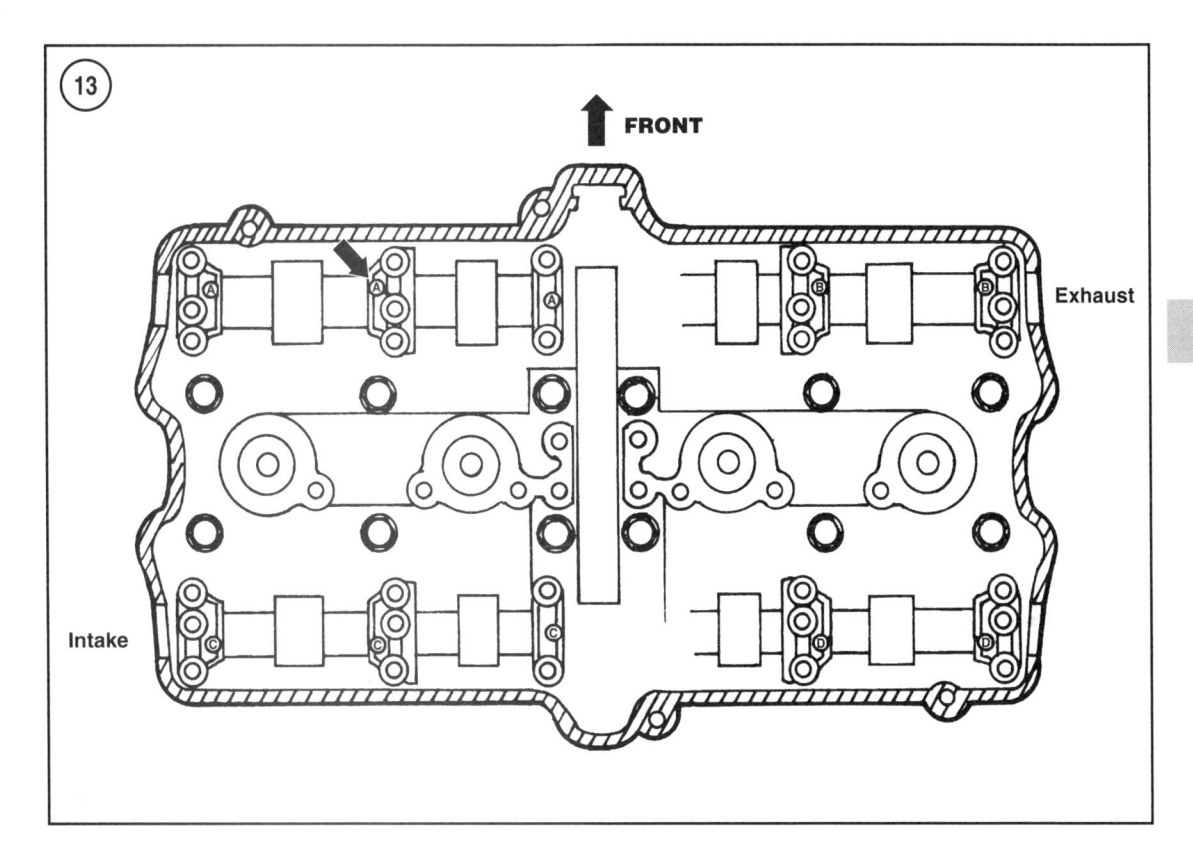

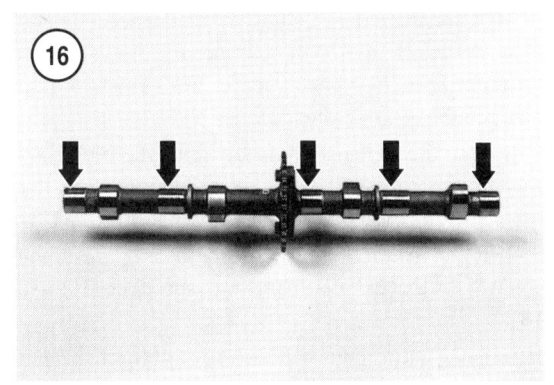

13

Intake / Exhaust / FRONT

14

15

16

each bolt, and torque the camshaft sprocket bolts to the specification in **Table 3**.

4. Apply a light but complete coat of molybdenum disulfide grease to each camshaft bearing journal (**Figure 16**) on both camshafts.

5. Coat all camshaft bearing surfaces in the cylinder head with clean engine oil.

6. Each camshaft is identified by an IN (intake) or EX (exhaust) embossed on the shaft. Also, the right side of each shaft is identified by a notch on the end of the camshaft.

CHAPTER FOUR

17

24th pin — FRONT ➔ — 1st pin

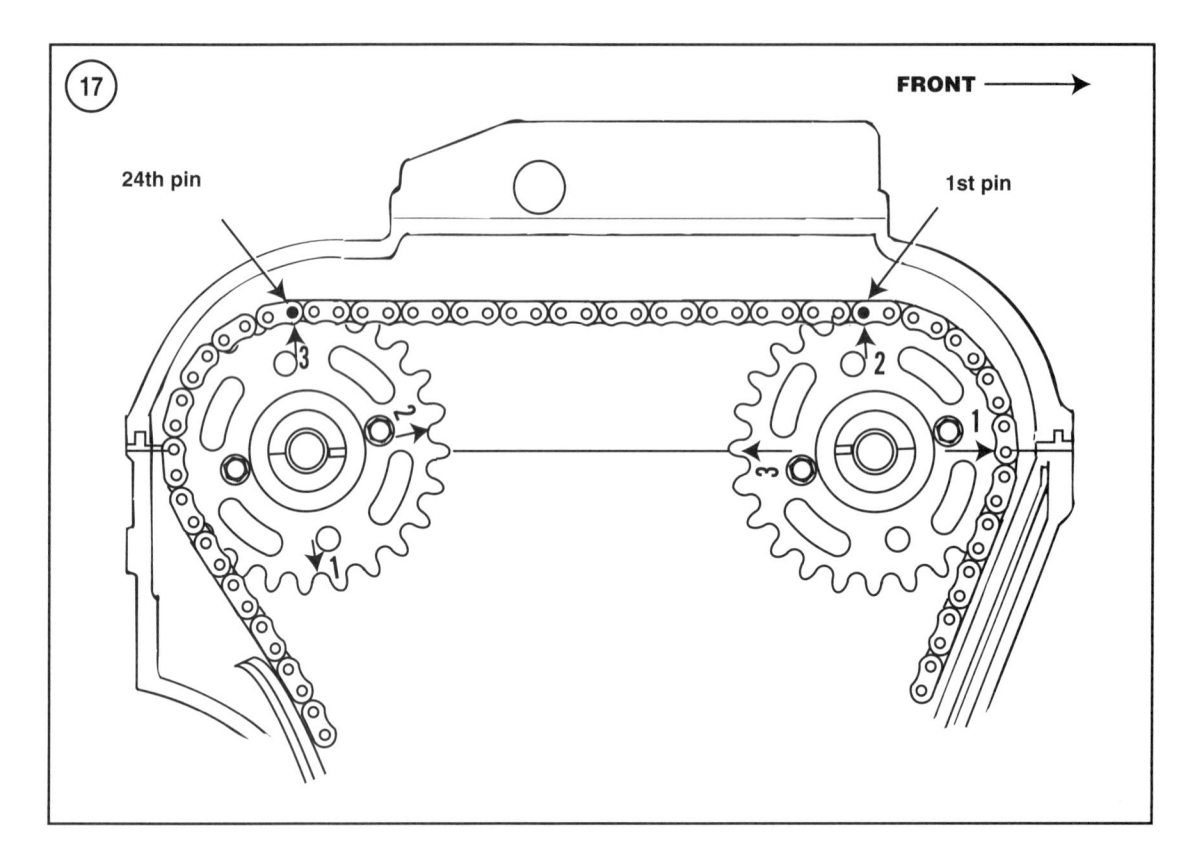

7. Position the exhaust camshaft so the notched end faces the right side of the engine. Fit the camshaft through the cam chain, and set the camshaft into place in the cylinder head.

8. Rotate the exhaust camshaft until the No. 1 arrow on the camshaft sprocket aligns with the top surface of the cylinder head as shown in **Figure 17**.

9. Lift the front of the cam chain and mesh the chain with the exhaust camshaft sprocket (**Figure 18**).

10. Use a white grease pencil to highlight the pin on the cam chain opposite the No. 2 arrow on the exhaust camshaft sprocket (**Figure 19**). This is the first pin.

11. Starting at this first pin, count rearward along the cam chain and identify the 24th pin (**Figure 17**). Also highlight this pin with a white grease pencil.

12. Recheck to make sure the No. 1 arrow on the exhaust camshaft sprocket (**Figure 17**) is still aligned with the top surface of the cylinder head. If the alignment is not correct, readjust the cam chain on the sprocket at this time.

13. Position the intake camshaft so the notch faces the right side of the engine. Install the camshaft

18

through the cam chain, and set the camshaft into place in the cylinder head.

14. Rotate the intake camshaft so the No. 3 arrow points straight up. Fit the cam chain onto the intake sprocket so the 24th pin is opposite the No. 3 arrow on the intake camshaft sprocket as shown in **Figure 20**.

15. Recheck the following:

    a. Make sure the T-mark on the signal generator rotor points to the center of the pickup coil (**Figure 10**).

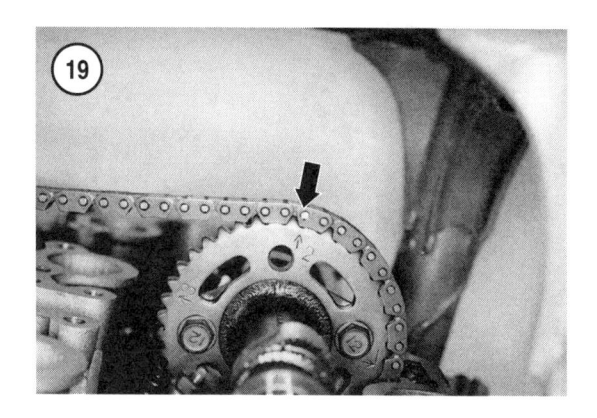

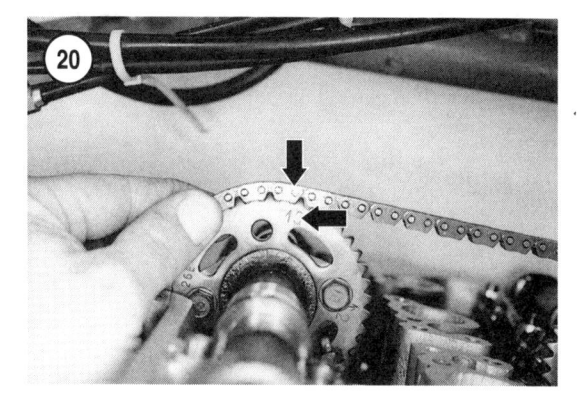

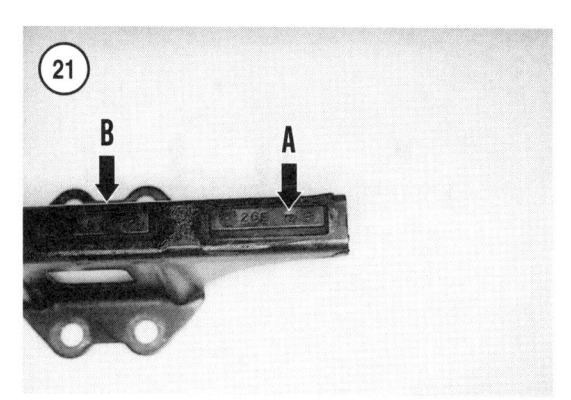

ENGINE TOP END

*proper location as shown in **Figure 13**.*

16. Install a locating dowel into each camshaft bearing cap and set the cap in its proper location in the cylinder head.

NOTE
The camshaft bearing cap bolts are identified with the numeral 9 embossed on the heads. Only use these bolts to install the camshaft bearing caps.

17. Loosely install the camshaft bearing cap bolts.

NOTE
A camshaft may move down slightly when the camshaft bearing cap bolts are tightened, and the cam chain could jump a tooth. Observe the cam chain while tightening the camshaft bearing cap bolts.

18. Following a crisscross pattern, evenly tighten the bolts on the exhaust camshaft in two to three stages, and then torque the camshaft bearing cap bolts to specification (**Table 3**).
19. Repeat this procedure and tighten the cap bolts on the intake camshaft to specification.
20. Install the cam chain tensioner as described in this chapter.
21. Install the upper cam chain guide so its locating arrow (A, **Figure 21**) points forward. Install the four mounting bolts, and torque them to specification.
22. Recheck the camshaft timing by performing the following:
    a. Be sure the No. 2 arrow on the exhaust camshaft sprocket still points to the first pin (**Figure 17**) on the cam chain.
    b. Be sure the No. 3 arrow on the intake camshaft sprocket points to the 24th pin (**Figure 17**) on the cam chain.
23. Fill the oil pockets in the cylinder head with new engine oil so the cam lobes are submerged in fresh oil.
24. Place a 19 mm wrench on the signal generator rotor and rotate the crankshaft clockwise several times.
25. Adjust the valves as described in Chapter Three.
26. Install the spark plugs.

b. Make sure the No. 1 arrow on the exhaust camshaft sprocket points to the top surface of the cylinder head and that its No. 2 arrow points to the first pin (**Figure 17**) on the cam chain.

c. Make sure the No. 3 arrow on the intake camshaft sprocket points to the 24th pin (**Figure 17**) on the cam chain.

NOTE
Each camshaft bearing cap is identified by a unique identification mark. Make sure each cap is installed in its

110 CHAPTER FOUR

27. Install the signal generator cover and a *new* gasket.
    a. Apply a light coat of gasket sealer to the groove in the rubber grommet (A, **Figure 22**).
    b. Also apply gasket sealer to the mating surfaces (B, **Figure 22**).
    c. Tighten the cover bolts securely. Make sure the bolt with the sealing washer is in the location noted during disassembly (**Figure 9**)
28. Install the cylinder head cover as described in this chapter.

Inspection

When measuring the camshafts in this section, compare the measurements to the specifications listed in **Table 2**. Replace parts that are out of specification or that show damage as described in this section.
1. Check the camshaft lobes for wear. Make sure the lobes are not scored and the edges are square.
2. Measure the height of each lobe (**Figure 23**) with a micrometer.
3. Check each camshaft bearing journal (**Figure 24**) for wear and scoring.
4. Measure the diameter of each camshaft bearing journal with a micrometer. Replace the camshaft if any journal diameter is out of specification. Record each camshaft journal diameter to determine the camshaft bearing clearance.
5. If the bearing journals are severely worn or damaged, check the camshaft bearing surfaces (**Figure 25**) in the cylinder head and in the camshaft bearing caps (**Figure 26**) for wear or scoring. If any of the bearing surfaces are worn or scored, replace the cylinder head assembly and camshaft bearing caps as a set.
6. Place each camshaft on a set of V-blocks, and check its runout with a dial indicator.

> *NOTE*
> *If the camshaft sprockets are worn, check the cam chain, chain guides and chain tensioner for damage.*

7. Inspect the camshaft sprocket for broken or chipped teeth. Also check the teeth for cracking or rounding. If the camshaft sprocket is damaged or severely worn, replace the camshaft. Also, inspect the timing sprocket mounted on the crankshaft as described in Chapter Five.
8. Inspect the sliding surface of the upper cam chain guide (B, **Figure 21**) for wear or damage.

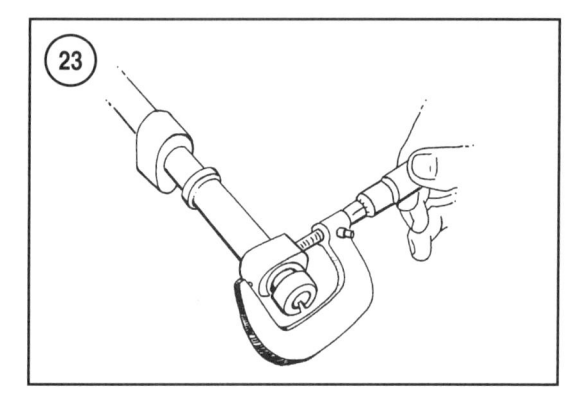

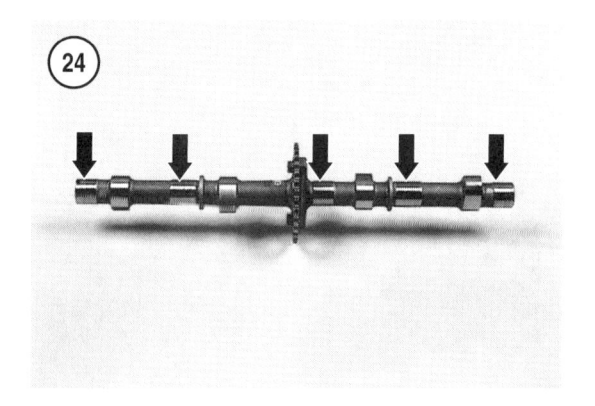

ENGINE TOP END

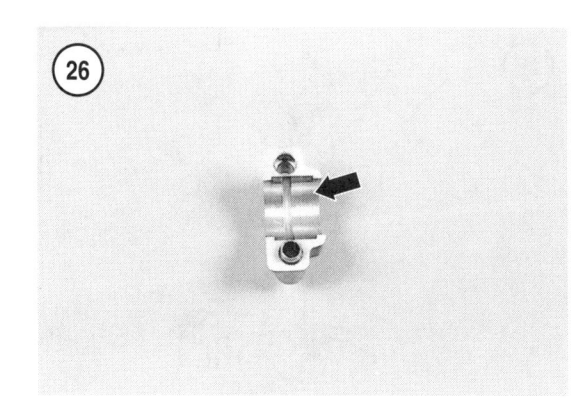

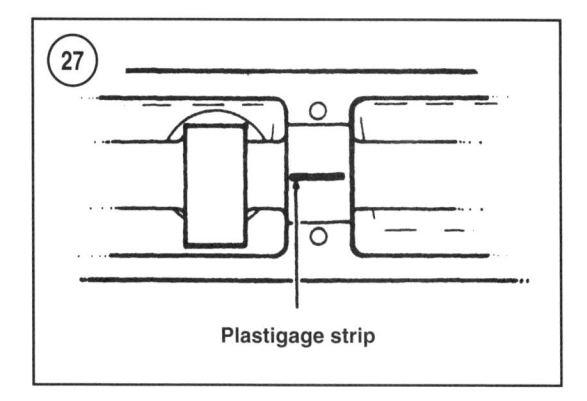

from the bearing surface of the cylinder head and camshaft bearing caps.

1. Do not install the drive chain onto the camshafts for this procedure.
2. Install the camshafts into the cylinder head in the correct location. Install the exhaust camshaft in the front of the engine and the intake camshaft in the rear. Be sure the notch on the end of each camshaft faces the right side of the engine.
3. Place a strip of Plastigage onto each bearing journal (**Figure 27**). The Plastigage must be parallel to the camshaft.

NOTE
*Each camshaft bearing cap is identified by a unique identification mark. Make sure each cap is installed in its proper location as shown in **Figure 13**.*

4. Install a locating dowel into each camshaft bearing cap, and set the cap in its proper location in the cylinder head.

NOTE
The camshaft bearing cap bolts are identified with the numeral 9 embossed on the heads. Only use these bolts to install the camshaft bearing caps.

5. Loosely install the camshaft bearing cap bolts.
6. Following a crisscross pattern, evenly tighten the bolts on the exhaust camshaft in two to three stages, and then torque the camshaft bearing cap bolts to specification (**Table 3**).
7. Repeat this procedure and tighten the cap bolts on the intake camshaft to specification.

CAUTION
Do not rotate the camshafts with the Plastigage in place.

8. Following a crisscross pattern, evenly loosen the bearing cap bolts in two to three stages.
9. Pull straight up and carefully remove each bearing cap.
10. Measure the flattened Plastigage (**Figure 28**) at the widest point, according to the manufacturer's instructions.

CAUTION
Be sure to remove all traces of Plastigage from the camshaft bearing caps and from the camshaft bearing

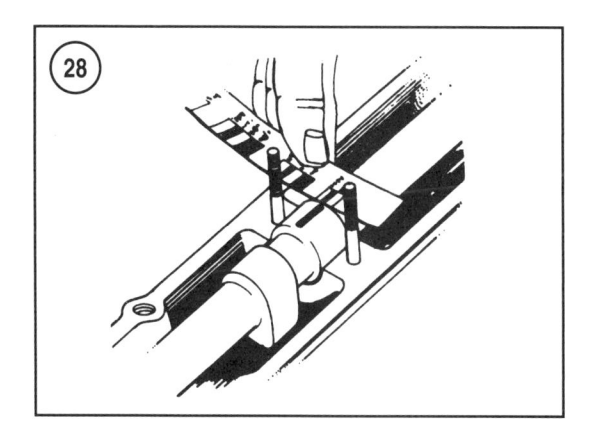

Also check both ends of the guide. Replace the cam chain guide as necessary.
9. Measure the camshaft bearing clearance as described below.

Camshaft Bearing Clearance Measurement

This procedure requires the use of Plastigage. The camshafts must be installed into the cylinder head. Before installing the camshafts, wipe all oil residue from each camshaft bearing journal and

journals. If any Plastigage is left in the engine, it can plug an oil control orifice and cause severe engine damage.

10. Remove *all* Plastigage from the camshafts and bearing caps.

11. If the camshaft bearing oil clearance is greater than specified in **Table 2**, perform the following:
   a. Remove both camshafts from the cylinder head.

   NOTE
   *Each camshaft bearing cap is identified by a unique identification mark. Be sure each cap is installed in its proper location as shown in **Figure 13**.*

   b. Place the bearing caps in their correct location in the cylinder head, and install the camshaft bearing cap bolts. Tighten the bolts to the specified torque.
   c. Use a bore gauge and measure the inside diameter of each camshaft journal holder (**Figure 29**). Record each measurement.
   d. Refer to the camshaft journal outside diameter dimensions taken during camshaft inspection (Step 4).
   e. Replace the camshaft if the outside diameter of a camshaft journal is outside the range specified in **Table 2**. Replace the cylinder head and the camshaft caps as a set if the inside diameter of a camshaft journal holder is out of specification.

CAM CHAIN TENSIONER

Removal/Installation

Refer to **Figure 30**.

1. Remove the spring holder bolt (A, **Figure 31**) and gasket from the cam chain tensioner.
2. Withdraw the spring (**Figure 32**) from the tensioner body.
3. Remove the cam chain tensioner bolts (B, **Figure 31**), and remove the tensioner body and gasket.
4. Inspect the chain tensioner as described below.

CAUTION
Reset the ratchet pushrod before installing the tensioner. Correct tension will not be applied to the cam chain unless the pushrod is reset.

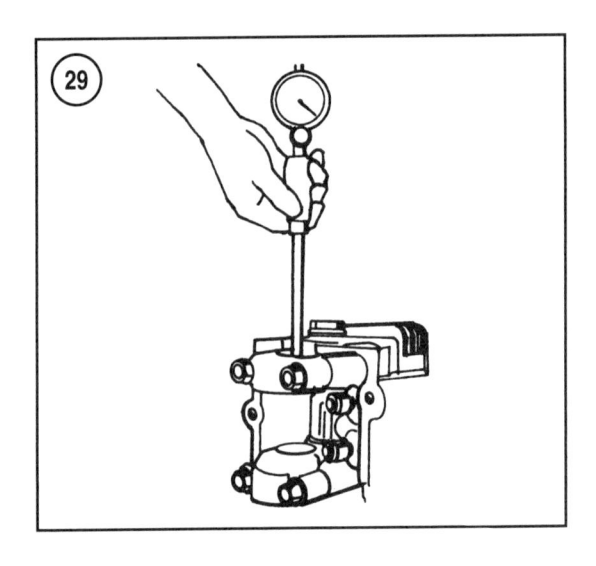

5. Reset the ratchet pushrod by performing the following:
   a. Push the spring ratchet pawl (A, **Figure 33**), and press the pushrod (B, **Figure 33**) all the way into the body.
   b. Release the ratchet pawl. The pushrod should stay within the body. If it does not, replace the tensioner body.

6. Fit the tensioner body and a *new* gasket onto the cylinder block.
7. Install the tensioner mounting bolts (B, **Figure 31**), and torque the bolts to the specification in **Table 3**.
8. Install the spring (**Figure 32**) into the tensioner body.
9. Install the spring holder bolt (A, **Figure 31**) and washer. Torque the spring holder bolt to specification.
10. Once the chain tensioner is installed, the cam chain will be slightly loose. To correct this, rotate the crankshaft clockwise slightly. A distinct click should be heard as the chain is tensioned.

Inspection

1. Release the ratchet pawl and check the movement of the pushrod. If it does not slide smoothly in and out of the housing, replace the tensioner body.
2. Check the condition of the spring, washer, and spring holder bolt (**Figure 34**). Replace any part that is worn or damaged.

ENGINE TOP END

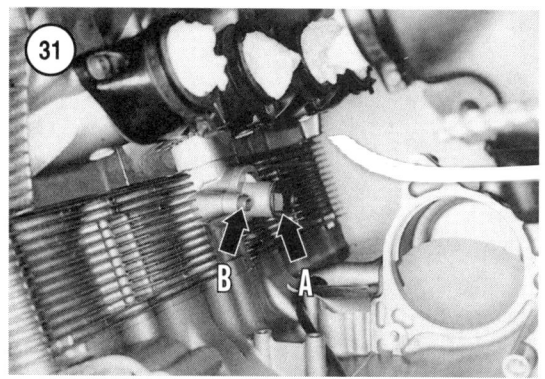

CAM CHAIN GUIDES AND TENSIONER

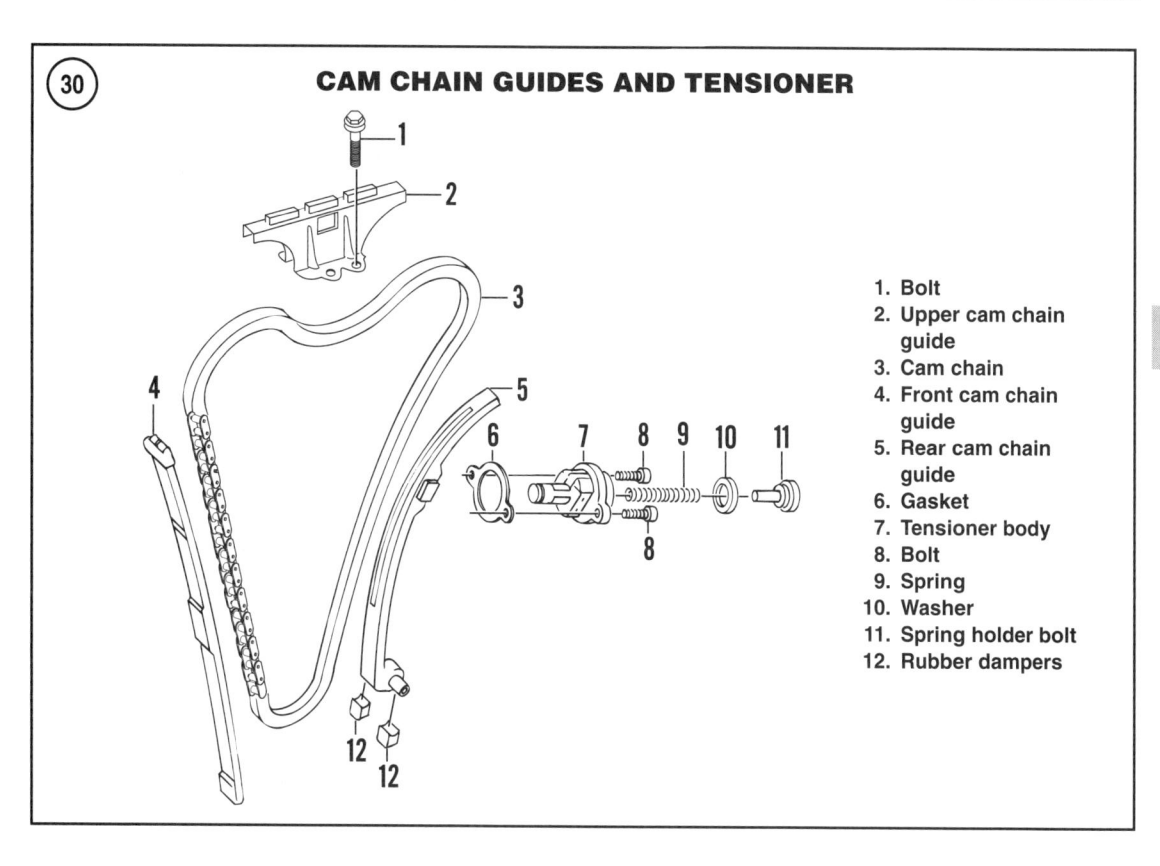

1. Bolt
2. Upper cam chain guide
3. Cam chain
4. Front cam chain guide
5. Rear cam chain guide
6. Gasket
7. Tensioner body
8. Bolt
9. Spring
10. Washer
11. Spring holder bolt
12. Rubber dampers

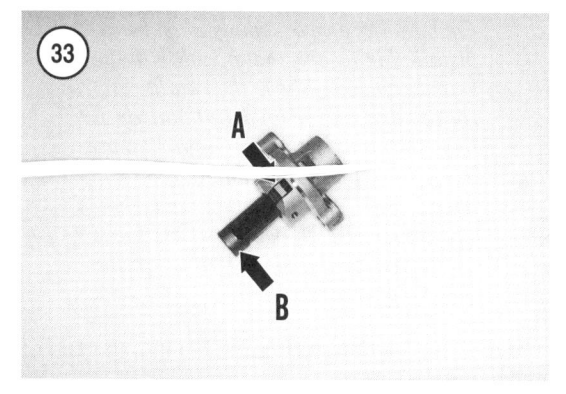

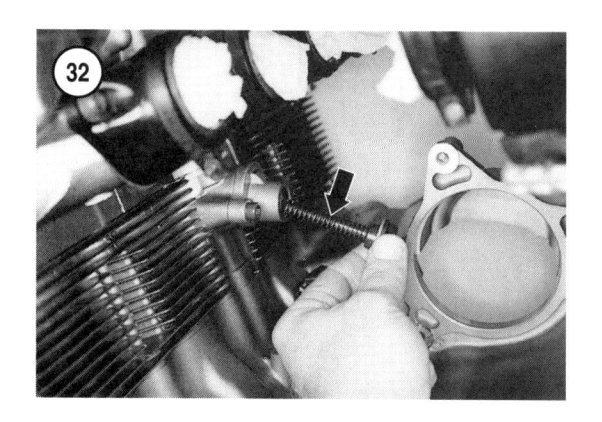

CAM CHAIN

A continuous cam chain is used on all models. Do not cut the chain; replacement link components are not available. Refer to crankshaft removal in Chapter Five for cam chain removal and inspection procedures.

ROCKER ARMS

NOTE
The rocker arms can be serviced while the engine is in the frame. This procedure is shown with the engine removed from the frame for clarity.

Removal

1. Remove both camshafts as described in this chapter.
2. Remove the rocker arm shaft bolt (**Figure 35**) from the cylinder head.
3. Unscrew cylinder head plug (**Figure 36**), and remove the plug and its washer.

NOTE
Each rocker arm assembly must be reinstalled in its original position in the cylinder head. Mark the shafts and rocker arms with an I (intake) or E (exhaust) and with the cylinder number. The cylinders are numbered from left to right, 1-4. The left and right sides refer to the position of the parts as viewed by the rider sitting on the seat facing forward.

4. Screw an 8 mm bolt (**Figure 37**) into the end of the rocker arm shaft.
5. Use the bolt to pull the rocker arm shaft out of the cylinder head.
6. Remove the rocker arms and springs.
7. Repeat this for all rocker arm shaft assemblies.
8. Wash all parts in solvent, and thoroughly dry them with compressed air.
9. Inspect the parts as described below.

Installation

1. Apply clean engine oil to the rocker arm shaft, rocker arm bore and the cylinder head.

ENGINE TOP END

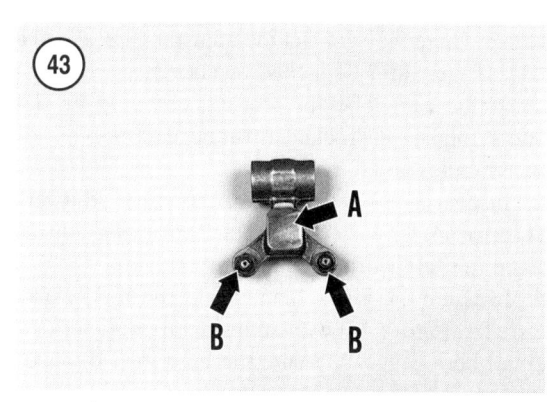

2. Refer to the marks made during disassembly so each rocker arm assembly will be reinstalled in its original location in the cylinder head.
3. Install the rocker arm (A, **Figure 38**) and the spring (B). The spring goes on the outboard side of the rocker arm, the side away from the cam chain tunnel.
4. Position the rocker arm shaft so the bolt hole (**Figure 39**) is vertical.
5. Partially install the rocker arm shaft into the cylinder head, through the spring, and then through the rocker arm bore.
6. Rotate the rocker arm shaft so the bolt hole (A, **Figure 40**) aligns with the bolt hole in the cylinder head (B, **Figure 40**). Pull the rocker arm back so the next rocker arm and spring can be installed.
7. Install the next rocker arm (A, **Figure 41**) and its spring (B, **Figure 41**). Make sure the spring is on the outboard side of the rocker arm, the side away from the cam chain tunnel.
8. Push the shaft into the cylinder head until it bottoms. If necessary, rotate the shaft slightly to align the shaft's bolt hole with the bolt hole (B, **Figure 40**) in the cylinder head.
9. Install the rocker arm shaft bolt, and tighten the bolt (**Figure 35**) to the torque specification in **Table 3**.
10. Inspect the sealing washer (**Figure 42**) on the cylinder head plug. Replace the washer if necessary.
11. Install the cylinder head plug and sealing washer. Torque the plug to specification.

Inspection

Compare all measurements to the specifications in **Table 2**. Replace parts that are damaged or out of specification.

1. Inspect the rocker arm pad where it contacts the cam lobe (A, **Figure 43**), and inspect the valve

stems where they contact the adjusters. (B, **Figure 43**). If the pad is scratched or unevenly worn, inspect the cam lobe for scoring, chipping or flat spots. Replace the rocker arm as necessary. If an adjuster end is pitted, replace it.

2. Inspect the opposite end of the valve adjusters (**Figure 44**) for wear or damage. Replace the adjusters if they are worn or damaged.

3. Measure the inside diameter of the rocker arm bore (A, **Figure 45**) with an inside micrometer or a small bore gauge. Measure the bore in two places that are at right angles to each other.

4. Inspect each rocker arm shaft for signs or wear or damage.

5. Measure the shaft's outside diameter (B, **Figure 45**) with a micrometer.

6. Check the rocker arm springs for cracks or distortion. Replace the springs as necessary.

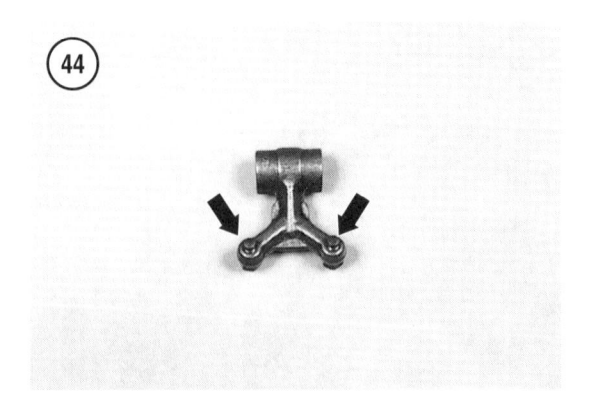

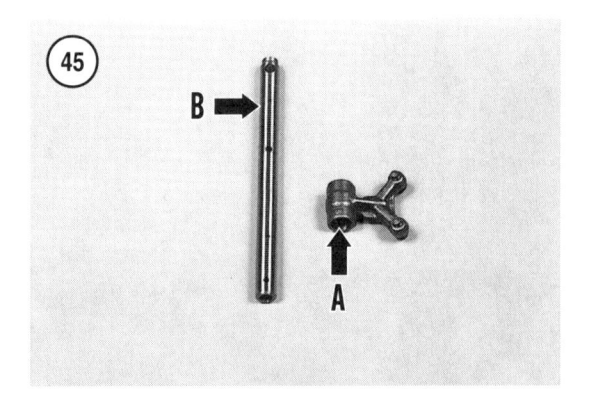

CYLINDER HEAD

The cylinder head can be serviced while the engine is in the frame. This procedure is shown with the engine out of the frame for photographic clarity.

CAUTION
To prevent warping and damage, remove the cylinder head only when the engine is at room temperature.

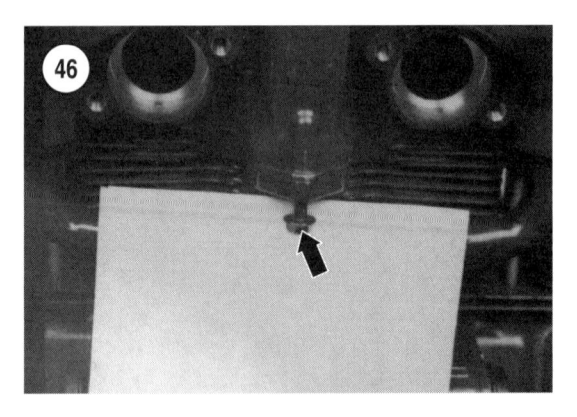

Removal

1. Remove the removable frame downtube as described in *Engine Removal* (Steps 20-26) in Chapter Five.
2. Remove the carburetors and exhaust system as described in Chapter Eight.
3. Remove the cylinder head cover as described in this chapter.
4. Remove the camshafts and rocker arm assemblies as described in this chapter.
5. Remove the 6 mm cylinder head bolt (**Figure 46**) that secures the cylinder head to the cylinder block.
6. Remove the front cam chain guide.

CAUTION
*Note that cylinder head nuts (**Figure 47**) are different. Nuts 1-8 (A, **Figure 48**) are acorn nuts. The four conventional nuts (9-12) must be reinstalled in the same location (B, **Figure 48**) during assembly.*

7. Following the reverse of the tightening sequence shown in **Figure 47**, evenly loosen the cylinder head nuts in two to three stages. Remove the nuts along with their washers.

CAUTION
The cooling fins are fragile and may be damaged if tapped or pried too

ENGINE TOP END 117

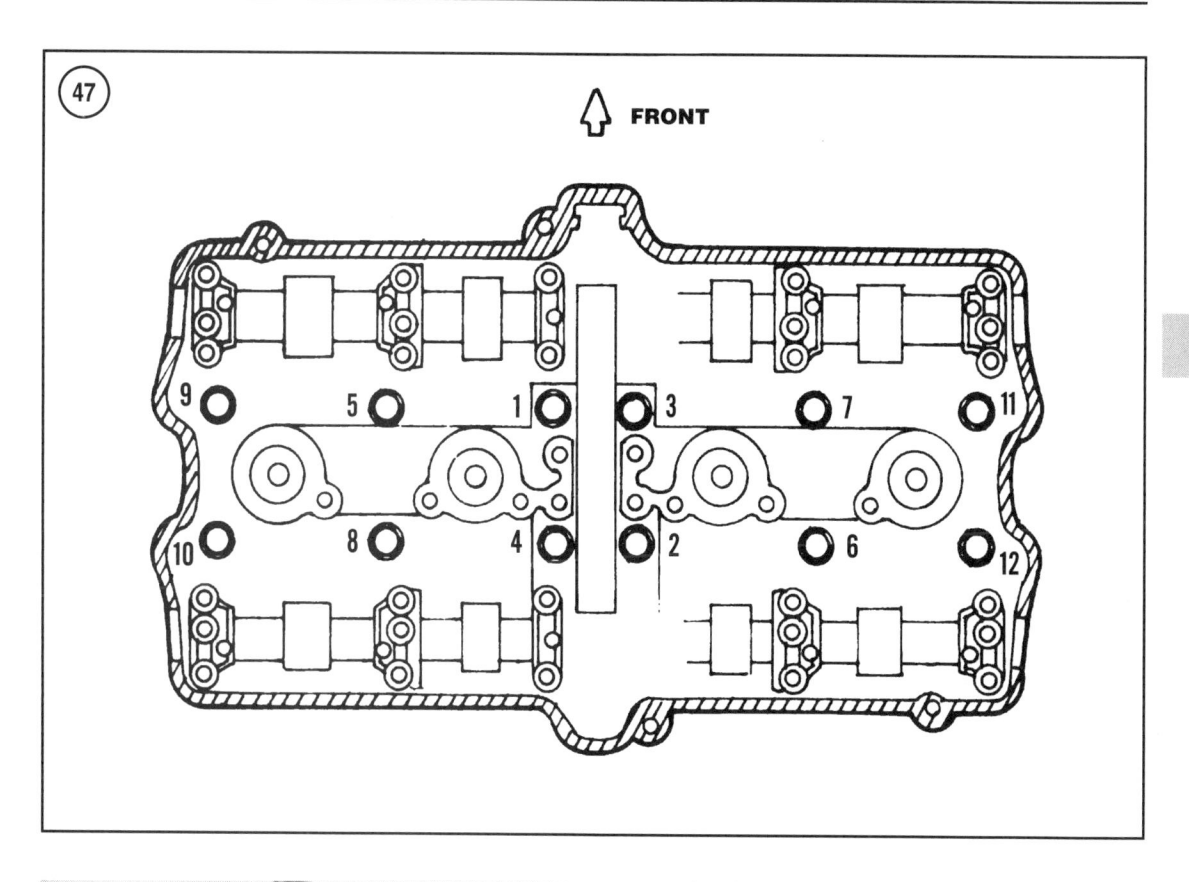

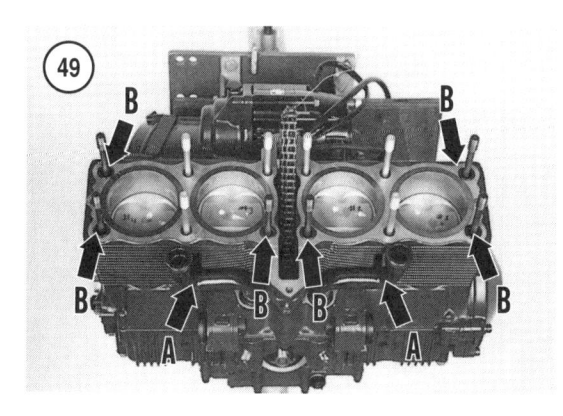

47

⇧ FRONT

9 5 1 3 7 11
10 8 4 2 6 12

48

49

hard. Never use a metal hammer to loosen the cylinder head.

8. Loosen the cylinder head by tapping around the perimeter with a soft-faced mallet. If necessary, gently pry the head loose.

9. Lift the cylinder head straight up, and remove the head from the cylinder and crankcase studs. Guide the cam chain through the cam chain tunnel in the cylinder head, and retie the wire to the exterior of the engine. This prevents the cam chain from falling into the crankcase.

10. Remove the cylinder head gasket. Do not lose the locating dowels.

11. Place a clean shop cloth into the cam chain tunnel in the cylinder block to keep objects and debris out of the crankcase.

12. Remove the external oil pipes (A, **Figure 49**) from the crankcase. *New* O-rings must be installed during assembly to prevent oil leaks.

13. Remove the six O-rings (B, **Figure 49**) from the cylinder block. These O-rings must be replaced during assembly.

14. Inspect the cylinder head as described below.

Installation

1. Apply Suzuki Super Grease A to *new* O-rings, and install the O-rings (**Figure 50**) at each end of both front external oil pipes.

2. Install both oil pipes (A, **Figure 49**) into the receptacles in the crankcase.

3. Apply Suzuki Super Grease A to *new* O-rings, and install the six O-rings (B, **Figure 49**) into the cylinder block.

4. If removed, install a locating dowel (**Figure 51**) at each end of the cylinder block.

5. Remove the shop rag from the cam chain tunnel in the cylinder block.

> *NOTE*
> *If a Suzuki gasket kit is being used, carefully inspect the cylinder head gasket. A small oil jet can become lodged between the layers of this gasket.*

6. Install a *new* cylinder head gasket so its UP mark (**Figure 52**) faces up.

7. Carefully slide the cylinder head onto the cylinder block. Feed the cam chain through the tunnel in the cylinder head, and secure the wire to the exterior of the engine (**Figure 53**).

8. Apply oil to the threads of the crankcase studs.

9. Install the cylinder head nuts and washers. Install the copper washers with the acorn nuts, and install the steel washers with the conventional nuts. Refer to **Figure 54** for the correct location of the conventional nuts and the acorn nuts.

10. Evenly tighten the cylinder head nuts in two-to-three stages. Following the tightening sequence shown in **Figure 47**, tighten the nuts to the torque specification in **Table 3**.

11. Install the 6 mm cylinder head bolt (**Figure 46**), and torque the bolt to specification.

12. Install the front cam chain guide (**Figure 55**).

13. Install the rocker arm assemblies and the camshafts as described in this chapter.

14. Adjust the valves as described in Chapter Three.

15. Install the carburetor and exhaust system as described in Chapter Eight.

16. Install the removable frame downtube as described *Engine Removal* in Chapter Five.

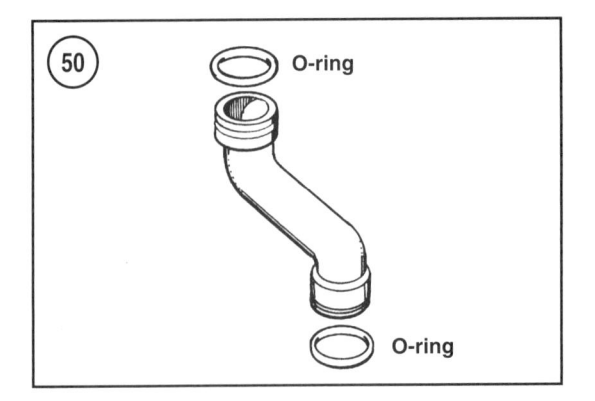

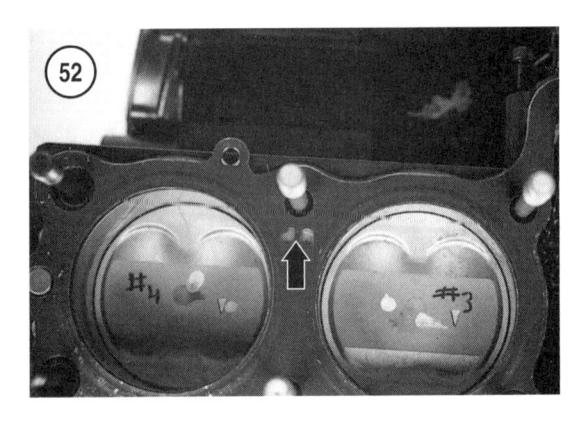

ENGINE TOP END

54

FRONT

A

B   B

55

56

Port

Solvent or kerosene

Combustion chamber

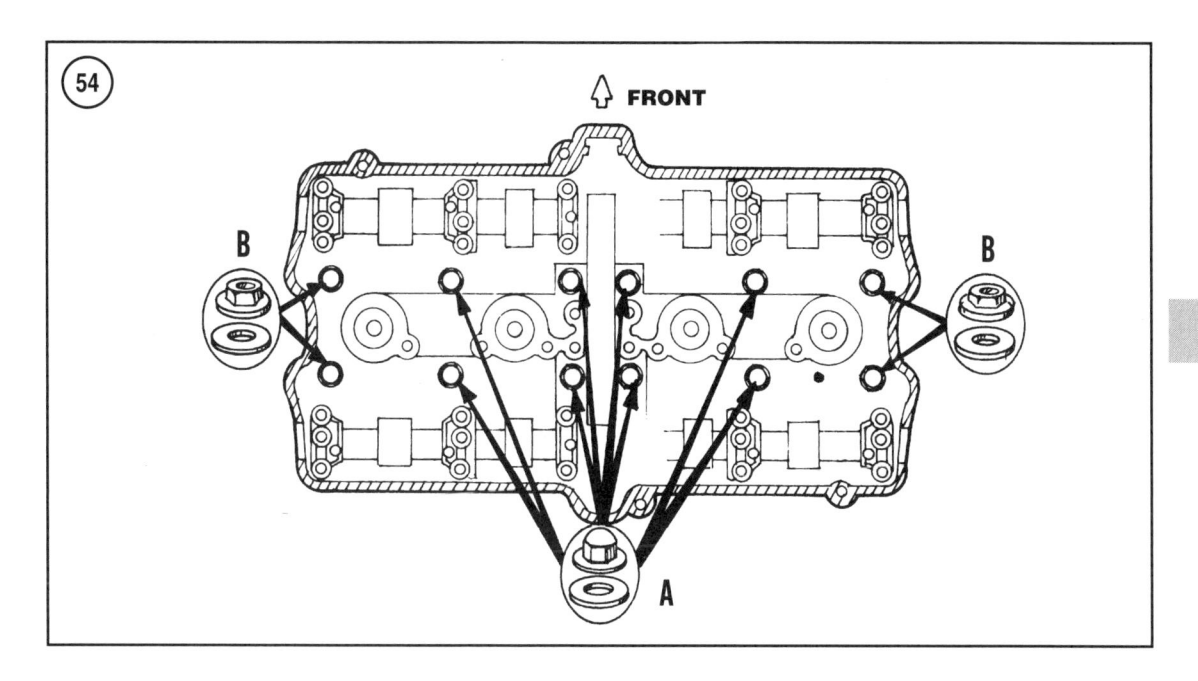

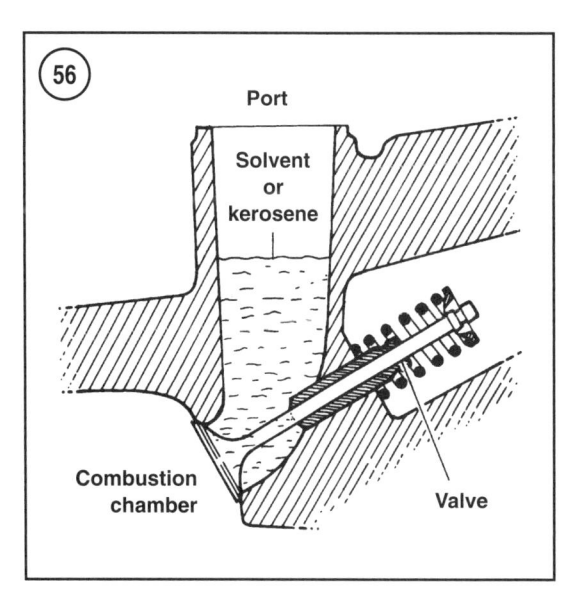

Valve

Cylinder Head Inspection

Compare all measurements to the specifications in **Table 2**. Replace any part that is damaged or out of specification.

1. Before cleaning the head or removing the valves, perform the following leak test:

   a. Position the cylinder head so the exhaust ports face up. Pour solvent or kerosene into each port opening (**Figure 56**).

   b. Turn the head over slightly, and check each exhaust valve area on the combustion chamber side. If the valve and seats are in good condition, there should be no leakage past the valve seats. If an area is wet, the valve seat is not sealing correctly. This can be caused by a damaged valve seat or valve face or by a bent or damaged valve. Remove the valve, and inspect the valve and seat for wear.

   c. Repeat this test for the intake valves.

2. Remove all traces of gasket residue from the cylinder head and cylinder block mating surfaces. Do not scratch the gasket surfaces.

> *CAUTION*
> *Cleaning the combustion chamber with the valves removed can damage the valve seat surfaces. A damaged or even slightly scratched valve seat will cause poor valve seating.*

3. *Without removing the valves*, remove all carbon deposits from the combustion chamber (**Figure 57**). Use a fine wire brush or wooden scraper. Take care not to damage the head, valves or spark plug threads.

NOTE
When using a tap to clean spark plug threads, coat the tap with an aluminum tap cutting fluid or kerosene.

NOTE
Aluminum spark plug threads are commonly damaged due to galling, cross-threading and overtightening. To prevent galling, apply an antiseize compound to the plug threads before installation. Do not overtighten the plug.

4. Examine the spark plug threads in the cylinder head for damage. If damage is minor or if the threads are dirty or clogged with carbon, use a spark plug thread tap to clean the threads. If thread damage is severe, the threads can be restored by installing a steel thread insert. Purchase thread insert kits from an automotive supply store or have the inserts installed by a Suzuki dealership or machine shop.

NOTE
If the cylinder head was bead-blasted, clean the head thoroughly with solvent and then with hot soapy water. Residual grit can be hard to get out of small crevices and other areas. Also chase each exposed thread with a tap to remove grit between the threads or the threads may be damaged later. Residue grit left in the engine will contaminate the oil and cause premature piston, ring and bearing wear.

5. After all carbon is removed from the combustion chambers and valve ports, and the spark plug thread hole is repaired, clean the entire head in solvent. Blow it dry with compressed air.

6. Check for cracks in the combustion chambers and the exhaust ports. A cracked head must be replaced.

CAUTION
Do not clean the piston crowns while the pistons are installed in the cylinders. Carbon will fall between the cyl-

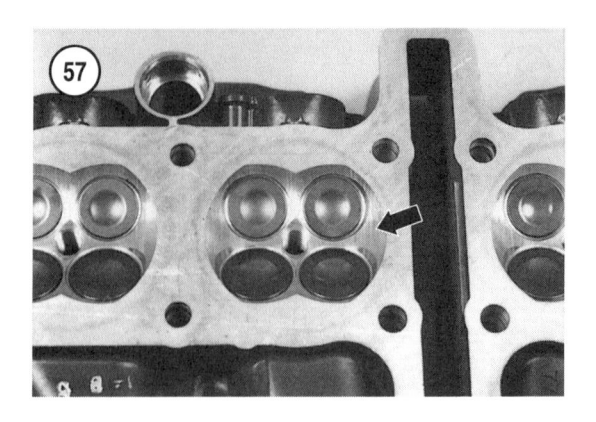

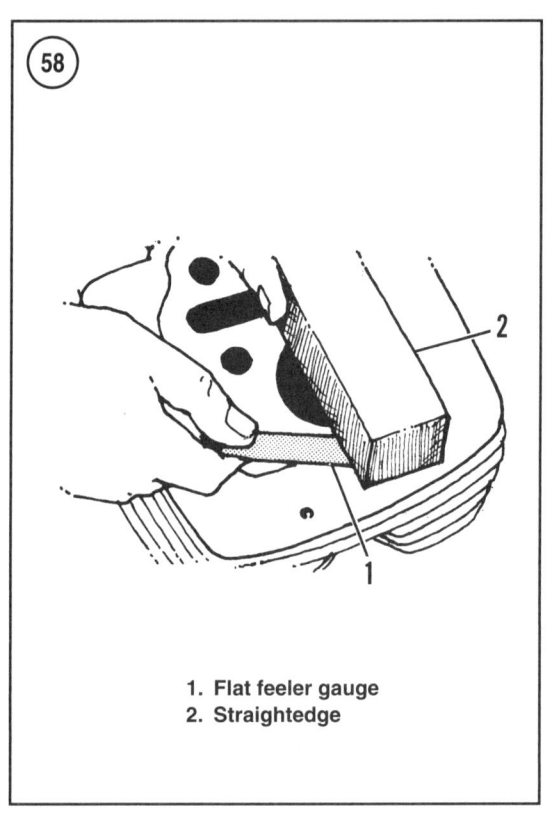

1. Flat feeler gauge
2. Straightedge

ENGINE TOP END

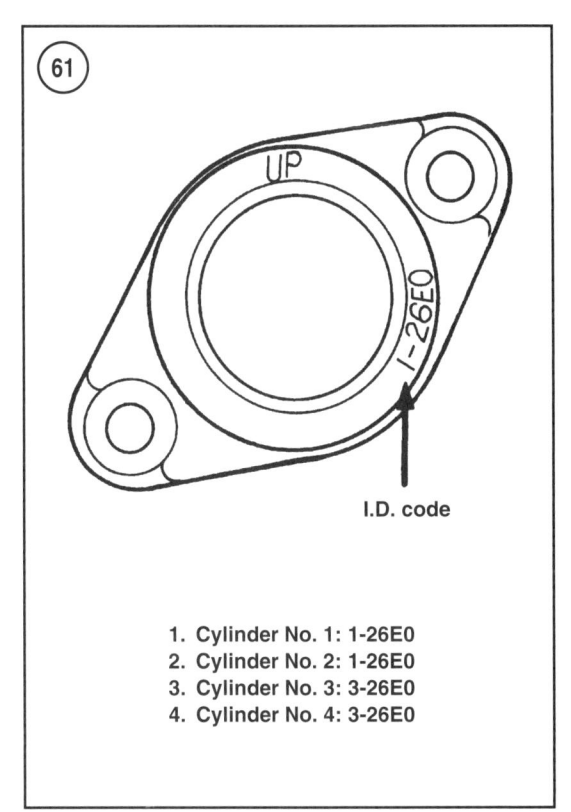

60

61

1. Cylinder No. 1: 1-26E0
2. Cylinder No. 2: 1-26E0
3. Cylinder No. 3: 3-26E0
4. Cylinder No. 4: 3-26E0

62

inder wall and piston and collect on the piston rings. Because carbon grit is very abrasive, premature cylinder, piston and ring wear will occur. If the piston crowns have heavy carbon deposits, remove the pistons as described later in this chapter and clean them. Excessive carbon buildup on the piston crowns reduces piston cooling, raises engine compression and causes overheating.

7. Examine the crown on all four pistons. A crown should show no signs of wear or damage. If a crown appears pecked or spongy-looking, also check the spark plug, valves and combustion chamber for aluminum deposits. If these deposits are found, the cylinder is overheating due to a lean fuel mixture or preignition.

8. Place a straightedge across the gasket surface at several points. Measure warp by attempting to insert a feeler gauge between the straightedge and cylinder head at each location (**Figure 58**). Maximum allowable warp is listed in **Table 2**. Warp or nicks in the cylinder head surface could cause an air leak and result in overheating. If warp exceeds the limit, the cylinder head must be resurfaced or replaced. Consult a Suzuki dealership or machine shop experienced in this type of work.

9. Inspect the hole in each oil pipe (**Figure 59**). Make sure it is clean and unobstructed. If necessary, remove the oil pipe. Clean it with solvent, dry it with compressed air, and install the pipe with its large end going in last (**Figure 60**).

NOTE
*Each intake manifold must be reinstalled in its original location. Mark each manifold prior to removal. If new intake manifolds are required, refer to **Figure 61** for correct identification numbers and cylinder location*

10. Inspect the intake manifolds (**Figure 62**) for cracks or other damage that would allow unfiltered air to enter the engine. If necessary, remove the intake manifolds and install *new* O-rings to prevent a vacuum leak. Lubricate the O-ring with Suzuki Super Grease A, and install each manifold in its original location. Tighten the screws securely.

11. Inspect the threads on the exhaust pipe mounting bolts for damage. Clean the threads with an appropriate size metric tap if necessary.

12. Check the valves and valve guides as described in this chapter.

VALVES AND VALVE COMPONENTS

Refer to **Figure 63** when servicing the valves.

Complete valve service requires a number of special tools and considerable skill to use them. Consequently, even experienced mechanics who perform their own service generally remove the cylinder head and have a machine shop or dealer perform the inspection and service.

The following procedures describe how to check for valve component wear and to determine what type of service is required. In most cases, the need for valve service is caused by poor valve seating, worn valve guides and burned valves. A valve spring compressor is required to remove and install the valves.

Valve Removal

1. Remove the cylinder head as described in this chapter.
2. Install a valve spring compressor (**Figure 64**) squarely over the valve spring retainer, and place the other end of the tool against the valve head.

> *CAUTION*
> *To avoid loss of spring tension, do not compress the spring any more than necessary to remove the valve keepers.*

3. Tighten the valve spring compressor until the valve keepers separate from the valve stem. Lift the valve keepers out through the valve spring compressor with a magnet or needlenose pliers.
4. Gradually loosen the valve spring compressor and remove it from the cylinder head.
5. Remove the spring retainer and the two valve springs.
6. Remove any burrs from the valve stem groove before removing the valve (**Figure 65**). Otherwise the valve guide will be damaged as the valve stem passes through it.
7. Remove the valve from the cylinder while rotating it slightly.
8. Remove the spring seat.
9. Pull the oil seal off the valve guide (B, **Figure 66**). Discard the oil seal.

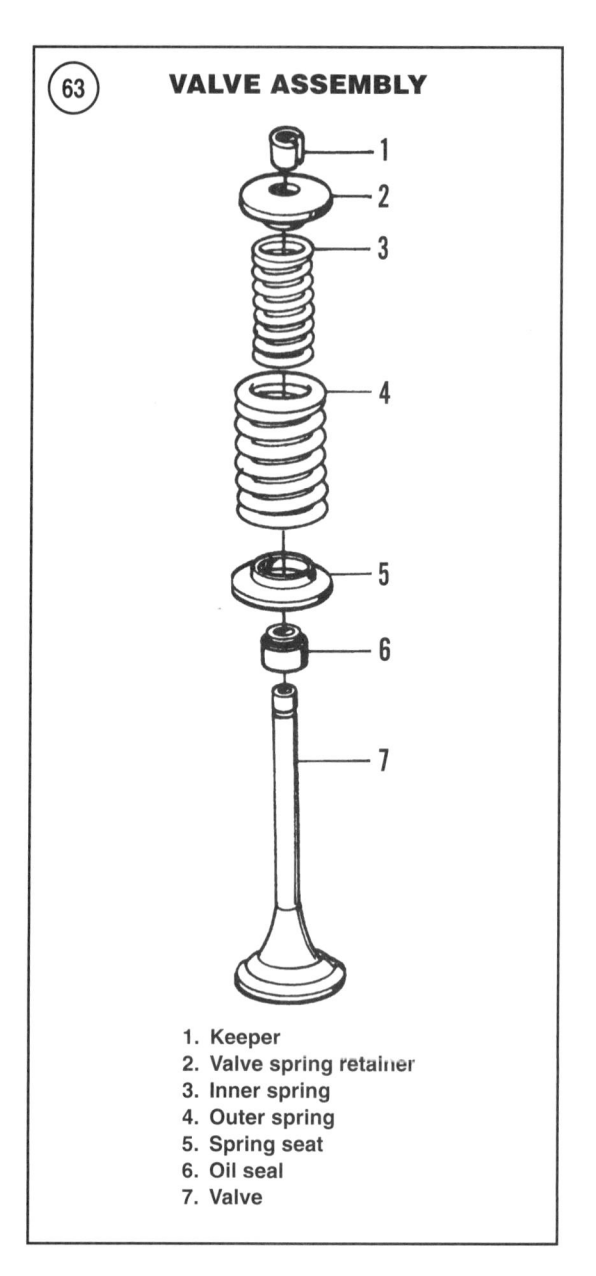

63 VALVE ASSEMBLY

1. Keeper
2. Valve spring retainer
3. Inner spring
4. Outer spring
5. Spring seat
6. Oil seal
7. Valve

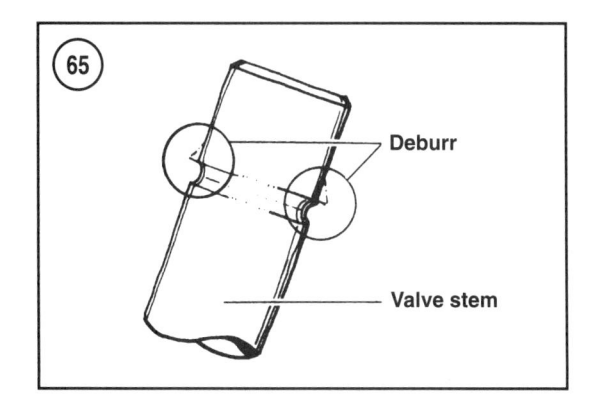

ENGINE TOP END

CAUTION
All component parts of each valve assembly must be kept together (Figure 67). Place each set in a divided carton, into separate small boxes or into small recloseable plastic bags. Label each valve set. Identify a valve set by its cylinder number and either intake or exhaust valves. This keeps parts from getting mixed up and makes installation simpler. Do not intermix components from the valve assemblies or excessive wear may result.

10. Repeat Steps 2-10 and remove the remaining valves. Keep all valve sets separate.

11. Remove each valve seat plate (A, **Figure 66**) from the exhaust side of the cylinder head.

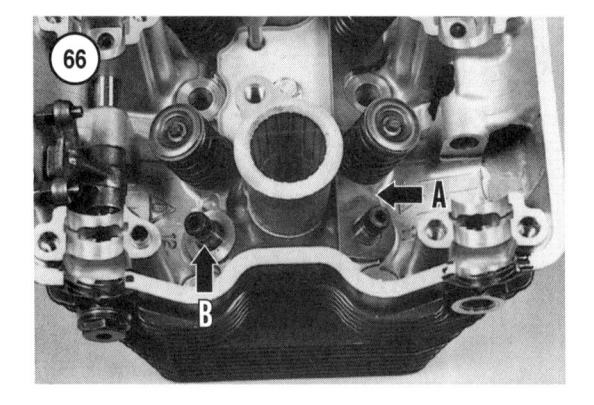

Valve Installation

1. Clean the end of the valve guides.
2. Install each valve seat plate (A, **Figure 66**) onto the exhaust side of the cylinder head.
3. Install the spring seat onto each valve guide.
4. Oil the inside of the *new* oil seal (B, **Figure 66**), and install the seal onto the valve guide.
5. Coat the valve stem with molybdenum disulfide paste. Install the valve partway into the guide. Slowly turn the valve as it enters the oil seal, and continue turning it until the valve is completely installed.
6. Position the valve springs with their *closer* wound coils (**Figure 68**) facing the cylinder head.
7. Install the outer valve spring, and make sure it is properly seated on the spring seat.
8. Install the inner valve spring, and make sure it is properly seated on the spring seat.
9. Install the spring retainer on top of the valve springs.

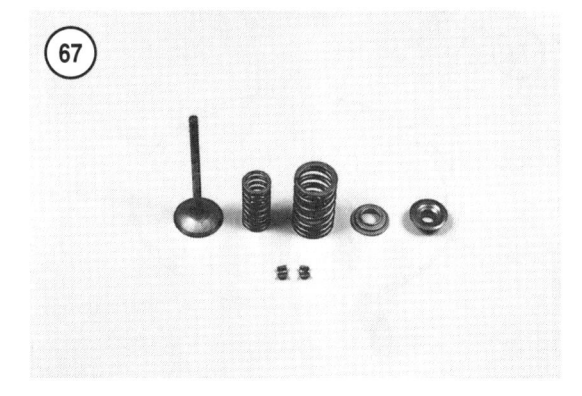

CAUTION
To avoid loss of spring tension, do not compress the springs any more than necessary to install the valve keepers.

10. Compress the valve springs with a valve spring compressor (**Figure 64**) and install the valve keepers.

11. Make sure both keepers are seated around the valve stem prior to releasing the compressor.

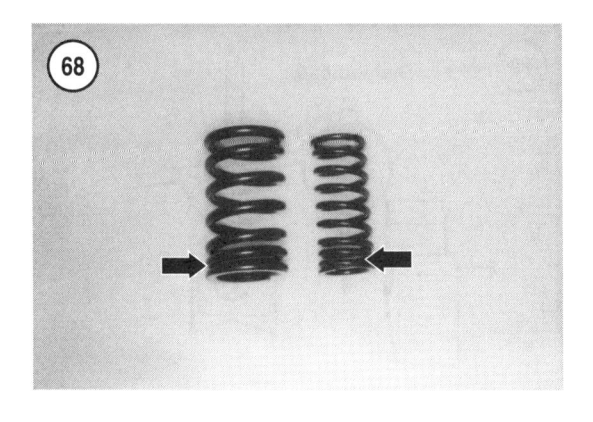

12. Slowly release the tension from the compressor and remove it. After removing the compressor, inspect the valve keepers to make sure they are properly seated (**Figure 69**). Tap the end of the valve stem with a drift and hammer. This ensures that the keepers are properly seated.

13. If the valve stem end has been resurfaced, check that the end of the valve (A, **Figure 70**) extends above the valve keepers (B, **Figure 70**). If it does not, replace the valve.

14. Repeat Steps 3-12 for the remaining valves.

15. Install the cylinder head as described in this chapter.

16. After installing the cylinder head, adjust the valve clearance as described in Chapter Three.

Valve Inspection

Compare all measurement to the specifications in **Table 2**. Replace any component that is out of specification, worn to the wear limit or damaged.

1. Clean the valves in solvent. Do not gouge or damage the valve seating surface.

2. Inspect the valve face (**Figure 71**). Minor roughness and pitting can be removed by lapping the valve as described in this chapter. Excessive unevenness to the contact surface is an indication that the valve is not serviceable.

3. Inspect the valve stem for wear and roughness. Measure the radial runout of the valve head as shown in **Figure 72**.

4. Measure the valve stem runout as shown in **Figure 73**.

5. Measure the valve stem outside diameter with a micrometer (**Figure 74**).
   a. If the valve stem is out of specification, discard the valve.
   b. If the valve stem is within specification, record the measurement so it can be used to determine valve stem-to-guide clearance in Step 9.

6. Measure the valve head thickness (**Figure 75**) with a vernier caliper.

7. Remove all carbon and varnish from the valve guides with a stiff spiral wire brush before measuring wear.

NOTE
If the required measuring tools are unavailable, proceed to Step 10.

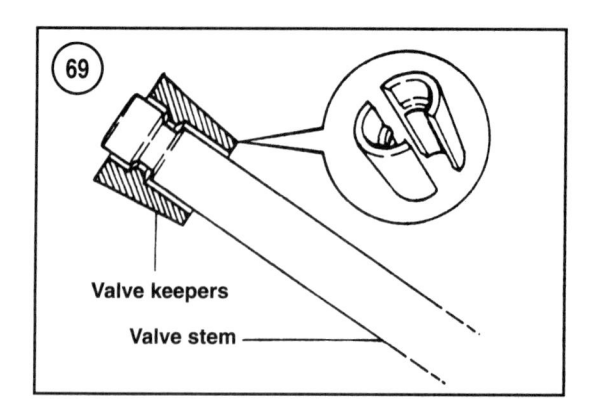

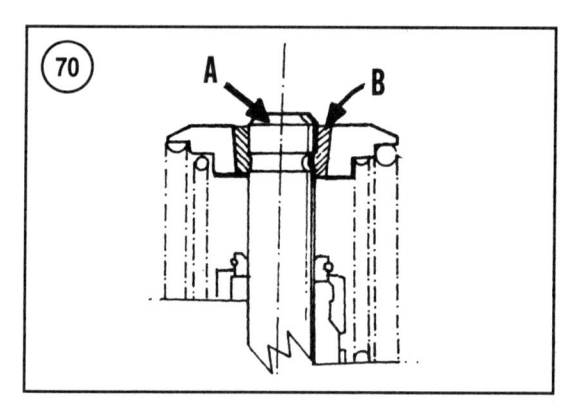

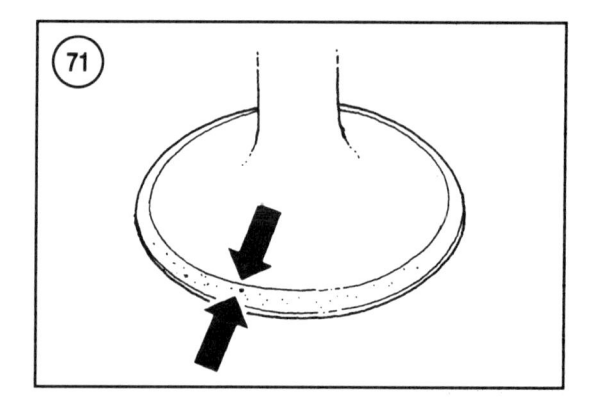

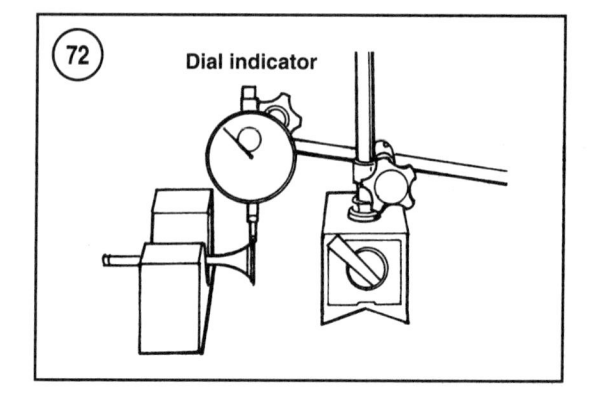

ENGINE TOP END

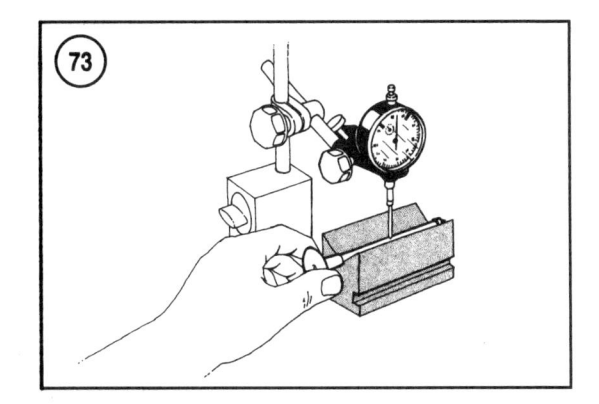

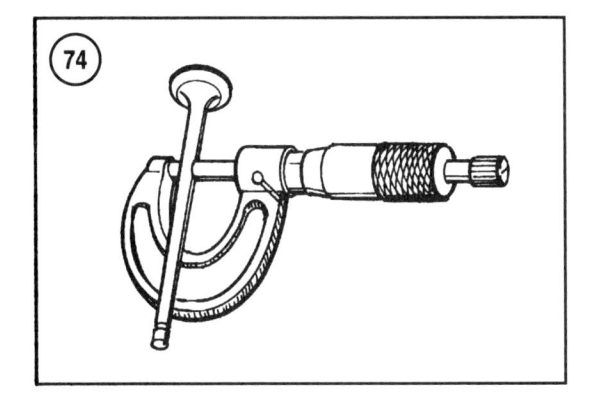

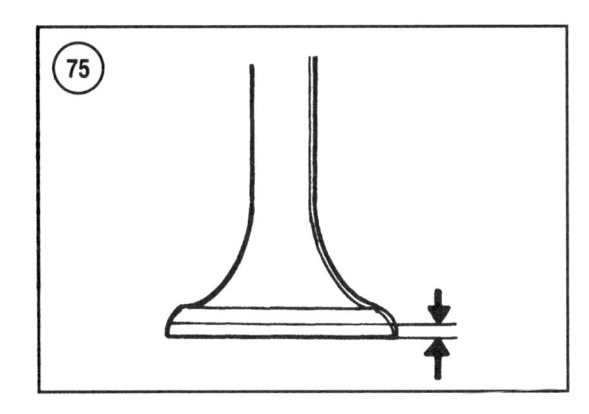

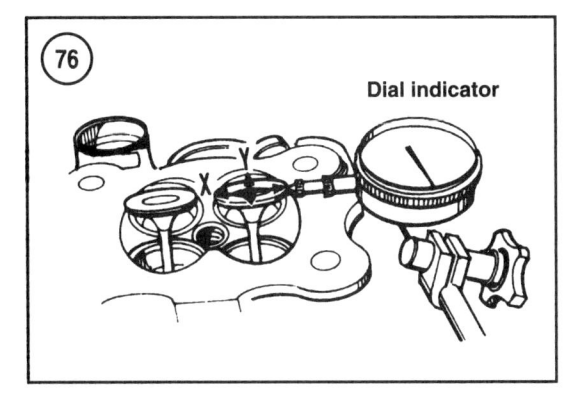

8. Measure the valve guide inside diameter with a small hole gauge. Measure the diameter at the top, center and bottom of the guide. Measure the small hole gauge, and compare the largest measurement to the specification in **Table 2**.
   a. If the valve guide is out of specification, replace it as described in this chapter.
   b. If the valve guide is within specification, record the measurement so it can be used to calculate valve stem-to-guide clearance in Step 9.

9. Subtract the valve stem outside diameter (Step 5) from the valve guide inside diameter (Step 8). The difference is the valve stem-to-guide clearance. If the clearance is out of specification, replace the valve and guide as a set.

10. If a small bore gauge is not available, measure the valve stem deflection by performing the following:
    a. Insert each valve into its guide.
    b. Hold the valve slightly off its seat (about 10 mm or 0.39 in.)
    c. Attach a dial indicator to the valve head (**Figure 76**) and rock the valve sideways in two directions 90° to each other. If the valve stem deflection in either direction exceeds the service limit in **Table 2** and the valve stem outside diameter is within specification, the valve guide is probably worn. However, as a final check, take the cylinder head to a Suzuki dealership or machine shop and have the valve guides measured.

11. Check the inner and outer valve springs as follows:
    a. Visually inspect each of the valve spring for cracks, distortion or other damage.
    b. Measure the valve spring free length with a vernier caliper.
    c. Repeat for each valve spring.
    d. Replace defective springs as a set (inner and outer).

12. Check the valve spring retainer and valve keepers for cracks or other damage.

13. Inspect the valve stem end for pitting or wear. If necessary, resurface the valve stem end, and measure the valve stem end length (**Figure 77**). The valve must be replaced if the valve stem end length is equal to or less than the wear limit specified in **Table 2**.

14. Inspect the valve seats. If worn or burned, they may be reconditioned as described in this chapter.

Valve Guide Replacement

The valve guides must be replaced when valve-to-stem clearance is excessive. Entrust this job to a Suzuki dealership, as special tools and considerable expertise are required. When a valve guide is replaced, the valve must also be replaced.

NOTE
Each intake manifold must be reinstalled in its original location. Mark each manifold prior to removal. If new intake manifolds are required, refer to Figure 61 for correct identification numbers and cylinder location

1. Remove the securing screws and remove all the intake manifolds from the cylinder head.

CAUTION
Do not heat the cylinder head with a torch (propane or acetylene). Never bring a flame into contact with the cylinder head. The direct heat will destroy the case hardening and may warp the head.

2. The valve guides are installed with a slight interference fit. Heat the cylinder head in a shop oven or on a hot plate. Heat the cylinder head to a temperature of 100-150° C (212-300° F). Use temperature indicator sticks, available at welding supply stores, to monitor the cylinder head temperature.
3. Place the new valve guides in the freezer. The cold temperature will reduce the guides' outside diameter and ease installation.

WARNING
Wear welding gloves when performing the following procedure. The cylinder head will be very hot.

4. Remove the cylinder head from the oven or hot plate. Place it on wooden blocks with the combustion chambers facing up.

CAUTION
Do not attempt to remove the valve guides if the head is not hot enough. Doing so may damage the valve guide bore.

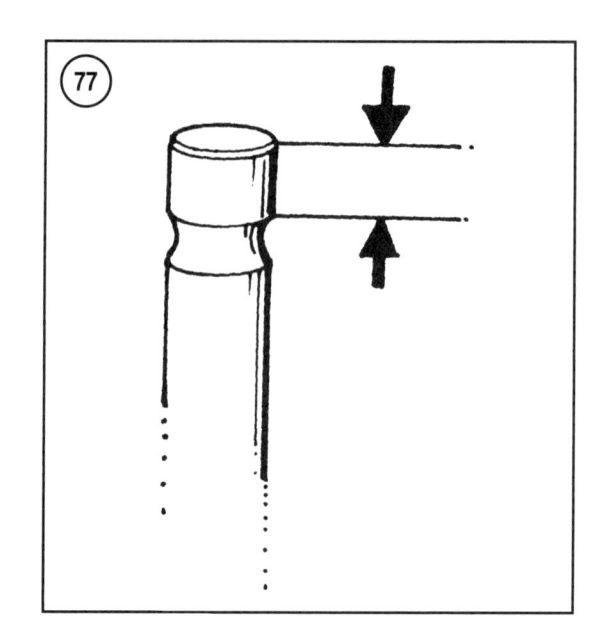

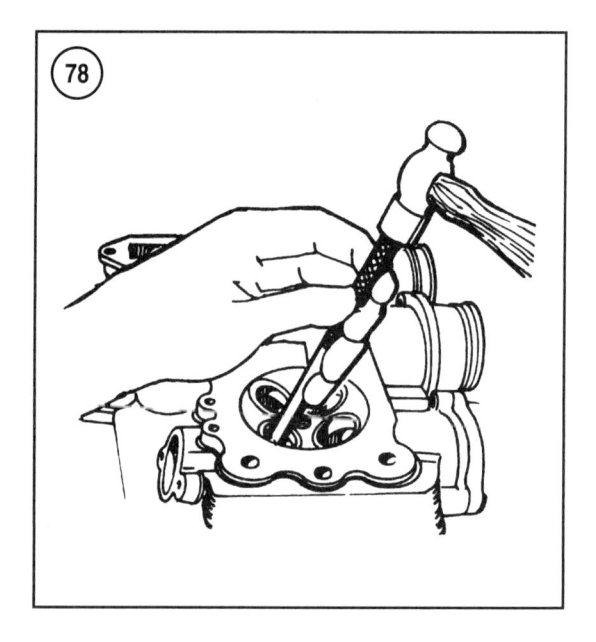

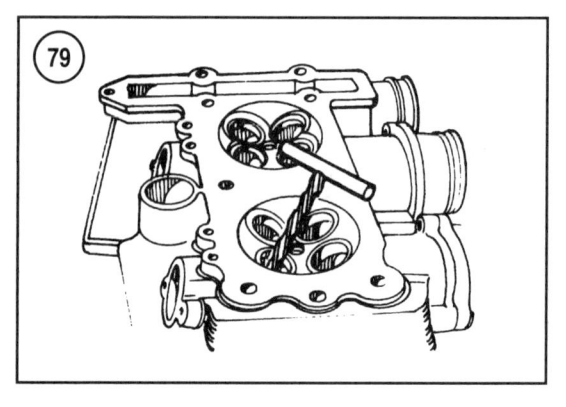

ENGINE TOP END

guide bore reamer (part No. 09916-34580) and reamer handle (part No. 09916-3452) or equivalent.

8. Rotate the reamer *clockwise* and withdraw it from the valve guide bore. Remove the reamer and handle.

9. Remove a *new* valve guide from the freezer, and install a *new* ring onto the guide.

10. Apply fresh engine oil to the *new* valve guide and to the valve guide bore in the cylinder head.

11. From the top side (valve side) of the cylinder head, drive the valve guide into place with a hammer and the Suzuki valve guide remover/installer (**Figure 80**). Drive the valve guide until the ring completely seats in the cylinder head.

12. After installation, ream the valve guide by performing the following:

   a. Use the Suzuki 5.0 mm valve guide reamer (part No. 09916-34570) and the reamer handle (part No. 09916-34542) or equivalent.
   b. Apply cutting oil to both the valve guide and the valve guide reamer.

CAUTION
*Always rotate the reamer **clockwise**. The valve guide will be damaged if the reamer is rotated counterclockwise.*

   c. Insert the reamer from the combustion chamber side and rotate it *clockwise* through the valve guide (**Figure 81**). Continue to rotate the reamer and work it down through the entire length of the valve guide. Apply additional cutting oil during this procedure.
   d. While rotating the reamer *clockwise*, withdraw the reamer from the valve guide.
   e. Measure the valve guide inside diameter with a small hole gauge. This measurement must be within the specification listed in **Table 2**.

13. Repeat for the other valve guides.

14. Thoroughly clean the cylinder head and valve guides with solvent to remove all metal particles. Clean the cylinder head with hot soapy water, rinse the head completely, and thoroughly dry it with compressed air.

15. Lubricate the valve guides with engine oil.

16. Recondition the valve seats as described in this chapter.

17. Install the intake manifolds in their original locations on the cylinder head. To prevent a vacuum leak, install a new O-ring with each intake manifold. If new intake manifolds are installed, refer to

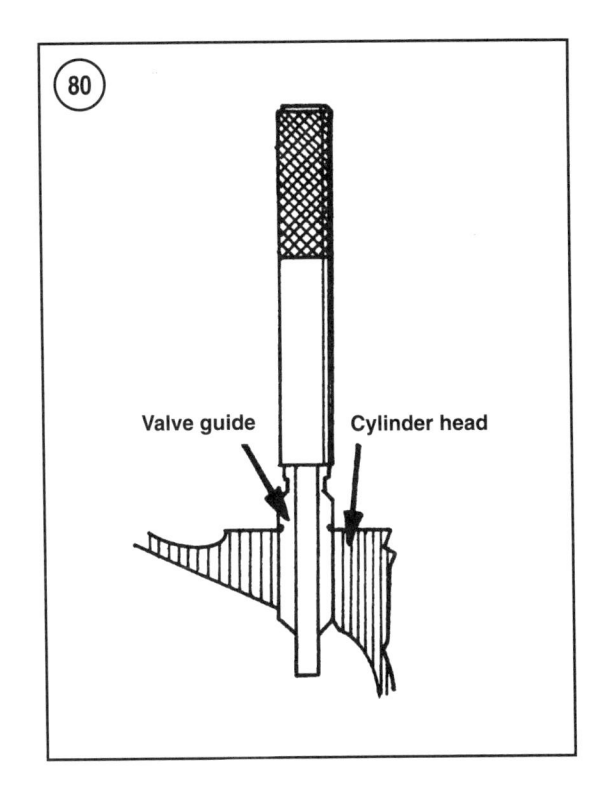

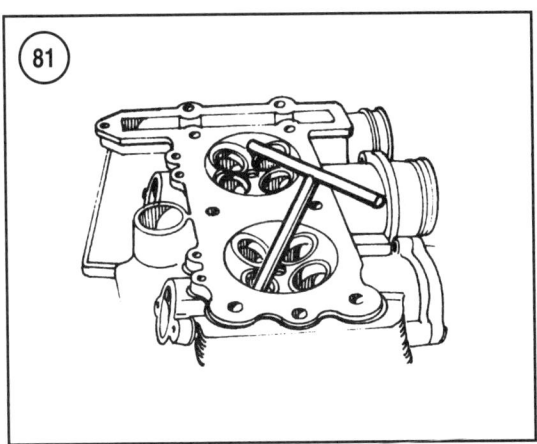

5. From the combustion side of the cylinder head, drive out the old valve guide (**Figure 78**) with a hammer and the Suzuki valve guide remover/installer (part No. 09916-44310) or equivalent.

6. Remove and discard the valve guide and the ring. Never reuse a valve guide or ring. They are no longer true nor within tolerance.

7. Insert the valve guide reamer from the combustion chamber side, and rotate the reamer *clockwise* through the valve guide bore (**Figure 79**). Continue to rotate the reamer and work it through the entire length of the bore. Use the Suzuki 10.8 mm valve

Figure 82 for correct identification numbers and cylinder location.

Valve Seat Inspection

The most accurate method for checking the valve seat is to use a marking compound, available from auto parts and tool stores. Marking compounds are used for locating high or irregular spots when checking or making close fits. Follow the manufacturer's directions.

NOTE
Because of the close operating tolerances within the valve assembly, the valve stem and guide must be within tolerance; otherwise, the inspection results will be inaccurate.

1. Remove the valves as described in this chapter.
2. Clean the valve seat in the cylinder head and valve mating areas with contact cleaner.
3. Thoroughly clean off all carbon deposits from the valve face with solvent or detergent. Dry the valve thoroughly.
4. Spread a thin layer of marking compound evenly on the valve face.
5. Moisten the end of a suction cup valve tool and attach it to the valve. Insert the valve into the guide.
6. Using the valve lapping tool, tap the valve against the valve seat with a light rotating motion in both directions (**Figure 83**).
7. Remove the valve and examine the impression left by the marking compound. If the impression (on the valve or on the cylinder head) is not even and continuous and if the valve seat width (**Figure 84**) is not within the specified tolerance, the valve seat must be reconditioned.
8. Closely examine the valve seat in the cylinder head. It should be smooth and even with a polished seating surface.
9. If the valve seat is good, install the valve as described in this chapter.
10. If the valve seat is not correct, have the valve seat(s) reconditioned.
11. Repeat for the other valves.

Valve Seat Reconditioning

Special valve cutters and considerable experience are required to properly recondition the valve seats

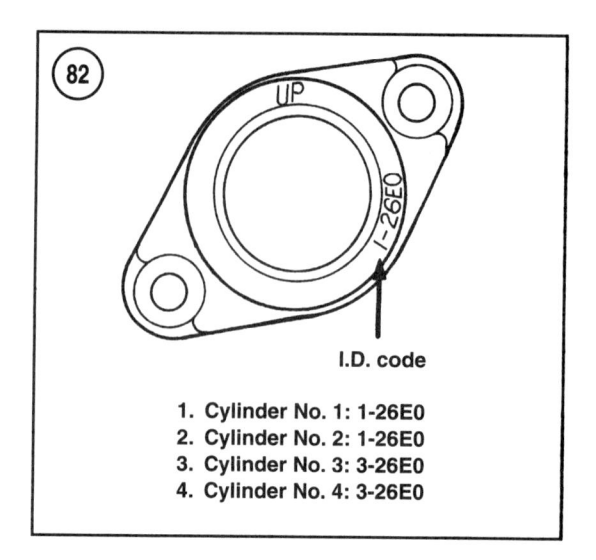

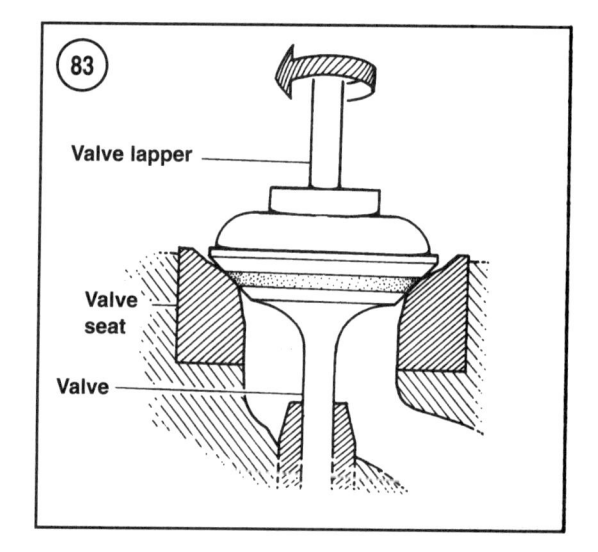

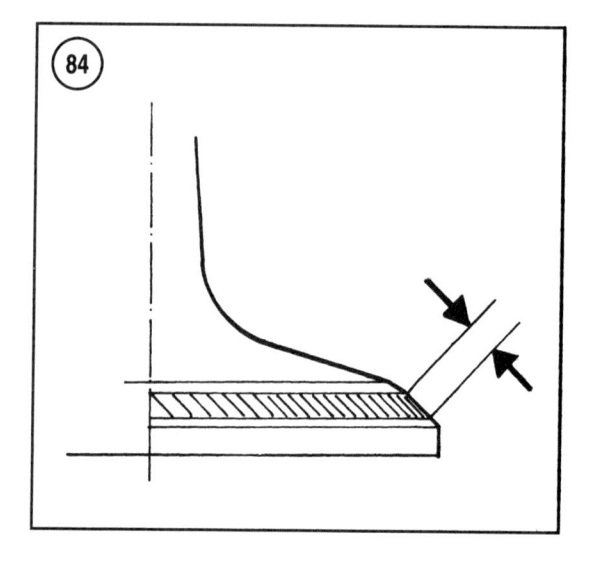

I.D. code

1. Cylinder No. 1: 1-26E0
2. Cylinder No. 2: 1-26E0
3. Cylinder No. 3: 3-26E0
4. Cylinder No. 4: 3-26E0

ENGINE TOP END

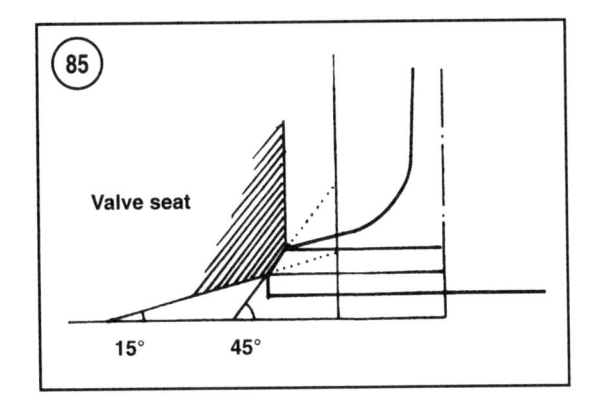

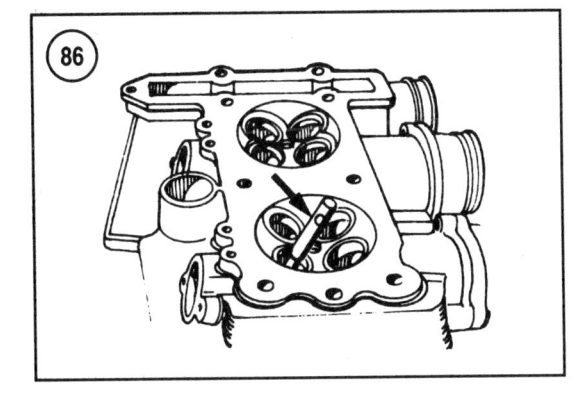

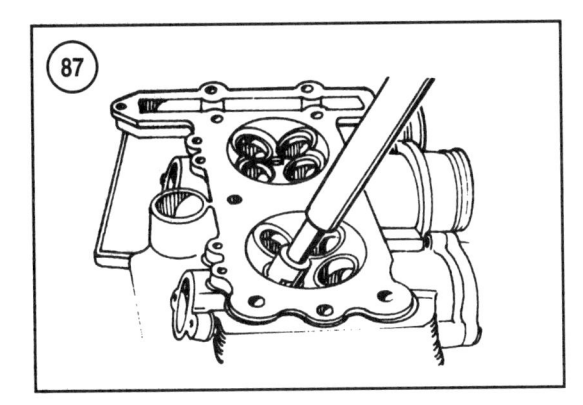

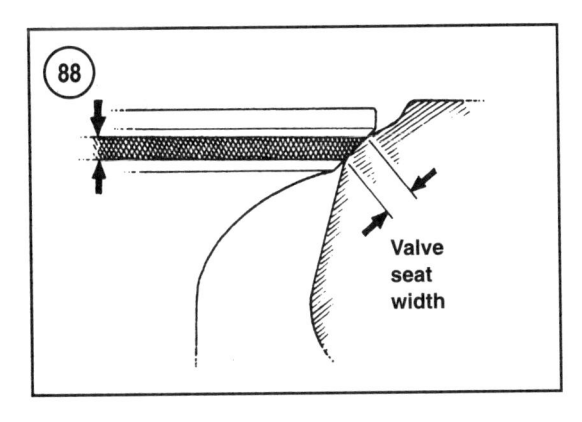

in the cylinder head. If these tools are unavailable, have a Suzuki dealership or machine shop perform the procedure. The following procedure is provided for those who choose to perform this task.

The Suzuki solid pilot (N-100-5.0) and valve cutters (N-121 or N-122) or equivalent are required to recondition the valve seats.

The valve seats for both the intake and exhaust valves are machined to the same angles. The valve contact surface is cut to a 45° angle and the area above the contact surface (closest to the combustion chamber) is cut to a 15° angle (**Figure 85**).

1. Carefully rotate and insert the solid pilot into the valve guide (**Figure 86**). Be sure the pilot is correctly seated.
2. Install the 45° cutter and T-handle onto the solid pilot.
3. Using the 45° cutter, descale and clean the valve seat with one or two turns (**Figure 87**).

> *CAUTION*
> *When cutting valve seats, work slowly. Measure the valve seat contact area in the cylinder head after each cut to make sure the contact area is correct and to avoid removing too much material. Over-cutting will sink the valve too far into the cylinder head, and the cylinder head will have to be replaced.*

4. If the seat is still pitted or burned, turn the 45° cutter additional turns until the surface is clean. Refer to the previous CAUTION to avoid removing too much material from the cylinder head.
5. Inspect the valve seat by performing the following:
   a. Spread a thin layer of marking compound evenly on the valve face.
   b. Moisten the end of a suction cup valve tool and attach it to the valve. Insert the valve into the guide.
   c. Using the valve lapping tool, tap the valve against the valve seat with a light rotating motion in both directions (**Figure 83**).
   d. Measure the valve seat width (**Figure 88**) with a vernier caliper. It should be within the range specified in **Table 2**.
6. If the contact area is too *high* on the valve (**Figure 84**) or if it is too wide, use the 15° cutter to remove a portion of the top area of the valve seat. This lowers and narrows the contact area on the valve.

7. If the contact area is too *low* on the valve or too narrow (**Figure 89**), use the 45° cutter to remove a portion of the lower area of the valve seat. This raises and widens the contact area on the valve.

8. Once the desired valve seat position and width are obtained, use the 45° cutter to lightly clean off any burrs that may have been caused by previous cuts.

CAUTION
Do not use any valve lapping compound after the final cut has been made.

9. Check that the finish has a smooth, velvety surface. It should not be shiny or polished. Final seating will take place when the engine is run.

10. Repeat for the remaining valve seats.

11. Thoroughly clean the cylinder head and all valve components in solvent or detergent and hot water.

12. Install the valve assemblies as described in this chapter. Check the seal at each valve seat by pouring solvent into the intake and exhaust ports (**Figure 90**). There should be no leaking past the seat in the combustion chamber. If leakage occurs, the combustion chamber will appear wet. If fluid leaks past any of the seats, the valve seats must be inspected for debris or burrs that are preventing a proper seal.

13. Apply a light coat of engine oil to all bare metal surfaces to prevent rust.

Valve Lapping

Valve lapping is a simple operation which can restore the valve seal without machining if the amount of wear or distortion is not too great.

Perform this procedure after determining that valve seat width and outside diameter are within specifications. A valve lapping tool (**Figure 83**) is required.

1. Smear a light coat of fine grade valve lapping compound onto the seating surface of the valve.
2. Insert the valve into the cylinder head.
3. Wet the suction cup of the lapping tool and stick in onto the head of the valve. Spin the tool in both directions while pressing it against the valve seat, and lap the valve to the seat. Every 5 to 10 seconds, rotate the valve 180° in the valve seat. Continue with this action until the mating surfaces on the valve and seat are smooth and equal in size.

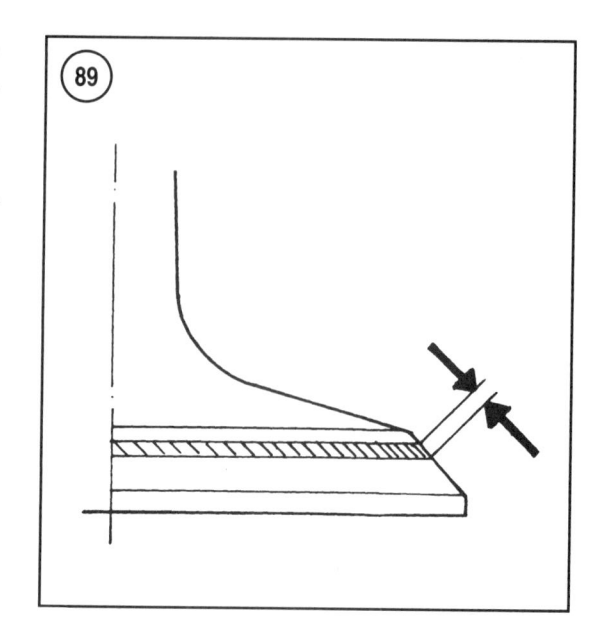

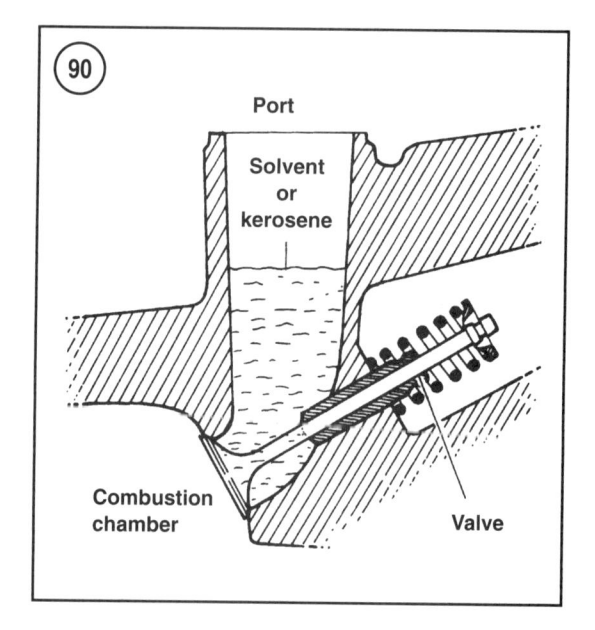

ENGINE TOP END

7. Install the valve assemblies as described in this chapter.

8. After the lapping has been completed and the valves have been reinstalled into the head, test the valve seats as described in Step 12 of *Valve Seat Reconditioning*. If fluid leaks past any of the seats, disassemble that valve assembly and repeat this procedure until there is no leakage.

NOTE
This solvent test does not ensure long-term durability or maximum power. It merely ensures maximum compression will be available on initial start-up after reassembly.

9. Apply a light coat of engine oil to all bare metal surfaces to prevent rust.

CYLINDER BLOCK

Removal

1. Remove the cylinder head as described in this chapter.
2. Remove the cylinder head gasket and the locating dowels.
3. If still installed, remove the external oil pipes (**Figure 91**) from the front of the crankcase.
4. On models with a PAIR system, remove the PAIR air pipes from the cylinder block as described in Chapter Eight.
5. Remove the bolts securing the oil hose assembly (**Figure 92**) to the crankcase and the oil hose assembly. Make sure the O-ring behind the oil hose fitting is removed from the crankcase.
6. Remove the cylinder base nut (**Figure 93**) from the stud at the front of the crankcase.

CAUTION
The cooling fins are fragile and may be damaged if tapped or pried too hard. Do not strike the fins with a metal-faced hammer.

7. Loosen the cylinder block by tapping around its perimeter with a soft-faced mallet. If necessary, pry the cylinder block loose from the crankcase.
8. Push the rear cam chain guide forward so it is out of the way.
9. Pull the cylinder block (**Figure 94**) straight up and off of the pistons and crankcase studs. Work the

4. Closely examine the valve seat in the cylinder head. It should have a smooth, evenly polished seating ring.

5. Repeat Steps 1-4 for the other valves.

6. Thoroughly clean the valves and cylinder head in solvent or detergent and hot water to remove all valve grinding compound. Dry the components thoroughly.

CAUTION
Any compound left on the valves or the cylinder head will cause excessive wear and damage.

cam chain wire through the cam chain tunnel in the cylinder block. Reattach the wire to the exterior of the crankcase.

10. Remove the base gasket.
11. Remove the locating dowels from the crankcase.
12. Use tweezers or needlenose pliers to remove the two oil jets (**Figure 95**) from the top of the crankcase. A jet is located adjacent to each rear crankcase stud on the left and right corners of the crankcase.
13. Inspect the cylinder block as described below.

Installation

A set of piston-holding fixtures and piston ring compressors make installation of the cylinder block over the pistons safer and easier. Cylinder block installation can be accomplished without these tools, but it is a lot more difficult and also increases the chance of damage to both the cylinder wall surfaces and to the piston rings and skirts. These tools are available from a Suzuki dealership or tool supplier.

1. Check the top surface of the crankcase and the bottom surface of the cylinder block. Both must be clean.
2. Install the two oil jets (**Figure 96**) adjacent to the rear crankcase stud on the left and right corners of the crankcase.
3. Install a *new* base gasket onto the crankcase. Make sure the UP mark on the gasket faces up as shown in **Figure 97**.
4. Install the locating dowels (**Figure 98**) onto the two front center crankcase studs.
5. Rotate the crankshaft so the No. 2 and No. 3 pistons are at top dead center. Install a piston-holding fixture on each of the two inside pistons.
6. Lubricate the cylinder walls, pistons and rings liberally with clean engine oil prior to installation.
7. Feed the cam chain and wire up through the cam chain tunnel in the cylinder block. Carefully align the cylinder block with the two raised pistons.
8. Slowly slide the cylinder block over the rear cam chain guide and lower the block down onto the No. 2 and No. 3 pistons until the liners *lightly* touch the top piston rings.
9. On the No. 2 and No. 3 pistons, compress each piston ring as it enters the cylinder bore. Slide the cylinder block all the way down until it passes by the piston rings (**Figure 99**).

ENGINE TOP END

Compress each piston ring as it enters the cylinder bore. Slide the cylinder block all the way down until it passes by the piston rings.

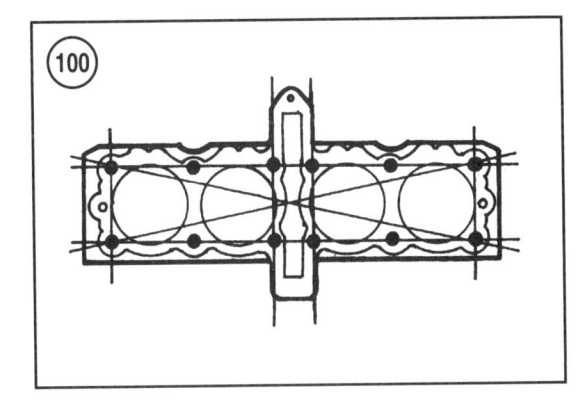

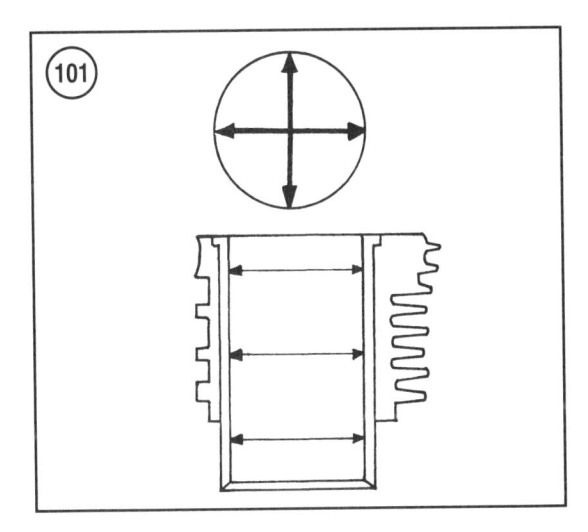

12. Carefully push the cylinder block down until it bottoms on the upper crankcase. Make sure the locating dowels correctly engage the cylinder block.

13. Install the cylinder base nut (**Figure 93**) onto the stud at the front of the crankcase. Torque the nut to the specification in **Table 3**.

14. Place a *new* O-ring into the fitting for the oil hose assembly, and secure the fitting (**Figure 92**) to the crankcase. Tighten the oil hose mounting bolts to specification.

15. On models with a PAIR system, install the PAIR air pipes onto the cylinder block as described in Chapter Eight.

16. Install the cylinder head and cylinder head cover as described in this chapter.

Inspection

A bore gauge and micrometer are required to accurately measure the cylinder bore. If these tools are not available, have the measurements performed by a Suzuki dealership or machine shop.

Compare all measurement to the specifications in **Table 2**. Replace or rebore the cylinder block if it is damaged or out of specification.

1. Soak any old gasket material with solvent. Remove all gasket residue from the cylinder block top and bottom gasket surfaces. If necessary, gently scrape away gasket residue. Both surfaces must be free of all residue.

2. Wash the cylinder block in solvent. Dry it with compressed air.

3. Check the cylinder block surfaces for cracks or damage.

4. Check the cylinder block for warp with a straightedge (**Figure 58**) and flat feeler gauge. Check for warp at several spots across the cylinder block (**Figure 100**). The block must be replaced if cylinder warp exceeds the limit.

5. Check the locating dowel holes for cracks or other damage.

6. Check each cylinder bore for deep scratches, scoring, or other visible damage.

7. Measure the inside diameter of each cylinder bore with a bore gauge or inside micrometer at the points shown in **Figure 101**. Measure in line with the piston pin and 90° to the pin. If any measure-

CAUTION
In the following step, do not damage the No. 2 and No. 3 pistons when the piston-holding fixtures are removed.

10. Support the cylinder block, and remove the piston-holding fixtures.

11. Slowly lower the cylinder block and insert the No.1 and No. 4 pistons into the cylinder bores.

ment is out of specification, the cylinder block must be rebored to the next oversize and new pistons and piston rings installed. Rebore all four cylinders even though only one may be worn.

CAUTION
*Never rebore a cylinder if the finished diameter will exceed the cylinder bore wear limit in **Table 2**.*

NOTE
Purchase the new pistons before boring the cylinders so the pistons can be measured and the cylinder bored to match.

8. Wash each cylinder bore in hot soapy water and rinse it completely. This is the only way to clean the cylinder walls of the fine grit material left from the bore or honing job. After washing the walls, run a clean white cloth through each cylinder. The cloth should show no traces of grit or other debris. If the cloth is dirty, rewash the cylinder walls. Once the cylinder walls are completely clean, lubricate them with clean engine oil to prevent rust.

PISTON AND PISTON RINGS

The pistons are made of an aluminum alloy. The piston pin is made of steel and is a precision fit in the pistons. The piston pins are held in place by a clip at each end.

Piston Removal

1. Remove the cylinder head and cylinder block as described in this chapter.
2. Identify the top of each piston by cylinder number (**Figure 102**). The No. 1 cylinder is on the left side. The pistons must be reinstalled onto the correct connecting rods and into the correct cylinder bores during installation.
3. Cover the crankcase below the piston with a clean shop cloth to keep the piston pin circlips from falling into the crankcase.
4. Before removing a piston, hold the rod tightly and rock the piston (**Figure 103**). Any rocking motion (do not confuse with the normal sliding motion) indicates wear on the piston pin, rod bushing, pin bore, or more likely, a combination of all three.

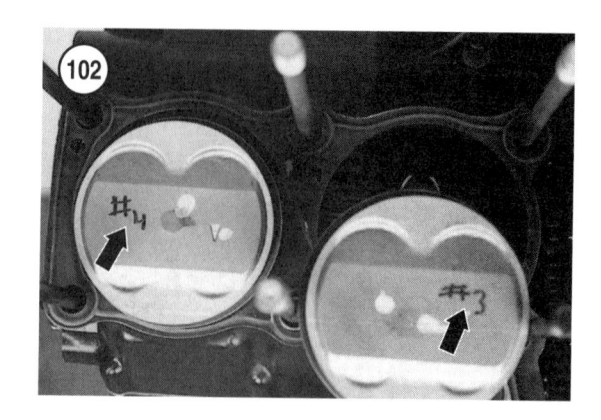

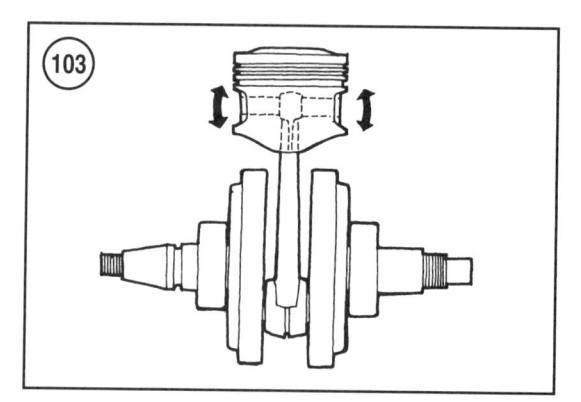

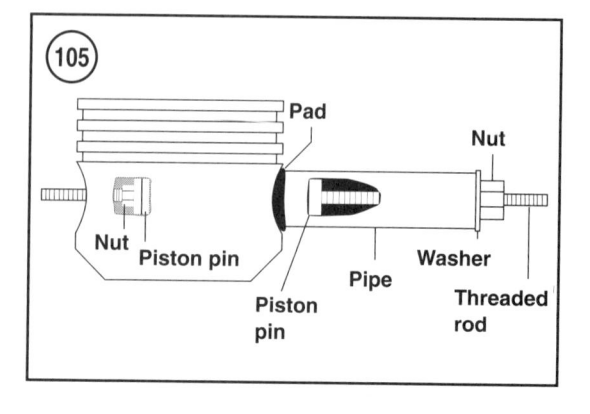

ENGINE TOP END

9. Inspect the pistons and piston pins as described in this chapter.

Piston Installation

1. Apply molybdenum disulfide grease to the inside of the connecting rod small end.

NOTE
The pistons must be installed with the arrow facing forward (the exhaust side of the engine).

2. Install a *new* circlip into the side of the piston that will face the center line of the cylinder block. Make sure the clip is correctly seated in the piston groove. The circlip ends must not align with the cutout in the piston (**Figure 106**).
3. Apply molybdenum disulfide grease to the piston pin, and slide the pin into the piston until the pin is flush with the piston pin boss (**Figure 107**).
4. Place the correct piston over the connecting rod.
   a. Refer to the reference numbers marked on the pistons during removal, and install the pistons onto their original connecting rods. If the cylinders were rebored, match each piston with the correct connecting rod.
   b. Install each piston so the arrow on the crown points to the exhaust side of the engine (the front).
5. Align the piston pin with the hole in the connecting rod. Push the piston pin through the connecting rod and into the other side of the piston. Do not use force when installing the piston pin. Push the pin until it clears the pin clip groove in the near side of the piston or until it touches the pin clip in the other side.
6. Once the pin is installed, check that the arrow on the piston crown points to the front (exhaust side) of the engine. Also make sure that the piston is installed on the correct connecting rod.
7. Install a *new* piston pin circlip into the other side of the pin boss. Make sure the circlip is seated correctly in the piston groove (**Figure 106**).
8. Check the installation by rocking the piston back and forth around the pin axis and from side to side along the axis. The piston should rotate freely back and forth but not from side to side.
9. Repeat Steps 1-8 for the remaining pistons.
10. If removed, install the piston rings as described in this chapter.

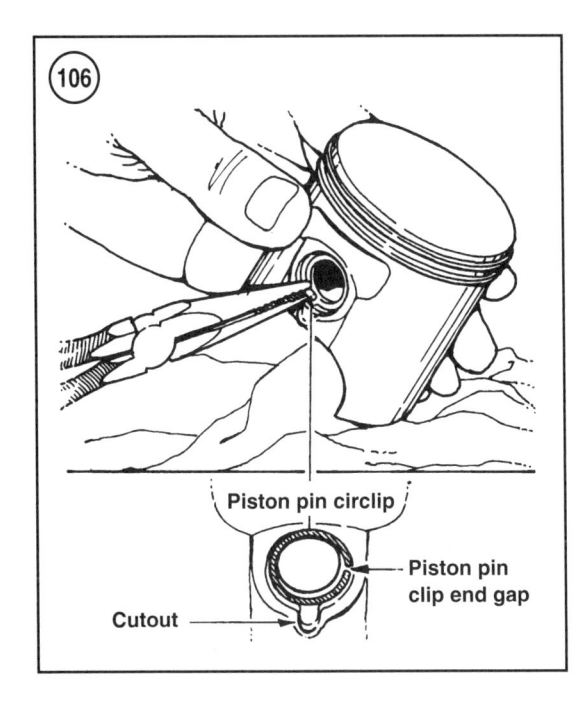

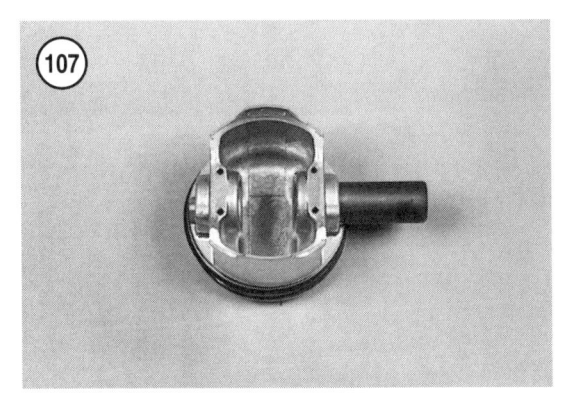

5. Remove the circlip from each side of the piston pin bore (**Figure 104**). When removing the clip, hold a thumb over one clip edge so the clip will not spring out.

CAUTION
Discard the piston circlips. New circlips must be installed during assembly.

6. Push the piston pin out of the bore by hand. If the pin is tight, remove it with a homemade tool (**Figure 105**). Do not drive the piston pin out with a hammer and pipe. This action could damage the piston pin, connecting rod or piston.
7. Lift the piston off the connecting rod.
8. Repeat for the other three pistons.

11. Install the cylinder block and cylinder head as described in this chapter.

Piston Inspection

1. If necessary, remove the piston rings as described in this chapter.

> *CAUTION*
> *Be careful not to gouge or otherwise damage the piston when removing carbon. Never use a wire brush to clean the piston skirt or ring grooves. Do not attempt to remove the carbon ridge from the sides of the piston above the top ring or from the cylinder bore near the top. Removal of carbon from these two areas may cause increased oil consumption.*

2. Carefully clean the carbon from the piston crown (**Figure 108**) with a soft scraper. Large carbon accumulations reduce piston cooling and result in detonation and piston damage. Renumber the piston as soon as it is cleaned so the piston can be properly identified during assembly.

3. After cleaning the piston, examine the crown. The crown should show no signs of wear or damage. If the crown appears pecked or spongy-looking, also check the spark plug, valves and combustion chamber for aluminum deposits. If these deposits are found, the engine is overheating.

4. Examine each ring groove for burrs, dented edges or other damage. Pay particular attention to the top compression ring groove. It usually wears more than the others. Because the oil rings are constantly bathed in oil, these rings and grooves wear little compared to compression rings and their grooves. If there is evidence of oil ring groove wear or if the oil ring assembly is tight and difficult to remove, the piston skirt may have collapsed due to excessive heat and is permanently deformed. Replace the piston.

5. Check the oil control holes (**Figure 109**) in the piston for carbon or oil sludge buildup. Clean the holes with wire and blow them clear with compressed air.

6. Check the piston skirt (**Figure 110**) for galling and abrasion that may have been caused by piston seizure. If a piston shows signs of partial seizure (bits of aluminum build-up on the piston skirt), re-

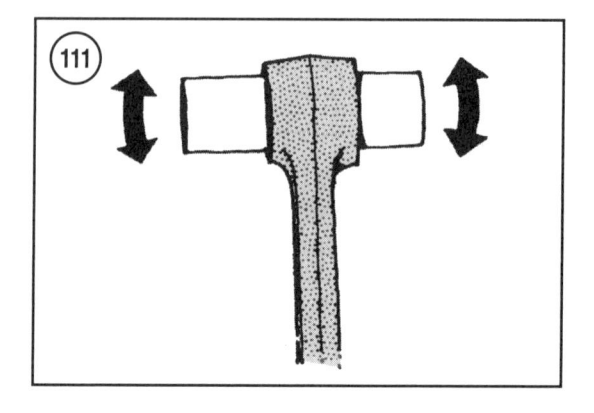

ENGINE TOP END

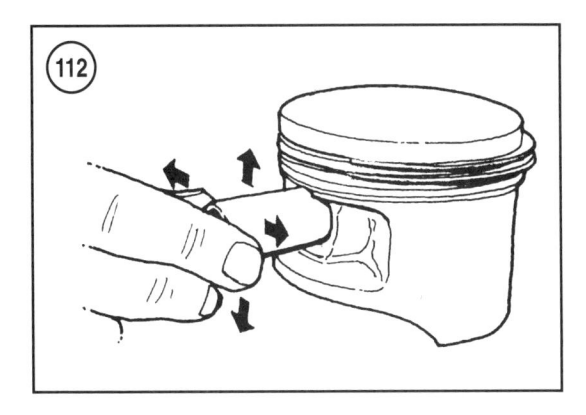

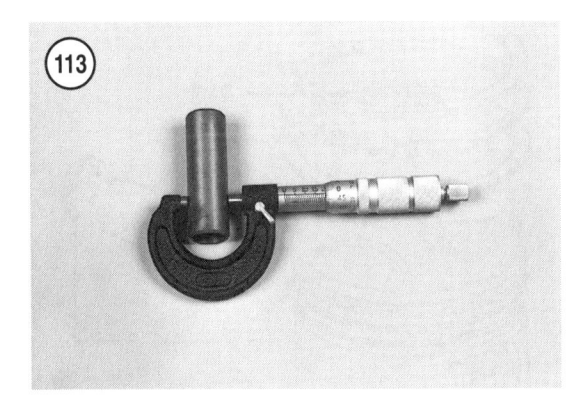

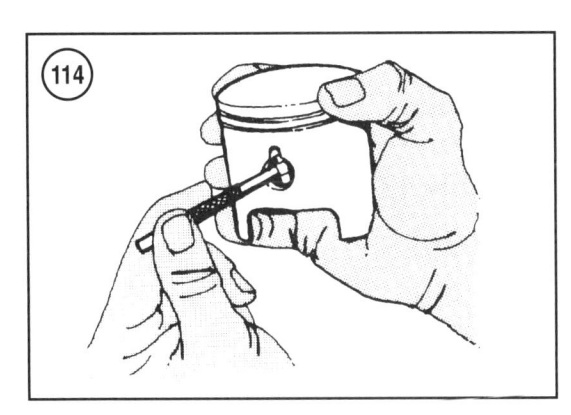

112

113

114

place the piston and rebore the cylinders, if necessary, to reduce the possibility of engine noise and further piston seizure.

NOTE
If the piston skirt is worn or scuffed unevenly from side to side, the connecting rod may be bent or twisted.

7. Check the circlip groove on each side for wear, cracks or other damage. If the grooves are questionable, check the circlip fit by installing a new circlip into each groove and then attempt to move the circlip from side to side. If the circlip has any side play, the groove is worn and the piston must be replaced.

8. Measure piston-to-cylinder clearance as described in *Piston Clearance* in this chapter.

9. If damage or wear indicates piston replacement, select a new piston as described under *Piston Clearance* in this chapter. If the piston, rings and cylinder are not damaged and are dimensionally correct, they can be reused.

Piston Pin Inspection

Compare all measurements to the specification in **Table 2**. Replace any part that is damaged, worn to the service limit or out of specification.

1. Clean the piston pin in solvent, and dry it thoroughly.
2. Inspect the piston pin for chrome flaking or cracks. Replace if necessary.
3. Oil the piston pin and install it into the connecting rod (**Figure 111**). Slowly rotate the piston pin and check for radial play.
4. Oil the piston pin and partially install it into the piston. Check the piston pin for excessive play (**Figure 112**).
5. Measure the piston pin outside diameter at three places with a micrometer (**Figure 113**). Replace the piston pin if any measurement is out of specification.
6. Measure the inside diameter of the piston pin bore (**Figure 114**) with a small hole gauge. Measure the small hole gauge with a micrometer.
7. Replace the piston pin and/or piston or connecting rod if necessary.

Piston Clearance

1. Make sure the piston skirt and cylinder wall are clean and dry.
2. Measure the cylinder bore with a bore gauge or inside micrometer. Measure the cylinder bore at the three positions, measured from the top surface, as shown in **Figure 101**. Measure in line with the piston pin and 90° to the pin. Record the bore dimensions.
3. Measure the piston outside diameter with a micrometer at a right angle to the piston pin bore. Mea-

115

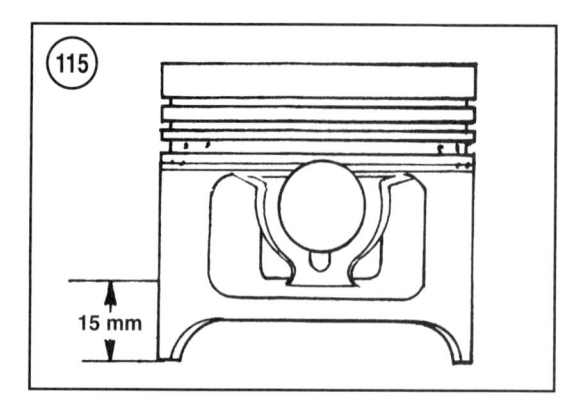

sure up 15 mm (0.590 in.) from the bottom edge of the piston skirt (**Figure 115**).

4. Subtract the piston outside diameter from the largest bore diameter; the difference is piston-to-cylinder clearance. If clearance exceeds the service limit specified in **Table 2**, replace the pistons and cylinder block.

Piston Ring
Inspection and Removal

The piston and ring assembly is a 3-ring type (**Figure 116**). The top and second rings are compression rings. The lower ring is an oil control ring assembly, consisting of two ring rails and an expander spacer.

When measuring the piston rings and pistons in this section, compare the actual measurements to the new and service limit specifications in **Table 2**. Replace parts that are out of specification or show damage as described in this section.

1. Measure the side clearance of each compression ring in its groove with a flat feeler gauge (**Figure 117**). If the clearance is greater than specified, replace the rings. If the clearance is still excessive with the new rings installed, replace the piston.

WARNING
The edges of all piston rings are very sharp. Be careful when handling them to avoid cutting fingers.

NOTE
Store the old rings in the order in which they are removed.

2. Remove the compression rings with a ring expander tool (**Figure 118**) or by spreading the ring

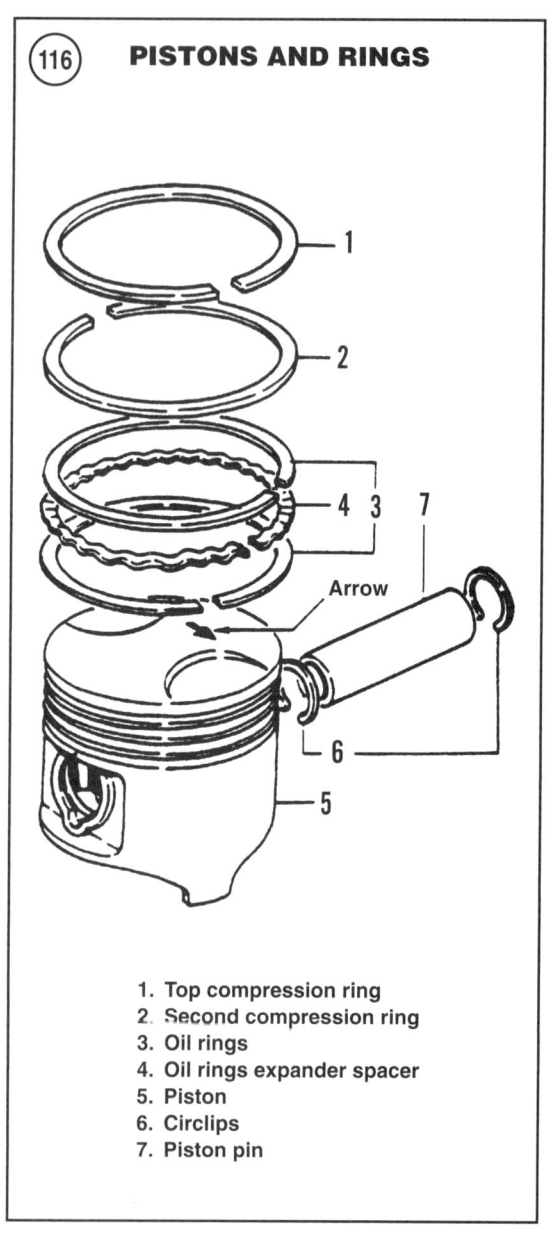

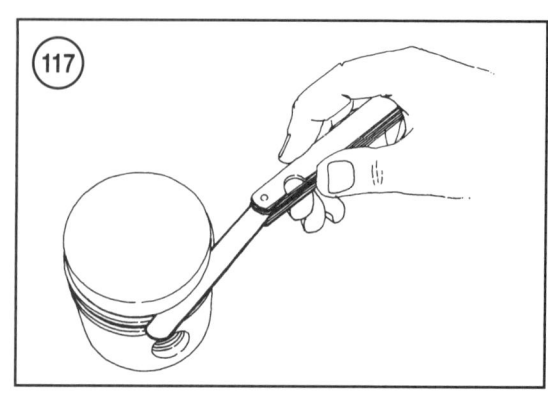

116 PISTONS AND RINGS

1. Top compression ring
2. Second compression ring
3. Oil rings
4. Oil rings expander spacer
5. Piston
6. Circlips
7. Piston pin

117

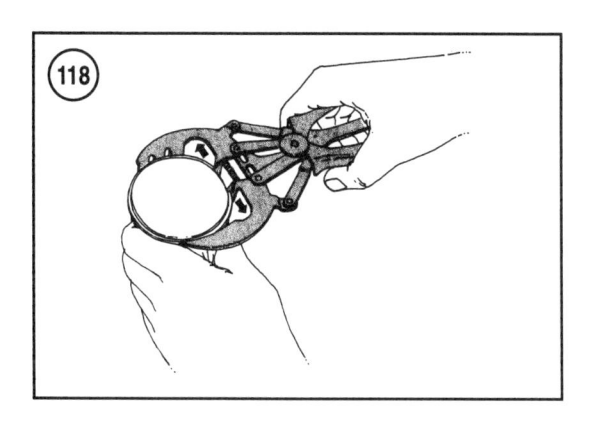

ENGINE TOP END

ends by hand and lifting the rings up evenly (**Figure 119**).

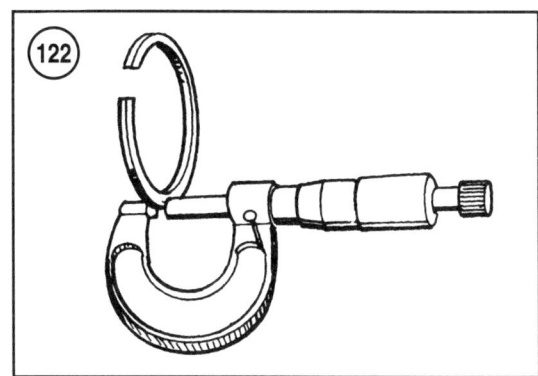

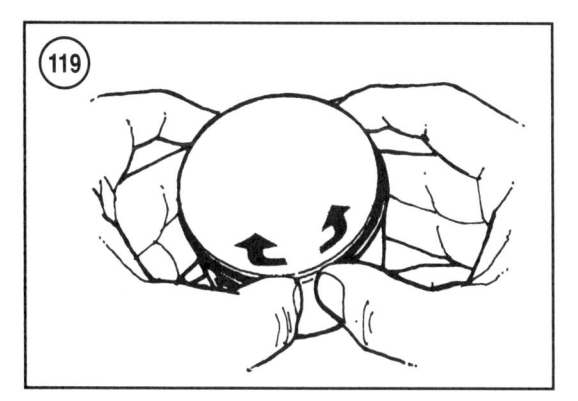

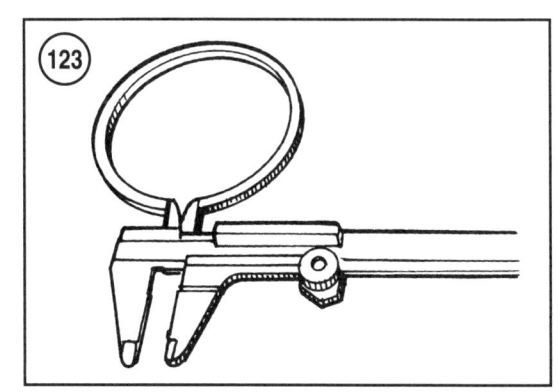

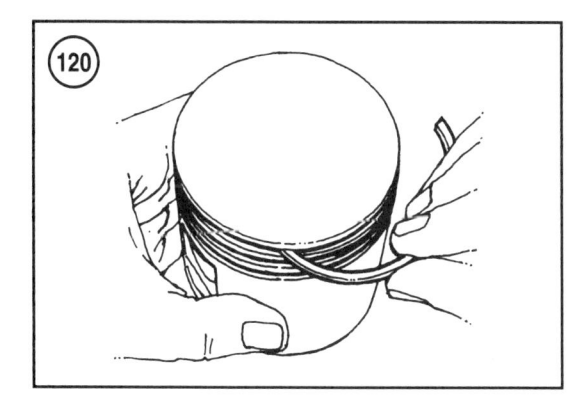

3. Remove the oil ring assembly by first removing the upper and then the lower ring rails. Then remove the expander spacer.

4. Using a broken piston ring, carefully remove carbon and oil residue from the piston ring grooves (**Figure 120**). Do not remove aluminum material from the ring grooves, as this will increase ring side clearance.

5. Roll each ring around its piston groove as shown in **Figure 121** to check for binding. Clean up minor imperfections with a fine-cut file.

6. Measure each compression ring groove width with a vernier caliper. Measure each groove at several points around the piston. Replace the piston if any groove is outside the specified range.

7. Inspect grooves carefully for burrs, nicks or broken or cracked lands. Replace the piston if necessary.

8. Measure the thickness of each compression ring with a micrometer (**Figure 122**). If the thickness is less than specified, replace the ring(s).

9. Measure the free end gap of each compression ring with a vernier caliper (**Figure 123**). If the free

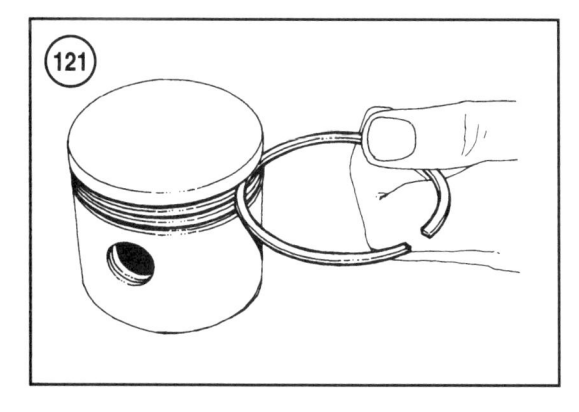

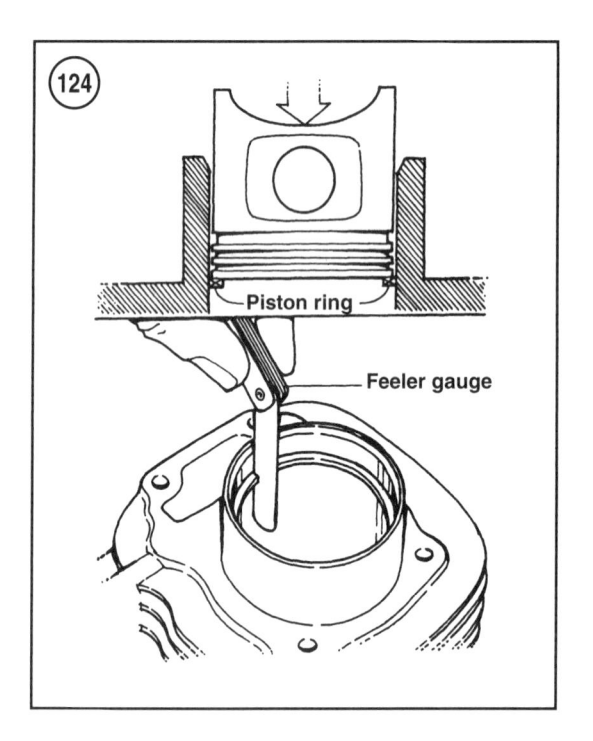

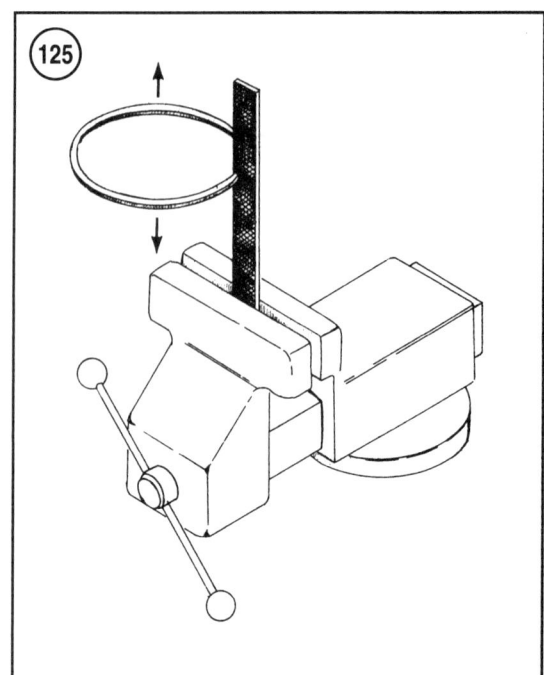

end gap exceeds the service limit, replace the ring(s).

10. Insert the ring into the bottom of the cylinder bore and square it with the cylinder wall by tapping it with the piston. Measure the end gap with a feeler gauge (**Figure 124**). Replace the rings if the end gap equals or exceeds the service limit. Also measure the end gap when installing new piston rings. If the gap on a new compression ring is smaller than specified, hold a small file in a vise, grip the ends of the ring by hand and enlarge the gap (**Figure 125**).

Piston Ring Installation

1. Clean the piston and rings. Dry them with compressed air.
2. Install piston rings as follows:

> *NOTE*
> *Install the piston rings—first the bottom, then the middle, and then the top ring, by carefully spreading the ends by hand and slipping the rings over the top of the piston. Remember that the piston rings must be installed with the manufacturer's marks facing toward the top of the piston. Incorrectly installed piston rings can wear rapdly and/or allow oil to escape past them.*

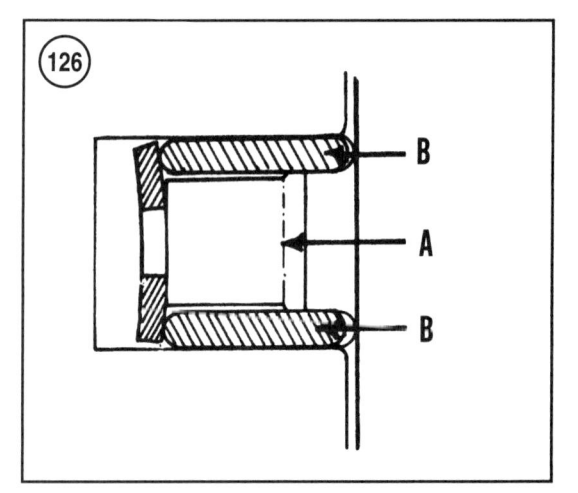

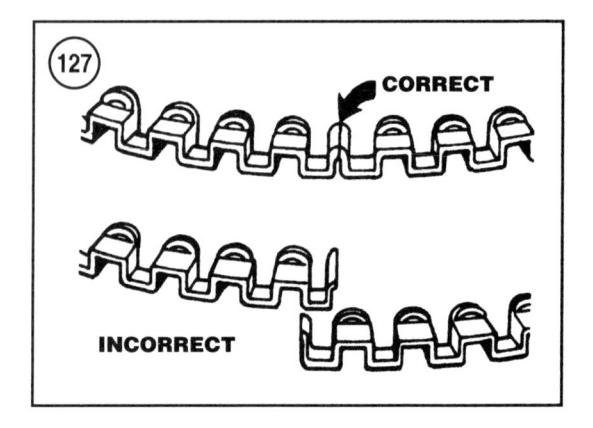

ENGINE TOP END

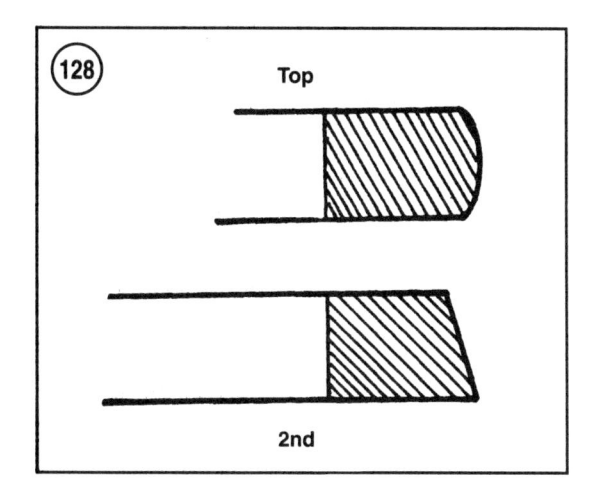

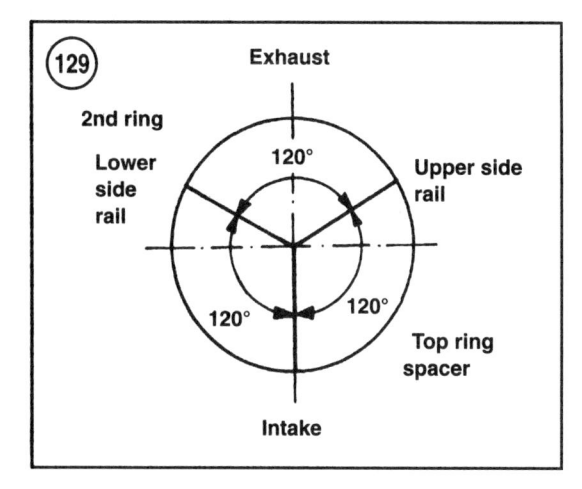

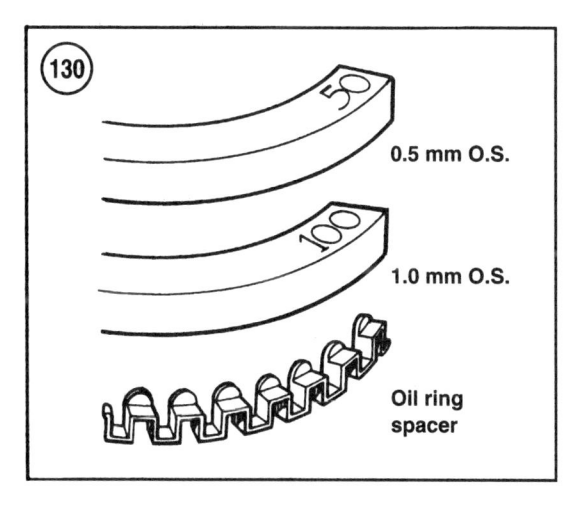

a. Install the oil control ring assembly into the bottom ring groove. Install the oil ring expander spacer first (A, **Figure 126**), and then install each ring rail (B, **Figure 126**). Make sure the ends of the expander spacer butt together (**Figure 127**). They should not overlap. If reassembling used parts, install the ring rails as they were removed.

NOTE
When installing aftermarket piston rings, follow the manufacturer's directions.

b. Install the second or middle compression ring with the manufacturer's RN mark facing up. This ring has a slight taper (**Figure 128**).
c. Install the top compression ring with the manufacturer's R mark facing up.

3. Make sure the rings are seated completely in their grooves all the way around the piston. Also check that the end gaps are distributed around the piston as shown in **Figure 129**. The ring gaps must not align with each other to prevent compression pressures from escaping past them.

4. If new rings are installed, the cylinders must be deglazed or honed. This helps seat the new rings. Refer honing service to a Suzuki dealership or competent machine shop. After honing, measure the ring end gap (**Figure 124**) for each compression ring.

5. When installing oversized compression rings, check the ring number (**Figure 130**) to ensure that the correct rings are installed. The ring oversize number should be the same as the piston oversize number.

6. A paint mark on the oil ring spacer identifies oversized oil rings. When installing oversized oil rings, check the color to ensure that the correct size oil rings are being installed.

  Standard size: no color
  0.5 mm oversize: red
  1.0 mm oversize: yellow

7. When new parts are installed, break the engine in as though it were new. Refer to *Engine Break-In* in Chapter Five.

Tables 1-3 are on the following pages.

Table 1 GENERAL ENGINE SPECIFICATIONS

Item	Specification
Engine type	DOHC inline 4 cylinder, TSCC 4-valve head
Bore × stroke	62.6 × 48.7 mm (2.465 × 1.917 in.)
Displacement	599cc (36.5 cu. in.)
Compression ratio	11.3:1
Compression pressure	
Standard	1000-1500 kPa (145-218 psi)
Wear limit	800 kPa (116 psi)
Ignition type	Electronic
Ignition timing	
1995	
Austria and Switzerland models	4 BTDC @ 1500 rpm
All models except Austria and Switzerland	13 BTDC @ 1500 rpm
1996	
USA, California, Austria and Switzerland models	4 BTDC @ 1500 rpm
All models except USA, California, Austria and Switzerland	13 BTDC @ 1500 rpm
1997-1999	
USA, California, and Switzerland models	4 BTDC @ 1500 rpm
All models except USA, California, and Switzerland	13 BTDC @ 1500 rpm
2000	
USA, California, and Canada models	4 BTDC @ 1200 rpm
Australia and European models	13 BTDC @ 1500 rpm
Firing order	1-2-4-3
Cooling system	Air/oil cooled
Lubrication system	Wet sump

Table 2 TOP END SPECIFICATIONS

Item	Standard mm (in.)	Wear limit mm (in.)
Camshaft		
Cam lobe height		
1995-1999 Switzerland models		
Intake	32.38-32.43 (1.2748-1.2764)	32.08 (1.2630)
Exhaust	32.10-32.14 (1.2638-1.2654)	31.80 (1.2520)
1995-1999 All models except Switzerland		
Intake	33.13-33.17 (1.3043-1.3059)	32.83 (1.2925)
Exhaust	32.85-32.89 (1.2933-1.2949)	32.55 (1.2815)
2000 models		
Intake	33.13-33.17 (1.3043-1.3059)	32.83 (1.2925)
Exhaust	32.85-32.89 (1.2933-1.2949)	32.55 (1.2815)
Journal oil clearance (bearing clearance)	0.032-0.066 (0.0013-0.0026)	0.150 (0.0059)
Journal outside diameter	21.959-21.980 (0.8645-0.8654)	–
Journal holder inside diameter	22.012-22.025 (0.8666-0.8671)	–
Camshaft runout	–	0.10 mm (0.004)

(continued)

ENGINE TOP END

Table 2 TOP END SPECIFICATIONS (continued)

Item	Standard mm (in.)	Wear limit mm (in.)
Rocker arm		
Bore inside diameter	12.000-12.018 (0.4724-0.4731)	–
Shaft outside diameter	11.973-11.984 (0.4714-0.4718)	–
Valves and valve springs		
Valve clearance (cold)		
Intake	0.10-0.15 (0.004-0.006)	–
Exhaust	0.18-0.23 (0.007-0.009)	–
Valve stem outside diameter		
Intake	4.965-4.980 (0.1955-0.1961)	–
Exhaust	4.955-4.970 (0.1950-0.1957)	–
Valve stem deflection	–	0.35 (0.014)
Valve stem runout	–	0.05 (0.002)
Valve stem end length	–	2.5 (0.10)
Valve guide inside diameter	5.000-5.012 (0.1969-0.1973)	–
Valve stem-to-guide clearance		
Intake	0.020-0.047 (0.0008-0.0019)	
Exhaust	0.030-0.057 (0.0012-0.0022)	
Valve head diameter		
Intake	23 (0.9)	–
Exhaust	20 (0.8)	–
Valve head thickness	–	0.5 (0.02)
Valve head radial runout	–	0.03 (0.001)
Valve seat width	0.9-1.1 (0.035-0.043)	–
Valve seat cutter angle		
Intake	15 and 45 degrees	
Exhaust	15 and 45 degrees	
Valve spring free length		
Inner	–	35.0 (1.38)
Outer	–	38.4 (1.51)
Valve spring tension		
Inner	5.6-6.6 kg @ 28 mm (12.3-14.6 lbs.@ 1.10 in.)	–
Outer	12.8-15.0 kg @ 31.5 mm (28.2-33.1 lbs.@ 1.24 in.)	
Cylinder head warp	–	0.20 (0.008)
Cylinder		
Bore	62.600-62.615 (2.4646-2.4652)	62.690 (2.4681)
Warp	–	0.20 (0.008)
Compression pressure	1000-1500 kPa (145-218 psi)	800 kPa (116 psi)
Maximum difference between cylinders		200 kPa (29 psi)
Piston		
Outside diameter*	62.555-62.570 (2.4628-2.4634)	62.480 (2.4598)
Piston-to-cylinder clearance	0.040-0.050 (0.0016-0.0020)	0.120 (0.0047)
Piston oversizes	0.5 mm and 1.0 mm	–
Piston pin bore inside diameter	18.002-18.008 (0.7087-0.7090)	18.030 (0.7098)
Piston pin outside diameter	17.996-18.000 (0.7085-0.7086)	17.980 (0.7079)
Piston rings		
Ring-to-groove clearance		
Top	–	0.180 (0.007)
Second	–	0.150 (0.006)
Ring thickness		
1995-1999 models		
Top	0.77-0.79 (0.030-0.031)	–
Second	0.97-0.99 (0.038-0.039)	–

(continued)

Table 2 TOP END SPECIFICATIONS (continued)

Item	Standard mm (in.)	Wear limit mm (in.)
Ring thickness (continued)		
2000 models		
Top	0.97-0.99 (0.038-0.039)	–
Second	0.77-0.79 (0.030-0.031)	–
Piston ring groove width		
1995-1999 models		
Top	0.81-0.83 (0.032-0.033)	–
Second	1.01-1.03 (0.039-0.040)	–
Oil ring	2.01-2.03 (0.0791-0.0799)	–
2000 models		
Top	1.02-1.04 (0.040-0.041)	–
Second	0.81-0.83 (0.032-0.033)	–
Oil ring	1.51-1.53 (0.059-0.060)	–
Ring end gap (installed)		
1995-1999		
Top	0.1-0.3 (0.004-0.012)	0.7 (0.03)
Second	0.3-0.5 (0.012-0.020)	0.7 (0.03)
2000		
Top	0.1-0.3 (0.004-0.012)	0.5 (0.02)
Second	0.3-0.5 (0.012-0.020)	0.7 (0.03)
Ring free gap		
1995-1999 models		
First	Approx. 8.6 (0.34)	6.9 (0.27)
Second	Approx. 6.7 (0.26)	5.4 (0.21)
2000 models		
First	Approx. 6.7 (0.26)	5.4 (0.21)
Second	Approx. 7.0 (0.28)	5.6 (0.22)

*Measured 15 mm (0.590 in.) from skirt bottom

Table 3 TOP END TORQUE SPECIFICATIONS

Item	N•m	in.-lb.	ft.-lb.
Cam chain guide mounting bolt	10	88	–
Cam chain tensioner mounting bolt	7	62	–
Cam chain tensioner spring holder bolt	35	–	26
Camshaft bearing cap bolt	10	88	–
Camshaft sprocket bolt	25	–	19
Cylinder base nut	9	80	–
Cylinder head banjo bolt	16	–	11.5
Cylinder head bolt, 6 mm	10	88	–
Cylinder head cover banjo bolt	16	–	11.5
Cylinder head cover bolt	14	–	10
Cylinder head cover oil fitting bolt	10	88	–
Cylinder head cover plug	15	–	11
Cylinder head nut, 10 mm	38	–	28
Cylinder head plug	28	–	20.5
Cylinder stud bolt	15	–	11
Exhaust pipe bolt	23	–	17
(continued)			

ENGINE TOP END

Table 3 TOP END TORQUE SPECIFICATIONS (continued)

Item	N•m	in.-lb.	ft.-lb.
Front lower mounting bolts			
55 mm (2.2 in.) long	55	–	41
Front upper mounting bolts			
55 mm (2.2 in.) long	55	–	41
Removable frame			
downtube mounting bolt	32	–	23
Muffler mounting bolt			
1995-1999 models	23	–	17
2000 models	29	–	21
Oil hose mounting bolt	10	88	–
Rocker arm shaft bolt	9	80	–
Rocker arm shaft set bolt	9	80	–
Spark plug (2000 models)	11	97	–
Valve adjuster locknut	10	88	–

CHAPTER FIVE

ENGINE LOWER END

This chapter describes service procedures for the following lower end components:
1. Crankcase assembly.
2. Crankshaft.
3. Connecting rods.
4. Starter clutch and gears
5. Oil cooler, oil pump and lubrication system.
6. Transmission shaft assemblies (removal and installation only).

Tables 1-7 appear at the end of the chapter.

SERVICING THE ENGINE IN FRAME

Refer to *Engine Service Notes* in Chapter Four.
Many components, including the following, can be serviced with the engine mounted in the frame. The motorcycle frame is an excellent holding fixture, especially for breaking loose stubborn bolts and nuts.
1. External gearshift mechanism.
2. Clutch.
3. Carburetor.
4. Alternator.
5. Starter motor and gears.
6. Exhaust system.
7. Signal generator.

ENGINE

Removal/Installation

1. Remove the fairing (Chapter Fourteen) on models so equipped.
2. Remove the seat and frame cover as described in Chapter Fourteen.

ENGINE LOWER END

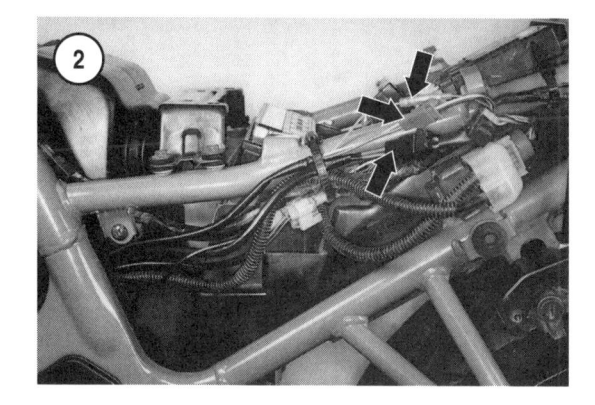

3. Remove the fuel tank as described in Chapter Eight.
4. Remove the battery as described in Chapter Three.
5. Remove the exhaust system as described in Chapter Eight.
6. Disconnect the crankcase breather hose (A, **Figure 1**) from the breather cover.
7. Remove the breather cover (B, **Figure 1**) and gasket from the top of the cylinder head cover.
8. Remove the carburetor assembly as described in Chapter Eight.
9. Drain the engine oil and remove the oil filter as described in Chapter Three.
10. Disconnect the spark plug leads and tie them up out of the way.
11. On models equipped with a PAIR system, disconnect the PAIR hoses.
12. Remove the engine drive sprocket as described in Chapter Ten.
13. Disconnect the following electrical connectors located on the left side of the rear frame. See **Figure 2**.
    a. Signal generator (2-pin connector, refer to wiring diagram for wire colors).
    b. Oil pressure switch (bullet connector, green/yellow wire).
    c. Sidestand switch (2-pin connector, green and black/white wires).
14A. On 1995-1999 models, disconnect the following connectors located on the left side of the rear frame.
    a. Neutral switch (1-pin connector, blue wire)
    b. Alternator (2-pin connector, red and orange wires).
14B. On 2000 models, disconnect the following connectors located on the left side of the rear frame.
    a. Neutral switch (4-pin connector; blue, red/black, green/blue and black/white wires).
    b. Speed sensor (3-pin connector; black/red, black and black/white wires).
    c. Disconnect the connector and the wire from the alternator.
15. Disconnect the starter motor lead from the starter motor.
16. Remove the oil cooler as described in this chapter.
17. If the engine is going to be disassembled, remove the following parts while the engine is still in the frame:
    a. Cylinder head (Chapter Four).
    b. Cylinder block (Chapter Four).
    c. Pistons (Chapter Four).
    d. Alternator and starter (Chapter Nine).
    e. Starter clutch and gears.
    f. Signal generator (Chapter Nine).
    g. Clutch assembly (Chapter Six).
    h. External shift mechanism (Chapter Seven).
18. Take a final look over the engine to make sure everything has been disconnected.
19. Place a suitable size jack, with a piece of wood to protect the crankcase, under the engine. Raise the jack and apply a small amount of jack pressure on the engine.

CAUTION
Continually adjust jack pressure during engine removal and installation to prevent damage to the mounting bolt threads and hardware.

20. Remove the nuts and the front pair of mounting bolts (A, **Figure 3**) from the removable frame downtube.

21. Remove the nuts and the upper pair of mounting bolts (B, **Figure 3**) from the removable frame downtube.

22. Remove the nuts and the lower pair of mounting bolts (C, **Figure 3**) from the removable frame downtube.

23. Remove the nuts and the rear pair of mounting bolts (**Figure 4**) from the removable frame downtube.

24. Remove the right, front lower mounting bolt (A, **Figure 5**) and remove the special nut (B, **Figure 5**) from behind the mounting boss; see **Figure 6**.

CAUTION
*Self-locking nuts are used on the upper rear through bolt (A, **Figure 7**), lower rear through bolt (D, **Figure 7**) and on the upper front engine mounting bolts (B, **Figure 7**). Discard these nuts during removal. They must be replaced.*

25. Disassemble the right, front upper mount. Remove the nut from the mounting bolt, and remove the front upper mounting bolt (D, **Figure 3**). Discard the nut. It cannot be reused.

26. Remove the removable frame downtube from the frame.

27. Disassemble the left, front upper mount. Remove the nut from the mounting bolt, and remove the front upper mounting bolt. Discard the nut. It cannot be reused.

28. Remove the nut (A, **Figure 8**) from the upper rear through bolt. Discard the nut. It cannot be reused.

29. Remove the nut (**Figure 9**) from the lower rear through bolt. Discard the nut. It cannot be reused.

30. Remove the left, front lower mounting bolt (A, **Figure 10**), and remove the special nut from behind the mounting boss. See **Figure 6**.

31. From the left side, remove the lower rear through bolt (B, **Figure 10**) and then remove the upper rear through bolt (C, **Figure 10**). Do not lose the spacer (B, **Figure 8**) that sits on the right end of the upper rear through bolt.

WARNING
Due to the weight of the engine, two people are required to safely remove the engine assembly from the frame.

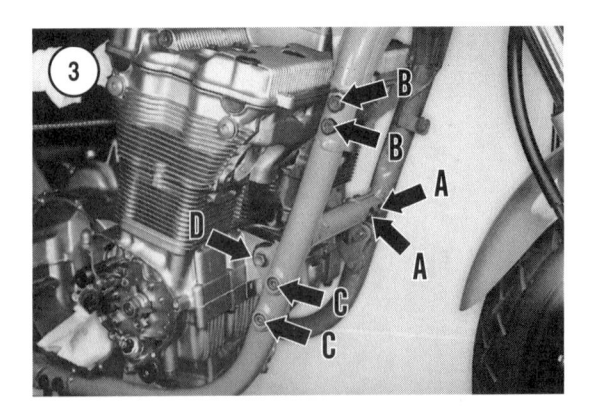

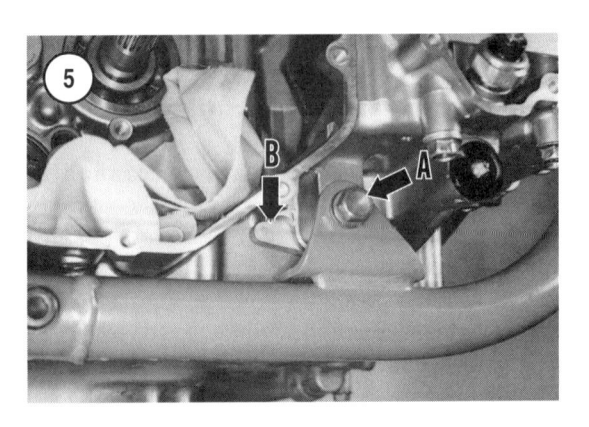

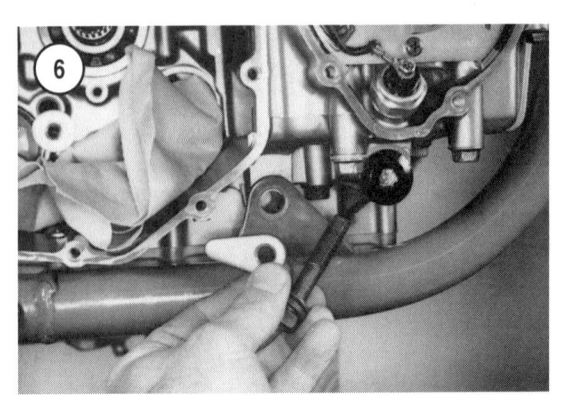

ENGINE LOWER END

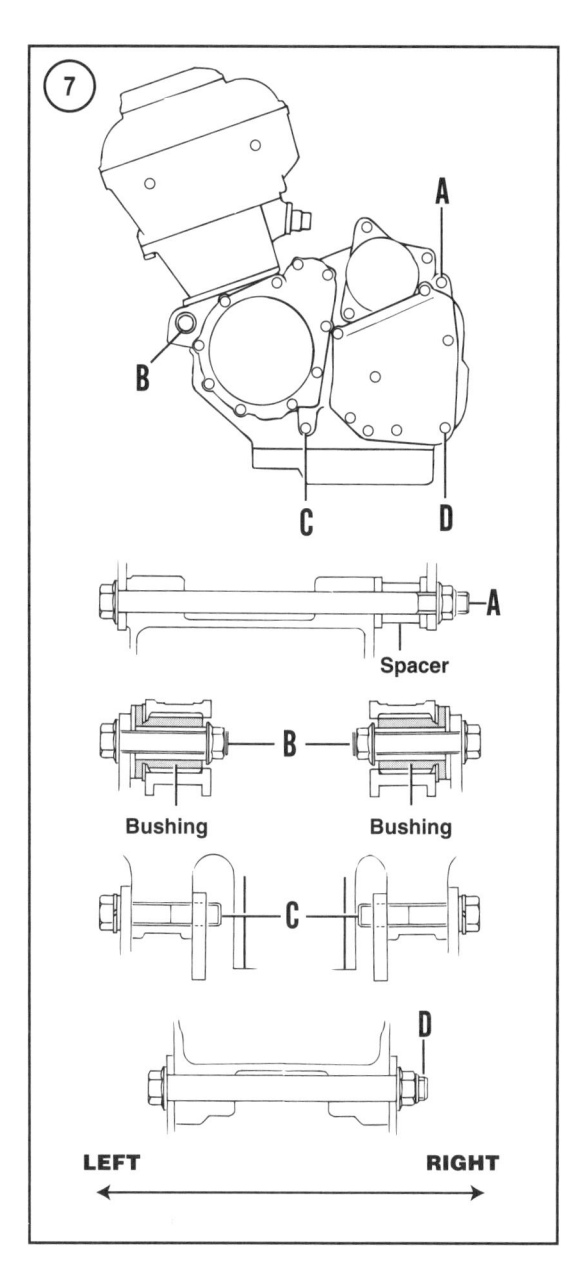

32. Gradually lower the engine and remove it from the right side of the frame.

33. Install the engine by reversing these removal steps. Note the following:

> *CAUTION*
> *Be sure to install **new** self-locking nuts on all of the engine mounting bolts. Never reuse a self-locking nut. These fasteners lose their locking abilities once they are removed. Do **not** try to use a locking agent and then reuse an old self-locking nut. This will not be sufficient to keep the nut in place.*

a. Make sure the air filter housing is in place on the engine before starting engine installation.
b. Tighten the mounting bolts to the torque specifications in **Table 2**.
c. Fill the engine with the recommended type and quantity of oil; refer to Chapter Three.
d. Adjust the clutch as described in Chapter Three.
e. Adjust the drive chain as described in Chapter Three.

150 CHAPTER FIVE

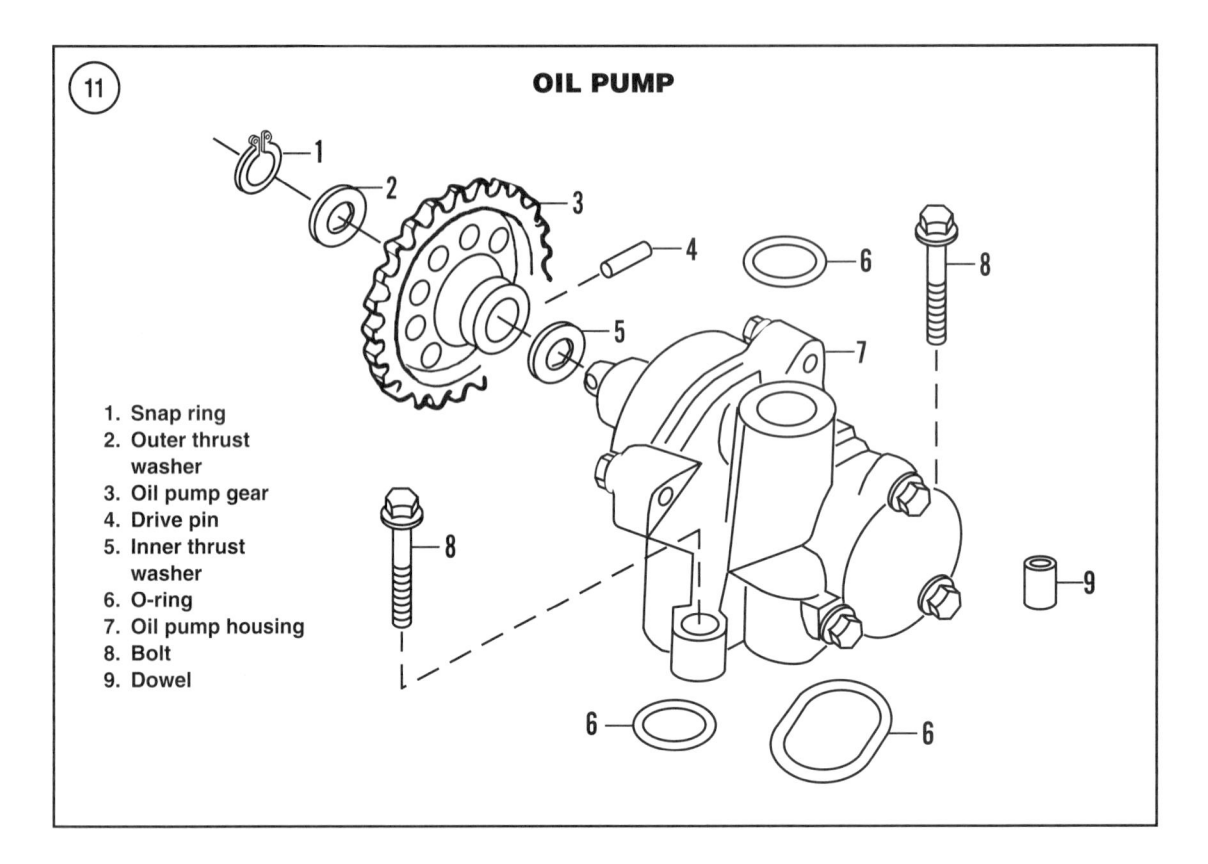

OIL PUMP ⑪

1. Snap ring
2. Outer thrust washer
3. Oil pump gear
4. Drive pin
5. Inner thrust washer
6. O-ring
7. Oil pump housing
8. Bolt
9. Dowel

f. Start the engine and check for leaks.

OIL PUMP

Removal/Installation

Refer to **Figure 11**.

1. Remove the engine and separate the crankcase as described in this chapter.

2. Remove the snap ring (**Figure 12**) and remove outer thrust washer from inside the oil pump gear.

3. Cover the crankcase opening so parts or debris will not fall into the crankcase.

NOTE
The drive pin is loosely installed in the oil pump shaft. Rotate the oil pump gear so the pin is horizontal before removing the gear. The pin could easily fall into the crankcase during oil pump gear removal.

4. Rotate the oil pump gear so the drive pin in the shaft is horizontal. Remove the oil pump gear (**Figure 13**) from the oil pump shaft.

ENGINE LOWER END

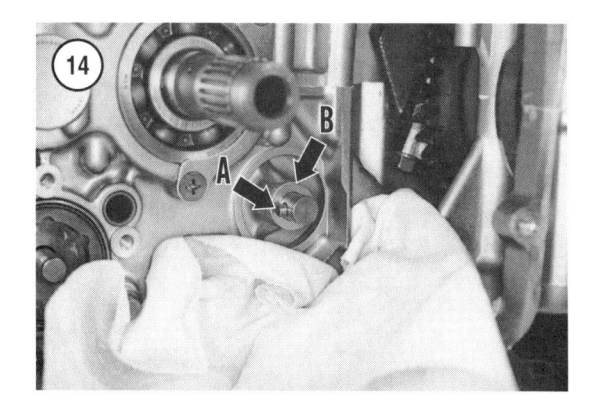

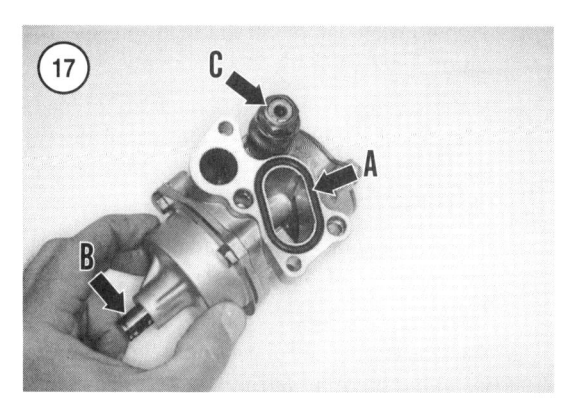

5. Remove the drive pin (A, **Figure 14**) and the inner thrust washer (B, **Figure 14**) from the pump shaft.
6. Remove the bolts (**Figure 15**) securing the oil pump to the crankcase and remove the oil pump assembly.
7. Remove the O-ring (A, **Figure 16**) and the locating dowels (B, **Figure 16**) from the crankcase.
8. Remove the O-ring (A, **Figure 17**) from the oil pump.
9. Inspect the oil pump as described in this chapter.

CAUTION
To prevent loss of oil pressure and to prevent an oil leak, always install new O-rings.

10. Install the locating dowels (B, **Figure 16**) and a *new* O-ring (A, **Figure 16**) in the crankcase.
11. Install a *new* O-ring (A, **Figure 17**) into the oil pump.
12. Set the oil pump into place in the crankcase.
13. Apply ThreeBond Threadlock No. 1342 to the threads of the oil pump mounting bolts, and torque the bolts to the specification in **Table 2**.
14. Install the inner thrust washer (B, **Figure 14**) onto the oil pump shaft, and then install the drive pin (A, **Figure 14**) through the shaft.
15. Align the notch in the oil pump gear with the drive pin, and install the oil pump gear (**Figure 13**) onto the pump shaft.
16. Install the outer thrust washer and the snap ring (**Figure 12**) into the recess in the oil pump gear. Be sure the snap ring is properly seated in the oil pump shaft.
17. Assemble the crankcase as described in this chapter.

Inspection

Replacement parts are not available for the oil pump. If the oil pump is not operating properly, replace the entire oil pump assembly.

CAUTION
Do not try to disassemble the oil pump. Replacement parts and lockwashers are not available.

1. Rotate the drive shaft (B, **Figure 17**). If there is any binding or signs of wear, replace the oil pump assembly.

2. Make sure the locking tabs on the lockwashers are in place and bent up against one side of the bolts securing the oil pump together. Refer to **Figure 18** and **Figure 19**.

3. Inspect the oil pump body for cracks or damage. Make sure all oil flow openings are clear.

4. Make sure the integral relief valve (C, **Figure 17**) is secured tightly to the oil pump body.

5. Inspect the teeth on the oil pump gear (A, **Figure 20**). Replace the gear if any teeth are damaged or missing.

6. Inspect the drive pin (B, **Figure 20**) for cracks, nicks or other signs of wear. If damage is found, replace the drive pin, and inspect the drive pin mating surfaces of the oil pump gear and the oil pump shaft.

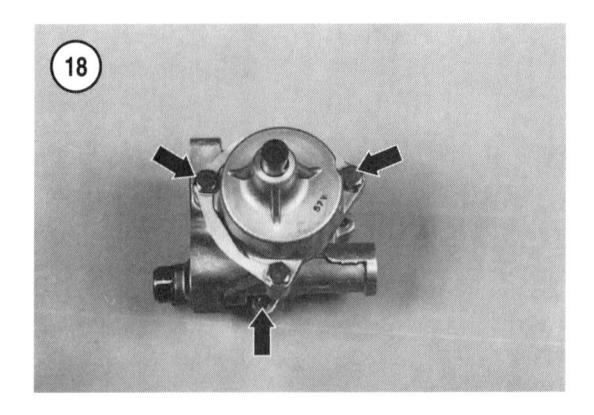

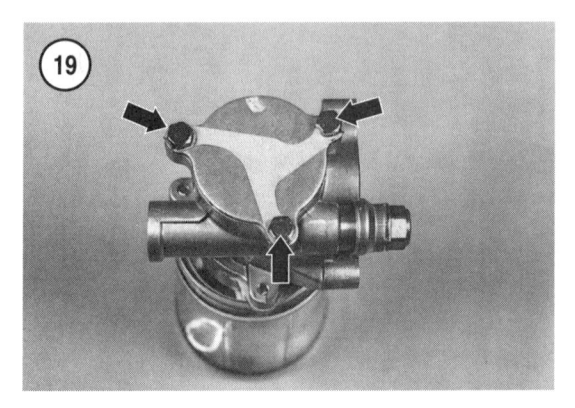

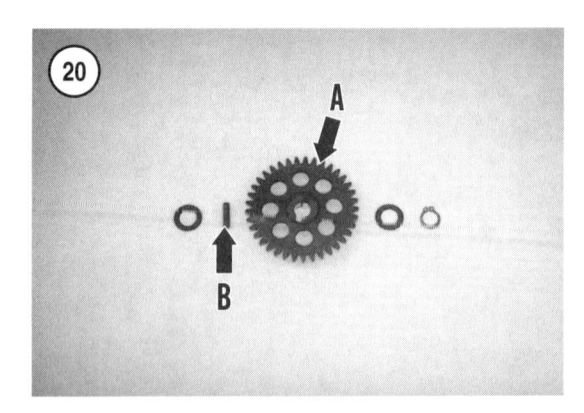

OIL COOLER

Removal/Installation

Refer to **Figure 21**.

1. Drain the engine oil as described in Chapter Three.

2. On models with fairings, remove the front fairing as described in Chapter Fourteen.

3. Place an oil pan beneath the lower fittings on the oil cooler hoses. The pan will catch oil that drains from the fittings as the hoses are removed.

4. Remove the union bolts and sealing washers (**Figure 22**) securing each oil line fitting to the front of the oil pan.

5. On models so equipped, remove the mounting bolt and remove the clamp (**Figure 23**) securing the right oil line to the frame.

6. Remove the bolts (**Figure 24**) securing the oil cooler mounts to the frame.

7. Pull the oil cooler up to release the lower locating tab from the damper in the frame receptacle, and remove the oil cooler from the frame. Do not lose the collar and damper inside each oil cooler mount.

8. Install by reversing these removal steps. Note the following:
   a. Clean all debris from the mating surfaces on the oil pan, the oil lines and oil cooler.
   b. Install *new* O-rings seals on the fittings on top of the oil lines. Tighten these bolts securely.
   c. Install a *new* sealing washer (**Figure 25**) on each side of the oil line fittings when installing each banjo bolt (**Figure 22**).
   d. Tighten each banjo bolt to the torque specification listed in **Table 2**.
   e. Make sure the collar and damper are in place in each oil cooler mount, and install the oil cooler mounting bolts (**Figure 24**). Torque the bolts to specification.
   f. Refill the engine with the recommended type and quantity of oil as described in Chapter Three.
   g. Start the engine and check for oil leaks before installing the front fairing.

ENGINE LOWER END

OIL COOLER

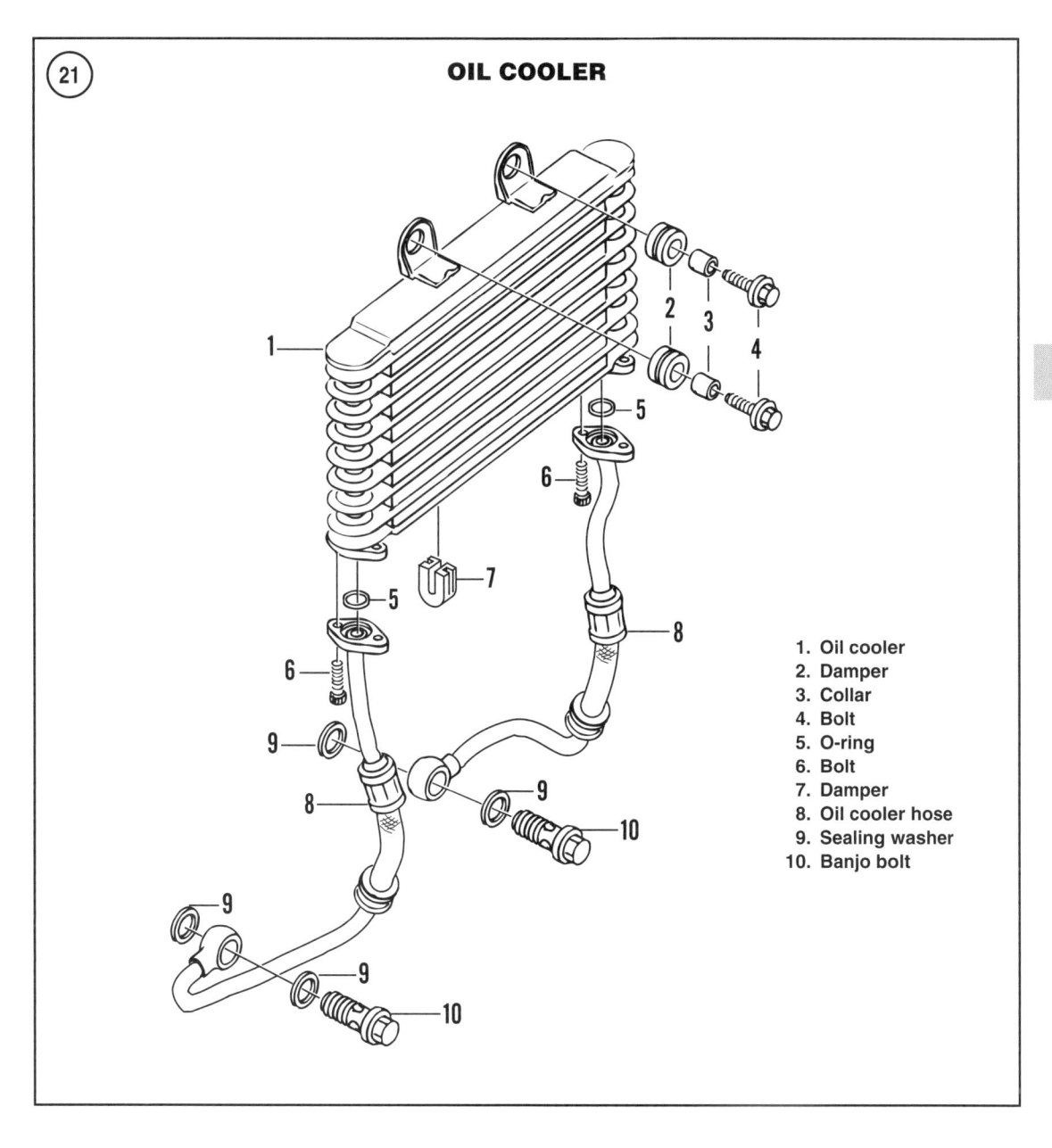

1. Oil cooler
2. Damper
3. Collar
4. Bolt
5. O-ring
6. Bolt
7. Damper
8. Oil cooler hose
9. Sealing washer
10. Banjo bolt

OIL PAN, OIL STRAINER AND OIL PRESSURE REGULATOR

Removal

NOTE
This procedure is shown with the engine removed from the frame for clarity. The oil pan can be removed with the engine installed in the frame.

1. If the engine is still installed in the frame, perform the following:
   a. Remove the exhaust system as described in Chapter Eight.
   b. Remove the banjo bolts (**Figure 22**) and sealing washers securing the oil cooler lines to the front of the oil pan.
2. Remove the oil pan bolts (**Figure 26**). Please note that a copper washer is installed under one bolt (A, **Figure 26**). A *new* copper washer must be installed under this bolt during installation.
3. Remove the oil pan and the gasket from the lower crankcase. Make sure a new one is installed during assembly.
4. Remove the oil strainer bolts (A, **Figure 27**). Remove the oil strainer (B, **Figure 27**) and its gasket from the crankcase.
5. Remove the shim (**Figure 28**) from the oil outlet, and then remove the outlet O-ring (**Figure 29**).
6. Inspect the oil pan, oil strainer, and oil pressure regulator as described below.

Installation

1. Apply a coat of Suzuki Super Grease A to a *new* O-ring, and install the O-ring (**Figure 29**) into the oil outlet in the crankcase.
2. Apply a coat of Suzuki Super Grease A to the shim, and install it on top of the oil outlet (**Figure 28**).
3. Install a *new* oil strainer gasket (**Figure 30**).
4. Set the oil strainer in place in the crankcase so the arrow stamped on the strainer cover points toward the front of the engine.
5. Install the oil strainer bolts (A, **Figure 27**) and tighten them securely.
6. Install a *new* oil pan gasket.
7. Install the oil pan and bolts. Install a *new* copper washer under the bolt shown in A, **Figure 26**.

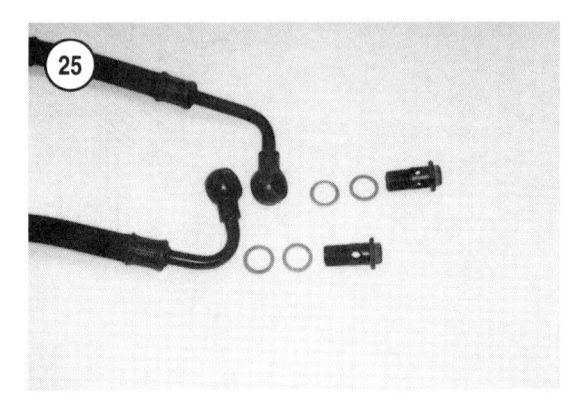

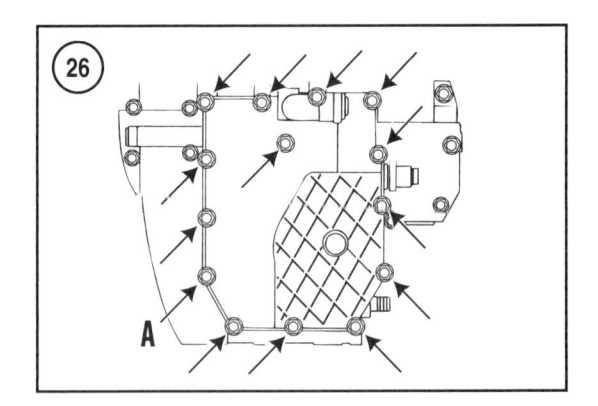

ENGINE LOWER END

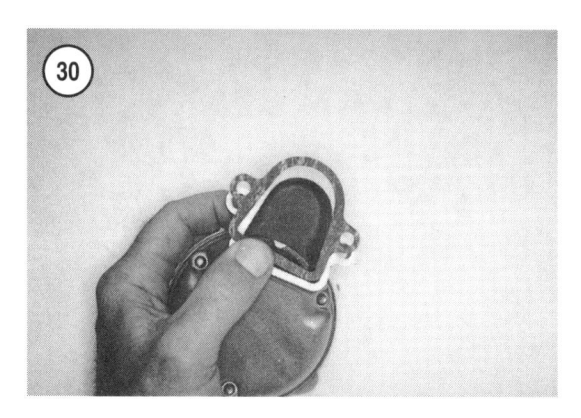

Tighten the oil pan bolts to the torque specification listed in **Table 2**.

8. Secure the oil cooler lines to the front of the oil pan. Use a *new* sealing washer on both sides of each oil fitting, and torque each banjo bolt (**Figure 22**) to specification.

Inspection and Cleaning

1. Remove all traces of gasket material from the gasket sealing surfaces of the oil pan and the crankcase. This will provide a good, leak-free surface for the oil pan gasket.
2. Remove the oil gallery plugs (A, **Figure 31**) and their gaskets from the oil pan.
3. Remove the oil pressure regulator (**Figure 32**) and washer from the oil pan.
4. Clean all debris from the oil-fitting mating surfaces on the oil pan.
5. Wash the oil pan in solvent. Clean out the oil galleries located behind the plug.
6. Thoroughly dry the pan with compressed air. Be sure to remove all solvent residue and any oil sludge loosened by the solvent. Any pieces of sludge left in any oil gallery may clog the gallery or oil control orifices in the lubrication system.
7. Make sure all oil control openings in the oil pan are clear.
8. Inspect the oil drain bolt threads in the oil pan (B, **Figure 31**). Clean the threads with the proper size metric thread tap if necessary.
9. Install the oil gallery plugs and gaskets into the oil pan. Tighten the plugs securely.
10. Inspect the oil pressure regulator by performing the following:
    a. Inserting a wooden dowel into the end of the oil pressure regulator (**Figure 33**).

b. Use the dowel to push and release the piston, and note the piston's movement.

c. Replace the oil pressure regulator if the piston does not move smoothly within the regulator.

11. Install the oil pressure regulator and washer into the oil pan. Tighten the regulator to the torque specification listed in **Table 2**.

12. Clean the oil strainer with solvent, and check the inlet screen (A, **Figure 34**) for broken areas or damage. If necessary, remove the mounting bolts (B, **Figure 34**), and install a new oil strainer onto the housing.

STARTER CLUTCH AND GEARS

Removal

The starter gears can be removed with the engine in the frame. This procedure is shown with the engine removed for clarity.

1. Drain the engine oil as described in Chapter Three.
2. Place an oil drain pan under the starter clutch cover.
3. Remove the bolts securing the starter clutch cover (A, **Figure 35**) to the crankcase, and remove the cover and gasket. Note the location of the bolt (B, **Figure 35**) with a copper washer under it. Install a *new* copper washer at this location during assembly.
4. Remove the locating dowel (A, **Figure 36**).
5. Remove the shaft (A, **Figure 37**) and the starter idler gear (B, **Figure 37**) from the crankcase.

6A. If the engine is installed in the frame, shift the transmission into gear. This prevents the gear from rotating while loosening the mounting bolt.

6B. If the engine is removed, hold the starter clutch with a Grabbit or a universal holding tool (**Figure 38**). Do not overtighten the tool as it may damage the gear.

7. Loosen, but do not remove, the starter clutch mounting bolt. The bolt must be left in place for use with the special tool in the next step.
8. Install the Suzuki rotor remover (part No. 09930-33720) onto the starter clutch (**Figure 39**), and loosen the starter clutch from the taper on the end of the crankshaft.
9. Remove the rotor remover, unscrew the starter clutch mounting bolt (A, **Figure 40**) and remove the starter clutch (B, **Figure 40**) from the crankshaft.

Installation

1. Clean the tapered end of the crankshaft and the mating surface of the starter clutch with an aerosol

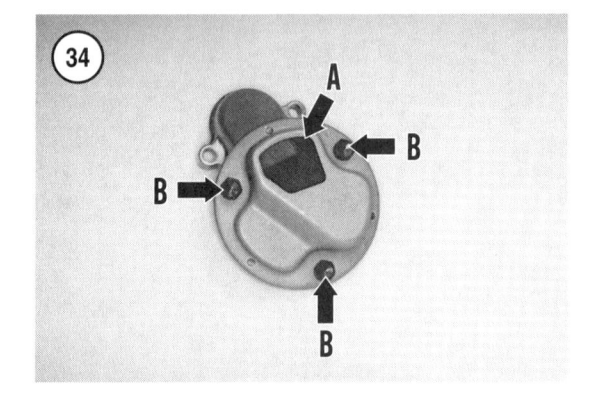

ENGINE LOWER END

parts cleaner to remove all traces of oil. Both surfaces must be dry and free of any residue.

2. Install the starter clutch (B, **Figure 40**) onto the crankshaft.

3. Apply ThreeBond Threadlock 1303 to the threads of the starter clutch mounting bolt, and install the bolt (A, **Figure 40**).

4. Hold the starter clutch with the same tool used during removal, and tighten the starter clutch mounting bolt to the torque specification in **Table 2**.

5. Install the starter idler gear (B, **Figure 37**) and shaft (A, **Figure 37**).

6. Apply a light coat of ThreeBond Liquid Gasket 1104, or equivalent, to the crankcase surfaces at the point where the upper and lower crankcase halves meet (B, **Figure 36**). This helps prevent an oil leak.

7. Install the locating dowel (A, **Figure 36**) into the crankcase.

8. Install a *new* gasket and the starter clutch cover (A, **Figure 35**) and evenly tighten the mounting bolts in a crisscross pattern. Install a *new* copper washer under the bolt shown in B, **Figure 35**. Tighten the bolts securely in a crisscross pattern.

9. Refill the engine with the recommended type and quantity of engine oil as described in Chapter Three.

Disassembly/Inspection/Assembly

1. Check the operation of the starter clutch by performing the following:
   a. Set the starter clutch down on the bench with the sprague clutch facing up.
   b. Rotate the sprague clutch (A, **Figure 41**) counterclockwise around the starter driven gear (B, **Figure 41**). The sprague clutch

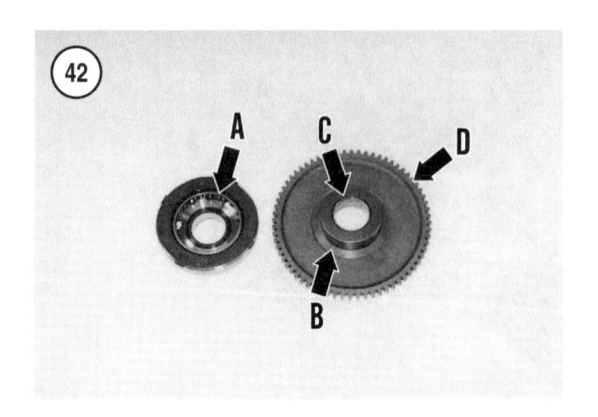

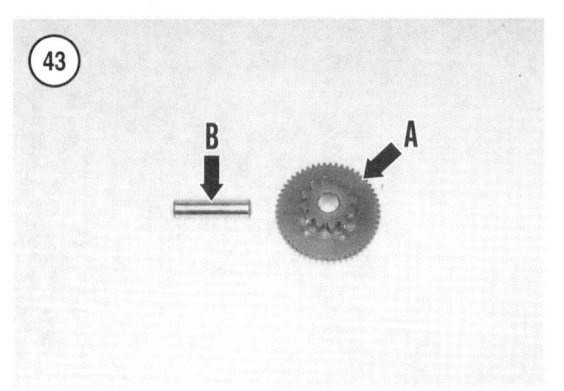

should rotate freely when turned counterclockwise.

   c. Rotate the sprague clutch (A, **Figure 41**) clockwise around the starter driven gear (B, **Figure 41**). The sprague clutch should engage the starter driven gear when turned in this direction.

   d. The starter clutch is faulty if it fails either test. Replace both the starter driven gear and sprague clutch as a set.

2. Lift the sprague clutch from the starter driven gear.

3. Check the rollers (A, **Figure 42**) in the sprague clutch for uneven or excessive wear.

4. Inspect the outer bearing surface (B, **Figure 42**) of the starter driven gear for wear or abrasion.

5. Inspect the inner bearing surface (C, **Figure 42**) of the starter driven gear for wear or abrasion.

6. Inspect the starter driven gear for chipped or missing teeth (D, **Figure 42**).

7. If either the sprague clutch or the starter driven gear is worn or damaged, replace both the starter driven gear and sprague clutch as a set.

8. Inspect the starter idler gear (A, **Figure 43**) for chipped for missing teeth. Look for uneven or excessive wear on the gear faces.

9. Inspect the starter idler gear shaft (B, **Figure 43**) for nicks, scratches, or signs of uneven wear.

10. Rotate the sprague clutch (A, **Figure 41**) counterclockwise, and install it onto the starter driven gear (B, **Figure 41**).

CRANKCASE

The engine must be removed from the frame in order to service the lower end.

ENGINE LOWER END

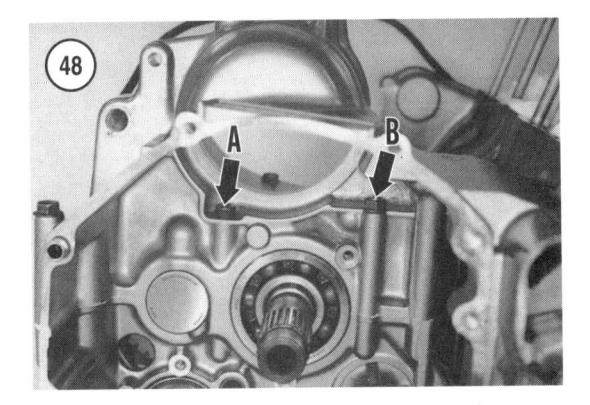

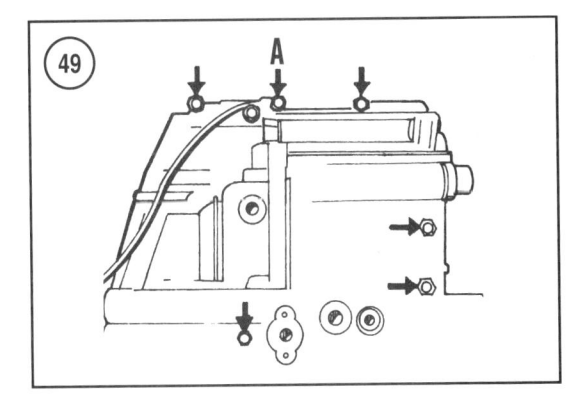

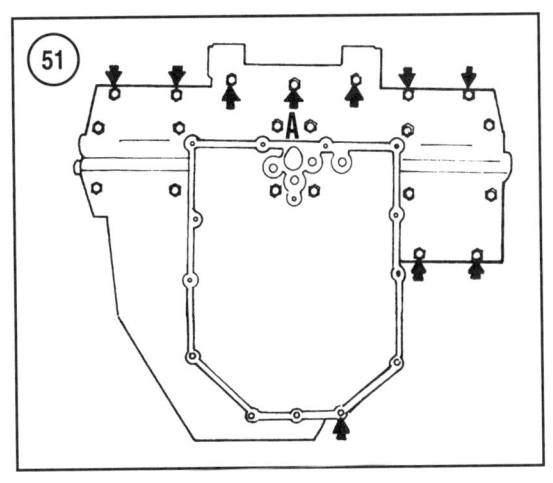

Disassembly

1. Remove the engine as described in this chapter.
2. Remove the engine sprocket as described in Chapter Seven.
3. Straighten the locking tabs, and remove the bolts securing the oil seal retainer (A, **Figure 44**). Remove the retainer.
4. Remove the mounting screws, and remove the neutral switch (B, **Figure 44**) along with its O-ring.
5. Remove the neutral switch contact (**Figure 45**) and its spring from the shift drum.
6. Remove the screws securing the mainshaft bearing retainer (**Figure 46**), and remove the bearing retainer.
7. Remove the upper crankcase plug bolt and washer (**Figure 47**). Removing this plug provides access to the upper crankcase bolt (A, **Figure 48**) located below it.
8. Remove the upper crankcase bolt (A, **Figure 48**) and upper crankcase nut (B, **Figure 48**).
9. Remove the upper crankcase bolts shown in **Figure 49**.
10. Place the engine upside down on wooden blocks. This protects the connecting rods and the crankcase studs.
11. Remove the oil pan and oil strainer as described in this chapter. Do not lose the copper washer under the pan bolt (A, **Figure 26**).
12. Remove the oil pan and gasket.
13. Remove lower crankcase nut (**Figure 50**) located beneath the mainshaft.

NOTE
*On 2000 models, note the sealing washer installed beneath one bolt (A, **Figure 51**). Install a new sealing*

washer at this location during assembly.

14. Remove the lower crankcase bolts shown in **Figure 51**. Do not forget the single bolt (**Figure 52**) at the rear corner.
15. Remove the bolt (A, **Figure 53**) securing the oil return pipe (B, **Figure 53**) to the crankcase and remove the pipe.
16. Remove the main oil gallery plug (**Figure 54**) and its O-ring.

NOTE
*A tightening sequence number is cast into the lower crankcase next to each main bearing bolt (**Figure 55**).*

17. Evenly loosen the main bearing bolts in descending order of the tightening sequence cast into the lower crankcase (**Figure 55**). Remove the bolts. Note the sealing washer installed under bolts 9 and 11. Install *new* washers with these bolts during assembly.
18. Remove the oil return pipe (C, **Figure 53**) that was held in place by main bearing bolt No. 1.
19. Double check that all of the upper and lower crankcase bolts have been removed.
20. Tap the lower crankcase with a plastic mallet and separate the two halves.

CAUTION
If it is necessary to pry the halves apart, do it very carefully. Do not damage the gasket surfaces. If any gasket surface is scratched or otherwise damaged, the cases will leak oil and have to be replaced.

21. Lift the lower crankcase off of the upper crankcase, and immediately turn the lower crankcase

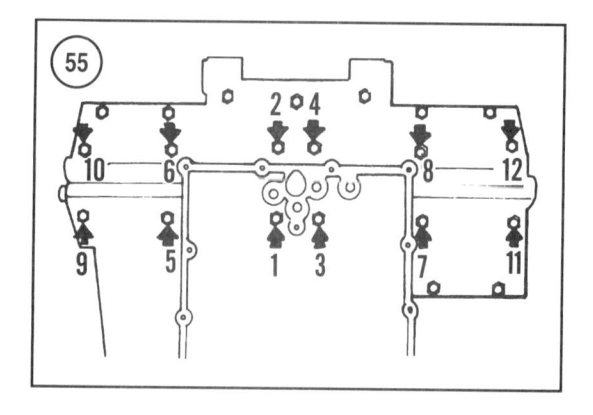

ENGINE LOWER END

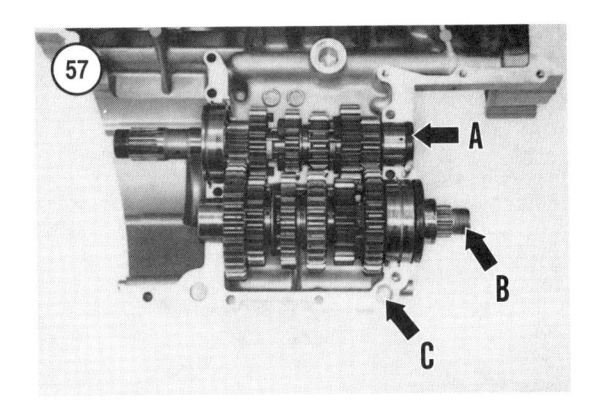

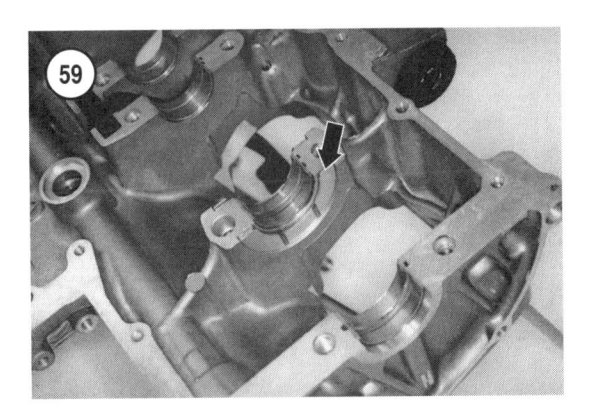

over. Be careful that the crankshaft main bearing inserts do not fall out of the lower case half. If any do, reinstall them immediately into their original locations if possible.

22. Remove the O-rings (A, **Figure 56**) from the oil galleries.

23. Remove the mainshaft assembly (A, **Figure 57**) and the countershaft assembly (B, **Figure 57**) from the upper crankcase half.

24. Remove the C-rings (A, **Figure 58**) and the transmission bearing locating dowels (B, **Figure 58**).

25. Lift the crankshaft/connecting rod assembly (B, **Figure 56**) out of the crankcase.

26. Remove the crankshaft side thrust bearings (**Figure 59**) from the upper crankcase half.

27. Remove the chain guide dampers (**Figure 60**), and then remove the rear cam chain guide (**Figure 61**).

28. Remove the oil pump as described in this chapter.

29. Remove the internal shift mechanism as described in Chapter Six.

30. Remove the crankshaft main bearing inserts as described in this chapter.

31. Inspect the crankcase as described in this chapter.

Assembly

NOTE
If reusing the old bearing inserts, make sure they are installed in the same locations noted during removal.

1. Install the crankshaft main bearing inserts into the crankcase halves as described in this chapter.

2. Install the internal shift mechanism as described in Chapter Six.

3. Install the oil pump as described in this chapter.

4. Install the rear cam chain guide (**Figure 61**) into the upper crankcase half.

5. Install the chain guide dampers (**Figure 60**) so the arrows point toward the front and rear of the engine.

6. Install *new* O-rings (A, **Figure 56**) into the oil galleries.

7. Install the crankshaft side thrust bearings (**Figure 62**) into the upper crankcase half with the grooved sides facing out (**Figure 59**).

8. If removed, install the cam chain onto the crankshaft timing gear.

9. Apply molybdenum disulfide oil to each crankshaft journal.

10. Install the crankshaft/connecting rod assembly (B, **Figure 56**) into the upper crankcase.

NOTE
Prior to installation, coat all bearing surfaces with assembly oil or fresh engine oil.

11. Install the C-rings (A, **Figure 58**) and the transmission bearing locating dowels (B, **Figure 58**).

12. Install the mainshaft assembly (A, **Figure 57**) by performing the following:
   a. Set the mainshaft assembly into the upper crankcase half so the large bearing properly engages the C-ring (A, **Figure 63**) and the small bearing engages the locating dowel.
   b. Rotate the large bearing so the locating pin (B, **Figure 63**) correctly engages the crankcase.
   c. If not yet installed, fit the end cap (**Figure 64**) into place on the end of the mainshaft.

13. Install the countershaft assembly (B, **Figure 57**) by performing the following:
   a. Set the countershaft assembly into the upper crankcase half so the large bearing properly engages the C-ring (A, **Figure 65**) and the small bearing engages the locating dowel.
   b. Rotate the large bearing so the locating pin (B, **Figure 65**) correctly engages the crankcase.

14. If removed, install the locating dowels into the upper crankcase half. Refer to C, **Figure 56** and C, **Figure 57**.

15. Make sure the crankshaft main bearing inserts are securely in place in the lower crankcase half.

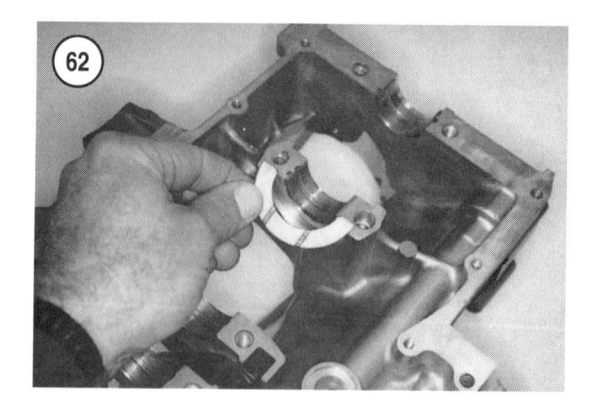

ENGINE LOWER END

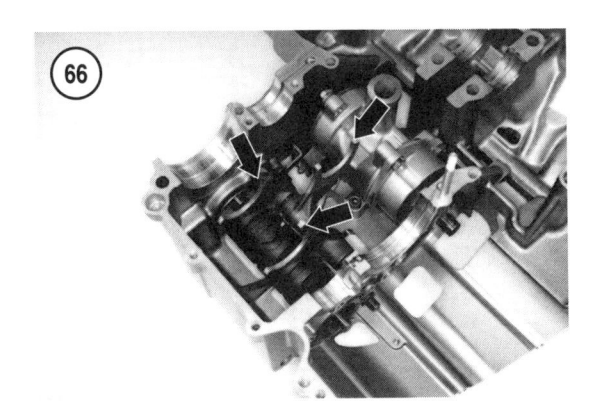

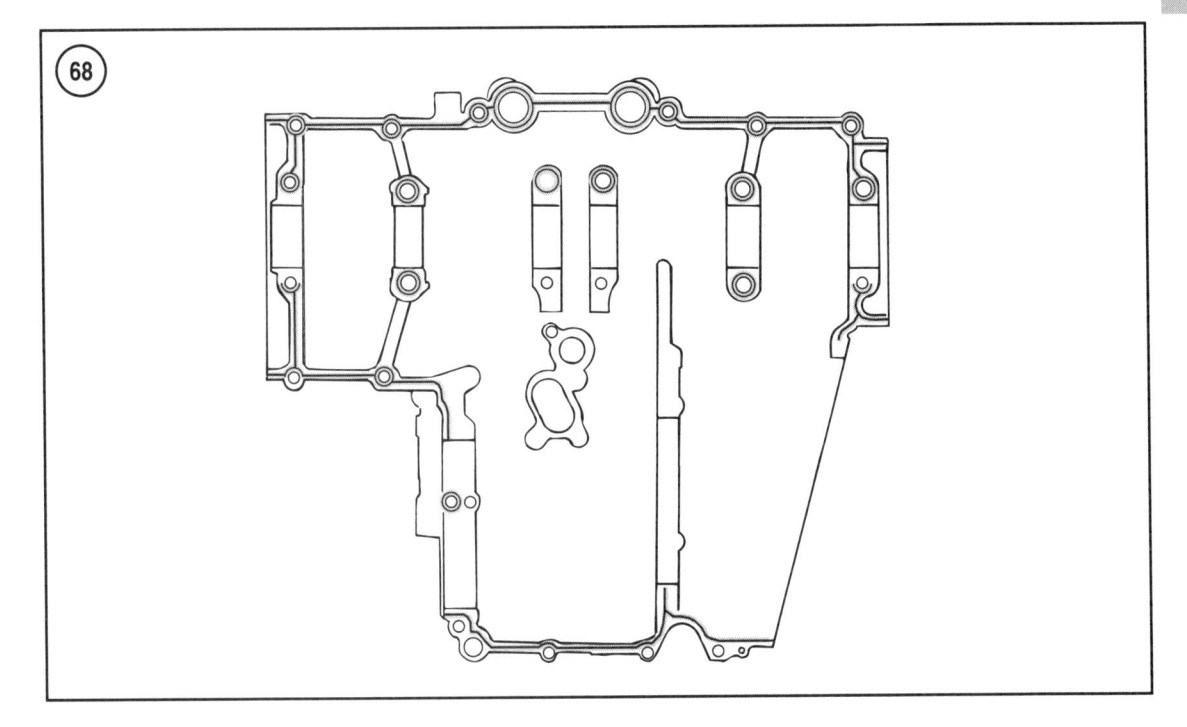

16. Shift the shift drum into NEUTRAL. The shift forks should be positioned as shown in **Figure 66**.

17. Level the upper case half so the transmission shafts parallel the workbench. This keeps the gears from sliding during lower case half installation.

18. Temporarily install a 6 mm bolt and washer (**Figure 67**) to keep the shift fork shaft in place. This step is not necessary if the external shift mechanism has been installed.

19. Check the shift fork and sliding gear alignment by partially lowering the lower crankcase half onto the upper half. Make sure that the sliding gears on the transmission shafts align with shift forks. Reposition the gears as necessary, and then remove the lower case half.

20. Make sure the case half mating surfaces are perfectly clean and dry. Clean them with electrical contact cleaner, and wipe them with a lint-free cloth.

NOTE
Use ThreeBond Liquid Gasket 1104, Gasgacinch Gasket Sealer, or an equivalent gasket sealer. When selecting a sealer, avoid thick and hard-setting materials.

21. Apply a light coat of gasket sealer to the mating surfaces of the lower crankcase half (**Figure 68**). Cover only flat surfaces. Do not apply gasket sealer to any curved bearing surfaces. Make the coating as

thin as possible, but make sure the gasket sealer completely covers the mating surfaces.

CAUTION
Crankcase halves should fit together without force. If the crankcase halves do not completely mate with one another, do not attempt to pull them together with the crankcase bolts. Separate the crankcase halves and investigate the cause of the interference. If the transmission shafts were disassembled, recheck to make sure that a gear is not installed backwards. Do not risk damage by trying to force the cases together.

22. Position the lower crankcase onto the upper crankcase. Set the front portion down first and lower the rear area into place. Make sure the shift forks properly engage their respective transmission gears and that the shift fork guide pins still engage in the shift drum grooves. Join both halves and tap them together lightly with a plastic mallet. Do **not** use a metal hammer. It will damage the case half.

23. If installed, remove the temporary 6 mm bolt and washer (**Figure 67**). Slowly spin the transmission shafts and shift the transmission with the shift drum (**Figure 69**). Make sure the shift forks are operating properly and that it is possible to shift through all gears. This is the time to find that something may be installed incorrectly—not after the crankcase is completely assembled.

24. Install the right oil return pipe (**Figure 70**) into the lower crankcase half. Make sure its mounting hole aligns with the crankcase hole for main bearing bolt No. 1.

NOTE
Prior to tightening the bolts, install all bolts and check that the bolt heads are all the same distance up from the bolt boss on the crankcase. If any bolts are higher or lower that the others, switch the bolts around until all are of the same height.

25. Apply a light coat of oil to the main bearing bolts and install the bolts. Place a *new* copper washer under bolts No. 9 and No. 11 (**Figure 71**).

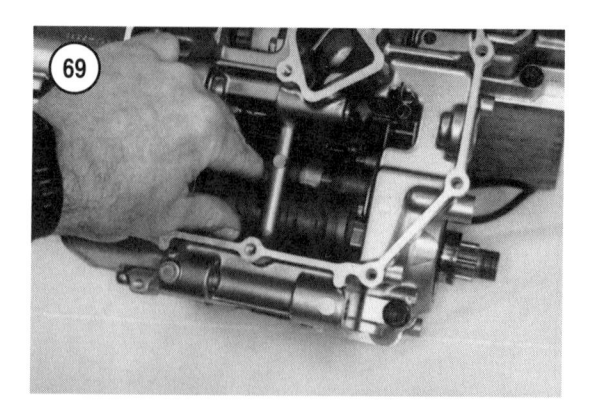

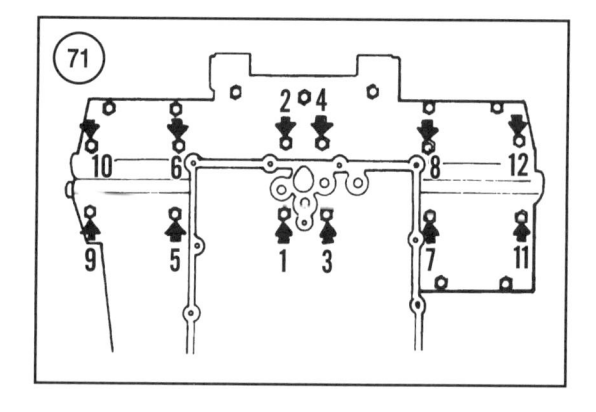

ENGINE LOWER END

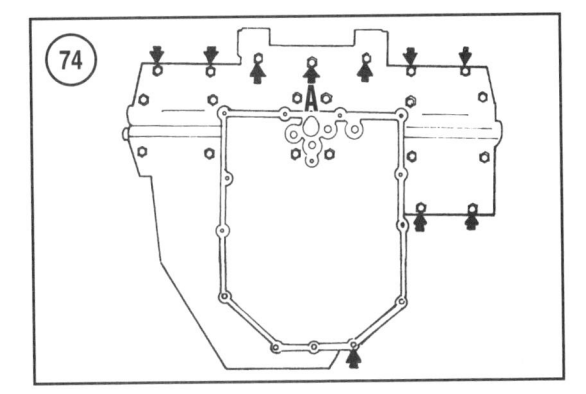

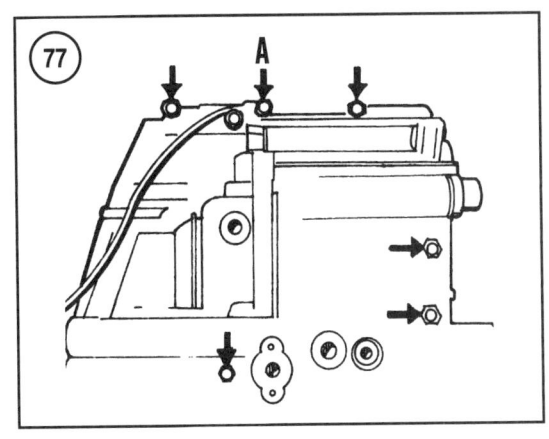

NOTE
A torque sequence number is cast into the lower crankcase next to each main bearing bolt (Figure 71).

26. Following the tightening sequence cast into the lower crankcase, evenly tighten the main bearing bolts. Tighten all bolts to the initial torque specification listed in **Table 2**, and then tighten all the bolts to the final torque specification.

27. Install the main oil gallery plug (**Figure 72**) and a *new* O-ring. Torque the plug to specification.

28. Set the oil return pipe (B, **Figure 73**) into the crankcase, and secure it with the bolt (A, **Figure 73**).

29. Check that the two oil seals are correctly seated against both case halves.

NOTE
On 2000 models, install a new sealing washer beneath the bolt shown in A, Figure 74.

30. Apply a light coat of oil to the crankcase bolts, and install the bolts into the lower crankcase (**Figure 74**). Do not forget the single bolt (**Figure 75**) at the rear corner. Tighten all the crankcase bolts to the initial torque specification and then to the final torque specification.

31. Install lower crankcase nut (**Figure 76**) located beneath the mainshaft.

32. Install the oil strainer and oil pan as described in this chapter.

33. Place the engine right side up on the workbench.

34. Install the upper crankcase bolts shown in **Figure 77**. Install the engine ground wire beneath bolt

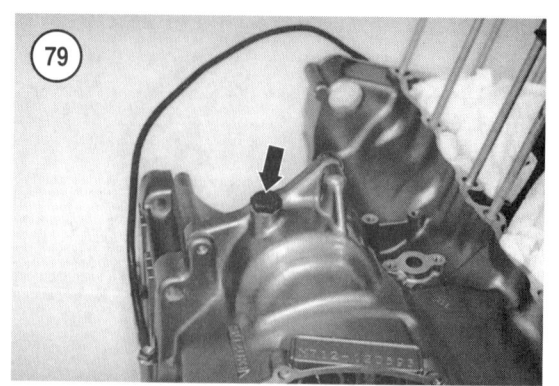

A, **Figure 77**. Also install the upper crankcase bolt (A, **Figure 78**) and upper crankcase nut (B, **Figure 78**). Apply a light coat of oil to the threads prior to installation, and torque the fasteners to the specification. First tighten the bolts and nut to their initial torque specifications and then to the final torque specification.

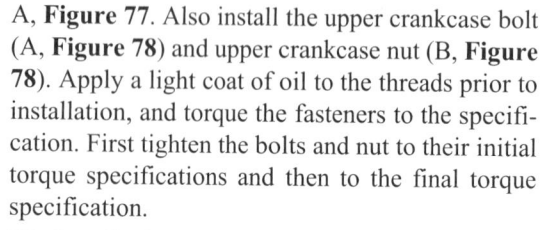

35. Install the upper crankcase plug bolt and washer (**Figure 79**). Tighten the plug securely.

36. Install the mainshaft bearing retainer (**Figure 80**). Apply a light coat of ThreeBond Threadlock 1342 to the mounting screw threads, and tighten the screws securely.

37. Install the neutral switch contact (**Figure 81**) and spring into the shift drum.

38. Install the neutral switch (B, **Figure 82**) along with a *new* O-ring.

39. Install the oil seal retainer (A, **Figure 82**) and bolts. Tighten the bolts securely, and then bend the locking tabs against one of the bolt flats. Make sure the neutral switch wire sits beneath the finger (C, **Figure 82**) on the seal retainer.

40. If the engine drive sprocket is going to be installed at this time, install it as described in Chapter Seven.

41. Install the engine as described in this chapter.

42. Install all exterior components removed as described in this and other related chapters.

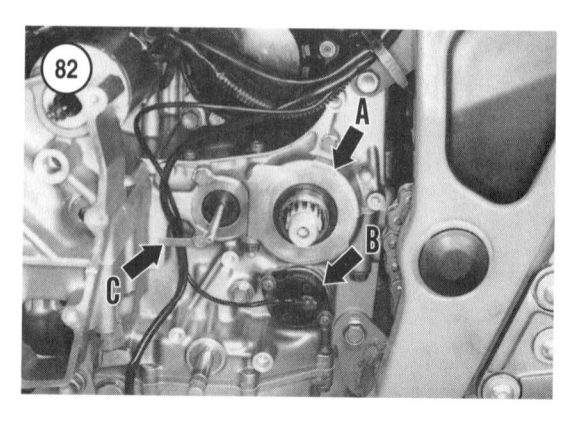

Inspection

1. Thoroughly clean the inside and outside of both crankcase halves with cleaning solvent. Dry them with compressed air. Make sure no solvent residue is left in the cases. It will contaminate the new engine oil.

ENGINE LOWER END

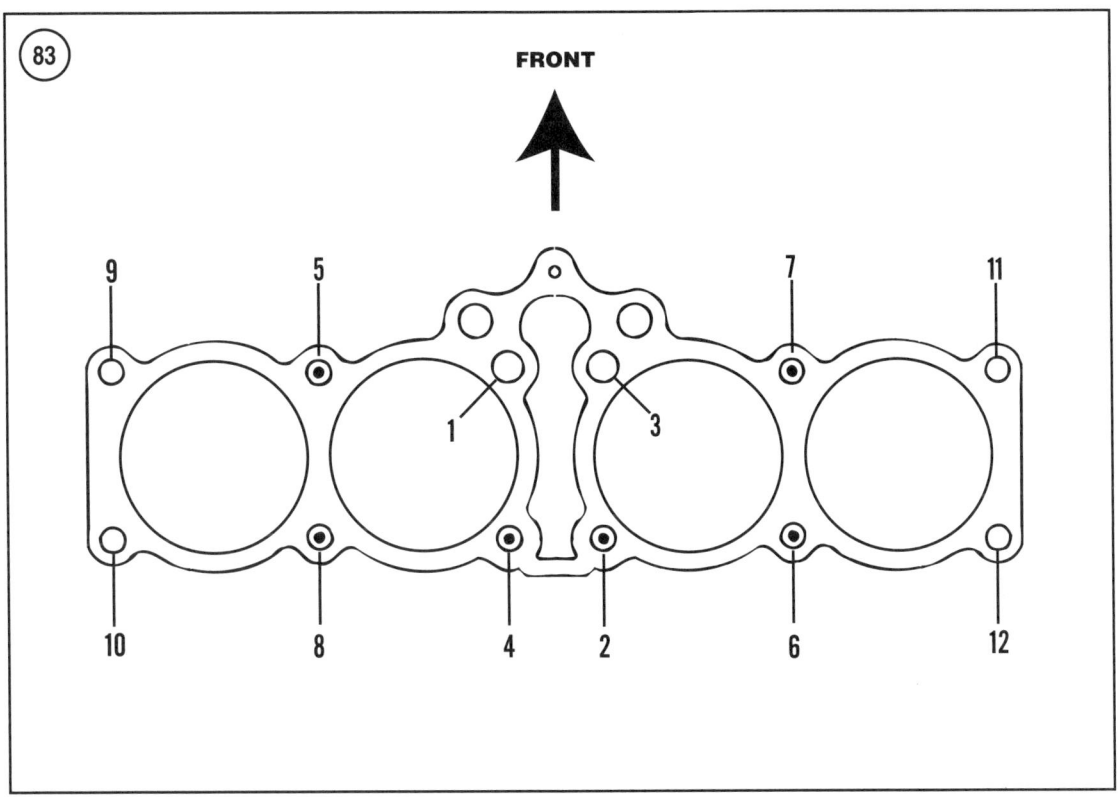

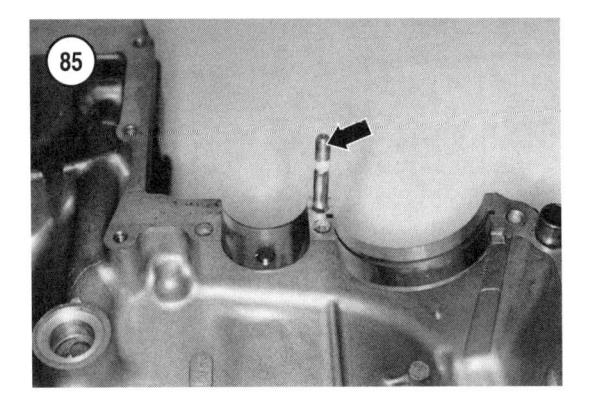

83

FRONT

2. Remove all old gasket sealing material from the mating surfaces on both case halves.

3. Carefully inspect the cases for cracks and fractures. Also check the areas around the stiffening ribs, around bearing bosses and threaded holes. If damage is found, have it repaired by a shop specializing in the repair of precision aluminum castings or replace the crankcase halves as a set.

NOTE
*There are two sizes of crankcase studs available. If a crankcase stud must be replaced, see a Suzuki dealership to get the proper size and color (silver or black) stud. If stud 7 shown in **Figure 83** must be replaced, apply Suzuki Bond 1207B to the threads, and torque the stud to specification.*

4. Make sure the crankcase studs are tight. If necessary, torque the studs to specification.

5. Inspect the threads of the crankcase-to-cylinder block threaded stud (**Figure 84**), as well as the studs in the upper crankcase (**Figure 85**) and in the lower crankcase (A, **Figure 86**). If necessary, clean the

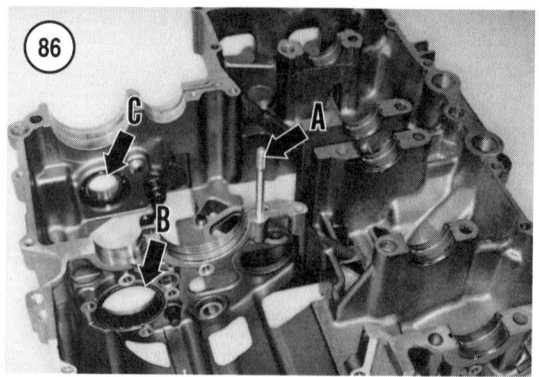

threads with the proper size metric die or replace the stud.

6. Make sure the transmission bearing locating pins (B, **Figure 87**) are in place and secure. Replace if necessary.

NOTE
*Three types of oil jets are used in the crankcase. See **Figure 88**.*

7. Use needlenose pliers to pull the two oil jets (A, **Figure 88**) from the cylinder mating surface on the upper crankcase (**Figure 89**).

8. Remove the four oil jets (B, **Figure 88**) from the bearing bosses in the upper crankcase (**Figure 90**) by performing the following:
   a. If still installed, remove the main bearing inserts as described in *Crankshaft*.
   b. Use a round punch to push the oil jets from the base side of the crankcase half (**Figure 91**), and remove the jets from inside the crankcase (**Figure 92**).

9. Unthread and remove the two threaded oil jets (C, **Figure 88**) from either side of the transmission compartment (**Figure 93**) in the lower crankcase.

10. Inspect the oil jets and O-rings (**Figure 94**). If any wear or damage is found, replace the jet. The O-rings cannot be replaced separately.

11. Make sure all oil control openings and galleries are clear.

12. Inspect the shift shaft oil seal (**Figure 95**). Replace it if necessary. Apply Suzuki Super Grease A to the lips of the new oil seal before installation.

Crankcase Bearings Removal/Installation

1. Turn the shift drum bearings by hand and check for damaged races, balls or needles. Refer to B and

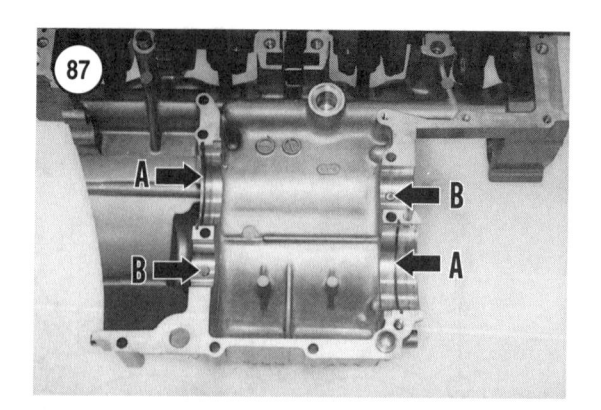

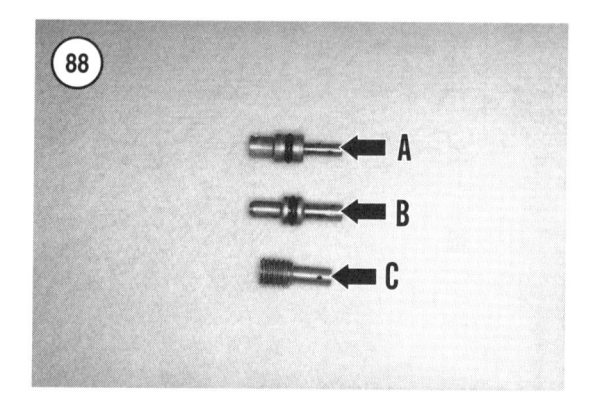

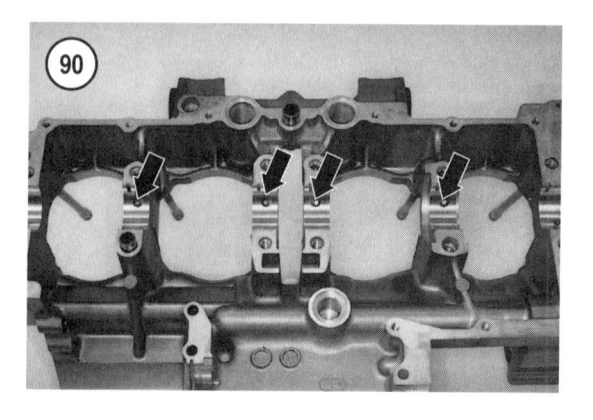

ENGINE LOWER END 169

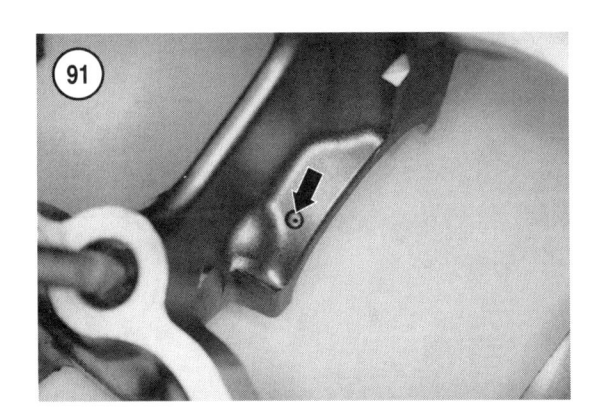

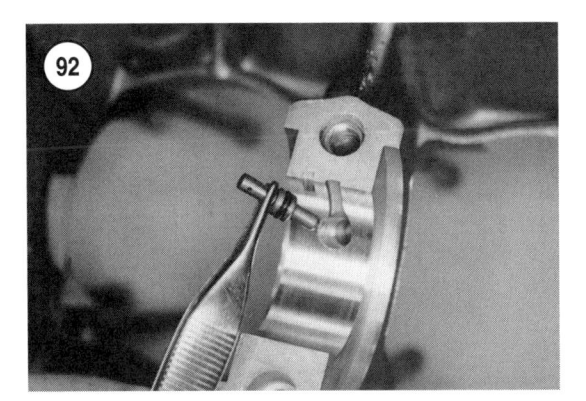

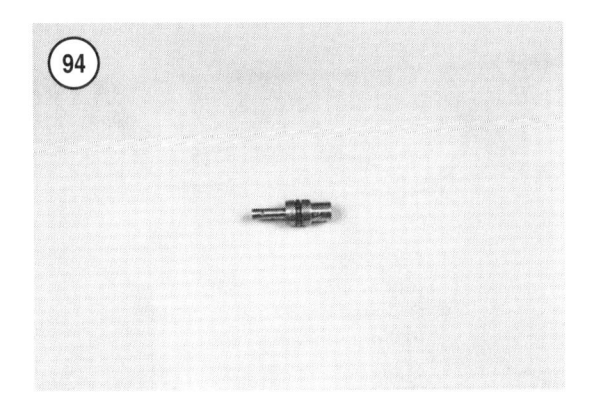

C, **Figure 86**. Replace a bearing if it has excessive side play. If the bearings are in good condition, oil the races or needles with fresh engine oil. If necessary, replace the bearings as follows.

NOTE
If bearing replacement is required, purchase the new bearing(s) and place them in a freezer for approximately two hours before installation. Chilling the bearings slightly reduces their overall diameter and heating the crankcase slightly increases the bearing boss's inside diameter. This makes bearing installation easier.

2. Remove the circlip securing the ball bearing into the inner surface of the crankcase.

WARNING
Before heating the crankcase half as described in Step 3, remove the shift shaft oil seal and thoroughly wash the crankcase in soap and water. Make sure no gasoline or solvent fumes are present.

3. The bearings are installed with a slight interference fit. The crankcase half must be heated in a shop oven to a temperature of about 100° C (212° F). To check the temperature of the case half, drop tiny drops of water on the case; if they sizzle and evaporate immediately, the temperature is correct.

WARNING
Wear insulated gloves (insulated kitchen mitts) when handling heated parts.

CAUTION
Do not heat the cases with a torch (propane or acetylene). Never bring a

flame into contact with the bearing or case. The direct heat will damage the case hardening of the bearing and may warp the case.

4. Remove the case from the oven, and place it on wood blocks. Hold onto the crankcase with kitchen mitts or heavy gloves—it is hot.

5. Carefully tap the bearing(s) out of the crankcase with a block of wood, socket or piece of pipe that matches the diameter of the bearing outer race.

NOTE
If a bearing is difficult to remove or install, do not take a chance on expensive crankcase damage. Have the work performed by a dealer or competent machine shop.

6. Reheat the crankcase half in the oven.

7. Remove the case from the oven and place on wood blocks. Hold onto the crankcase with kitchen mitts or heavy gloves—it is hot.

8. While the crankcase is still hot, press each new bearing into place in the crankcase by hand until it seats completely. Do not hammer it in. If the bearing will not seat, remove it and cool it again. Reheat the crankcase and install the bearing again.

9. Install the circlip retaining the ball bearing. Make sure the circlip is seated correctly in the groove.

CRANKSHAFT

Removal/Installation

1. Disassemble the crankcase as described in this chapter.

2. Remove the crankshaft/connecting rod assembly (**Figure 96**) and the cam chain from the upper crankcase half.

NOTE
In Step 3, No. 1 refers to the left-most bearing in a case half. This is the bearing that sits to the left (or outside) of the No. 1 cylinder. Number the bearings 1-6, counting from left to right across the engine. "Left" refers to the engine as it sits in the frame – not as it sits on the bench.

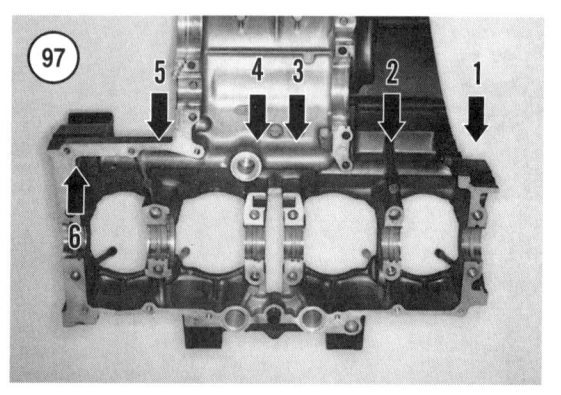

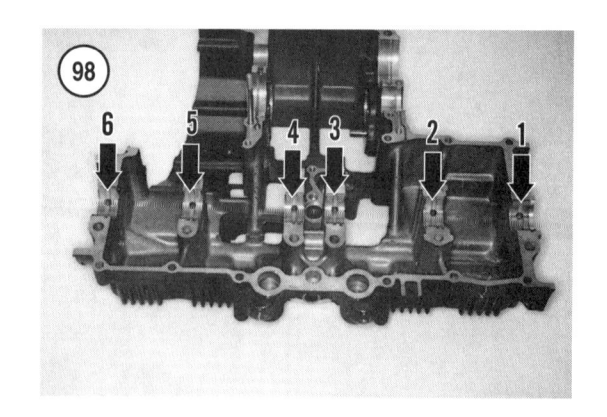

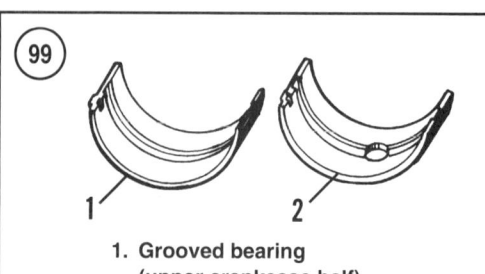

1. Grooved bearing (upper crankcase half)
2. Grooved bearing with oil hole (lower crankcase half)

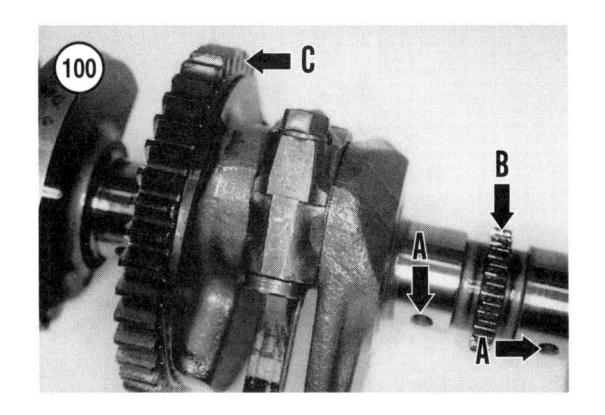

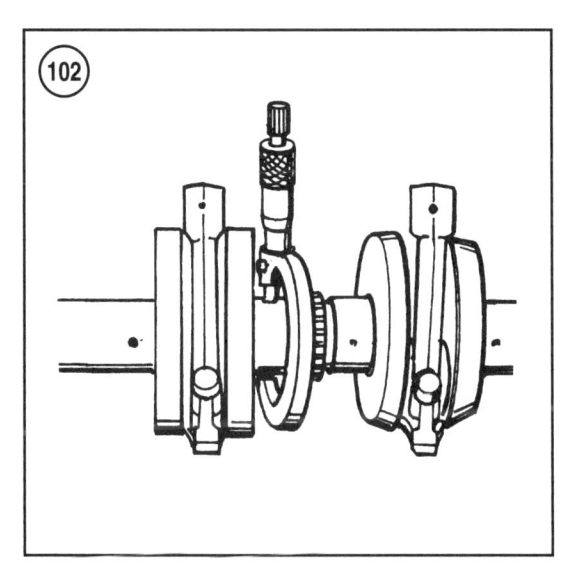

ENGINE LOWER END

can be reinstalled in their original locations. Remember that the inserts with an oil hole go into the lower crankcase (**Figure 99**).

CAUTION
If the old bearings are reused, they must be installed in their original locations.

4. Inspect the crankshaft and main bearings as described in this chapter.

5. Install the crankshaft/connecting rod assembly and camshaft chain (**Figure 96**) into the upper crankcase half.

6. Assemble the crankcase as described earlier in this chapter.

Inspection

Compare all measurements to the specifications in **Table 1**. Replace any component that is damaged or out of specification.

1. Clean the crankshaft thoroughly with solvent. Clean the oil holes (A, **Figure 100**) with rifle cleaning brushes. Flush thoroughly, and dry the crankshaft with compressed air. Lightly oil all bearing journal surfaces immediately to prevent rust.

2. Carefully inspect each main bearing journal (**Figure 101**) for scratches, ridges, scoring or nicks. Very small nicks and scratches may be removed with crocus cloth. More serious damage must be removed by grinding. Entrust this job to a machine shop.

3. Inspect the timing sprocket teeth (B, **Figure 100**). If damaged, replace the crankshaft.

4. Inspect the primary drive gear teeth (C, **Figure 100**). If damaged, replace the crankshaft.

5. If the surface finish on all main bearing journals is satisfactory, measure the journal outside diameter with a micrometer (**Figure 102**).

6. Set the crankshaft on V-blocks, and use a dial indicator to check crankshaft runout. See **Figure 103**.

7. Make sure the dowel pin (**Figure 104**) is secure in the end of the crankshaft.

8. Check the crankshaft main bearing clearance as described below.

3. If the main bearing inserts are going to be removed for cleaning, perform the following;
   a. Remove each main bearing insert from its bearing boss in the upper (**Figure 97**) and lower (**Figure 98**) crankcase halves.
   b. Mark the backside of the inserts with a 1, 2, 3, 4, 5 or 6 and U (upper) or L (lower) so they

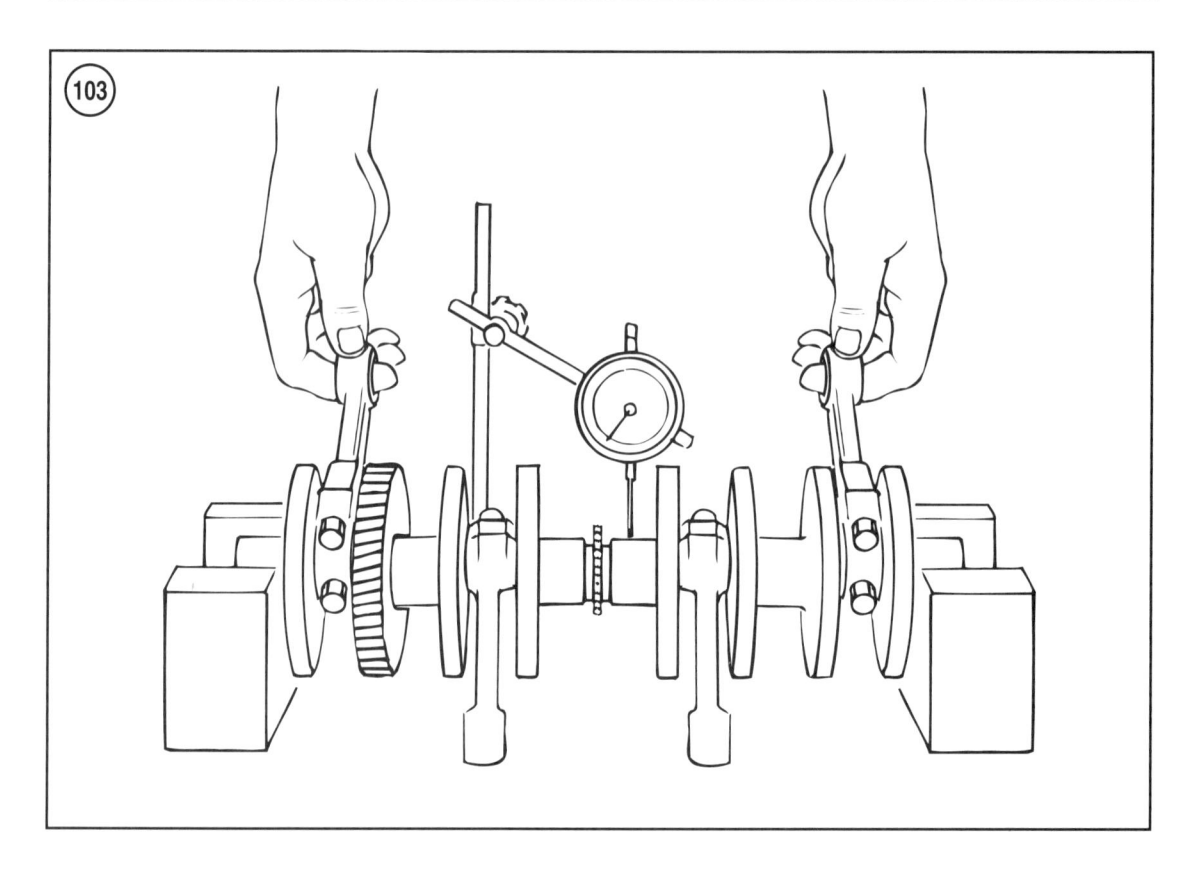

Crankshaft Main Bearing Clearance Measurement

1. Check each main bearing insert (A, **Figure 105**) for evidence of wear, abrasion, and scoring. If the bearings are good, they may be reused. If any insert is questionable, replace the entire set.
2. Clean the bearing surfaces of the main bearing inserts, and clean the crankshaft journals.
3. Place the upper crankcase on a workbench upside down on wooden blocks. This will protect the protruding connecting rod ends and the crankcase studs.
4. Install the existing main bearing inserts into their original positions in the upper (**Figure 97**) and lower (**Figure 98**) crankcase. Carefully press each insert into place by hand. Be sure the tab on the insert (B, **Figure 105**) locks into the cutout in the bearing boss. Remember that the inserts with a hole go into the lower crankcase.
5. Install the crankshaft into the upper crankcase (**Figure 96**).
6. Place a piece of Plastigage over each main bearing journal. Each piece of Plastigage must parallel the crankshaft (**Figure 106**). Do not place any Plastigage over an oil hole in the crankshaft.

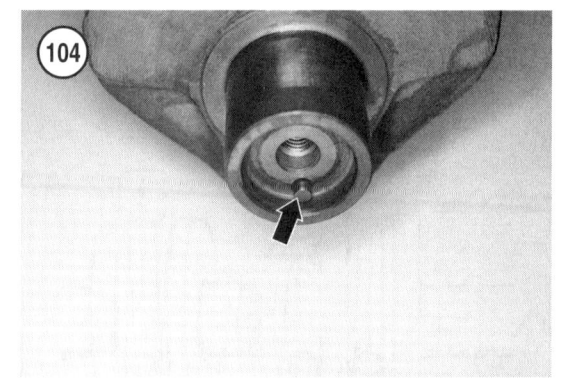

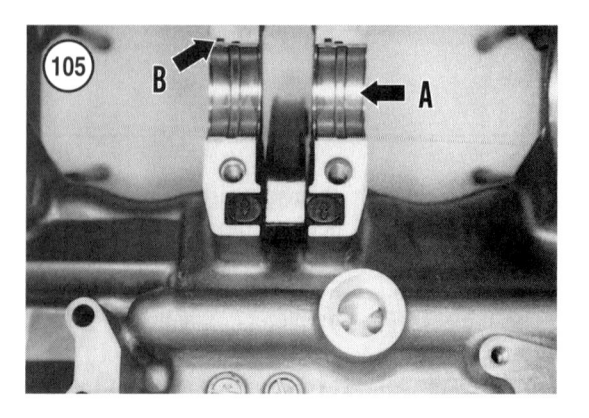

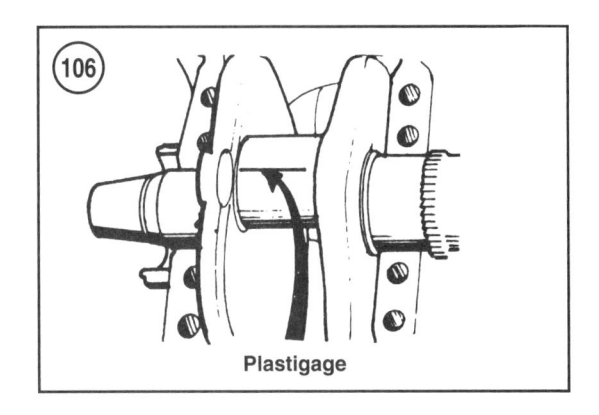

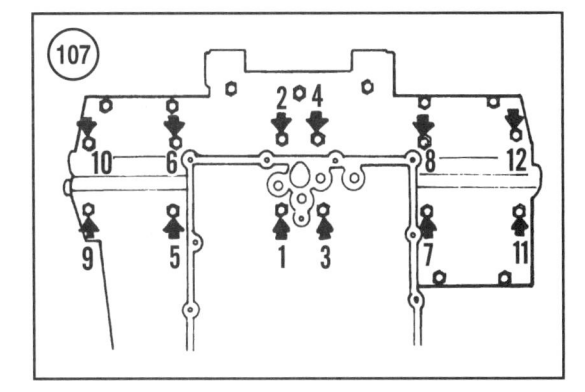

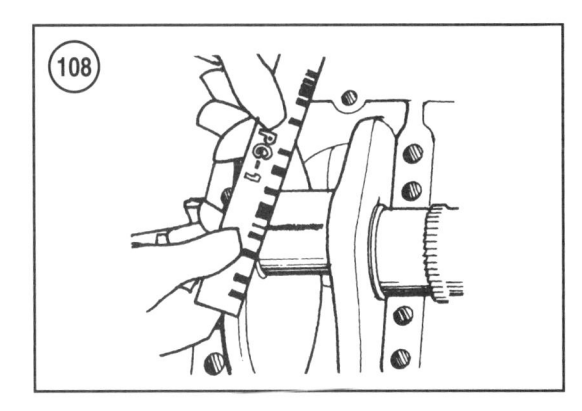

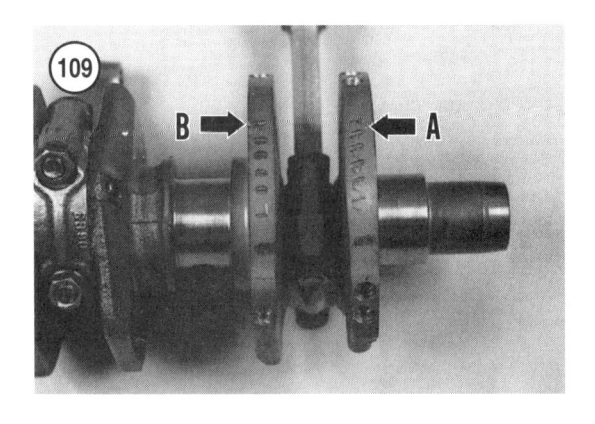

ENGINE LOWER END

CAUTION
Do not rotate the crankshaft while the Plastigage is in place.

7. Position the lower crankcase onto the upper crankcase. Set the front portion down first and lower the rear. If the transmission shafts are still installed, make sure the shift forks properly engage their respective transmission gears and that the guide pins still engage the shift drum grooves. Join both halves and lightly tap them together with a plastic mallet—do not use a metal hammer as it will damage the case.

CAUTION
Crankcase halves should fit together without force. If the crankcase halves do not fit together, do not attempt to pull them together with the crankcase bolts. Separate the crankcase halves and find the cause of the interference. If the transmission shafts were disassembled, check them to make sure that a gear is not installed backwards. Do not risk damage by forcing the cases together.

8. Apply a light coat of oil to the main bearing bolts, and install the bolts. Place a *new* copper washer under bolts No. 9 and No. 11 (**Figure 107**).
9. Following the tightening sequence cast into the lower crankcase (**Figure 107**), evenly tighten the main bearing bolts. First tighten all the bolts to the initial torque specification listed in **Table 2**, and then tighten them all to the final torque specification.
10. Loosen each main bearing bolt in the descending order of the numbers cast into the lower crankcase (**Figure 107**). Remove the bolts.
11. Carefully remove the lower crankcase half.
12. Measure the width of the flattened Plastigage according to manufacturer's instructions. Measure the Plastigage (**Figure 108**) at its widest point.
13. If any crankshaft main bearing clearance exceeds the wear limit specified in **Table 2**, replace the entire set of main bearings. Select the new main bearings as described below in this chapter.
14. Remove the Plastigage strips from the main bearing journals.

Main Bearing Selection

1. The crankshaft main bearing journals are identified by an A, B or C (A, **Figure 109**) stamped into

CRANKSHAFT MAIN BEARING JOURNAL IDENTIFICATION

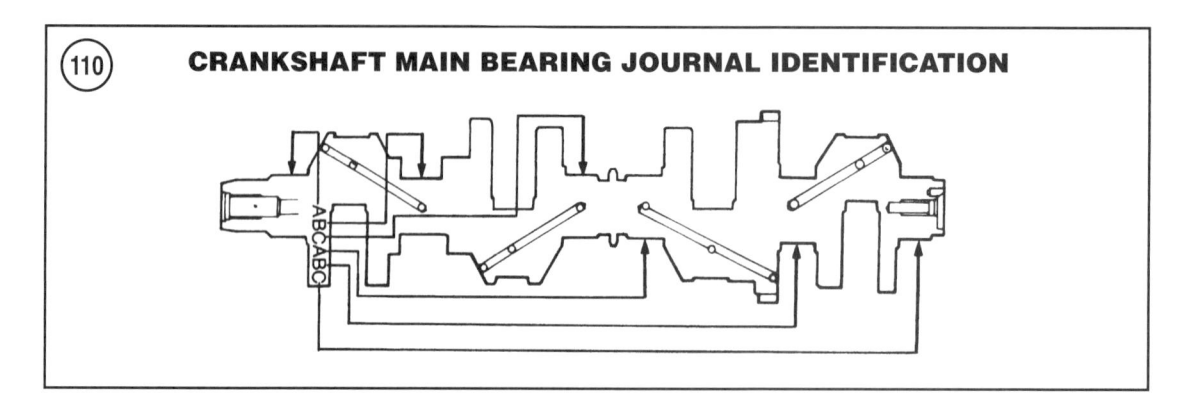

the crank web. The stamped letters relate to the journals as shown in **Figure 110**. The series of numbers (B, **Figure 109**) stamped into the crankweb refer to connecting rod bearing selection.

2. The crankcase main bearing codes (A or B) are stamped on the rear surface of the upper crankcase. Refer to **Figure 111**. The stamped letters are in the same order as the bearing boss locations in the crankcase.

3. Bearing inserts are identified by color codes (**Figure 112**). Refer to **Table 3**, and select new bearings by cross-referencing the crankshaft journal codes (A, **Figure 109**) with the crankcase bearing boss codes (**Figure 111**). **Table 3** gives the bearing color, part number and thickness. Always replace bearing inserts as a set.

4. After installing new bearing inserts, recheck the clearance by repeating the procedure described in this chapter. If the clearance is still out of specifications, either the crankcases or the crankshaft is worn beyond the service limit and requires replacement.

Crankshaft Side Thrust Clearance Inspection

1. Disassemble the crankcase as described in this chapter.

2. Leave the crankshaft and both right and left thrust bearings in place in the upper case half (**Figure 113**).

3. Push the crankshaft to the left until there is no clearance between the crankshaft and the right thrust bearing (**Figure 114**).

4. Install a flat feeler gauge between the left thrust bearing and the machined surface of the crankshaft. Refer to **Figure 115** and **Figure 116**. The measurement should equal the crankshaft thrust clearance specification in **Table 1**. If the crankshaft thrust clearance is greater than specified, perform the following:

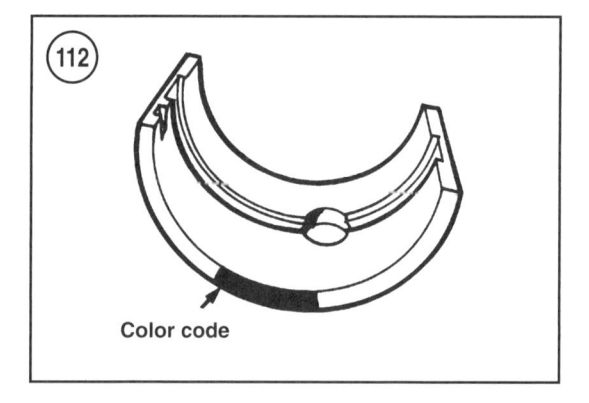

ENGINE LOWER END

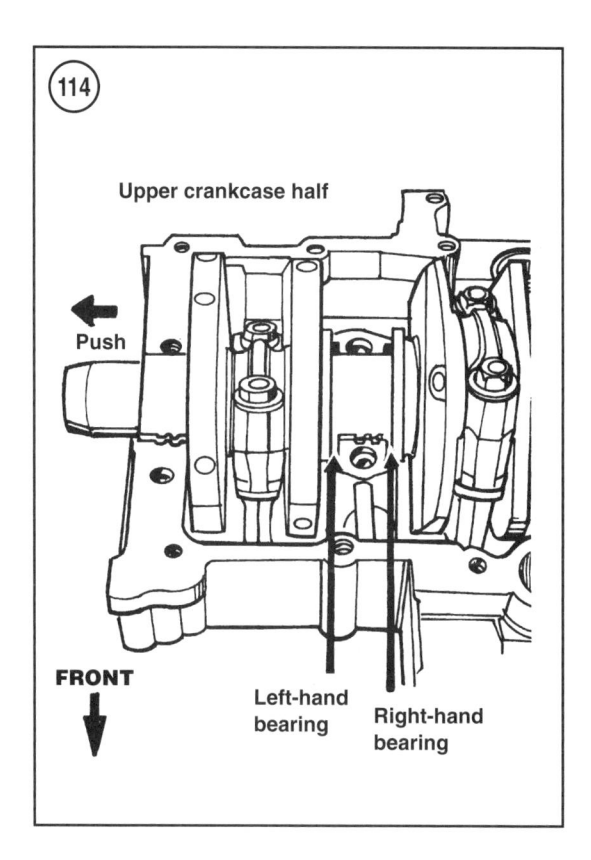

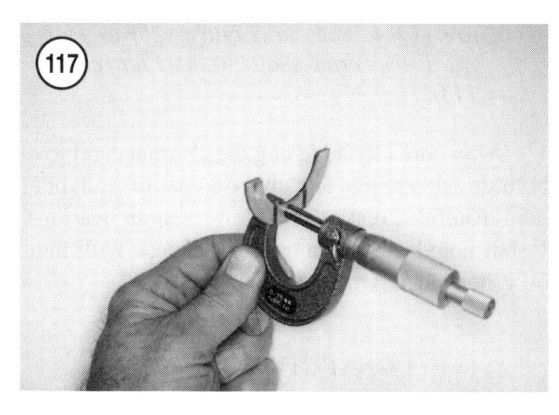

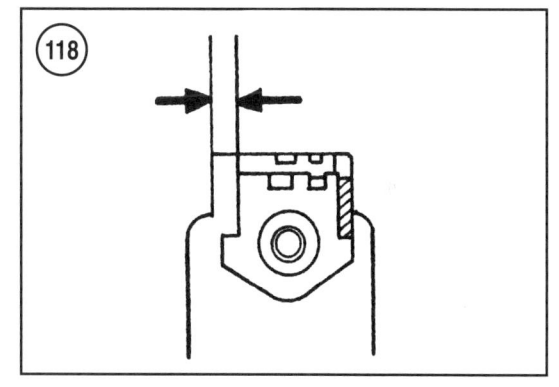

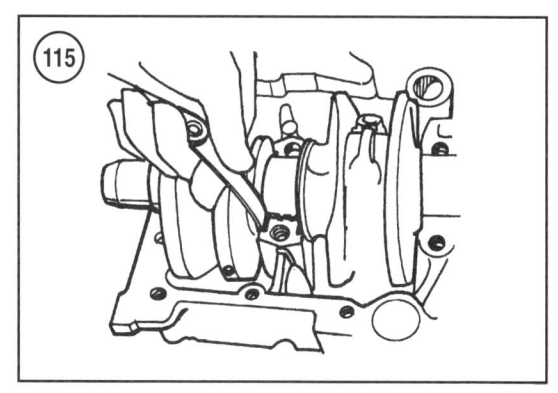

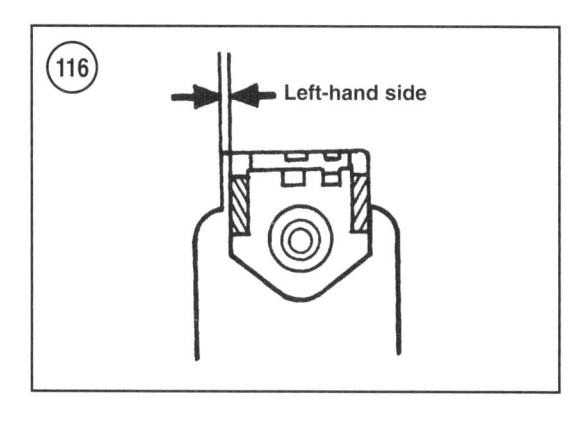

114 Upper crankcase half — Push — FRONT — Left-hand bearing — Right-hand bearing

115

116 Left-hand side

117

118

a. Remove the right thrust bearing and measure its thickness with a micrometer (**Figure 117**).
b. If the thickness is within specification, proceed to Step 6. If the thickness is less than specified, replace the right thrust bearing with a new one and repeat Step 3 and Step 4.

5. Install the right thrust bearing, and measure the thrust bearing clearance.

6. If the clearance is still greater than specified, remove the left thrust bearing.

7. Use a flat feeler gauge to measure the clearance between the machined surface of the crankshaft and the left surface of the crankcase boss (**Figure 118**).

8. Refer to **Table 5** and select the correct thrust bearing based on the clearance measured in Step 7.

9. Install the new left thrust bearing, and then repeat Step 3 and Step 4.

10. If the clearance cannot be brought into specification with different thrust bearings, replace the crankshaft.

CAUTION
*Install both the right and left thrust bearings with their oil grooves (**Fig-***

ure 119) *facing out* (**Figure 120**) *toward the crankshaft web* (**Figure 113**).

11. After correctly adjusting the clearance, remove both thrust bearings and apply a coat of molybdenum disulfide grease to each side of both bearings. Install both bearings into the crankcase with their oil groove facing the crankshaft web.

CONNECTING RODS

Removal/Installation

1. Disassemble the crankcase as described in this chapter.
2. Lift the crankshaft/connecting rod assembly and cam chain.
3. Measure the connecting rod side clearance by inserting a flat feeler gauge between a connecting rod and either crankshaft machined web (**Figure 121**). Record the clearance for each connecting rod, and compare the measurements to the specifications listed in **Table 1**. If the clearance exceeds the wear limit, inspect the connecting rod width and the crankshaft pin width as described in this chapter.

NOTE
Before disassembling the connecting rods, mark each rod and cap with that rod's cylinder number. Cylinders are numbered 1-4, counting left to right. "Left" refers to the engine as it sits in the frame, not how it may sit on the bench.

4. Remove the connecting rod cap nuts (**Figure 122**) and separate the rods from the crankshaft. Keep each cap with its original rod so the code on the end of the cap mates with the mark on the rod (**Figure 123**).

NOTE
Keep each bearing insert in its original location in the crankcase, rod or rod cap. If the bearing inserts are reused, they must be installed in their original locations to prevent rapid wear.

5. Inspect the connecting rods and bearings as described in this chapter.

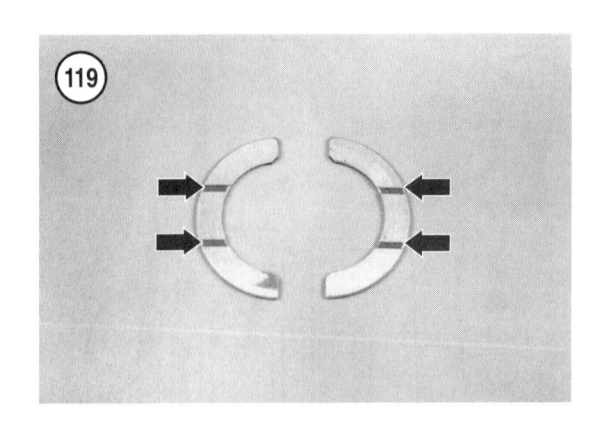

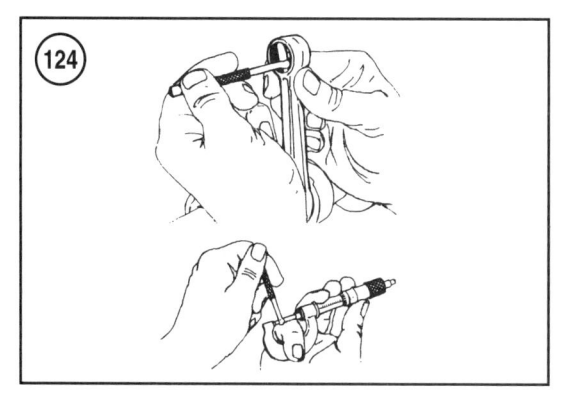

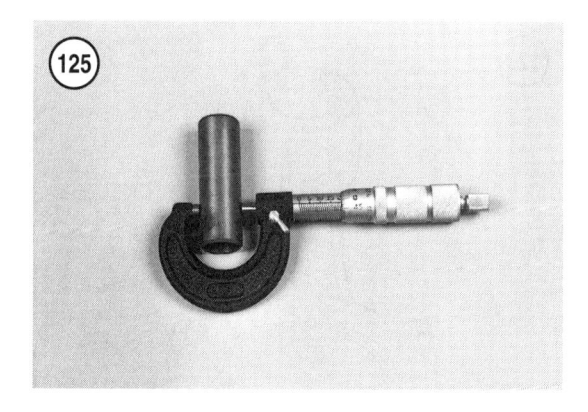

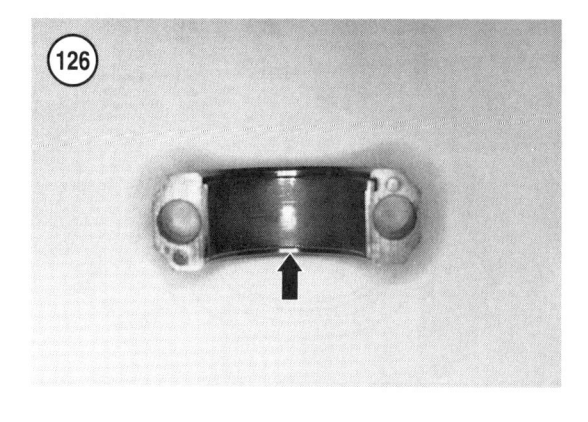

ENGINE LOWER END

6. If new bearing inserts will be installed, check the bearing clearance as described in this chapter.

7. Apply a light even coat of molybdenum disulfide grease to the crankpin and to the connecting rod bearing inserts.

8. Install the connecting rod onto the crankshaft, being careful to not damage the bearing surface of the crankpin with the threaded studs on the connecting rod.

9. Match the code on the end of the cap with the code on the connecting rod (**Figure 123**), and install the cap.

10. Apply a light coat of molybdenum disulfide grease to the threads of the connecting rod studs, and install the cap nuts (**Figure 122**). Tighten both connecting rod cap nuts to the initial torque specification listed in **Table 2** and then to the final torque.

11. After the connecting rods are installed and the cap nuts tightened to the correct torque, rotate the crankshaft several times and make sure there is no binding.

Connecting Rod Inspection

CAUTION
Never try to remove the connecting rod studs. If loosened and retightened, the bearing cap will never fit properly.

Compare all measurements to the specifications in **Table 1**. Replace the connecting rod assembly if any part is damaged or out of specification.

1. Carefully inspect each crankpin for scratches, ridges, scoring or nicks. Very small nicks and scratches may be removed with crocus cloth. Have more serious damage removed by a machine shop.

2. Check each connecting rod for obvious damage such as cracks and burns. Check the threads of the connecting rod studs for thread damage or stretching.

3. Check the piston pin bushing for wear or scoring.

4. Measure the small end inner diameter with a small hole gauge (**Figure 124**), and measure the gauge with a micrometer.

5. Measure the piston pin outer diameter with a micrometer (**Figure 125**).

6. Take the connecting rods to a machine shop, and check the alignment for twisting and bending.

7. Examine the bearing inserts (**Figure 126**) for wear, scoring or burning. They are reusable if in

good condition. If discarding an insert, make a note of the bearing color code on the side of the insert. A previous owner may have used undersize bearings.
8. Refer to the connecting rod bearing clearances measured during removal. If the connecting bearing clearance exceeds the service limit, perform the following:
   a. Measure the width of the connecting rod big end with a micrometer (**Figure 127**). If the width is less than specified, replace the connecting rod assembly.
   b. Measure the crankpin width with a dial caliper (**Figure 128**). If the width is greater than specified, replace the crankshaft.

Connecting Rod Bearing Clearance Measurement

1. Check the inserts in each connecting rod for evidence of wear, abrasion, and scoring. If the bearings are good, they may be reused. If any insert is questionable, replace both inserts in that connecting rod as a set.
2. Clean the bearing surfaces of the crankpin and the bearing inserts.
3. Install the rod bearing inserts in the connecting rod and bearing cap (**Figure 126**). Make sure the tab on the insert locks into the cutout in the cap or in the connecting rod (**Figure 129**). Carefully press each insert into place by hand. Make sure the insert is locked in place correctly.
4. Install the connecting rod onto the crankshaft, being careful not to damage the bearing surface of the crankpin with the threaded studs.
5. Place a piece of Plastigage over the crankpin parallel to the crankshaft (**Figure 130**). Do not place the Plastigage material over an oil hole in the crankshaft.

CAUTION
Do not rotate the crankshaft while the Plastigage is in place.

6. Match the mark on the end of the cap with the mark on the rod (**Figure 123**), and install the cap.
7. Apply a light coat of molybdenum disulfide grease to threads of the connecting rod studs, and install the cap nuts. Tighten both cap nuts to the initial torque specification and then to the final torque.
8. Loosen the cap nuts, and carefully remove the cap from the connecting rod.

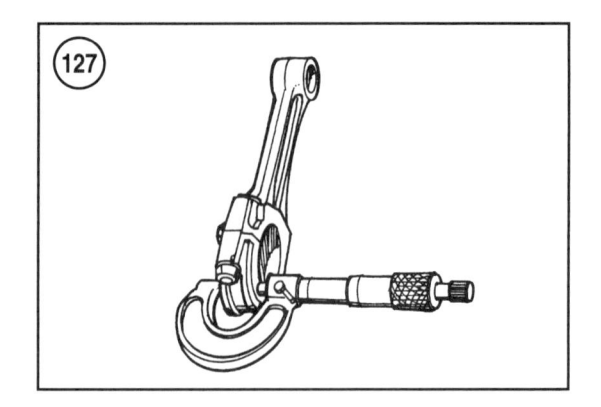

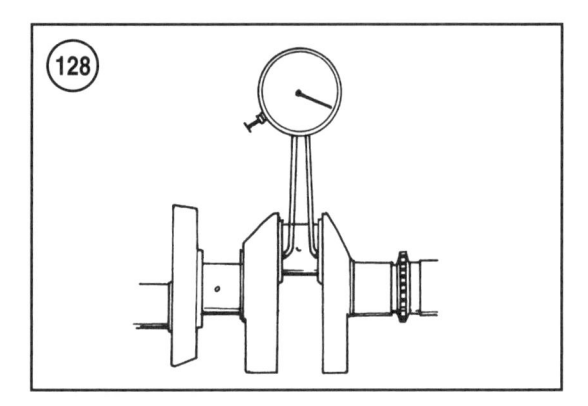

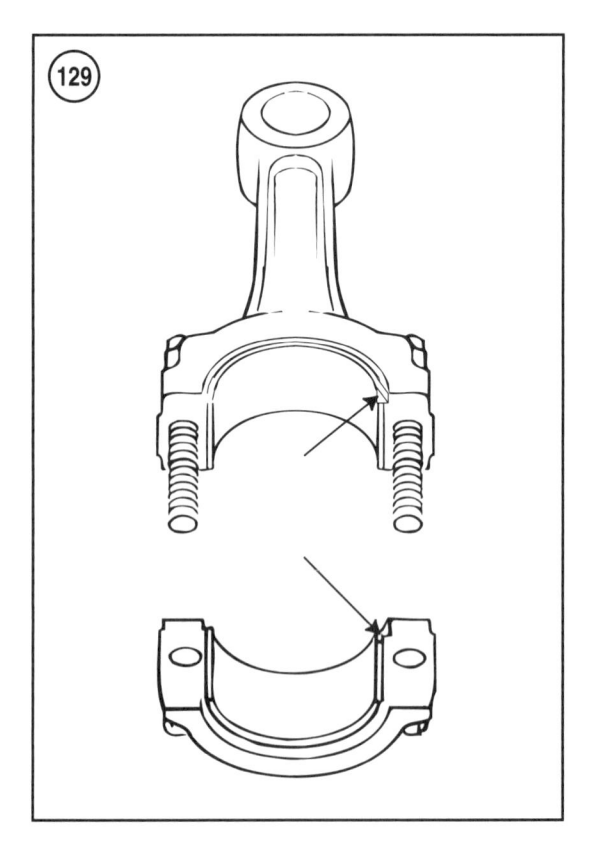

ENGINE LOWER END

Figure 130

Figure 131

Figure 132

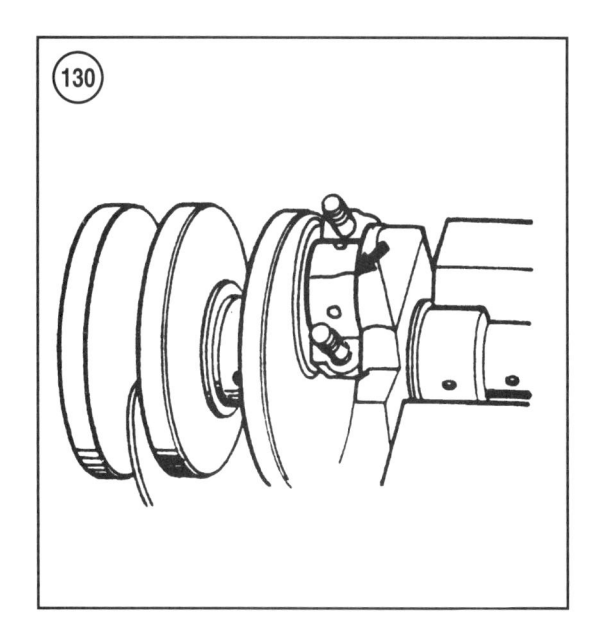

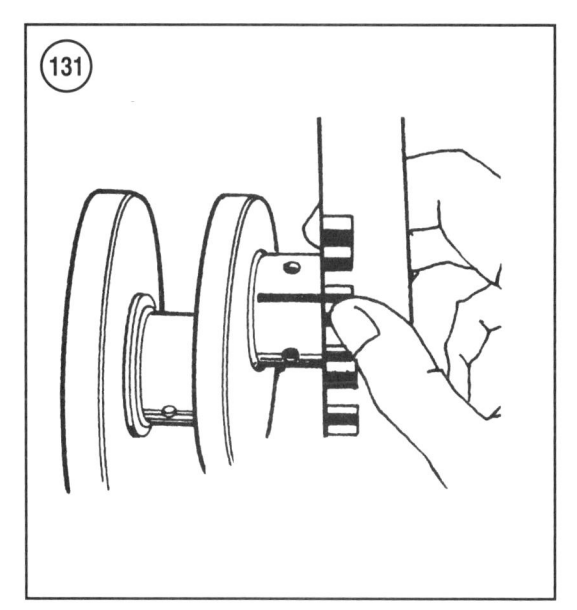

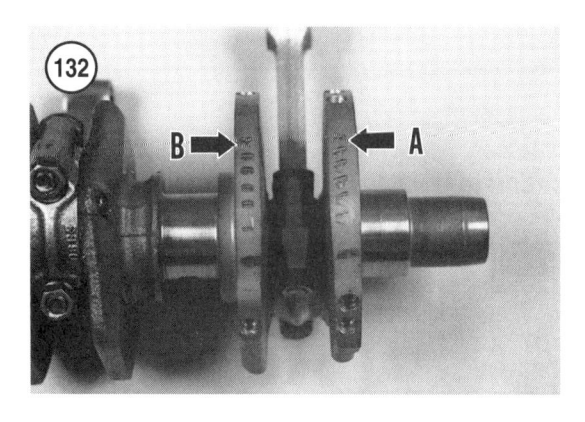

9. Measure the width of the flattened Plastigage according to manufacturer's instructions. Measure at both ends of the Plastigage strip (**Figure 131**), and record the widest measurement.

10. If the connecting rod bearing clearance exceeds the wear limit, select new bearings as described in this chapter.

11. Remove the Plastigage strips from the main bearing journals.

Connecting Rod Bearing Selection

1. A series of code numbers stamped onto the crankweb (B, **Figure 132**) indicate the outside diameter of the crankpins. Refer to **Figure 133** to determine the outside diameter code number for each particular crankpin.

2. The connecting rod code (1 or 2) marked on the side of each connecting rod and cap (**Figure 123**) indicates the inside diameter of the connecting rod.

3. Bearing inserts are identified by color codes (**Figure 134**). Refer to **Table 6** and select a new set of bearing inserts by cross-referencing the connecting rod inner diameter code (**Figure 123**) with the crankpin outer diameter code (B, **Figure 132**). Always replace bearing inserts as a set.

4. After installing new bearing inserts, recheck the clearance by repeating the procedure described above in this chapter. If the clearance is still out of specifications, either the connecting rod or the crankshaft is worn beyond the service limit and requires replacement.

BREAK-IN

Following cylinder servicing (for example, boring, honing or new rings) and major lower end work, the engine should be broken in as though it were new. The performance and service life of the engine greatly depend upon a careful and sensible break-in, particularly during the first 800 km (500 miles) of operation.

For the first 800 km (500 miles) of operation, keep the engine speed below 6000 rpm. Avoid prolonged, steady running at one engine speed, no matter how moderate, and avoid hard acceleration.

During the period of 800-1600 km (500-1000 miles) of service, keep the engine speed below 9000 rpm. Again, hard acceleration, as well as prolonged,

CHAPTER FIVE

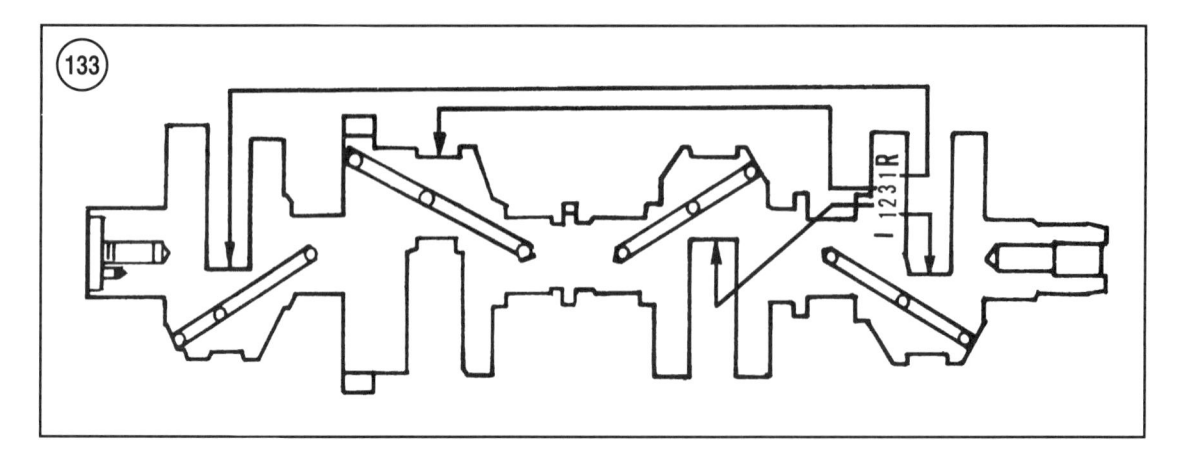

(133)

steady running at one engine speed should be avoided.

After 1600 km (1000 miles) of operation, the engine can be operated at full throttle. However, keep the engine speed below 12,000 rpm.

During break-in, always take the time to warm up a cold engine before increasing the engine speed or shifting the transmission into gear. This allows the lubrication system time to circulate oil throughout the engine.

At no time, either during or after break-in, should the oil level be allowed to drop below the low level line on the oil inspection window. The oil will become overheated, resulting in insufficient lubrication and increased wear.

1000 km (600 Mile) Service

It is essential that the oil and filter be changed after the first 1000 km (600 miles). In addition, it is a good idea to change the oil and filter at the completion of break-in (about 1600 km/1,000 miles) to ensure that all of the particles produced during break-in are removed from the lubrication system. The small added expense is a smart investment that will result in increased engine life.

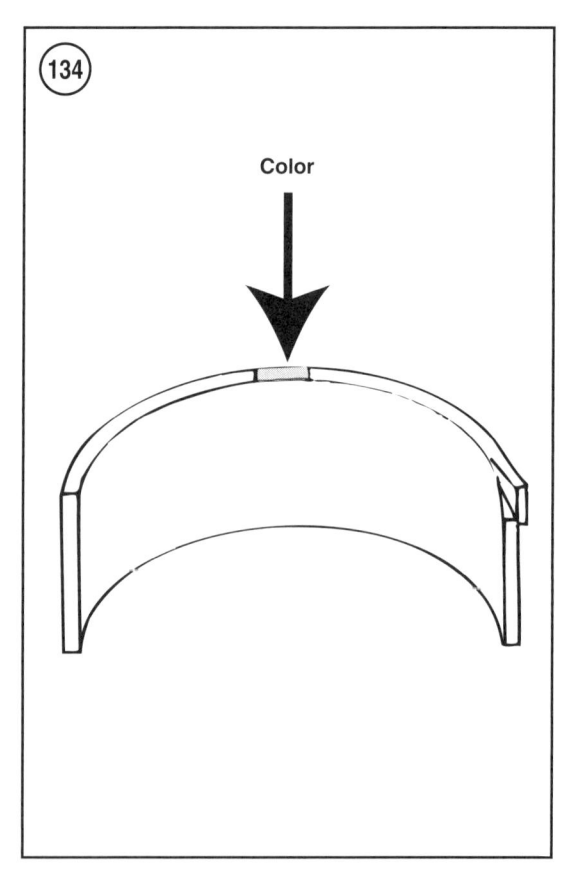

(134) Color

Table 1 LOWER END SPECIFICATIONS

Item	Standard mm (in.)	Wear limit mm (in.)
Connecting rod		
Piston pin end inside diameter	18.010-18.018 (0.7091-0.7094)	18.040 (0.7102)
Side clearance	0.10-0.20 (0.004-0.008)	0.30 (0.010)
Crankpin end width	20.95-21.00 (0.825-0.827)	
	(continued)	

ENGINE LOWER END

Table 1 LOWER END SPECIFICATIONS (continued)

Item	Standard mm (in.)	Wear limit mm (in.)
Connecting rod bearing clearance	0.032-0.056 (0.0013-0.0022)	0.080 (0.0031)
Connecting rod inside diameter		
Code 1	37.000-37.008 (1.4567-1.4570)	
Code 2	37.008-37.016 (1.4570-1.4573)	
Crankshaft		
Crankpin width	21.10-21.15 (0.831-0.833)	–
Crankpin standard outside diameter	33.976-34.000 (1.3376-1.3386)	–
Crankpin outside diameter		
Code 1	33.992-34.000 (1.3383-1.3386)	–
Code 2	33.984-33.992 (1.3380-1.3383)	–
Code 3	33.976-33.984 (1.3376-1.3380)	–
Crankshaft main bearing clearance	0.020-0.044 ((0.0008-0.0017)	0.080 (0.0031)
Crankshaft journal width (1995-1999 models)	24.00-24.05 (0.945-0.947)	–
Crankshaft journal standard diameter	31.976-32.000 (1.2589-1.2598)	–
Code A	31.992-32.000 (1.2595-1.2598)	–
Code B	31.984-31.992 (1.2592-1.2595)	–
Code C	31.976-31.984 (1.2589-1.2592)	–
Crankshaft runout	–	0.05 (0.002)
Crankshaft thrust clearance	0.04-0.09 (0.002-0.004)	–
Crankshaft right thrust bearing		
1995-1997 models		
Thickness	2.445-2.465 (0.0963-0.0970)	–
Color code	Brown	–
Part No.	12228-19C00	–
1998-2000 models		
Thickness	2.425-2.450 (0.0955-0.0965)	–
Color code	Green	–
Part No.	12228-43414	–
Crankcase-main-bearing boss inside diameter		
Code A	35.000-35.008 (1.3780-1.3783)	–
Code B	35.008-35.016 (1.3783-1.3786)	–
Oil pressure @ 60° C (140° F)	300-600 kPa (43-87 psi) @ 3000 rpm	

Table 2 LOWER END TORQUE SPECIFICATIONS

Item	N•m	in.-lb.	ft.-lb.
Alternator driven gear nut			
1995-1999 models	60	–	44
2000 models	55	–	40.5
Connecting rod cap nut			
Initial	20	–	15
Final	35	–	26
Crankcase bolt and nut			
6 mm			–
Initial	6	53	–
(continued)			

Table 2 LOWER END TORQUE SPECIFICATIONS (continued)

Item	N•m	in.-lb.	ft.-lb.
Crankcase bolt and nut (continued)			
6 mm			
Final			
1995-1999 models	13	115	–
2000 models	11	97	–
8 mm			
Initial	13	115	–
Final		–	
1995-1999 models	22	–	16
2000 models	23	–	17
Crankcase stud	15	–	11
Engine sprocket nut	115	–	85
Main bearing bolts			
Initial	13	115	–
Final			
1995-1999 models	22	–	16
2000 models	23	–	17
Main oil gallery plug	40	–	29.5
Front upper mounting bolts			
55 mm (2.2 in.) long	55	–	40.5
Front lower mounting bolts			
55 mm (2.2 in.) long	55	–	40.5
Rear lower through bolt			
10 × 130 mm	75	–	55
Rear upper through bolt			
10 × 180 mm	75	–	55
Removable frame			
downtube mounting bolt	32	–	23
Oil cooler banjo bolt			
1995-1999	28	–	21
2000 models	23	–	17
Oil cooler hose			
mounting bolt	10	88	–
Oil cooler mounting bolt	11	97	–
Oil drain bolt	23	–	17
Oil pan bolt	14	–	10
Oil pressure regulator	28	–	21
Oil pressure switch	14	–	10
Oil pump mounting bolt	10	88	–
Signal generator bolt	25	–	18
Speed sensor rotor bolt	13	115	–
Starter clutch			
mounting bolt	150	–	110

Table 3 CRANKSHAFT MAIN BEARING INSERT SELECTION

Crankshaft journal code	A	B	C
Crankcase bearing boss code			
A	Green	Black	Brown
B	Black	Brown	Yellow

ENGINE LOWER END

Table 4 CRANKSHAFT INSERT COLOR, PART NO., THICKNESS

Year/color	Specification mm (in.)	Part No.
1995-1999 models		
Green	1.486-1.490 (0.0585-0.0587)	12229-27A00-0A0
Black	1.490-1.494 (0.0587-0.0588)	12229-27A00-0B0
Brown	1.494-1.498 (0.0588-0.0590)	12229-27A00-0C0
Yellow	1.498-1.502 (0.0590-0.0591)	12229-27A00-0D0
2000 models		
Green		
Upper insert	1.486-1.490 (0.0585-0.0587)	12229-27A10-0A0
Lower insert	1.486-1.490 (0.0585-0.0587)	12229-27A00-0A0
Black		
Upper insert	1.490-1.494 (0.0587-0.0588)	12229-27A10-0B0
Lower insert	1.490-1.494 (0.0587-0.0588)	12229-27A00-0B0
Brown		
Upper insert	1.494-1.498 (0.0588-0.0590)	12229-27A10-0C0
Lower insert	1.494-1.498 (0.0588-0.0590)	12229-27A00-0C0
Yellow		
Upper insert	1.498-1.502 (0.0590-0.0591)	12229-27A10-0D0
Lower insert	1.498-1.502 (0.0590-0.0591)	12229-27A00-0D0

Table 5 THRUST BEARING SELECTION

Clearance before inserting left thrust bearing mm (in.)	Color	Part No.	Thrust bearing thickness
2.415-2.440 (0.0951-0961)	Red	12228-43411	2.350-2.375 (0.0925-0.935)
2.440-2.465 (0.0961-0.0970)	Black	12228-43412	2.375-2.400 (0.0935-0.0945)
2.465-2.490 (0.0970-0.0980)	Blue	12228-43413	2.400-2.425 (0.0945-0.0955)
2.490-2.515 (0.0980-0.0990)	Green	12228-43414	2.425-2.450 (0.0955-0.0965)
2.515-2.540 (0.0990-0.1000)	Yellow	12228-43415	2.450-2.475 (0.0965-0.0974)
2.540-2.565 (0.1000-0.1010)	White	12228-43416	2.475-2.500 (0.0974-0.0984)

Table 6 CONNECTING ROD BEARING INSERT SELECTION

Crankpin O.D. code Connecting rod I.D. code	1	2	3
1	Green	Black	Brown
2	Black	Brown	Yellow

Table 7 CONNECTING ROD INSERT COLOR, THICKNESS, PART NO.

Year/Color	Specification	Part No.
1995-1999 models		
Green	1.480-1.484 (0.0583-0.0584)	12164-17E01-0A0
Black	1.484-1.488 (0.0584-0.0586)	12164-17E01-0B0
Brown	1.488-1.492 (0.0586-0.0587)	12164-17E01-0C0
Yellow	1.492-1.496 (0.0587-0.0589)	12164-17E01-0D0
	(continued)	

Table 7 CONNECTING ROD INSERT COLOR, THICKNESS, PART NO. (continued)

Year/color	Specification	Part No.
2000 models		
Green	1.480-1.484 (0.0583-0.0584)	12164-26E00-0A0
Black	1.484-1.488 (0.0584-0.0586)	12164-26E00-0B0
Brown	1.488-1.492 (0.0586-0.0587)	12164-26E00-0C0
Yellow	1.492-1.496 (0.0587-0.0589)	12164-26E00-0D0

CHAPTER SIX

CLUTCH

This chapter provides complete service procedures for the clutch and clutch release mechanism. When inspecting clutch components, compare any measurements to the clutch specifications in **Table 1**. Replace components that are damaged, worn to the wear limit or out of specification. During assembly, tighten fasteners to the torque specifications listed in **Table 2**. **Table 1** and **Table 2** are located at the end of this chapter.

The clutch is a wet (operates in the engine oil) multi-plate design. The clutch assembly is located on the right side of the engine, with the inner clutch hub splined to the transmission mainshaft. The outer housing rotates freely on the mainshaft, and is geared to the crankshaft.

Release operation is accomplished via a pushrod/push piece assembly operating on the pressure plate. The pushrods pass through the transmission mainshaft and are activated by the clutch cable pulling on the clutch lifter mechanism mounted in the drive sprocket cover on the left side of the engine. Routine adjustment to compensate for cable stretch is covered in Chapter Three.

CLUTCH

Removal/Disassembly

The clutch assembly can be removed with the engine in the frame. This procedure is shown with the

186

CHAPTER SIX

① CLUTCH

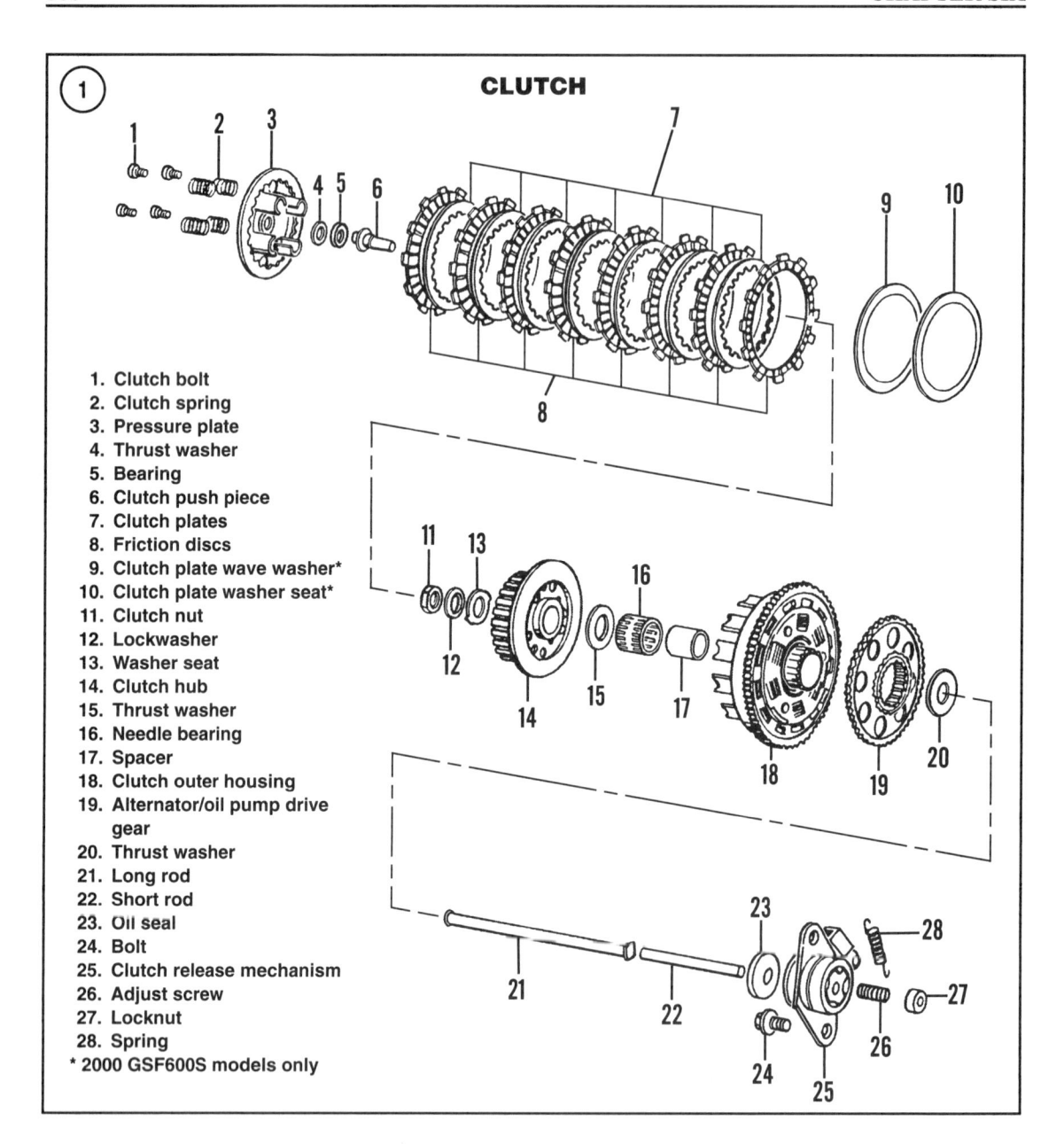

1. Clutch bolt
2. Clutch spring
3. Pressure plate
4. Thrust washer
5. Bearing
6. Clutch push piece
7. Clutch plates
8. Friction discs
9. Clutch plate wave washer*
10. Clutch plate washer seat*
11. Clutch nut
12. Lockwasher
13. Washer seat
14. Clutch hub
15. Thrust washer
16. Needle bearing
17. Spacer
18. Clutch outer housing
19. Alternator/oil pump drive gear
20. Thrust washer
21. Long rod
22. Short rod
23. Oil seal
24. Bolt
25. Clutch release mechanism
26. Adjust screw
27. Locknut
28. Spring

* 2000 GSF600S models only

CLUTCH

engine removed and partially disassembled for clarity.

Refer to **Figure 1**.

1. Drain the engine oil as described in Chapter Three.
2. Shift the transmission into gear.

NOTE
The clutch release mechanism is located inside the engine sprocket cover on the left side of the engine.

3. Remove the engine sprocket cover as described in Chapter Seven.
4. Remove the clutch cover bolts. Note the gaskets installed beneath the two front clutch cover bolts (A, **Figure 2**). During assembly, install new gaskets with these bolts.
5. Remove the clutch cover (B, **Figure 2**) and gasket (A, **Figure 3**). Do not lose the two locating dowels (B, **Figure 3**).
6. Remove the starter clutch cover as described in Chapter Five.
7. Hold the starter clutch with a Suzuki starter clutch holder (part No. 09920-34810) or a universal holding tool. Using a crisscross pattern, loosen each clutch spring bolt (A, **Figure 4**).
8. Remove the clutch spring bolts.
9. Remove each clutch spring (A, **Figure 5**), and then remove the pressure plate (B, **Figure 5**).
10. Remove the thrust washer (A, **Figure 6**), bearing (B, **Figure 6**) and clutch push piece (**Figure 7**).
11. Remove the friction discs and clutch plates (A, **Figure 8**).
12. On 2000 models, remove the clutch plate wave washer and the clutch plate washer seat from the clutch hub (**Figure 1**).

13. If necessary, remove the short pushrod (B, **Figure 8**) from the right side of the mainshaft, and remove the long pushrod (**Figure 9**) from the left side.

> *CAUTION*
> *Do not clamp the Grabbit on too tightly. It could damage the grooves in the clutch hub.*

14. Hold the clutch hub with a Grabbit or similar tool, and remove the clutch nut (**Figure 10**).
15. Remove the lockwasher (A, **Figure 11**) and the washer seat (B, **Figure 11**). During assembly, install a new washer.
16. Remove the clutch hub (C, **Figure 11**) from the mainshaft.
17. Remove the thrust washer (**Figure 12**).
18. Slide the clutch outer housing forward enough to expose the ends of the needle bearing and spacer.
19. Hold onto the clutch outer housing and remove the needle bearing (**Figure 13**) and the spacer (A, **Figure 14**).
20. Remove the clutch outer housing (B, **Figure 14**). The alternator/oil pump drive gear should come off with the clutch outer housing.
21. Remove the thrust washer (**Figure 15**).
22. Inspect all components as described in this chapter.

Assembly/Installation

> *CAUTION*
> *Two thrust washers are used on the clutch assembly. The larger diameter thrust washer with the beveled side (A, Figure 16) is installed in Step 1 and the smaller diameter thrust washer (B, Figure 16) is installed in Step 7. These thrust washers must be installed in the correct location for proper clutch operation.*

1. Install the larger thrust washer (**Figure 15**) so its beveled side faces in towards the crankcase.
2. Install the alternator/oil pump drive gear (A, **Figure 17**) onto the back of the clutch outer housing.
3. Slide the clutch outer housing assembly onto the mainshaft (B, **Figure 14**).
4. Apply clean engine oil to the needle bearing and the spacer.

CLUTCH

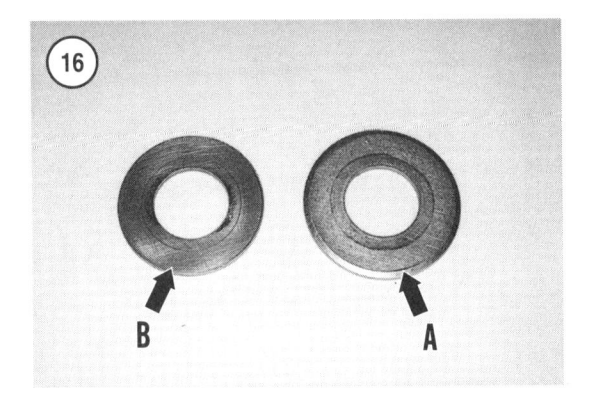

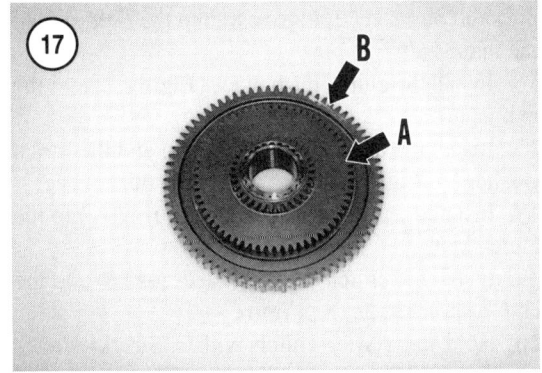

5. Hold onto the clutch outer housing, and install the spacer (A, **Figure 14**) and the needle bearing (**Figure 13**).
6. Push the clutch outer housing toward the crankcase until it stops. Make sure the primary driven gear on the back of the outer housing properly engages the primary drive gear on the crankshaft.
7. Install the thrust washer (**Figure 12**), and seat it against the clutch outer housing.
8. Install the clutch hub (C, **Figure 11**) so it bottoms against the outer housing.
9. Install the washer seat (B, **Figure 11**) and a *new* lockwasher (A, **Figure 11**). Make sure the beveled side of the lockwasher faces away from the clutch hub.
10. Install the clutch nut (**Figure 10**).
11. Hold the clutch hub with a Grabbit or similar tool, and torque the clutch nut to the specification in **Table 2**.
12. On 2000 models, install the clutch plate washer seat and the clutch plate wave washer if they were removed. See **Figure 1**.

NOTE
If new friction discs and clutch plates are being installed, apply new engine oil to all surfaces to avoid clutch lockup when the clutch is used for the first time.

13. Install a friction disc onto the clutch hub, and then install a clutch plate.
14. Continue to alternately install a friction disc and then a clutch plate until all are installed. The last item installed is a friction disc (A, **Figure 8**).
15. If removed, install the pushrods. Apply Suzuki Super Grease A to the long pushrod, and install it into the left side of the mainshaft (**Figure 9**). Install

the short pushrod (B, **Figure 8**) into the right side of the mainshaft.

16. Install the clutch push piece (**Figure 7**) into the mainshaft.

17. Install the bearing (B, **Figure 6**) and the thrust washer (A, **Figure 6**) onto the clutch push piece.

18. Install the pressure plate (B, **Figure 5**) onto the clutch hub.

19. Install the clutch springs (A, **Figure 5**) and the clutch spring bolts (A, **Figure 4**)

20. Hold the starter clutch with a Suzuki starter clutch holder (part No. 09920-34810) or a universal holding tool. Using a crisscross pattern, torque each clutch spring bolt to the specification in **Table 2**.

21. Apply a light coat of ThreeBond Liquid Gasket 1104, or equivalent, to the crankcase mating surfaces where the upper and lower crankcase halves meet (B, **Figure 4**). This prevents an oil leak.

22. Install a *new* clutch cover gasket (A, **Figure 3**). Make sure the locating dowels (B, **Figure 3**) are in place.

NOTE
*Install a new gasket under each of the two clutch cover bolts (A, **Figure 2**) at the front of the cover. Oil will leak from the cover if new gaskets are not used.*

23. Install the clutch cover (B, **Figure 2**) and the bolts. Tighten the bolts securely. Include a *new* gasket under the two clutch cover bolts (A, **Figure 2**).

24. Adjust the clutch as described in Chapter Three.

25. Add engine oil as described in Chapter Three.

Inspection

Compare all measurements to the specifications in **Table 1**. Replace any part that is damaged, worn to the wear limit or out of specification.

1. Separate the alternator/oil pump drive gear (A, **Figure 17**) from the back of the clutch outer housing.

2. Clean all clutch parts in a petroleum-based solvent such as kerosene, and thoroughly dry them with compressed air.

3. Measure the free length of each clutch spring, as shown in **Figure 18**.

4. Measure the thickness of each friction disc at several places around the disc, as shown in **Figure 19**.

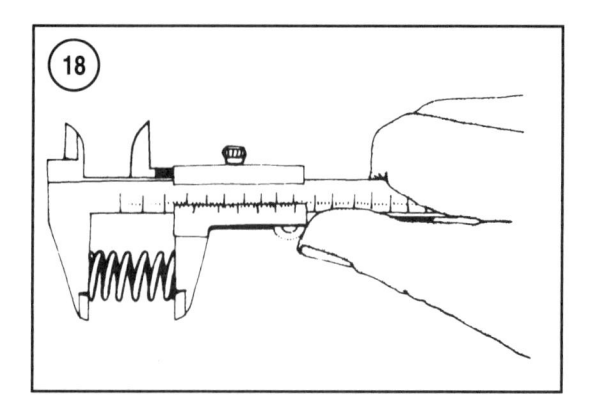

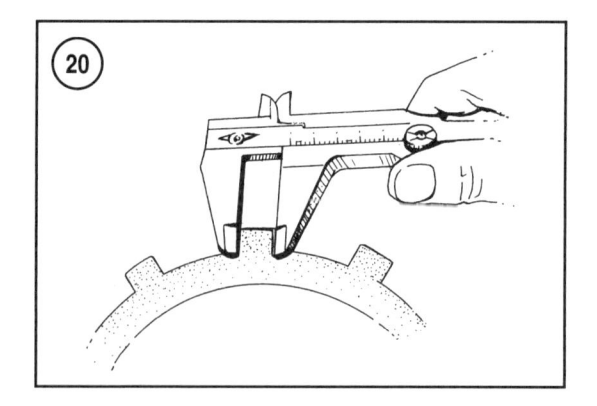

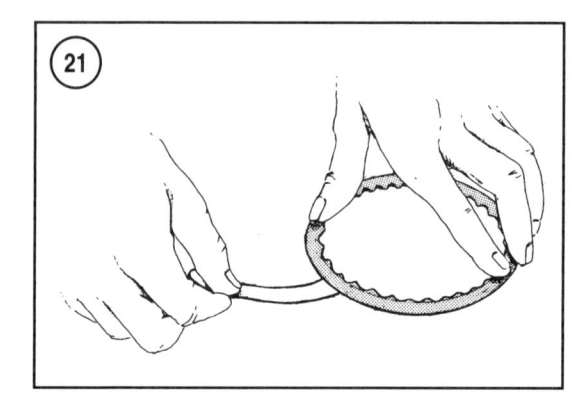

CLUTCH

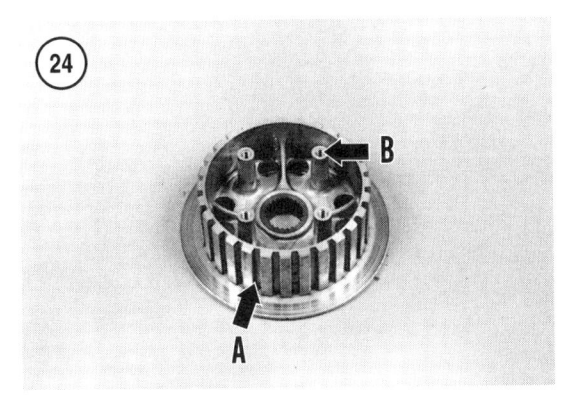

5. Measure the friction-disc claw width (**Figure 20**) at several places on each friction disc.
6. Check the clutch plates for warp with a flat feeler gauge on a surface plate or a piece of plate glass (**Figure 21**).

NOTE
If any of the friction discs, clutch plates or clutch springs require replacement, consider replacing all of them as a set to retain maximum clutch performance.

7. Inspect the slots in the clutch outer housing (A, **Figure 22**) for cracks, nicks or galling where they come in contact with the friction disc claws. If any severe damage is evident, replace the housing.
8. Inspect the gear teeth (B, **Figure 17**) on the clutch outer housing for damage. Remove any small nicks with an oilstone. If damage is severe, replace the clutch outer housing. Also check the teeth on the primary drive gear of the crankshaft; if damaged, the driven gear may also need replacing.
9. Inspect the damper springs on the clutch outer housing. If they are sagged or broken, replace the housing.
10. Inspect the outer splines of the clutch outer housing (**Figure 23**) and the inner splines of the alternator/oil pump drive gear for damage. Remove any small nicks with an oilstone. If damage is severe, replace the clutch outer housing and/or the alternator/oil pump drive gear.
11. Inspect the gear teeth on the alternator/oil pump drive gear (A, **Figure 17**) for damage. Remove any small nicks with an oilstone. If damage is severe, replace the alternator/oil pump drive gear.
12. Inspect the grooves (A, **Figure 24**) and studs (B) in the clutch hub. If either show signs of wear or galling, replace the clutch hub.
13. Inspect the inner splines in the clutch hub for damage. Remove any small nicks with an oilstone. If damage is severe, replace the clutch hub.
14. Inspect the grooves and studs in the clutch pressure plate (B, **Figure 22**). If either show signs of wear or galling, replace the clutch pressure plate.
15. Inspect the spring receptacles in the clutch pressure plate for wear or damage. Replace the clutch pressure plate if necessary.
16. Check the inner bearing surface (**Figure 25**) of the clutch outer housing for signs of wear or damage. Replace the clutch outer housing if necessary.

17. Check the needle bearing (A, **Figure 26**). Make sure it rotates smoothly with no signs of wear or damage. Replace the bearing if necessary.
18. Check the inner and outer surfaces of the spacer (B, **Figure 26**) for signs of wear or damage. Replace the spacer if necessary.
19. Install the spacer into the needle bearing, rotate the spacer within the bearing and check for wear. Replace either/or both parts if necessary.
20. Check the clutch push piece (A, **Figure 27**) for wear or damage. Replace it if necessary.
21. Check the clutch release bearing (B, **Figure 27**). Make sure it rotates smoothly with no signs of wear or damage. Replace the clutch release bearing if necessary.
22. Inspect the clutch pushrods (**Figure 28**) for bending. Roll each rod on a surface plate or piece of plate glass. If a rod is bent or deformed in any way, it must be replaced. Otherwise it may hang up inside the transmission shaft and cause erratic clutch operation.

CLUTCH RELEASE MECHANISM

The clutch release mechanism is mounted inside the engine sprocket cover.

Removal/Installation

1. Loosen the locknut and the barrel adjuster at the clutch hand lever.
2. At the engine sprocket cover, slide the rubber cover (A, **Figure 29**) up onto the clutch cable and completely unscrew the clutch adjustment locknut (B, **Figure 29**).
3. Remove the engine sprocket cover as described in Chapter Seven.
4. Unhook the return spring (A, **Figure 30**) from the clutch release arm.
5. Disconnect the lower clutch cable end from the anchor (B, **Figure 30**) on the clutch release arm.
6. Remove the bolts (C, **Figure 30**) securing the clutch release mechanism to the cover, and remove the mechanism from the engine sprocket cover.
7. Install by reversing these removal steps, while noting the following:
   a. Install the clutch release mechanism, and tighten the bolts securely.
   b. Adjust the clutch as described in Chapter Three.

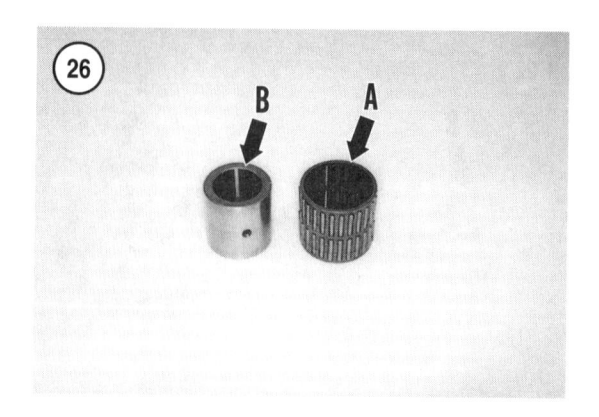

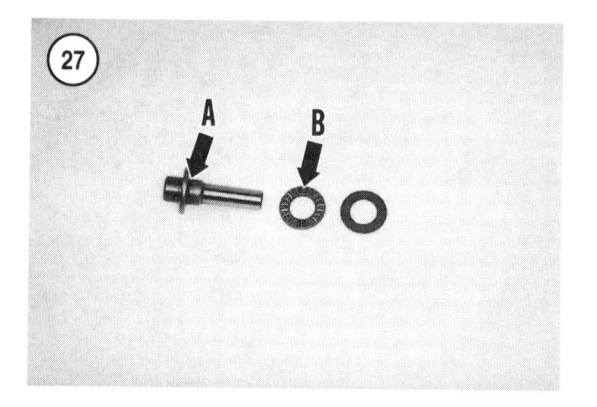

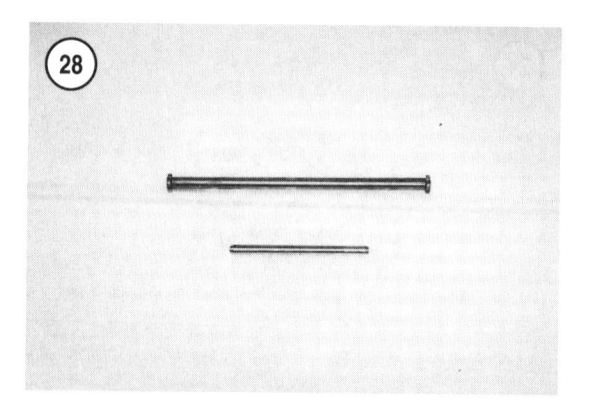

CLUTCH CABLE REPLACEMENT

1. On models with fairings, remove the fairing as described in Chapter Fourteen.
2. Loosen the locknut and the adjusting barrel at the clutch hand lever.
3. At the engine sprocket cover, slide the rubber cover (A, **Figure 29**) up onto the clutch cable and completely unscrew the clutch adjustment locknut (B, **Figure 29**).
4. Remove the engine sprocket cover as described in Chapter Seven.

CLUTCH

NOTE
Prior to removing the cable, make a drawing of the cable routing through the frame, including the location of each cable tie. It is very easy to forget how the cable was routed once it has been removed. The new cable must follow the same path as the old cable.

9. Remove any cable ties securing the clutch cable to the frame.
10. Remove the old clutch cable by pulling it from the top (upper cable end). Continue until the cable is removed from the frame, leaving the attached piece of string in its mounting position.
11. Untie the string from the old cable.
12. Connect the upper cable end of the new cable to the clutch lever.
13. Tie the string onto the bottom end of the new clutch cable.
14. Slowly pull the string and cable to install the cable along the path of the original clutch cable. Continue until the clutch cable is correctly routed through the engine and frame. Untie and remove the string.
15. Visually check the entire length of the clutch cable as it runs through the frame and engine. Make sure there are no kinks or sharp bends. Straighten out the cable if necessary.
16. Feed the cable through the engine sprocket cover, and connect the lower end of the clutch cable to the anchor (B, **Figure 30**) on the clutch release arm.
17. Install any cable ties needed to secure the clutch cable to the frame.
18. Adjust the clutch as described in Chapter Three.

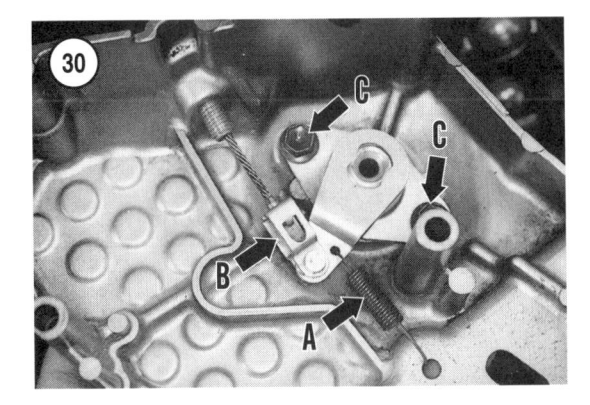

5. Disconnect the clutch cable from the anchor (B, **Figure 30**) on the clutch release arm and remove the cable from the engine sprocket cover.
6. Tie a piece of heavy string onto the end of the old cable. Cut the string to a length that is longer than the new clutch cable.
7. Tie the lower end of the string to the frame or engine component.
8. Disconnect the upper cable end from the anchor on the clutch lever.

Table 1 CLUTCH SPECIFICATIONS

Item	Standard	Wear limit
Friction disc		
Quantity	8	–
Thickness		
1995-1999 models	2.65-2.95 mm (0.104-0.116 in.)	2.35 mm (0.93 in.)
2000 models	2.92-3.08 mm (0.115-0.121 in.)	2.62 mm (0.103 in.)
Claw width		
1995-1999 models	–	15.0 mm (0.59 in.)
2000 models	15.9-16.0 mm (0.626-0.630 in.)	15.1 mm (0.594 in.)
(continued)		

Table 1 CLUTCH SPECIFICATIONS (continued)

Item	Standard	Wear limit
Clutch plate		
Quantity	7	–
Warp	–	0.1 mm (0.004 in.)
Clutch spring free length	–	
1995-1999 models	–	69.5 mm (2.74 in.)
2000 models	–	47.6 mm (1.87 in.)
Clutch release screw		
1995-1999 models	1/2-1/4 turns back	–
2000 models		
Clutch lever free play	10-15 mm (0.4-0.6 in.)	–

Table 2 CLUTCH TORQUE SPECIFICATIONS

Item	N•m	in.-lb.	ft.-lb.
Clutch hub nut			
1995-1999 models	90	–	66
2000 models	95	–	70
Clutch spring bolt	12	106	–

CHAPTER SEVEN

TRANSMISSION AND GEARSHIFT MECHANISMS

This chapter provides complete service procedures for the transmission and the external and the internal shift mechanisms. During inspection, compare any measurements to the gearshift specifications in **Table 2**. Replace any component that is damaged, worn to the wear limit or out of specification. During assembly, tighten fasteners to the torque specifications listed in **Table 3**. **Tables 1-3** appear at the end of this chapter.

ENGINE DRIVE SPROCKET COVER

The drive chain is an endless type. There is no master link. To remove the drive chain, remove the engine sprocket from the countershaft and remove the swing arm as described in Chapter Twelve.

Removal/Installation

1. Loosen the shift lever clamp bolt (A, **Figure 1**) and remove the shift lever (B, **Figure 1**) from the shift shaft.
2. Remove the bolts (**Figure 2**) securing the engine sprocket cover and move the cover out of the way. Do not lose the dowels installed behind the cover.
3. Suspend the cover from the frame with a wire or bungee cord. The clutch cable does not have to be disconnected unless the cover must be completely removed. The same applies to the speed sensor on

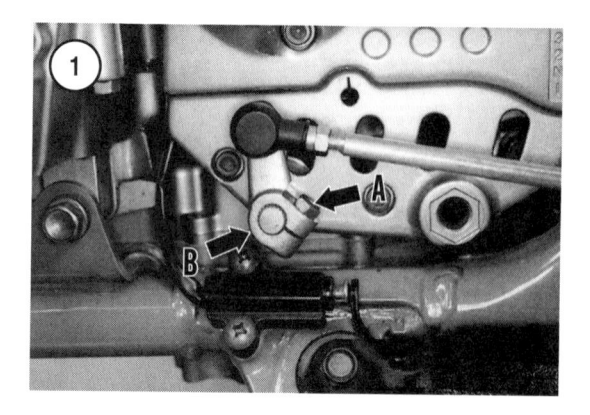

2000 models. Leave the sensor mounted on the engine sprocket cover unless the cover must be completely removed.

4. Installation is the reverse of removal. Note the following:

NOTE
*When installing the sprocket cover with the rear wheel removed, make sure the upper chain run sits on top of the upper bolt boss (**Figure 3**). When the chain is disconnected from the rear sprocket, it lies down so the cover can be installed incorrectly.*

 a. If removed, reinstall the dowels into the crankcase.
 b. Install the shift lever onto the shift shaft so the split in the shift lever clamp aligns with the punch mark on the end of the shift shaft.
 c. Tighten the clamp bolt securely.

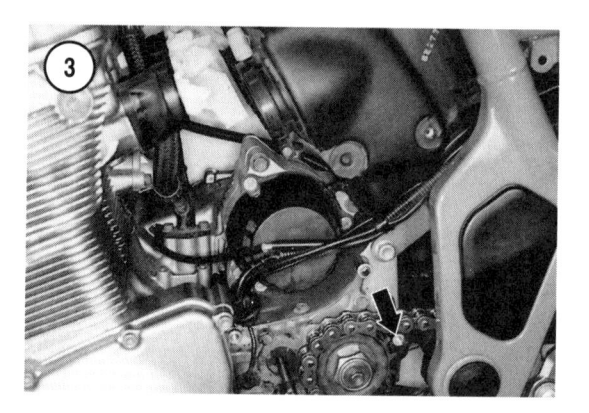

ENGINE DRIVE SPROCKET

1. Remove the engine sprocket cover as described in this chapter.
2. Have an assistant apply the rear brake and perform the following:
3. On 1995-1999 models, remove the bolt (A, **Figure 4**) and washer (B, **Figure 4**) from the center of the sprocket nut.
4. Loosen and remove the drive sprocket nut (A, **Figure 5**) and the lockwasher (B, **Figure 5**).
5. Provide slack in the drive chain by performing the following:
 a. Remove the cotter pin (A, **Figure 6**) and loosen the rear axle nut (B, **Figure 6**). 
 b. Loosen the drive chain adjuster (C, **Figure 6**) on each side of the swing arm.
 c. Push the rear wheel forward to provide slack in the drive chain.
6. Remove the drive chain from the engine sprocket.
7. Slide the engine sprocket off the countershaft.
8. Inspect the engine sprocket as described below.
9. Install by reversing these removal steps. Note the following:

TRANSMISSION AND GEARSHIFT MECHANISMS

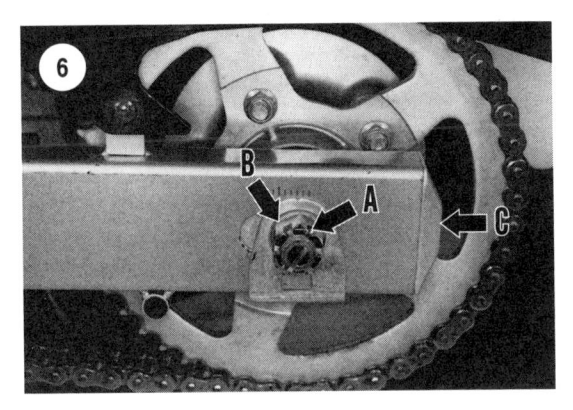

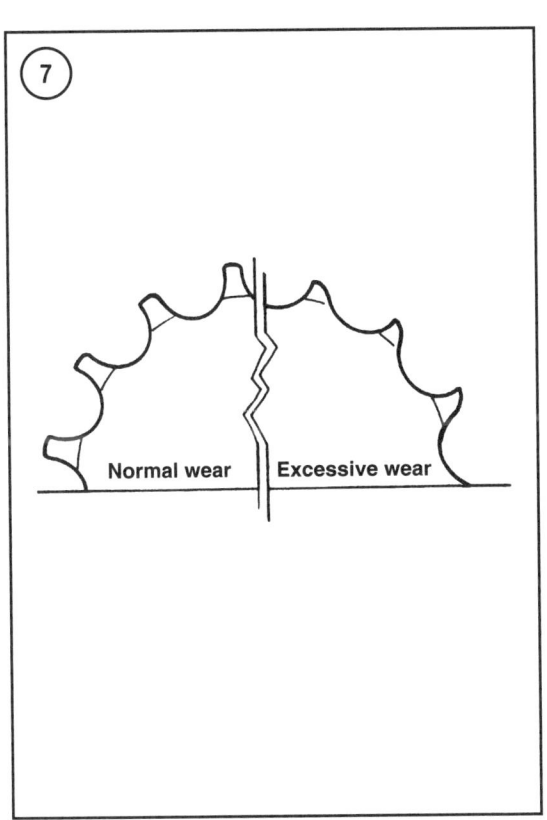

a. Position the drive chain onto the engine sprocket and then slide the sprocket onto the countershaft.
b. Install a *new* sprocket lockwasher.
c. Install the sprocket nut. Tighten the nut to the torque specification in **Table 3**.
d. On 1995-1999 models, tighten the sprocket nut stopper bolt to the torque specification.
e. Adjust the drive chain as described in Chapter Three.

Inspection

Inspect the sprocket teeth (**Figure 7**). If the teeth are visibly worn or undercut, replace the engine sprocket, rear sprocket and drive chain. Never replace any one sprocket or the chain separately. Worn parts will cause rapid wear of the new components.

EXTERNAL GEARSHIFT MECHANISM

The shift ratchet mechanism is located on the right side of the crankcase. The shift lever is subject to a lot of abuse. If the motorcycle has been in a hard spill, the gearshift lever may have been hit and the shift shaft bent. It is very hard to straighten the shaft without subjecting the crankcase halves to abnormal stress. If the shaft is bent enough to prevent it from being withdrawn from the crankcase, there is little recourse but to cut the shaft off with a hacksaw very close to the crankcase. It is much cheaper in the long run to replace the shift shaft than to risk damaging a very expensive crankcase assembly.

Removal

Refer to **Figure 8**.
1. Remove the engine sprocket cover as described in this chapter.
2. Remove the clutch assembly as described in Chapter Six.
3. Remove the snap ring (**Figure 9**) and the washer from the left side of the shift shaft.

NOTE
During operation, residue thrown from the chain collects on the shift shaft end. Clean the exposed end of

EXTERNAL SHIFT MECHANISM

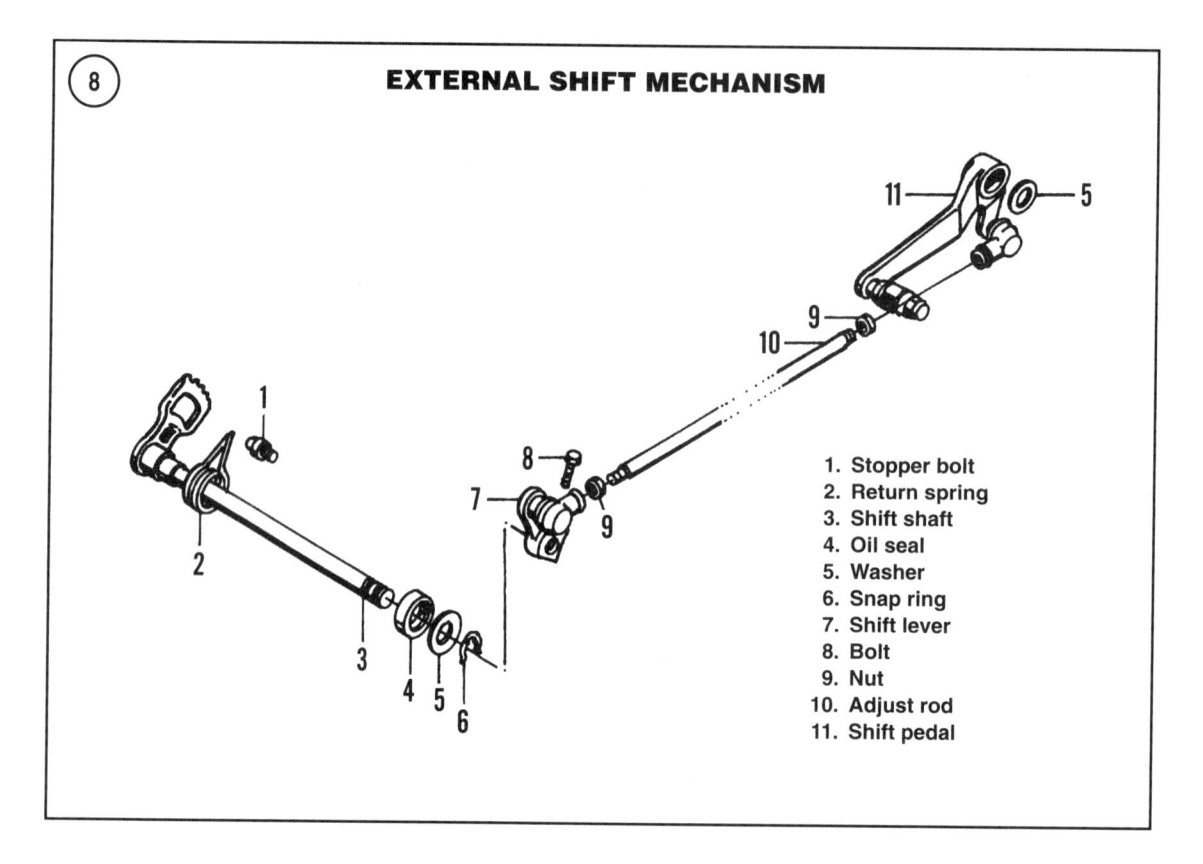

1. Stopper bolt
2. Return spring
3. Shift shaft
4. Oil seal
5. Washer
6. Snap ring
7. Shift lever
8. Bolt
9. Nut
10. Adjust rod
11. Shift pedal

the shift shaft before removing it through the oil seal.

4. Pull the shift shaft (A, **Figure 10**) from the right side of the crankcase. See the information regarding a *bent shift shaft* in the introductory paragraph of this procedure.

5. Remove the screws securing the pawl retainer (A, **Figure 11**), and remove the pawl retainer.

6. Remove the screws securing the cam guide (B, **Figure 11**), and remove the cam guide.

7. Remove the cam gear assembly (**Figure 12**) from the end of the shift drum. Do not lose the pawls, springs and pins in the assembly. Store these small parts in a recloseable plastic bag to avoid misplacing them.

8. Inspect the external shift mechanism as described below.

Installation

1. Compress the spring-loaded shift pawls by hand (**Figure 13**) and install the cam gear assembly into the shift drum as shown in **Figure 12**.

TRANSMISSION AND GEARSHIFT MECHANISMS

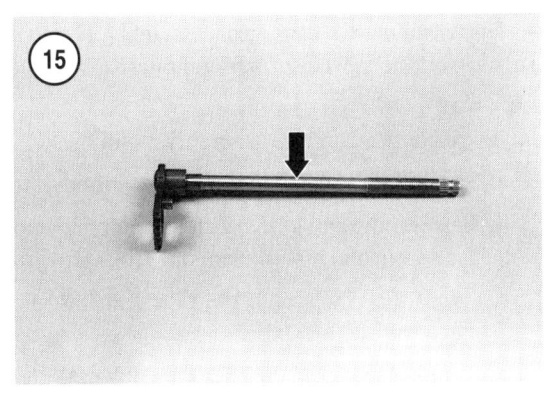

2. Set the cam guide (B, **Figure 11**) into place on the crankcase. Apply a small amount of ThreeBond Threadlock 1342 to the mounting screws and tighten the screws securely.

3. Set the pawl retainer (A, **Figure 11**) into place. Apply a small amount of ThreeBond Threadlock 1342 to the mounting screws and tighten the screws securely.

4. Apply clean engine oil to the shift shaft and slide the shift shaft part way into the crankcase.

5. Align the center of the cam gear with the center of the shift shaft gear (A, **Figure 10**) and then push the shaft assembly all the way into the crankcase. Make sure the arms of the return spring straddle the stopper bolt (B, **Figure 10**) in the crankcase.

6. On the other side of the crankcase, install the washer and the snap ring (**Figure 9**) onto the shift shaft. Make sure the snap ring is correctly seated in the shaft groove.

7. Install the clutch assembly as described in Chapter Six.

8. Install the engine sprocket cover as described in this chapter.

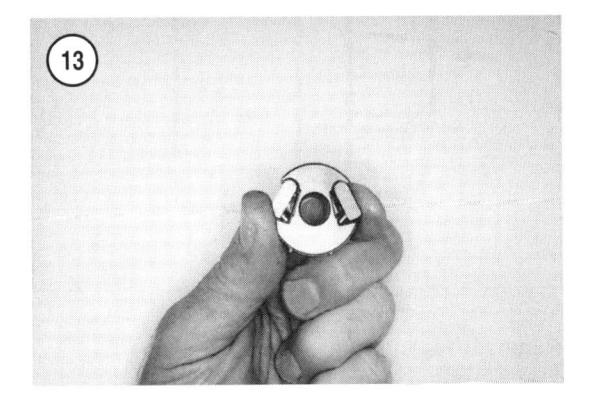

Inspection

1. Inspect the return spring (A, **Figure 14**) on the shift shaft assembly. If broken or weak it must be replaced.

2. Inspect the gear teeth (B, **Figure 14**) on the shift shaft assembly. If a tooth is broken or worn, replace the shift shaft assembly.

3. Inspect the shift shaft assembly (**Figure 15**) for wear or other damage. Make sure it is straight. Replace it if necessary.

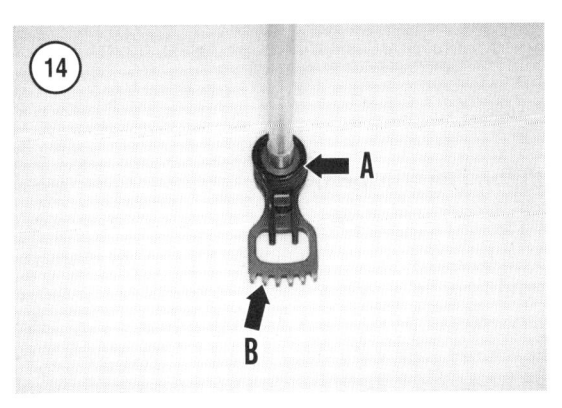

4. Disassemble the cam gear assembly (**Figure 16**). Inspect the pawls, springs and pins for wear or damage.

5. Assemble the cam gear assembly as follows:

   a. Install the springs into the cam gear body.

   b. Position the pawl pins with the rounded end facing out and install them onto the springs.

   c. Install the pawls onto the pins and into the cam gear body.

   d. The pin grooves in the pawls are offset. When the pawls are installed correctly the wider shoulder (A, **Figure 17**) must face toward the outside of the cam gear body.

   e. Hold the pawls in place and place the assembly into an aerosol spray can top.

TRANSMISSION

Servicing the transmission and internal gearshift components requires removing the engine and separating the crankcase as described in Chapter Five. Once the crankcase has been disassembled, the transmission assemblies, shift drum and shift fork assemblies can then be removed from the crankcase.

These overhaul procedures refer to the transmission mainshaft and countershaft. The term mainshaft refers to the transmission input shaft. The mainshaft is connected to the clutch outer housing, which is driven by the primary drive gear on the crankshaft. The term countershaft refers to the transmission output shaft. The countershaft drives the engine sprocket.

NOTE
Suzuki terminology for the transmission shafts is different than most manufacturers. Suzuki refers to the mainshaft (input) as the countershaft and the countershaft (output) as the driveshaft. Most manufacturers, and the procedures in this manual, refer to the input shaft as the mainshaft and the output shaft as the countershaft. Notice that this is opposite of Suzuki's parts information and keep this in mind when ordering replacement parts.

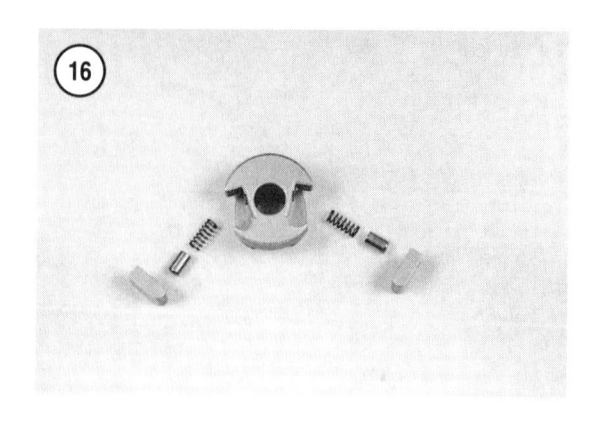

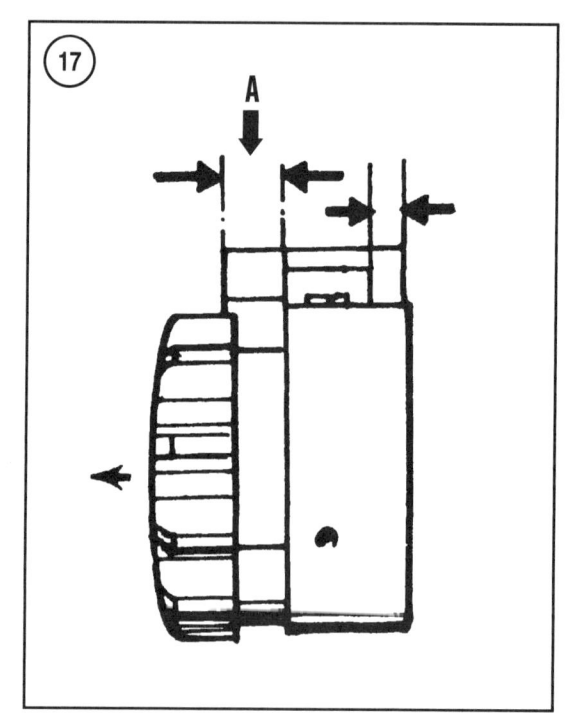

Removal/Installation

Remove and install the transmission mainshaft and countershaft assemblies as described in Chapter Five.

Preliminary Inspection

1. Clean and inspect the assemblies prior to disassembling them. Place the assembled shaft into a large can or plastic bucket and thoroughly clean the assembly with a petroleum-based solvent, such as kerosene, and a stiff brush. Dry the assembly with

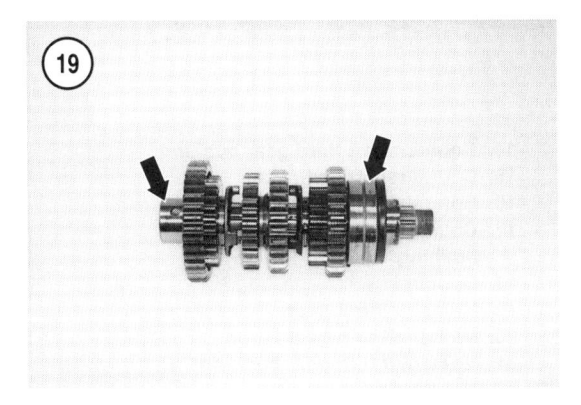

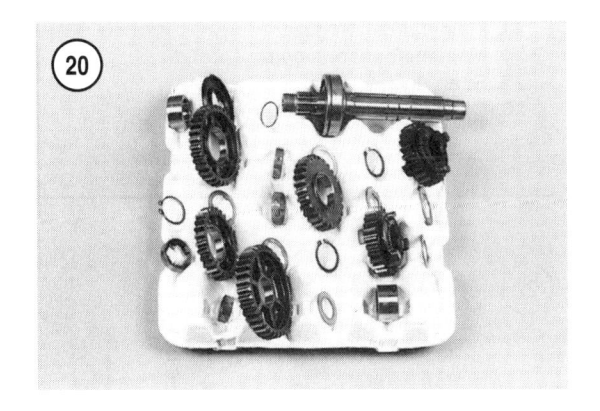

TRANSMISSION AND GEARSHIFT MECHANISMS

2. Carefully check the engagement dogs. If any are chipped, worn, rounded or missing, the affected gear must be replaced.

3. Rotate the transmission bearings by hand. Refer to **Figure 18** and **Figure 19**. Check for roughness, noise and radial play. Replace any bearing that is suspect.

4. Slide the clutch pushrods into the mainshaft and check for binding. If binding occurs, check the pushrods for bending or damage. If they are in good condition, inspect the mainshaft tunnel for debris. Clean out the tunnel if necessary.

5. If the transmission shafts are satisfactory and are not going to be disassembled, apply assembly oil or engine oil to all components and reinstall them into the crankcase as described in Chapter Five.

NOTE
If disassembling a used, high mileage transmission for the first time, pay particular attention to any additional shims not shown in the illustrations or photographs. To compensate for wear, additional shims may have been installed during a previous repair. If the transmission is being reassembled with the old parts, install these shims in their original locations since the shims have developed a wear pattern. If new parts are being used, discard the additional shims.

Transmission Service Notes

1. As each part is removed from the shaft, set it in an egg crate in the exact order of removal and with the same orientation the part had when installed on the shaft. This is an easy way to remember the correct relationship of all parts (**Figure 20**).

2. The snap rings fit tightly on the transmission shafts. It is recommended that all snap rings be replaced during assembly.

3. Snap rings will turn and fold over, making removal and installation difficult. To ease replacement, open a snap ring with a pair of snap ring pliers. At the same time grasp the back of the snap ring with another pair of pliers, and remove the snap ring. Repeat for installation.

compressed air or let it sit on rags to drip dry. Do this for both shaft assemblies.

2. Visually inspect the components for excessive wear. Check the gear teeth for chips, burrs or pitting. Clean up minor damage with an oilstone. Replace any components with damage that cannot be cleaned up.

NOTE
Replace defective gears and their mating gears on the other shaft as well, even though they may not show as much wear or damage.

CHAPTER SEVEN

TRANSMISSION

21

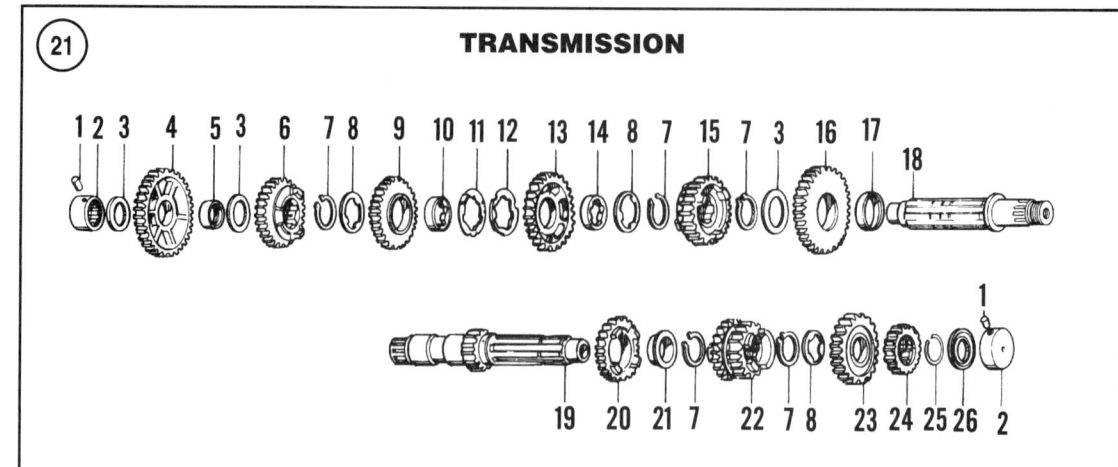

1. Locating pin
2. Needle bearing
3. Thrust washer
4. Countershaft first gear
5. Countershaft first gear bushing
6. Countershaft fifth gear
7. Snap ring
8. Splined washer
9. Countershaft fourth gear
10. Countershaft fourth gear bushing
11. Lockwasher No. 2
12. Lockwasher No. 1
13. Countershaft third gear
14. Countershaft third gear bushing
15. Countershaft sixth gear
16. Countershaft second gear
17. Countershaft second gear bushing
18. Countershaft
19. Mainshaft/first gear
20. Mainshaft fifth gear
21. Mainshaft fifth gear bushing
22. Mainshaft third/fourth combination gear
23. Mainshaft sixth gear
24. Mainshaft second gear
25. Snap ring
26. Oil seal

Countershaft Disassembly

Refer to **Figure 21**.

1. If not cleaned during *Preliminary Inspection*, place the assembled shaft into a large can or plastic bucket. Thoroughly clean it with solvent and a stiff brush. Dry the shaft assembly with compressed air or let it sit on rags to dry.

2. Remove the outer bearing race, needle bearing and thrust washer. Do not lose the locating dowel in the outer bearing race.

3. Slide first gear, first gear bushing and the thrust washer off the countershaft.

4. Slide off the fifth gear.

5. Remove the snap ring and splined washer.

6. Slide off the fourth gear and fourth gear bushing.

7. Slide off the lockwasher No. 2.

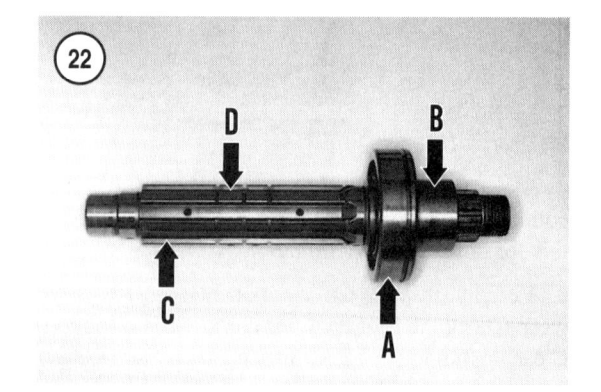

8. Rotate the lockwasher No. 1 in either direction to disengage its tangs from the grooves on the countershaft. Slide off the lockwasher No. 1.

9. Slide off the third gear and third gear bushing.

10. Slide off the splined washer.

TRANSMISSION AND GEARSHIFT MECHANISMS

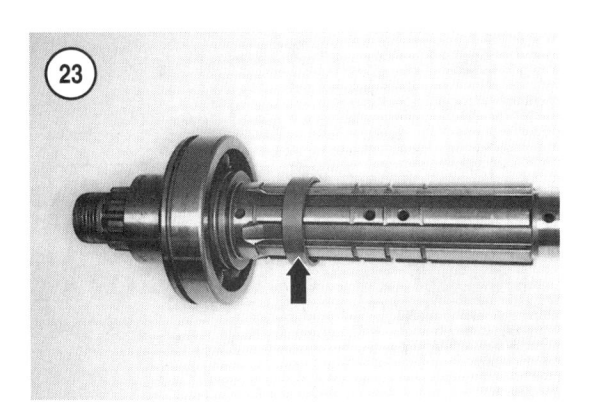

11. Remove the snap ring.
12. Slide off the sixth gear.
13. Remove the snap ring and the thrust washer.
14. Slide off the second gear and second gear bushing.
15. Remove the oil seal and spacer from the other end of the countershaft.
16. If necessary, remove the ball bearing from the countershaft.
17. Inspect the components as described in *Transmission Inspection*.

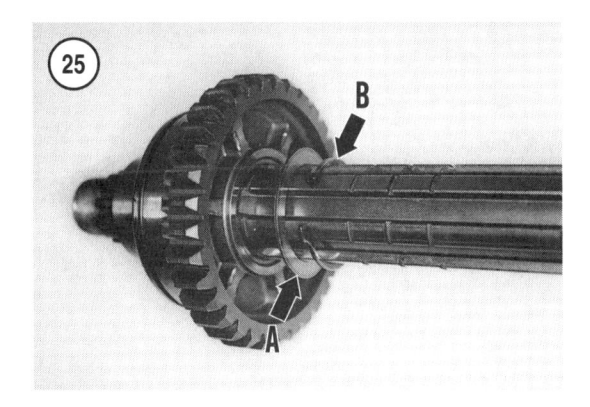

Countershaft Assembly

NOTE
Install new snap rings during assembly to ensure proper gear alignment. Do not expand a snap ring more than necessary to slide it over the shaft.

1. Apply a light coat of molybdenum oil to all sliding surfaces prior to installing any parts.
2. If removed, install the ball bearing (A, **Figure 22**) and the spacer (B, **Figure 22**).
3. Slide second gear bushing (**Figure 23**) onto the countershaft and install second gear (**Figure 24**). The gear's engagement slots should face out, away from the bearing.
4. Install on the thrust washer (A, **Figure 25**) and then the snap ring (B, **Figure 25**). Make sure the snap ring is correctly seated in the circlip groove (**Figure 26**).
5. Install sixth gear (**Figure 27**) so its shift-fork groove faces out, away from second gear.
6. Install the snap ring (A, **Figure 28**) so it is properly seated in the snap ring groove.
7. Install the splined washer (B, **Figure 28**) and the third gear bushing (C, **Figure 28**). Make sure the oil hole in the bushing aligns with the oil hole in the

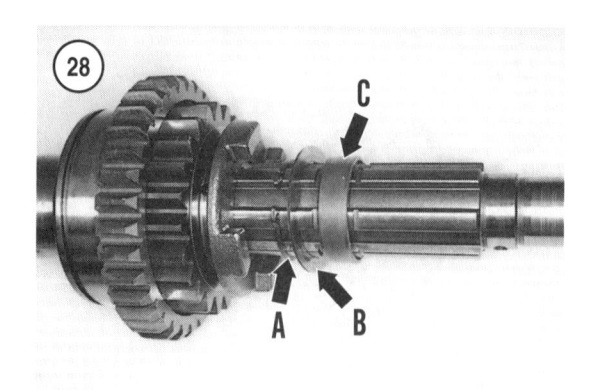

countershaft. These holes must align to ensure proper gear lubrication.

8. Install third gear (**Figure 29**) so its engagement slots face in toward sixth gear.

9. Install lockwasher No. 1 (**Figure 30**). Rotate the lockwasher in either direction so the tangs on the lockwasher engage the grooves in the countershaft (**Figure 31**).

10. Install lockwasher No. 2 (**Figure 32**), and press it into place. The tangs on lockwasher No. 2 should engage the cutouts in lockwasher No. 1 (**Figure 33**).

TRANSMISSION AND GEARSHIFT MECHANISMS

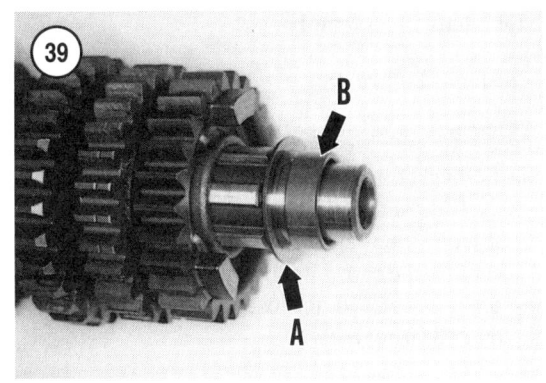

11. Align the oil hole in the fourth gear bushing (A, **Figure 34**) with the oil hole in the countershaft (B, **Figure 34**) and slide the bushing into place. This alignment is necessary for proper gear lubrication.

12. Install the fourth gear (**Figure 35**) so its engagement slots face out.

13. Install the splined washer (A, **Figure 36**) and the snap ring (B, **Figure 36**). Make sure the snap ring is correctly seated in the circlip groove (**Figure 37**).

14. Install fifth gear (**Figure 38**) so its shift fork groove faces in toward fourth gear.

15. Slide on the thrust washer (A, **Figure 39**) and the first gear bushing (B, **Figure 39**).

16. Slide on the first gear (**Figure 40**) so its flat side faces out, away from fifth gear.

17. Install the thrust washer (**Figure 41**) and the needle bearing (**Figure 42**).

18. Apply a light coat of Suzuki Super Grease A to the lips of a *new* oil seal, and install the oil seal (**Figure 43**) onto the other end of the countershaft.

19. Refer to **Figure 44** for correct placement of all gears. Make sure all snap rings are correctly seated in the countershaft grooves.

20. Make sure each gear properly engages an adjoining gear where applicable.

Mainshaft Disassembly

Refer to **Figure 45**.

1. If not cleaned during *Preliminary Inspection*, place the assembled mainshaft into a large can or plastic bucket, and thoroughly clean the assembly with solvent and a stiff brush. Dry with compressed air or let it sit on rags to dry.
2. Remove the cap, outer bearing race, needle bearing and oil seal. Do not lose the locating dowel in the outer bearing race.

> *NOTE*
> *The snap ring is recessed inside the second gear. Steps 3-5 must be performed to expose this snap ring for removal.*

3. Slide the third-fourth combination gear away from the sixth and second gears to expose the snap ring and splined washer.
4. Using angled snap ring pliers, open the snap ring (**Figure 46**), and slide the snap ring and the splined washer away from the sixth and second gears.
5. Slide sixth and second gears toward the third-fourth combination gear and expose the snap ring under the second gear. If necessary, use the sixth and second gears to tap the sixth-gear snap ring and splined washer inward until the circlip is exposed.
6. Remove the circlip (A, **Figure 47**), and remove second gear (B, **Figure 47**).
7. Remove the sixth gear.
8. Remove the splined washer and the snap ring.
9. Slide off the third-fourth combination gear.
10. Remove the snap ring.
11. Slide off the fifth gear and fifth gear bushing.
12. If necessary, remove the ball bearing (A, **Figure 48**) from the mainshaft.
13. Inspect the components as described in *Transmission Inspection*.

Mainshaft Assembly

> *NOTE*
> *The first gear (B, Figure 48) is part of the mainshaft. If the gear is defective, replace the mainshaft.*

1. Apply a light coat of molybdenum oil to all sliding surfaces prior to installing any parts.
2. Install fifth gear onto the mainshaft so the gear's engagement dogs face out, away from first gear (A, **Figure 49**).

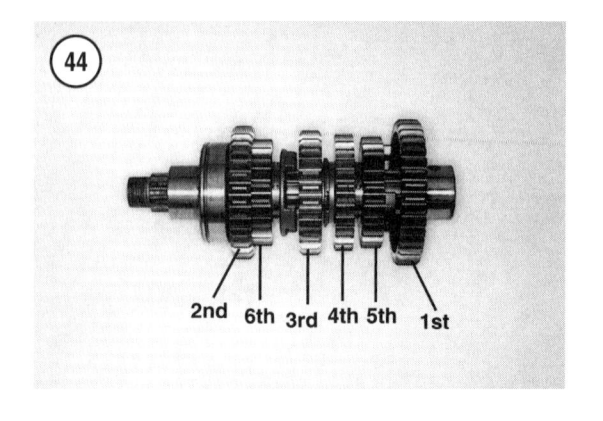

TRANSMISSION AND GEARSHIFT MECHANISMS

⑤ TRANSMISSION

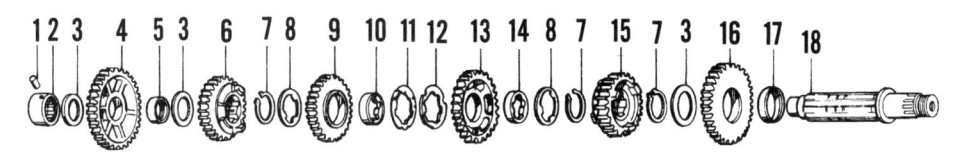

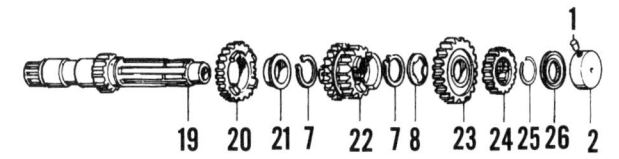

1. Locating pin
2. Needle bearing
3. Thrust washer
4. Countershaft first gear
5. Countershaft first gear bushing
6. Countershaft fifth gear
7. Snap ring
8. Splined washer
9. Countershaft fourth gear
10. Countershaft fourth gear bushing
11. Lockwasher No. 2
12. Lockwasher No. 1
13. Countershaft third gear
14. Countershaft third gear bushing
15. Countershaft sixth gear
16. Countershaft second gear
17. Countershaft second gear bushing
18. Countershaft
19. Mainshaft/first gear
20. Mainshaft fifth gear
21. Mainshaft fifth gear bushing
22. Mainshaft third/fourth combination gear
23. Mainshaft sixth gear
24. Mainshaft second gear
25. Circlip
26. Oil seal

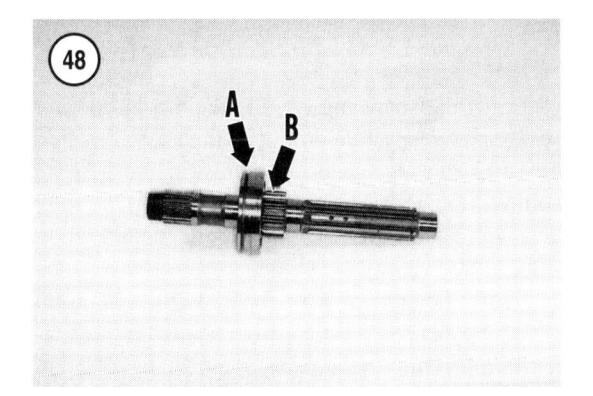

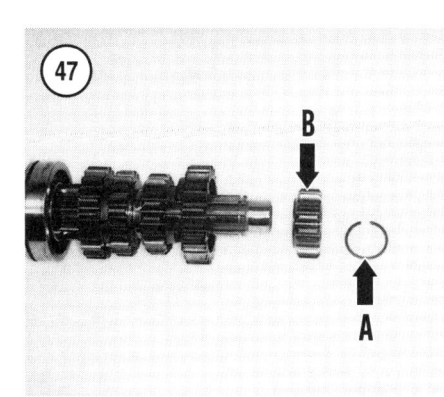

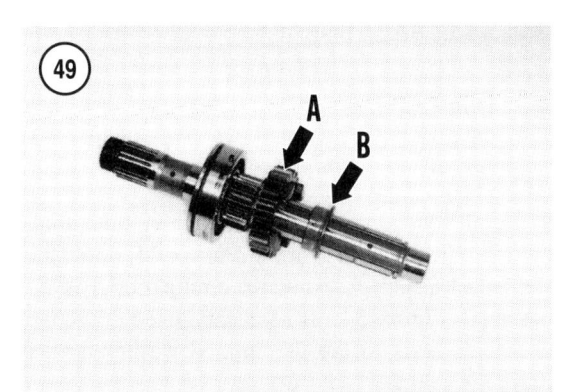

3. Position the fifth gear bushing with the flange side going on last. Slide the fifth gear bushing (B, **Figure 49**) onto the mainshaft and push it all the way into the fifth gear.

4. Install the snap ring so its flat side faces out away from fifth gear. Make sure the snap ring is correctly seated (**Figure 50**) in the snap ring groove.

5. Install third-fourth combination gear with the larger diameter fourth gear (**Figure 51**) going on first.

NOTE
*In Step 6 **do not** seat the snap ring in its respective groove at this time. It will be positioned correctly in Step 13.*

6. Install the snap ring (A, **Figure 52**) but do *not* seat it in its respective groove in the shaft. Position the snap ring so its faces in toward third-fourth combination gear. Move the snap ring *past the snap ring groove* toward the third-fourth combination gear.

7. Install the splined washer (B, **Figure 52**), and slide it up against the snap ring installed in Step 6.

8. Install sixth gear so its engagement dogs face in toward the third-fourth combination gear (**Figure 53**).

NOTE
After the second gear is installed on the shaft, the outermost snap ring groove in the shaft must be exposed.

9. Install second gear with its shoulder side going on first. Slide second gear (A, **Figure 54**) down the shaft toward sixth gear until the circlip groove is exposed (B, **Figure 54**). If necessary, use the second and sixth gears to tap the splined washer farther down the shaft.

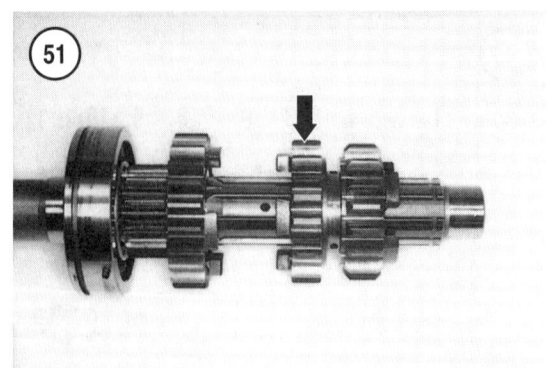

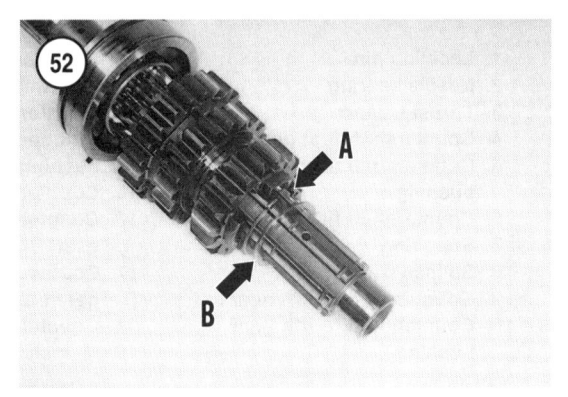

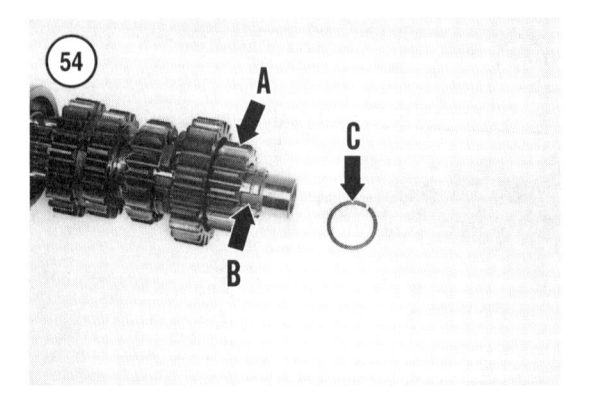

TRANSMISSION AND GEARSHIFT MECHANISMS

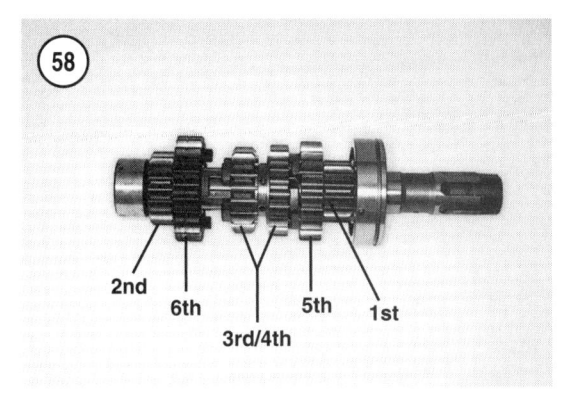

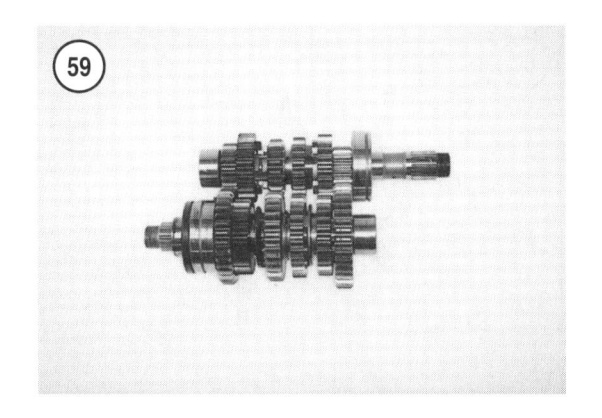

10. Install the circlip (C, **Figure 54**). Make sure it is correctly seated in the mainshaft groove (**Figure 55**).
11. Slide the second and sixth gears against the circlip at the end of the shaft to expose the snap ring and splined washer installed in Step 6.
12. Slide the splined washer toward the sixth gear.
13. Using angled snap ring pliers, move the snap ring into its respective groove. See **Figure 46**. Make sure it is correctly seated in the mainshaft groove.
14. After the snap ring is installed, spin the sixth gear to make sure it rotates correctly and that the splined washer and snap ring are installed correctly. Reposition the snap ring if necessary.
15. Lubricate the oil seal with Suzuki Super Grease A and install the oil seal with the dished side facing out (**Figure 56**).
16. Install the needle bearing (**Figure 57**).
17. Refer to **Figure 58** for correct placement of all gears. Make sure the circlip and snap rings are correctly seated in the mainshaft grooves. Check that each gear properly engages an adjoining gear where applicable.
18. After both transmission shafts have been assembled, mesh the two assemblies together in the correct position (**Figure 59**). Check that each gear properly engages its mate on the opposite shaft. This is the last check prior to installing the shaft assemblies into the crankcase; make sure they are correctly assembled.

Transmission Inspection

NOTE
Replace defective gears and their mating gears on the other shaft as well, even though they may not show as much wear or damage.

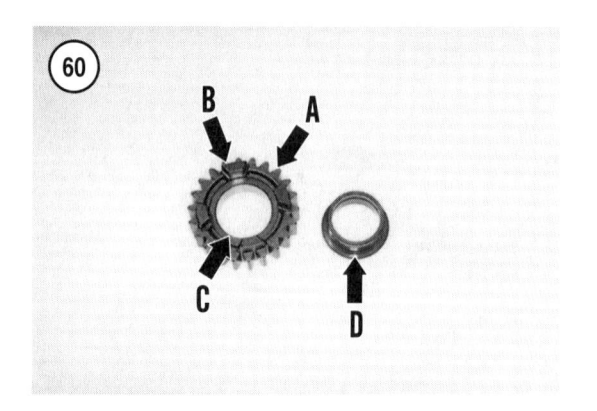

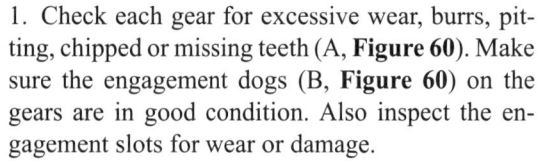

1. Check each gear for excessive wear, burrs, pitting, chipped or missing teeth (A, **Figure 60**). Make sure the engagement dogs (B, **Figure 60**) on the gears are in good condition. Also inspect the engagement slots for wear or damage.
2. On splined gears, check the inner splines (**Figure 61**) for excessive wear or damage. Replace the gear if necessary.
3. On gears with bushings, inspect the inner surface of the gear (C, **Figure 60**) for wear, pitting or damage. Insert the bushing into the gear and check for smooth operation.
4. Check each bushing (D, **Figure 60**) for excessive wear, pitting or damage. Replace any bushing if necessary.
5. On splined bushings, check the inner splines (**Figure 62**) for excessive wear or damage. Replace if necessary.
6. Make sure that all gears and bushings slide smoothly on the shaft splines.
7. Inspect countershaft lockwashers No. 1 and No. 2 (**Figure 63**) for wear, cracks, or damage. Replace if necessary.
8. Inspect the washers for bending wear or damage. Replace if necessary.
9. Check the needle bearing (**Figure 64**). Make sure the needles rotate smoothly with no signs of wear or damage. Replace the needle bearing as necessary.
10. Inspect the ball bearing (A, **Figure 65**). Make sure the bearing rotates smoothly with no binding.
11. Inspect the splines (B, **Figure 65**) and snap ring grooves (C, **Figure 65**) in a shaft. If any are damaged, replace the shaft.
12. Inspect the clutch hub splines (A, **Figure 66**) and clutch nut threads (B, **Figure 66**) on the end of the mainshaft. If any of the splines are damaged, the shaft must be replaced.

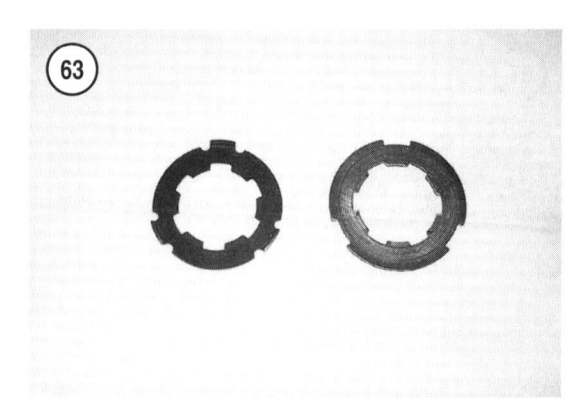

TRANSMISSION AND GEARSHIFT MECHANISMS

INTERNAL SHIFT MECHANISM

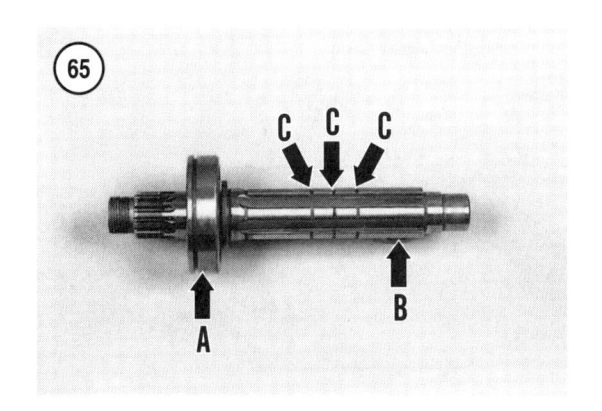

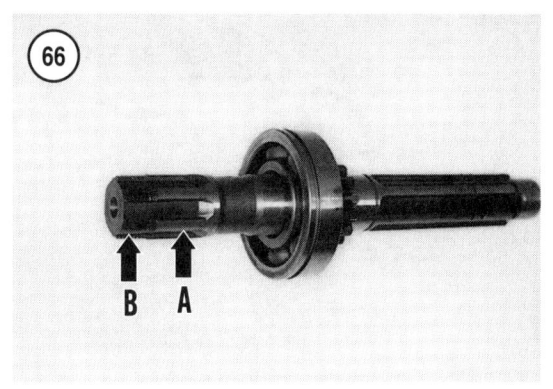

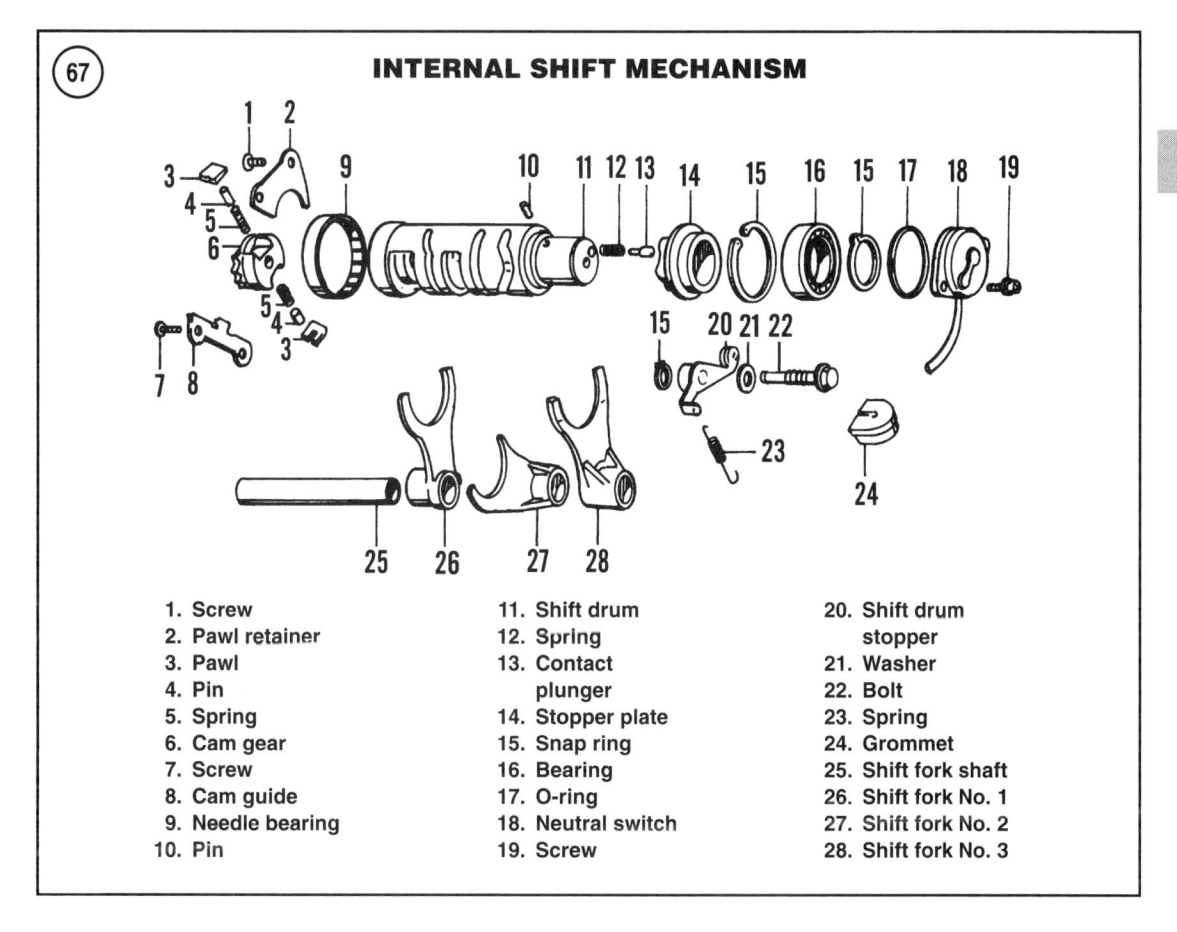

1. Screw
2. Pawl retainer
3. Pawl
4. Pin
5. Spring
6. Cam gear
7. Screw
8. Cam guide
9. Needle bearing
10. Pin
11. Shift drum
12. Spring
13. Contact plunger
14. Stopper plate
15. Snap ring
16. Bearing
17. O-ring
18. Neutral switch
19. Screw
20. Shift drum stopper
21. Washer
22. Bolt
23. Spring
24. Grommet
25. Shift fork shaft
26. Shift fork No. 1
27. Shift fork No. 2
28. Shift fork No. 3

13. Inspect the shift fork-to-gear clearance as described in *Internal Gearshift Mechanism*.

INTERNAL GEARSHIFT MECHANISM

The internal shift mechanism consists of the shift drum and shift forks. To service the internal shift mechanism, it is necessary to remove the engine and split the crankcase as described in Chapter Five.

Removal/Disassembly

Refer to **Figure 67**.

1. Remove the engine and split the crankcase as described in Chapter Five.

2. Remove the transmission assemblies as described in Chapter Five.

3. Remove the external gearshift mechanism as described in this chapter.

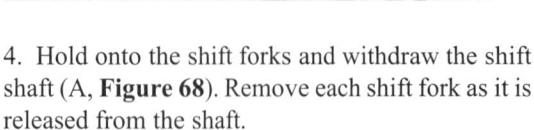

4. Hold onto the shift forks and withdraw the shift shaft (A, **Figure 68**). Remove each shift fork as it is released from the shaft.

5. Turn the crankcase over.

6. Unhook the shift drum stopper spring (A, **Figure 69**) from the boss in the crankcase.

7. Turn the crankcase over.

8. Remove the snap ring (A, **Figure 70**) securing the shift drum stopper (B, **Figure 70**) to the crankcase stud. Remove the shift drum stopper and washer from the stud.

9. If still installed, remove the neutral switch (**Figure 71**) and its O-ring from the receptacle in the crankcase.

10. Remove the switch contact plunger and spring (**Figure 72**) from the end of the shift drum.

11. Remove the snap ring (**Figure 73**) securing the shift drum into the crankcase.

12. Partially withdraw the shift drum (A, **Figure 74**), and remove the stopper plate (B, **Figure 74**) from the end of the drum.

13. Carefully withdraw the shift drum the rest of the way from the crankcase.

14. Thoroughly clean all parts in solvent, and dry them with compressed air.

15. Inspect the internal shift mechanism components as described in *Inspection*.

Assembly/Installation

1. Apply a light coat of engine oil to the shift fork shafts, the inside bores of the shift forks, the shift drum bearing surfaces and to the bearings in the crankcase prior to installing any parts.

2. Make sure the locating pin (**Figure 75**) is in place in the shift drum.

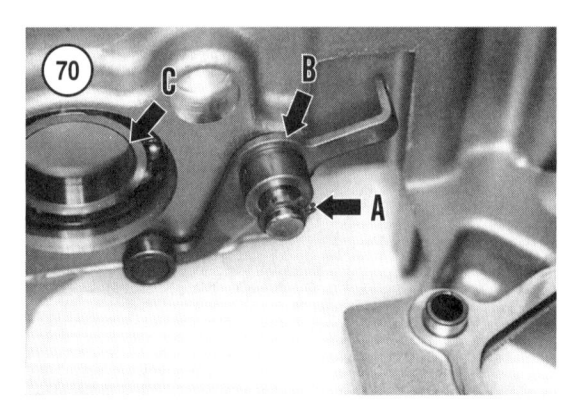

TRANSMISSION AND GEARSHIFT MECHANISMS

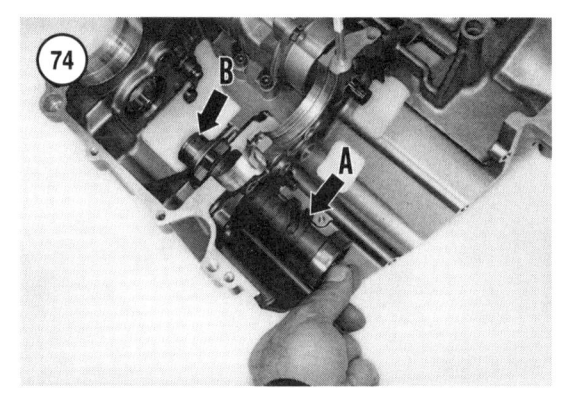

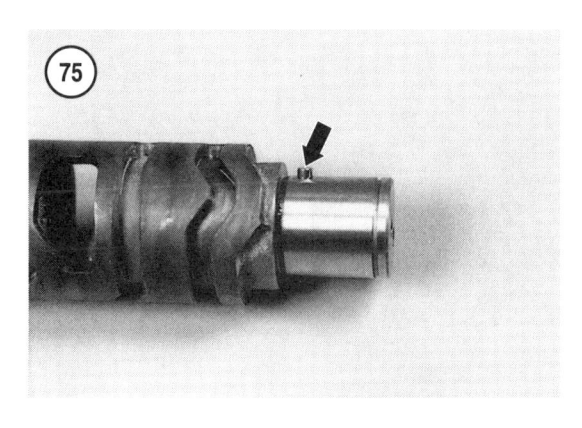

3. Install the shift drum part way into the crankcase (A, **Figure 74**).

4. Position the stopper plate with the flange side going on last and install the stopper plate (B, **Figure 74**). Align the pin groove in the stopper plate with the locating pin in the shift drum (see **Figure 76**) and push the stopper plate onto the drum until the plate bottoms.

5. Push the shift drum the rest of the way into the crankcase until its stops. See **Figure 77**. Make sure the shift drum rotates smoothly with no binding.

6. Install the snap ring (**Figure 73**) securing the shift drum into the crankcase. Make sure the snap ring is correctly seated in the shift drum groove (**Figure 78**).

7. Install the neutral switch contact spring and plunger (**Figure 72**) into the end of the gearshift drum.

8. Install a *new* O-ring into the receptacle in the crankcase and install the neutral switch (**Figure 71**). Tighten the screws securely.

9. Install the washer and shift drum stopper (B, **Figure 70**) onto the crankcase stud. Secure them in place with the snap ring. Make sure the snap ring (A, **Figure 70**) is correctly seated in the groove.

10. If removed, hook the shift drum stopper spring onto the shift drum stopper.

11. Turn the crankcase over.
12. Hook the shift drum stopper spring (A, **Figure 69**) onto the mounting boss in the crankcase.
13. Rotate the shift drum back and forth and make sure the shift drum stopper roller rides correctly on the stopper plate.
14. Rotate the shift drum to the NEUTRAL position and make sure the shift drum stopper roller is correctly seated in the neutral detent of the stopper plate (B, **Figure 69**).
15. Turn the crankcase over.
16. Partially install the shift fork shaft (A, **Figure 68**) into the crankcase.
17. Hold the No. 1 shift fork (B, **Figure 68**) in position and push the shift fork shaft through it. Make sure the fork guide pin engages its respective groove in the shift drum.
18. Hold the No. 2 shift fork (C, **Figure 68**) in position and push the shift fork shaft through it. Make sure the guide pin engages its respective groove in the shift drum.
19. Hold the No. 3 shift fork in position and push the shift fork shaft through it. Make sure the guide pin is indexed into its respective groove in the shift drum.
20. Push the shift fork all the way through each shift fork until the shaft bottoms in the crankcase boss.
21. Make sure the shift fork guide pins are correctly meshed with the grooves in the shift drum (**Figure 79**).
22. The shift fork shaft can slide out of the crankcase at this point. To prevent this from happening, install the external shift mechanism as described in this chapter or temporarily install a spare 6 mm bolt and washer (**Figure 80**).
23. Install the transmission assemblies as described in this chapter.
24. Assemble the crankcase as described in Chapter Five.

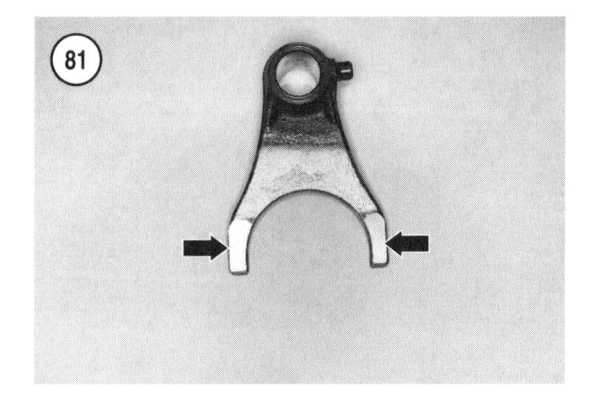

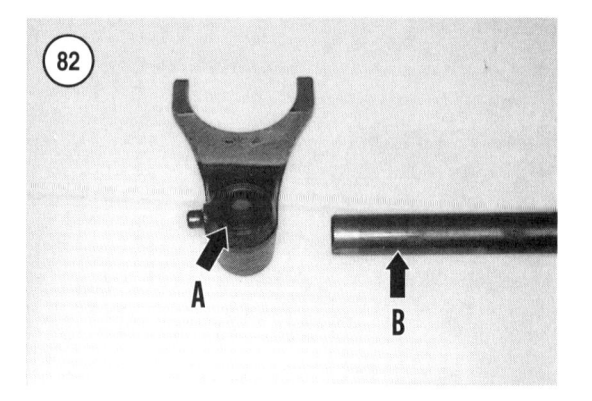

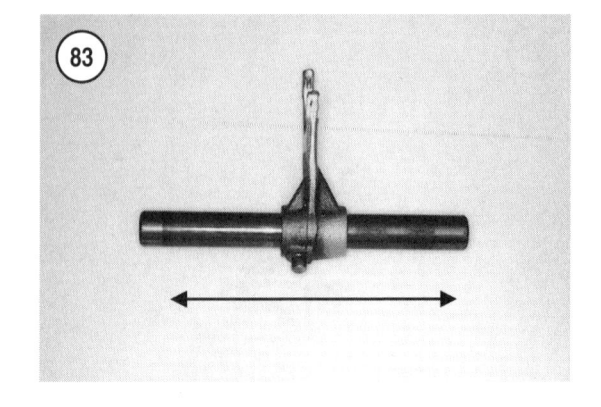

TRANSMISSION AND GEARSHIFT MECHANISMS

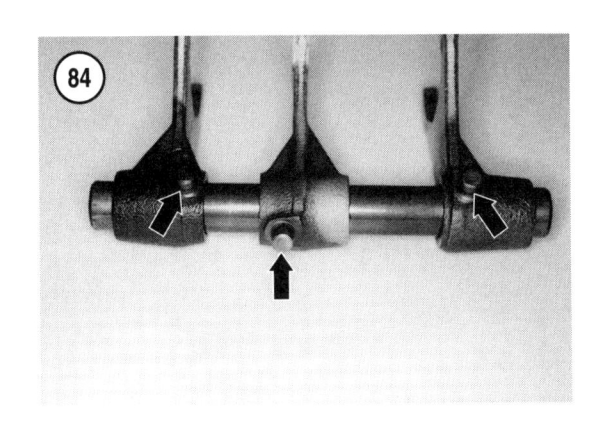

25. Install the engine as described in Chapter Five.

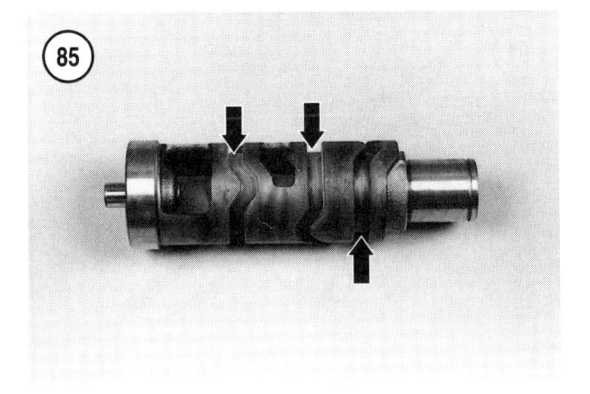

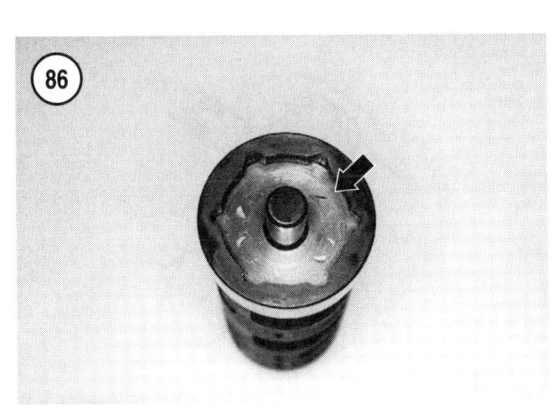

Inspection

Compare any measurements to the specification in **Table 2**. Replace any part that is damaged, worn to the wear limit or out of specification.

1. Inspect each shift fork for signs of wear or cracking. Check for any arc-shaped wear or burned marks on the fingers of the shift forks (**Figure 81**). This indicates that the shift fork has come in contact with the gear. The fork fingers have become excessively worn and the fork must be replaced.

2. Check the bore of each shift fork (A, **Figure 82**) and the shift fork shaft (B, **Figure 82**) for burrs, wear or pitting. Replace any worn parts.

3. Install each shift fork onto the shaft (**Figure 83**) and make sure it moves freely on the shaft with no binding.

4. Check the guide pin (**Figure 84**) on each shift fork for wear or damage. Replace the shift fork(s) as necessary.

5. Roll the shift fork shaft on a flat surface such as a piece of plate glass and check for any bends. If the shaft is bent, it must be replaced.

6. Check the grooves in the shift drum (**Figure 85**) for wear or roughness. If any groove profiles have excessive wear or damage, replace the shift drum.

7. Inspect the cam gear receptacle (**Figure 86**) in the end of the shift drum for wear or damage. Replace the shift drum if necessary.

8. Check the shift drum stopper plate (**Figure 87**) for wear; replace as necessary.

9. Check the neutral switch contact plunger and spring (**Figure 88**) for wear or damage. If the spring has sagged, replace it.

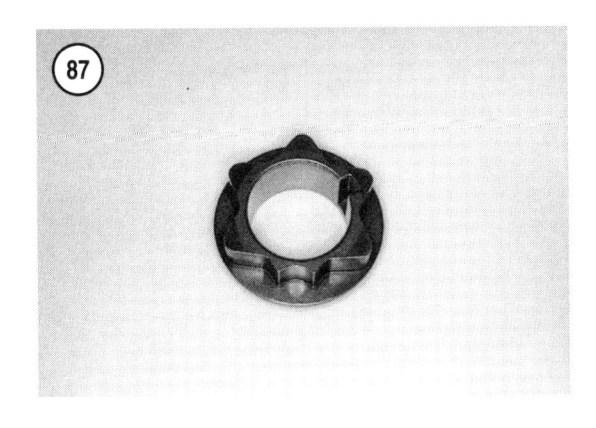

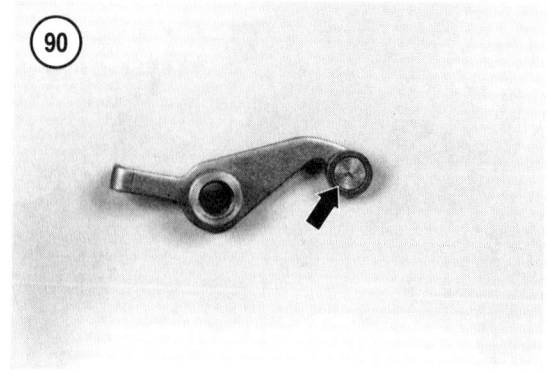

10. Make sure the locating pin (**Figure 75**) fits tightly in the shift drum. If the pin is loose, replace it.

11. Check the shift drum bearings. Refer to C, **Figure 70** and **Figure 89**. Make sure they operate smoothly with no signs of wear or damage. If damaged, replace the bearing as described in Chapter Five.

12. Inspect the roller (**Figure 90**) on the end of the shift drum stopper. If worn or damaged, replace the shift drum stopper.

CAUTION
Replace worn shift forks. Worn forks can cause the transmission to slip out of gear, leading to more serious and expensive damage.

13. Inspect the shift fork-to-gear clearance as follows:

   a. Install each shift fork into the shift fork groove in its respective gear. Use a flat feeler gauge and measure the clearance between the fork and the gear as shown in **Figure 91**.

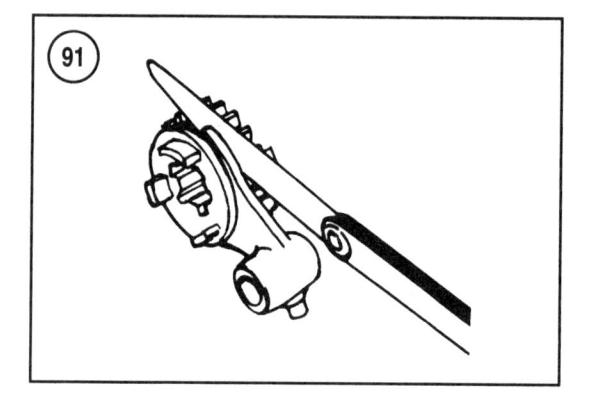

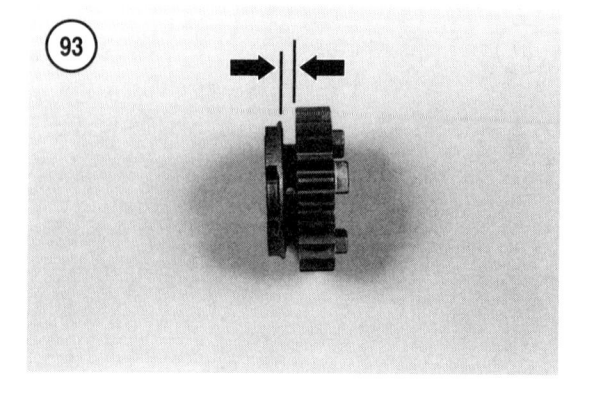

   b. If the clearance is greater than specification, measure the thickness of the shift fork fingers with a micrometer (**Figure 92**). If the thickness is out of specification, replace the shift fork.

   c. If the shift fork thickness is within tolerance, measure the shift fork groove width (**Figure 93**) in each gear. Replace the gear(s) if the groove width is out of specification.

TRANSMISSION AND GEARSHIFT MECHANISMS

Table 1 TRANSMISSION SPECIFICATIONS

Item	Standard
Transmission gear ratios	
First gear	3.083 (37/12)
Second gear	2.062 (33/16)
Third gear	1.647 (28/17)
Fourth gear	1.400 (28/20)
Fifth gear	1.227 (27/22)
Sixth gear	1.095 (23/21)
Primary reduction ratio	1.744 (75/43)
Final reduction ratio	
1995-1999 all models except USA and California	3.133 (47/15)
1996-1999 USA and California models	3.200 (48/15)
2000 models	3.133 (47/15)

Table 2 GEARSHIFT SPECIFICATIONS

Item	Standard mm (in.)	Wear limit mm (in.)
Shift fork-to-groove clearance	0.1-0.3 (0.004-0.012)	0.50 (0.020)
Shift fork groove width		
No. 1 and No. 3 (countershaft fifth and sixth gears)	4.8-4.9 (0.189-0.193)	—
No. 2 (mainshaft third-fourth combination gear)	5.0-5.1 (0.197-0.201)	—
Shift fork thickness		
No. 1 and No. 3	4.6-4.7 (0.181-0.185)	—
No. 2	4.8-4.9 (0.189-0.193)	—
Shift lever height		
1995-1999 models	35 (1.38)	—
2000 models	55 (2.2)	—

Table 3 ENGINE SPROCKET TORQUE SPECIFICATIONS

Item	N•m	in.-lb.	ft.-lb.
Engine sprocket nut	115	—	85
Engine sprocket nut stopper bolt	11	97	—

CHAPTER EIGHT

FUEL, EMISSION CONTROL AND EXHAUST SYSTEMS

This chapter includes service procedures for all parts of the fuel, emission and exhaust systems. Air filter service is covered in Chapter Three.

Refer to **Tables 1-8** at the end of this chapter for carburetor and torque specifications.

The fuel system consists of the fuel tank, the fuel valve, four carburetors and an air filter. The exhaust system consists of a 4-into-1 exhaust pipe and a muffler assembly.

The emission controls consist of crankcase emission system, an evaporative emission control system on California models, as well as the PAIR (Air Supply) System on 1995-1999 California and Switzerland models and on all 2000 models.

CARBURETOR OPERATION

For proper operation, a gasoline engine must be supplied with air and fuel mixed in proper proportions. A mixture with an excessive amount of fuel is said to be rich. A lean mixture is one which contains insufficient fuel. A properly adjusted carburetor supplies the proper air/fuel mixture under all operating conditions.

Each carburetor consists of several major systems. A float and float valve mechanism maintain a constant fuel level in the float bowls. The pilot system supplies fuel at low speeds. The main fuel system supplies fuel at medium and high speeds. A

FUEL, EMISSION CONTROL AND EXHAUST SYSTEMS

CARBURETOR FITTINGS (1995-1999 MODELS)

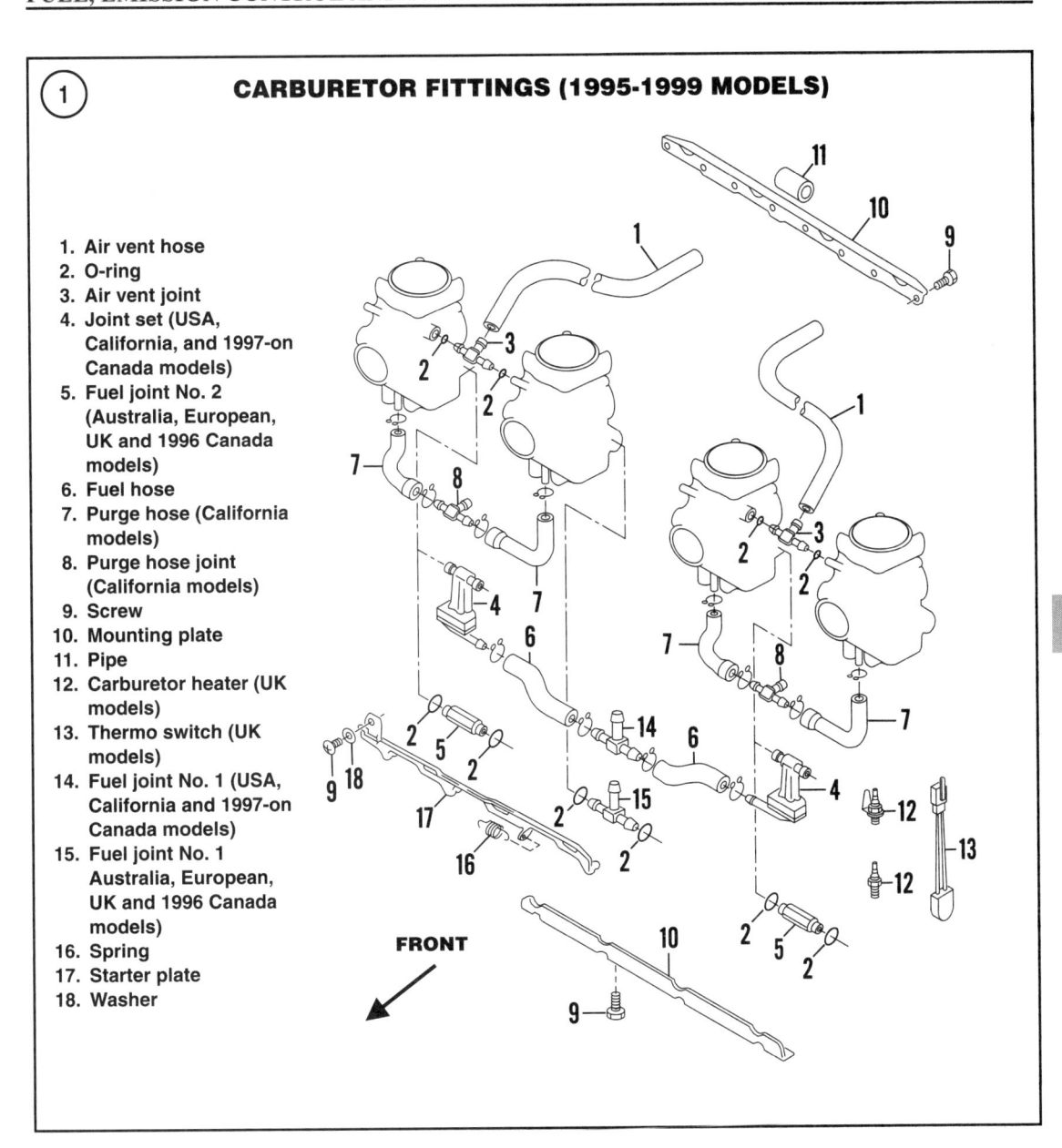

1. Air vent hose
2. O-ring
3. Air vent joint
4. Joint set (USA, California, and 1997-on Canada models)
5. Fuel joint No. 2 (Australia, European, UK and 1996 Canada models)
6. Fuel hose
7. Purge hose (California models)
8. Purge hose joint (California models)
9. Screw
10. Mounting plate
11. Pipe
12. Carburetor heater (UK models)
13. Thermo switch (UK models)
14. Fuel joint No. 1 (USA, California and 1997-on Canada models)
15. Fuel joint No. 1 Australia, European, UK and 1996 Canada models)
16. Spring
17. Starter plate
18. Washer

starter (choke) system supplies the rich mixture needed to start a cold engine.

CARBURETOR SERVICE

If poor engine performance, hesitation and little or no response to mixture adjustment is observed, and all other factors that could affect performance are correct, perform major carburetor service (removal and cleaning) as described in this chapter. Alterations in jet size, throttle slide cutaway and jet needle position should only be attempted by those experienced in this type of tuning work. Do not adjust or modify the carburetors in an attempt to fix a drivability problem caused by another system. Refer to *Carburetor Rejetting* in this chapter.

CARBURETOR ASSEMBLY

Removal/installation

When performing this procedure, refer to **Figure 1** for 1995-1999 models or to **Figure 2** for 2000 models.

CHAPTER EIGHT

CARBURETOR FITTINGS (2000 MODELS)

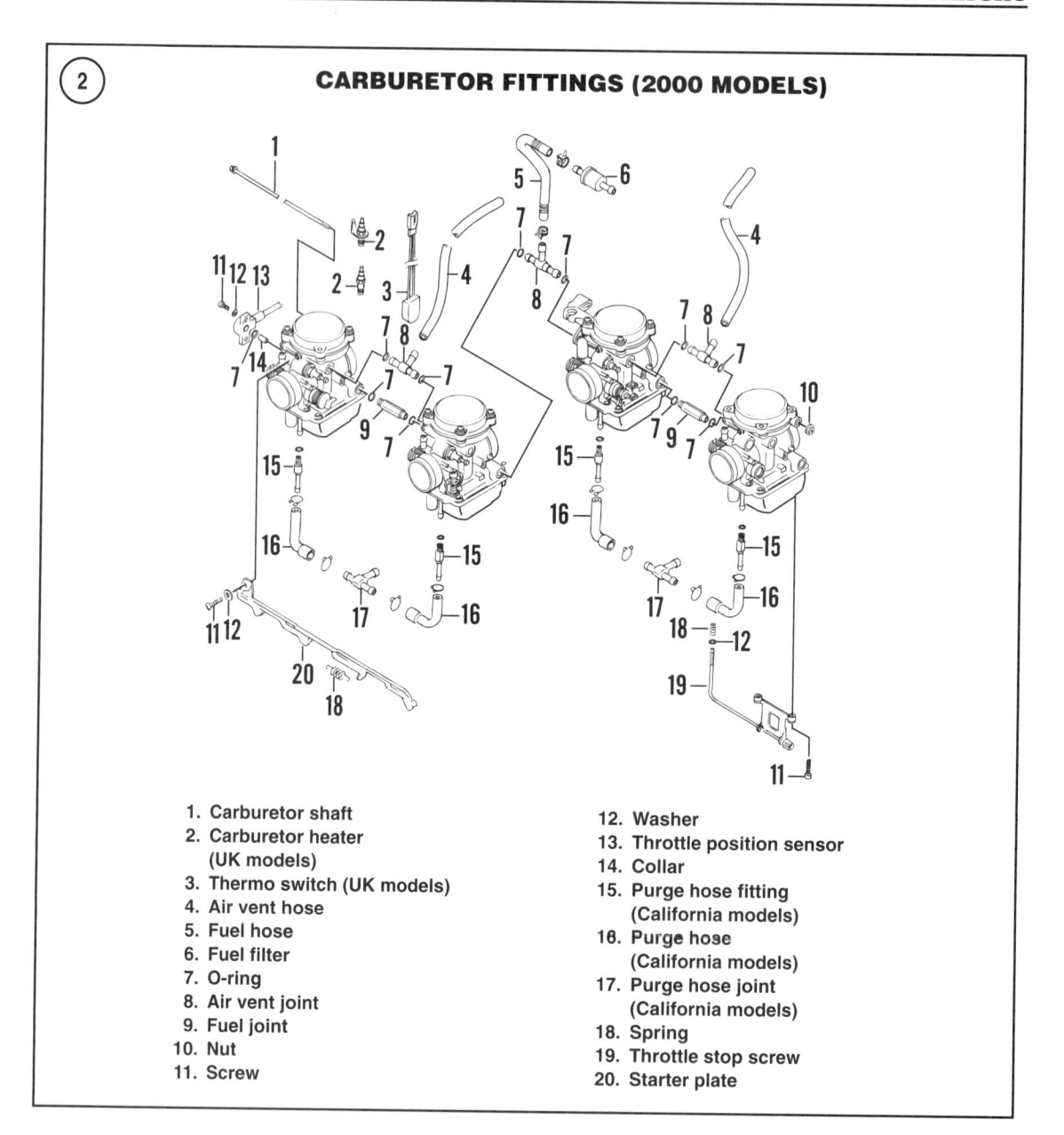

1. Carburetor shaft
2. Carburetor heater (UK models)
3. Thermo switch (UK models)
4. Air vent hose
5. Fuel hose
6. Fuel filter
7. O-ring
8. Air vent joint
9. Fuel joint
10. Nut
11. Screw
12. Washer
13. Throttle position sensor
14. Collar
15. Purge hose fitting (California models)
16. Purge hose (California models)
17. Purge hose joint (California models)
18. Spring
19. Throttle stop screw
20. Starter plate

Remove all four carburetors as an assembled unit.

1. On models with a fairing, remove the fairing as described in Chapter Fourteen.
2. Remove the seat as described in Chapter Fourteen.
3. Remove the fuel tank as described in this chapter.
4. Disconnect the negative battery cable.
5. Remove the left and right air filter housing covers by performing the following:

   a. Remove the mounting screw (**Figure 3**).

FUEL, EMISSION CONTROL AND EXHAUST SYSTEMS

11. Remove the air filter housing mounting screw (B, **Figure 5**) on each side.
12. Move the air filter housing rearward slightly and disengage each air duct from the carburetor inlet.
13. Loosen the carburetor clamp screw (C, **Figure 5**) on each intake manifold.
14. Pull the carburetor assembly rearward and disengage each carburetor from its intake manifold.
15. Drape a heavy towel over the frame and set the carburetor assembly on the towel.
16. Remove the choke cable by performing the following:
    a. Remove the mounting screw (A, **Figure 6**) and lift the choke cable bracket from the starter plate.
    b. Disconnect the choke cable end from the anchor (B, **Figure 6**) on the starter plate.

NOTE
Label the throttle pull and return cables before disconnecting them so they can be reinstalled in the proper position during assembly. When the carburetor assembly is installed in the engine, the pull cable is the rear-most cable. The return cable is the front cable.

17. Disconnect the throttle cable from the throttle wheel by performing the following:
    a. Loosen the return cable locknut (A, **Figure 7**).
    b. Loosen the return cable adjuster (B, **Figure 7**) until there is sufficient slack.
    c. Disconnect the cable end (C, **Figure 7**) from the throttle wheel.
    d. Repeat this procedure for the pull cable.
18. Stuff a clean cloth into each intake duct on the cylinder head to prevent the entry of debris.

CAUTION
Do not try to remove a cover by pulling its top out from the frame. Doing so will break the cover. Disconnect the bottom of the cover from the damper and then lower the cover from the frame pin.

  b. Pull the bottom of the cover out from the frame to disconnect the cover from the rubber damper.
  c. Lower the cover down to disconnect it from the frame pin and remove the cover.
6. Disconnect the crankcase breather hose (**Figure 4**) from the air filter housing.
7. On California models, disconnect each EVAP purge hose from its fitting on the bottom of the carburetor assembly.
8. On 1995-1999 California and Switzerland models and on 2000 models, disconnect the PAIR vacuum hose from the fitting on the No. 3 carburetor.
9. On 2000 models, disconnect the throttle position sensor electrical lead.
10. Loosen the carburetor clamp screw (A, **Figure 5**) on each air duct from the air filter housing.

CHAPTER EIGHT

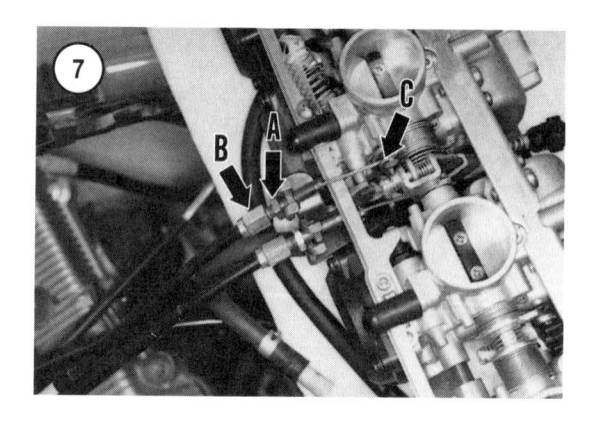

CARBURETOR

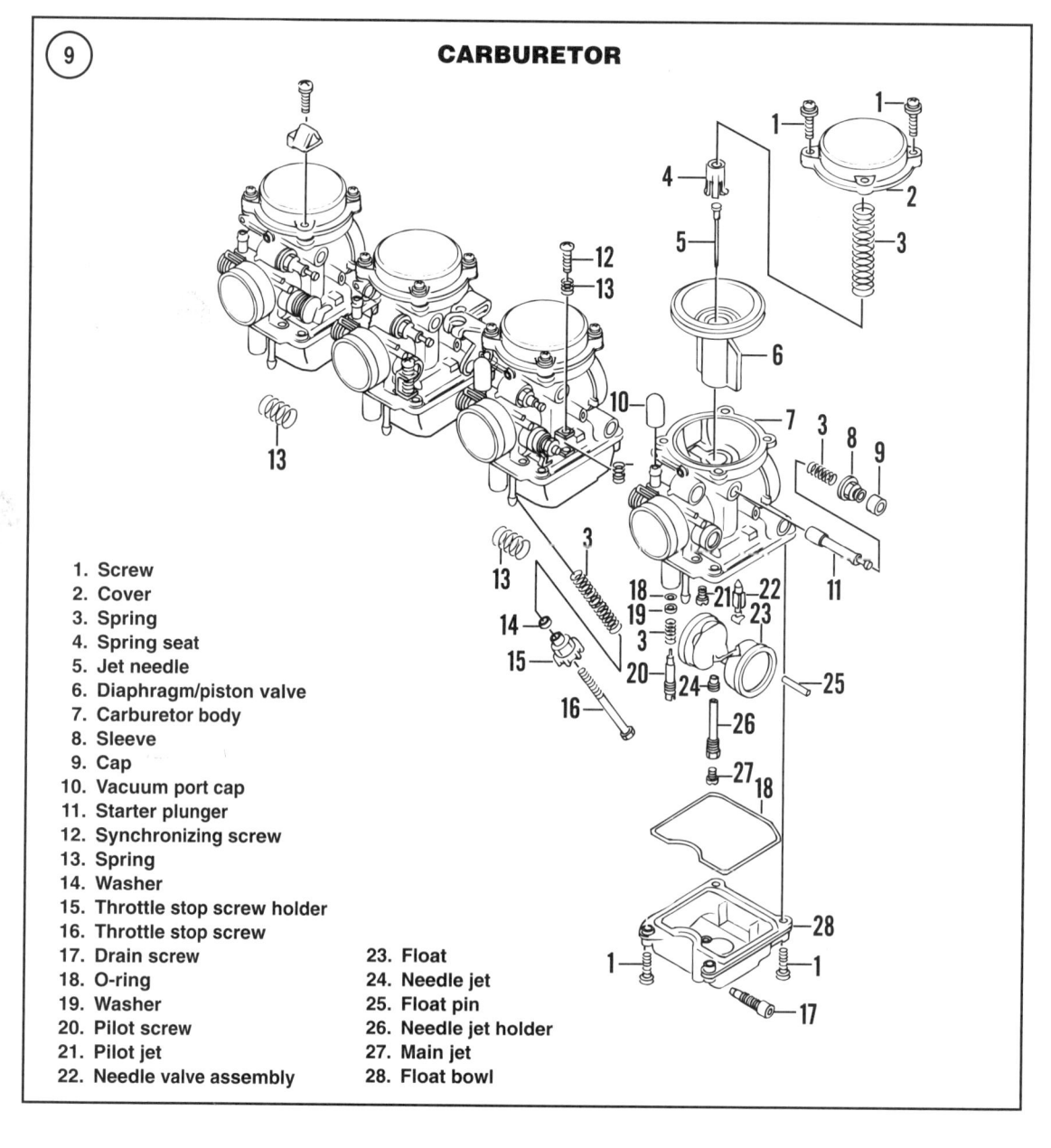

1. Screw
2. Cover
3. Spring
4. Spring seat
5. Jet needle
6. Diaphragm/piston valve
7. Carburetor body
8. Sleeve
9. Cap
10. Vacuum port cap
11. Starter plunger
12. Synchronizing screw
13. Spring
14. Washer
15. Throttle stop screw holder
16. Throttle stop screw
17. Drain screw
18. O-ring
19. Washer
20. Pilot screw
21. Pilot jet
22. Needle valve assembly
23. Float
24. Needle jet
25. Float pin
26. Needle jet holder
27. Main jet
28. Float bowl

FUEL, EMISSION CONTROL AND EXHAUST SYSTEMS

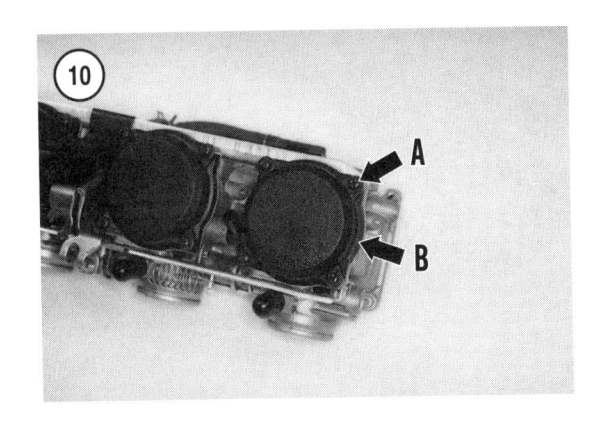

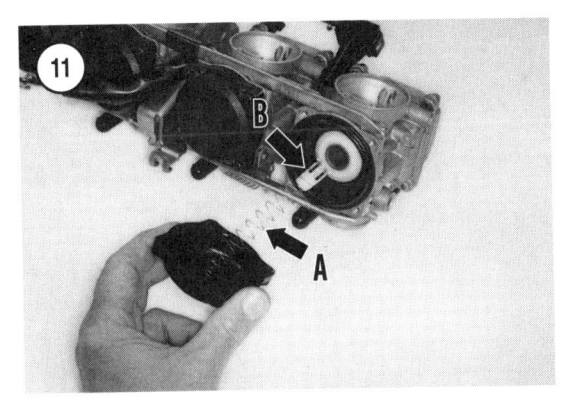

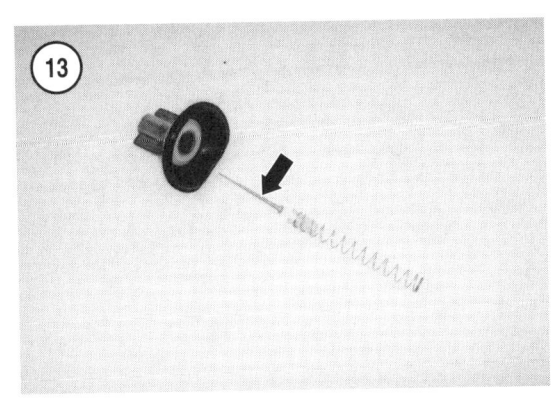

CAUTION
*The tip of the pilot screw extends into the bore on the engine side of each carburetor. See **Figure 8**. The exposed tips are fragile and can easily be broken. Handle the carburetors carefully so the pilot screws are not damaged.*

19. Install by reversing these removal steps. Pay attention to the following:

   a. Make sure the carburetors are fully seated forward in the intake manifolds on the cylinder head. A solid bottoming out will be felt when they are correctly seated.
   b. Make sure each carburetor clamp screw is tight to avoid a vacuum leak and possible valve damage due to a lean fuel mixture.
   c. Adjust the throttle cable and choke cable as described in Chapter Three.

CARBURETOR

Individual Carburetor Disassembly

NOTE
*The throttle position sensor is preset by the manufacturer. Do not remove it. If removal is necessary, make an alignment mark on the sensor relating to the centerline of the mounting screws. Make corresponding alignment marks on the carburetor body so the sensor can be precisely installed **in the same position**.*

Disassemble only one carburetor at a time to prevent accidental interchange of parts. Refer to **Figure 9** for this procedure.

1. Remove the top-cover screws (A, **Figure 10**), and remove the cover (B, **Figure 10**). Watch for the spring (A, **Figure 11**) and spring seat (B, **Figure 11**) beneath the cover.
2A. On 1995-1999 models, remove the spring and spring seat (**Figure 11**).
2B. On 2000 models, remove the spring.
3. Remove the diaphragm/piston valve (**Figure 12**) from the carburetor.
4A. On 1995-1999 models, remove the jet needle (**Figure 13**) from the diaphragm/piston valve.
4B. On 2000 models, disassemble the diaphragm/piston valve by performing the following:

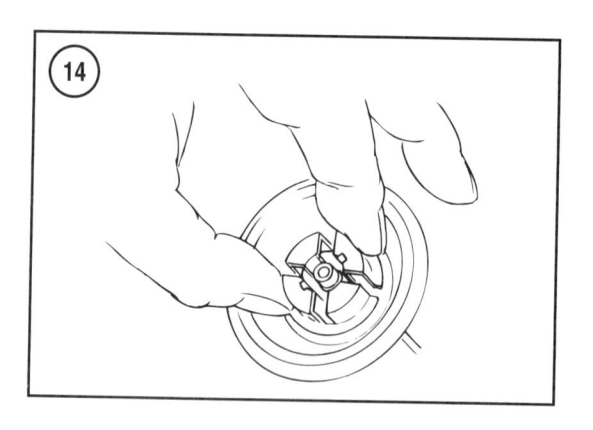

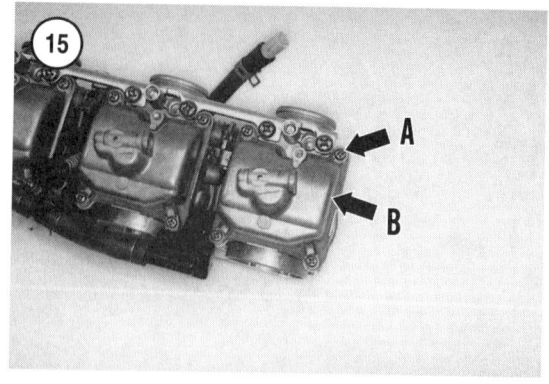

a. Squeeze the opposing tangs on the jet needle stopper (**Figure 14**) and remove the stopper from the diaphragm/piston valve.

b. Remove the jet needle and two washers. One washer is thicker than the other. Note the relative positions of these washers. They must be reinstalled in their original positions.

5. Remove the float bowl screws (A, **Figure 15**), and remove the float bowl (B, **Figure 15**) and float bowl O-ring (**Figure 16**). Make sure a new O-ring is installed during assembly.

6. Carefully remove the float pivot pin (**Figure 17**) from the posts in the carburetor body.

7. Remove the float assembly by carefully pulling it straight up. Do not lose the needle valve (A, **Figure 18**) hanging from the float tang.

8A. On U.S.A., California, Canada and some European models, the pilot screw assembly is located under a plug (A, **Figure 19**) that should not to be removed. If removal is necessary, refer to *Pilot Screw* later in this chapter.

8B. On models without a pilot-screw plug, screw the pilot screw in until it *lightly seats* while counting and recording the number of turns. The pilot screw must be reinstalled to this same position during assembly. Unscrew and remove the pilot screw, spring, washer and O-ring.

9. Unscrew and remove the pilot jet (B, **Figure 19**).

10. On 2000 models, remove the starter jet (C, **Figure 19**).

11. Remove the main jet (**Figure 20**) from the end of the needle jet holder.

12. Remove the needle jet holder (**Figure 21**).

13. Remove the needle jet (**Figure 22**). Note that the needle jet has a convex and a concave end. The convex end of the needle jet faces the top of the car-

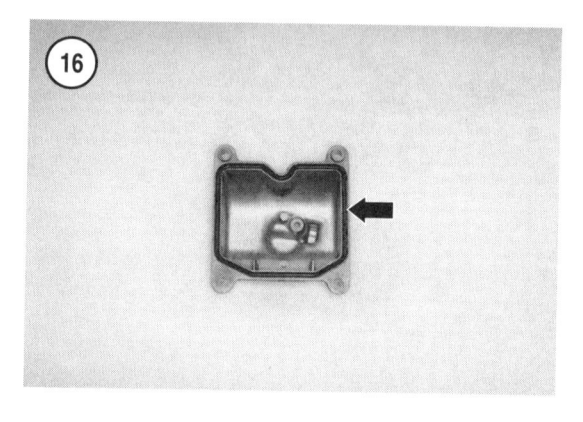

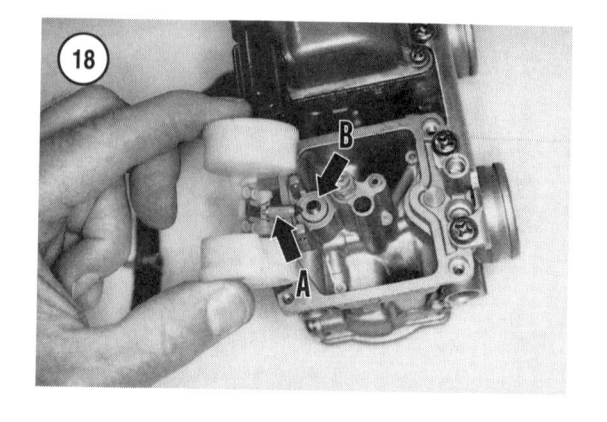

FUEL, EMISSION CONTROL AND EXHAUST SYSTEMS

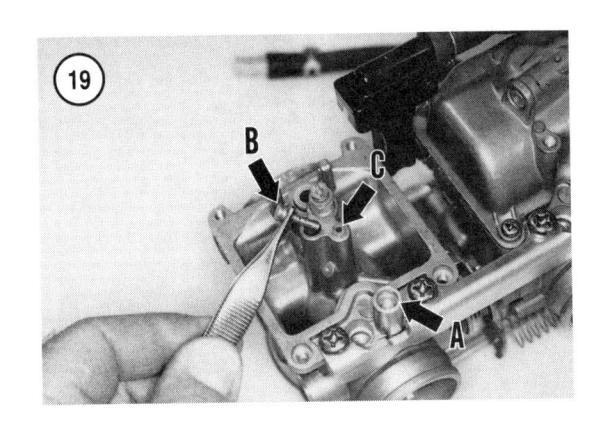

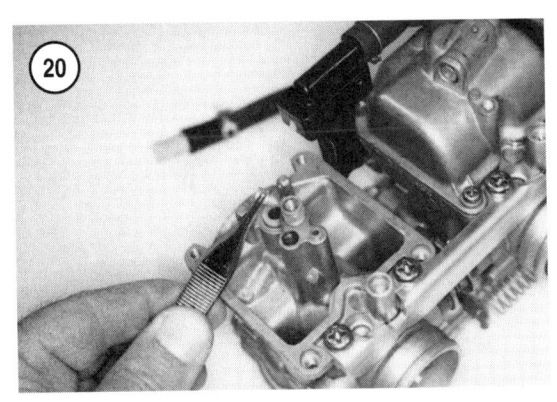

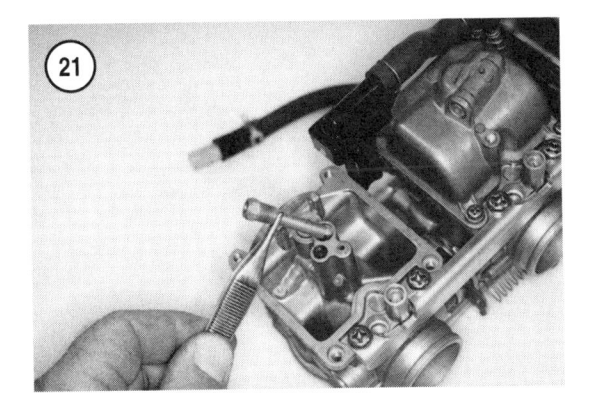

buretor. The needle jet will have to be reinstalled with this same orientation during assembly.

NOTE
*Further disassembly is neither necessary nor recommended. Do not remove the throttle shaft and butterfly assemblies (**Figure 23**). If these parts are damaged, the carburetor will have to be replaced, as these items are not available separately.*

14. Clean and inspect all parts as described in this chapter.

15. Assemble the carburetor by reversing these disassembly steps while noting the following:

   a. Install the needle jet (**Figure 22**) so its convex end faces up toward the top of the carburetor.
   b. On 2000 models, make sure the washer and E-clip are installed in place on the jet needle.
   c. Install the diaphragm/piston valve into the carburetor body so the side with the detent (**Figure 12**) faces the air filter housing side of the carburetor. Make sure the diaphragm is seated in the carburetor body (**Figure 24**).

d. Install the spring and top cap. Before installing the top cover screws, insert a finger into the venturi and move the piston valve (**Figure 25**) up. The piston valve should rise all the way up into the bore and slide back down immediately with no binding. If it binds or if the movement is sluggish, chances are the diaphragm did not seat correctly or the spring is not centered.

e. When installing the float bowl, install a *new* O-ring.

f. Check and adjust the float height as described in this chapter.

g. After the assembly and installation are completed, adjust the carburetors as described in this chapter and in Chapter Three.

Cleaning and Inspection

CAUTION
The carburetor bodies are equipped with plastic parts that cannot be removed. Do not dip the carburetor body, O-rings, float assembly, needle valve or piston valve/diaphragm into carburetor cleaner or other harsh solutions that can damage these parts. Suzuki does not recommend the use of a caustic carburetor cleaning solvent. Instead, clean the carburetors and related parts in a petroleum-based solvent.

1. Initially clean all parts in a mild petroleum-based cleaning solution. Wash the parts in hot soap and water, and rinse them with cold water. Blow dry the parts with compressed air.

CAUTION
*If compressed air is not available, allow the parts to air dry or use a clean lint-free cloth. Do **not** use a paper towel to dry carburetor parts. The small paper particles could plug openings in the carburetor housing or jets.*

2. Allow the carburetors to dry thoroughly before assembly. Blow out the jets and the needle jet holder with compressed air.

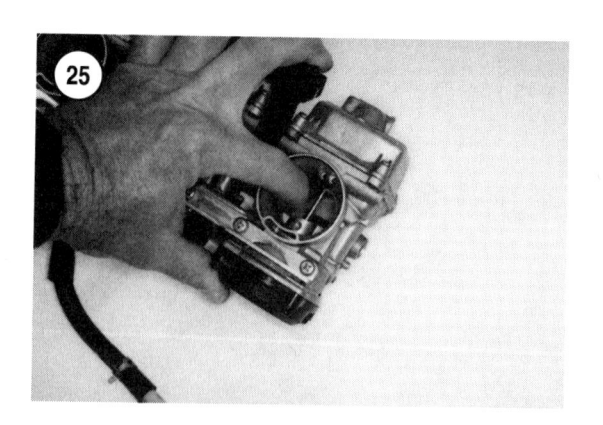

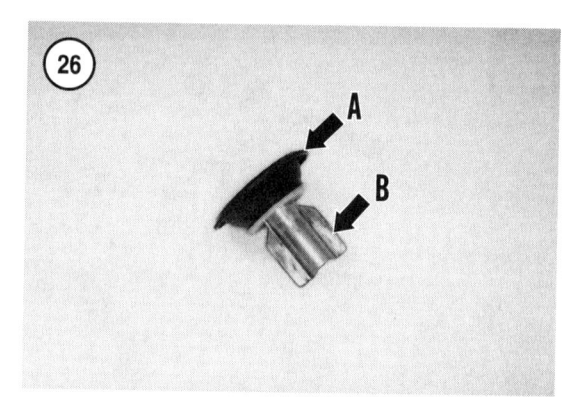

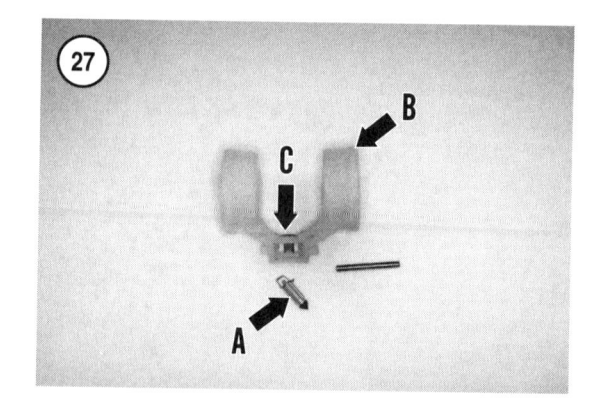

CAUTION
*Do **not** use wire or drill bits to clean jets. Even minor gouges in a jet can alter flow rate and change the air/fuel mixture.*

3. Make sure the drain screw is in good condition and does not leak. Replace the drain screw if necessary.

4. Inspect the diaphragm (A, **Figure 26**) for cracks, deterioration or other damage. Check the piston valve sides (B, **Figure 26**) for excessive wear. In-

FUEL, EMISSION CONTROL AND EXHAUST SYSTEMS

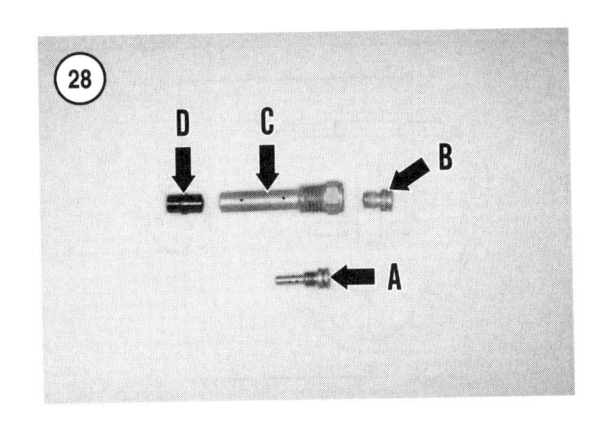

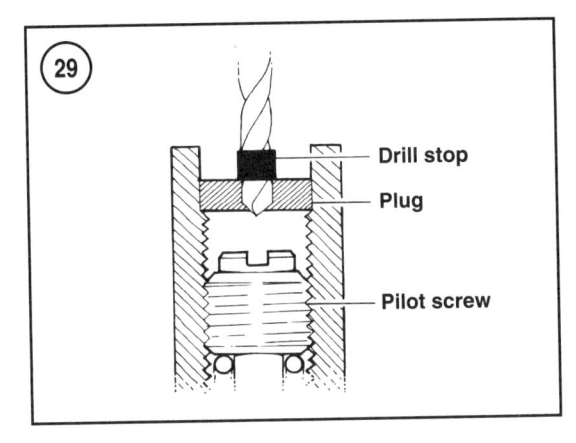

28

D C B A

29

- Drill stop
- Plug
- Pilot screw

stall the piston valve into the carburetor body and move it up and down in the bore. The piston valve should move smoothly with no binding or excessive play. Replace the piston valve and/or carburetor if necessary.

5. Inspect the tapered end of the needle valve for steps, uneven wear or other damage (A, **Figure 27**).
6. Inspect the needle valve seat (B, **Figure 18**) for steps, uneven wear or other damage. Insert the needle valve into the valve seat and slowly move it back and forth, checking for smooth operation. If either part is worn or damaged, replace both parts as a pair for maximum performance.
7. Inspect the float (B, **Figure 27**) for deterioration or damage. Place the float in a container of water and push it down. If the float sinks or if bubbles appear (indicating a leak), the float must be replaced.
8. Inspect the pilot jet (A, **Figure 28**), main jet (B), needle jet holder (C) and needle jet. Make sure all holes are open and no part is worn or damaged. Replace the worn or unserviceable parts.
9. On 2000 models, inspect the jet needle stopper assembly (**Figure 14**) for deterioration or damage.

10. Inspect the jet needle taper (**Figure 13**) for steps, uneven wear or other damage. On 2000 models, make sure the E-clip is securely in place.
11. If removed, inspect the pilot screw O-ring. Replace the O-ring if it has become hard or is starting to deteriorate.
12. Make sure all openings in the carburetor housing are clear. Clean them out if they are plugged in any way and then apply compressed air to all openings.
13. Check the top cover for cracks or damage and replace it if necessary.
14. Make sure the screws in the throttle plate (**Figure 23**) are tight.
15. Inspect the carburetor body for internal or external damage. If damaged, replace the carburetor assembly. The body cannot be replaced separately.
16. Move the throttle wheel back and forth from stop to stop. The throttle lever should move smoothly and return under spring tension. If it does not move freely or if it sticks in any position, replace the carburetor.

PILOT SCREW

Removal/Installation (U.S.A., California, Canada and some European Models)

The pilot screws on these models are sealed. A plug has been installed at the top of the pilot screw bore to prevent routine adjustment. The pilot screw does not require adjustment unless the carburetor is overhauled, the pilot screw has been incorrectly adjusted or a pilot screw requires replacement. The following procedure describes how to remove and install the pilot screw in these models.

1. Set a stop 6 mm from the end of a 1/8 inch drill bit. See **Figure 29**.
2. Carefully drill a hole in the plug at the top of the pilot screw bore on the carburetor body as shown in **Figure 29**. Do not drill too deeply. The pilot screw will be difficult to remove if the head is damaged.
3. Screw a sheet metal screw into the plug, and pull the plug from the bore.
4. Screw the pilot screw in until it *lightly seats*, while counting and recording the number of turns. The pilot screw must be reinstalled in the same position during assembly.
5. Remove the pilot screw, spring, washer and O-ring from the carburetor body.

8

6. Inspect the O-ring at the end of the pilot screw. Replace the screw and/or O-ring if damaged or worn (grooved).
7. Install the pilot screw in the same position noted during removal Step 3 or to the specification listed in the appropriate table.
8. Install new plugs by tapping them into place with a punch.
9. Repeat this procedure for the other carburetors, if necessary. Make sure to keep components from each carburetor separate.

THROTTLE POSITION SENSOR (2000 MODELS)

Inspection

1. Remove the fuel tank as described in this chapter.
2. Disconnect the electrical connector from the throttle position sensor.
3. Set an ohmmeter to the R × 1 k scale. If using an analog meter, calibrate the meter as described in Chapter One.
4. With the throttle lever fully-closed, measure the resistance across the two terminals on the sensor side of the connector as shown in **Figure 30**.
5. Replace the throttle position sensor if the resistance does not equal the fully-closed specification listed in **Table 7**.

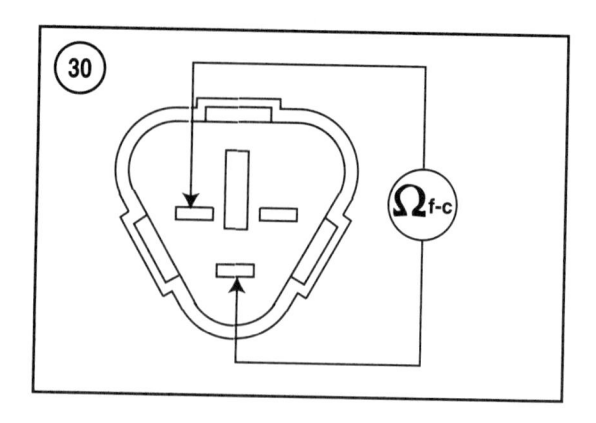

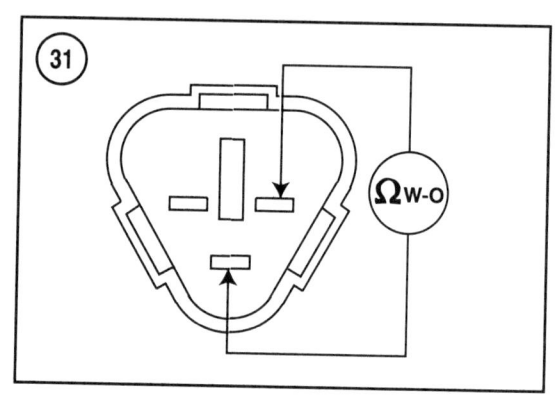

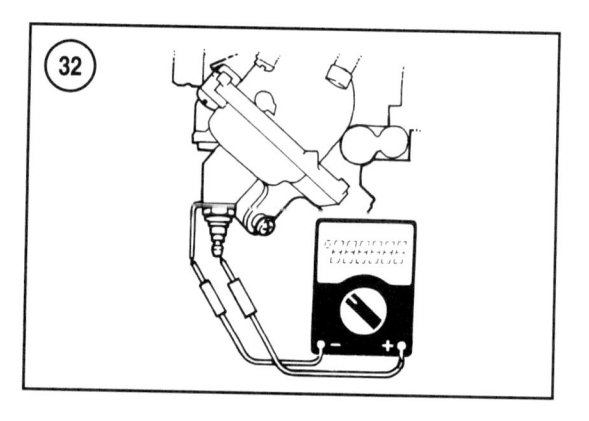

Adjustment

1. Remove the carburetor assembly as described in this chapter.
2. Set an ohmmeter to the R × 1 k scale. If using an analog meter, calibrate the meter as described in Chapter One.
3. With the throttle lever fully-closed, measure the resistance across the two terminals on the sensor side of the connector as shown in **Figure 30**. The resistance should equal the fully-closed resistance specified in **Table 7**.
4. Use the throttle lever to fully open the throttle.
5. While holding the throttle in the wide-open position, measure the resistance across the two terminals in the sensor side of the connector as shown in **Figure 31**. This value should equal the wide-open resistance specification in **Table 7**.
6. If the wide-open resistance is not within the specified value, loosen the mounting screws on the throttle position sensor. Slightly rotate the sensor until the wide-open resistance is within specification, and then tighten the sensor mounting screws securely.

CARBURETOR HEATER (UK MODELS)

Removal/Installation

1. Remove the carburetor assembly as described in this chapter.
2. Disconnect the electrical lead from the carburetor heater.

FUEL, EMISSION CONTROL AND EXHAUST SYSTEMS

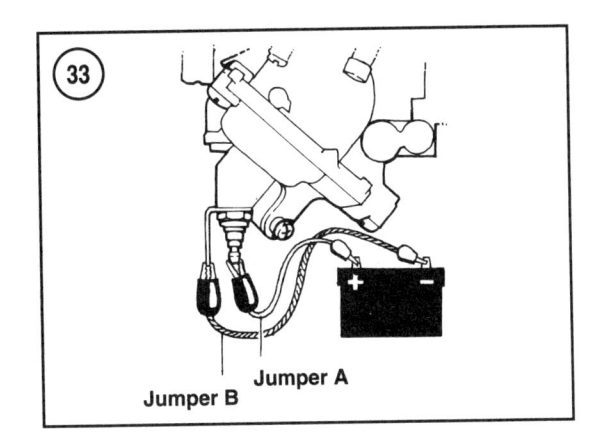

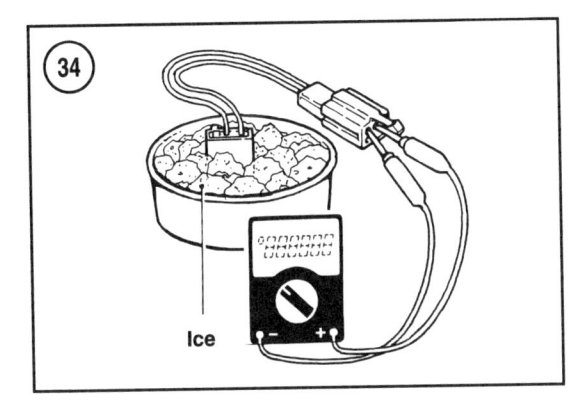

Figure 33
Jumper A
Jumper B

Figure 34
Ice

3. Unscrew and remove the carburetor heater from the bottom of the float bowl.
4. Repeat the above procedure for the remaining carburetor heaters.
5. Installation is the reverse of removal. Pay attention to the following:
   a. Apply Suzuki thermo grease (part No. 99000-59029) or equivalent to the tip of the carburetor heater.
   b. Torque the carburetor heater to the specification in **Table 8**.

Inspection

1. Remove the carburetor assembly as described in this chapter.
2. Disconnect the electrical lead from the carburetor heater on the bottom of the float bowl.
3A. On 1997-1999 models, check the resistance of the heater coil by performing the following:

NOTE
The carburetor heater must be cold when performing this resistance test.

   a. Set an ohmmeter to the R × 10 scale. If using an analog meter, calibrate the meter as described in Chapter One.
   b. Connect the ohmmeter negative test lead to the spade connector on the heater and connect the positive test lead to the heater body as shown in **Figure 32**.
   c. Replace the heater if the resistance is outside the range specified in **Table 7**.

3B. On 2000 models, use a battery to check the carburetor heater operation by performing the following:

CAUTION
Electrical arcing may occur when connecting the jumpers in the following test. Connect the jumpers in the described order so any arcing will take place away from the carburetors.

   a. Connect one end of jumper A to the battery positive terminal, and then connect the other end of jumper A to the carburetor body as shown in **Figure 33**.
   b. Connect one end of jumper B to the spade connector on the carburetor heater, and then connect the other end of jumper B to the battery negative terminal.

CAUTION
Do not touch the carburetor heater directly. It can burn.

   c. After 5 minutes, check the temperature of the float bowl by hand. It should be warm. Replace the carburetor heater if the float bowl does not heat up.
   d. Disconnect the jumper B from the negative battery terminal and then from the carburetor heater. Then disconnect jumper A.

4. Repeat this test for the remaining carburetor heaters.

Carburetor Thermo-Switch Inspection (U.K. Models)

The thermo switch is located under the fuel tank.
1. Unplug the thermo-switch connector from the wiring harness.
2. Remove the thermo switch, and immerse it in a pan of ice.
3. After the switch has sat in the ice for about five minutes, check the continuity across the two terminals in the thermo-switch connector **Figure 34**.

CARBURETOR FITTINGS (1995-1999 MODELS)

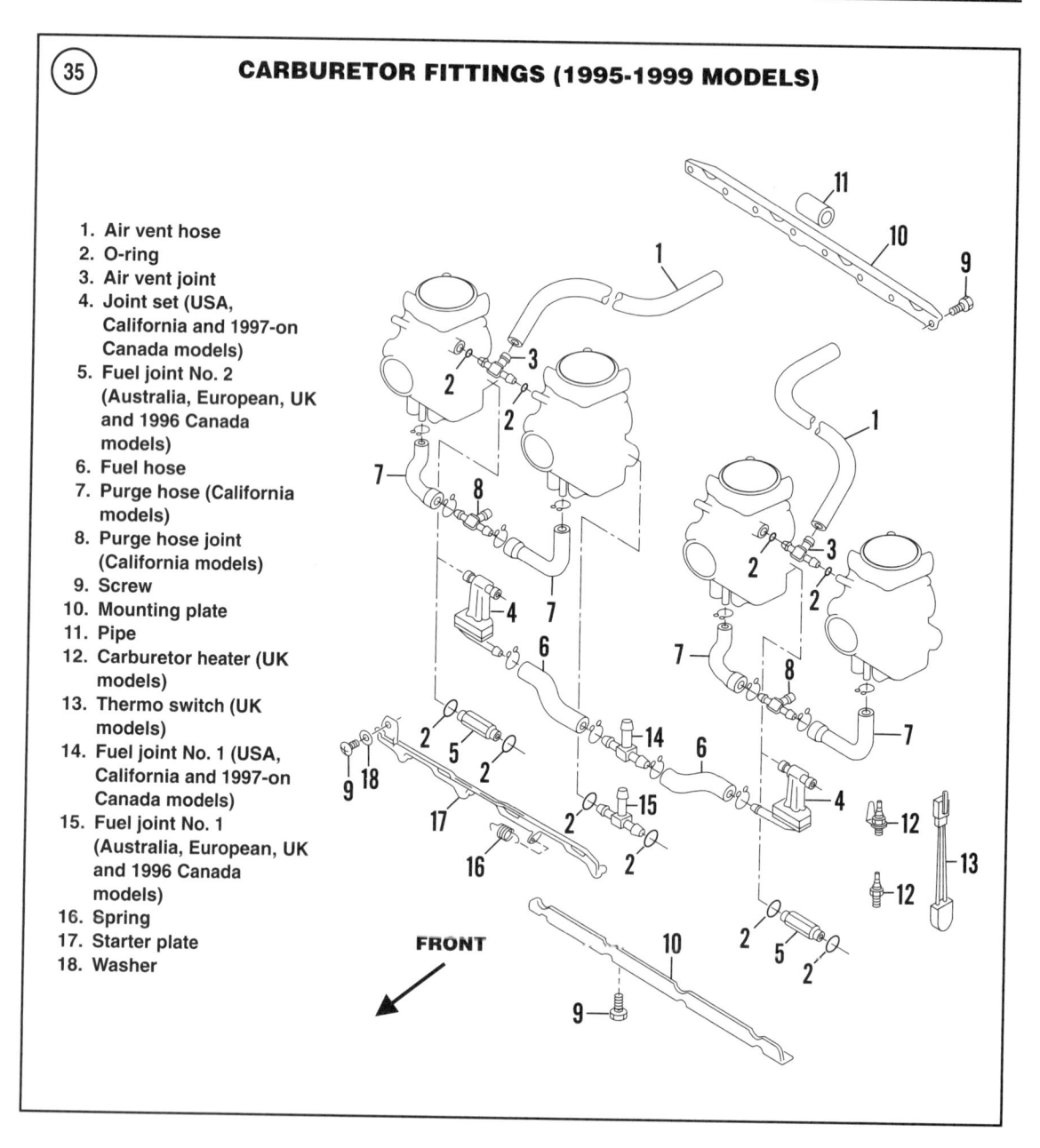

1. Air vent hose
2. O-ring
3. Air vent joint
4. Joint set (USA, California and 1997-on Canada models)
5. Fuel joint No. 2 (Australia, European, UK and 1996 Canada models)
6. Fuel hose
7. Purge hose (California models)
8. Purge hose joint (California models)
9. Screw
10. Mounting plate
11. Pipe
12. Carburetor heater (UK models)
13. Thermo switch (UK models)
14. Fuel joint No. 1 (USA, California and 1997-on Canada models)
15. Fuel joint No. 1 (Australia, European, UK and 1996 Canada models)
16. Spring
17. Starter plate
18. Washer

4. The chilled switch should have zero or very low resistance. Replace the switch if it has infinite or very high resistance.

CARBURETOR SEPARATION

Refer to **Figure 35** when separating the carburetors on 1995-1999 models; refer to **Figure 36** for 2000 models.

1. Remove the carburetor assembly as described in this chapter.

2. If still installed, remove any fuel, air and vacuum hoses from the carburetors. Label each hose and fitting so the hoses can be reinstalled in their original locations during assembly.

3. Disengage the spring (A, **Figure 37**) from the starter plate.

4. Remove the mounting screws (B, **Figure 37**) from the starter plate.

5. Disengage the starter plate fingers from the starter valve plungers, and remove the starter plate (C, **Figure 37**).

FUEL, EMISSION CONTROL AND EXHAUST SYSTEMS

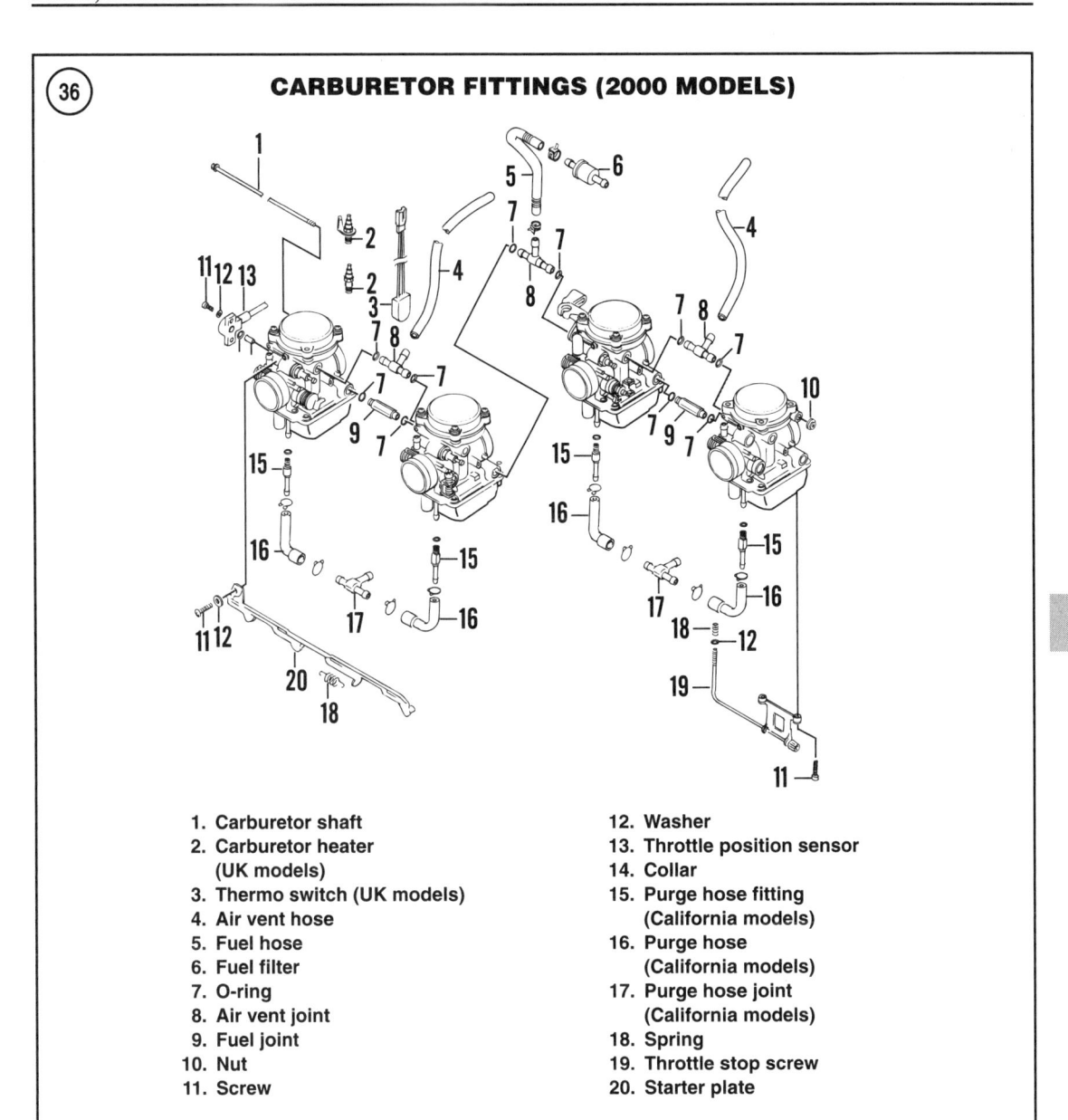

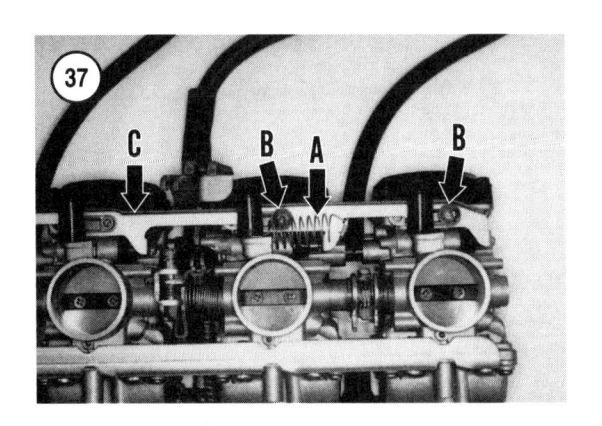

36 CARBURETOR FITTINGS (2000 MODELS)

1. Carburetor shaft
2. Carburetor heater (UK models)
3. Thermo switch (UK models)
4. Air vent hose
5. Fuel hose
6. Fuel filter
7. O-ring
8. Air vent joint
9. Fuel joint
10. Nut
11. Screw
12. Washer
13. Throttle position sensor
14. Collar
15. Purge hose fitting (California models)
16. Purge hose (California models)
17. Purge hose joint (California models)
18. Spring
19. Throttle stop screw
20. Starter plate

NOTE
The Phillips head screws in the next step had a threadlocking agent applied prior to assembly. Use an impact driver to loosen the screws to avoid rounding off the screw head slots.

6A. On 1995-1999 models, remove the screws securing the upper mounting plate (A, **Figure 38**) and the lower mounting plate (**Figure 39**).

6B. On 2000 models, remove the nut from the upper and lower carburetor shaft, and remove each shaft.

7. On 1996-1999 U.S.A and California models and on 1997-1999 Canada models, slide the hose clamps down the fuel hose and off the fuel T-fitting (B, **Figure 38**).
8. Disconnect the fuel T-fitting from one of the carburetors and separate the No. 1 and No. 2 carburetors from the No. 3 and No. 4 carburetors.
9. Slide the hose clamps in toward the center of the fuel and air vent hoses. Disconnect the fuel hose and the air vent hose from one of the carburetors.
10. Carefully pull the two carburetor bodies apart. Separate the following components from their respective ports on the carburetors.
    a. The air vent joint (**Figure 40**) on all models. Remove the O-rings. Make sure new ones are installed during assembly.
    b. The joint set (**Figure 41**) on 1996-1999 U.S.A and California models and on 1997-1999 Canada models.
    c. The fuel joint on 1995-1999 Australian, U.K. and European models and on 2000 models. Remove the O-rings. Make sure new ones are installed during assembly.
11. Assemble the carburetors by reversing these disassembly steps, noting the following:
    a. Install *new* O-rings on the fuel joints and air vent joints connecting the carburetors.
    b. Place the carburetor assembly on a piece of plate glass.
    c. Press down on all four carburetors to align them and tighten the upper and lower interconnecting bolts and nuts securely.
    d. Connect the air, fuel and vacuum hoses to the proper fittings as noted during disassembly.

FLOAT HEIGHT ADJUSTMENT

The carburetor assembly has to be removed and partially disassembled for this adjustment.
1. Remove the carburetor assembly as described in this chapter.
2. Remove the screws (A, **Figure 15**) securing the float bowls and remove the bowl (B, **Figure 15**).
3. Hold the carburetor assembly with the carburetor inclined until the float arm just touches the float needle—not pushing it down. Use a float level gauge, vernier caliper or small ruler and measure the distance from the carburetor body to the bottom surface of the float body (**Figure 42**). The correct float height is listed in **Tables 1-6**.

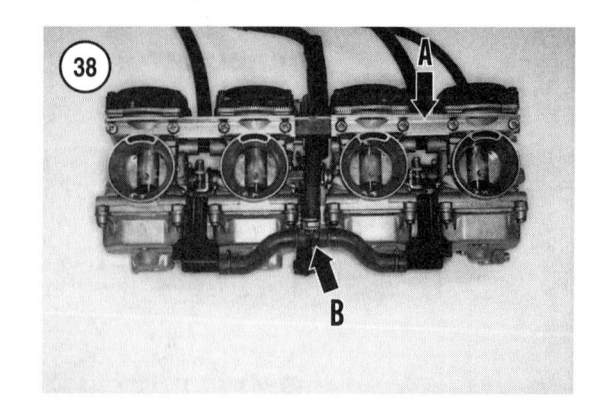

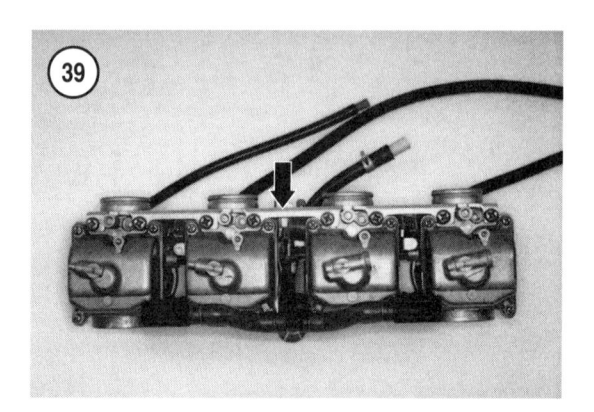

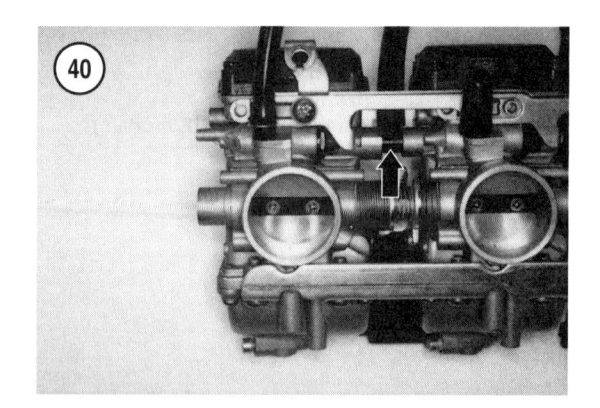

FUEL, EMISSION CONTROL AND EXHAUST SYSTEMS

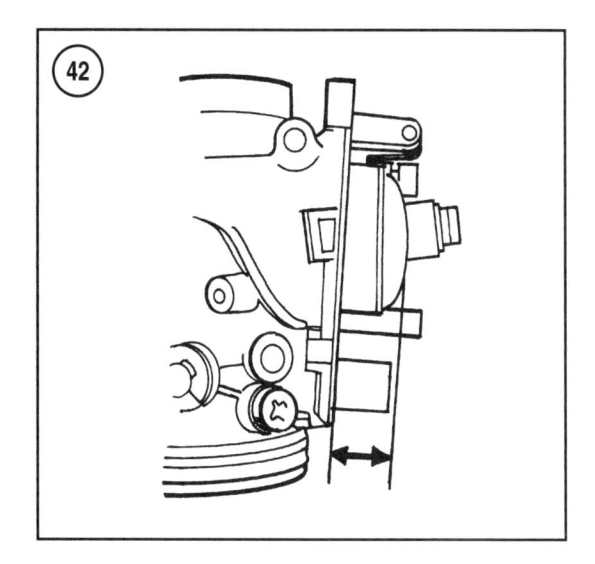

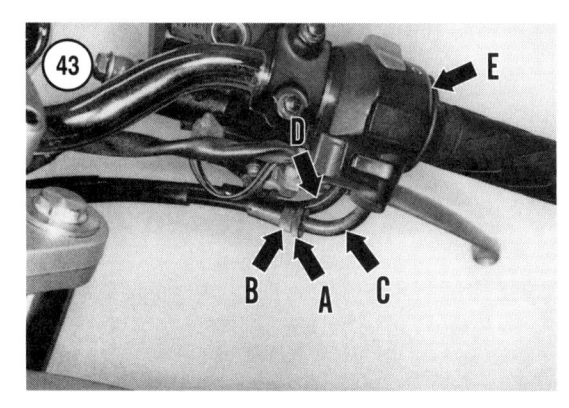

4. Adjust by carefully bending the tang (C, **Figure 27**) on the float arm. If the float height measurement is too small, the result will be a rich air/fuel mixture. If it is too large, the mixture will be lean.

NOTE
The floats on all carburetors must be adjusted to the same height to maintain the same air/fuel mixture.

5. Reassemble and install the carburetors.

Carburetor Rejetting

If rejetting is necessary, check with a dealer or motorcycle performance tuner for jet-size recommendations for specific conditions. Change jet sizes in increments of one. After each change, test ride the motorcycle and inspect the spark plugs as described in *Reading Spark Plugs* (Chapter Three).

Do not attempt to solve poor-running symptoms by rejetting the carburetors. Observe the following steps to determine if rejetting is necessary.

1. If the following conditions hold true, chances are that rejetting is not necessary.
    a. The engine has held a good tune in the past with standard jetting.
    b. The engine has not been modified.
    c. The motorcycle is being operated in the same geographical region under the same general climate conditions as in the past.
    d. The motorcycle is being operated at the same speeds.
2. If any of the following conditions hold true, rejetting may be necessary.
    a. A non-standard type of air filter element is installed.
    b. A non-standard exhaust system is installed.
    c. Any of the top end engine components (such as pistons, camshafts, valves or compression ratio) have been modified.
    d. The motorcycle is in use at considerably higher or lower altitudes or in a considerably hotter or colder climate than in the past.
    e. The motorcycle is being operated at considerably higher speeds than before and changing to colder spark plugs does not solve the problem.
    f. Someone has previously changed the carburetor jetting.
    g. The motorcycle has never held a satisfactory engine tune.

THROTTLE CABLE REPLACEMENT

1. Remove the seat as described Chapter Fourteen.
2. Remove the carburetor assembly as described in this chapter. Set the carburetor on a heavy towel on the frame.
3. At the throttle grip, loosen the cable locknut (A, **Figure 43**) on the return cable (C, **Figure 43**). Turn the adjuster (B, **Figure 43**) to achieve the maximum amount of slack in the return cable.
4. Repeat the procedure in Step 3, and create the maximum amount of slack in the pull cable (D, **Figure 43**).
5. Remove the screws securing the right switch assembly (E, **Figure 43**) and disengage the return cable from the throttle grip.

6. At the carburetor assembly, loosen the locknut (A, **Figure 44**) on the return cable and turn the adjuster (B, **Figure 44**) to create the needed slack.

7. Disconnect the return cable end (C, **Figure 44**) from the throttle wheel and disengage the cable from the carburetor bracket.

8. Tie a 7-ft. (2 m) piece of heavy string or cord to the carburetor end of the return cable. Wrap this end with masking or duct tape. Do not use an excessive amount of tape, as it must be pulled through the frame during removal. Tie the other end of the string to the frame.

9. Visually inspect the route the cable takes through the frame. Loosen any cable ties the cable must pass through.

10. At the throttle grip end of the cable, carefully pull the cable (and attached string) out through the frame. Make sure the attached string follows the same path as the cable through the frame.

11. Remove the tape and untie the string from the old cable.

12. Lubricate a new return cable as described in Chapter Three.

13. Connect the end of the new return cable to the throttle wheel.

14. Tie the string to the carburetor end of the new return cable and wrap it with tape.

15. Carefully pull the string back through the frame, routing the new cable along the same path as the old cable.

16. Remove the tape and untie the string from the cable and the frame.

17. Attach the end of the new return cable to the carburetor throttle wheel (C, **Figure 44**).

18. Fit the cable through the carburetor bracket and finger-tighten the locknut (A, **Figure 44**).

19. Repeat Steps 5-18 to remove and install a new pull cable.

20. Install the right switch housing and tighten the screws securely.

21. Operate the throttle grip and make sure the carburetor throttle linkage is operating correctly, with no binding. If operation is incorrect or there is binding, carefully check that the cables are attached correctly and there are no tight bends in the cables.

22. Tighten any cable ties that were loosened.

23. Install the carburetor assembly, fuel tank and seat.

24. Adjust the throttle cable as described in Chapter Three.

25. Test ride the motorcycle slowly at first and make sure the throttle is operating correctly.

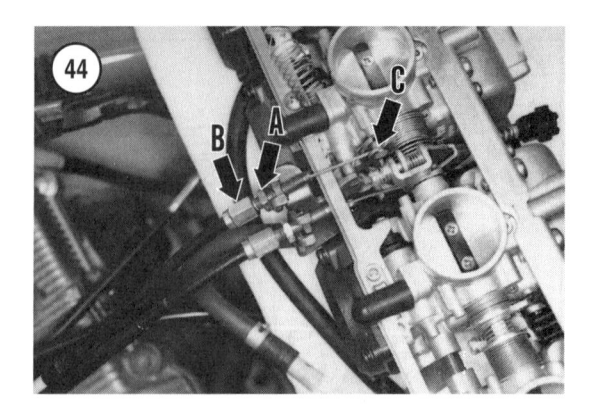

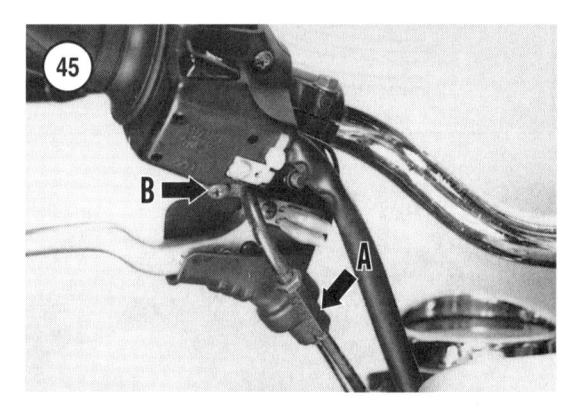

STARTER CABLE REPLACEMENT

1. Remove the fuel tank as described in this chapter.

2. At the clutch lever, loosen the locknut and turn the adjuster (A, **Figure 45**) to create any needed slack. Note that the starter cable bracket is secured under one of the housing mounting screws (B, **Figure 45**). The bracket must be reinstalled in the same manner during assembly.

3. Remove the screws securing the left handlebar switch housing together. Separate the housing halves and disengage the starter cable from the choke lever.

FUEL, EMISSION CONTROL AND EXHAUST SYSTEMS

47 AIR FILTER HOUSING (1995-1999 MODELS)

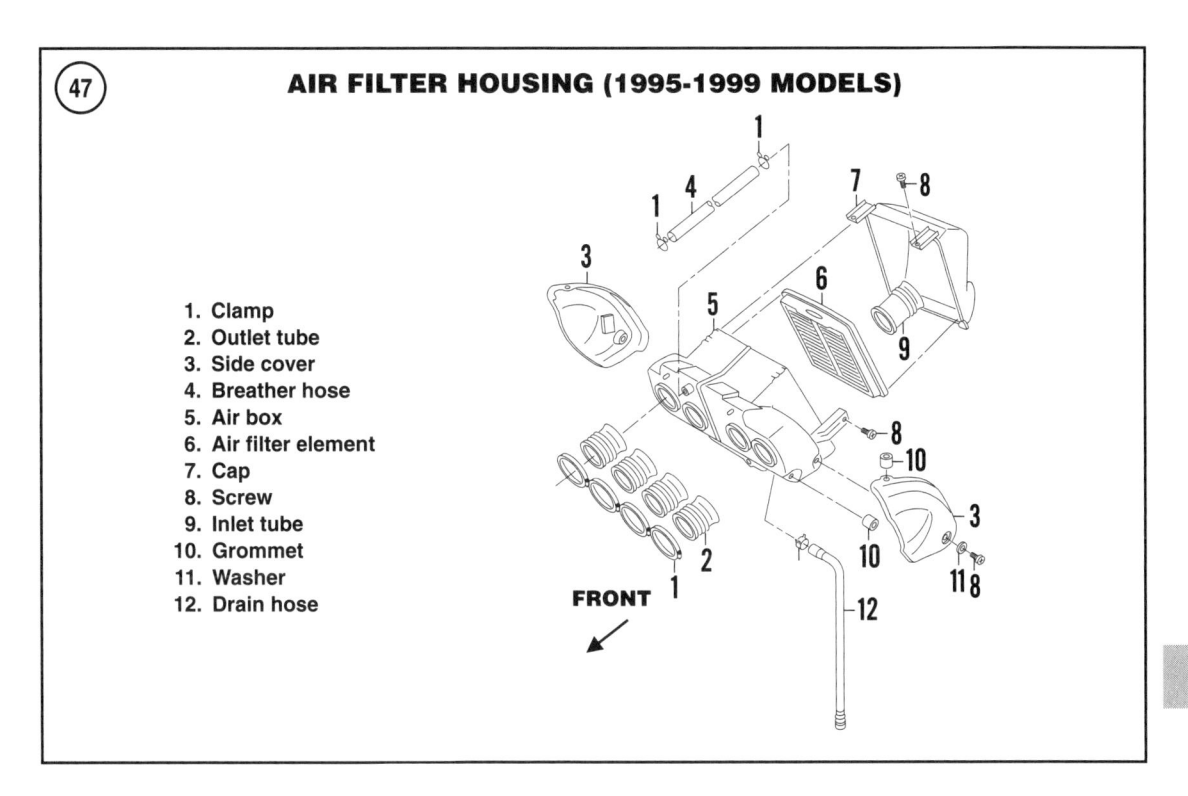

1. Clamp
2. Outlet tube
3. Side cover
4. Breather hose
5. Air box
6. Air filter element
7. Cap
8. Screw
9. Inlet tube
10. Grommet
11. Washer
12. Drain hose

FRONT

4. At the carburetor, remove the mounting screw (A, **Figure 46**) and remove the starter cable clamp from the starter plate.

5. Disengage the end of the starter cable from the anchor (B, **Figure 46**) on the starter plate.

6. Tie a 7-ft. (2 m) piece of heavy string or cord to the carburetor end of starter cable. Wrap this end with masking or duct tape. Do not use an excessive amount of tape, as it must be pulled through the frame during removal. Tie the other end of the string to the frame.

7. Visually inspect the route the cable takes through the frame. Loosen any cable ties the cable must pass through.

8. At the choke lever end of the cable, carefully pull the cable (and attached string) out through the frame. Make sure the attached string follows the same path as the cable through the frame.

9. Remove the tape and untie the string from the cable.

10. Lubricate a new starter cable as described in Chapter Three.

11. Connect the end of the new starter cable to the choke lever.

12. Tie the string to the carburetor end of the new starter cable and wrap it with tape.

13. Carefully pull the string back through the frame, routing the new cable along the same path as the old cable.

14. Reverse Steps 1-5 to install the new cable while noting the following:

   a. Connect the cable and choke lever to the switch housing.

   b. Align the switch housing locating pin with the hole in the handlebar and fit the switch in place on the handlebar. Tighten the screws securely. Make sure the starter cable bracket is secured under the mounting screw (B, **Figure 45**).

   c. Operate the choke lever and make sure the link is operating correctly without binding. If the operation is incorrect or there is binding, carefully check that the cable is attached correctly and that there are no tight bends in the cable.

   d. Start the engine and let it idle. Turn the handlebar from side to side and listen to the engine. The engine speed should not increase when the handlebars turn. If it does, the cable is improperly routed. Correct the problem before riding.

AIR FILTER HOUSING

Removal/Installation

When performing this procedure, refer to **Figure 47** for 1995-1999 models or **Figure 48** for 2000 models.

CHAPTER EIGHT

AIR FILTER HOUSING (2000 MODELS)

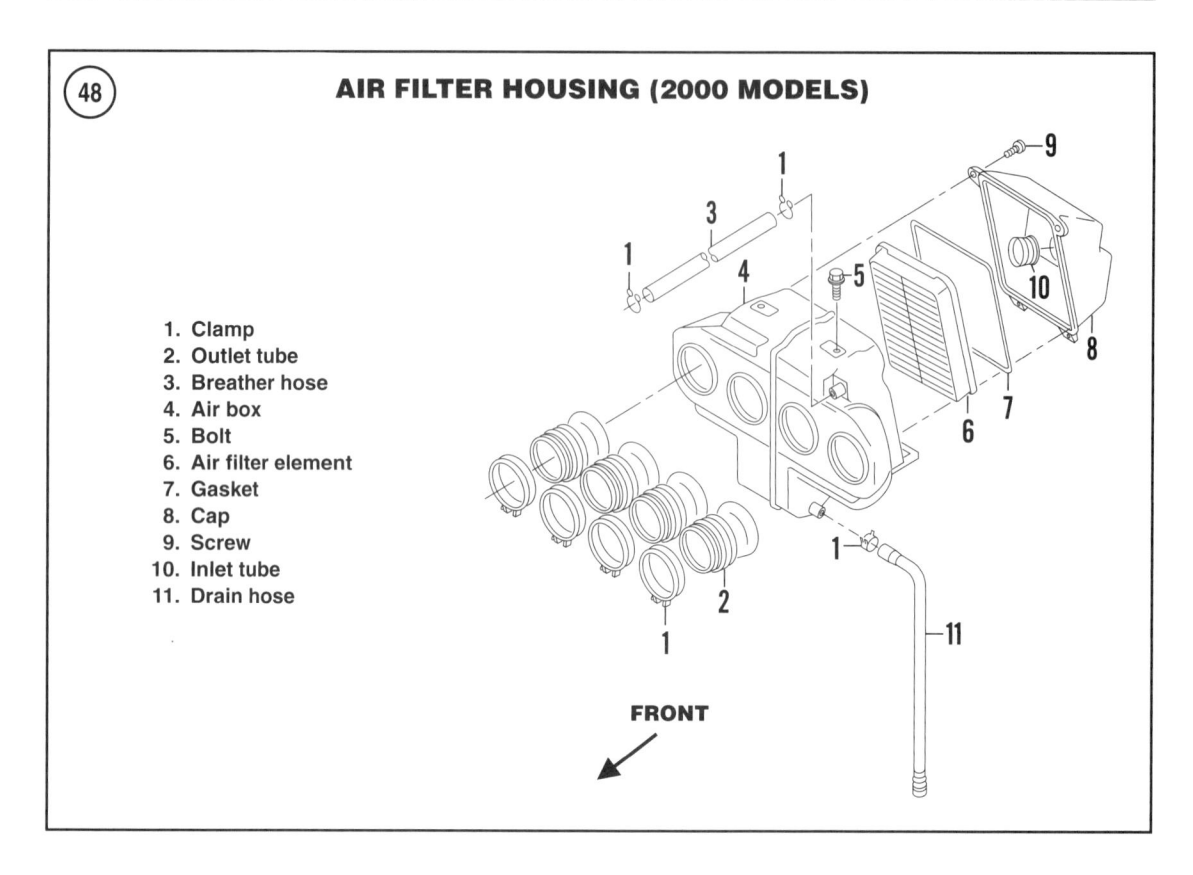

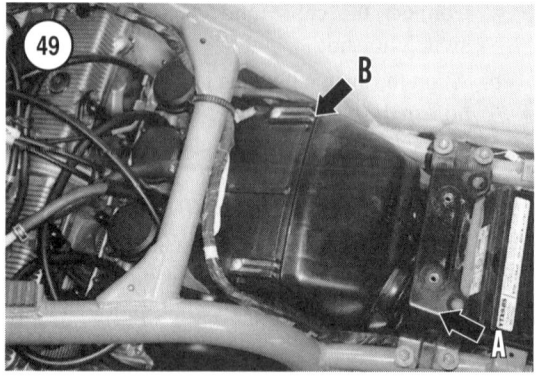

1. Clamp
2. Outlet tube
3. Breather hose
4. Air box
5. Bolt
6. Air filter element
7. Gasket
8. Cap
9. Screw
10. Inlet tube
11. Drain hose

1. Remove the seat and the rear frame cover as described in Chapter Fourteen.

2. Remove the fuel tank as described in this chapter.

3. Remove the fuel-tank mounting bracket (A, **Figure 49**) from the frame.

4. Disconnect the crankcase breather hose (A, **Figure 50**) from the fitting on the air filter housing.

5. Release the carburetor air vent hoses (B, **Figure 50**) from the retainer under the fuel-tank mounting bracket.

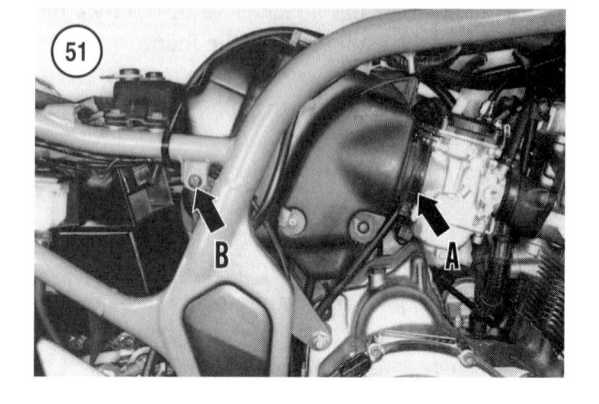

FUEL, EMISSION CONTROL AND EXHAUST SYSTEMS

FUEL TANK (1995-1999 MODELS)

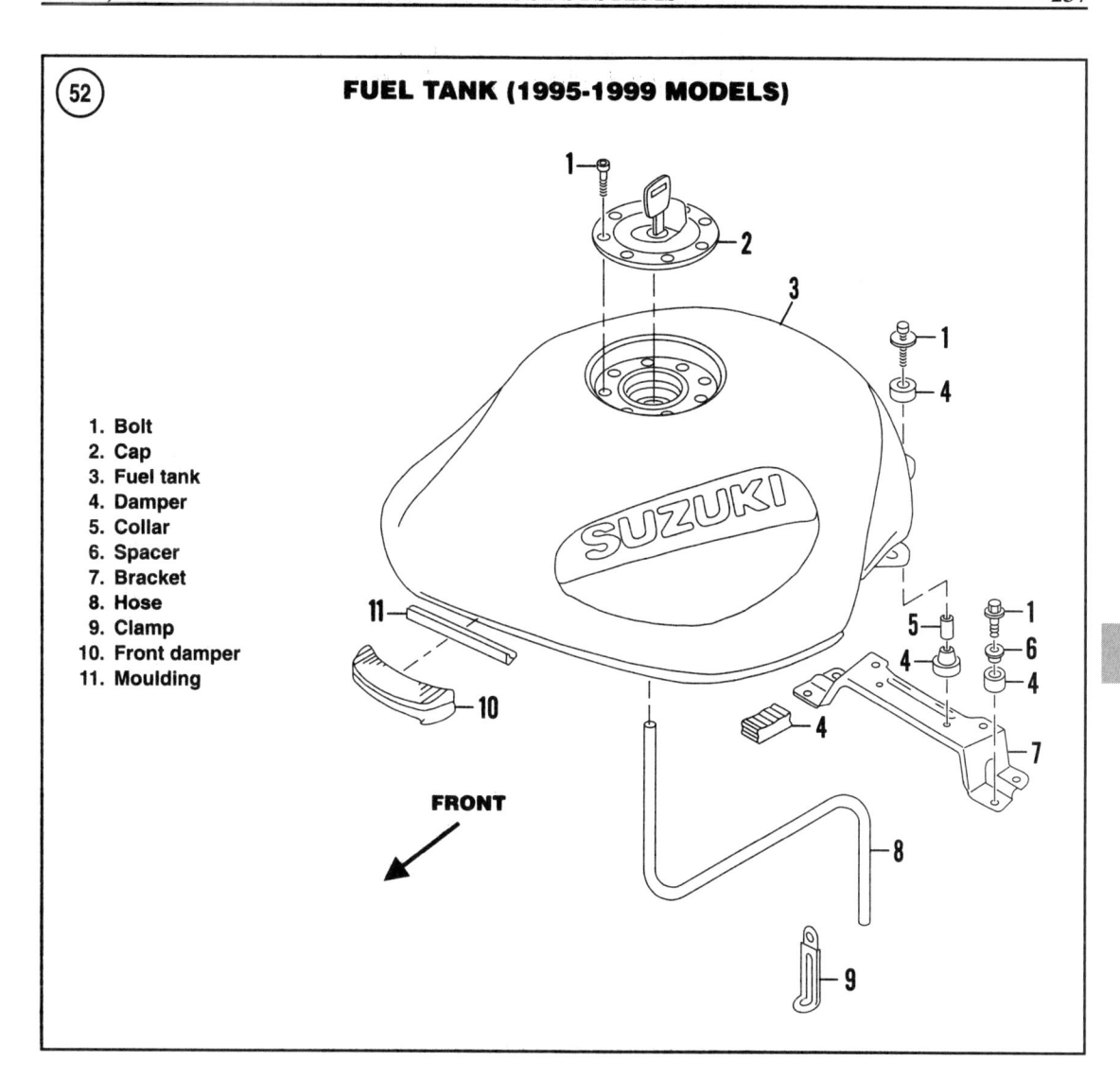

1. Bolt
2. Cap
3. Fuel tank
4. Damper
5. Collar
6. Spacer
7. Bracket
8. Hose
9. Clamp
10. Front damper
11. Moulding

6. On 1995-1999 California and Switzerland models and on 2000 models, disconnect the PAIR air cleaner hose from the fitting on the air filter housing.

7. Loosen the clamp screw (A, **Figure 51**) on each air duct and slide the clamps rearward away from the carburetors.

8. Remove the air-filter-housing mounting bolt (B, **Figure 51**) on each side.

9. Pull the air filter housing (B, **Figure 49**) rearward and disengage each air duct from the four carburetors.

10. Install by reversing these removal steps, noting the following:

   a. Make sure the air filter housing air ducts are fully seated against the carburetor inlets. A solid bottoming out will be felt when they are correctly seated.

   b. Make sure the carburetor clamp screws are tight to avoid a vacuum leak and possible engine damage due to a lean fuel mixture.

FUEL TANK

Removal/Installation

When performing this procedure, refer to **Figure 52** for 1995-1999 models or **Figure 53** for 2000 models.

1. Remove the seat and rear frame cover as described in Chapter Fourteen.
2. Disconnect the negative battery cable.

FUEL TANK (2000 MODELS)

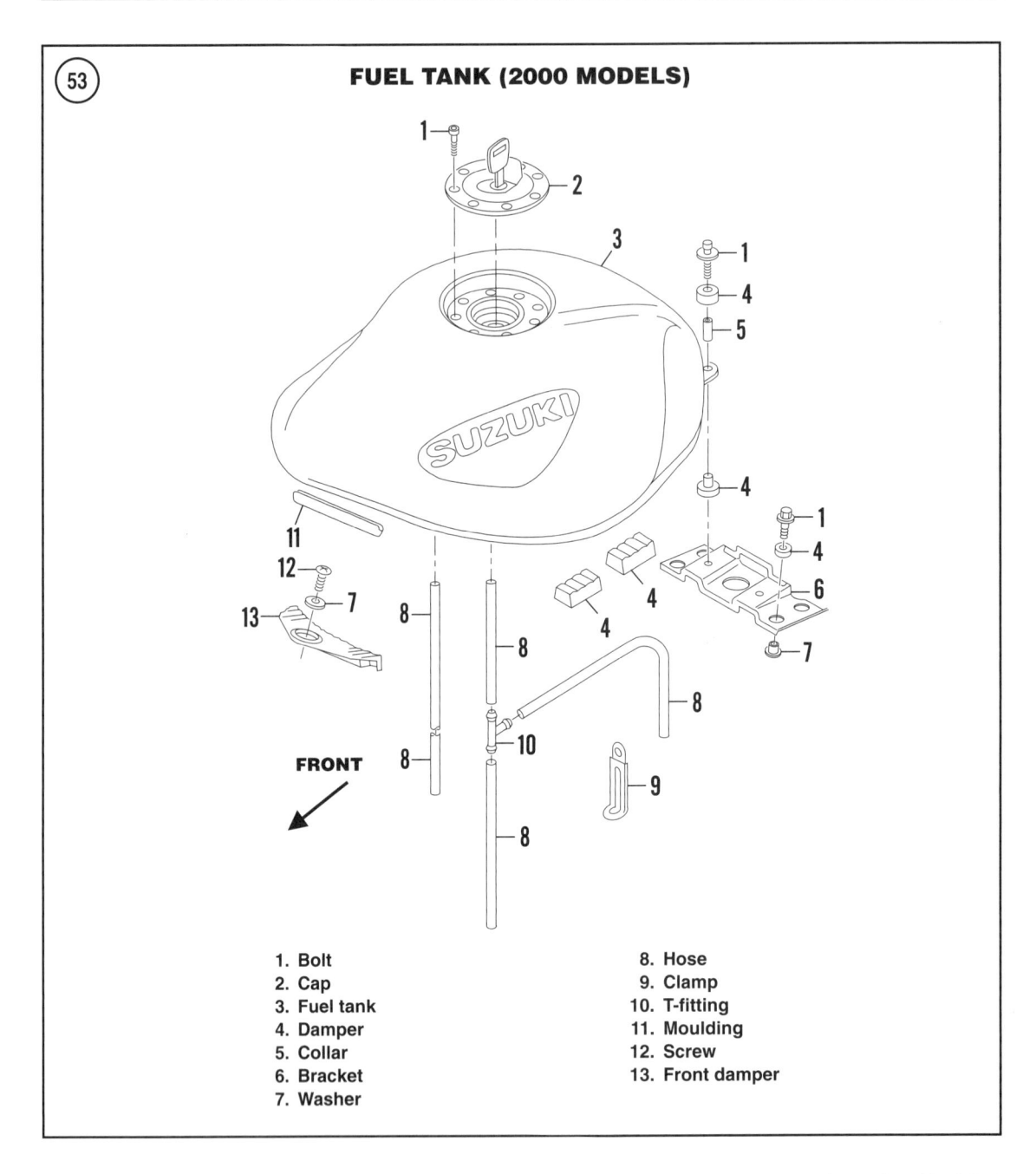

Figure 53

1. Bolt
2. Cap
3. Fuel tank
4. Damper
5. Collar
6. Bracket
7. Washer
8. Hose
9. Clamp
10. T-fitting
11. Moulding
12. Screw
13. Front damper

3. Turn the fuel valve to the ON position.
4. Remove the fuel tank mounting bolts (**Figure 54**).
5. On 2000 models, remove the mounting screw and remove the control knob (**Figure 55**) from the fuel valve.
6. Slide the fuel tank rearward, and tilt it up.
7. Disconnect the fuel line (A, **Figure 56**) and vacuum line (B, **Figure 56**) from the fuel valve. Plug the end of the lines with golf tees to prevent the entry of debris and to prevent any loss of residual fuel in the line.
8. Disconnect the drain hose (**Figure 57**) from the fuel tank.
9. On 2000 models, disconnect the breather hose from the fuel tank.
10. On 1996-1999 California models, disconnect the evaporative emission system breather line from the fuel tank.
11. Pull the tank rearward and out from the frame.

FUEL, EMISSION CONTROL AND EXHAUST SYSTEMS 239

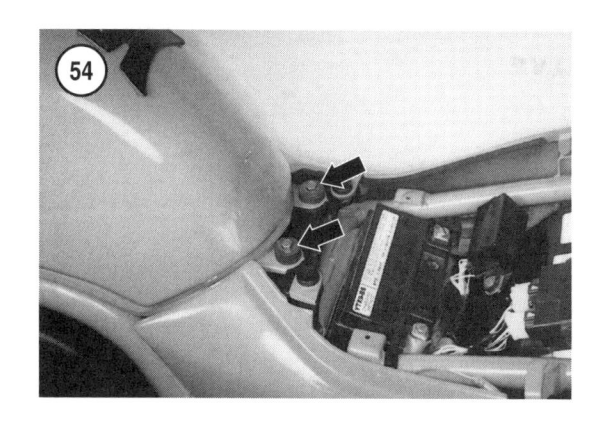

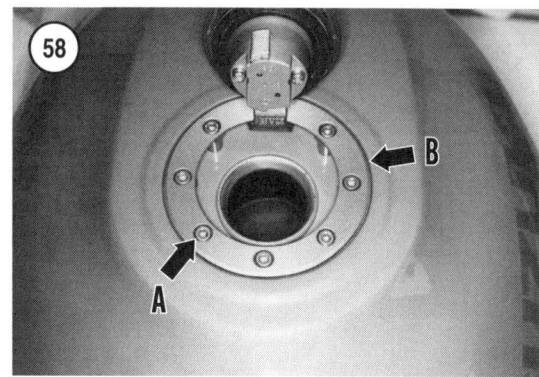

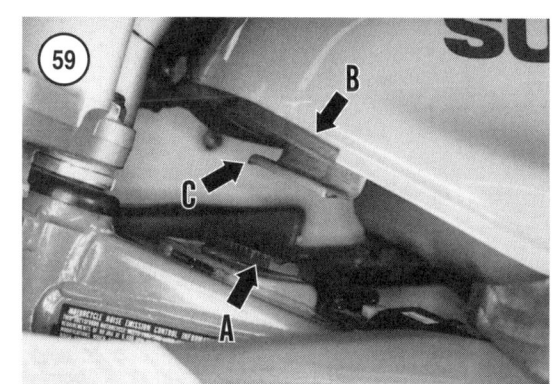

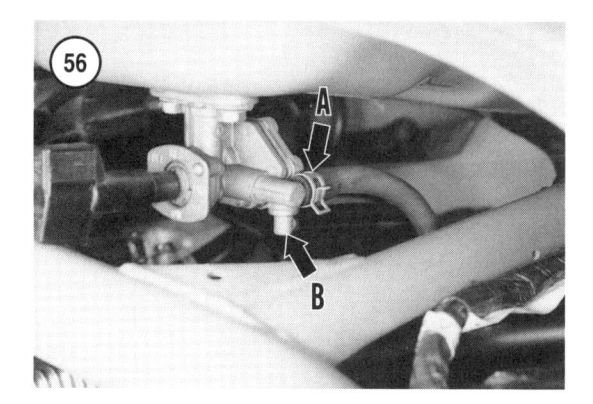

12. If necessary, remove the filler cap as follows:
    a. Remove the bolts (A, **Figure 58**) securing the filler cap assembly.
    b. Remove the filler cap (B, **Figure 58**) from the fuel tank.
13. Install by reversing these removal steps, noting the following:
    a. Inspect the rubber damper (A, **Figure 59**) where the front of the fuel tank attaches to the frame, and inspect the damper on the fuel tank (B, **Figure 59**). Replace either damper if it is damaged or starting to deteriorate.
    b. Make sure the fuel line (A, **Figure 56**) is secure on the fuel valve.
    c. Make sure the tang at the front of the tank (C, **Figure 59**) is secured under the frame stop.
    d. Start the engine and check for fuel leaks.

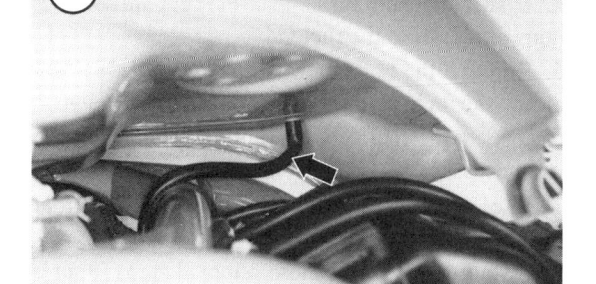

FUEL VALVE

Removal/Installation

WARNING
Some fuel may spill out of the tank during the following procedure. Work

FUEL VALVE

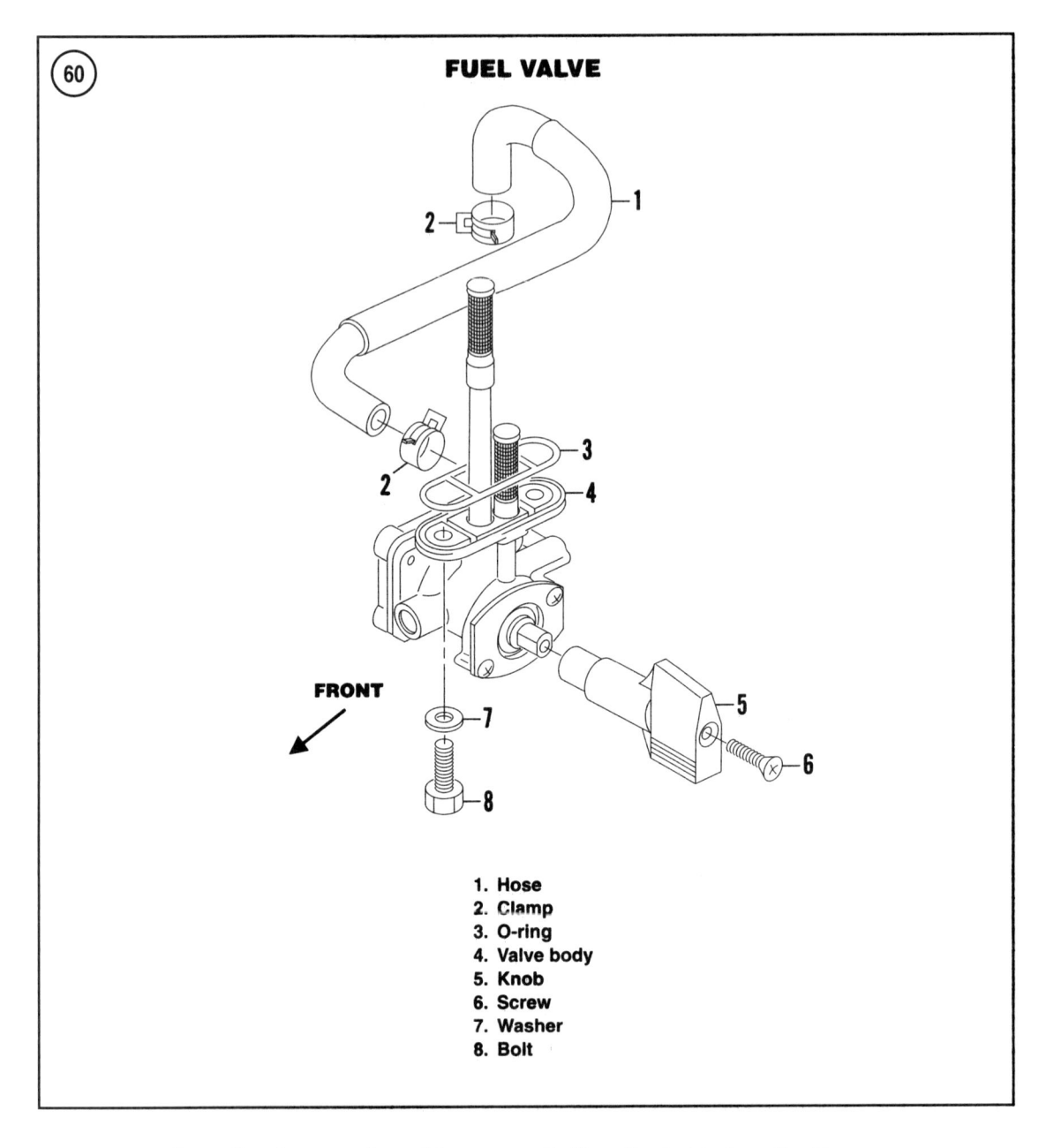

1. Hose
2. Clamp
3. O-ring
4. Valve body
5. Knob
6. Screw
7. Washer
8. Bolt

in a well-ventilated area at least 50 feet from any sparks or flames, including gas appliance pilot lights. Do not allow anyone to smoke in the area. Have a BC-rated fire extinguisher on hand.

Refer to **Figure 60**.

1. Remove the fuel tank as described in this chapter.
2. Cover the work bench with a blanket or several towels to protect the surface of the fuel tank.
3. Turn the fuel tank on its side.
4. If still attached, disconnect the fuel and/or vacuum line(s) from the fuel valve.
5. Remove the bolts and washers (**Figure 61**) securing the fuel valve to the fuel tank and the valve.
6. Inspect the fuel valve mounting O-ring; replace it if necessary.
7. Use compressed air to clean the filter screen at the end of the fuel intake on the fuel valve.
8. Install by reversing these removal steps. Pour a small amount of gasoline into the tank after install-

FUEL, EMISSION CONTROL AND EXHAUST SYSTEMS

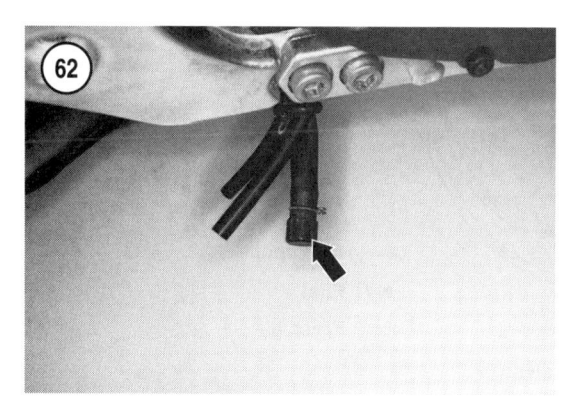

ing the valve and check for leaks. If a leak is present, solve the problem immediately.

FUEL FILTER

The Bandit is equipped with a small fuel filter screen in the fuel valve. 2000 models are also equipped with an inline filter in the fuel line located above the carburetor assembly. If the inline filter is dirty, replace it. Install the new filter so the direction arrow on the filter points toward the carburetors. The arrow should always point in the direction of fuel flow.

Consider installing an inline fuel filter on 1995-1999 models.

An inline fuel filter (A.C. part No. GF453 or equivalent) is available at most auto and motorcycle supply stores. Cut out a section of the fuel line from the fuel valve to the carburetor assembly equivalent to length of the filter so the fuel line does not kink and restrict fuel flow. Insert the fuel filter and secure the fuel line to each end of the filter. Make sure the direction arrow on the filter points to the carburetor side of the fuel line.

CRANKCASE BREATHER SYSTEM

All models are equipped with a closed crankcase breather system. The system routs the engine combustion gases into the air filter housing where they are burned in the engine.

Inspection/Cleaning

Make sure the hose clamps at each end of the hose are tight. Check the hose for deterioration. Replace it as necessary.

Remove the drain plug (**Figure 62**) on the end of the air filter housing drain hose and drain out all residue. Perform this procedure more frequently if a considerable amount of riding is done at full throttle or in the rain.

EVAPORATIVE EMISSION CONTROL SYSTEM (CALIFORNIA MODELS ONLY)

The evaporative emissions control system (**Figure 63**) captures fuel vapors and stores them so they will not be released into the atmosphere. The fuel vapors are routed through the rollover valve and stored in the charcoal canister, located on right side of the rear frame. When the engine is started, the stored vapors are drawn from the canister. They pass through the purge control valves, flow onto the carburetors and then into the engine, where they are burned.

When removing a hose from any component in the system, mark the hose and the fitting with a piece of masking tape so they can be properly identified during assembly. There are so many vacuum hoses on these models that reconnecting the hoses can be very confusing.

Refer to **Figure 64** for 1996-1999 models or to **Figure 65** for 2000 GSF600S models. A hose routing diagram also appears on the Emission Control label located under the seat.

Inspection

Make sure all evaporative emission control hoses are correctly routed, properly attached to the different components and that all hose clamps are tight. Check all hoses for deterioration and replace them as necessary. Due to the number of hoses, when re-

CHAPTER EIGHT

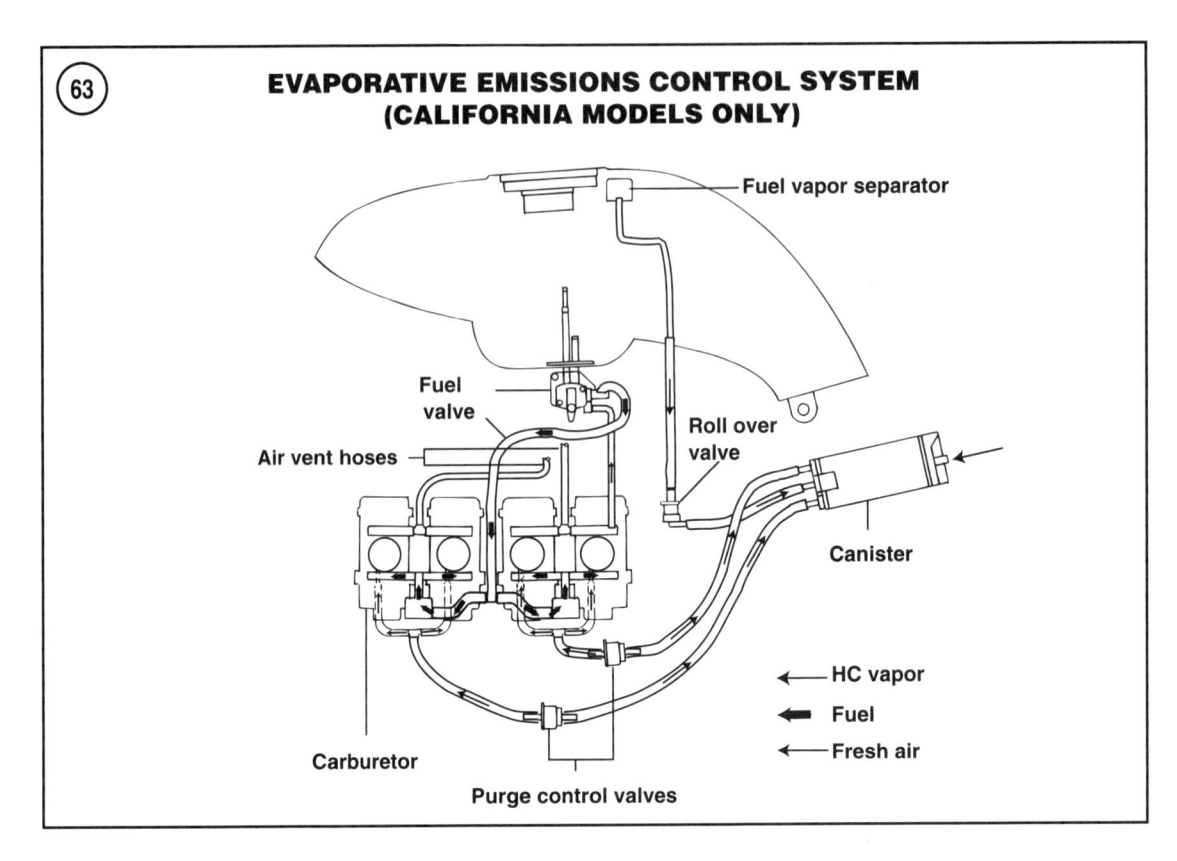

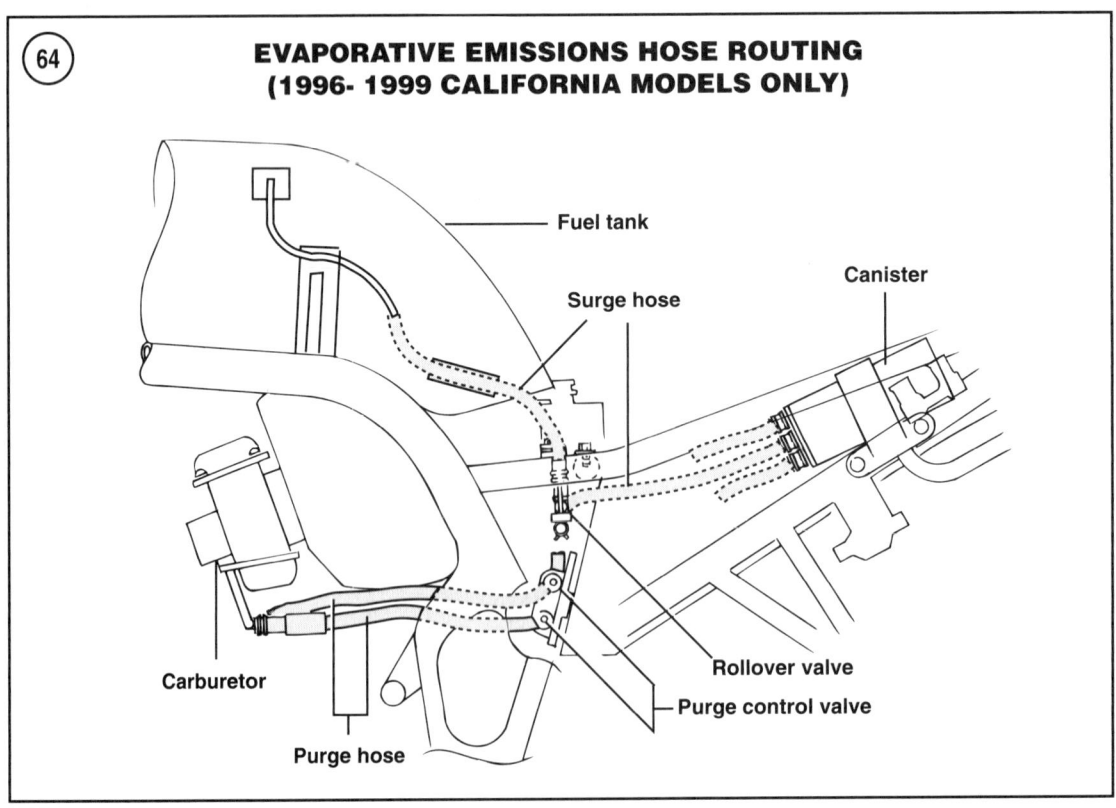

63 EVAPORATIVE EMISSIONS CONTROL SYSTEM (CALIFORNIA MODELS ONLY)

- Fuel vapor separator
- Fuel valve
- Air vent hoses
- Roll over valve
- Canister
- ← HC vapor
- ← Fuel
- ← Fresh air
- Carburetor
- Purge control valves

64 EVAPORATIVE EMISSIONS HOSE ROUTING (1996-1999 CALIFORNIA MODELS ONLY)

- Fuel tank
- Surge hose
- Canister
- Carburetor
- Purge hose
- Rollover valve
- Purge control valve

FUEL, EMISSION CONTROL AND EXHAUST SYSTEMS

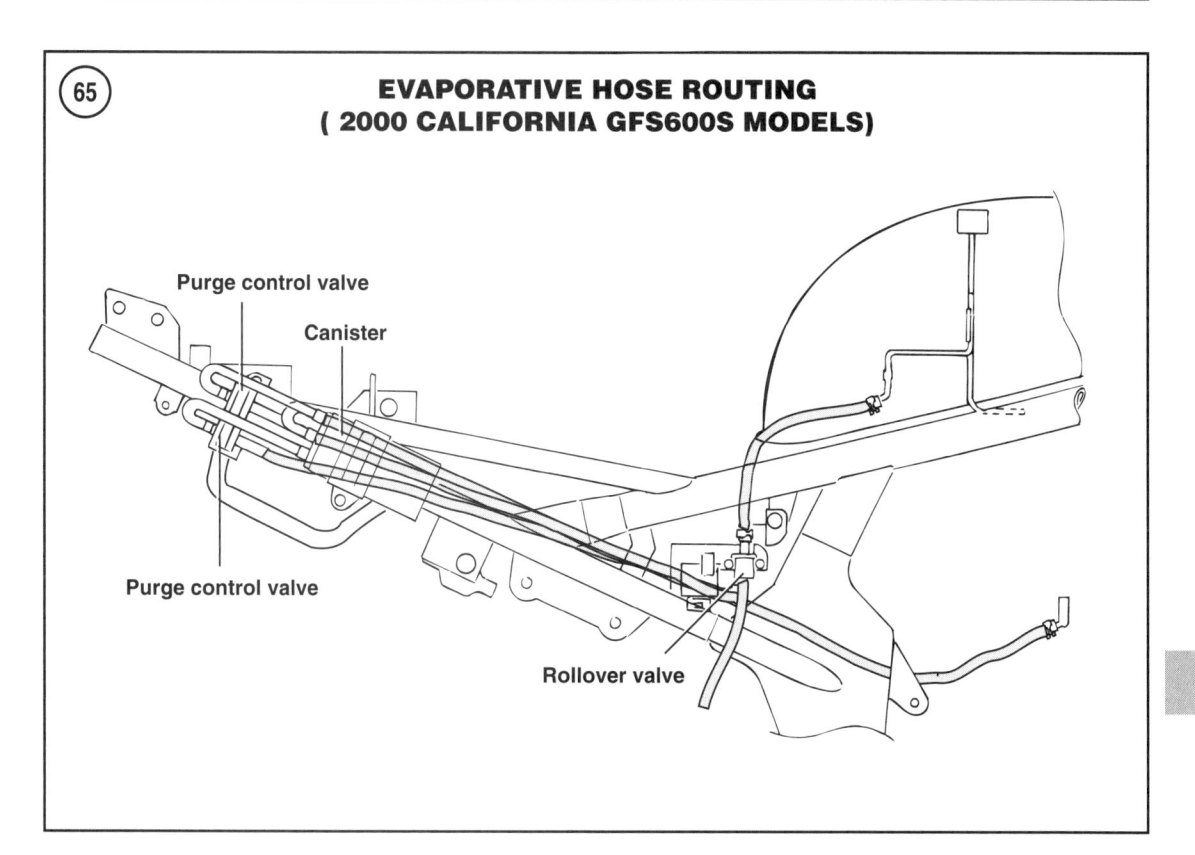

65 **EVAPORATIVE HOSE ROUTING (2000 CALIFORNIA GFS600S MODELS)**

Purge control valve
Canister
Purge control valve
Rollover valve

moving a hose from any component in the system, mark the hose and the fitting with a piece of masking tape so they can be properly identified during assembly.

PURGE CONTROL VALVES AND CHARCOAL CANISTER

Removal/Installation

1. Remove the fuel tank as described in this chapter.
2. Remove the seat and right rear frame cover as described in Chapter Fourteen.

NOTE
Prior to removing the hoses from the purge control valves and the charcoal canister, mark the hose and the fitting with a piece of masking tape. Make sure to clearly identify each hose and its fitting.

3. Remove the bolts, lockwashers and washers securing the charcoal canister and the purge control valves to the frame and remove the canister assembly. Refer to **Figure 66** for 1996-1999 models and to **Figure 67** for 2000 GSF600S models.

4. Disconnect the hoses going to the charcoal canister and to each purge control valve.

5. Install by reversing these removal steps, noting the following:
   a. Make sure to install the hoses onto the correct fittings on the charcoal canister and on the purge control valves.
   b. Make sure the hoses are not kinked, twisted or in contact with any sharp surfaces.

PAIR SYSTEM (1995-1999 CALIFORNIA and SWITZERLAND, 2000 MODELS)

The PAIR (Air Supply) System uses vacuum pulses from the carburetor to introduce fresh air into the exhaust ports (**Figure 68**). On 1995-1999 models, the system consists of a PAIR control valve, two reed valves, an air cleaner, and air and vacuum hoses. On 2000 models, the air cleaner, control

244 CHAPTER EIGHT

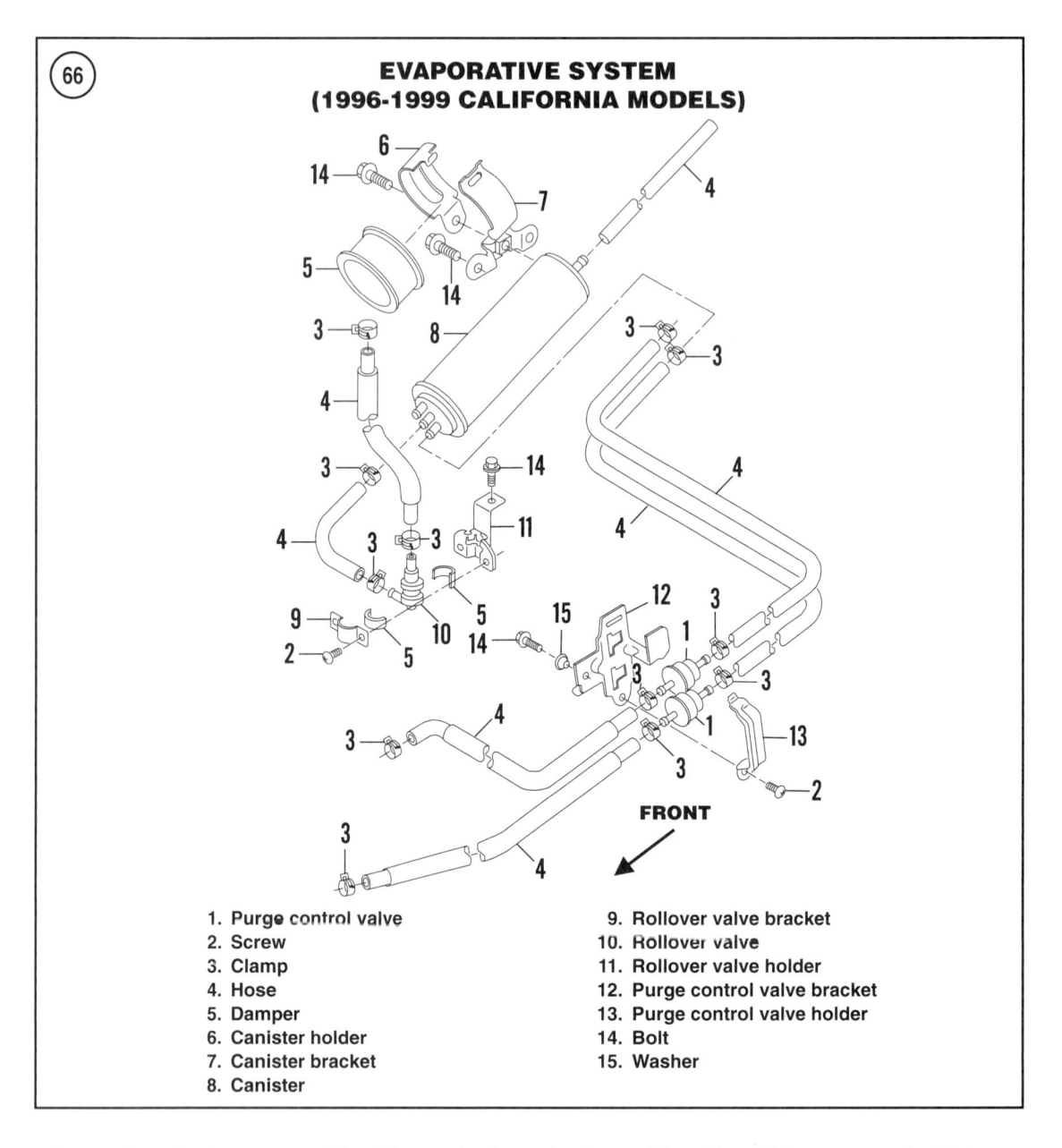

**EVAPORATIVE SYSTEM
(1996-1999 CALIFORNIA MODELS)**

66

1. Purge control valve
2. Screw
3. Clamp
4. Hose
5. Damper
6. Canister holder
7. Canister bracket
8. Canister
9. Rollover valve bracket
10. Rollover valve
11. Rollover valve holder
12. Purge control valve bracket
13. Purge control valve holder
14. Bolt
15. Washer

valve, and reed valves are combined into a single PAIR valve assembly.

Make sure all air and vacuum hoses are correctly routed and securely attached to their respective fittings. Inspect the hoses and replace any if necessary.

Removal/Installation

Refer to **Figure 69** for 1995-1999 California and Switzerland models or **Figure 70** for 2000 models.

1. On models with a fairing, remove the fairing as described in Chapter Fourteen.

2. Remove the exhaust system and the fuel tank as described in this chapter.

3. Remove the oil cooler as described in Chapter Five.

*NOTE
Label each hose and its fitting during disassembly. This ensures that each hose will be connected to the correct fitting during assembly.*

FUEL, EMISSION CONTROL AND EXHAUST SYSTEMS

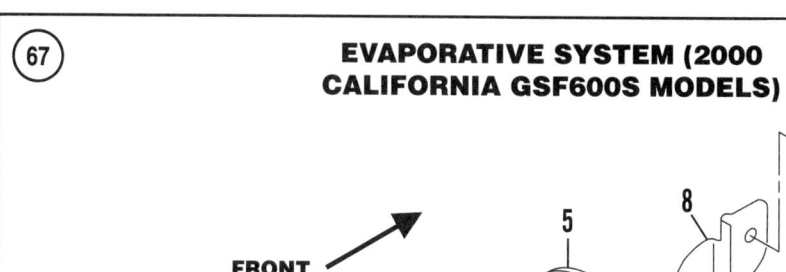

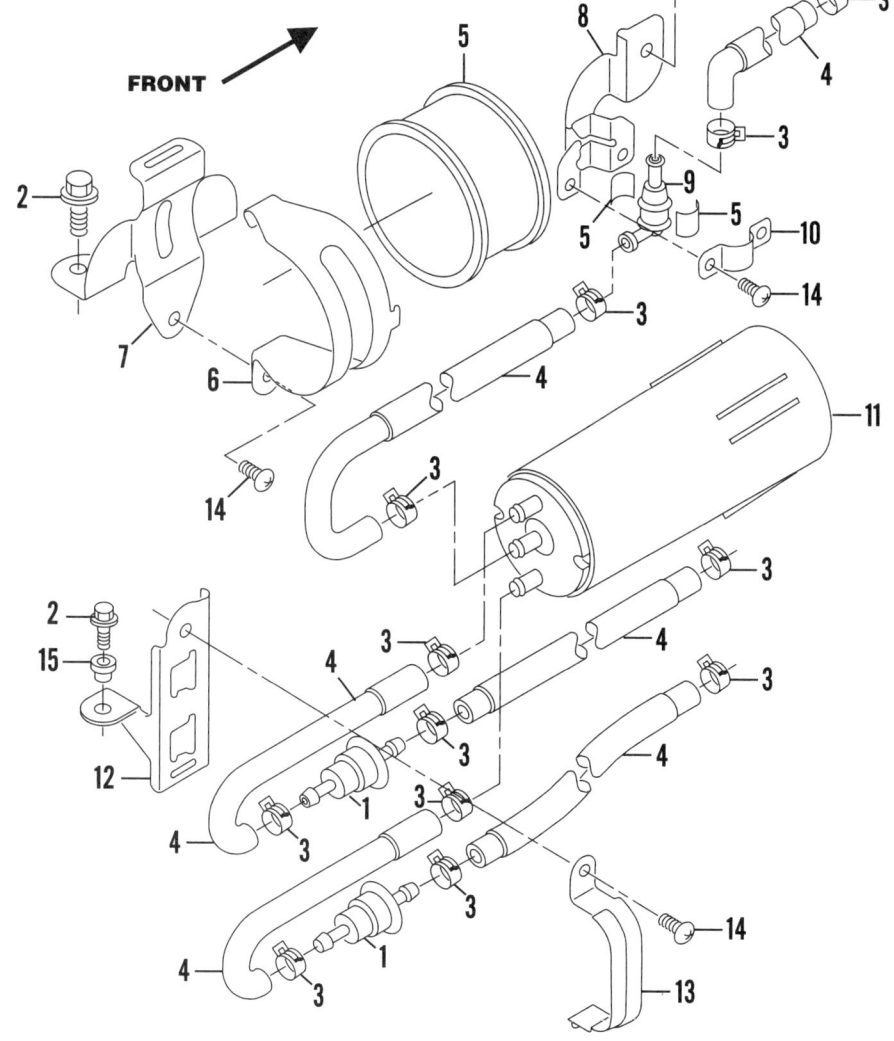

⑥⑦ EVAPORATIVE SYSTEM (2000 CALIFORNIA GSF600S MODELS)

1. Purge control valve
2. Bolt
3. Clamp
4. Hose
5. Damper
6. Canister holder
7. Canister bracket
8. Rollover valve bracket
9. Rollover valve
10. Rollover valve holder
11. Canister
12. Purge control valve holder
13. Purge control valve bracket
14. Screw
15. Washer

PAIR SYSTEM

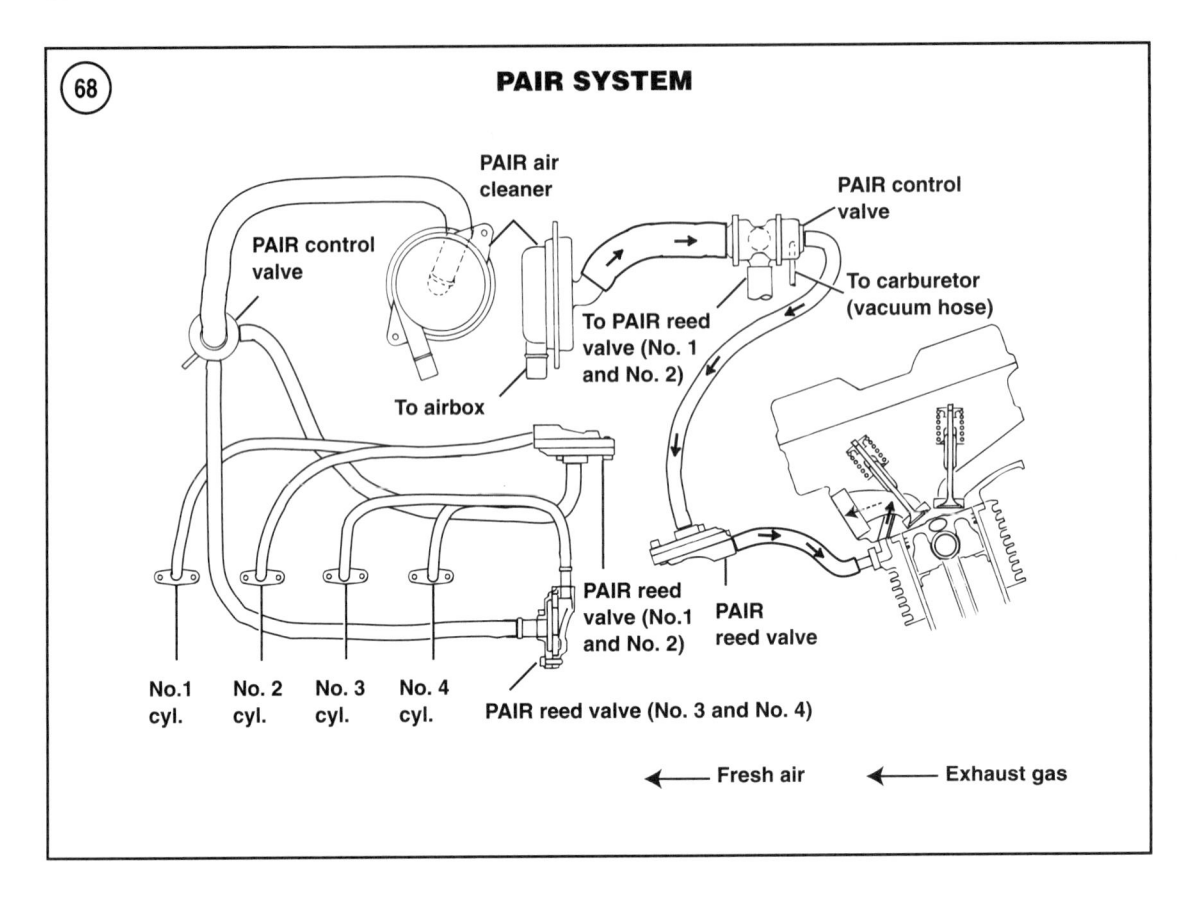

Figure 68: PAIR System diagram showing PAIR air cleaner, PAIR control valve, PAIR reed valves (No.1 and No.2, No.3 and No.4), connections to airbox, carburetor (vacuum hose), and cylinders No.1–No.4. Arrows indicate fresh air and exhaust gas flow.

4. Loosen the hose clamps and disconnect the hoses from their respective fittings. Label each hose and its fitting.

5A. On 1995-1999 models, remove the PAIR assembly by performing the following (see **Figure 71**):

   a. Disconnect the PAIR vacuum hose on the side of the control valve.
   b. Disconnect the PAIR air hose from the fitting on the PAIR air cleaner.
   c. Disconnect the two reed valve hoses from each reed valve.
   d. Remove the bolts securing the PAIR bracket. Lift the bracket and the PAIR assembly from the frame.
   e. Install by reversing these removal steps.

5B. On 2000 models, remove the PAIR valve assembly by performing the following (see **Figure 72**):

   a. Disconnect the PAIR vacuum hose from the PAIR valve assembly.
   b. Disconnect the PAIR air hose from the PAIR valve assembly.
   c. Disconnect the reed valve hoses from the outlets on each reed valve.
   d. Remove the mounting bolt and remove the PAIR valve assembly from the mounting bracket.
   e. Install by reversing these removal steps. Tighten the PAIR valve assembly mounting screw to the specification in **Table 8**.

6. To remove the air pipe(s), perform the following:

   a. Disconnect the PAIR valve hose from the lower end of the air pipe.
   b. Remove the nuts securing the air pipe to the cylinder.
   c. Remove the air pipe and gasket.
   d. Install by reversing these removal steps. Install a *new* gasket and tighten the nuts to the specification in **Table 8**.

7. Install the exhaust system and fuel tank as described in this chapter.

8. Install the oil cooler as described in Chapter Five.

9. Install the fairing as described in Chapter Fourteen.

FUEL, EMISSION CONTROL AND EXHAUST SYSTEMS

PAIR SYSTEM (1995-1999 CALIFORNIA AND SWITZERLAND MODELS)

1. Hose
2. Control valve
3. Bolt
4. PAIR air cleaner
5. Mounting bracket
6. Reed valve
7. Clamp
8. Stud
9. Gasket
10. Nut
11. Air pipe

CHAPTER EIGHT

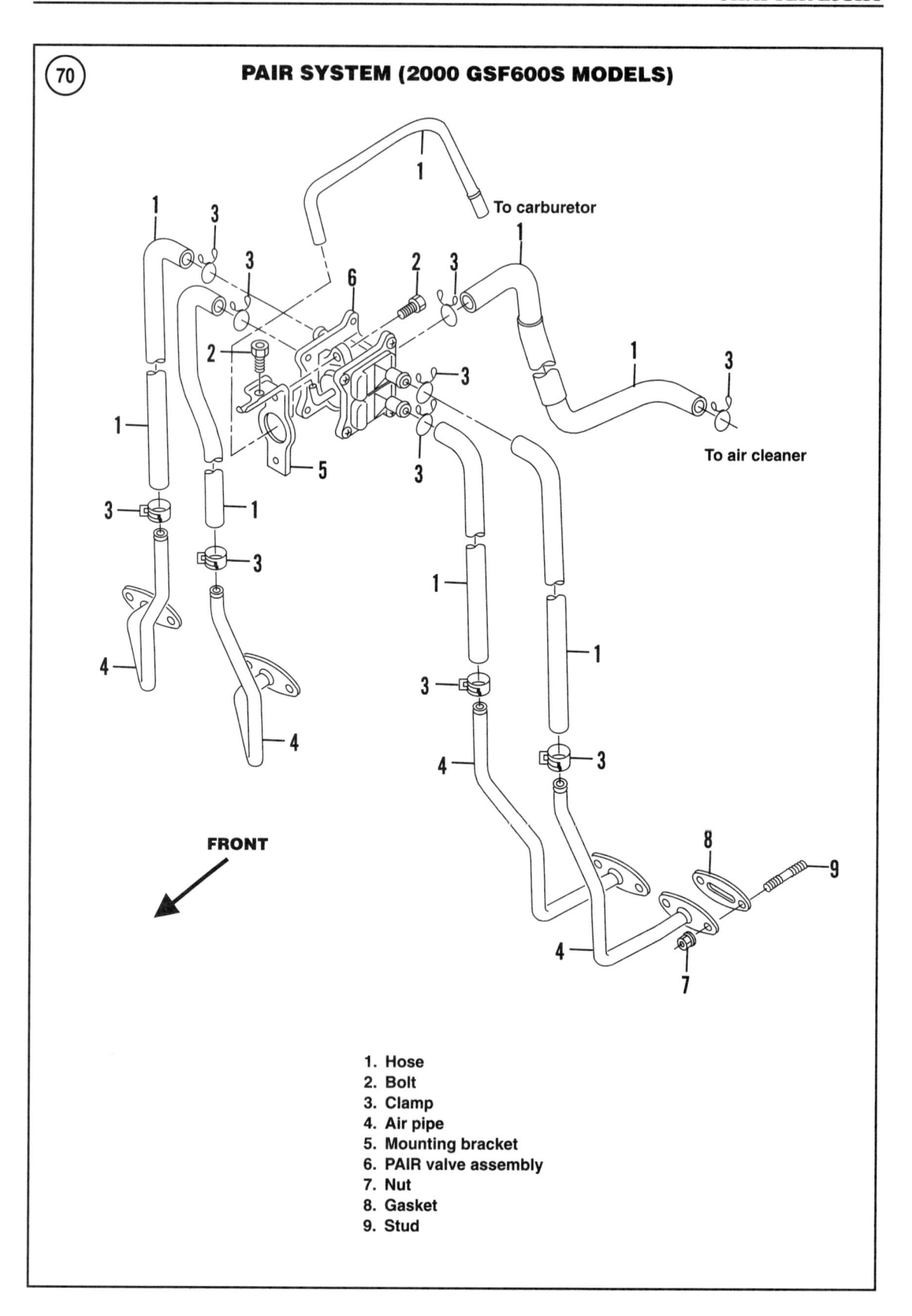

⑦ PAIR SYSTEM (2000 GSF600S MODELS)

To carburetor

To air cleaner

FRONT

1. Hose
2. Bolt
3. Clamp
4. Air pipe
5. Mounting bracket
6. PAIR valve assembly
7. Nut
8. Gasket
9. Stud

FUEL, EMISSION CONTROL AND EXHAUST SYSTEMS

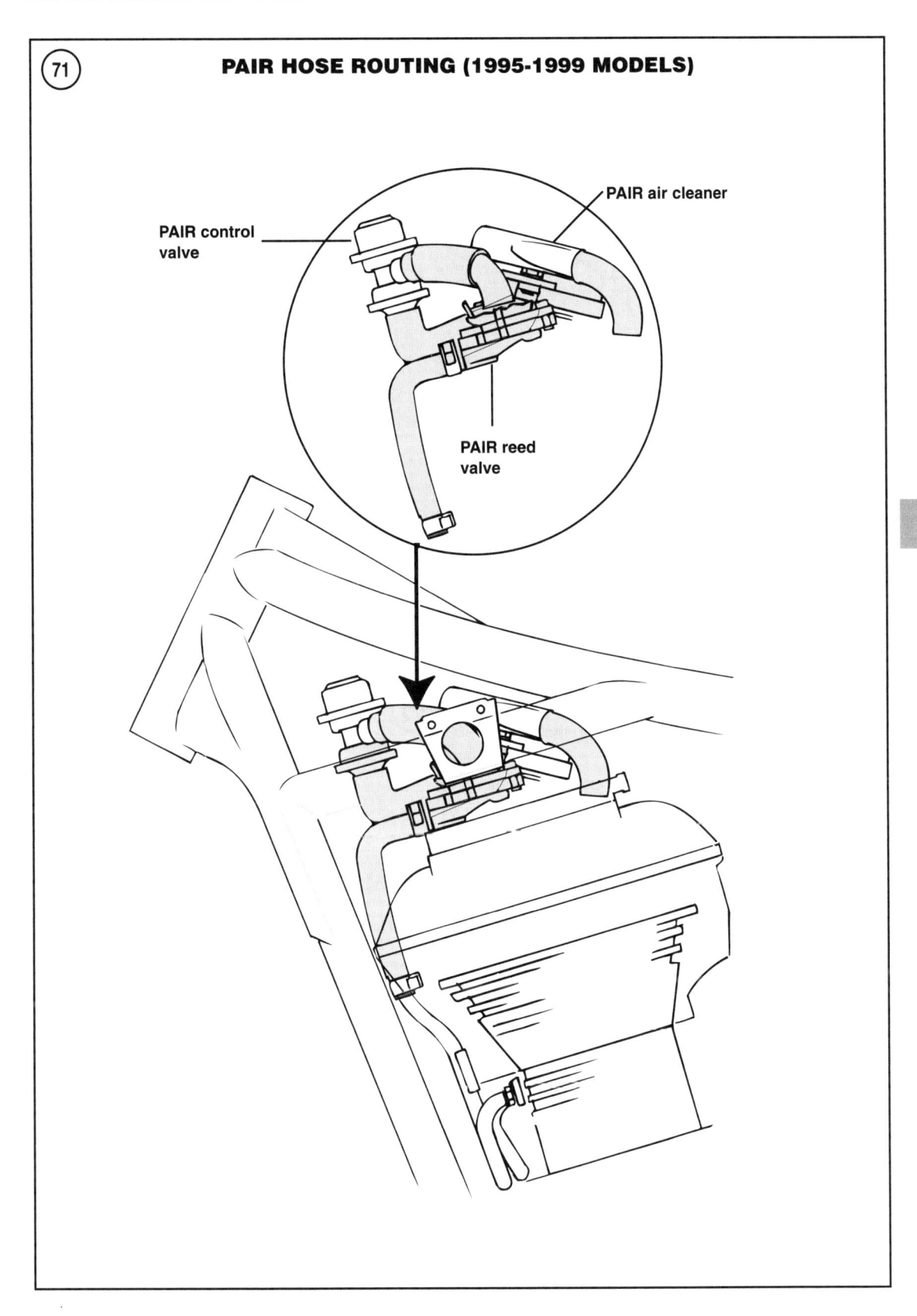

PAIR HOSE ROUTING (1995-1999 MODELS)

⑦¹

- PAIR control valve
- PAIR air cleaner
- PAIR reed valve

PAIR HOSE ROUTING (2000 MODELS)

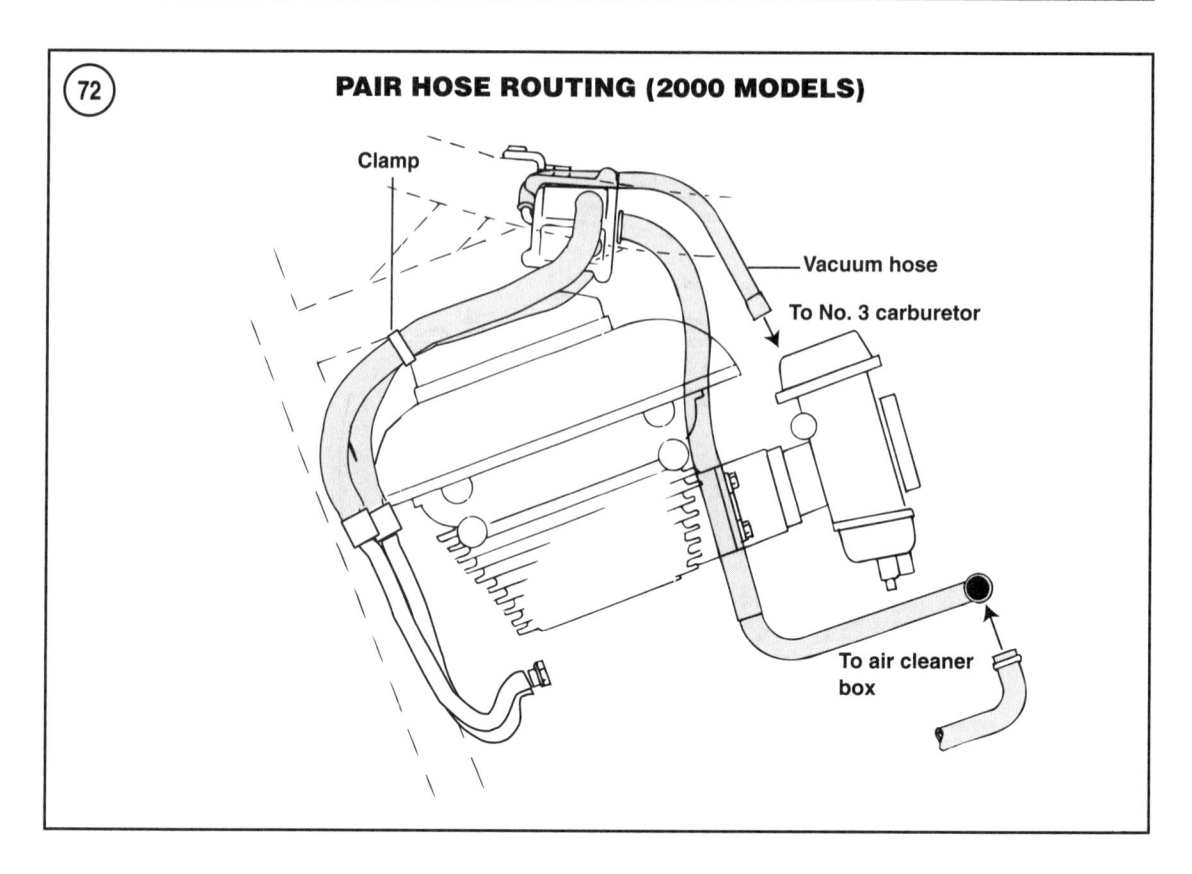

Inspection (1995-1999 models)

1. Inspect the reed valve by performing the following:
    a. Remove the mounting screws and remove the reed valve from the PAIR mounting bracket.
    b. Remove the cover bolts (A, **Figure 73**) from the reed valve and remove the cover (B).
    c. Remove the reed valve from the reed-valve body (**Figure 74**).
    d. Inspect the reed valve for carbon deposits. Replace the reed valve if deposits are found.
    e. Repeat Steps 1-3 for the other reed valve.
2. Inspect the control valve by performing the following:
    a. Blow air into the inlet port on the bottom of the control valve (**Figure 75**).
    b. Air should flow from the two control-valve outlet ports. Replace the control valve if it does not.
    c. Connect a vacuum pump to the vacuum fitting on the top of the control valve. See **Figure 76**.

CAUTION
Vacuum pressure applied in the following step should not exceed the

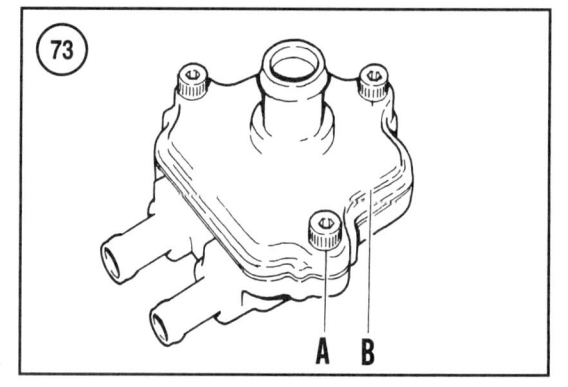

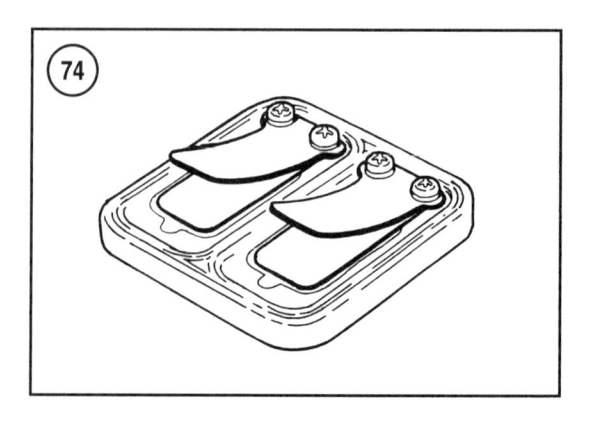

FUEL, EMISSION CONTROL AND EXHAUST SYSTEMS

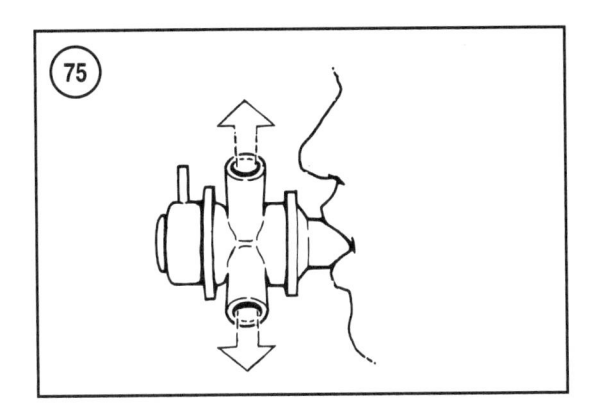

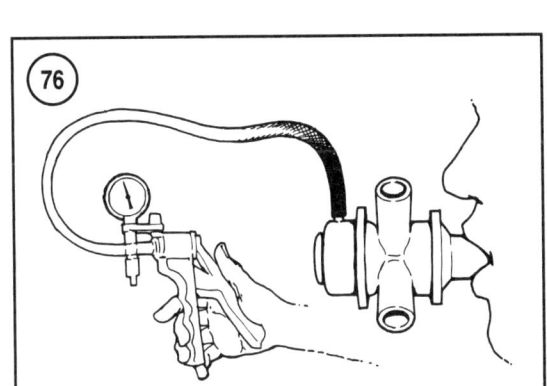

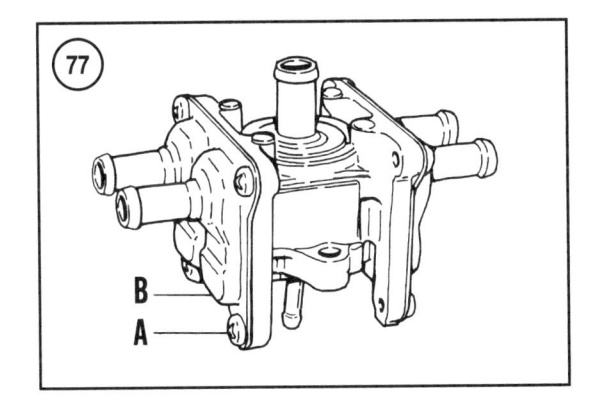

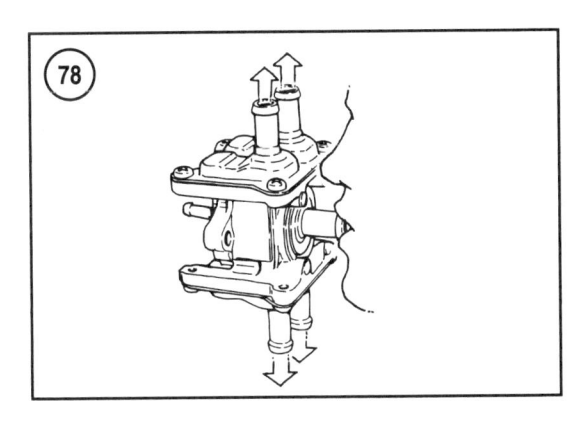

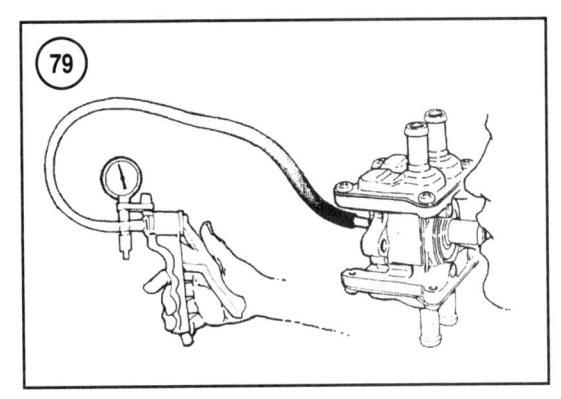

value specified in **Table 7**. The control valve could be damaged if excessive vacuum pressure is applied.

  d. Slowly apply vacuum to the control valve until the vacuum pressure is within the range specified in **Table 7**.
  e. Blow into the control valve inlet port. Air should not flow from the outlet ports when the applied vacuum is within the vacuum pressure range specified in **Table 7**. If it does, replace the control valve.

Inspection (2000 models)

1. Inspect the reed valve by performing the following:
   a. Remove the cover screws (A, **Figure 77**) from the reed valve and remove the cover (B, **Figure 77**).
   b. Remove the reed valve from the reed-valve body (**Figure 74**).
   c. Inspect the reed valve for carbon deposits. Replace the reed valve if deposits are found.
   d. Repeat Steps 1-3 for the other reed valve.
2. Inspect the control valve by performing the following:
   a. Blow air into the inlet port on the bottom of the control valve (**Figure 78**).
   b. Air should flow from the two control-valve outlet ports. Replace the control valve if it does not.
   c. Connect a vacuum pump to the vacuum fitting on the top of the control valve. See **Figure 79**.

CAUTION
*Vacuum pressure applied in the following step should not exceed the value specified in **Table 7**. The control*

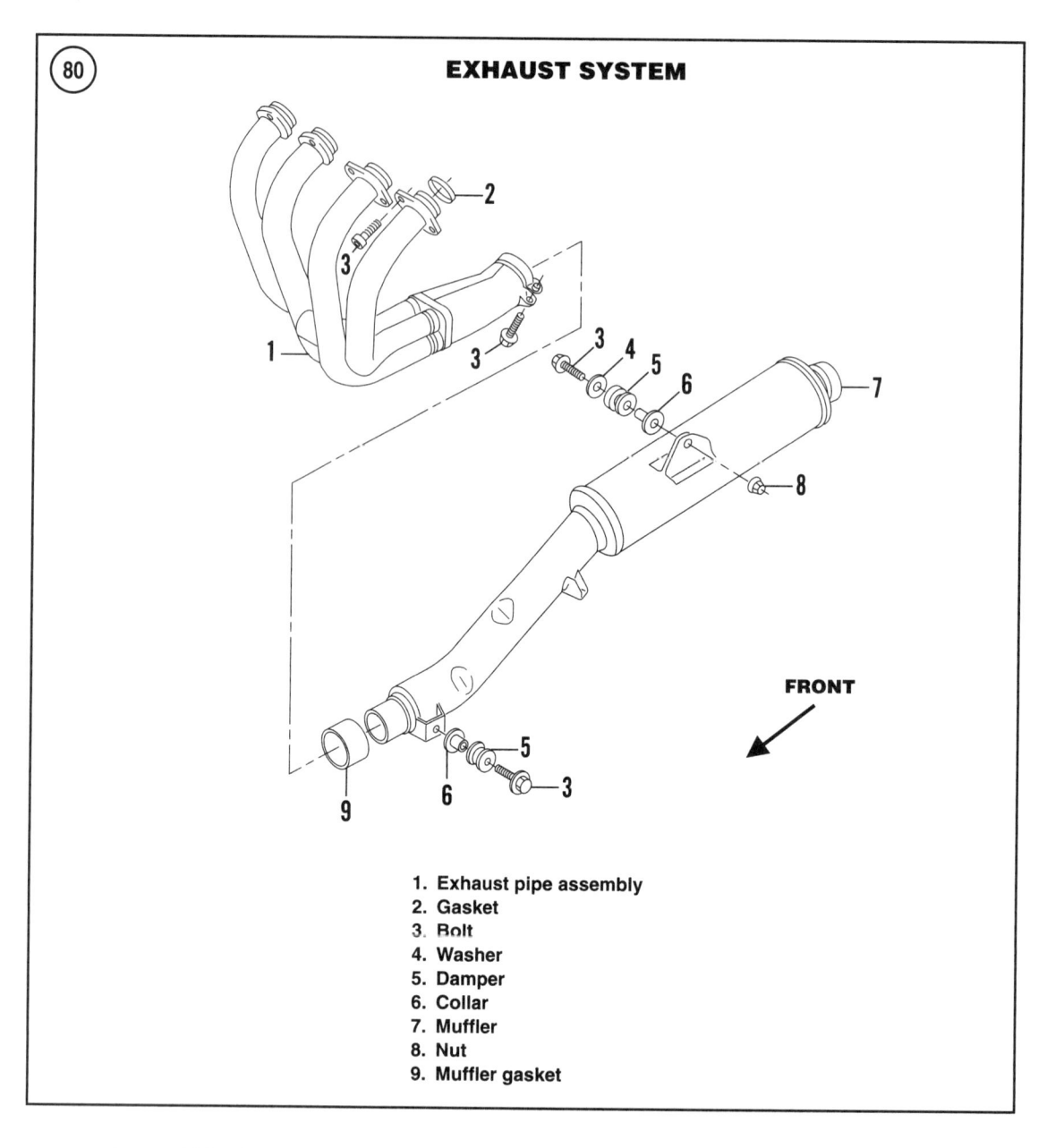

EXHAUST SYSTEM

80

1. Exhaust pipe assembly
2. Gasket
3. Bolt
4. Washer
5. Damper
6. Collar
7. Muffler
8. Nut
9. Muffler gasket

valve could be damaged if excessive vacuum pressure is applied.

d. Slowly apply vacuum to the control valve until the vacuum pressure is within the range specified.

e. Blow into the control valve inlet port. Air should not flow from the outlet ports when the applied vacuum is within the vacuum pressure range specified in **Table 7**. If it does, replace the control valve.

FUEL, EMISSION CONTROL AND EXHAUST SYSTEMS

4. Pull the muffler out from exhaust pipe and remove the muffler. Remove the exhaust pipe gasket.
5. Check the rubber grommet at the rear mounting bracket. Replace the rubber grommet if it is starting to harden or deteriorate.
6. Installation is the reverse of removal.
   a. Install a *new* exhaust pipe gasket.
   b. Tighten the fasteners to the specifications in **Table 8**.
   c. After installation is complete, start the engine and check for exhaust leaks.

Exhaust Pipe Removal/Installation

Refer to **Figure 80**.
1. Securely support the motorcycle on level ground.
2. Remove the oil cooler as described in Chapter Five.
3. Remove the muffler as previously described in this chapter.
4. Remove the two header bolts (**Figure 83**) from each exhaust port.
5. Pull the exhaust pipe assembly forward and out of the cylinder head and then remove the exhaust pipe assembly from the motorcycle. Remove the sealing gaskets from the exhaust ports in each cylinder.
6. Inspect the mounting bracket on the muffler for cracks or damage.
7. Check the exhaust pipe-to-cylinder head flange for corrosion, burned areas or damage.
8. Inspect all of the welds for leakage or corrosion.
9. Install a *new* exhaust pipe sealing gasket into each exhaust port. Apply a small amount of heavy grease to the gaskets to hold them in place.
10. Install the exhaust pipe assembly onto the cylinder head and frame.
11. Install the exhaust header bolts (**Figure 83**). Finger-tighten them at this time.
12. Install the muffler as previously described in this chapter. Finger-tighten the hardware at this time.
13. Tighten the exhaust system fasteners to the specification in **Table 8**, using the following sequence:
   a. Exhaust header bolts.
   b. Exhaust pipe-to-muffler clamp bolt.
   c. Muffler mounting bolt.
14. After installation is complete, start the engine and check for exhaust leaks.

EXHAUST SYSTEM

The exhaust system is a vital performance component. Because of its design, it is a vulnerable piece of equipment. Check the exhaust system for deep dents and fractures. Repair them or replace the defective component immediately. Check the muffler frame mounting flanges for fractures and loose bolts. Check the cylinder head mounting flanges for tightness. A loose exhaust pipe connection can rob the engine of power.

Muffler Removal/Installation

Refer to **Figure 80**.
1. Securely support the motorcycle on level ground.
2. Loosen the clamp bolt (**Figure 81**) securing the muffler to the exhaust pipe assembly.
3. Remove the nut from the muffler mount (**Figure 82**) that secures the muffler to the rear footpeg. Remove the bolt and washer. Do not lose the collar or damper from this mount.

Table 1 CARBURETOR SPECIFICATIONS (1995 MODELS)

Item	Specification
Carburetor model	Keihin CVK32
Carburetor type	Constant velocity
Bore size	32 mm
Carburetor identification	
U.K. France, Italy, Belgium and Spain models	26E0
Switzerland models	26E2
Germany models	26E3
Germany U-type models	26E4
Idle speed	
All models except Switzerland	1100-1300 rpm
Switzerland models	1150-1300 rpm
Float height	16-18 mm (0.63-0.71 in.)
Main jet	
All models except Switzerland	
Carburetors No. 1 & No. 4	No. 98
Carburetors No. 2 & No. 3	No. 100
Switzerland models	
Carburetors No. 1 & No. 4	No. 100
Carburetors No. 2 & No. 3	No. 102
Main air jet	No. 90
Jet needle	
All models except Switzerland	N1QJ
Switzerland models	N76L
Pilot jet	No. 35
Pilot air jet	No. 150
Valve seat	2.4 mm
Pilot screw	
All models except Switzerland	1 7/8 turns out
Switzerland models	2 1/8 turns out
Throttle cable free play	0.5-1.0 mm (0.02-0.04 in.)
Choke cable free play	0.5-1.0 mm (0.02-0.04 in.)

Table 2 CARBURETOR SPECIFICATIONS (1996 MODELS)

Item	Specification
Carburetor model	Keihin CVK32
Carburetor type	Constant velocity
Bore size	32 mm
Carburetor identification	
U.S.A. models	26E1
California models	26E5
Canada, U.K. France, Italy, Belgium, Spain, Netherlands and Brazil models	26E0
Switzerland models	26E2
Australia, Germany, Denmark, Finland, Norway and Sweden models	26E3
Germany U-type models	26E4
Idle speed	
All models except Switzerland	1100-1300 rpm
Switzerland models	
GSF600	1100-1300 rpm
GSF600S	1150-1300 rpm
Float height	16-18 mm (0.63-0.71 in.)
(continued)	

FUEL, EMISSION CONTROL AND EXHAUST SYSTEMS

Table 2 CARBURETOR SPECIFICATIONS (1996 MODELS) (continued)

Item	Specification
Main jet	
All models except Switzerland	
Carburetors No. 1 & No. 4	No. 98
Carburetors No. 2 & No. 3	No. 100
Switzerland models	
Carburetors No. 1 & No. 4	No. 100
Carburetors No. 2 & No. 3	No. 102
Main air jet	No. 90
Jet needle	
U.S.A. models	N1QA
California and Switzerland models	N76L
All models except U.S.A., California and Switzerland	N1QJ
Pilot jet	No. 35
Pilot air jet (GSF600ST)	
U.S.A. models	No. 155
All models except U.S.A.	No. 150
Valve seat (GSF600ST)	2.4 mm
Pilot screw	
U.S.A. and California models	Pre-set
All models except U.S.A., California and Switzerland	1 7/8 turns out
Switzerland models	2 1/8 turns out
Throttle cable free play	0.5-1.0 mm (0.02-0.04 in.)
Choke cable free play	0.5-1.0 mm (0.02-0.04 in.)

Table 3 CARBURETOR SPECIFICATIONS (1997 MODELS)

Item	Specification
Carburetor model	Keihin CVK32
Carburetor type	Constant velocity
Bore size	32 mm
Carburetor identification	
U.S.A. and Canada models	26E1
California models	26E5
U.K. models	26E7
France, Italy, Belgium, Spain, and Netherlands models	26E0
Brazil models	26E6
Switzerland models	26E2
Australia, and Germany, Denmark, Finland, Norway and Sweden models	26E3
Germany U-type models	26E4
Idle speed	
All models except Switzerland	1100-1300 rpm
Switzerland models	1150-1300 rpm
Float height	16-18 mm (0.63-0.71 in.)
Main jet	
All models except Switzerland	
Carburetors No. 1 & No. 4	No. 98
Carburetors No. 2 & No. 3	No. 100
Switzerland models	
Carburetors No. 1 & No. 4	No. 100
Carburetors No. 2 & No. 3	No. 102
(continued)	

Table 3 CARBURETOR SPECIFICATIONS (1997 MODELS) (continued)

Item	Specification
Main air jet	No. 90
Jet needle	
U.S.A. and Canada models	N1QA
California and Switzerland models	N76L
All models except U.S.A., California, Canada and Switzerland models	N1QJ
Pilot jet	No. 35
Pilot air jet (Germany U-type and Switzerland models)	No. 150
Valve seat (Germany U-type and Switzerland models)	2.4 mm
Pilot screw	
U.S.A., California and Canada models	Pre-set
All models except U.S.A., California and Canada models	1 7/8 turns out
Switzerland models	2 1/8 turns out
Throttle cable free play	0.5-1.0 mm (0.02-0.04 in.)
Choke cable free play	0.5-1.0 mm (0.02-0.04 in.)

Table 4 CARBURETOR SPECIFICATIONS (1998 MODELS)

Item	Specification
Carburetor model	Keihin CVK32
Carburetor type	Constant velocity
Bore size	32 mm
Carburetor identification	
U.S.A. and Canada models	26E1
California models	26E5
U.K. models	26E7
France, Italy, Belgium, Spain and Netherlands models	26E0
Switzerland models	26E2
Australia and Germany (non U-type), Denmark, Finland, Norway and Sweden models	26E3
Brazil models	26E6
Germany U-type models	26E4
Idle speed	
All models except Switzerland	1100-1300 rpm
Switzerland models	1150-1300 rpm
Float height	16-18 mm (0.63-0.71 in.)
Main jet	
All models except Switzerland	
Carburetors No. 1 & No. 4	No. 98
Carburetors No. 2 & No. 3	No. 100
Switzerland models	
Carburetors No. 1 & No. 4	No. 100
Carburetors No. 2 & No. 3	No. 102
Main air jet	No. 90
Jet needle	
U.S.A. and Canada models	N1QA
California and Switzerland models	N76L
All models except U.S.A., California, Canada and Switzerland models	N1QJ

(continued)

FUEL, EMISSION CONTROL AND EXHAUST SYSTEMS

Table 4 CARBURETOR SPECIFICATIONS (1998 MODELS) (continued)

Item	Specification
Pilot jet	No. 35
Pilot screw	
U.S.A. California and Canada models	Pre-set
All models except U.S.A., California, Canada and Switzerland	1 7/8 turns out
Switzerland models	2 1/8 turns out
Throttle cable free play	0.5-1.0 mm (0.02-0.04 in.)
Choke cable free play	0.5-1.0 mm (0.02-0.04 in.)

Table 5 CARBURETOR SPECIFICATIONS (1999 MODELS)

Item	Specification
Carburetor model	Keihin CVK32
Carburetor type	Constant velocity
Bore size	32 mm
Carburetor identification	
U.S.A. and Canada models	26E1
California models	26E5
U.K. models	26E7
France, Italy, Belgium, Spain, and Netherlands models	26E0
Switzerland models	26E2
Australia, Germany, Denmark, Finland, Norway and Sweden models	26E3
Brazil models	26E6
Germany U-type models	26E4
Idle speed	
All models except Switzerland	1100-1300 rpm
Switzerland models	1150-1300 rpm
Float height	16-18 mm (0.63-0.71 in.)
Main jet	
All models except Switzerland	
Carburetors No. 1 & No. 4	No. 98
Carburetors No. 2 & No. 3	No. 100
Switzerland models	
Carburetors No. 1 & No. 4	No. 100
Carburetors No. 2 & No. 3	No. 102
Main air jet	No. 90
Jet needle	
U.S.A. and Canada models	N1QA
California and Switzerland models	N76L
All models except U.S.A., California, Canada and Switzerland models	N1QJ
Pilot jet	No. 35
Pilot screw	
U.S.A. California and Canada models	Pre-set
All models except U.S.A., California, Canada and Switzerland	1 7/8 turns out
Switzerland models	2 1/8 turns out
Throttle cable free play	0.5-1.0 mm (0.02-0.04 in.)
Choke cable free play	0.5-1.0 mm (0.02-0.04 in.)

Table 6 CARBURETOR SPECIFICATIONS (2000 MODELS)

Item	Specification
Carburetor model	Keihin CVR32SS
Carburetor type	Constant velocity
Bore size	32 mm
Carburetor identification	31F2
U.S.A., and Canada models	31F2
California models	31F3
U.K. and European models	31F0
European U-type models	31F1
Idle speed	1100-1300 rpm
Float height	16-18 mm (0.63-0.71 in.)
Main jet	No. 92
Jet needle	N1QL
Needle jet	3.4
Pilot jet	No. 35
Throttle valve	11
Pilot screw	
USA, California, Canada models	Pre-set (1 7/8 turns out)
U.K. and European models	Pre-set (1 3/4 turns out)
European U-type models	Pre-set (1 7/8 turns out)
Throttle cable free play	2.0-4.0 mm (0.08-0.16 in.)
Choke cable free play	0.5-1.0 mm (0.02-0.04 in.)

Table 7 CARBURETOR TEST SPECIFICATIONS

Item	Specification
Carburetor heater coil resistance	
(1997-1999 U.K models)	12-18 ohms
Throttle position sensor (2000 models)	
Fully-closed resistance	Approximately 5 k ohms
Wide-open resistance	3.09-4.63 k ohms
PAIR Control Valve Vacuum Pressure	
1995-1999 California and Switzerland models	47-73 kPa (350-550 mm Hg, 13.8-21.7 in. Hg)
2000 models	44-65.3 kPa (330-490 mm Hg, 10.6-17.7 in. Hg)

Table 8 TORQUE SPECIFICATIONS

Item	N•m	in.-lb.	ft.-lb.
Carburetor heater			
(U.K. models)	3	26.5	–
Exhaust pipe bolt	23	–	17
Muffler mounting bolt			
1995-1999 models	23	–	17
2000 models	29	–	21
PAIR air pipe nuts	10	88	
PAIR valve assembly mounting bolt			
(2000 models)	10	88	–

CHAPTER NINE

ELECTRICAL SYSTEM

This chapter covers service and test procedures for most of the electrical system. Battery and spark plug information is covered in Chapter Three.

Electrical system specifications are in **Tables 1-3** at the end of the chapter. Wiring diagrams are located at the end of the book. The systems and components covered in this chapter are:

1. Charging.
2. Ignition.
3. Starting.
4. Lighting.
5. Switches.
6. Combination meter.
7. Horn.
8. Fuses.

PRELIMINARY INFORMATION

Resistance Testing

Resistance readings will vary with temperature. The resistance increases when the temperature increases and decreases when the temperature decreases.

Specifications for resistance are based on tests performed at a specific temperature [68° F (20° C)]. If a component is warm or hot let it cool to room temperature. If a component is tested at a temperature that varies from the specification test temperature, a false reading may result.

The manufacturer specifies using the Suzuki Multi Circuit Tester (part No. 09900-25008) for accurate resistance tests. Due to the specific resistance values of the semiconductors in this meter, using another meter may provide inaccurate results.

An equivalent tool is the Motion Pro IgnitionMate (part No. 08-0193). However, the test procedures in this chapter use the Suzuki Multi Circuit Tester. If an alternative meter is being used, follow that manufacturer's instructions.

Make sure the battery of any tester being used is in good condition. The battery of an ohmmeter is the source for the current that is applied to the circuit being tested; accurate results depend on the battery having sufficient voltage.

NOTE
When using an analog ohmmeter, always calibrate the meter between each resistance test by touching the test leads together and zeroing the meter.

Electrical Component Replacement

Most parts suppliers do not accept returns on electrical components. If the exact cause of any electrical system malfunction has not been determined, do not attempt to remedy the problem with guesswork and unnecessary parts replacement. If possible, have the suspect component or system tested by a professional technician *before* purchasing electrical components.

Electrical Component/Connector Location and Service

The location of electrical connectors can vary between model years. On 1995-1999 models, many electrical connectors can be found on the left side of the frame, behind the rear frame cover. On 2000 models, they are behind the left side cover.

The position of the connectors may have been changed during previous repairs. Always confirm the wire colors to and from the connector and follow the wiring harness to the various components when performing tests.

Moisture can enter many of the electrical connectors and cause corrosion, which may cause a poor electrical connection. This may result in component failure and a possible breakdown on the road. To prevent moisture from entering into the various connectors, disconnect them and after making sure the terminals are clean, pack the connector with dielectric grease. Do not use a substitute that may interfere with current flow. Dielectric grease is specifically formulated to seal the connector and not increase current resistance. For best results, the compound should fill the entire inner area of the connector. It is recommended that each time a connector is unplugged, that it be cleaned and sealed with dielectric grease.

Ground connections are often overlooked during troubleshooting. Make sure they are corrosion free and tight. Apply dielectric grease to the terminals before reconnecting them.

NEGATIVE BATTERY TERMINAL

Many of the procedures in this chapter require disconnecting the negative battery cable as a safety precaution. This procedure is described below.
1. Turn the ignition switch OFF.
2. Remove the seat as described in Chapter Fourteen. On 2000 models, remove the document tray.
3. Disconnect the negative battery cable from the battery terminal (**Figure 1**).
4. Move the negative cable out of the way so it will not accidentally make contact with the negative battery terminal.
5. Once the procedure is completed, connect the negative battery cable to the terminal, and tighten the bolt securely.
6. Install the seat as described in Chapter Fourteen.

CHARGING SYSTEM

The charging system consists of the battery, alternator, solid-state voltage regulator and rectifier (**Figure 2**). Alternating current generated by the al-

ELECTRICAL SYSTEM

CHARGING SYSTEM

1995-1999 MODELS

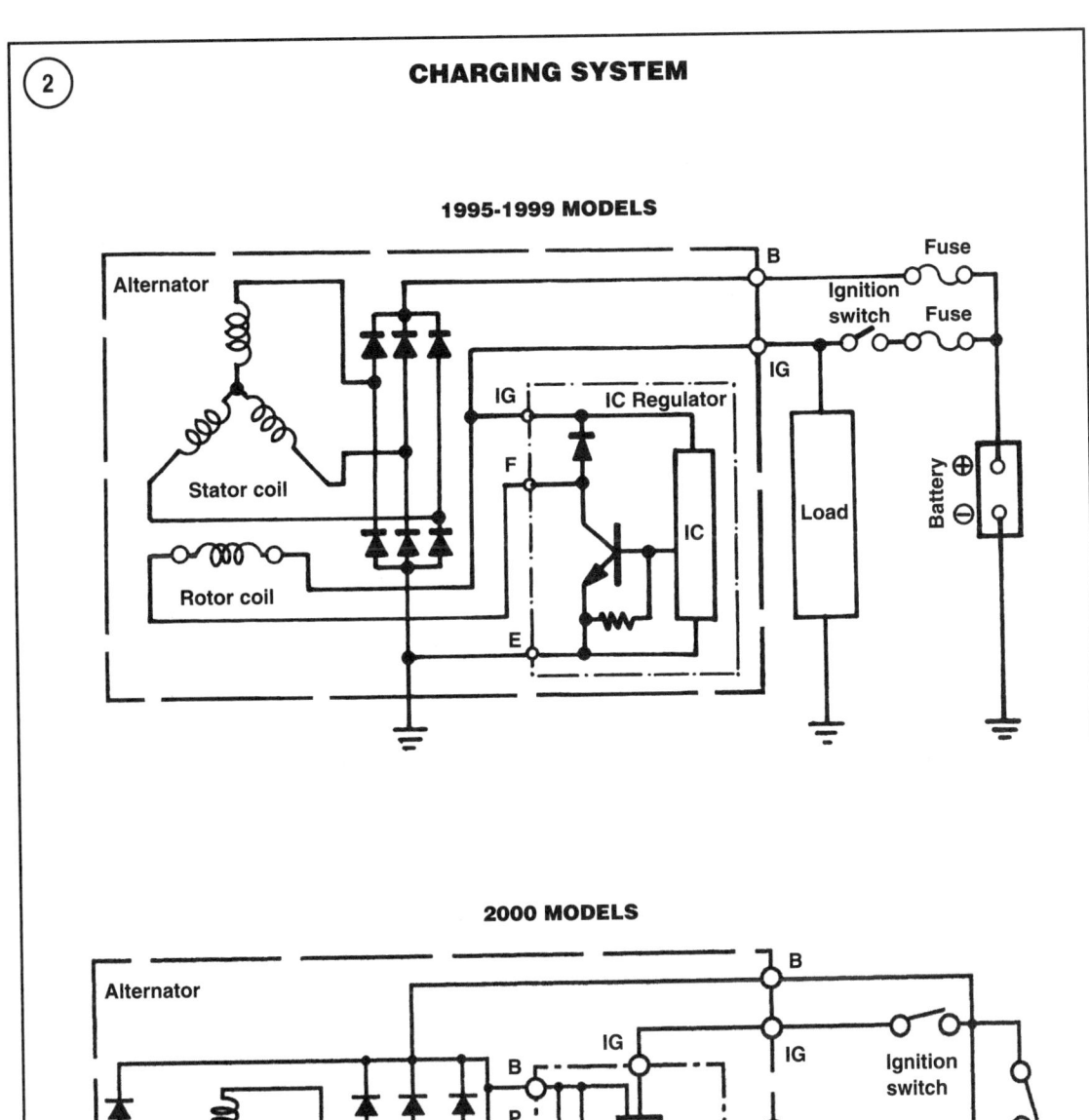

2000 MODELS

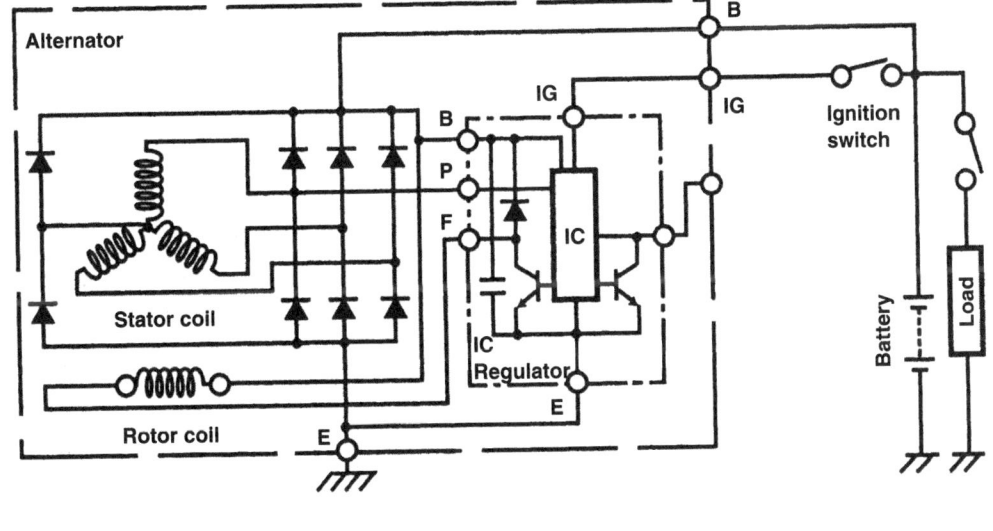

ternator is rectified to direct current. The voltage regulator maintains the voltage to the battery and electrical loads (for example, lights and ignition) at a constant voltage regardless of variations in engine speed and load.

Troubleshooting

Refer to Chapter Two.

Current Draw Test

Perform this test prior to performing the regulated voltage test.
1. Turn the ignition switch OFF.
2. Remove the seat as described in Chapter Fourteen. On 2000 models, remove the document tray.
3. Disconnect the negative battery cable (**Figure 1**) from the battery terminal.

CAUTION
Before connecting the ammeter into the circuit in Step 4, set the meter to its highest amperage scale. This will prevent a possible large current flow from damaging the meter or blowing the meter's fuse, if so equipped.

4. Connect the ammeter between the battery negative cable and the negative terminal of the battery (**Figure 3**). Switch the ammeter from its highest to lowest amperage scale while reading the meter. If the needle swings even the slightest amount, there is a current draw on the system. If current exceeds 1 mA, the battery will eventually discharge.
5. If the current draw exceeds 1 mA, the probable causes are:
   a. Short circuit in the system.
   b. Loose, dirty or faulty electrical system connectors in the charging system wiring harness system.
   c. Damaged battery.
6. To locate a short circuit, refer to the wiring diagrams at the end of this book. Continue to measure the current draw while disconnecting different connectors in the electrical system one by one. When the current draw returns to normal, that circuit contains the short. Continue testing the defective circuit until the problem is identified.
7. Disconnect the ammeter test leads and reconnect the negative battery cable.

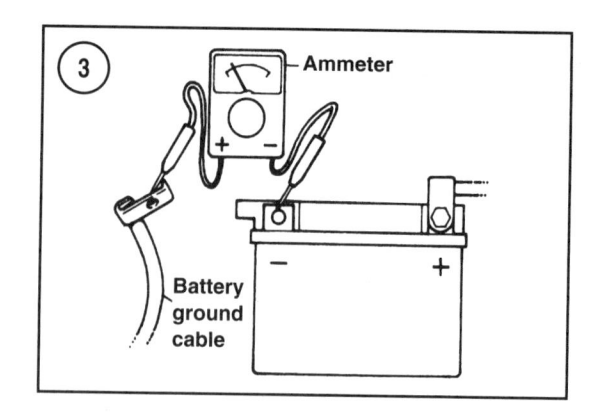

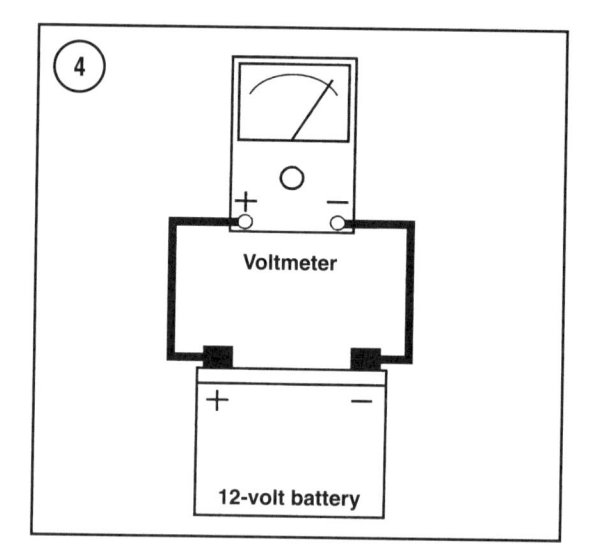

Regulated Voltage Test

Whenever charging system trouble is suspected, make sure the battery is fully charged and in good condition before performing any tests. Clean and test the battery as described in Chapter Three. Make sure all electrical connectors are tight and free of corrosion.

ELECTRICAL SYSTEM

than specified, test the alternator and the IC regulator as described in this chapter.

6. If the regulated voltage is too high, the IC regulator is probably at fault. Inspect the IC regulator as described in this chapter.

7. After the test is completed, disconnect the voltmeter and shut off the engine.

ALTERNATOR

The IC regulator and rectifier are built into the alternator. These two components can be removed and replaced separately.

Removal/Installation

1. Remove the seat as described in Chapter Fourteen. On 2000 models, remove the document tray.
2. Remove the engine drive sprocket as described in Chapter Seven.
3. Disconnect the negative battery cable (**Figure 1**).
4A. On 1995-1999 models, perform the following:
   a. Remove the left rear frame cover as described in Chapter Fourteen.
   b. Disconnect the 2-pin alternator connector (containing 1 red wire and 1 orange wire) among the electrical connectors on the left side of the rear frame. See **Figure 5**.
   c. Remove the starter motor as described in this chapter.
4B. On 2000 models, perform the following:
   a. Disconnect the connector from its mate on the alternator (A, **Figure 6**).
   b. Pull back the rubber boot, and disconnect the electrical lead from the alternator terminal (B, **Figure 6**).
5. Remove the alternator mounting bolts (**Figure 7**). Carefully pull the alternator from the crankcase.
6. Install by reversing these removal steps, noting the following:
   a. Inspect the O-ring (A, **Figure 8**) on the alternator housing. Replace the O-ring if it is starting to harden or deteriorate.
   b. Inspect the gear teeth (B, **Figure 8**) for wear or damage. Check for chipped or missing teeth. If damaged, replace the gear.
   c. Tighten the alternator mounting bolts to the torque specification in **Table 3**.
   d. Make sure the electrical connector is corrosion-free and secure.

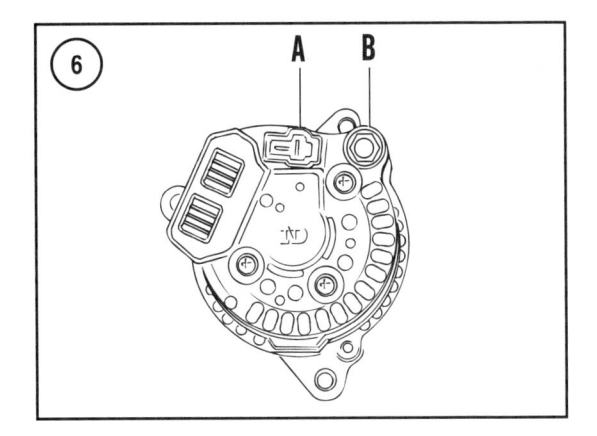

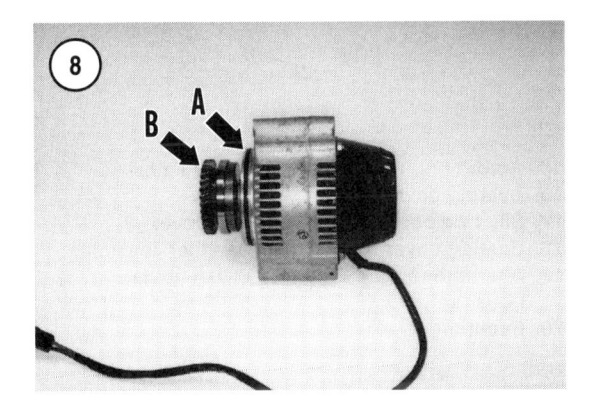

1. Start the engine and let it reach normal operating temperature; shut off the engine.

2. Remove the seat as described in Chapter Fourteen. On 2000 models, remove the document tray.

3. Start the engine and let it idle.

4. Connect a 0-15 DC voltmeter to the negative battery and positive terminals (**Figure 4**).

5. Increase engine speed to 5000 rpm, and measure the voltage. It should be within the regulated voltage range specified in **Table 1**. If the voltage is less

CHAPTER NINE

ALTERNATOR (1995-1999 MODELS)

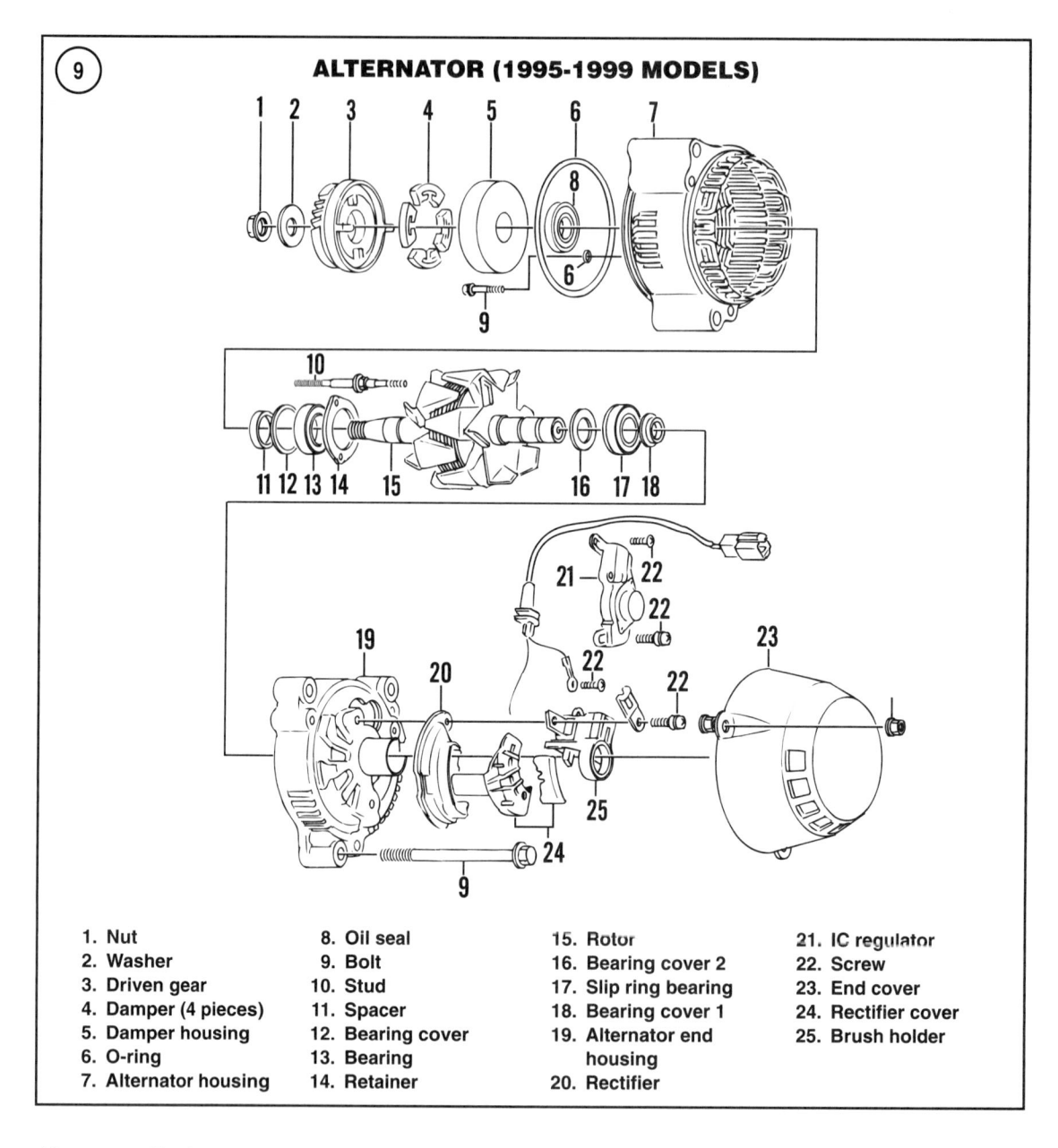

1. Nut
2. Washer
3. Driven gear
4. Damper (4 pieces)
5. Damper housing
6. O-ring
7. Alternator housing
8. Oil seal
9. Bolt
10. Stud
11. Spacer
12. Bearing cover
13. Bearing
14. Retainer
15. Rotor
16. Bearing cover 2
17. Slip ring bearing
18. Bearing cover 1
19. Alternator end housing
20. Rectifier
21. IC regulator
22. Screw
23. End cover
24. Rectifier cover
25. Brush holder

Alternator Testing

The alternator must be partially disassembled to perform these tests. Refer to **Figure 9** for 1995-1999 models and to **Figure 10** for 2000 models.

1. Remove the screws securing the end cover (**Figure 11**) and remove the end cover.
2. To remove the brush holder and IC regulator, perform the following:

  a. Remove the screw (A, **Figure 12**) securing the electrical lead to the brush holder.

  b. Remove the screws (B, **Figure 12**) securing the brush holder and IC regulator. Remove these items.

CAUTION
In the following step, do not apply excessive heat from the soldering gun when unsoldering the wires. Excess heat can destroy the components within the rectifier. Place the soldering gun on the terminal just long enough to melt the solder and remove

ELECTRICAL SYSTEM

ALTERNATOR (2000 MODELS)

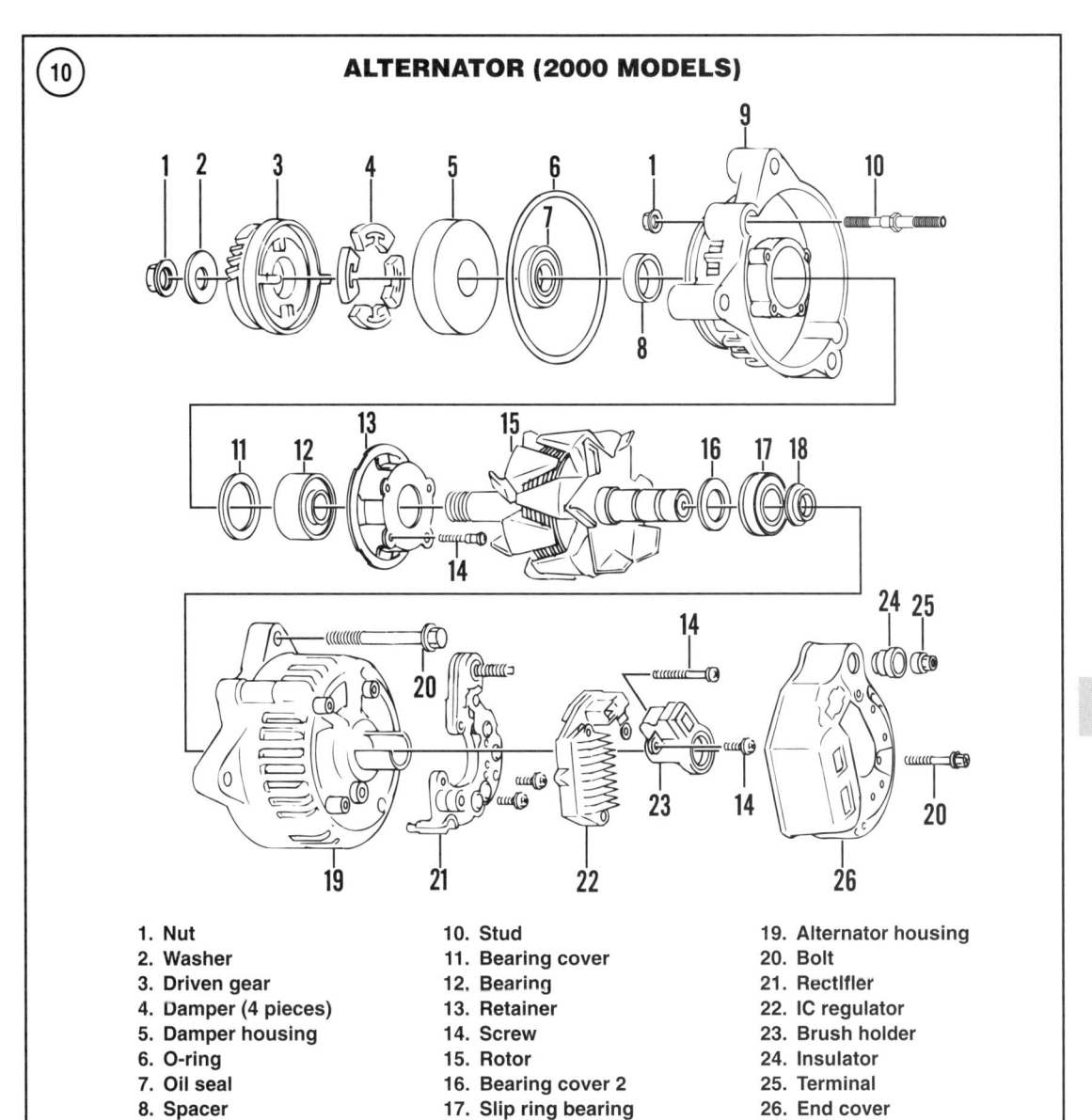

1. Nut
2. Washer
3. Driven gear
4. Damper (4 pieces)
5. Damper housing
6. O-ring
7. Oil seal
8. Spacer
9. End housing
10. Stud
11. Bearing cover
12. Bearing
13. Retainer
14. Screw
15. Rotor
16. Bearing cover 2
17. Slip ring bearing
18. Bearing cover 1
19. Alternator housing
20. Bolt
21. Rectifier
22. IC regulator
23. Brush holder
24. Insulator
25. Terminal
26. End cover

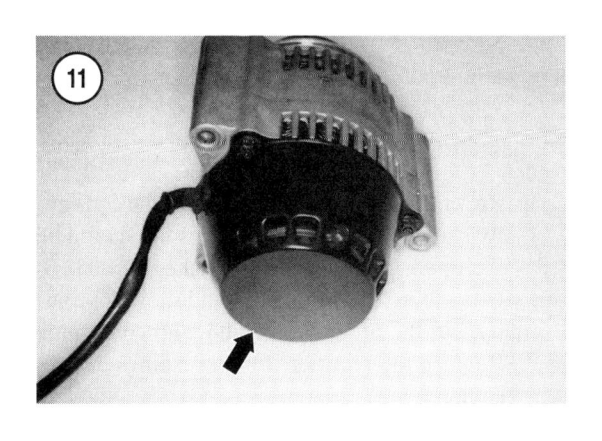

the wire. *Remove the solder gun immediately.*

3A. On 1995-1999 models, perform the following:
   a. Use a solder gun and unsolder the stator coil electrical wires (A, **Figure 13**) and battery lead wire connector (B, **Figure 13**) from the rectifier.
   b. Remove the rectifier from the alternator.
3B. On 2000 models, perform the following:
   a. Remove the stator coil mounting screws.
   b. Use needlenose pliers to straighten out the stator coil wires P1, P2, P3 and P4 shown in **Figure 14**.
   c. Remove the rectifier from the alternator.

NOTE
Stator and rotor removal requires special tools and a press. If these components require replacement, have the procedures performed by a Suzuki dealership.

4. Test the stator coil by performing the following:
   a. Set an ohmmeter to the R × 10 scale and check the continuity between the stator wires.
   b. There should be continuity (low resistance) between the wires shown in **Figure 15** on 1995-1999 models or **Figure 16** on 2000 models. If there is no continuity (infinite resistance), the stator assembly is faulty and must be replaced.
5. Test the rotor by performing the following:
   a. Set an ohmmeter to the R × 10 scale and check the continuity between the two slip rings (**Figure 17**) on the end of the rotor assembly.
   b. There should be continuity (low resistance) between the two slip rings. If there is no continuity (infinite resistance), the rotor assembly is faulty and must be replaced.
6. Measure the outside diameter of the slip ring. If the slip ring is worn to the wear limit, replace the rotor assembly.
7. Test the rectifier, by performing the following:
   a. Set an ohmmeter to the R × 10 scale. For the following continuity tests, refer to **Figure 18** for 1995-1999 models and to **Figure 19** for 2000 models.
   b. Check the continuity between terminal B and ground. Note the continuity shown on the meter.
   c. Reverse the connections and note the continuity shown on the meter. The results should be the opposite of the reading taken in Step B. One of the test readings should show continuity, but the other should show no continuity. Replace the rectifier if both readings are the same.

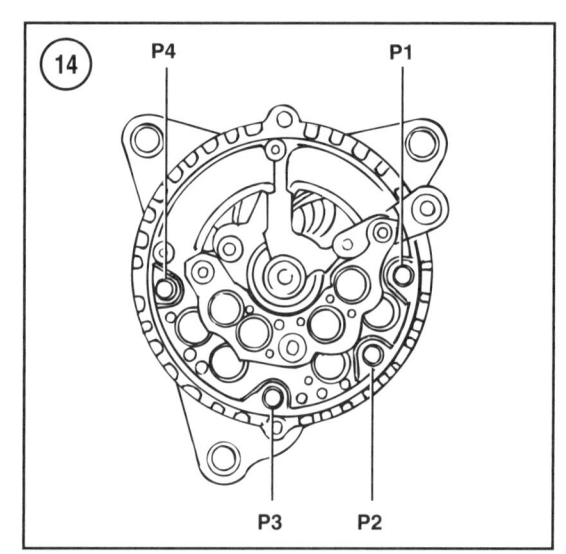

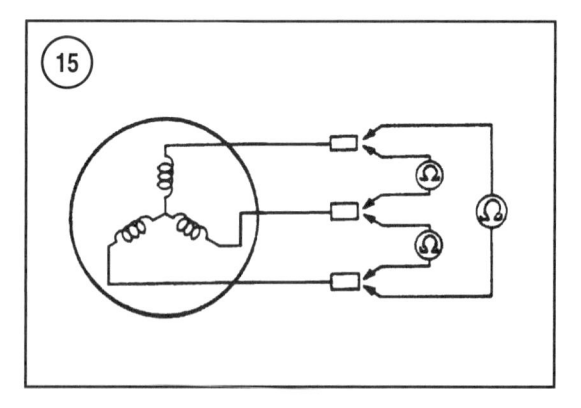

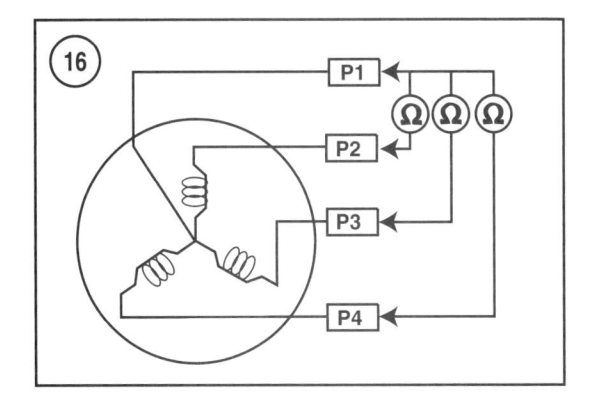

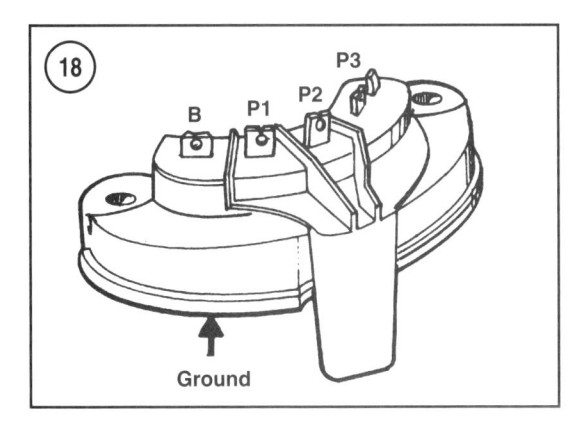

ELECTRICAL SYSTEM

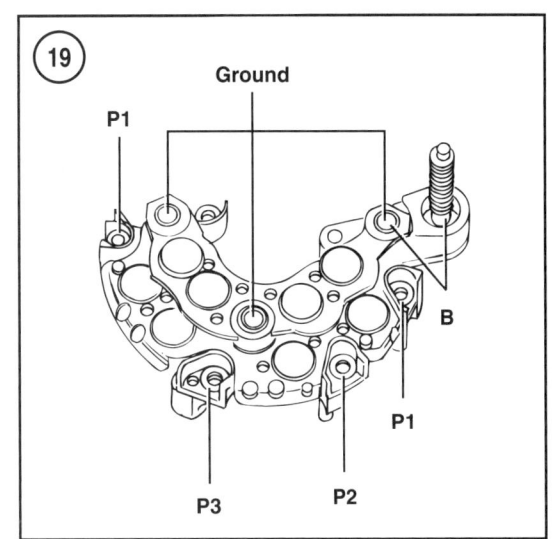

b. Make sure all electrical connectors are free of corrosion and are tight.

IC Regulator Testing (1995-1999 Models)

Tools

Special test equipment and expertise are required to test the IC voltage regulator in 1995-1999 models. If the required tools and expertise are not available, have the voltage regulator tested by a Suzuki dealer.

The following components are required for this test:
1. A variable DC power source.
2. A 0-25 volt DC voltmeter.
3. A switch.
4. A 12 volts/3.4 watt bulb (for example, a turn signal indicator bulb and socket).
5. Jumper wires.

d. Repeat this test (steps 7a-c) between terminal B and each of the P terminals. There should be continuity in one direction and no continuity in the other. Replace the rectifier if both readings are the same.

8. Reassemble the alternator by reversing these steps, noting the following:

   a. On 1995-1999 models, solder the stator coil electrical wires (A, **Figure 13**) and battery lead wire connector (B, **Figure 13**) onto the rectifier portion of the alternator.

Test

1. Remove the screws securing the end cover (**Figure 11**) and remove the end cover.
2. Remove the brush holder and IC regulator by performing the following:

   a. Remove the screw (A, **Figure 12**) securing the electrical lead to the brush holder and the IC regulator.

   b. Remove the screws (B, **Figure 12**) securing the brush holder and IC regulator, and remove these items.

268

20 IC REGULATOR

Bulb (12V 3.4W)

Switch

Variable DC power source

Voltmeter

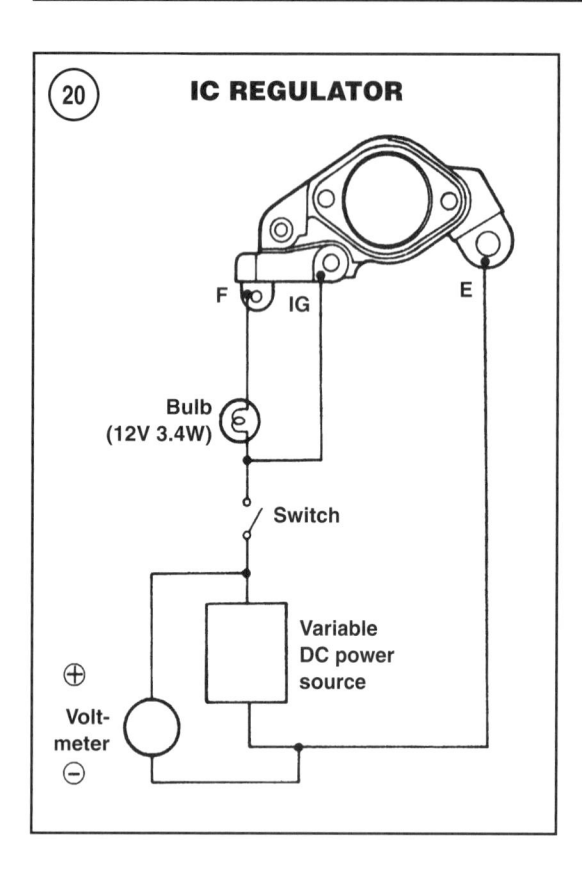

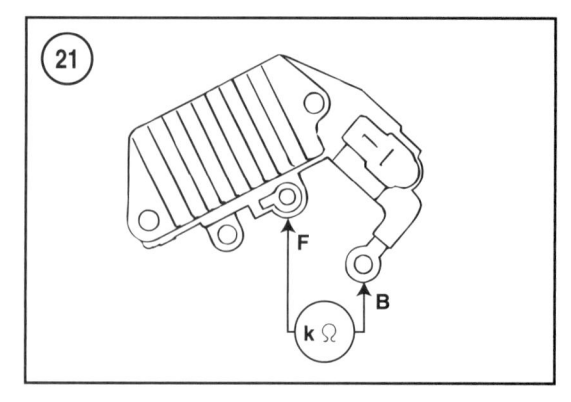

3. Connect the test equipment to the IC regulator as shown in **Figure 20**.
4. Turn the variable power supply to 12 volts, and turn the switch to the ON position.
5. The test light should be ON. If the light is ON, the regulator is working. If the light is OFF, the regulator is defective and must be replaced.
6. Increase the voltage on the variable power supply to 14.5 volts. The test light should go OFF. If the light goes OFF, the regulator is working. If the light stays ON, the regulator is defective and must be replaced.
7. Turn the power supply OFF, and disconnect the regulator from the jumper wires.
8. Reassemble by reversing these steps.

IC Regulator Testing (2000 Models)

1. Remove the screws securing the end cover (**Figure 11**) and remove the end cover.
2. Remove the brush holder and IC regulator by performing the following:
   a. Remove the screw (A, **Figure 12**) securing the electrical lead to the brush holder and the IC regulator.

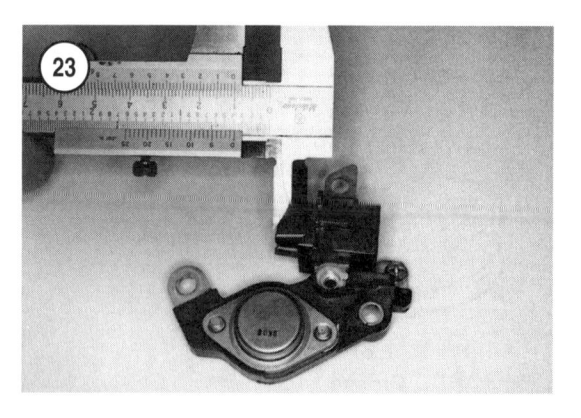

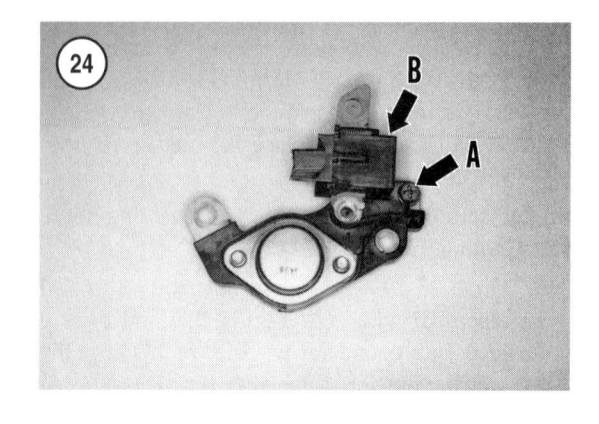

ELECTRICAL SYSTEM

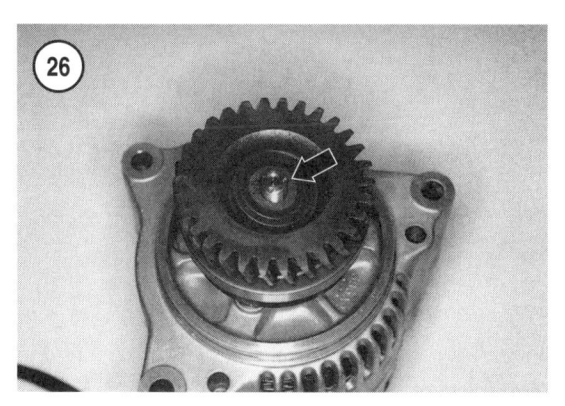

b. Remove the screws (B, **Figure 12**) securing the brush holder and IC regulator, and remove these items.

3. Check the continuity between the rotor coil terminal (F, **Figure 21**) and the battery terminal (B, **Figure 21**) by performing the following:
    a. Set an ohmmeter to the R × 1k scale.
    b. Connect one test lead to the F terminal on the IC regulator. Connect the other test lead to the B terminal. Note the reading shown on the meter.
    c. Reverse the test leads and again note the reading shown on the meter. The IC regulator should have continuity in one direction, but no continuity in the other. Replace the IC regulator if both readings are the same.

Brush Inspection

1. Remove the screws securing the end cover (**Figure 11**) and remove the end cover.
2. To remove the brush holder and IC regulator, perform the following:
    a. Remove the screw (A, **Figure 12**) securing the electrical lead to the brush holder and the IC regulator.
    b. Remove the screws (B, **Figure 12**) securing the brush holder and IC regulator and remove these items.
3. Remove the cover (**Figure 22**) from the brush holder.
4. Use a small scale or vernier caliper to measure the brush length (**Figure 23**). If worn to the service limit listed in **Table 1** or less, replace the brush assembly.
5. If necessary, remove the screw (A, **Figure 24**) securing the brush assembly (B, **Figure 24**) and remove it from the IC regulator.
6. Reassemble by reversing these steps.

Driven Gear and Damper
Removal/Inspection/Installation

1. Place the driven gear in a vise with soft jaws.
2. Remove the driven gear nut (**Figure 25**).
3. Remove the washer (**Figure 26**).
4. Remove the driven gear (**Figure 27**) and damper from the alternator.
5. Inspect the damper housing for wear or damage. Inspect the damper bosses (**Figure 28**) for wear or damage. Replace the damper housing if necessary.

6. Remove the rubber dampers (**Figure 29**) from the driven gear. Inspect the dampers for wear or deterioration. Replace the dampers as a set if any is worn.
7. Inspect the driven gear (**Figure 30**) for wear, chipped or missing teeth. Replace the driven gear if necessary.
8. Inspect the damper bosses (**Figure 31**) in the backside of the driven gear for wear or damage. Replace the driven gear if necessary.
9. Install by reversing these removal steps, noting the following:
   a. Apply molybdenum disulfide grease to the damper surface (**Figure 29**) prior to installation.
   b. Tighten the alternator driven gear nut to the torque specification listed in **Table 3**. After the nut is tightened, use a centerpunch and stake the nut in place (**Figure 32**).

IGNITION SYSTEM

The models covered in this manual are equipped with two very similar transistorized electronic ignition systems, which include a signal generator as well as an igniter unit with an 8-bit central processing unit, 4 MHz ceramic vibrator and a ROM unit (Read only Memory). The difference between the two ignition systems is the addition of a throttle position sensor on 2000 models. See **Figure 33** and **Figure 34**.

Both systems use no breaker points and are non-adjustable, but the timing should be checked to make sure all ignition components within the system are operating correctly. The ignition system is operated by the digital microprocessor within the igniter unit. The ignition advance curve is pre-programmed into the igniter unit's ROM and is closely matched to the spark timing of the engine's ignition requirements. This advance curve cannot be modified to improve performance.

A safe-guard feature is built into both ignition systems to prevent the accidental over-revving of the engine. If the engine speed exceeds 12,000 rpm, the system interrupts the primary current to the No. 1 and No. 4 spark plugs.

CAUTION
Please note that this is not a no-load system. Engine speed can exceed 12,000 rpm without a load, which can

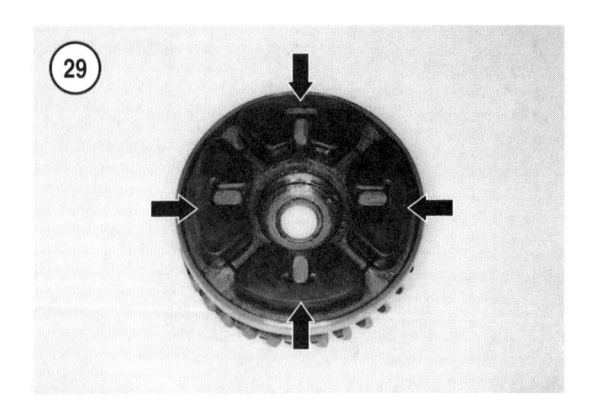

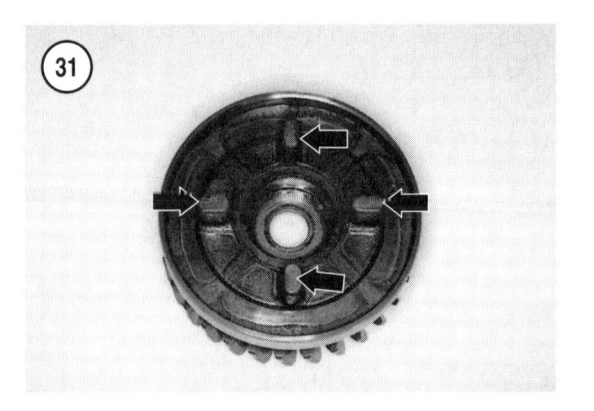

# ELECTRICAL SYSTEM

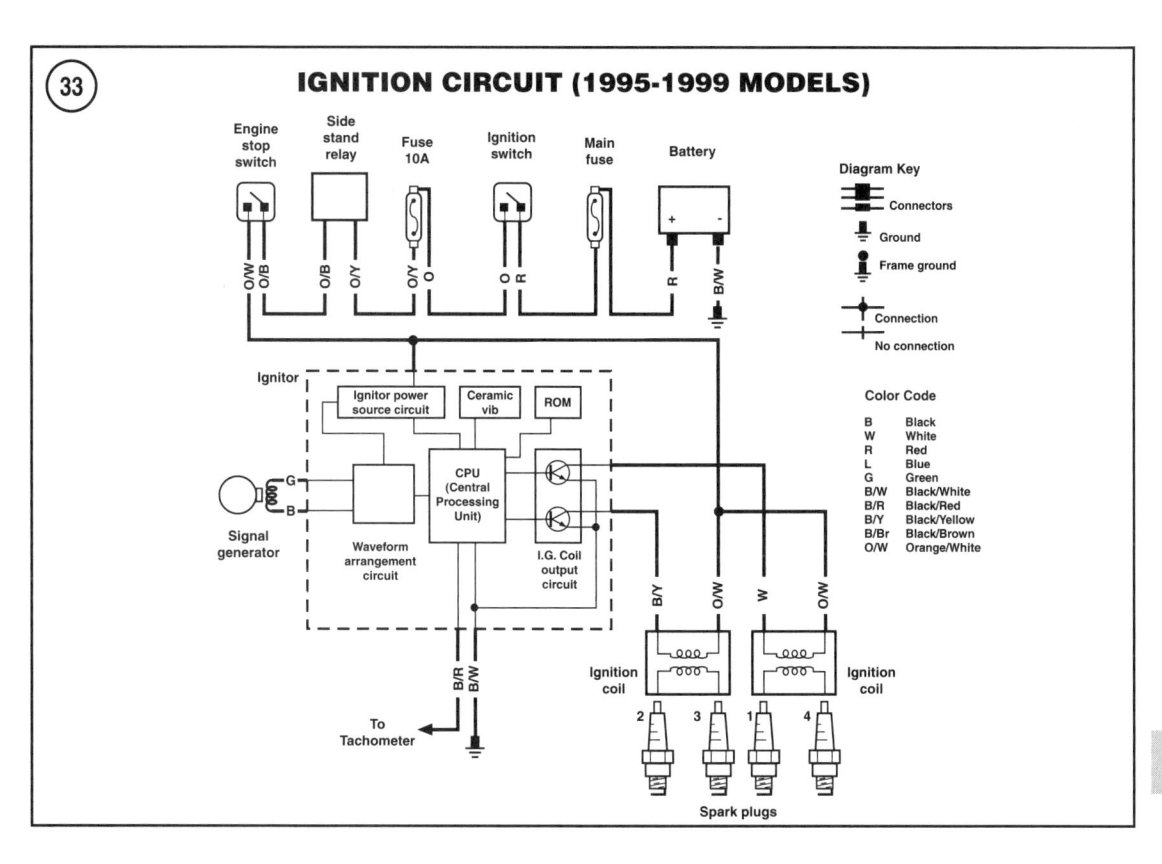

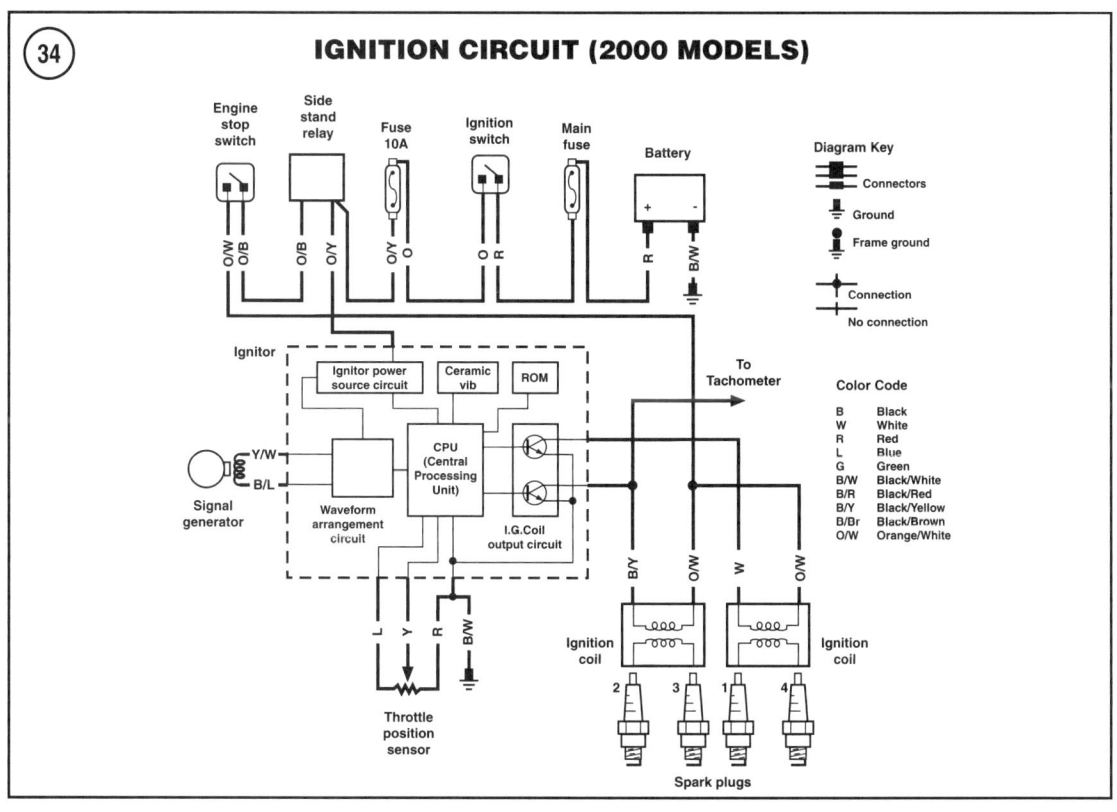

33 **IGNITION CIRCUIT (1995-1999 MODELS)**

34 **IGNITION CIRCUIT (2000 MODELS)**

lead to engine damage. Avoid operating the engine above 12,000 rpm without load.

The signal generator is mounted on the right end of the crankshaft. As the signal generator rotor is turned by the crankshaft, the rotor sends a signal to the igniter unit. This signal turns the igniter unit transistor alternately ON and OFF. As the transistor turns ON and OFF, the current passing through the primary windings of the ignition coil also turns ON and OFF. This induces a secondary current in the ignition coils secondary windings and produces the current necessary to fire the spark plugs.

Ignition System Precautions

To protect the ignition system from damage, observe the following precautions:
1. Never disconnect any of the electrical connections while the engine is running.
2. Keep all connections between the various units clean and tight. Make sure that the wiring connectors are pushed together firmly to help keep out moisture.
3. Do not substitute another type of ignition coil.

Troubleshooting

Refer to Chapter Two.

Signal Generator

Peak voltage test (2000 models)

Peak voltage test results are based on the use of the Suzuki Multi-Circuit Tester (part No. 09900-25008) with the peak voltage adapter. If these tools are not available, refer testing to a Suzuki dealership.
1. Remove the rear frame cover as described in Chapter Fourteen.
2. Disconnect the igniter connector (A, **Figure 35**) from the igniter unit.
3. Turn the tester's knob to voltage.
4. Connect the negative test probe to the yellow/white terminal (green, 95-99 models) on the connector, and connect the positive test probe to the black/blue terminal (black, 95-99 models). See **Figure 36**.

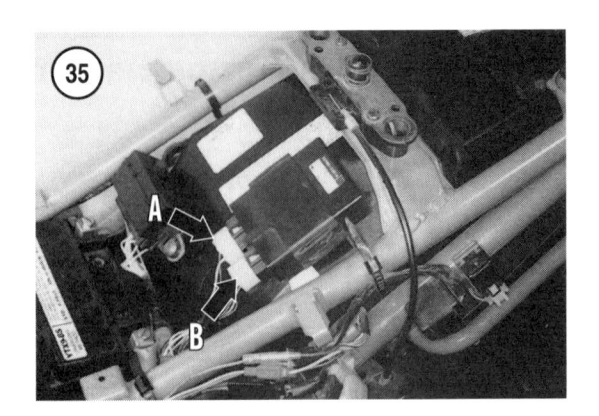

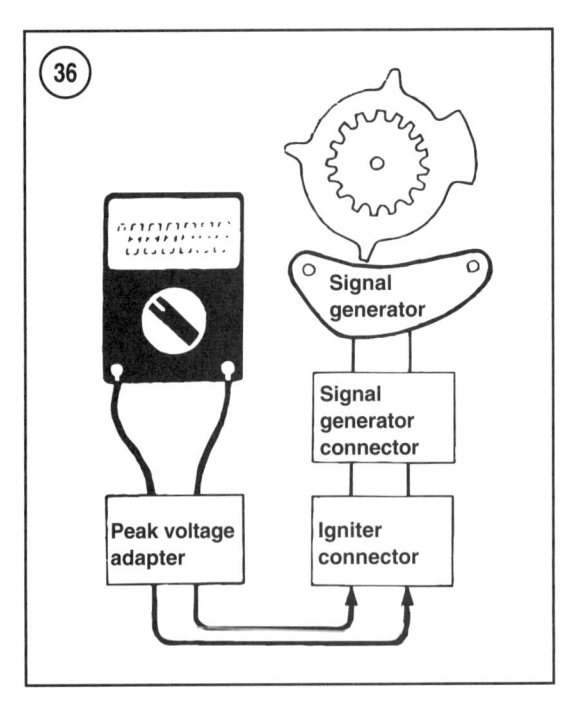

5. Shift the transmission into neutral and turn the ignition switch ON.

WARNING
High voltage is present during ignition system operation. Do not touch ignition components, wires or test leads while cranking or running the engine.

6. Press the starter button and crank the engine for a few seconds while reading the meter. Record the highest meter reading.

NOTE
*All peak voltage specifications are **minimum** values. If the measured*

ELECTRICAL SYSTEM

c. Connect the negative test probe to the yellow terminal on the signal generator side of the connector, and connect the positive test probe to the blue terminal.
d. Shift the transmission into neutral and turn the ignition switch ON.
e. Press the starter button and crank the engine for a few seconds while reading the meter. Record the highest meter reading.

8. If the peak voltage measured at the signal generator connector is normal but the peak voltage at the igniter connector is less than the minimum specified value, replace the wiring.

9. If the peak voltage at both the signal generator connector and the igniter connector are less than the minimum value specified in **Table 1**, replace the signal generator.

10. If the test results are acceptable, reconnect the electrical connector. Make sure the electrical connector is corrosion-free and secure.

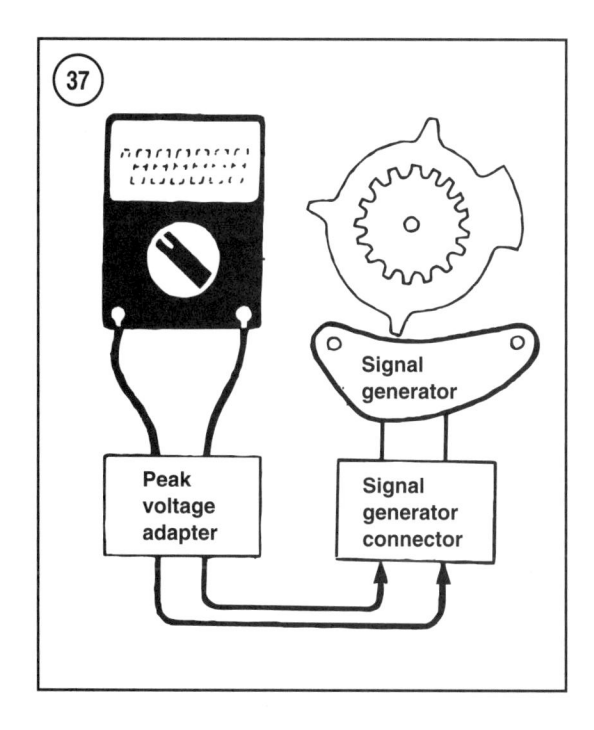

voltage meets or exceeds the specification, the test results are satisfactory. On some components, the voltage may greatly exceed the minimum specification.

7. If the signal generator peak voltage is less than the specified value, check the peak voltage at the signal generator coupler (**Figure 37**) by performing the following:

a. Remove the left side cover as described in Chapter Fourteen.
b. Disconnect the 3-pin signal generator connector (1 blue wire, 1 yellow wire and 1 green/yellow wire on the signal generator side of the connector) from the main harness.

Signal generator resistance test

Suzuki specifies the use of the Suzuki Multi-Circuit Tester (part No. 09900-25008) for accurate resistance reading when testing the regulator/rectifier unit. Refer to the *Preliminary Information* section at the beginning of this chapter regarding this tester.

1A. On 1995-1999 models, remove the seat and the left rear-frame cover as described in Chapter Fourteen.
1B. On 2000 models, remove the left side cover as described in Chapter Fourteen.
2. Disconnect the signal generator connector from the main harness. See **Figure 38**.
   a. On 1995-1999 models, the signal generator is a two-pin connector with one black wire and one green wire on the device side of the connector.
   b. On 2000 models, the signal generator connector is a three-pin connector with one yellow, one blue, and one green/yellow wire on the device side. The yellow and blue terminals are the signal generator terminals.
3. Set an ohmmeter to the R × 100 scale, and check the resistance between the signal generator terminals in the device side of the connector. If the signal generator coil resistance is outside the specified range, replace the signal generator.

4. On 2000 models, check the continuity between the blue terminal on the device side of the connector and ground. There should be no continuity (infinite resistance). If the signal generator has continuity to ground, replace the signal generator.

Removal/Installation

1A. On 1995-1999 models, remove the seat and the left rear-frame cover as described in Chapter Fourteen.
1B. On 2000 models, remove the left side cover as described in Chapter Fourteen.
2. Disconnect the signal-generator connector from the wiring harness.
   a. On 1995-1999 models, the signal generator is a two-pin connector with one black wire and one green wire on the device side of the connector.
   b. On 2000 models, the signal generator connector is a three-pin connector with one yellow, one blue, and one green/yellow wire on the device side.
3. Remove the signal generator cover bolts, and remove the cover and its gasket. One cover bolt has a sealing washer installed beneath it. Note the position of this bolt. It must be reinstalled in the same location during assembly. See **Figure 39**.
4. Disconnect the oil pressure switch wire (A, **Figure 40**).
5. Hold onto the signal generator rotor with a wrench and loosen the signal generator rotor bolt (**Figure 41**). Remove the rotor. See **Figure 42**.
6. Remove the mounting screws securing the signal generator stator plate (B, **Figure 40**) to the crankcase.
7. Carefully remove the rubber grommet (C, **Figure 40**) from the crankcase. Pull the electrical wires through the opening in the crankcase (**Figure 43**) and remove the stator plate assembly.
8. Install by reversing these removal steps, noting the following:
   a. Install the rotor so the notch on the back of the rotor (A, **Figure 42**) engages the locating pin (B, **Figure 42**) in the crankshaft.
   b. Hold onto the signal generator rotor with a wrench, and torque the signal generator rotor bolt (**Figure 41**) to specification (**Table 2**).
   c. Apply a light coat of gasket sealer to the groove in the rubber grommet.

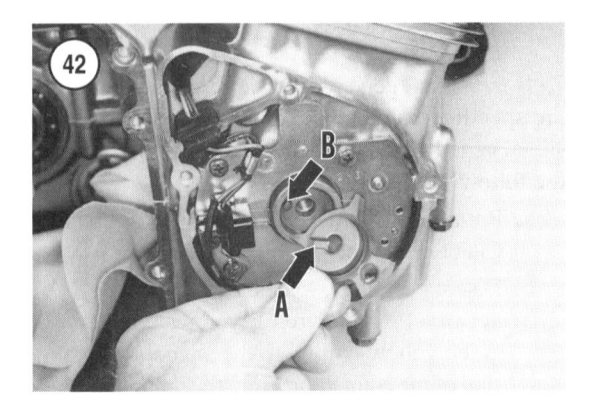

ELECTRICAL SYSTEM

tor/rectifier unit. Refer to the *Preliminary Information* section at the beginning of this chapter regarding this tester.

Primary peak voltage test (2000 models)

The Suzuki Multi-Circuit Tester (part No. 09900-25008) with the peak voltage adapter, the Motion Pro IgnitionMate (part No. 08-0193), or an equivalent peak voltage tester is required for this test.

1. Remove the fuel tank as described in Chapter Eight.
2. Remove all four spark plugs as described in Chapter Three.
3. Connect a new spark plug to each plug cap.
4. Ground all four spark plugs to the crankcase.

WARNING
High voltage is present during ignition system operation. Do not touch ignition components, wires or test leads while cranking or running the engine.

NOTE
*All peak voltage specifications are **minimum** values. If the measured voltage meets or exceeds the specification, the test results are satisfactory. On some components, the voltage may greatly exceed the minimum specification.*

5. Check the peak voltage for the No. 1 and No. 4 cylinders by performing the following:
   a. Turn the tester knob to voltage.
   b. Connect the positive test probe to the white terminal on the left ignition coil and connect the negative test probe to ground. See **Figure 44**.
   c. Shift the transmission into neutral and turn the ignition switch ON.
   d. Press the starter button and crank the engine for a few seconds while reading the meter. Record the highest meter reading.
6. Check the peak voltage for the No. 2 and No. 3 cylinders, perform the following:
   a. Turn the tester knob to voltage.
   b. Connect the positive test probe to the black/yellow terminal on the right ignition

---

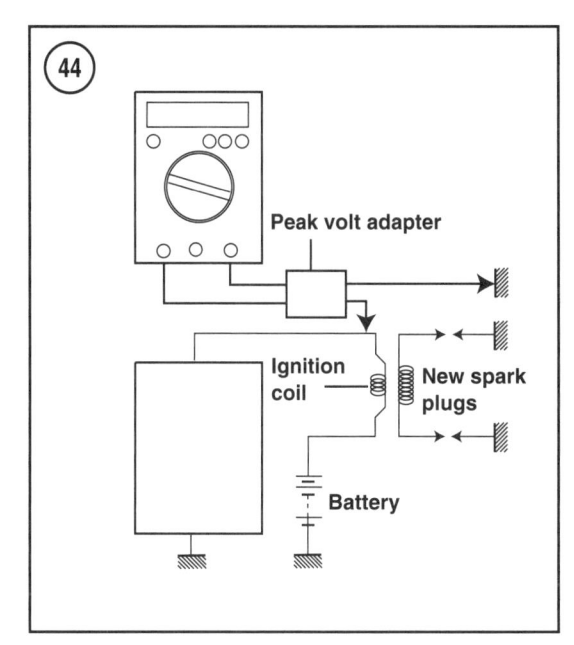

d. Install a *new* signal generator cover gasket and install the cover. Make sure the bolt with the sealing washer is installed in the location noted during disassembly. See **Figure 39**.
e. Make sure the electrical connector is corrosion-free and secure.

Ignition Coil

The ignition coil is a form of transformer which develops the high voltage required to jump the spark plug gap. The only maintenance required is keeping the electrical connections clean and tight, making sure both coils are mounted securely.

Suzuki specifies the use of the Suzuki Multi-Circuit Tester (part No. 09900-25008) for accurate resistance reading when testing the regula-

coil and connect the negative test probe to ground. See **Figure 44**.

c. Shift the transmission into neutral and turn the ignition switch ON.

d. Press the starter button and crank the engine for a few seconds while reading the meter. Record the highest meter reading.

7. If the peak voltage reading on either ignition coil is less than specified, measure the resistance on that ignition coil.

Resistance test

The Suzuki Multi-Circuit Tester (part No. 09900-25008) is required for accurate resistance testing of the ignition coil/plug cap. Refer to *Preliminary Information* section at the beginning of this chapter.

1. Disconnect all ignition coil wires (including the spark plug leads from the spark plugs) before testing.
2. Set an ohmmeter to the R × 1 scale and measure the primary coil resistance between the positive and the negative terminals on the top of the ignition coil (**Figure 45**). Record the measured resistance.
3. Set the ohmmeter to the R × 1,000 scale and measure the secondary coil resistance between the two spark plug leads (with the spark plug caps attached). Record the measured resistance.
4. If either measurement does not meet specification, the coil must be replaced. If the coil exhibits visible damage, replace it.
5. Reconnect all ignition coil wires to the ignition coil.
6. Repeat this procedure for the other ignition coil.

Removal/Installation

1. Remove the seat as described in Chapter Fourteen.
2. Disconnect the negative battery cable.
3. Remove the fuel tank as described in Chapter Eight.

NOTE
On the original equipment ignition coils and high voltage leads, the spark plug cylinder number is marked on each lead to ensure that the correct leads go to the correct cylinders during assembly. If these marks are no longer legible or are missing, mark each lead with its cylinder number. From left to right, the cylinders are numbered No. 1, No. 2, No. 3 and No. 4.

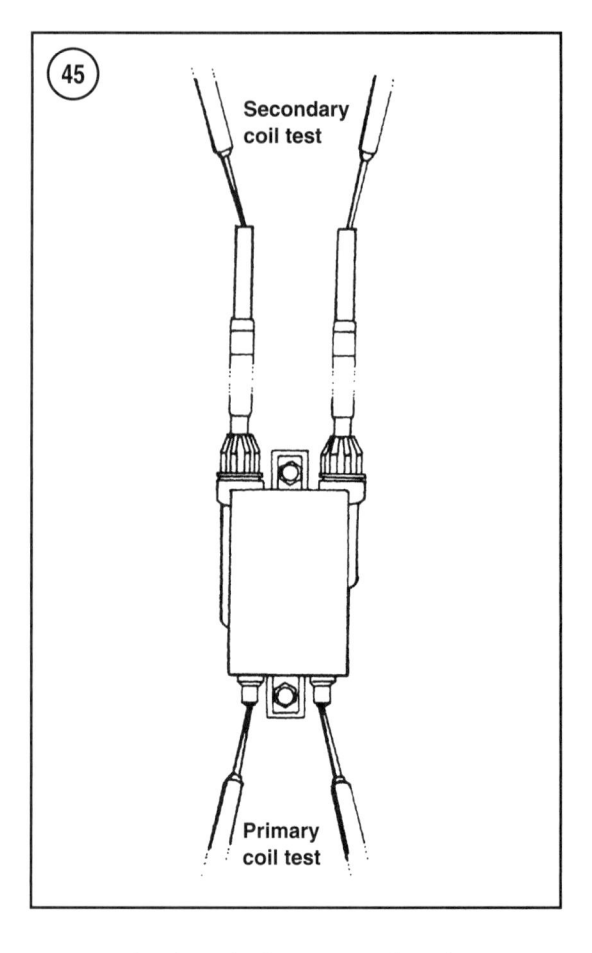

4. Disconnect the high voltage lead (A, **Figure 46**) from each spark plug.

NOTE
In Step 5, remove only the necessary components to provide easy access to the ignition coils.

5. On 2000 models, remove the PAIR assembly as described in Chapter Eight.
6. Remove the screws securing the ignition coil (B, **Figure 46**) to the frame.
7. Carefully pull the ignition coil away from the frame and disconnect the primary electrical wires from the coil.
8. If necessary, repeat Steps 6-7 for the other ignition coil.
9. Install by reversing these removal steps. Make sure all electrical connections are corrosion-free and secure.

ELECTRICAL SYSTEM

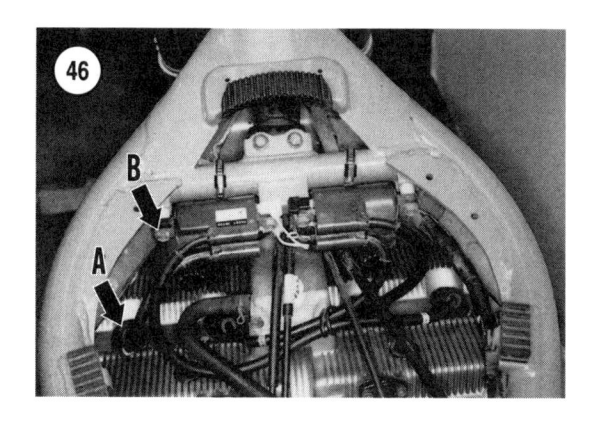

46

Igniter Unit

Input voltage test

1. Remove the seat as described in Chapter Fourteen.
2A. On 1995-1999 models, connect the probes of a voltmeter to the orange/white terminal and to the black/white terminal of the igniter connectors (A & B, **Figure 35**).
2B. On 2000 models, connect the probes of a voltmeter to the orange/yellow terminal and to the black/white terminal of the igniter connectors (A & B, **Figure 35**).
3. Turn the ignition switch ON, and check the voltage on the meter. It should read battery voltage.

NOTE
*Further testing of the igniter unit requires the Suzuki Digital Igniter Checker (part No. 09931-94490). Refer this testing to a Suzuki dealership. Most parts suppliers do not accept returns on electrical components. If the exact cause of any electrical system malfunction has not been determined, do not attempt to remedy the problem with guesswork and possibly unnecessary parts replacement. If possible, have the suspect component or system tested by a professional technician **before** purchasing electrical components.*

Replacement

1. Remove the seat and rear frame covers as described in Chapter Fourteen. On 2000 models, remove the document tray.
2. Disconnect the negative battery cable.
3. Disconnect both igniter connectors (A & B, **Figure 35**) from the igniter.
4. Remove the igniter unit from its rubber damper.
5. Install a new igniter unit into the damper. Attach both electrical wire connectors to it. Make sure both electrical connectors are corrosion-free and secure.
6. Install all parts removed.

STARTING SYSTEM

The starting system consists of the starter motor, starter relay, clutch switch, sidestand switch, sidestand relay (which is a combined turn signal/sidestand relay on 2000 models), neutral switch, engine stop switch and the starter button. When the starter button is pressed, it engages the starter relay that completes the circuit, allowing electricity to flow from the battery to the starter motor.

Figure 47 is a schematic of the starting system for 1995-1996 non-U.S.A., California and Canada models. **Figure 48** is a starting system schematic for 1996 U.S.A., California and Canada models and 1997-1999 models. **Figure 49** is a schematic of the starting system on 2000 models.

CAUTION
Do not operate the starter for more than 5 seconds at a time. Let it cool approximately 10 seconds between starting attempts.

Troubleshooting

Refer to Chapter Two.

STARTER MOTOR

Removal/Installation

1. Remove the seat as described in Chapter Fourteen.
2. Disconnect the negative battery cable.
3. Slide back the rubber boot on the electrical cable connector (A, **Figure 50**).
4. Disconnect the electrical cable from the starter motor terminal.
5. Remove the starter motor mounting bolts (B, **Figure 50**) and withdraw the starter from the top of the crankcase.
6. Inspect the O-ring (A, **Figure 51**). O-rings tend to harden after prolonged use and heat and therefore

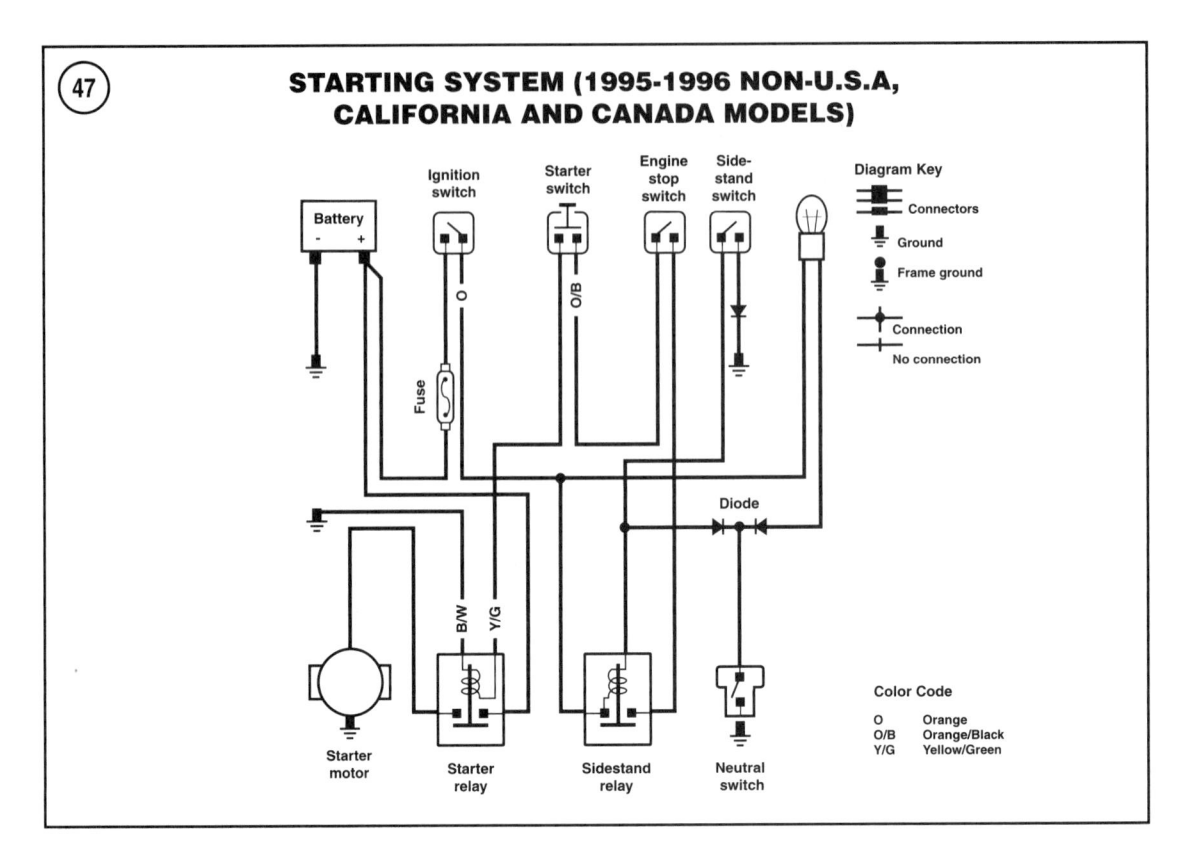

278 CHAPTER NINE

47 STARTING SYSTEM (1995-1996 NON-U.S.A, CALIFORNIA AND CANADA MODELS)

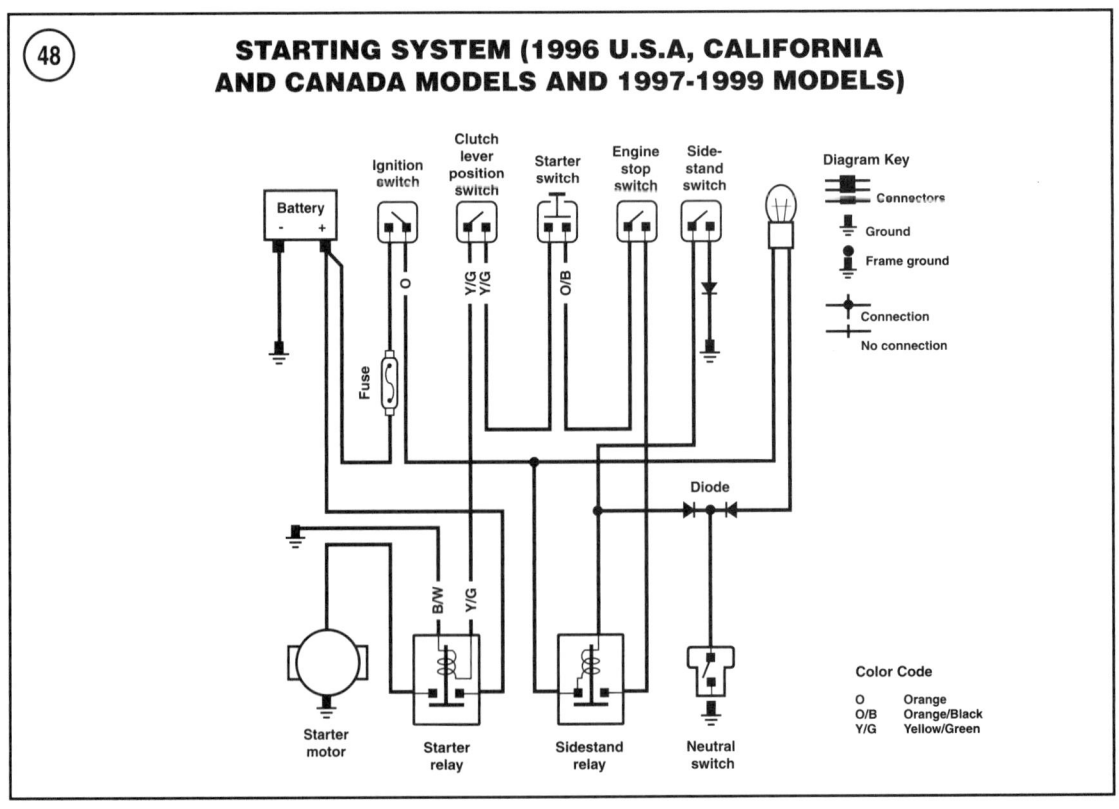

48 STARTING SYSTEM (1996 U.S.A, CALIFORNIA AND CANADA MODELS AND 1997-1999 MODELS)

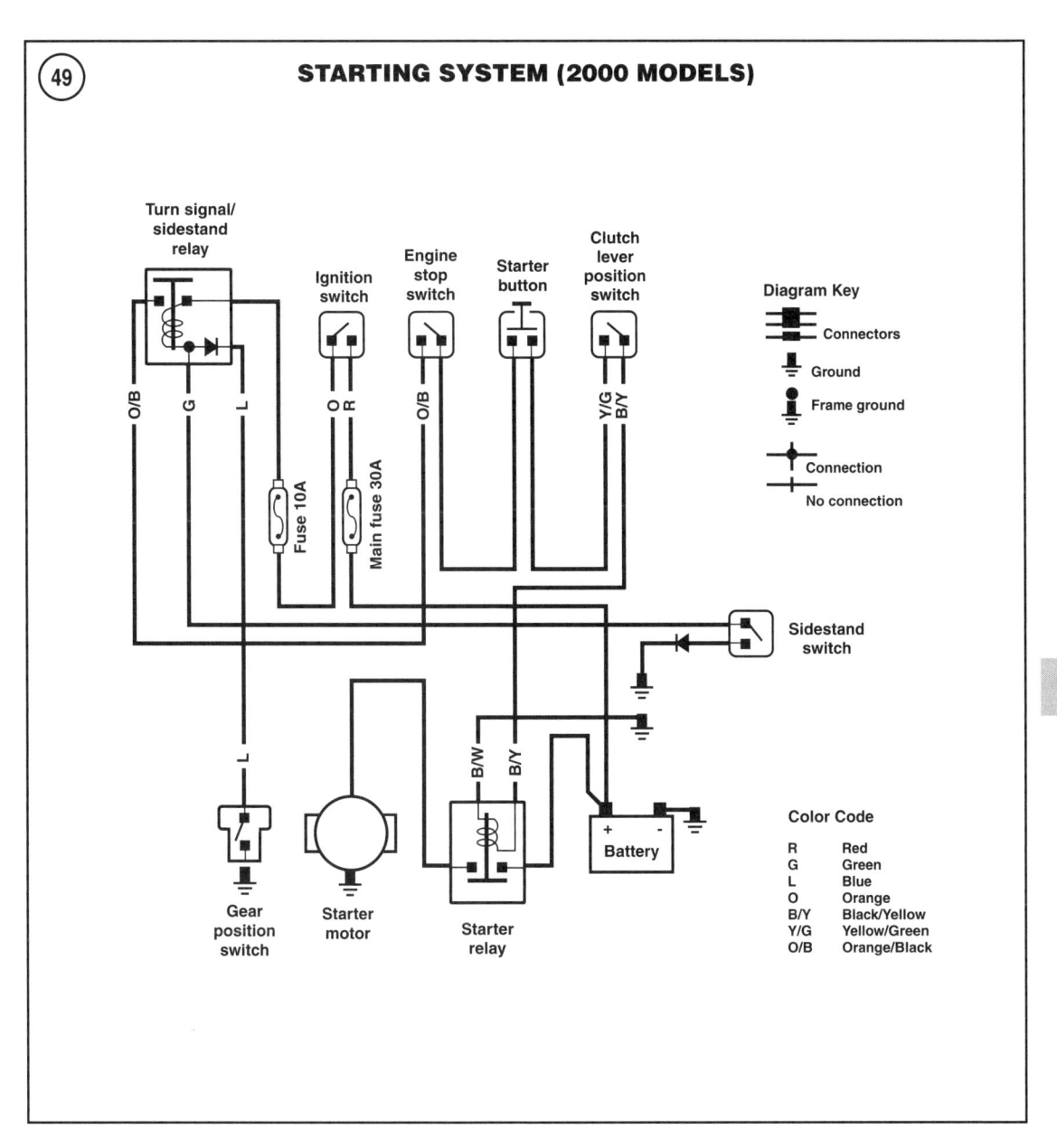

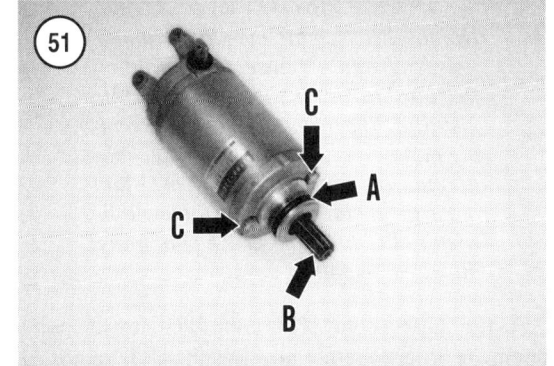

ELECTRICAL SYSTEM

49 STARTING SYSTEM (2000 MODELS)

STARTER MOTOR

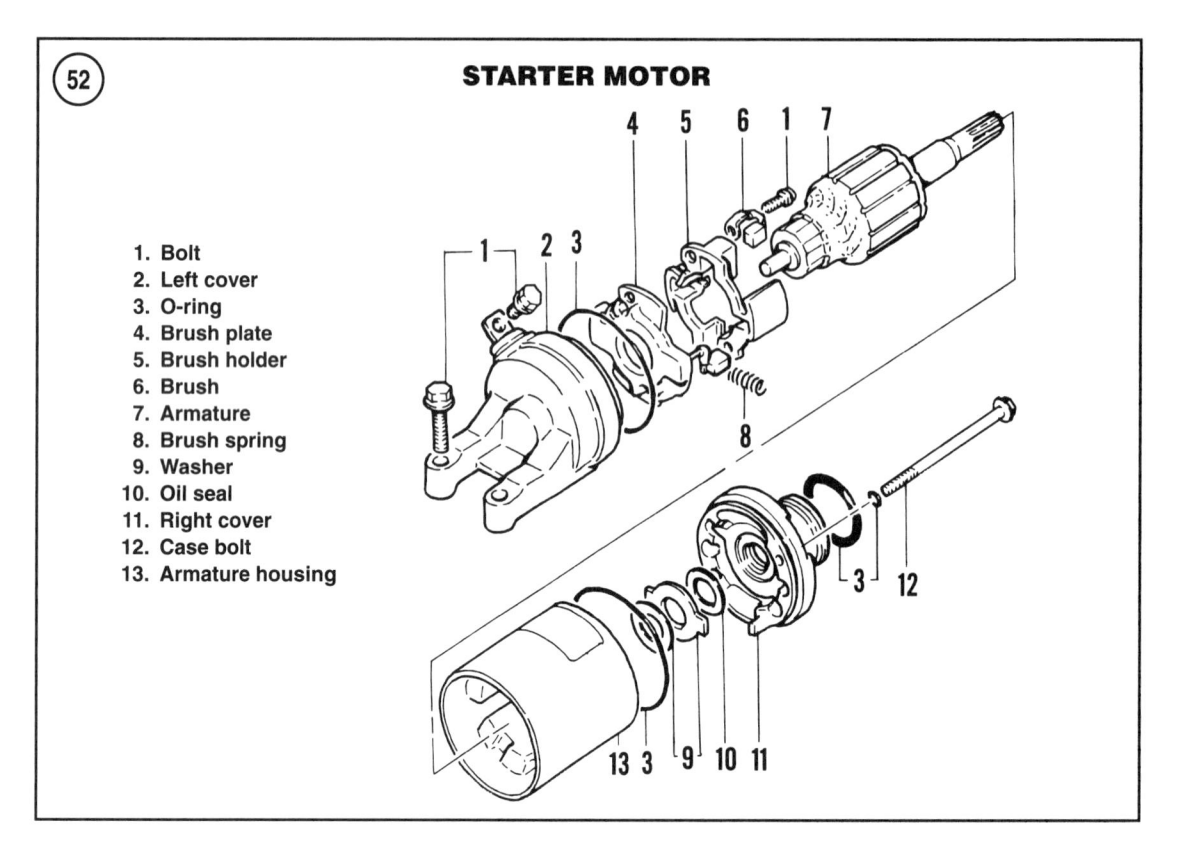

1. Bolt
2. Left cover
3. O-ring
4. Brush plate
5. Brush holder
6. Brush
7. Armature
8. Brush spring
9. Washer
10. Oil seal
11. Right cover
12. Case bolt
13. Armature housing

lose their ability to seal properly. Replace the O-ring as necessary.

7. Inspect the gear (B, **Figure 51**) for chipped or missing teeth. If damaged, the starter assembly must be replaced.

8. Install by reversing these removal steps. Torque the mounting bolts and the terminal bolt to the specifications in **Table 3**.

Disassembly

Refer to **Figure 52**.

NOTE
Do not disassemble the starter motor unless absolutely necessary. Holding the four brushes in their holders while installing the armature during assembly can be difficult. If the starter motor must be disassembled, an assistant or surgical clamps (hemostats) will be required to hold the brushes in place during assembly.

As the starter motor is disassembled, lay the parts out in the order of removal. As each part is removed

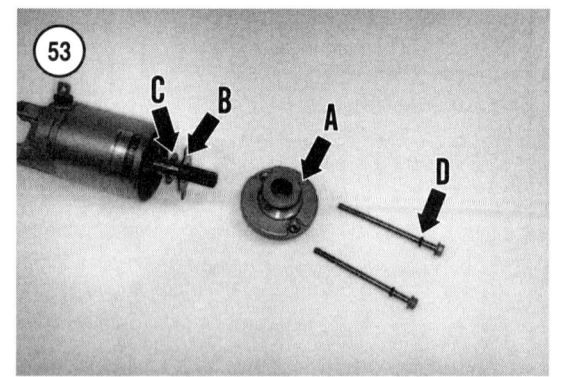

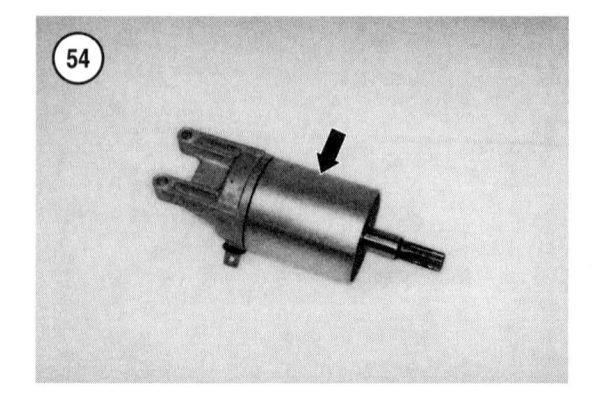

ELECTRICAL SYSTEM

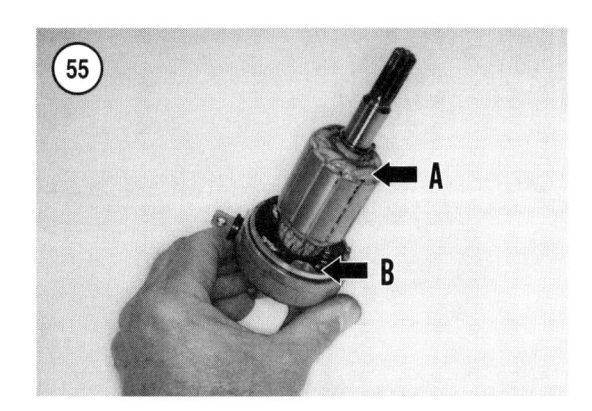

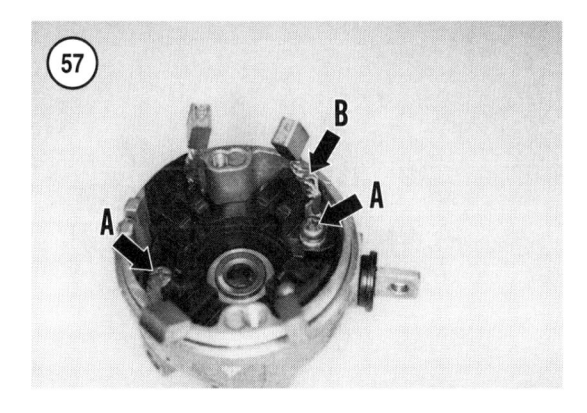

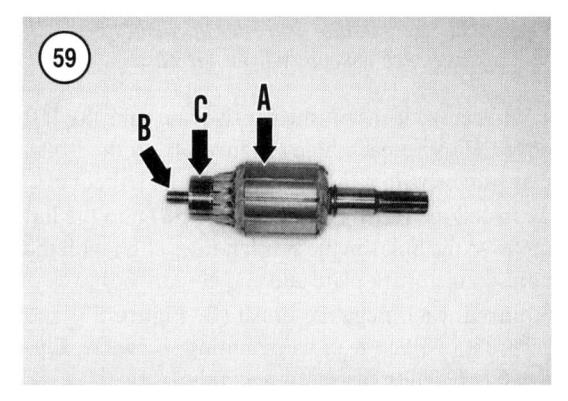

from the starter, set it next to the one previously removed. This is an easy way to remember the correct relationship of all parts.

1. Remove each case screw (C, **Figure 51**) and its O-ring.
2. Remove the right cover (A, **Figure 53**) from the armature housing.
3. Slide the washers (B and C, **Figure 53**) off the armature shaft.
4. Slide the housing (**Figure 54**) off the armature.
5. Lift the armature (A, **Figure 55**) from the brush plate assembly in the left cover (B, **Figure 55**).
6. Remove the four brush springs (**Figure 56**) from their respective slots in the brush holder.
7. Remove the two brush mounting screws (A, **Figure 57**) and remove the two negative brushes (B, **Figure 57**).
8. Remove the brush holder (**Figure 58**) from the left cover. Leave the brush plate and positive brushes in the left cover.

CAUTION
Do not immerse the wire windings in the case or the armature coil (A, Figure 59) in solvent, as the insulation may be damaged. Wipe the windings with a cloth lightly moistened with solvent and dry thoroughly.

9. Clean all grease, dirt and carbon from all components.
10. Inspect all starter components as described in this chapter.

Assembly

NOTE
In the next step, reinstall all parts in the same order noted during removal.

This is essential in order to insulate this brush assembly from the case.

1. If removed, install the brush plate into the left cover. Be sure each hole (**Figure 60**) in the brush plate aligns with a threaded hole in the left cover.
2. Install the brush holder (**Figure 58**) into the left cover so the holes in the brush holder align with the holes in the brush plate and end cover.
3. Install each negative brush (B, **Figure 57**) and secure it in place with its mounting screw (A, **Figure 57**). Tighten the screw securely.
4. Apply molybdenum disulfide paste onto the small shaft (B, **Figure 59**) of the armature.
5. Install the four brush springs (**Figure 56**) by sliding each spring into its slot in the brush holder.
6. Slide each brush into its place in the brush holder.
7. Press each brush back into its holder so there is sufficient clearance for the commutator. Hold the armature upright, and insert the commutator end of the armature (A, **Figure 55**) into the left cover (B, **Figure 55**). Do not damage the brushes during this step. Hold back the brushes as the commutator passes by them. Be sure all brushes are in correct contact with the armature. Push the assembly down until it bottoms out.
8. Keep the assembly in this position and slowly rotate the armature coil assembly to make sure it rotates freely with the brushes in place.

NOTE
Hold the armature coil and left cover together during the next step. The magnets within the armature housing will try to pull the armature out of the left cover and disengage the brushes.

9. Install an O-ring (**Figure 61**) onto the housing recess.
10. Install the housing over the armature coil assembly and onto the left cover (A, **Figure 62**). Align the case notch with the left cover notch (C, **Figure 62**).
11. Install the plain washer (C, **Figure 53**) onto the armature shaft.
12. Apply Suzuki Super Grease A (part No. 99000-25030) to the lips of the oil seal in the right cover and install the armed washer into the cover. Align the washer arms with the slots in the cover as shown in **Figure 63**.

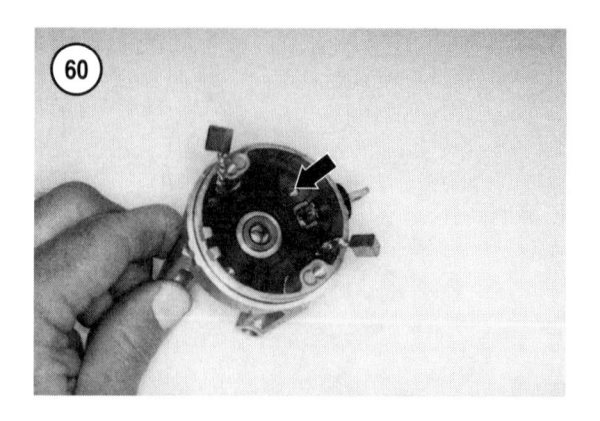

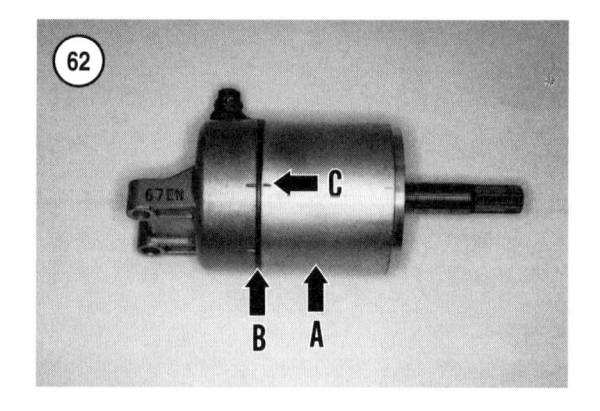

ELECTRICAL SYSTEM

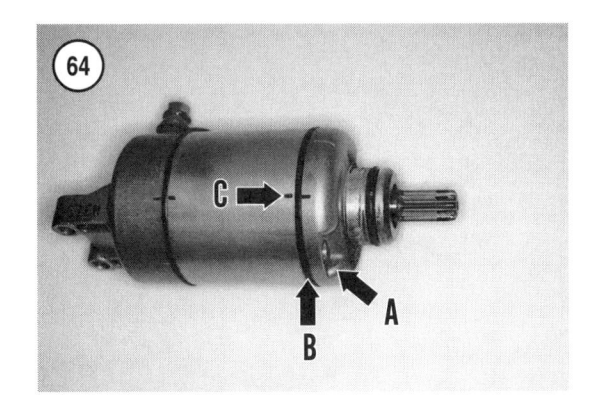

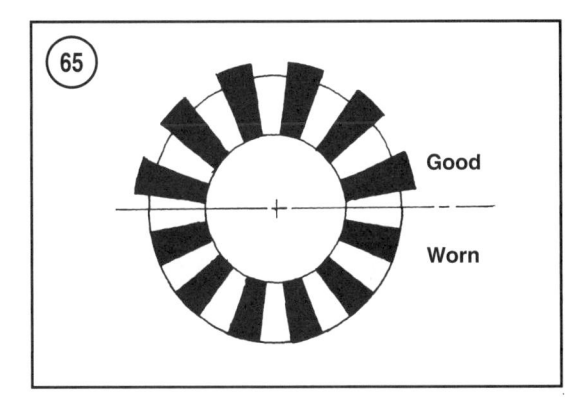

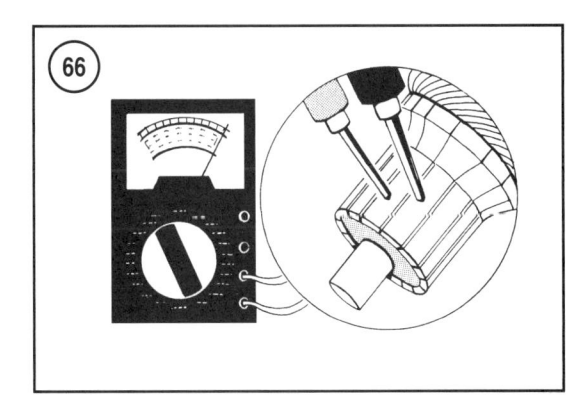

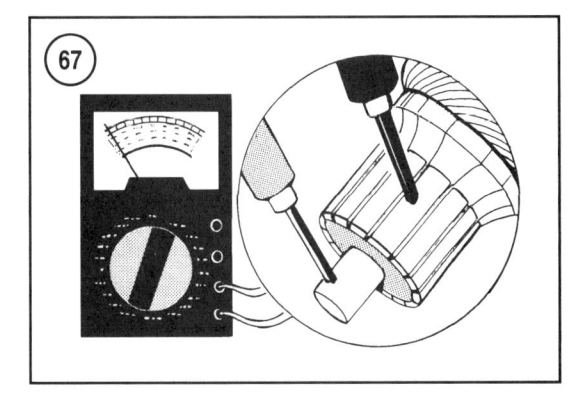

13. Install an O-ring onto the recess in the armature housing.
14. Install the right cover (A, **Figure 64**) onto the housing. Align the lines on the housing with the line on the cover.
15. Install the O-ring (D, **Figure 53**) onto the case screws and apply a light coat of clean engine oil to each O-ring.
16. Install the case bolts (C, **Figure 51**) and tighten them securely. After the bolts are tightened, check the seams to ensure the end covers are pulled tight against the case.

Inspection

1. Inspect each brush for abnormal wear. Service specifications are not available from Suzuki. Replace the brushes as necessary.
2. Inspect the commutator (C, **Figure 59**). The mica in a good commutator is below the surface of the copper bars. On a worn commutator, the mica and copper bars may be worn to the same level (**Figure 65**). If necessary, have the commutator serviced by a dealership or electrical repair shop.
3. Check the entire length of the armature coil assembly for straightness or heat damage. Rotate the ball bearing and check for roughness or binding.
4. Inspect the armature shaft where it contacts the bushing (B, **Figure 59**). Check for wear, burrs or damage.
5. Inspect the commutator copper bars (C, **Figure 59**) for discoloration. If a pair of bars are discolored, grounded armature coils are indicated.
6. Use an ohmmeter and perform the following:
    a. Check for continuity between the commutator bars (**Figure 66**); there should be continuity (indicated resistance) between pairs of bars.
    b. Check for continuity between the commutator bars and the shaft (**Figure 67**); there should be no continuity (infinite resistance).
    c. If the armature fails either of these tests, replace it.
7. Inspect the oil seal (**Figure 68**) in the right cover for wear, hardness or damage. If the oil seal is worn or damaged, replace it.
8. Inspect the O-ring (A, **Figure 51**) on the right cover for wear, hardness or damage. Replace the O-ring if necessary.

9. Inspect the needle bearing in the right cover. It must turn smoothly without excessive play or noise. Replace the cover as necessary.
10. Inspect the bushing in the left cover for wear or damage. The bushing cannot be replaced. If it is damaged, replace the left cover.
11. Inspect the magnets within the armature housing assembly. Make sure they have not picked up any small metal particles. If so, remove them prior to assembly. Also inspect the armature housing for loose, chipped or damaged magnets.
12. Inspect the brush holder and springs for wear or damage. If necessary, replace the holder or springs.
13. Inspect both end covers for wear or damage. Replace either end cover if it is damaged.
14. Check the long case screws for thread damage. Clean the threads with the appropriate size metric die if necessary. Inspect the O-ring seals for hardness, deterioration or damage. Replace as necessary.

STARTER RELAY

Removal/Installation

On 1995-1999 models, the starter relay is located on the left side of the frame, behind the rear frame cover. On 2000 models, the relay is located behind the left side cover.

1A. On 1995-1999 models, remove the seat and the left rear-frame cover as described in Chapter Fourteen.
1B. On 2000 models, remove the left side cover as described in Chapter Fourteen.
2. Disconnect the negative battery cable as described in this chapter.
3. Remove the cover from the starter relay.
4. Disconnect the starter relay primary connector (A, **Figure 69**).
5. Disconnect the terminal screws (B, **Figure 69**) and remove the black starter motor lead and the red battery lead. Remove the relay.
6. Install by reversing these removal steps while noting the following:
   a. Install both electrical cables to the relay and tighten the nuts securely.
   b. Make sure the electrical connectors are on tight and that the rubber boot is properly installed to keep out moisture.
   c. Install the cover.

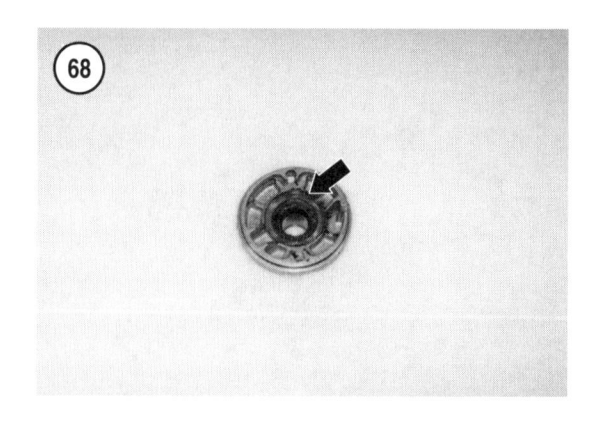

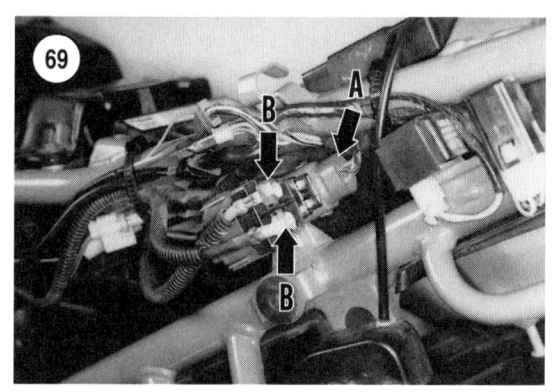

Starter Relay Voltage Test

1A. On 1995-1999 models, remove the seat and the left rear-frame cover as described in Chapter Fourteen.
1B. On 2000 models, remove the left side cover as described in Chapter Fourteen.
2. Remove the cover from the starter relay.
3A. On 1995-1999 models, connect a voltmeter's positive test lead to the yellow/green terminal on the starter relay. Connect the negative test lead to the black/white terminal.
3B. On 2000 models, connect a voltmeter's positive test lead to the black/yellow terminal on the starter relay. Connect the negative test lead to the black/white terminal.
4. Make sure the engine stop switch is in the RUN position.
5. Shift the transmission to neutral and disengage the clutch.
6. Press the starter button and read the voltage displayed on the voltmeter. It should show battery voltage.
7. Turn the ignition OFF, and disconnect the voltmeter.

ELECTRICAL SYSTEM

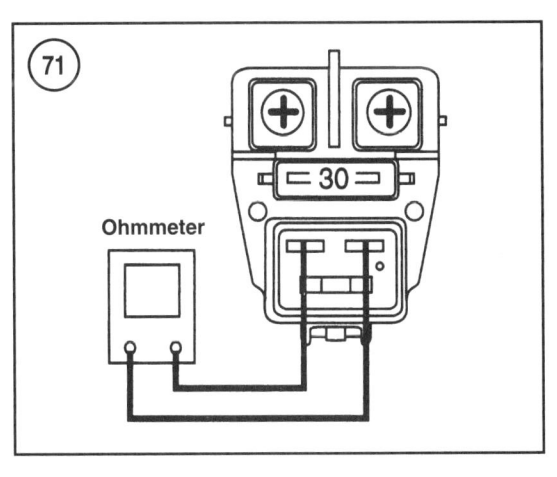

Starter Relay Continuity and Resistance Test

1A. On 1995-1999 models, remove the seat and the left rear-frame cover as described in Chapter Fourteen.

1B. On 2000 models, remove the left side cover as described in Chapter Fourteen.

2. Disconnect the negative battery cable as described in this chapter.

3. Remove the cover from the starter relay.

4. Disconnect the starter relay primary connector (A, **Figure 69**).

5. Disconnect the terminal screws (B, **Figure 69**) and remove the black starter motor lead and the red battery lead from the starter relay. Remove the relay.

6. Connect an ohmmeter and a 12-volt battery to the starter relay terminals as shown in **Figure 70**. When the battery is connected, there should be continuity (low to zero ohms) across the two load terminals. When the battery is disconnected, there should be no continuity (infinity).

7. Connect an ohmmeter to the starter relay terminals as shown in **Figure 71** and measure the resistance across these terminals. If the resistance is outside the specified range in **Table 1**, replace the starter relay.

LIGHTING SYSTEM

The lighting system consists of a headlight, taillight/brake light, directional lights, indicator lights and meter illumination lights. **Table 2** lists replacement bulbs for these components.

Always use the correct wattage bulb as indicated in this section. The use of a larger wattage bulb will give a dim light and a smaller wattage bulb will burn out prematurely.

Headlight Bulb Replacement

> *WARNING*
> *If the headlight has just burned out or has just been turned off, it will be **very** hot! Do not touch the bulb. Wait for the bulb to cool before removing it.*

> *CAUTION*
> *All models are equipped with quartz-halogen bulbs. Do not touch the bulb glass. Traces of oil on the bulb will drastically reduce the life of the bulb. Clean the bulb with a cloth moistened in alcohol or lacquer thinner.*

CHAPTER NINE

HEADLIGHT (1995-1999 GFS600 MODELS)

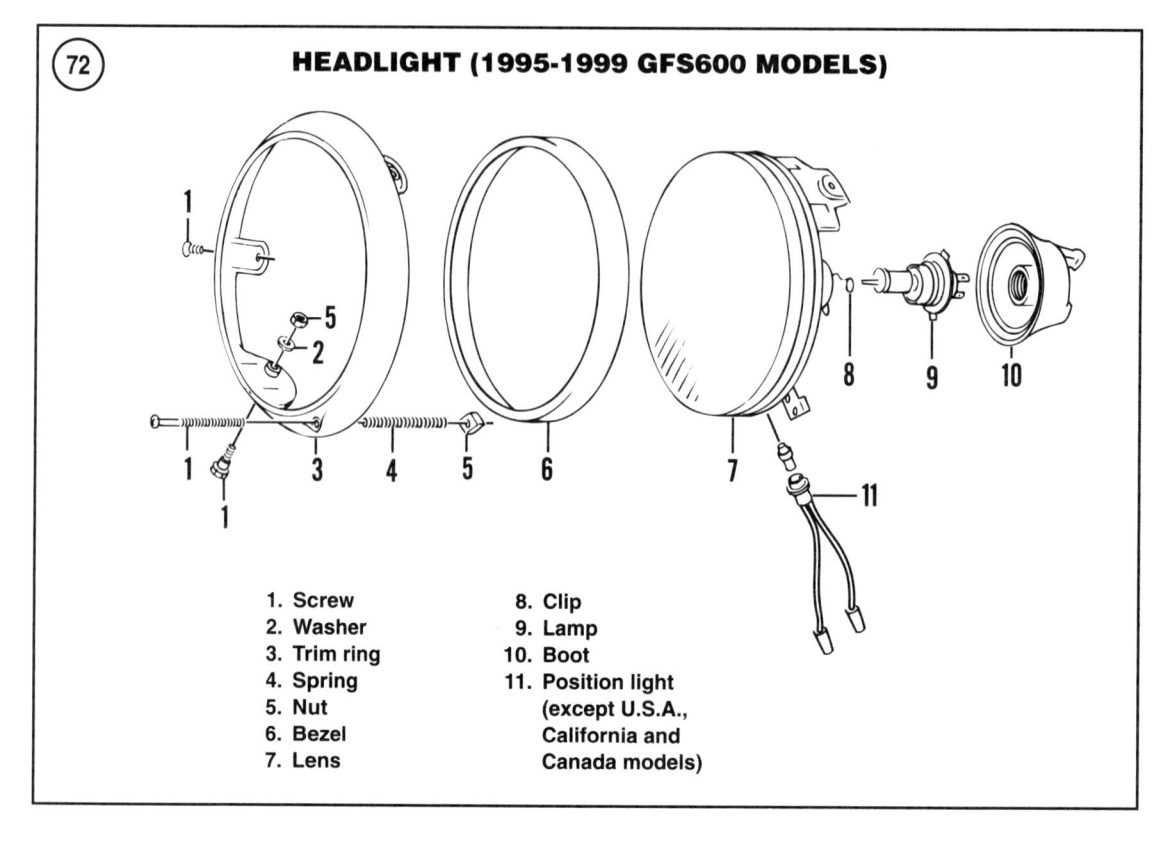

1. Screw
2. Washer
3. Trim ring
4. Spring
5. Nut
6. Bezel
7. Lens
8. Clip
9. Lamp
10. Boot
11. Position light (except U.S.A., California and Canada models)

Refer to **Figures 72-75** as appropriate for this procedure:

1. On GSF600 models, remove the headlight assembly as described in this chapter.

2A. On all models except 2000 GSF600S, perform the following:

   a. Disconnect the socket (A, **Figure 76**) from the bulb and remove the rubber boot (B, **Figure 76**).

   b. Unhook the retaining clip (A, **Figure 77**) from the bulb.

   c. Remove the light bulb and install a new bulb.

2B. On 2000 GSF600S models, disconnect the socket, turn the bulb counterclockwise and remove it.

3. Install by reversing these removal steps.

4. Be sure to position the rubber boot (B, **Figure 76**) with the TOP mark facing up.

Headlight Assembly
Removal/Installation (GSF600 models)

Refer to **Figure 72** when removing the headlight on 1995-1999 GSF600 models. Refer to **Figure 73** for 2000 GSF600 models.

1. Remove the screws securing the trim ring to the headlight housing.

2. Remove the lens assembly from the housing.

3. Install by reversing these removal steps.

4. Adjust the headlight as described in this chapter.

Headlight Assembly
Removal/Installation (GSF600S models)

1. Remove the front fairing as described in Chapter Fourteen.

2. If still connected, disconnect the headlight connector from the headlight.

3. On models with a position light, disconnect the position light connector.

4. Remove the fasteners (**Figure 78**) securing the headlight housing to the front fairing assembly and remove the housing.

5. Install by reversing these removal steps, noting the following:

   a. Tighten all screws securely. Do not overtighten the screws. The plastic mounting tabs on the housing may fracture.

   b. Adjust the headlight as described in this chapter.

ELECTRICAL SYSTEM

73

HEADLIGHT (2000 GFS600 MODELS)

1. Mounting ear
2. Bracket
3. Bolt
4. Damper
5. Collar
6. Nut
7. Housing
8. Washer
9. Spring
10. Vertical adjuster
11. Adjuster plate
12. Horizontal adjuster
13. Screw
14. Trim ring
15. Lens
16. Lamp
17. Boot
18. Position light

74

HEADLIGHT (1996-1999 GFS600S MODELS)

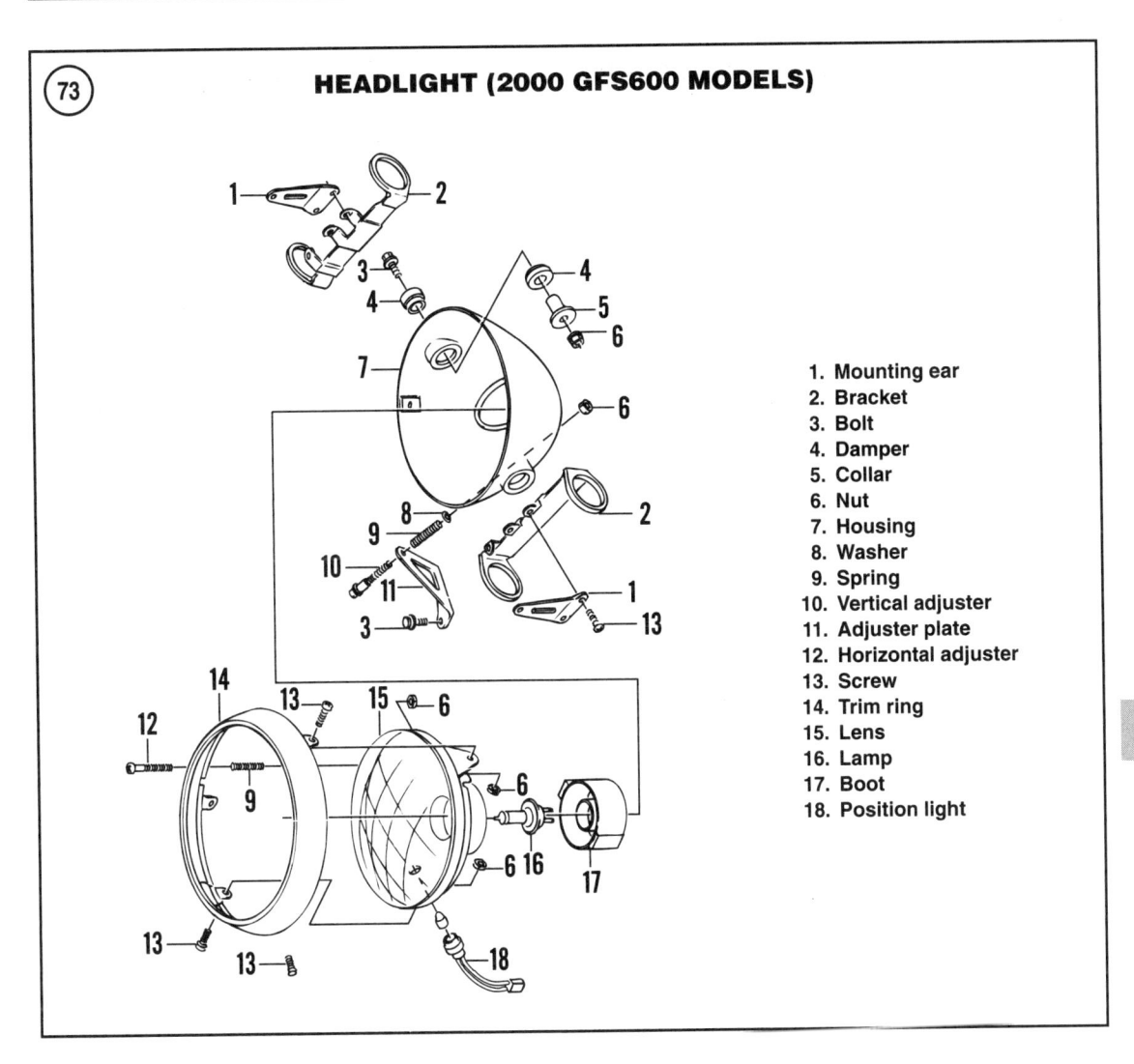

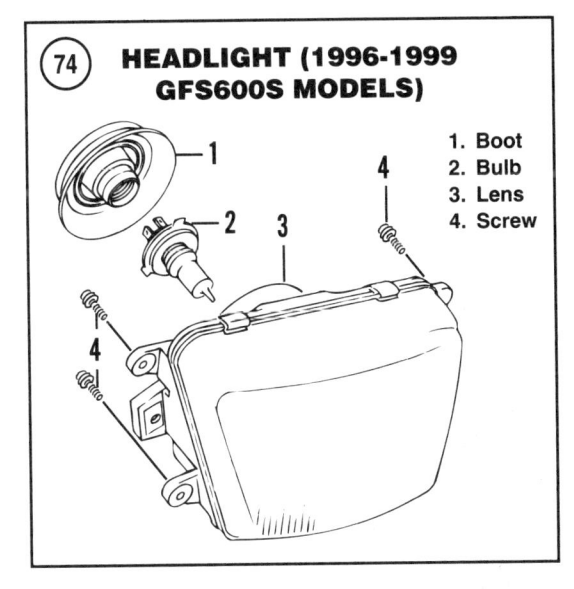

1. Boot
2. Bulb
3. Lens
4. Screw

Headlight Adjustment

Adjust the headlight horizontally and vertically according to area Department of Motor Vehicle regulations.

1995-1999 GSF600 models

To adjust the headlight, turn the adjuster on the front of the trim ring either clockwise or counterclockwise until the aim is correct.

2000 GSF600 models

To adjust the headlight horizontally, turn the adjuster on the front of the trim ring either clockwise

75 HEADLIGHT (2000 GSF MODELS)

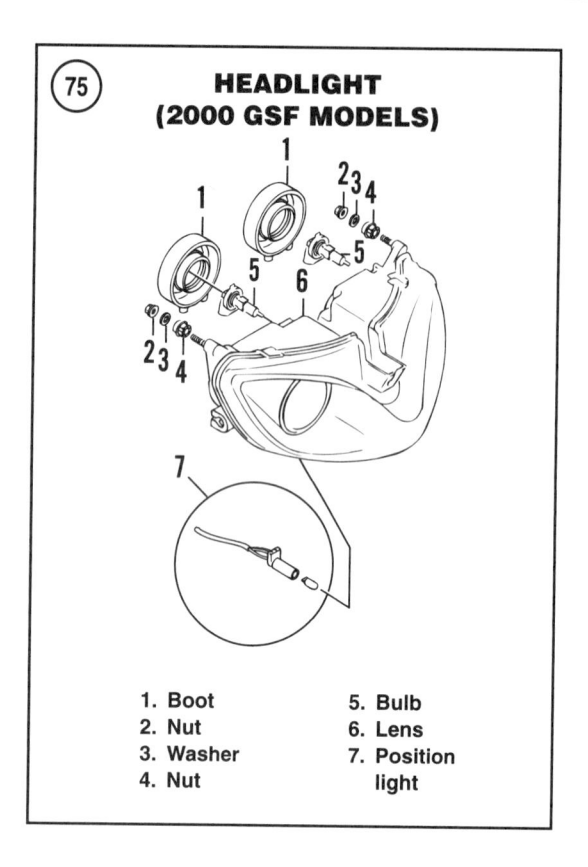

1. Boot
2. Nut
3. Washer
4. Nut
5. Bulb
6. Lens
7. Position light

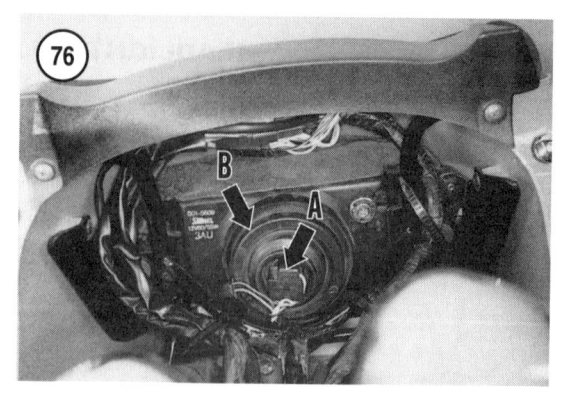

or counterclockwise until the aim is correct. See **Figure 73**.

To adjust the headlight vertically, turn the adjuster beneath the trim ring.

1996-1999 GSF600S models

Adjust the headlight from the rear of the headlight assembly.

To adjust the headlight horizontally, turn the upper screw (B, **Figure 77**). Turn the screw either clockwise or counterclockwise until the aim is correct.

For vertical adjustment, turn the lower screw (C, **Figure 77**) clockwise or counterclockwise.

2000 GSF600S models

Adjust the headlight from the rear of the headlight assembly.

To adjust the headlight horizontally, turn the upper screw clockwise or counterclockwise until the aim is correct.

For vertical adjustment, turn the lower screw clockwise or counterclockwise.

Taillight/Brake Light Bulb Replacement

Refer to **Figure 79** for 1995-1999 models or **Figure 80** for 2000 models.

1. Remove the seat as described in Chapter Fourteen.
2. On 1995-1999 models, remove the tail piece as described in Chapter Fourteen.

ELECTRICAL SYSTEM

TAILLIGHT AND LICENSE PLATE LIGHT (1995-1999 MODELS)

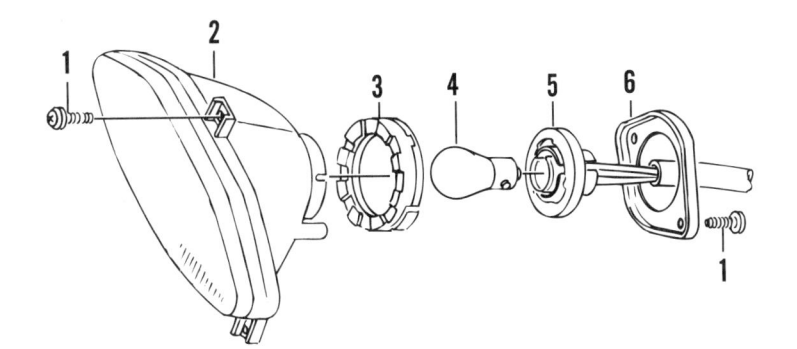

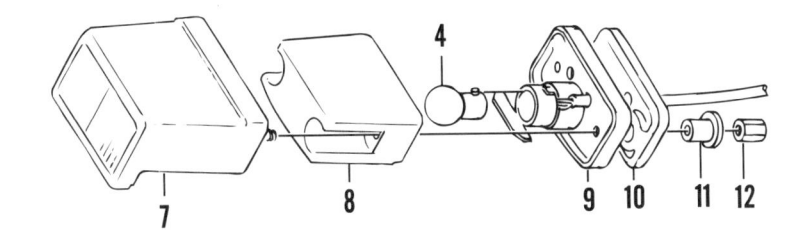

1. Screw
2. Taillight housing
3. Grommet
4. Bulb
5. Socket
6. Plate
7. Lens cover
8. Lens
9. License plate housing
10. Damper
11. Spacer
12. Nut

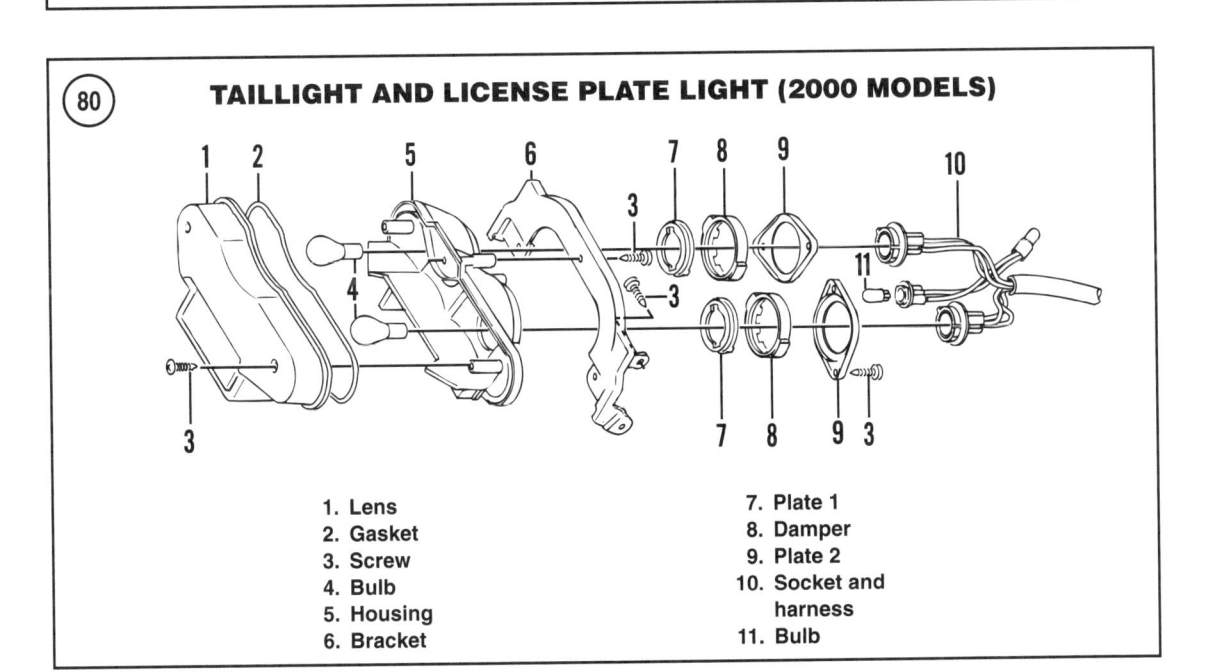

TAILLIGHT AND LICENSE PLATE LIGHT (2000 MODELS)

1. Lens
2. Gasket
3. Screw
4. Bulb
5. Housing
6. Bracket
7. Plate 1
8. Damper
9. Plate 2
10. Socket and harness
11. Bulb

3. Reach into the rear frame cover area, turn the bulb socket assembly (A, **Figure 81**) counterclockwise and remove the socket assembly from the backside of the taillight/brake light lens assembly.

4. Push the bulb into the socket and turn the bulb counterclockwise. Remove the bulb from the socket.

5. Replace the bulb(s) and install the socket assembly(ies).

6. Reinstall all removed parts.

License Plate Light Bulb Replacement (1995-1999 Models)

Refer to **Figure 79**.

1. Remove the seat as described in Chapter Fourteen.

2. Working up under the rear frame cover, remove the nuts (B, **Figure 81**), and then remove the lens and the lens cover.

3. Push the bulb (**Figure 82**) into the socket and turn the bulb counterclockwise. Remove the bulb from the socket.

4. Replace the bulb.

5. Install all items removed.

License Plate Light Bulb Replacement (2000 Models)

Perform the *Taillight/Brake Light Bulb Replacement* procedure described in this chapter.

Turn Signal Bulb Replacement

Refer to **Figure 83** for 1995-1999 models or **Figure 84** for 2000 models.

1. Remove the screws securing the lens to the turn-signal housing, and remove the lens.

2. Wash the lens with a mild detergent and wipe dry.

3. Push the bulb into the socket and turn the bulb counterclockwise. Remove the bulb from the socket.

4. Replace the bulb.

5. Install the lens. Do not overtighten the screws, as the lens may crack.

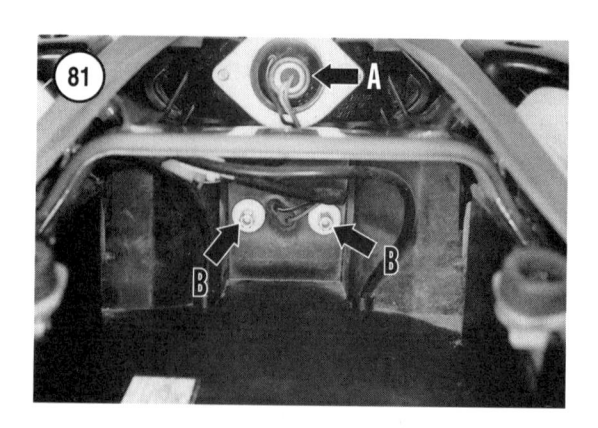

Turn Signal Assembly Removal/Installation

Refer to **Figure 83** for 1995-1999 models or to **Figure 84** for 2000 models.

1. Disconnect the electrical connector.

2. Unscrew the nut and carefully slide it off the electrical wires and connector.

3. Remove the turn signal assembly from the motorcycle.

4. Install by reversing these removal steps, noting the following:

   a. When installing a front turn signal onto GSF600S models, make sure the rubber grommet is properly seated in the fairing receptacle.

   b. Make sure the electrical connectors are free of corrosion and secure.

Speedometer and Tachometer Illumination Light and Indicator Light Replacement

1. On GSF600S models, remove the front fairing as described in Chapter Fourteen.

ELECTRICAL SYSTEM

83 TURN SIGNALS (1995-1999 MODELS)

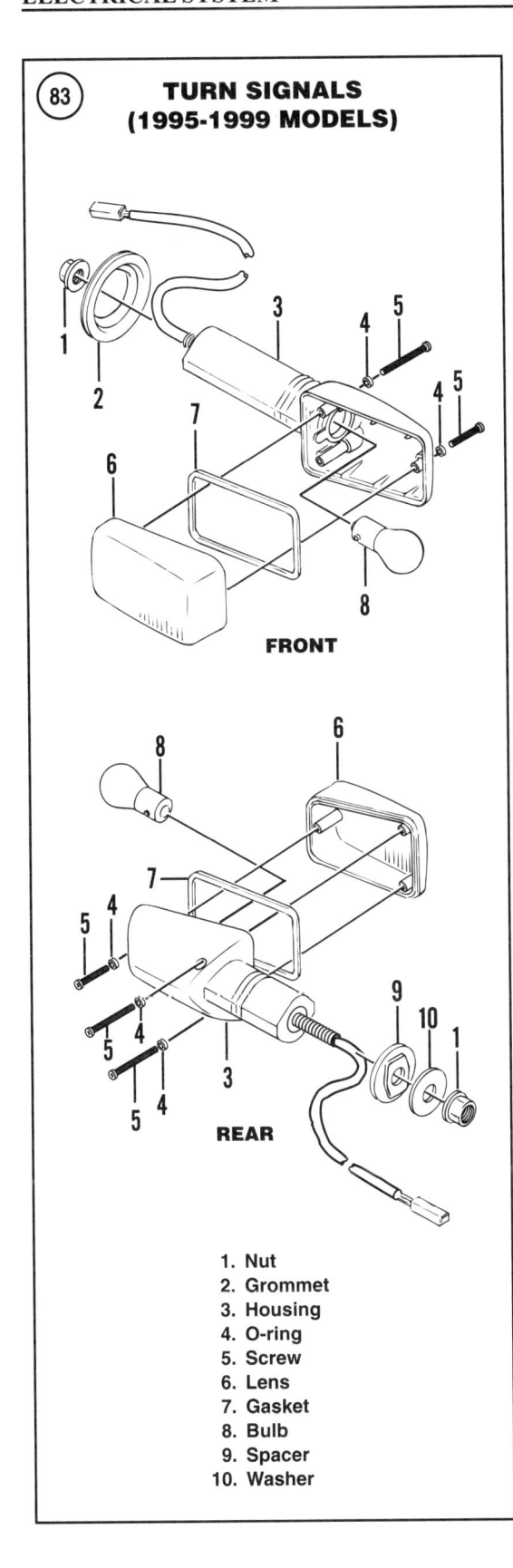

FRONT

REAR

1. Nut
2. Grommet
3. Housing
4. O-ring
5. Screw
6. Lens
7. Gasket
8. Bulb
9. Spacer
10. Washer

84 TURN SIGNALS (2000 MODELS)

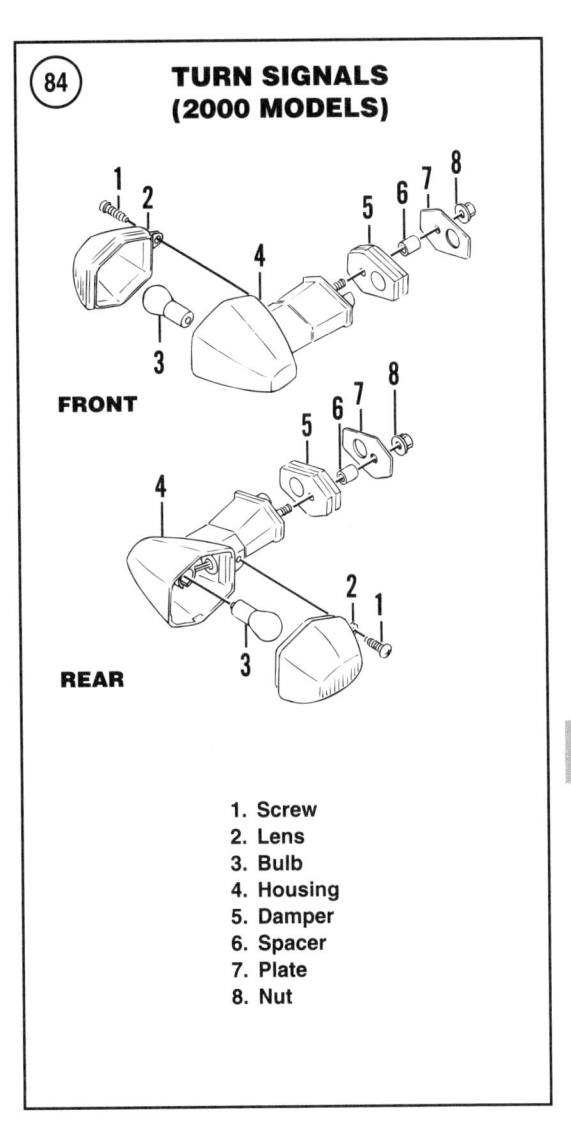

FRONT

REAR

1. Screw
2. Lens
3. Bulb
4. Housing
5. Damper
6. Spacer
7. Plate
8. Nut

2. Carefully pull the defective lamp holder/electrical wire assembly from the backside of the housing.
3. Remove and replace the defective bulb.

NOTE
If a new bulb will not work, check the wire connections for loose or broken wires. Also check the bulb socket for corrosion. Replace as necessary.

4. Push the lamp socket/electrical wire assembly back into the housing. Make sure it is completely seated to prevent the entry of moisture.
5. On GSF600S models, install the front fairing as described in Chapter Fourteen.

85 IGNITION SWITCH (1995-1999 MODELS)

Position \ Color	R	O	Gr	Br	O/Y	B/W
OFF						
ON	•—•		•—•		•—•	
LOCK						
PARK	•—————————•					

86 IGNITION SWITCH (2000 MODELS)

Position \ Color	R	O	Gr	Br	O/Y	B/W
ON	•—•	•—•		•—•		
OFF						
LOCK						
PARK	•—————————•					

87 LIGHTING SWITCH (EXCEPT U.S.A., CALIFORNIA AND CANADA)

Position \ Color	O/L	Gr	O/R	Y/W
OFF				
•		•—•		
ON	•—•			•—•

88 DIMMER SWITCH

Position \ Color	Y/W	W	Y
HI	•—————•		
LO	•—•		

89 TURN SIGNAL SWITCH

Position \ Color	G	Sb	B
L		•—•	
PUSH			
R	•—————•		

90 PASSING LIGHT SWITCH (EXCEPT CANADA AND U.S.)

Position \ Color	O/R	Y
•		
PUSH	•—•	

SWITCHES

Check and Testing

Switches can be tested for continuity with an ohmmeter (see Chapter One), or a test light at the switch connector plug by operating the switch in each of its operating positions and comparing the results with its switch operation diagram. For example, **Figure 85** shows a continuity diagram for the ignition switch for 1995-1999 models. The horizontal line indicates which terminals should show continuity when the switch is in a given position.

When the ignition switch in is in the PARK position, for example, there should be continuity between the red and brown terminals. This is indicated by the line on the operation diagram shown in **Figure 85**. An ohmmeter connected between these two terminals should indicate little or no resistance or a test light should light. When the ignition switch is in the OFF position, there should be no continuity between any of the terminals.

If the switch or button does not perform properly, replace it. Refer to **Figures 85-101** for each individual switch.

ELECTRICAL SYSTEM

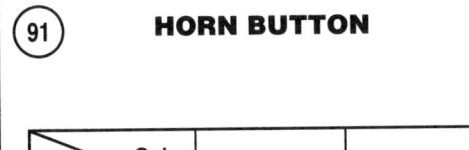

91. HORN BUTTON

Position \ Color	B/L	B/W
•		
PUSH	•——	——•

92. STARTER BUTTON

Position \ Color	O/W	Y/G
•		
PUSH	•——	——•

93. ENGINE STOP SWITCH

Position \ Color	O/B	O/W
•		
PUSH	•——	——•

94. FRONT BRAKE SWITCH (1995-1999 MODELS)

Position \ Color	B	B
OFF		
ON	•——	——•

95. FRONT BRAKE SWITCH (2000 MODELS)

Position \ Color	B/R	B
OFF		
ON	•——	——•

96. REAR BRAKE LIGHT SWITCH

Position \ Color	O/G	W/B
OFF		
ON	•——	——•

97. CLUTCH SWITCH (1996-1999 U.S.A., CALIFORNIA AND CANADA GSF600S MODELS)

Position \ Color	Y/G	Y/G
OFF		
ON	•——	——•

98. CLUTCH SWITCH (1997-ON MODELS EXCEPT U.S.A., CALIFORNIA AND CANADA GSF600S MODELS)

Position \ Color	B/Y	B/Y
FREE		
•	•——	——•

99 OIL PRESSURE SWITCH

Position \ Color	G/Y	Ground
ON (engine is stopped)	•——————•	
OFF (engine is running)		

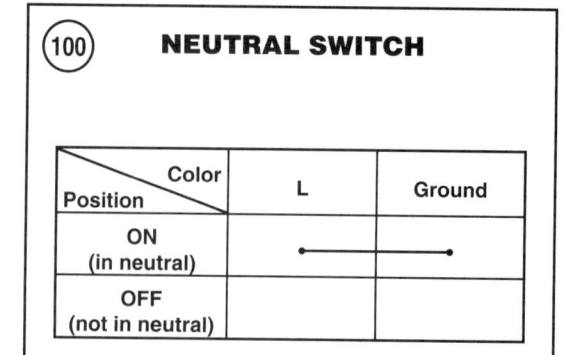

100 NEUTRAL SWITCH

Position \ Color	L	Ground
ON (in neutral)	•——————•	
OFF (not in neutral)		

101 SIDE-STAND SWITCH

Position \ Color	G	B/W
ON (Up position)	•——————•	
OFF (Down position)		

When testing switches, note the following:
1. First check the fuse as described in *Fuse* in this chapter.
2. Check the battery as described in *Battery* in Chapter Three. Charge the battery to the correct state of charge, if required.
3. Disconnect the negative battery cable from the battery if the switch connectors are not disconnected in the circuit.

CAUTION
Do not attempt to start the engine with the battery disconnected.

4. When separating two connectors, pull the connector housings and not the wires.
5. After locating a defective circuit, check the connectors to make sure they are clean and properly connected. Check all wires going into a connector housing to make sure each wire is properly positioned and that the wire end is not loose.
6. When reconnecting electrical connector halves, push them together until they click or snap into place.

Ignition Switch Removal/Installation

1. On models with a fairing, remove the front fairing as described in Chapter Fourteen.
2. On the left side, disconnect the 6-pin ignition switch connector (**Figure 102**) from the wiring harness.

NOTE
The ignition switch is held in place with two special Torx bolts. On this type of bolt, the head either shears off or rounds off as a theft deterrent.

3. Remove the ignition switch mounting bolts from the upper fork bridge as follows:

 a. Center punch a dimple into the bolt shoulder.
 b. Place the center punch in this dimple.
 c. Use a hammer to carefully tap the bolt counterclockwise, and remove the bolt.
 d. If the bolt cannot be loosened this way, drill a small hole in the center of the bolt and use a screw extractor to loosen and remove the bolt.

4. Remove the switch assembly (**Figure 103**).
5. Install the new ignition switch onto the upper fork bridge and install new Torx bolts. Tighten the bolts until the bolt head shears off or rounds off to the point where the tool slips off the head.
6. Reconnect the 6-pin electrical connector. Make sure the electrical connector is free of corrosion and is tight.
7. If removed, install the front fairing as described in Chapter Fourteen.

Right Handlebar Switch Housing Replacement

The right handlebar switches are not available individually. If any portion of the switch assembly is faulty, the entire switch housing must be replaced.

ELECTRICAL SYSTEM

1. Engine stop switch.
2. Start button.
3. Front brake light switch (electrical connectors only–the switch is separate).
4. Headlight switch (except U.S.A, California and Canada models).

Replacement

1. Remove the seat as described in Chapter Fourteen.
2. Disconnect the negative battery cable as described in this chapter.
3. Remove the fuel tank as described in Chapter Eight.
4A. On 1995-1996 models, perform the following:
   a. Unhook the tie wrap and locate the right-handlebar-switch 8-pin electrical connector. Refer to the appropriate wiring diagram at the end of this book to identify the wire colors in this connector.
   b. Disconnect the single electrical connector with a yellow/green wire. This wire goes from the starter switch to the clutch switch on U.S.A., California and Canada models. It goes from the starter switch to the starter relay on other 1995-1996 models.

4B. On 1997-on, unhook the tie wrap and locate the right handlebar switch 9-pin electrical connector. Refer to the appropriate wiring diagram at the end of this book to identify the wire colors in this connector.

5. Disconnect the two connectors (A, **Figure 104**) from the front brake switch.
6. Remove the electrical wire harness from any clips on the frame and carefully pull the harness out from the frame.
7. Remove the screws securing the right handlebar switch housing together and remove the switch assembly (B, **Figure 104**).
8. Assembly is the reverse of removal. Note the following.
   a. Install a new switch and tighten the screws securely. Do not overtighten the screws or the plastic switch housing may crack.
   b. Make sure the electrical connectors are corrosion-free and secure. Install the tie wrap to hold the electrical wires to the front of the frame. The wires must be retained in this manner to allow room for the fuel tank.
   c. Check the operation of the front brake switch before riding.

Left Handlebar Switch Housing

The clutch switch is the only switch in the left handlebar assembly that can be replaced separately. The others are not availble individually. If one is damaged, replace the switch housing assembly. The

left handlebar switch assembly includes the following switches:
 1. Headlight dimmer switch.
 2. Turn signal switch.
 3. Horn button.
 4. Passing button (except U.S.A., California and Canada models).
 5. Connectors for the clutch switch.

Replacement

1. Disconnect the negative battery cable as described in this chapter.
2. Remove the fuel tank as described in Chapter Eight.
3. Unhook the tie wrap and remove any plastic clamps securing the left handlebar switch cable to the frame.
4A. On 1995-1996 models, locate and disconnect the left handlebar switch 9-pin electrical connector. Refer to the appropriate wiring diagram at the end of this book to identify the wire colors in this connector.
4B. On 1997-on models, locate and disconnect the left handlebar switch 11-pin electrical connector. Refer to the appropriate wiring diagram at the end of this book to identify the wire colors in this connector.
5. On models with a clutch switch, disconnect the two connectors (A, **Figure 105**) from the clutch switch on the clutch lever.
6. Remove the screws securing the left handlebar switch housing together and separate the housing halves. Note that the starter cable bracket is secured under one of these screws (B, **Figure 105**). The bracket will have to be reinstalled in the same manner during assembly.
7. Disconnect the starter cable from the choke lever and remove the switch housing.
8. Install by reversing these removal steps while noting the following:
 a. Connect the starter cable to the choke lever in the switch housing.
 b. Align the locating pin with the hole in the handlebar. Install the switch onto the handlebar and tighten the screws securely.
 c. Make sure the electrical connectors are corrosion-free and secure.
 d. Check the operation of each switch mounted in the left handlebar switch.
 e. Operate the choke lever and make sure the linkage is operating correctly without binding. If operation is incorrect or if there is binding, carefully check that the cable is attached correctly and that there are no tight bends in the cable.

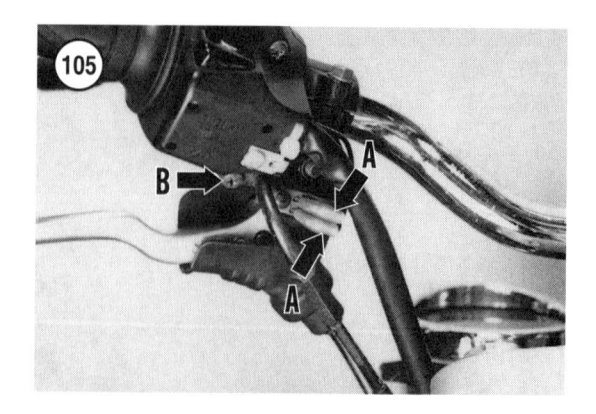

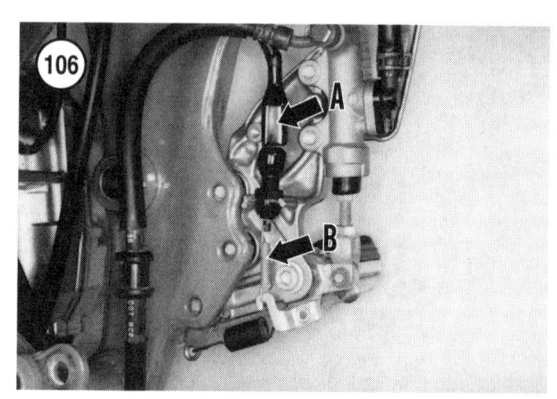

Clutch Switch Removal/Installation (1996 U.S.A., California and Canada Models and all 1997-On Models)

1. Disconnect the two connectors (A, **Figure 105**) from the clutch switch.

ELECTRICAL SYSTEM

4. Disconnect the spring (B, **Figure 106**) from the switch body.
5. Loosen the locknut, and remove the switch from the mounting boss on the frame.
6. Installation is the reverse of removal. Adjust the new switch as described in Chapter Three.

Neutral Switch Removal/Installation

1. Remove the engine drive sprocket and cover as described in Chapter Seven.
2. Remove any tie wraps securing the electrical wire to the frame.
3. Follow the single black wire from the neutral switch (**Figure 107**) to the electrical connector and disconnect the connector.

NOTE
Step 4 and Step 5 are shown with the engine removed from the frame and partially disassembled for clarity. It is not necessary to remove the engine from the frame for this procedure.

4. Remove the screws securing the neutral switch and remove the neutral switch assembly.
5. The O-ring (**Figure 108**) may come out with the neutral switch or it may remain in the crankcase. Remove the O-ring. A new one must be installed during assembly.
6. Do not lose the switch contact plunger and spring (**Figure 109**) from the end of the shift drum.
7. Carefully remove the electrical wire. Note how the wire is routed through the engine. The wire from the new switch must follow the same path.
8. Install by reversing these removal steps, noting the following:
   a. Install a *new* O-ring (**Figure 108**).
   b. Make sure the electrical connector is corrosion-free and secure.
   c. Attach any tie wraps securing the electrical wire to the frame.

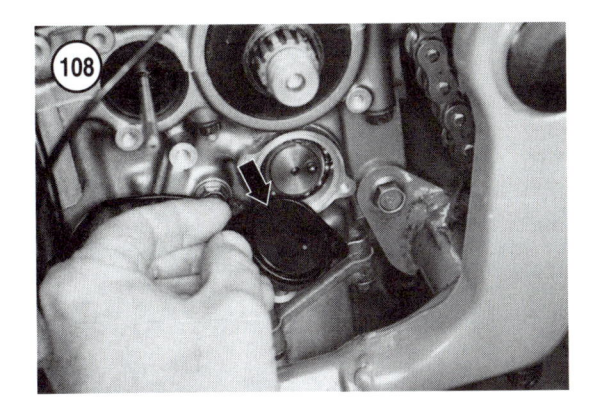

2. Remove the two switch mounting screws and remove the switch from the clutch lever.
3. Secure the new switch to the clutch lever and connect the clutch switch connectors (A, **Figure 105**).

Front Brake Switch Removal/Installation

1. Disconnect the two connectors (A, **Figure 104**) from the front brake switch.
2. Remove the two switch mounting screws and remove the switch from the brake lever.
3. Secure the new switch to the brake lever and connect the front brake switch connectors.

Rear Brake Switch Removal/Installation

1. Remove the rear wheel as described in Chapter Ten.
2. Roll back the rubber boot from the brake switch body (A, **Figure 106**).
3. Disconnect the harness connector from the switch body.

Sidestand Switch Removal/Installation

1. Securely support the motorcycle on level ground.

2A. On 1995-1999 models, remove the seat and the left rear-frame cover as described in Chapter Fourteen.

2B. On 2000 models, remove the left side cover as described in Chapter Fourteen.

3. Disconnect the 2-pin sidestand switch connector (one green wire and one black/white wire) from the wiring harness. (D, **Figure 110**)

4. Remove the screws securing the sidestand switch (**Figure 111**) to the frame and remove the switch. Note how the cable is routed through the frame. The cable for the new switch must follow the same path.

5. Installation is the reverse of removal.
   a. Tighten the sidestand switch mounting screws securely.
   b. Route the electrical wire harness through the frame and install the tie wraps securing the harness to the frame.

Sidestand Switch Inspection (2000 Models)

1. Remove the left side cover.
2. Disconnect the 2-pin sidestand switch connector (one green wire and one black/white wire) from the wiring harness.
3. Set the Suzuki multi tester (part No. 09900-25008) to diode test.
4. Connect the positive test probe to the green terminal on the switch side of the connector, and connect the negative test probe to the black/white terminal.
5. Move the sidestand up and note the reading on the meter. Move the sidestand down and note the voltage reading.
6. Replace the switch if either reading is outside the test voltage range listed in **Table 1**.

Oil Pressure Switch Removal/Installation

NOTE
Make sure the oil level is at the proper level before testing the oil pressure switch.

1. Drain the engine oil as described in Chapter Three.
2. Remove the signal generator cover bolts, and remove the cover and its gasket. One cover bolt has a sealing washer installed beneath it. Note the position of this bolt. It must be reinstalled in the same location during assembly. See **Figure 112**.

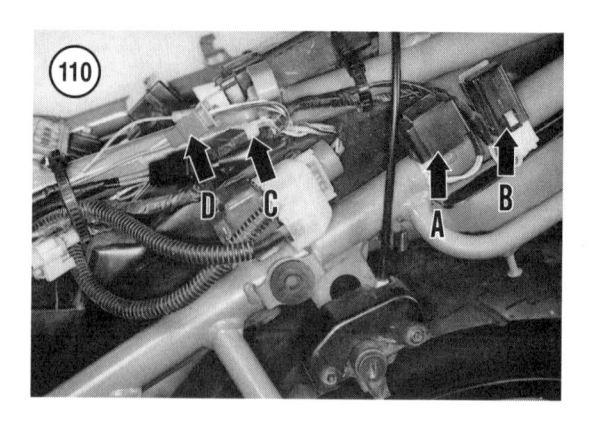

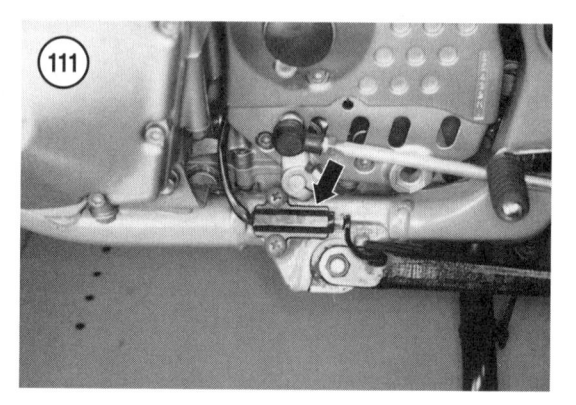

3. Disconnect the oil pressure switch wire (A, **Figure 113**).
4. Unscrew the oil pressure switch from the crankcase.
5. Install the oil pressure switch by reversing these removal steps, noting the following:
   a. Apply a light coat of gasket sealer to the switch threads prior to installation. Install the switch and torque the switch to the specification in **Table 3**.
   b. Apply a light coat of gasket sealer to the groove in the rubber grommet (B, **Figure 113**).

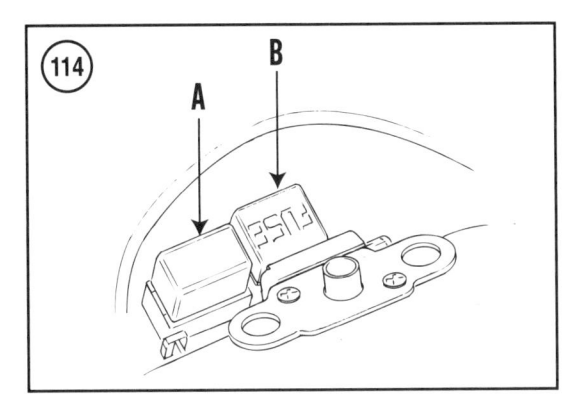

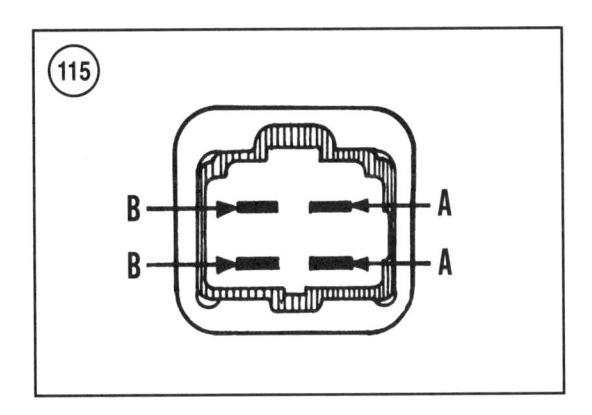

ELECTRICAL SYSTEM

Turn Signal Relay Testing

If a turn signal lamp does not light, first inspect for a blown bulb. If the bulb is good, check the turn signal switch and all electrical connections within the turn signal circuit.

If all of these items are in good working order, replace the turn signal relay on 1995-1999 models. On 2000 models, replace the turn-signal/sidestand relay.

Turn Signal Relay Replacement (1995-1999 Models)

1. Turn the handlebar all the way to the left to gain access to the relay.
2. Unhook the turn signal relay (A, **Figure 110**) from the frame clip.
3. Disconnect the turn signal relay electrical connector and remove the relay.
4. Connect the connector to the new relay and install the relay onto the frame clip.

Turn Signal/Sidestand Relay Replacement (2000 Models)

The turn signal/sidestand relay sits behind the seat-latch mechanism. See A, **Figure 114**.

1. Remove the seat as described in Chapter Fourteen.
2. Remove the turn signal/sidestand relay from the mounting clip.
3. Disconnect the electrical connector from the relay assembly.
4. Connect the connector to a new relay assembly.
5. Fit the relay assembly onto the mounting clip.

Sidestand Relay Testing (1995-1999 Models)

1. Remove the seats and rear frame cover as described in Chapter Fourteen.
2. Disconnect the negative battery cable as described in this chapter.
3. Pull straight up and remove the sidestand relay (B, **Figure 110**) from the rubber mount on the rear frame.
4. Disconnect the electrical connector from the relay.
5. Connect a 12-volt battery to the A terminals on the relay (**Figure 115**).

c. Install a new signal generator cover gasket and install the cover. Make sure the bolt with the sealing washer is installed in the location noted during disassembly. See **Figure 112**.

RELAYS

On 2000 models, the turn-signal relay, sidestand relay and diode are combined into the turn signal/sidestand relay.

6. Use an ohmmeter and check the continuity between the B terminals on the relay. There should be continuity.

7. If the relay fails this test, the relay is faulty and must be replaced. If the relay passes this test, reconnect the electrical connector and install the relay onto the rubber mount on the rear frame.

Diode Testing (1995-1999 Models)

1. Remove the seats and rear frame cover as described in Chapter Fourteen.

2. Disconnect the negative battery cable as described in this chapter.

3. Disconnect the electrical connector from the diode (C, **Figure 110**) and remove the diode.

4. Use an ohmmeter to check the continuity between terminals 1 and 2 (**Figure 116**) in the diode. Reverse the test probes and again check the continuity. The diode should have continuity in one direction but no continuity in the other. Replace the diode if these two readings are the same.

5. Use an ohmmeter to check the continuity between terminals 2 and 3 (**Figure 116**). Reverse the test probes and again check the continuity. The diode should have continuity in one direction but no continuity in the other. Replace the diode if these two readings are the same.

6. If the diode fails this test, it must be replaced. If the diode passes this test, reconnect the electrical connector and install the relay onto the rubber mount on the rear frame.

Diode Testing (2000 Models)

1. Remove the turn signal/sidestand relay as decribed in this chapter.

2. Set the Suzuki Multi-Circuit Tester (part No. 09900-25008) to diode test.

3. Refer to **Figure 117**, and measure the voltage across the diode terminals indicated in **Figure 118**.

4. Replace the turn signal/sidestand relay if any measurement is outside the range specified in **Figure 118**.

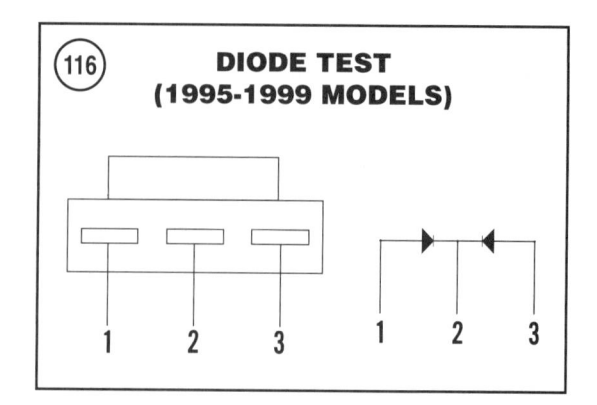

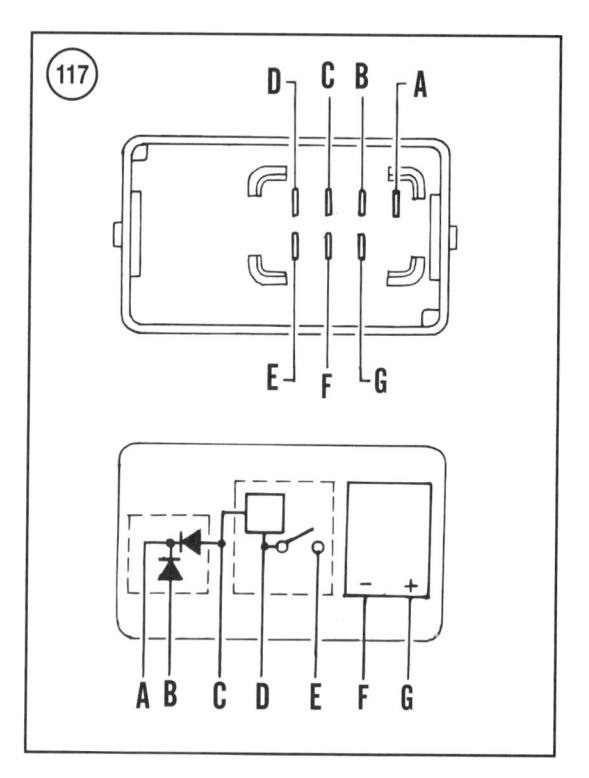

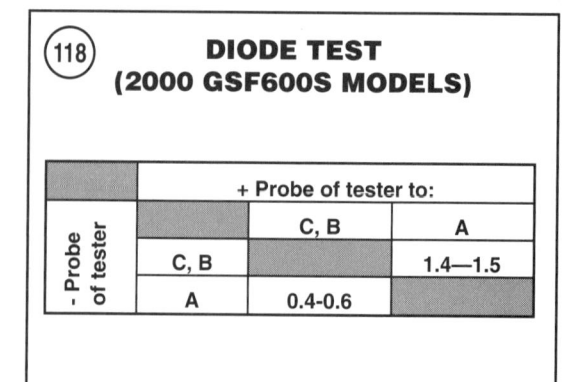

(116) **DIODE TEST (1995-1999 MODELS)**

(117)

(118) **DIODE TEST (2000 GSF600S MODELS)**

	+ Probe of tester to:	
− Probe of tester		C, B	A
	C, B		1.4—1.5
	A	0.4-0.6	

ELECTRICAL SYSTEM

COMBINATION METER INSPECTION (1995-1999 MODELS) (119)

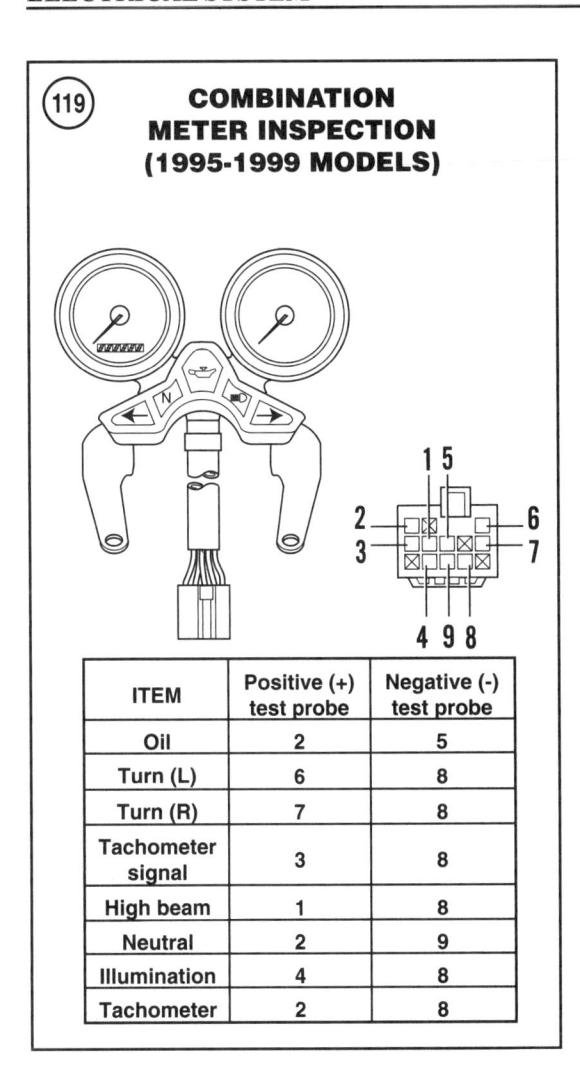

ITEM	Positive (+) test probe	Negative (−) test probe
Oil	2	5
Turn (L)	6	8
Turn (R)	7	8
Tachometer signal	3	8
High beam	1	8
Neutral	2	9
Illumination	4	8
Tachometer	2	8

COMBINATION METER INSPECTION (2000 MODELS) (120)

ITEM	Positive (+) test probe	Negative (−) test probe
Oil	14	3
Turn (L)	13	10
Turn (R)	8	10
Tachometer	2	16
High beam	12	10
Neutral	14	11
Illumination	7	10

COMBINATION METER

Inspection

1. Disconnect the combination meter connector from the wiring harness. On 2000 models, disconnect both connectors from the wiring harness.
2. Refer to the table in **Figure 119** or **Figure 120**, and check the continuity in the affected circuit.
   a. Set an ohmmeter to the R × 1 scale and connect the test probes to the terminals indicated in the table.
   b. The circuit should have continuity.
3. If the circuit does not have continuity, replace the indicator bulb and repeat the continuity test.
4. If the circuit still does not have continuity, inspect the connector for loose or broken wires.
5. If this does not resolve the problem, replace the combination meter.

Removal/Installation (1995-1999 Models)

Refer to **Figure 121**.

1. Disconnect the negative battery cable.
2A. On GSF600S models, remove the fairing as described in Chapter Fourteen.
2B. On GSF600 models, remove the headlight assembly and disconnect the combination meter 10-pin connector.
3. Unscrew the speedometer drive cable (A, **Figure 122**) from the back of the speedometer.
4. Remove the hardware (B, **Figure 122**) securing the mounting bracket to the lower surface of the fork bridge.
5. Remove the combination meter assembly.
6. Install by reversing these removal steps. Make sure the electrical connectors are corrosion-free and secure.

COMBINATION METER (1995-1999 MODELS)

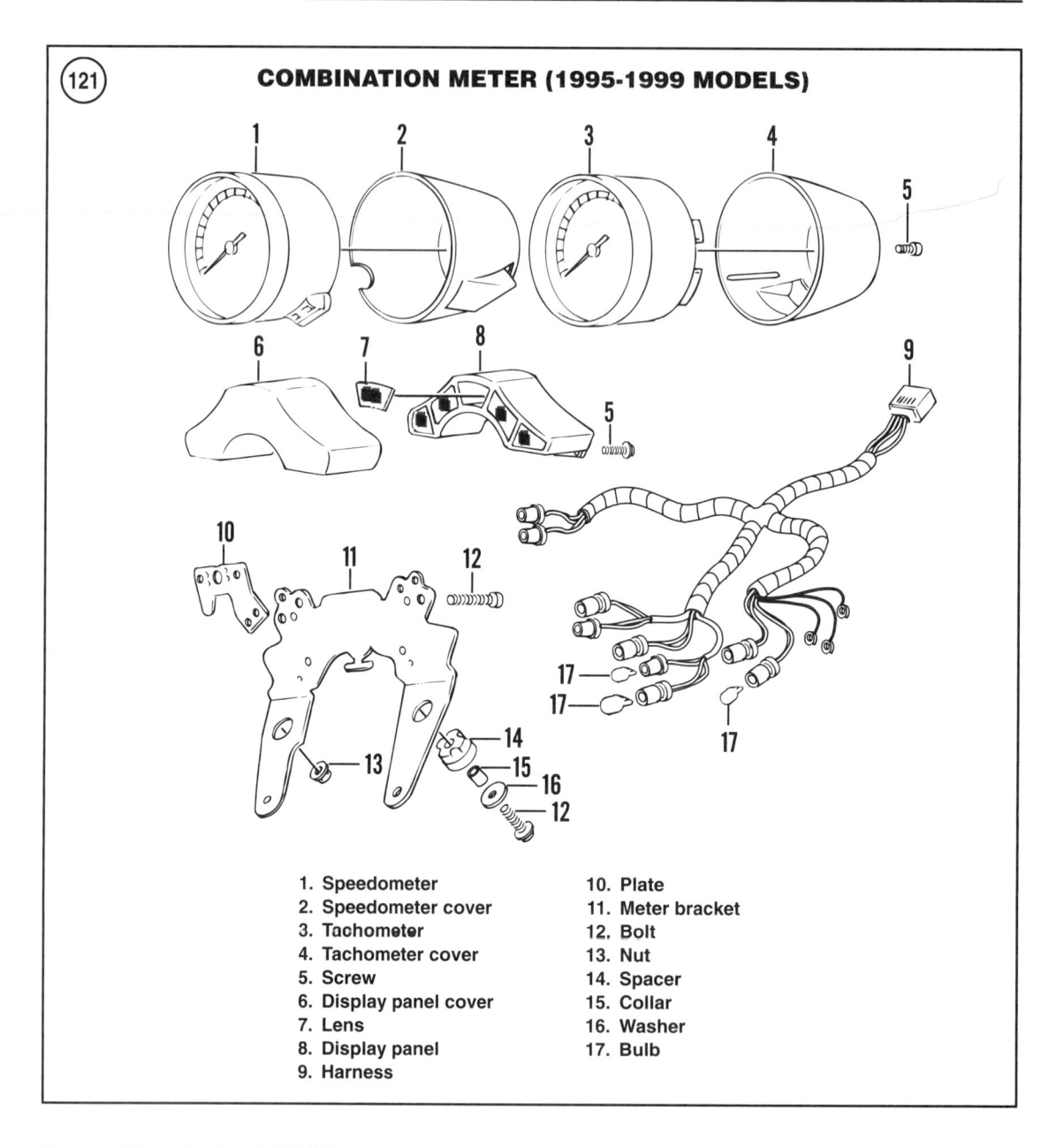

1. Speedometer
2. Speedometer cover
3. Tachometer
4. Tachometer cover
5. Screw
6. Display panel cover
7. Lens
8. Display panel
9. Harness
10. Plate
11. Meter bracket
12. Bolt
13. Nut
14. Spacer
15. Collar
16. Washer
17. Bulb

Removal/Installation (2000 Models)

Refer to **Figure 123**.

1. On GSF600S models, remove the fairing as described in Chapter Fourteen.

2. Remove the headlight assembly as described in this chapter.

3. Disconnect the two combination meter 10-pin and 4-pin connectors.

4. Remove the nuts securing the combination meter to the bracket and remove the meter.

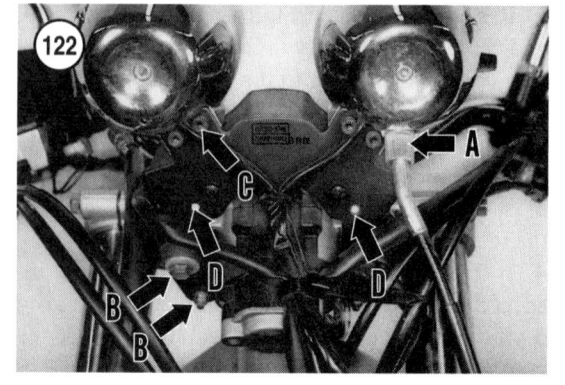

ELECTRICAL SYSTEM

(123) COMBINATION METER (1995-1999 MODELS)

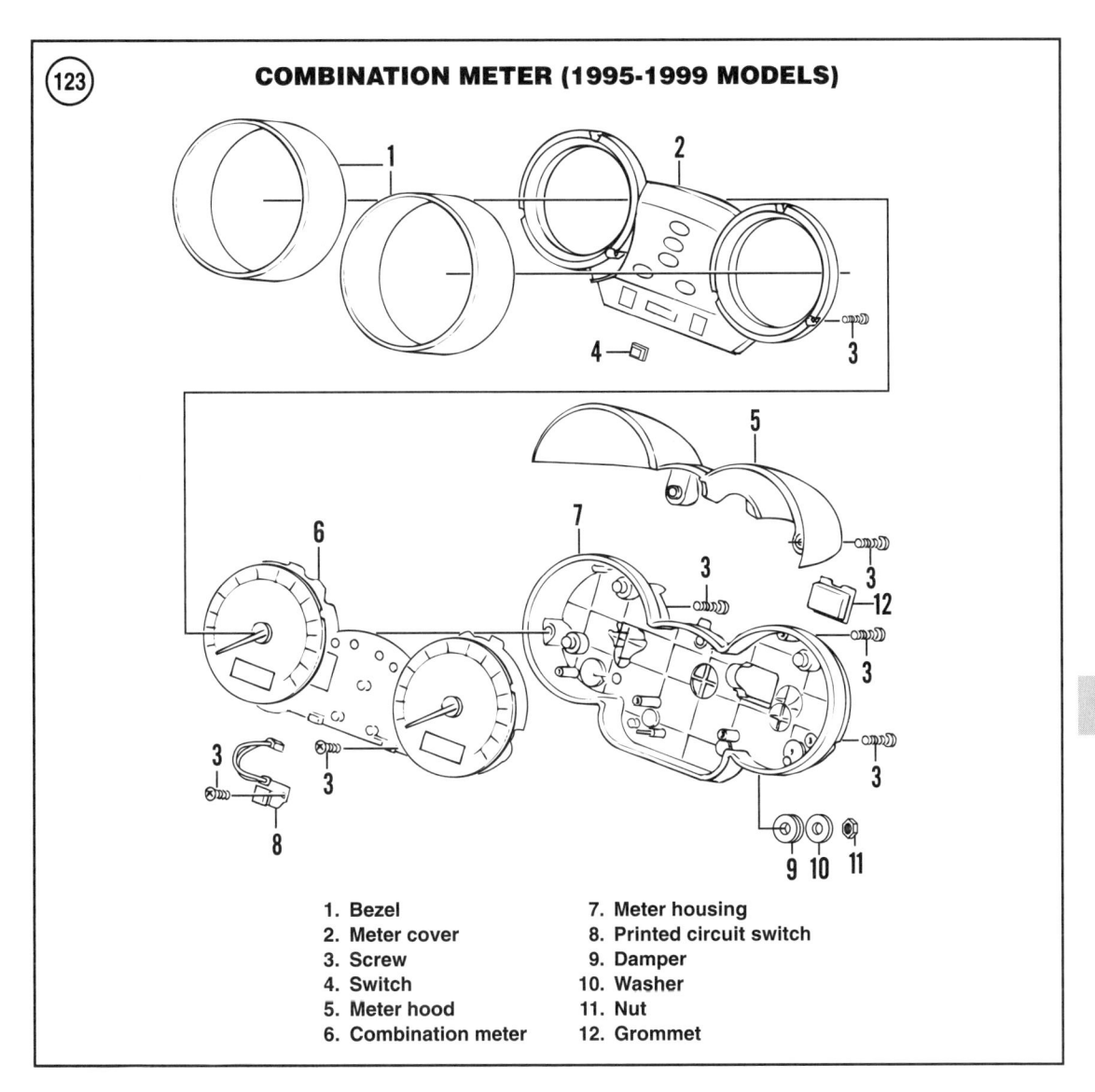

1. Bezel
2. Meter cover
3. Screw
4. Switch
5. Meter hood
6. Combination meter
7. Meter housing
8. Printed circuit switch
9. Damper
10. Washer
11. Nut
12. Grommet

Indicator Light Replacement (1995-1999 Models)

Refer to **Figure 121**.

1A. On GSF600S models, remove the fairing as described in Chapter Fourteen.

1B. On GSF600 models, remove the headlight assembly and disconnect the combination meter 10-pin connector.

2. Cut the cable ties securing the wiring behind the combination meter.

3. Lift the display panel cover and replace the bulb.

4. Installation is the reverse of removal. Remember to install new cable ties.

Speedometer Inspection (2000 Models)

If the speedometer, odometer or tripmeter does not function properly, inspect the speed sensor and its connectors as described in this chapter. If the speed sensor functions properly, replace the combination meter.

Speed Sensor Inspection (2000 Models)

1. Remove the left side cover as described in Chapter Fourteen.

2. Disconnect the 3-pin speed sensor connector (one black/red wire, one black/white wire and one black wire on the sensor side).

3. Remove the mounting screw, and remove the speed sensor from the engine sprocket cover.
4. Connect the negative battery terminal to the black/white terminal in the sensor side of the connector and connect the positive battery terminal to the black terminal. See **Figure 124**.
5. Connect a 10 k ohm resistor to the black/red and black terminals on the sensor side of the connector.
6. Connect a voltmeter across the resistor as shown in **Figure 124**.
7. Touch the pick-up surface of the sensor with a screwdriver and watch the voltmeter. The voltage reading should change from 0 to 12 volts or from 12 to 0 volts. If it does not, replace the sensor.

Oil Pressure Indicator Inspection (2000 Models)

1. Remove the signal generator cover bolts, and remove the cover and its gasket. One cover bolt has a sealing washer installed beneath it. Note the position of this bolt. It must be reinstalled in the same location during assembly. See **Figure 112**.
2. Disconnect the oil pressure switch wire (A, **Figure 113**).
3. Turn the ignition switch ON.
4. Ground the oil pressure wire and watch the oil pressure indicator. It should turn on.
5. If the oil pressure indicator does not turn on, check all electrical connections. If the connections are clean and tight, replace the oil pressure indicator lamp.
6. Install the signal generator cover by performing the following:
    a. Apply a light coat of gasket sealer to the groove in the rubber grommet (B, **Figure 113**).
    b. Install a new signal generator cover gasket and install the cover. Make sure the bolt with the sealing washer is installed in the location noted during disassembly. See **Figure 112**.

Speedometer/Tachometer Removal/Installation (1995-1999 Models)

Refer to **Figure 121**.
1A. On GSF600S models, remove the front fairing as described in Chapter Fourteen.
1B. On GSF600 models, remove the headlight assembly as described in this chapter.

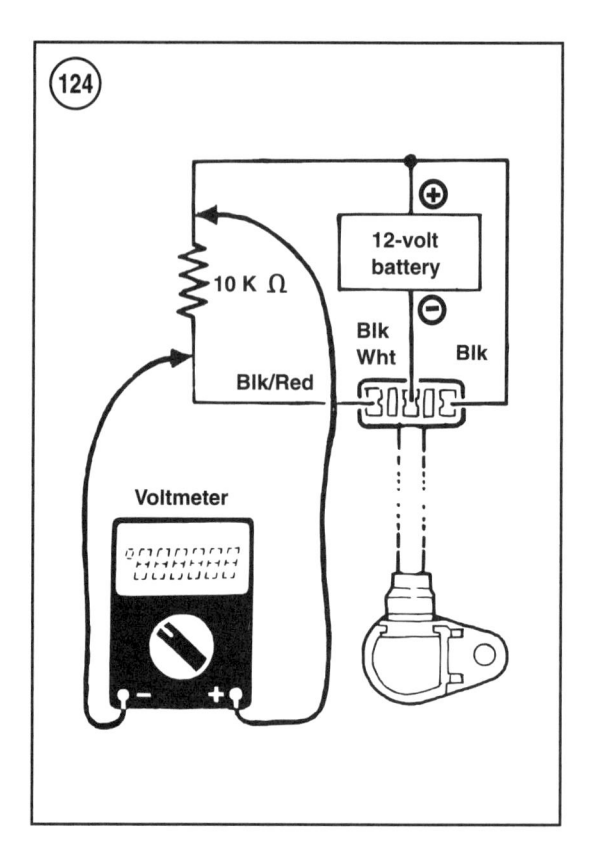

2. If removing the speedometer, unscrew the speedometer drive cable (A, **Figure 122**) from the back of the speedometer.
3. Remove the mounting bolts (C, **Figure 122**) securing the meter to the back of the combination meter.
4. Remove the screw from the rear of the cover (A, **Figure 125**) and remove the meter from its cover.
5. If the meter is being replaced, remove the indicator bulb socket (A, **Figure 126**) and remove the screws (B, **Figure 126**) securing the wiring to the meter.

ELECTRICAL SYSTEM

Horn Removal/Installation

1. The horn is mounted in various locations as follows:
   a. On 1995-1999 GSF600S models, the horn is mounted to the middle of the front fairing (**Figure 127**).
   b. On 2000 GSF600S models, the horn is mounted to the left side of the fairing.
   c. On GSF600 models, the horn is mounted to the lower fork bridge.
2. On GSF600S models, remove the front fairing as described in Chapter Fourteen.
3. Disconnect the electrical connectors from the spade connectors on the horn.
4. Remove the horn mounting bolt (**Figure 127**) and remove the horn.
5. Install by reversing these removal steps. Make sure the electrical connector is corrosion-free and secure.

FUSES

On 1995-1999 models, the fuse box is located under the seat, just behind the battery (**Figure 128**). On 2000 models, it is located behind the seat latch (B, **Figure 114**).

Whenever a fuse blows, determine the reason for the failure before replacing the fuse. Usually, the trouble is a short circuit in the wiring. This may be caused by worn-through insulation or a disconnected wire shorted to ground.

> **CAUTION**
> *Never substitute metal foil or wire for a fuse. Never use a higher amperage fuse than specified. An overload could result in a fire and complete loss of the motorcycle.*

> **CAUTION**
> *When replacing a fuse, make sure the ignition switch is in the OFF position. This will lessen the chance of a short circuit.*

6. Installation is the reverse of removal. Make sure the mounting boss on the meter aligns with the cutout in the meter cover (B, **Figure 125**) and then install the meter cover bolt (A, **Figure 125**).

Horn Testing

1. Disconnect the horn wires from the harness.
2. Connect a 12-volt battery to the horn.
3. If the horn is good it will sound. If not, replace it.

Fuse Replacement

1. Remove the seat as described in Chapter Fourteen.
2. Remove the fuse box cover.

3. Remove the fuse and inspect it. There is a spare fuse inside the fuse box.
4. Install the new fuse and push it all the way down until it seats completely, then install the cover.
5. Install the seat.
6. Replace the spare fuse as soon as possible.

MAIN FUSE

A 30-amp main fuse protects all electrical circuits. This fuse is located on the starter relay (**Figure 129**). On 1995-1999 models, the starter relay is on the left side behind the rear frame cover. On 2000 models, the relay is behind the left side cover.

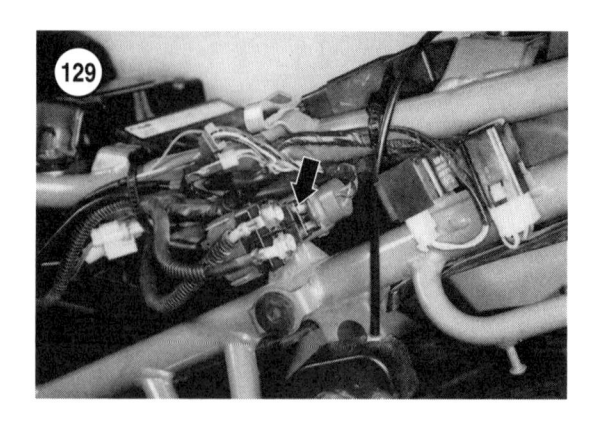

WIRING DIAGRAMS

Wiring diagrams for all models are located at the end of this book.

Table 1 ELECTRICAL SYSTEM SPECIFICATIONS

Battery	
Type	YT9-BS Maintenance free (sealed)
Capacity	12 volt 8 amp hour
Alternator	
Type	Three-phase AC
Regulated voltage (charging voltage)	
1995-1999 models	13.5 V @ 5000 rpm
2000 models	13.6-14.4 V @ 5000 rpm
Maximum output (2000 models)	More than 550 W @ 5000 rpm
Rotor slip ring outside diameter	
wear limit	14.0 mm (0.55 in.)
Brush length wear limit	4.5 mm (0.18 in.)
Pickup coil resistance	
(signal generator coil resistance)	Approx. 135-200 ohms
Ignition system	
Type	Fully transistorized
Firing order	1-2-4-3
Ignition timing	
1995	
Austria and Switzerland models	4 BTDC @ 1500 rpm
All models except Austria	
and Switzerland	13 BTDC @ 1500 rpm
1996	
USA, California, Austria	
and Switzerland models	4 BTDC @ 1500 rpm
All models except USA, California,	
Austria and Switzerland	13 BTDC @ 1500 rpm
1997-1999	
USA, California and	
Switzerland models	4 BTDC @ 1500 rpm
All models except USA, California	
and Switzerland	13 BTDC @ 1500 rpm
2000	
USA, California and Canada models	4 BTDC @ 1200 rpm
Australia, U.K. and European models	13 BTDC @ 1500 rpm
(continued)	

ELECTRICAL SYSTEM

Table 1 ELECTRICAL SYSTEM SPECIFICATIONS (continued)

Signal generator	
Resistance	Approx. 135-200 ohms
Peak voltage (2000 models)	More than 1.0 V
Peak voltage (1995-1999 models)	N/A
Ignition coil resistance	
Primary	2-4 ohms
Secondary	30-40 k ohms
Ignition coil primary peak voltage (2000 models)	More than 140 V
Starter relay resistance	
1995-1999 models	3-5 ohms
2000 models	3-6 ohms
Sidestand switch test voltage (2000 models)	
Up position (on)	0.4-0.6 volts
Down position (off)	1.4-1.5 volts
Fuse size	
Headlight (high and low beam)	15 amp
Turn signal	15 amp
Ignition	10 amp
Taillight	10 amp
Main	30 amp

Table 2 REPLACEMENT BULBS

Item	Voltage/wattage
Headlight (high/low beam)	
1995-1999 models	12 V 50/55 W
2000 models	12 V 60/50 W
Position light*	
1995-1999 models	12 V 4 W
2000 models	12 V 5 W
Tail/brake light	
1995-1999	12 V 5/21 W
2000 models	12 V 5/21 W × 2
Turn signal	12 V 21 W
License plate light	12 V 5 W
Tachometer light	
1995-1996 models	12 V 1.7 W
1997-1999 models	12 V 0.84 W
2000 models	LED
Speedometer light	
1995-1996 models	12 V 1.7 W
1997-1999 models	12 V 0.84 W
2000 models	LED
Neutral indicator light	
1995-1999 models	12 V 3 W
2000 models	LED
High beam indicator light	
1995-1999 models	12 V 1.7 W
2000 GSF600S models	LED
Turn signal indicator light	
1995-1999 models	12 V 3.4 W
2000 models	LED
Oil pressure indicator light	
1995-1999 models	12 V 3.4 W
2000	LED

*Not used on U.S.A. California, Canada and Australia models

Table 3 ELECTRICAL SYSTEM TORQUE SPECIFICATIONS

Item	N•m	in.-lb.	ft.-lb.
Alternator driven gear nut			
1995-1999 models	60	–	44
2000 models	55	–	40.5
Alternator mounting bolt	25	–	18
Oil pressure switch	14	–	10
Starter motor terminal bolt	3	26.5	
Starter motor mounting bolt	6	53	–
Stator mounting bolt	3	26.5	–
Starter relay terminal bolt	5	44	–
Signal generator rotor bolt	25	–	18

CHAPTER TEN

WHEELS, TIRES AND DRIVE CHAIN

This chapter describes repair and maintenance procedures for the front and rear wheels, tires and the drive chain.

When inspecting any of the components addressed in this chapter, compare all measurements to the wheel, tire and drive chain specifications in **Table 1**. Replace any component that is damaged, worn to the wear limit or out of specification. During assembly, tighten fasteners to the torque specifications in **Table 2**. **Tables 1-2** appear at the end of this chapter.

MOTORCYCLE STAND

Many procedures in this chapter require that the motorcycle be supported with a wheel off the ground. A quality motorcycle front end stand (**Figure 1**) or a swing arm stand does this safely and ef-

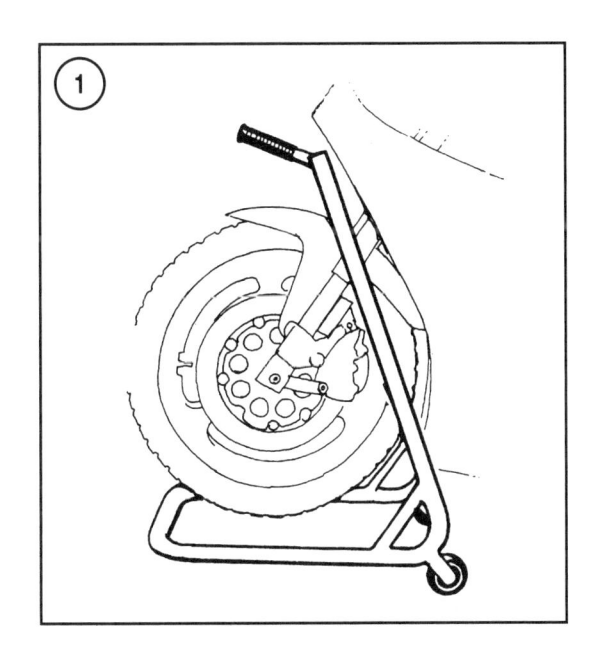

FRONT WHEEL (1995-1999 MODELS)

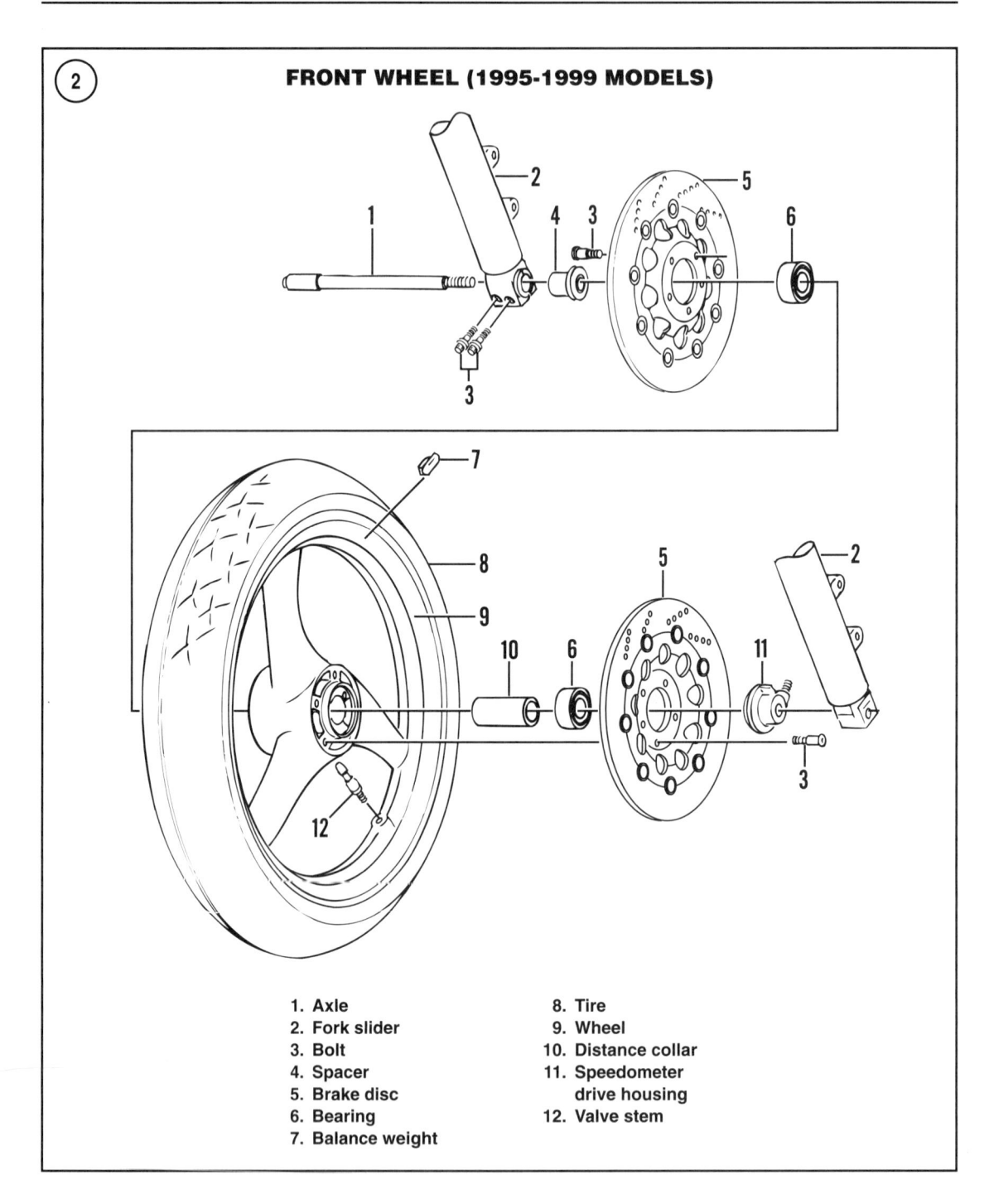

1. Axle
2. Fork slider
3. Bolt
4. Spacer
5. Brake disc
6. Bearing
7. Balance weight
8. Tire
9. Wheel
10. Distance collar
11. Speedometer drive housing
12. Valve stem

fectively. Before purchasing or using a stand, check the manufacturer's instructions to make sure the stand is designed for these models. If the motorcycle or the stand require any adjustment or accessories, perform the required modifications before lifting the motorcycle. When using a stand, have an assistant standing by.

An adjustable centerstand can also be used to support the motorcycle with a wheel off the ground. Again, check the manufacturer's instructions and perform any necessary modifications before supporting the motorcycle with an adjustable centerstand. A means to tie down one end of the motorcycle may also be required.

WHEELS, TIRES AND DRIVE CHAIN

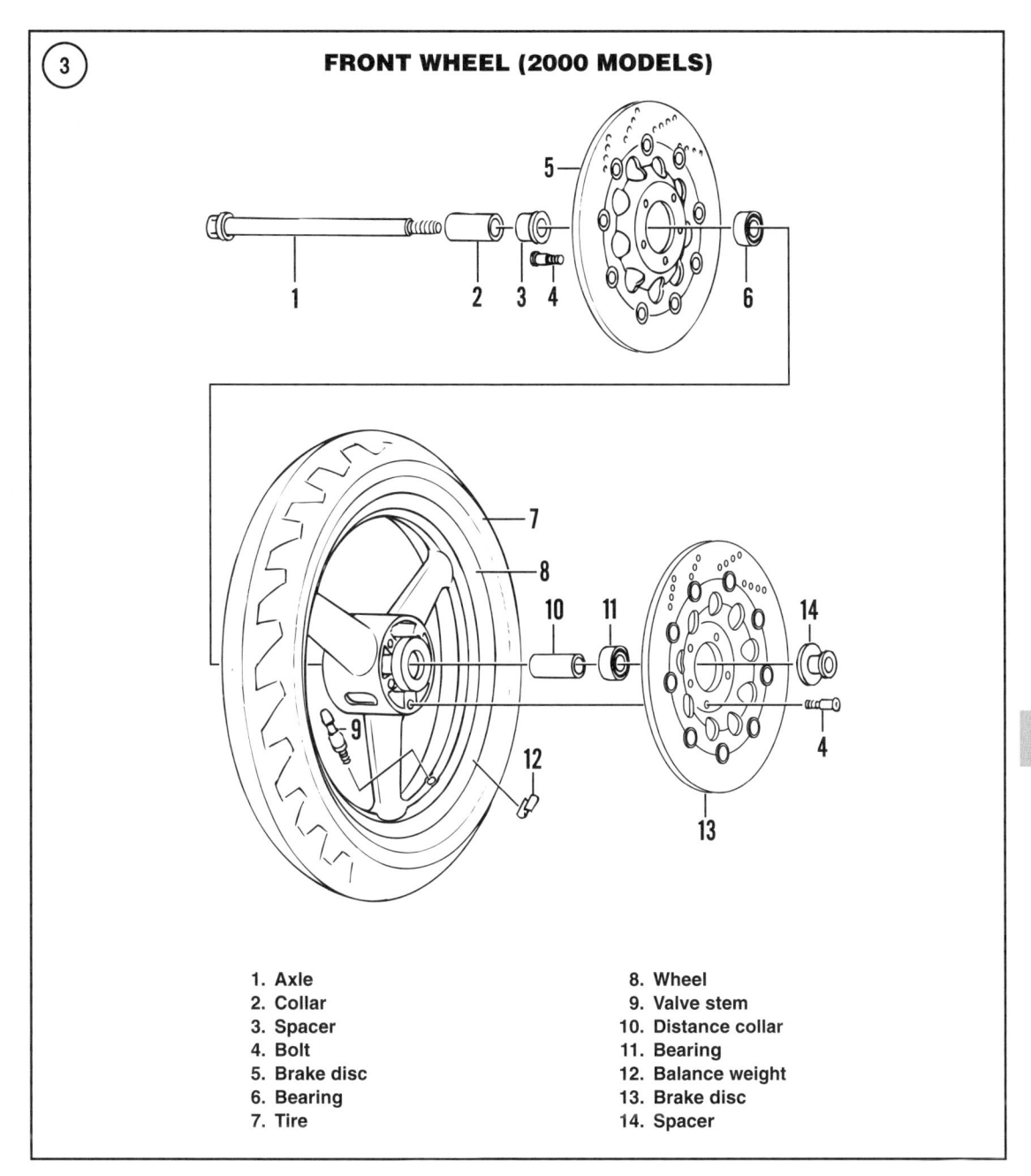

③ FRONT WHEEL (2000 MODELS)

1. Axle
2. Collar
3. Spacer
4. Bolt
5. Brake disc
6. Bearing
7. Tire
8. Wheel
9. Valve stem
10. Distance collar
11. Bearing
12. Balance weight
13. Brake disc
14. Spacer

Regardless of the method used to lift the motorcycle, be sure it is properly supported before walking away.

FRONT WHEEL

Refer to **Figure 2** when servicing the front wheel on 1995-1999 models. Refer to **Figure 3** when servicing 2000 models.

Removal

CAUTION
Use care when removing, handling and installing a wheel with disc brake rotors. The thin rotor can be easily damaged when subjected to side impact loads. If the rotor is knocked out of true by a side impact, a pulse will be felt at the brake lever when brak-

ing. Motorcycle rotors are too thin to be trued and must be replaced. Protect the rotors when transporting a wheel to a dealership or tire specialist for tire service. Do not place a wheel in a car trunk or pickup bed without protecting both rotors from side impact.

1. Support the motorcycle on the centerstand.
2. Shift the transmission into gear to prevent the motorcycle from rolling in either direction.

NOTE
Insert a piece of vinyl tubing or wood between the pads of each caliper once the caliper is removed. That way if the brake lever is inadvertently squeezed, the pistons will not be forced out of the cylinder. If this does happen, the caliper may have to be disassembled to reseat the pistons and the system will have to be bled.

3. Remove both brake calipers as described in Chapter Thirteen.
4. On 1995-1999 models, remove the speedometer cable (**Figure 4**) from the speedometer drive housing.
5. On the right fork leg, loosen both axle pinch bolts (A, **Figure 5**) and then loosen the front axle (B, **Figure 5**).

CAUTION
If using a jack, place a piece of wood on the jack pad to protect the oil pan.

6. Place a suitable size jack or wooden blocks under the oil pan to support the motorcycle securely with the front wheel off the ground.
7. Completely unscrew the axle from the left fork slider and remove the axle.
8. Pull the wheel down and forward, and remove the wheel from the front fork.
9. Remove the spacer (**Figure 6**) from the right side of the wheel. On 2000 models, remove a spacer from the right and left sides of the wheel.
10A. On 1995-1999 models, remove the speedometer gearbox from the left side of the hub.
10B. On 2000 models, do not lose the collar from the right fork leg.

CAUTION
Set the tire sidewalls on two wooden blocks. Do not set the wheel down on

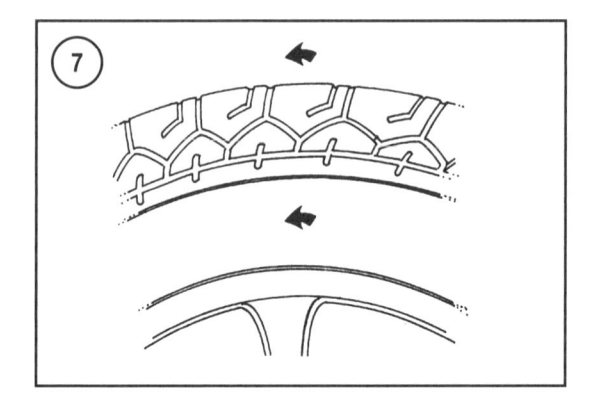

WHEELS, TIRES AND DRIVE CHAIN

2. Correctly position the wheel so the directional arrow points in the direction of normal wheel rotation (**Figure 7**).

3A. On 1995-1999 models, align the arms of the speedometer drive gear with the cutouts in the front hub and install the speedometer drive housing onto the left side of the hub. See **Figure 8**.

3B. On 2000 models, make sure the collar is in place in the right fork leg.

4. Fit the spacer into place on the right side of the hub (**Figure 6**). On 2000 models, fit a spacer into the right and left sides of the hub. Make sure the cover on the spacer completely seals the bearing in the hub.

5. Apply a light coat of grease to the front axle.

6. Position the wheel between the fork legs, lift the wheel and insert the front axle through the right fork slider, the spacer, the wheel hub and into the left fork slider.

7. On 1995-1999 models, rotate the speedometer drive housing until it rests against the boss (**Figure 9**) on the left fork slider.

8. Screw the axle (B, **Figure 5**) into the left fork slider and torque the axle to the specification in **Table 2**.

9. Install both brake calipers as described in Chapter Thirteen.

10. Remove the jack or wooden block(s) from under the oil pan.

11. Apply the front brake, push down hard on the handlebars and pump the fork four or five times to seat the front axle.

12. Torque the front axle pinch bolts (A, **Figure 5**) to specification.

13. Shift the transmission into neutral.

14. Roll the motorcycle back and forth several times. Apply the front brake as many times as necessary to make sure all brake pads seat against the brake disc correctly.

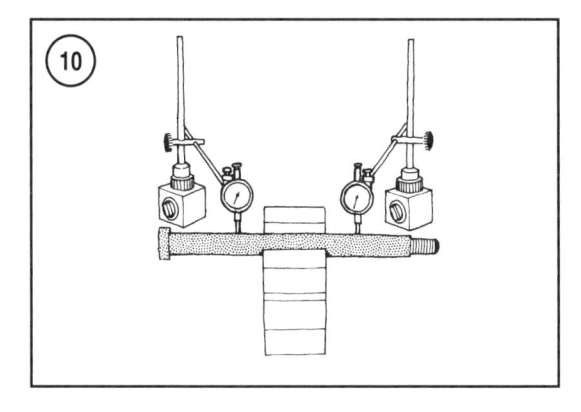

the disc surface. The disc could be scratched or warped.

11. Inspect the wheel as described in this chapter.

Installation

1. Make sure the bearing surfaces of each fork slider, the spacer, the collar (2000 models) and the axle are free of burrs and nicks.

Inspection

1. Remove any corrosion from the front axle with a piece of fine emery cloth. Clean the axle with solvent, and then wipe the axle clean with a lint-free cloth.

2. Set the axle on V-blocks and place the tip of a dial indicator in the middle of the axle (**Figure 10**). Rotate the axle and check its runout. If axle runout

exceeds the specified value, replace the axle; do not attempt to straighten it.

3. Check the brake disc bolts (A, **Figure 11**) for tightness on each disc. Torque the brake disc bolts to specification if necessary.

4. Check rim runout as follows:
   a. Measure the radial (up and down) runout of the wheel rim with a dial indicator (A, **Figure 12**). If runout exceeds the specification in **Table 1**, check the wheel bearings.
   b. Measure the axial (side to side) runout of the wheel rim with a dial indicator (B, **Figure 12**). If runout exceeds specification, check the wheel bearings.
   c. If necessary, replace the front wheel bearings as described in *Front and Rear Hubs* in this chapter.

5. Inspect the wheel rim for dents, bending or cracks. Check the rim and rim sealing surface for scratches that are deeper than 0.5 mm (0.01 in.). If any of these conditions are present, replace the rim.

6. Inspect the cover on the spacer (**Figure 6**). Replace the spacer if the cover is bent, buckled or otherwise damaged.

7. Since both front calipers are off the discs at this time, check the brake pads for wear. Refer to Chapter Thirteen.

Speedometer Drive Housing Inspection and Lubrication (1995-1999 models)

NOTE
The speedometer drive housing is a sealed assembly. No replacement parts are available. If any part of the housing is defective, the entire assembly must be replaced.

1. Remove the front wheel as described in this chapter.
2. Inspect the seal (A, **Figure 13**) for leakage.
3. Inspect the arms (B, **Figure 13**) of the speedometer drive gear for wear or damage.
4. Inspect the cutouts (B, **Figure 11**) in the front hub for wear or damage. Repair the hub or replace the wheel.
5. Install the front wheel as described in this chapter.

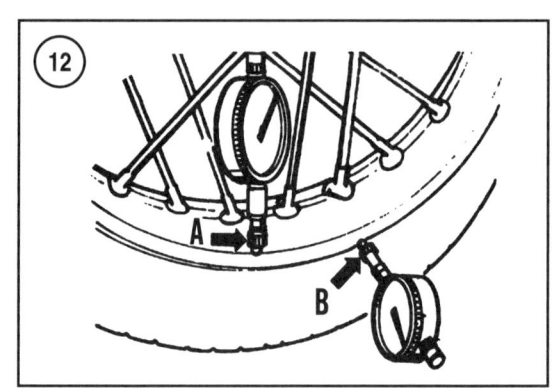

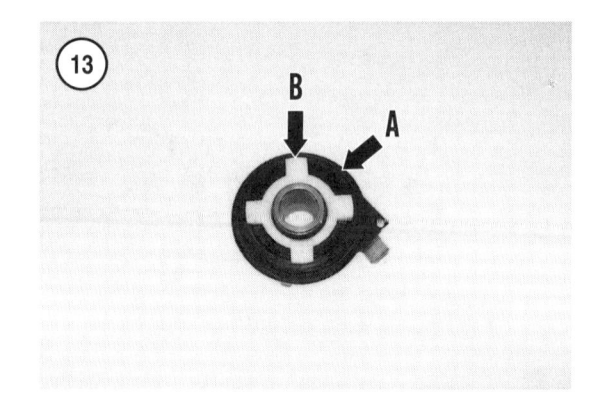

REAR WHEEL

Removal

NOTE
Insert a piece of vinyl tubing or wood into the caliper in place of the brake disc. That way if the brake pedal is inadvertently pressed, the pistons will not be forced out of the cylinders. If this does happen, the caliper may have to be disassembled to reseat the

WHEELS, TIRES AND DRIVE CHAIN

REAR WHEEL (1995-1999 MODELS)

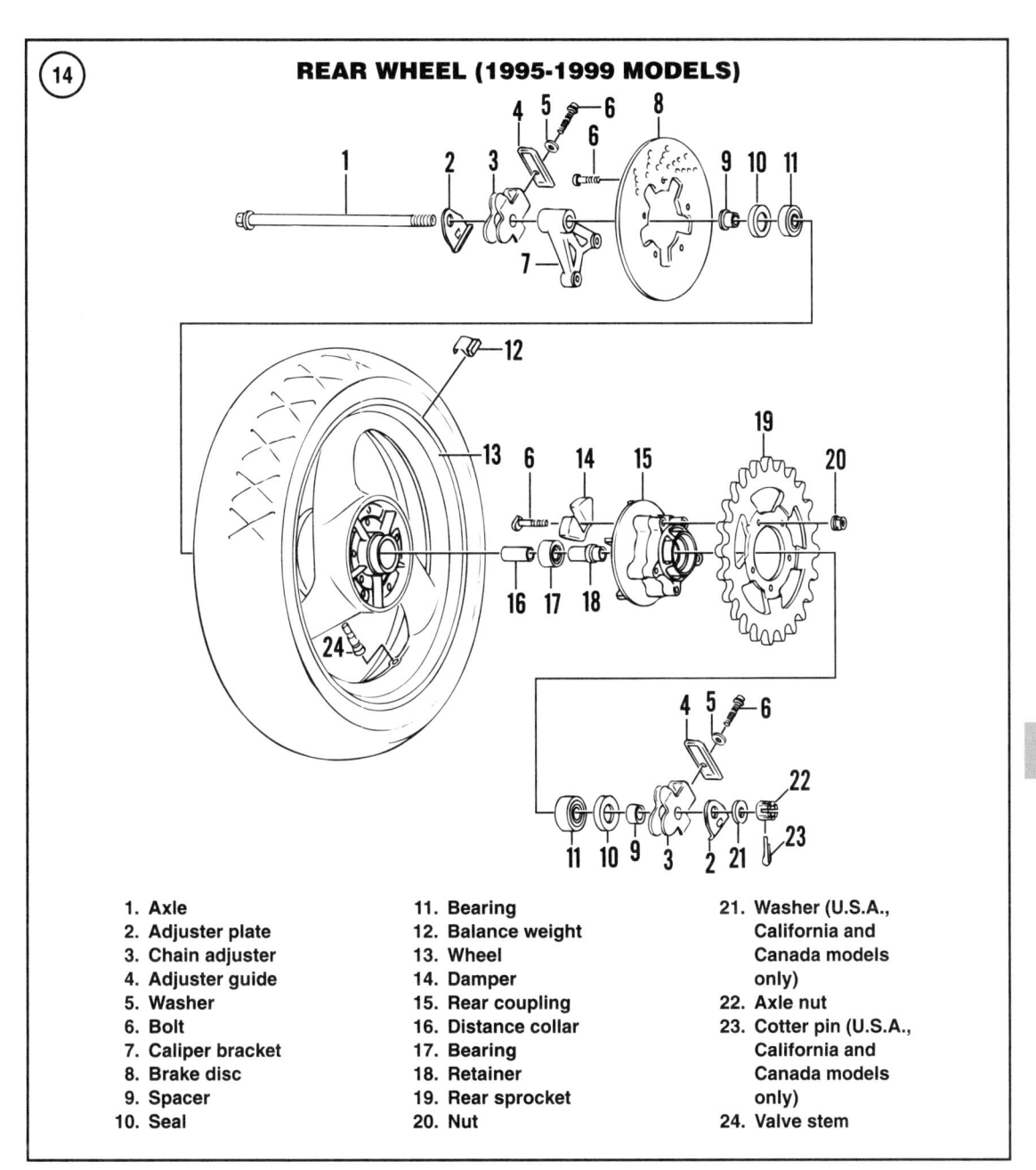

1. Axle
2. Adjuster plate
3. Chain adjuster
4. Adjuster guide
5. Washer
6. Bolt
7. Caliper bracket
8. Brake disc
9. Spacer
10. Seal
11. Bearing
12. Balance weight
13. Wheel
14. Damper
15. Rear coupling
16. Distance collar
17. Bearing
18. Retainer
19. Rear sprocket
20. Nut
21. Washer (U.S.A., California and Canada models only)
22. Axle nut
23. Cotter pin (U.S.A., California and Canada models only)
24. Valve stem

pistons and the system will have to be bled.

NOTE
The rear wheel can be removed and reinstalled with the rear caliper in place on the caliper bracket. However, installation is much easier if the rear caliper is removed from the bracket. Refer to **Figure 14** *when servicing the rear wheel on 1995-1999 models. Refer to* **Figure 15** *for 2000 models.*

1. Remove the brake caliper from the mounting bracket as described in Chapter Thirteen.

NOTE
On 1995-1999 models, the rear axle nut is on the left side of the motorcycle. On 2000 models, it is on the right.

REAR WHEEL (2000 MODELS)

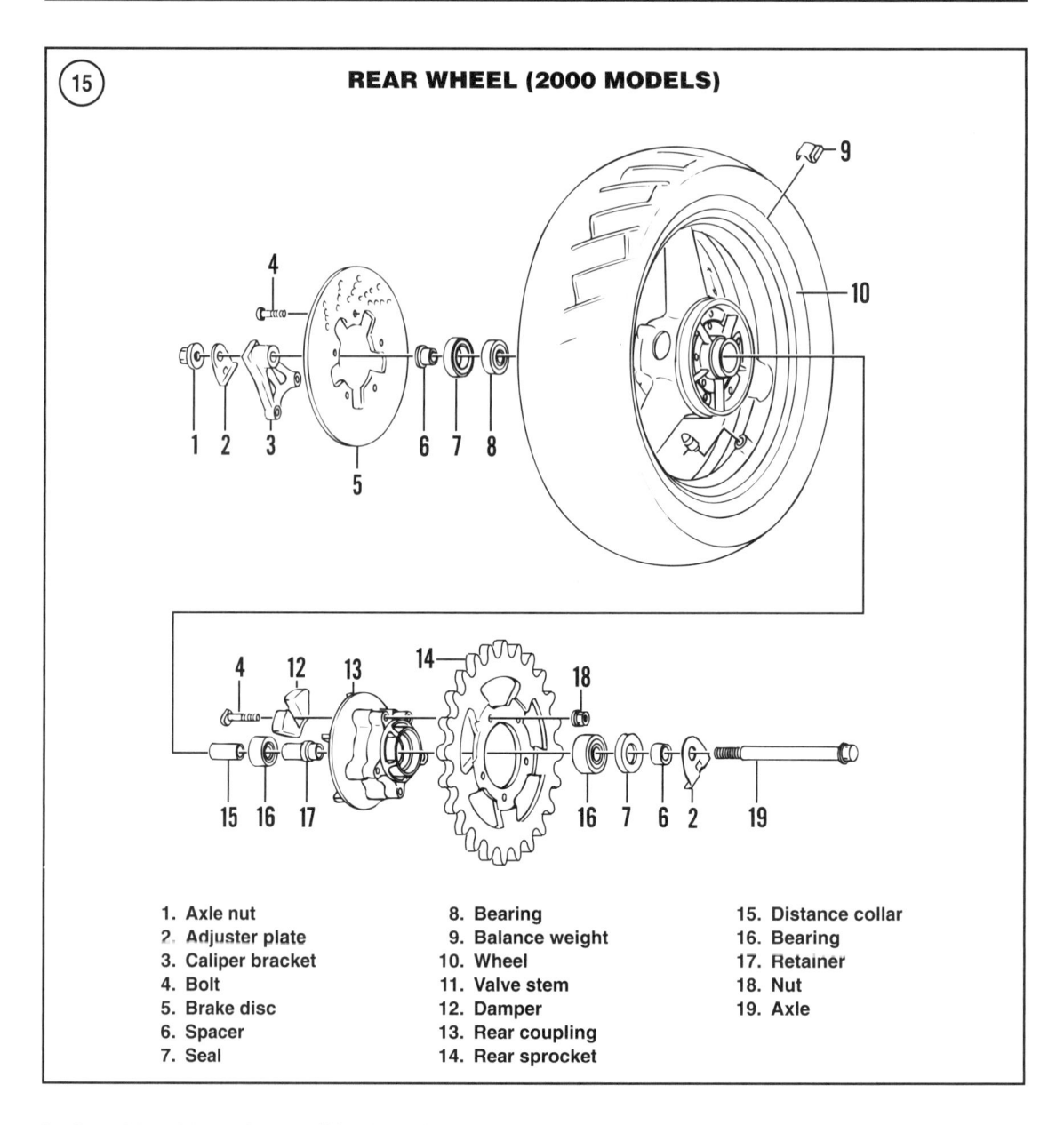

1. Axle nut
2. Adjuster plate
3. Caliper bracket
4. Bolt
5. Brake disc
6. Spacer
7. Seal
8. Bearing
9. Balance weight
10. Wheel
11. Valve stem
12. Damper
13. Rear coupling
14. Rear sprocket
15. Distance collar
16. Bearing
17. Retainer
18. Nut
19. Axle

2. On 1995-1999 U.S.A, California and Canada models, remove the cotter pin (A, **Figure 16**) from the rear axle nut. Discard the cotter pin. A new one must be installed during assembly.

3. Have an assistant apply the rear brake, and then loosen the axle nut (B, **Figure 6**).

4. Block the front wheel so the motorcycle will not roll in either direction while it is on a jack or wooden blocks.

CAUTION
If using a jack, place a piece of wood on the jack pad to protect the oil pan.

5. Place a suitable size jack or wooden blocks under the oil pan to support the motorcycle securely with the rear wheel off the ground.

WARNING
If the motorcycle has just been run, the muffler will be very HOT. If possible, wait for the muffler to cool down. If not, wear heavy gloves.

6. Loosen the chain adjuster (C, **Figure 16**) on each side of the swing arm and provide the maximum amount of slack in the drive chain.

WHEELS, TIRES AND DRIVE CHAIN

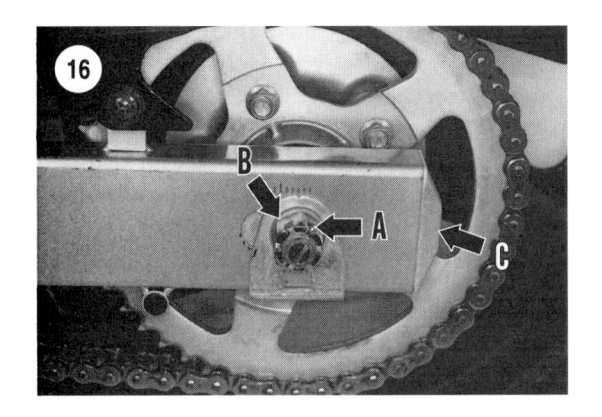

7. Remove the rear axle nut. On 1995-1999 U.S.A, California and Canada models, remove the washer.

8. Remove the chain adjuster plate from the axle end (**Figure 17**).

9A. On 1995-1999 models, remove the rear axle (**Figure 18**) and axle plate from the right side of the motorcycle.

9B. On 2000 models, remove the rear axle and axle plate from the left side.

10. Remove the caliper bracket from the right side of the motorcycle.

11. Remove the chain adjuster assembly (**Figure 19**) from each side of the swing arm.

12. Push the wheel forward and remove the drive chain from the rear sprocket.

13. Pull the wheel rearward and remove the wheel.

14. Remove each spacer from the left (**Figure 20**) and right (**Figure 21**) sides of the wheel.

CAUTION
Set the tire sidewalls onto two wooden blocks. Do not set the wheel down on the disc surface as it may get scratched or warped.

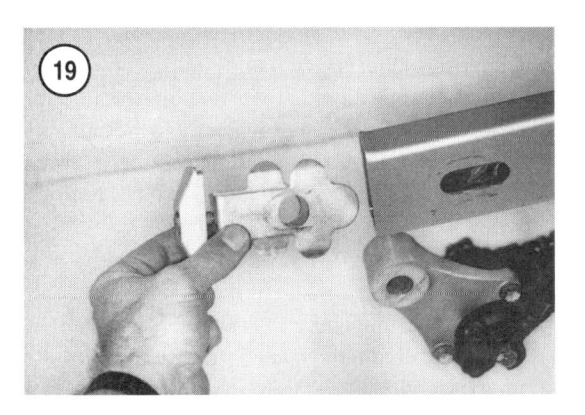

15. Inspect the wheel as described in this chapter.

Installation

1. Make sure all contact surfaces on the axle, swing arm and axle spacers are free of dirt and burrs.
2. Apply a light coat of grease to the axle, bearings, spacers and grease seals.
3. Install a chain adjuster assembly into each side of the swing arm (**Figure 19**).
4. Make sure the left (**Figure 20**) and right (**Figure 21**) axle spacers are installed on each side of the rear hub.
5. Position the wheel into place and roll it forward. Install the drive chain onto the rear sprocket.
6. Fit the caliper bracket into place between the wheel and the swing arm. Make sure the right axle spacer is still in place.
7. Raise the rear wheel up and into alignment with the swing arm.
8A. On 1995-1999 models, install the rear axle and adjuster plate (**Figure 18**) from the right side. Insert the axle through the adjuster plate, swing arm, the caliper bracket, the rear wheel and out through the left side of the swing arm. Push the axle all the way in until it bottoms against the swing arm. See **Figure 22**.
8B. On 2000 models, install the axle from the left side. Insert the axle through the adjuster plate, swing arm, the rear wheel, the caliper bracket and out through the right side of the swing arm.
9. Install the adjuster plate onto the end of the axle (**Figure 17**).
10. On 1995-1999 U.S.A. California and Canada models, install the washer onto the end of the axle.
11. Install the rear axle nut (B, **Figure 16**). Finger-tighten the nut at this time.
12. Adjust the drive chain as described in Chapter Three.
13. Torque the axle nut to specification.
14. On U.S.A., California and Canada models, install a *new* cotter pin onto the rear axle nut (A, **Figure 16**), and bend both ends over completely.
15. Install the rear caliper as described in Chapter Thirteen.
16. Remove the jack or wooden block(s) from under the oil pan. Remove the blocks from the front wheel.
17. Roll the motorcycle back and forth several times. Apply the rear brake as many times as necessary to make sure the brake pads seat against the brake disc correctly.

Inspection

NOTE
The rear wheel hub is equipped with a single seal that is located on the right side of the hub. The other seal is located in the rear coupling assembly on the left side.

1. If still in place, remove the left (**Figure 20**) and right (**Figure 21**) axle spacers from the hub.
2. Clean the axle, spacers and caliper bracket in solvent to remove all old grease and dirt. Make sure all axle contact surfaces are clean and free of dirt and old grease prior to installation. If these surfaces are not cleaned, the axle may be difficult to remove later on.
3. Place the axle on V-blocks and place the tip of a dial indicator in the middle of the axle (**Figure 10**). Rotate the axle and check the runout. If axle runout exceeds specification, replace the axle; do not attempt to straighten it.

WHEELS, TIRES AND DRIVE CHAIN

4. Check the brake disc bolts for tightness (A, **Figure 11**). Tighten the bolts to the torque specification the in **Table 2** if necessary.
5. Check the rear sprocket nuts (**Figure 23**) for tightness. Tighten the nuts to the torque specification if necessary.
6. Check rim runout as follows:
   a. Measure the radial (up and down) runout of the wheel rim with a dial indicator (A, **Figure 12**). If runout exceeds specification, check the wheel bearings.
   b. Measure the axial (side to side) runout of the wheel rim with a dial indicator (B, **Figure 12**). If runout exceeds specification, check the wheel bearings.
   c. If necessary, replace the rear wheel and/or rear coupling bearings as described in *Front and Rear Hubs* in this chapter.
7. Inspect the wheel rim for dents, bending or cracks. Check the rim and rim sealing surface for scratches that are deeper than 0.5 mm (0.01 in.). If any of these conditions are present, replace the rim.
8. Since the rear caliper is off the disc, check the brake pads for wear. Refer to Chapter Thirteen.

REAR COUPLING AND REAR SPROCKET

Removal/Disassembly/Assembly/Installation

1. Remove the rear wheel as described in this chapter.
2. If still in place, remove the left axle spacer (**Figure 20**).
3. If the rear sprocket is going to be removed, loosen and remove the nuts (**Figure 23**) securing the rear sprocket to the rear coupling at this time.

NOTE
If the rear coupling assembly is difficult to remove from the hub, tap on the backside of the sprocket (from the opposite side of the wheel through the wheel spokes) with the wooden handle of a hammer. Tap evenly around the perimeter of the sprocket until the coupling assembly is free of the hub and the rubber dampers.

4. Pull straight up and remove the rear coupling assembly from the rear hub.
5. Remove the inner retainer (**Figure 24**) from the rear coupling assembly.
6. Install by reversing these removal steps while noting the following:
   a. Align the rear coupling bosses (A, **Figure 25**) with the rubber damper receptacles and install the rear coupling.
   b. If removed, install the rear sprocket so the side with the stamping faces out away from the rear coupling.

CAUTION
On a new machine or after a new rear sprocket has been installed, check the torque on the rear sprocket nuts after 10 minutes of riding and after each 10-minute riding period until the nuts have seated and remain tight. Failure to keep the sprocket nuts correctly tightened will damage the rear hub.

   c. Tighten the rear sprocket nuts to torque specification after the assembly has been reinstalled in the rear wheel.

Inspection

1. Inspect the rubber dampers (B, **Figure 25**) for signs of damage or deterioration. If damaged, replace as a complete set.
2. Inspect the raised webs (C, **Figure 25**) in the rear hub. Check for cracks or wear. If any damage is visible, replace the rear wheel.
3. Inspect the rear coupling assembly for cracks or damage, replace if necessary.
4. Inspect the rear sprocket teeth. If the teeth are visibly worn or undercut (**Figure 26**), replace the rear sprocket as described in this chapter.

CAUTION
If the rear sprocket requires replacement, also replace the engine sprocket and the drive chain. Never install a new drive chain over worn sprockets or worn drive chain over new sprockets. The old part will wear out the new part prematurely.

5. If the rear sprocket requires replacement, also inspect the drive chain (Chapter Three) and engine sprocket (Chapter Seven). They also may be worn and need replacing.
6. Inspect the bearing for excessive axial play and radial play (**Figure 27**). Replace the bearing if it has an excess amount of free play.
7. On a non-sealed bearing, check the balls for evidence of wear, pitting or excessive heat (bluish tint). Turn the inner race by hand. The bearing must turn smoothly without excessive play or noise. A questionable bearing should be replaced. When replacing the bearing, be sure to take the old bearing along to ensure a perfect match.

NOTE
Fully sealed bearings are available from many bearing specialty shops. Fully sealed bearings provide better protection from dirt and moisture that passes through worn or damaged oil seals.

FRONT AND REAR HUBS

Preliminary Inspection

Inspect each wheel bearing prior to removing it from the wheel hub.

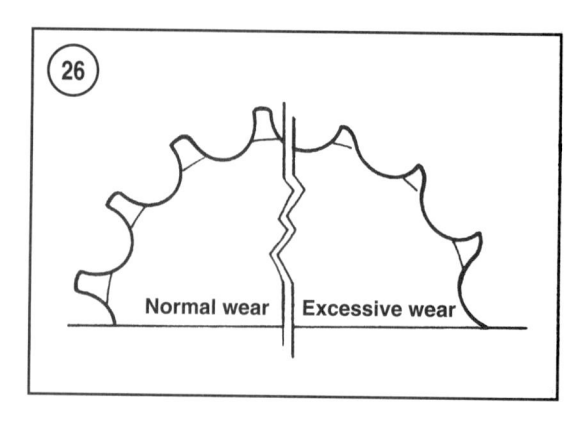

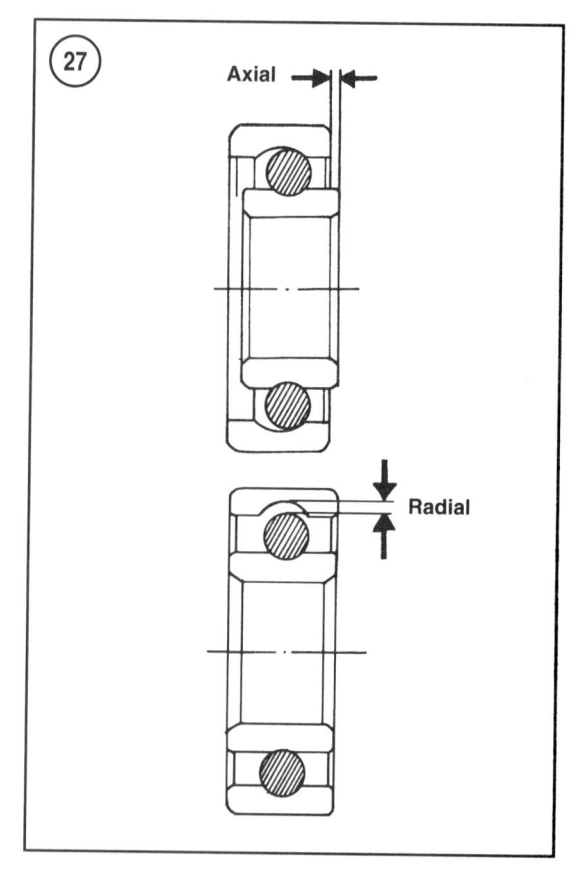

CAUTION
Do not remove the wheel bearings for inspection purposes. The bearings will be damaged during removal. Remove the wheel bearings only if they are to be replaced.

1. Perform Steps 1-3 of *Disassembly* in the following procedure.
2. Turn each bearing by hand. The bearings **must** turn smoothly with no roughness.

WHEELS, TIRES AND DRIVE CHAIN

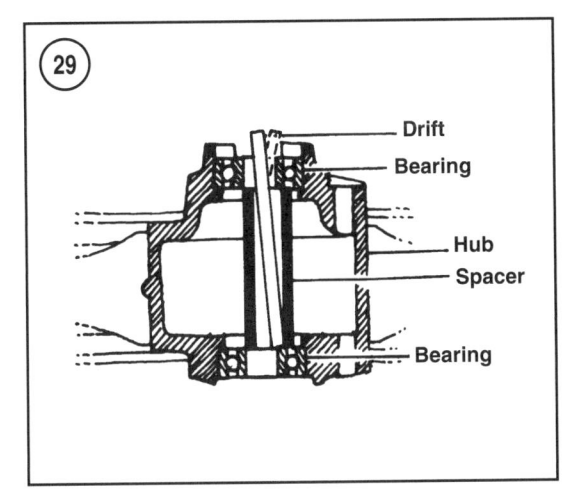

28

29
- Drift
- Bearing
- Hub
- Spacer
- Bearing

3. Inspect the play of the inner race of each wheel bearing. Check for excessive axial play and radial play (**Figure 27**). Replace the bearing if it has an excessive amount of free play.

4. On non-sealed bearings, check the balls for evidence of wear, pitting or excessive heat (bluish tint). Replace the bearings if necessary; always replace bearings as a complete set. When replacing the bearings, be sure to take the old bearings along to ensure a perfect match.

NOTE
Fully sealed bearings are available from many bearing specialty shops. Fully sealed bearings provide better protection from dirt and moisture.

Disassembly

This procedure applies to both the front- and rear-wheel hub assemblies. Any differences between the two hubs are identified.

1A. Remove the front wheel as described in this chapter. Refer to **Figure 2** (1995-1999 models) or **Figure 3** (2000 models).

1B. Remove the rear wheel as described in this chapter. Refer to **Figure 14** (1995-1999 models) or **Figure 15** (2000 models).

2. On the rear wheel perform the following:
   a. If still in place, remove the left and right spacers from the hub.
   b. Remove the rear coupling from the hub as described in this chapter.
   c. Carefully pry the seal (A, **Figure 28**) out of the right side of the rear hub and from the rear coupler. Place a shop cloth under the seal remover to protect the hub and coupling.

3. If necessary, remove the brake disc bolts (B, **Figure 28**) and remove the disc(s) from the wheel.

4. Before proceeding further, inspect the wheel bearings (C, **Figure 11**) as described in this chapter. If they must be replaced, proceed as follows.

5A. If the special tools are not used, perform the following:
   a. To remove the right and left bearings and distance collar, insert a soft aluminum or brass drift into one side of the hub.
   b. Push the distance collar over to one side and place the drift on the inner race of the lower bearing.
   c. Tap the bearing out of the hub with a hammer, working around the perimeter of the inner race (**Figure 29**). Remove the bearing and distance collar.
   d. Repeat for the bearing on the other side.

WARNING
Be sure to wear safety glasses while using the wheel bearing remover set.

NOTE
The Kowa Seiki Wheel Bearing Remover set can be ordered by a Suzuki dealership through K & L Supply Co. in Santa Clara, Ca.

5B. To remove the bearings with the Kowa Seiki Wheel Bearing Remover set, perform the following:
   a. Select the correct size remover head tool, and insert it into the bearing.
   b. Turn the wheel over and insert the remover shaft into the backside of the adapter. Tap the shaft and force it into the slit in the adapter

(**Figure 30**). This will force the adapter against the bearing inner race.
   c. Tap on the end of the shaft with a hammer and drive the bearing out of the hub. Remove the bearing and the distance collar.
   d. Repeat for the bearing on the other side.
6. Clean the inside and the outside of the hub with solvent. Dry with compressed air.

Assembly

CAUTION
*Always reinstall **new** bearings and seals. The bearings and seals are damaged during removal and must not be reused.*

NOTE
Replace bearings as a set. If any one bearing in a wheel is worn, replace all the bearings in that wheel. On the front wheel, replace both wheel bearings. On the rear wheel replace both wheel bearings as well as the rear coupling bearing.

1. On non-sealed bearings, pack the bearings with Suzuki Super Grease A or an equivalent good quality, waterproof bearing grease. To pack the bearings, spread some grease in the palm of your hand and scrape the open side of the bearing across your palm until the bearing is completely packed full of grease. Spin the bearing a few times to determine if there are any open areas; repack if necessary.
2. Blow any debris out of the hub prior to installing the new bearings.
3. Apply a light coat of wheel bearing grease to the bearing seating areas of the hub. This will make bearing installation easier.

CAUTION
Install non-sealed bearings with the single sealed side facing outward. Tap the bearings squarely into place, tapping on the outer race only. Do not tap on the inner race or the bearing might be damaged. Be sure that the bearings are completely seated.

4A. A Suzuki bearing installer (part No. 09924-84510) can be used to install the *front wheel bearings* as follows:

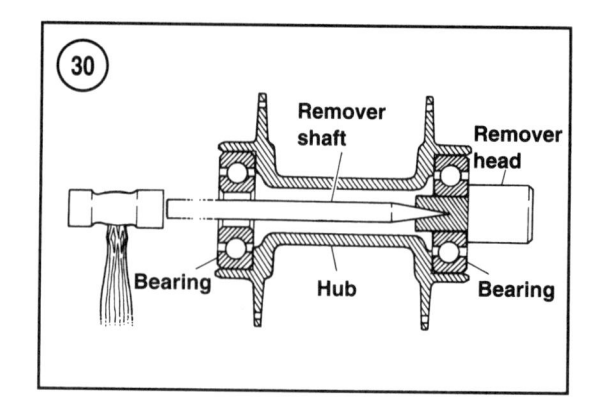

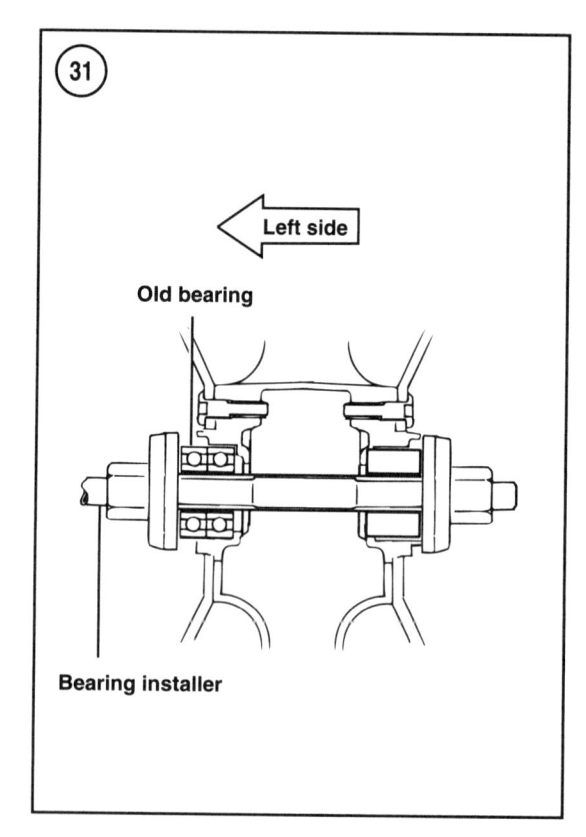

WHEELS, TIRES AND DRIVE CHAIN

NOTE
Install the left bearing into the hub first, and then install the right bearing.

a. Position the left bearing onto the hub with the sealed side facing out.
b. Set the old bearing on top of the new bearing and install the bearing installer as shown in **Figure 31**.
c. Tighten the bearing installer (**Figure 32**) and pull the left bearing into the hub until it is completely seated. Remove the bearing installer.
d. Turn the wheel over (right side up) on the workbench and install the distance collar.
e. Position the right bearing onto the hub with the sealed side facing out.
f. Set the old bearing on top of the new bearing and install the bearing installer as shown in **Figure 33**.
g. Tighten the bearing installer and pull the right bearing into the hub until there is a slight clearance between the inner race and the distance collar (**Figure 34**).

NOTE
Suzuki does not provide a specification for the slight clearance between the bearing and the distance collar. The important thing is that these two parts are not pressed up against each other.

h. Remove the bearing installer.

4B. The Suzuki bearing installer (part No. 09941-34513) can be used to install the *rear wheel bearings* as follows:

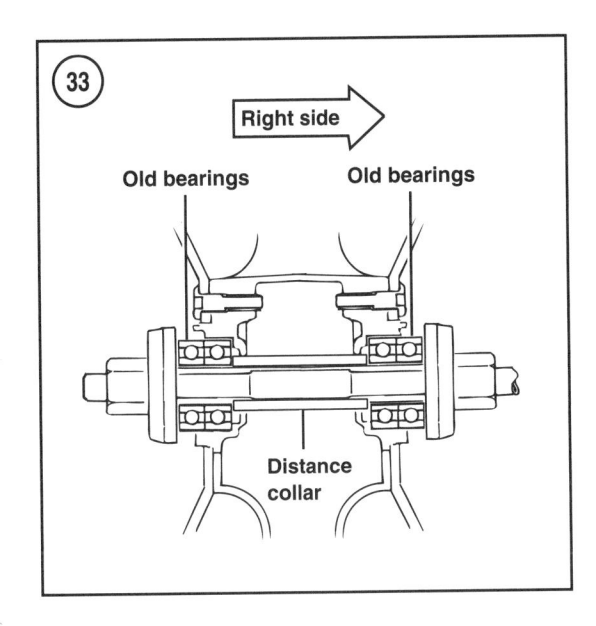

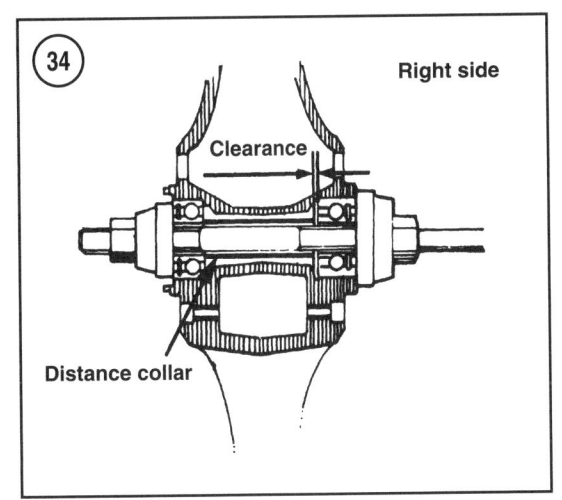

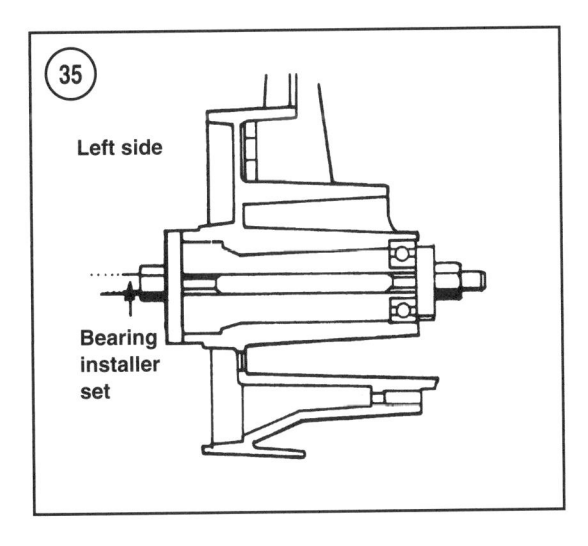

NOTE
Install the right bearing into the hub first and then install the left bearing.

a. Set the right bearing into the hub with the sealed side facing out and install the bearing installer as shown in **Figure 35**.
b. Tighten the bearing installer (**Figure 32**) and pull the right bearing into the hub until it is completely seated. Remove the bearing installer.
c. Turn the wheel over (left side up) on the workbench and install the distance collar.

d. Set the left bearing into the hub with the sealed side facing out and install the bearing installer as shown in **Figure 36**.

e. Tighten the bearing installer and pull the left bearing into the hub until there is a slight clearance between the inner race and the distance collar.

NOTE
Suzuki does not provide a specification for the slight clearance between the bearing and the distance collar. The important thing is that these two parts are not pressed up against each other.

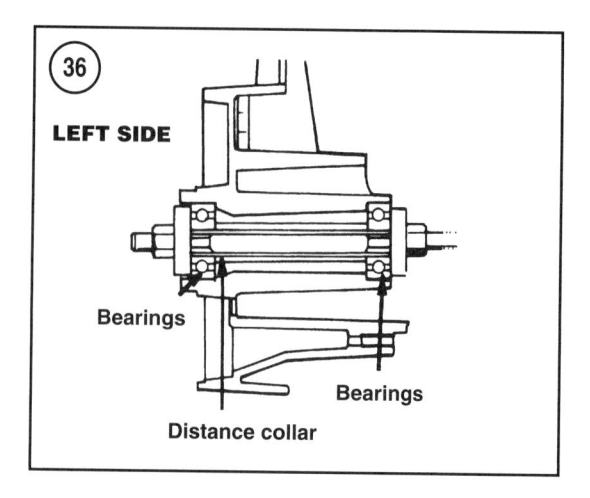

f. Remove the bearing installer.

4C. The Suzuki bearing installer (part No. 09913-75520) can be used to install the bearing into the rear coupling.

a. Set the bearing into the coupling with the sealed side facing out.

b. Place the bearing installer on top of the bearing.

c. Tap the installer and drive the bearing squarely into place in the rear coupling. Make sure that the bearing is completely seated.

4D. If special tools are not used, perform the following:

NOTE
On the front wheel, install the left bearing first; on the rear wheel, install the right bearing first.

a. Using a socket that matches the outer race diameter, tap the first bearing (left bearing on front wheel; right bearing on rear wheel) squarely into place in the hub. Tap on the outer race only (**Figure 37**). Do not tap on the inner race or the bearing might be damaged. Make sure that the bearing is completely seated.

b. Turn the wheel over on the workbench and install the distance collar.

c. Use the same tool set-up and drive the second bearing (right bearing on the front wheel; left bearing on the rear wheel) into the hub until there is a slight clearance (**Figure 34**) between the inner race and the distance collar.

NOTE
Suzuki does not provide a specification for the slight clearance between the bearing and the distance collar. The important thing is that these two parts are not pressed up against each other.

d. Using a socket that matches the outer race diameter, tap the rear coupling bearing squarely into place in the rear coupling. Tap on the outer race only (**Figure 37**). Do not tap on the inner race or the bearing might be damaged. Be sure that the bearing is completely seated.

5. Install a *new* seal into the right wheel hub or into the rear coupling by performing the following:

a. Pack grease to the lips of the new seal.

b. Position the seal with the manufacturer's marks facing out.

c. Use a tool with the same diameter as the seal (**Figure 38**) and drive the seal into the mounting bore until it is flush with the top surface of the bore or until it bottoms.

6. If the brake disc was removed, perform the following:

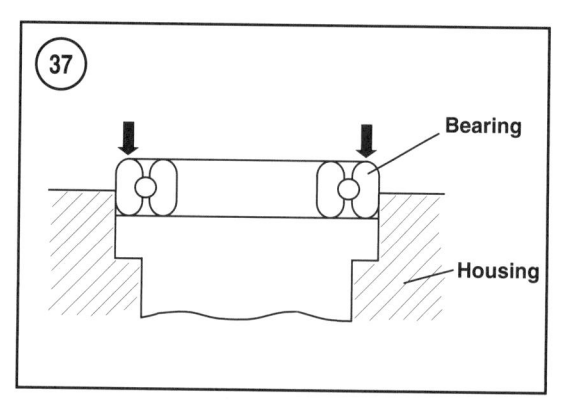

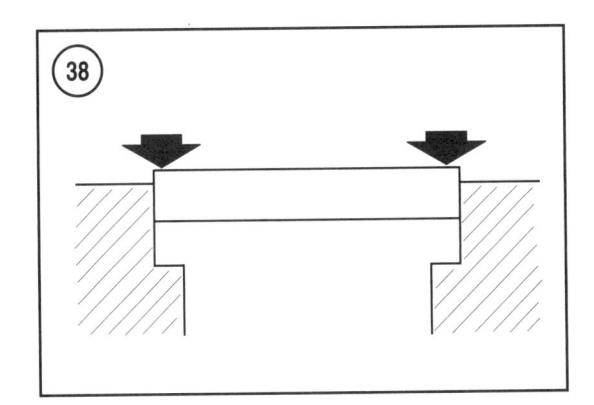

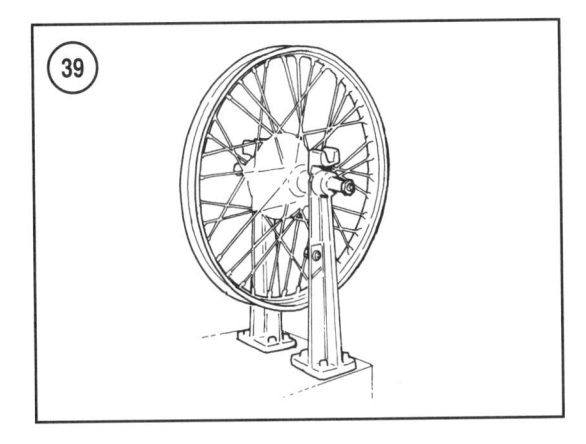

WHEELS, TIRES AND DRIVE CHAIN

ership. These kits contain test weights and strips of adhesive-backed weights that can be cut to the desired weight and attached to the rim.

Before attempting to balance the wheel, make sure that the wheel bearings are in good condition and properly lubricated. Also make sure that the brakes do not drag. The wheel must rotate freely.

NOTE
When balancing the wheels, do so with the brake disc(s) and the rear coupling attached. These components rotate with the wheel and they affect the balance.

1A. Remove the front wheel as described in this chapter.
1B. Remove the rear wheel as described in this chapter.
2. Mount the wheel on a fixture such as the one shown in **Figure 39** so the wheel can rotate freely.
3. Give the wheel a spin and let it coast to a stop. Mark the tire at the lowest point with chalk or light colored crayon.
4. Spin the wheel several more times. If the wheel keeps coming to rest at the same point, it is out of balance.
5. Attach a test weight to the upper (or light) side of the wheel.
6. Experiment with different weights until the wheel, when spun, comes to rest at a different position each time.
7. Remove the test weight, thoroughly clean the rim surface and then install the correct size weight onto the rim. Make sure it is secured in place so it will not fly off when riding.

a. Apply a small amount of a locking compound such as ThreeBond No. TB1360 or Loctite No. 271 to the brake disc bolt threads prior to installation.
b. Install the brake disc. Tighten the brake disc bolts to the torque specifications listed in **Table 2**.
7. Install the rear coupler onto the rear wheel.
8A. Install the front wheel as described in this chapter.
8B. Install the rear wheel as described in this chapter.

WHEELS

Wheel Balance

An unbalanced wheel is unsafe. Depending upon the degree of imbalance and the speed of the motorcycle, the rider may experience anything from a mild vibration to a violent shimmy that could lead to loss of control.

The balance weights attach to the rim on the Bandit. Weight kits are available from motorcycle deal-

TIRES

Tire wear and performance are greatly affected by tire pressure. Have a good tire gauge on hand and make a habit of frequent pressure checks. Maintain the tire inflation pressure recommended in **Table 1** for original equipment tires. If using another tire brand, follow their recommendation.

Follow a sensible break-in period when running on new tires. New tires will exhibit significantly less adhesion ability. Do not subject a new tire to hard cornering, hard acceleration or hard braking for the first 100 miles (160 km).

Removal

The original equipment cast alloy wheels are designed for use with tubeless tires only. These wheels can easily be damaged during tire removal. Take special care to avoid scratching and gouging the outer rim surface, especially when using tire irons. Insert scraps of leather between the tire iron and the rim to protect the rim from damage.

When removing a tubeless tire, take care not to damage the tire beads, inner liner of the tire or the wheel rim flange. Use tire levers or flat-handle tire irons with rounded heads.

Many experienced riders who perform most of their own service work choose to have tire service performed by a Suzuki dealership or sportbike specialist.

CAUTION
Suzuki recommends that the tires be removed with a tire changer. Due to the large and rigid tires, tire removal with tire irons can be difficult and result in rim damage. On the other hand, a pneumatic tire changer can easily break the beads loose as well as remove and install the tire without damaging the cast wheel. The following procedure is provided if this alternative is not chosen.

NOTE
To make tire removal easier, warming the tire will make it softer and more pliable. Place the wheel and tire assembly in the sun. If possible, place the wheel assembly in a completely closed vehicle. At the same time, place the new tire in the same location.

1A. Remove the front wheel as described in this chapter.

1B. Remove the rear wheel as described in this chapter.

2. If not already marked by the tire manufacturer, mark the valve stem location on the tire (**Figure 40**), so the tire can be installed in the same location for easier balancing.

3. Remove the valve core from the valve stem and deflate the tire.

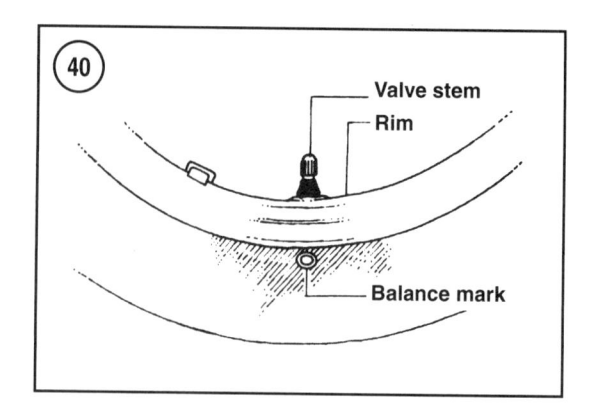

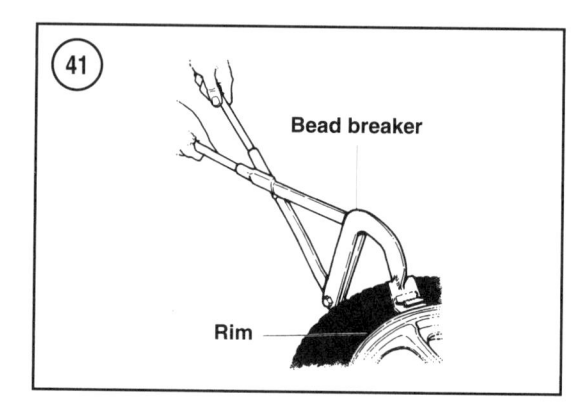

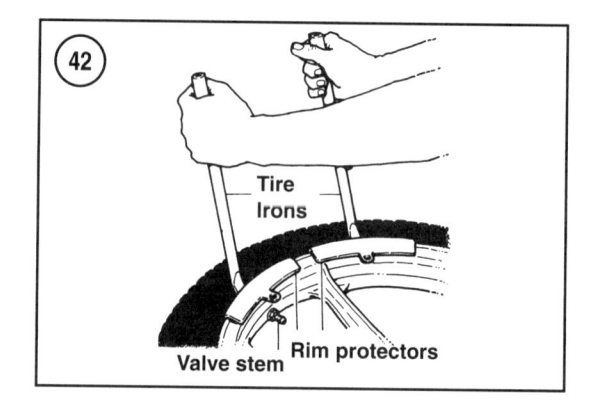

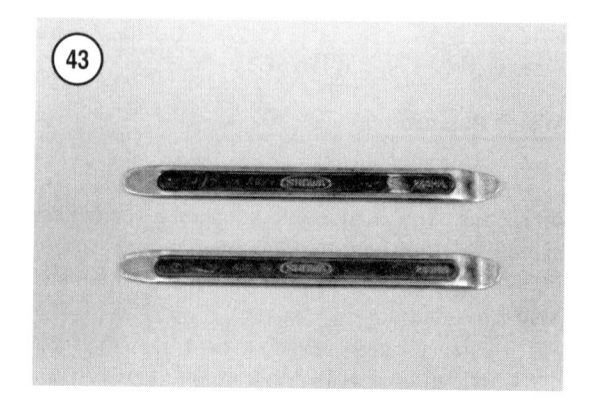

WHEELS, TIRES AND DRIVE CHAIN

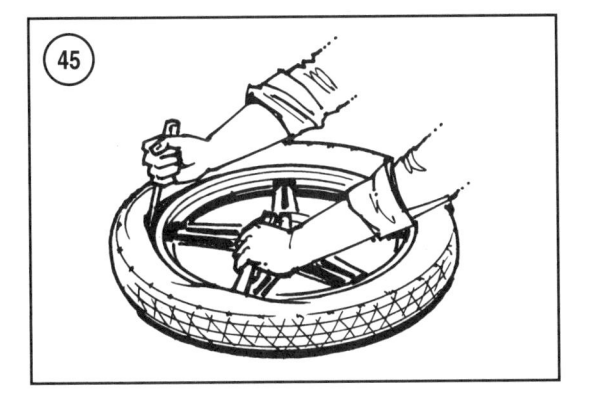

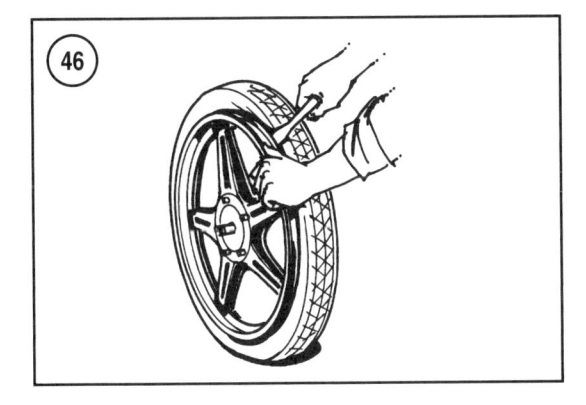

NOTE
*Removal of tubeless tires from their rims can be difficult because of the exceptionally tight tire bead-to-rim seal. Breaking the bead seal may require the use of a special tool (**Figure 41**). If the seal does not break loose, take the wheel to a motorcycle dealership or repair shop and have them break it loose on a tire changing machine.*

CAUTION
The inner rim and bead area are the sealing surfaces on the tubeless tire. Do not scratch the inside of the rim or damage the tire bead.

4. Press the entire bead on both sides of the tire away from the rim and into the center of the rim.
5. Lubricate both beads with soapy water.

CAUTION
*Use rim protectors (**Figure 42**) or insert scraps of leather between the tire iron and the rim to protect the rim from damage.*

NOTE
*Use only quality tire irons without sharp edges (**Figure 43**). If necessary, file the ends of the tire irons to remove rough edges.*

6. Insert a tire iron under the top bead next to the valve stem (**Figure 44**). Force the bead on the opposite side of the tire into the center of the rim and pry the bead over the rim with the tire iron.
7. Insert a second tire iron next to the first iron to hold the bead over the rim. Then work around the tire with the first tire iron, prying the bead over the rim (**Figure 45**).
8. Stand the wheel upright. Insert a tire iron between the second bead and the side of the rim that the first bead was pried over (**Figure 46**). Force the bead on the opposite side from the tire iron into the center of the rim. Pry the back bead off the rim, working around as with the first.
9. Inspect the valve stem seal. Because rubber deteriorates with age, it is advisable to replace the valve stem when replacing the tire.
10. Remove the old valve stem and discard it. Inspect the valve stem hole (**Figure 47**) in the rim. Remove any dirt or corrosion from the hole and wipe it

dry with a clean cloth. Install a *new* valve stem and make sure it is properly seated in the rim.

11. Carefully inspect the tire and wheel rim for any damage as described in the following section.

Inspection

1. Wipe off the inner surfaces of the wheel rim. Clean off any rubber residue or any oxidation.

> *WARNING*
> *Carefully consider whether a tire should be replaced. If there is any doubt about the quality of the existing tire, replace it with a new one. Do not take a chance on a tire failure at any speed.*

2. If any one of the following is observed; replace the tire:
    a. A puncture or split whose total length or diameter exceeds 6 mm (0.24 in.).
    b. A scratch or split on the side wall.
    c. Any type of ply separation.
    d. Tread separation or excessive abnormal wear pattern.
    e. Tread depth of less than the minimum value specified in **Table 1** on original equipment tires. Aftermarket tires' tread depth minimum may vary.
    f. Scratches on either sealing bead.
    g. The cord is cut in any place.
    h. Flat spots in the tread from skidding.
    i. Any abnormality in the inner liner.

3. Inspect the valve stem hole in the rim. Remove any dirt or corrosion from the hole and wipe it dry with a clean cloth.

Installation

1. Inspect the valve stem core rubber seal (**Figure 48**) for hardness or deterioration. Replace the valve core if necessary.

2. A new tire may have balancing rubbers inside. These are not patches and must be left in place. Most tires are marked with a colored spot near the bead (**Figure 40**) that indicates a lighter point on the tire. Place this next to the valve stem.

3. Lubricate both beads of the tire with soapy water.

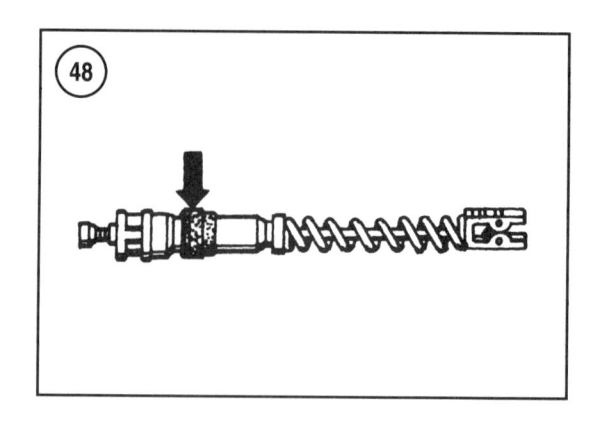

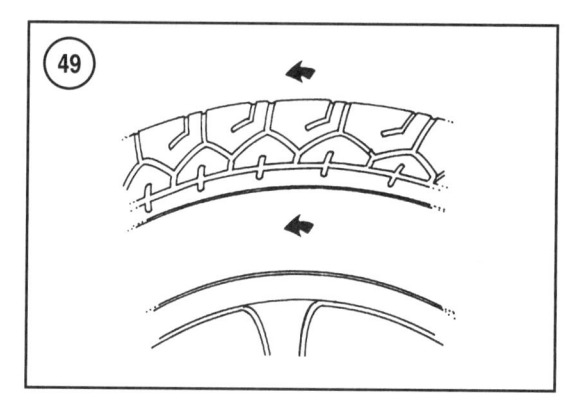

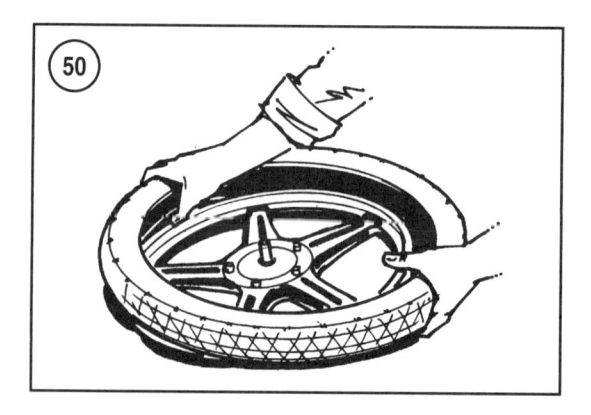

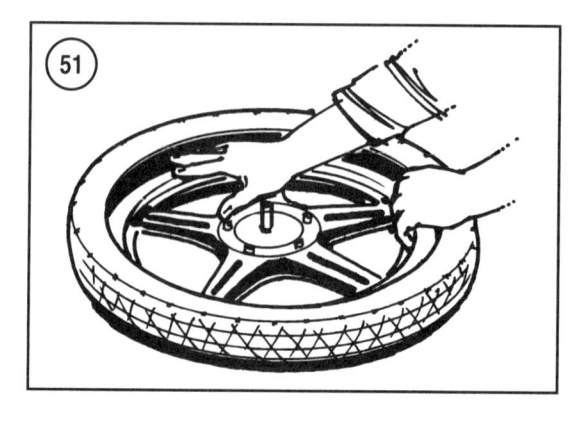

WHEELS, TIRES AND DRIVE CHAIN

per bead remains outside the rim (**Figure 50**). Work around the tire in both directions and press the lower bead, by hand, into the center of the rim (**Figure 51**). Use a tire iron for the last few inches of bead (**Figure 52**).

7. Press the upper bead into the rim opposite the valve stem. Working on both sides of this initial point, pry the bead into the rim with a tire tool and work around the rim to the valve stem (**Figure 53**). If the tire wants to pull up on one side, either use another tire iron or one knee to hold the tire in place. The last few inches are usually the toughest to install. If possible, continue to push the tire into the rim by hand. Relubricate the bead if necessary. If the tire bead wants to pull out from under the rim, use both knees to hold the tire in place. If necessary, use a tire iron for the last few inches.

8. Bounce the wheel several times, rotating it each time. This will force the tire bead against the rim flanges.

9. Once the tire beads are in contact with the rim, place an inflatable band around the circumference of the tire. Slowly inflate the band until the tire beads are pressed against the rim. Inflate the tire enough to seat it. Deflate the band and remove it.

WARNING
In the next step, never exceed 400 kPa (56 psi) inflation pressure as the tire could burst, causing severe injury. Never stand directly over a tire while inflating it.

10. After inflating the tire, check to see that the beads are fully seated and that the rim lines (**Figure 54**) are the same distance from the rim all the way around the tire. If the beads will not seat, deflate the tire and lubricate the rim and beads with soapy water.

11. Reinflate the tire to the required pressure as listed in **Table 1**. Install the valve stem cap.

12. Balance the wheel as described in this chapter.

13A. Install the front wheel as described in this chapter.

13B. Install the rear wheel as described in this chapter.

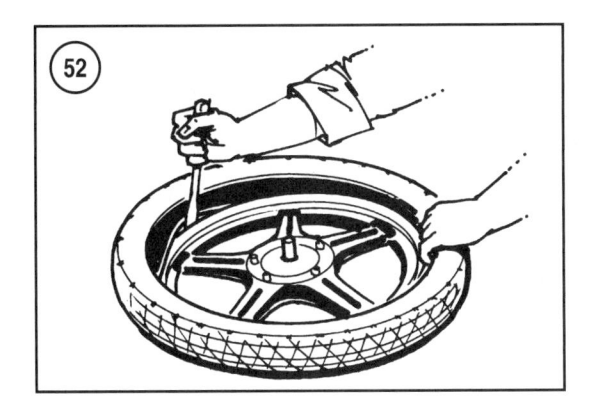

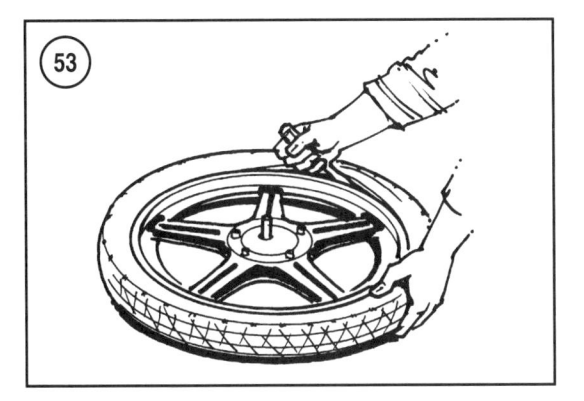

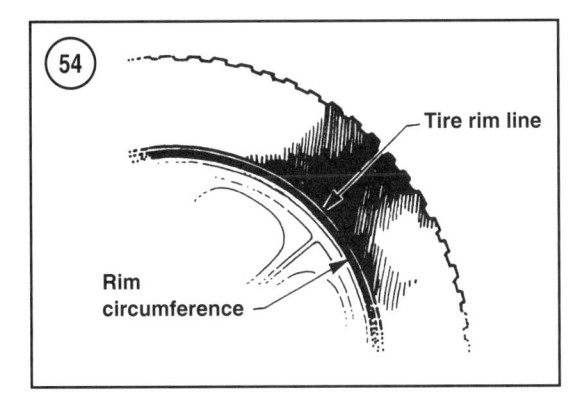

4. When installing the tire on the rim, make sure the correct tire, either front or rear, is installed on the correct wheel. Also install the tire so the direction arrow faces the normal direction of wheel rotation (**Figure 49**).

5. If remounting the old tire, align the mark made during removal with the valve stem. If a new tire is being installed, align the colored stop near the bead (indicating the lightest point of the tire) with the valve stem. See **Figure 40**.

6. Place the backside of the tire onto the rim so the lower bead sits in the center of the rim while the up-

TIRE REPAIRS

NOTE
Changing or patching on the road is very difficult. A can of pressurized tire

sealant may inflate the tire and seal the hole, although this is only a temporary fix.

WARNING
Do not install an inner tube inside a tubeless tire. The tube will cause abnormal heat buildup in the tire.

Tubeless tires have the word "TUBELESS" molded into the sidewall and the rims have "SUITABLE FOR TUBELESS TIRES" or equivalent (**Figure 55**) cast on them.

If the tire is punctured, remove it from the rim, inspect the inside of the tire and apply a combination plug/patch from inside the tire (**Figure 56**). Never attempt to repair a tubeless motorcycle tire using a plug or cord patch applied from outside the tire. This type of repair might be acceptable for automobiles, but they are not safe on a motorcycle tire, especially on a high-performance motorcycle like the Bandit.

After repairing a tubeless tire, do not exceed 30 mph (50 kph) for the first 24 hours. Do not exceed 80 mph (130 kph) and never race (canyon or otherwise) on a repaired tubeless tire. The patch could work loose because of tire flex and heat, resulting in a serious accident.

Repair

Do not rely on a plug or cord patch applied from outside the tire. Use a combination plug/patch applied from inside the tire (**Figure 56**).

1. Remove the tire from the wheel rim as described in this chapter.
2. Inspect the rim inner flange. Smooth any scratches on the sealing surface with emery cloth. If a scratch is deeper than 0.5 mm (0.020 in.), the wheel should be replaced.
3. Inspect the tire inside and out. Replace a tire if any of the following conditions are found:
   a. A puncture larger than 6 mm (1/4 in) diameter.
   b. A punctured or damaged side wall.
   c. More than two punctures in the tire.
   d. Tread depth less than the minimum value specified in **Table 1**.
   e. Ply or tread separation.
   f. Flat spots.
   g. Scratches on the bead.
   h. Cuts in the cord.
4. Apply the plug/patch following the manufacturer's instructions with the patch kit.

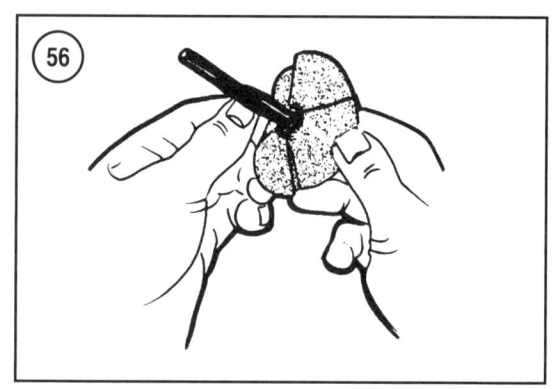

DRIVE CHAIN

Removal/Installation

1. Remove the swing arm as described in Chapter Twelve.
2. Remove the engine sprocket cover as described in Chapter Seven.
3. Slide the drive chain off the engine sprocket and remove it from the motorcycle.
4. Inspect the chain as described in Chapter Three.
5. Installation is the reverse of removal. Adjust the chain as described in Chapter Three.

WHEELS, TIRES AND DRIVE CHAIN

Table 1 WHEELS, TIRES AND DRIVE CHAIN SPECIFICATIONS

Item	Specification
Wheel rim size	
1995-1999 models	
Front	J17 × MT 3.00
Rear	J17 × MT 4.50
2000 models	
Front	J17 × MT 3.50
Rear	J17 × MT 4.50
Rim runout limit	
Axial	2.0 mm (0.08 in.)
Radial	2.0 mm (0.08 in.)
Axle runout limit	
Front	0.25 mm (0.010 in.)
Rear	0.25 mm (0.010 in.)
Tire size	
1995-1999 GSF600 models	
Front	110/70-17 54H
Rear	150/70-17 69H
1996-1999 GSF600S models	
U.S.A., California and Canada models	
Front	110/70-17 54H
Rear	150/70-17 69H
All models except U.S.A., California and Canada models	
Front	110/70 ZR17
Rear	150/70 ZR17
2000 models	
Front	120/60 ZR17 (55W)
Rear	160/60 ZR17 (69W)
Tire tread minimum depth	
Front	1.6 mm (0.06 in.)
Rear	2.0 mm (0.08 in.)
Tire pressure (cold)*	
Front	
Solo	225 kPa (33 psi)
Rider and passenger	225 kPa (33 psi)
Rear	
Solo	250 kPa (36 psi)
Rider and passenger	250 kPa (36 psi)
Drive chain	
Type	
1995-1999 models	
All models except U.S.A and California	RK50MFOZ$_1$ (110 links, continuous)
U.S.A and California models	RK50MFOZ$_1$ (112 links, continuous)
2000 models	RK50MFOZ$_1$ (112 links, continuous)
21-pin length	319.4 mm (12.6 in.)
Chain slack	25-35 mm (0.98-1.38 in.)

*Tire inflation pressure is for original equipment tires. Aftermarket tires may require different inflation pressure. The use of tires other than those specified by Suzuki may cause instability.

Table 2 WHEELS, TIRES AND DRIVE CHAIN TORQUE SPECIFICATIONS

Item	N•m	in.-lb.	ft.-lb.
Brake disc bolt	23	–	17
Engine sprocket nut	115	–	85

(continued)

Table 2 WHEELS, TIRES AND DRIVE CHAIN TORQUE SPECIFICATIONS (continued)

Item	N•m	in.-lb.	ft.-lb.
Engine sprocket nut			
stopper bolt	11	97	–
Front axle	65	–	48
Front axle pinch bolt	23	–	17
Rear axle nut	100	–	74
Rear caliper			
mounting bolt	25	–	18
Rear sprocket nut			
1995-1999 models	60	–	44
2000 models	50	–	37
Rear torque link nut	35	–	26
Speedometer sensor			
rotor bolt			
(2000 models)	13	115	–

CHAPTER ELEVEN

FRONT SUSPENSION AND STEERING

This chapter describes repair and maintenance procedures for the front fork and steering components. Front wheel removal, front hub service, tire changing, tire repair and wheel balancing are covered in Chapter Ten.

When inspecting components described in this chapter, compare all measurements to the front suspension specifications listed in **Table 1**. Replace any component that is damaged, worn to the wear limit or out of specification. During assembly, tighten fasteners to the torque specifications in **Table 2**.

Table 1 and **Table 2** are located at the end of this chapter.

HANDLEBAR

Removal/Installation

NOTE
This procedure is shown with the fairing removed for clarity.

CAUTION
Cover the frame and fuel tank with a heavy cloth or plastic tarp to protect it from brake fluid spills. Brake fluid destroys plastic, painted and plated sur-

faces. Wash off spilled brake fluid immediately.

NOTE
If handlebar replacement is not required, proceed to Step 12.

1. Remove the master cylinder clamp bolts (A, **Figure 1**). Remove the clamp and the master cylinder from the handlebar. Secure the master cylinder to the frame with a bungee cord. Be sure the master cylinder is in an upright position. Do not disconnect the hydraulic brake line.

2. Remove the two screws, and separate the halves of the right handlebar switch assembly (B, **Figure 1**). Remove the switch assembly from the handlebar.

3. Disconnect the throttle pull cable and the return cable from the throttle grip (C, **Figure 1**).

4. Remove the screw securing the right balance set (D, **Figure 1**) and remove the parts from the handlebar end.

5. Remove the throttle grip from the handlebar.

6. Slide back the clutch adjuster boot (A, **Figure 2**). Loosen the adjuster locknut (B, **Figure 2**) and turn the adjuster (C, **Figure 2**) to slacken the clutch cable. Disconnect the clutch cable from the hand lever.

7. Disconnect the electrical leads from the clutch switch (A, **Figure 3**).

8. Remove the screws securing the left switch assembly together and separate the switch assembly. Note that the starter cable bracket is secured under one of these screws (B, **Figure 3**). The bracket will have to be reinstalled in the same manner during assembly.

9. Disconnect the choke lever and cable from the switch housing.

10. Remove the screw securing the left balance set (A, **Figure 4**) and remove the parts from the handlebar end. Remove the left handlebar grip (B, **Figure 4**) as described in this chapter.

11. Loosen the clamp bolt (C, **Figure 4**) and remove the clutch lever assembly from the handlebar.

12. Remove the caps (**Figure 5**) from the upper handlebar holders.

13. Remove the clamp bolts and remove the upper handlebar holders.

14. Lift the handlebar from the lower handlebar holders.

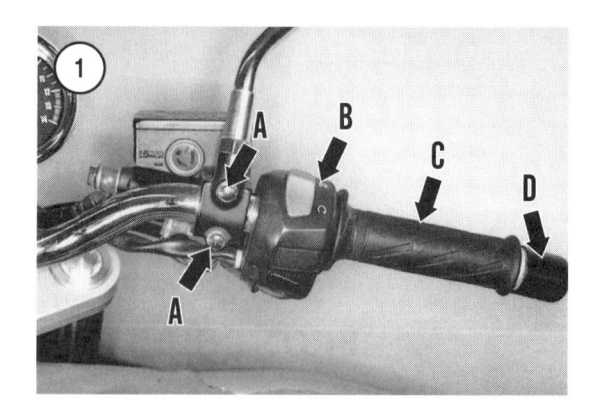

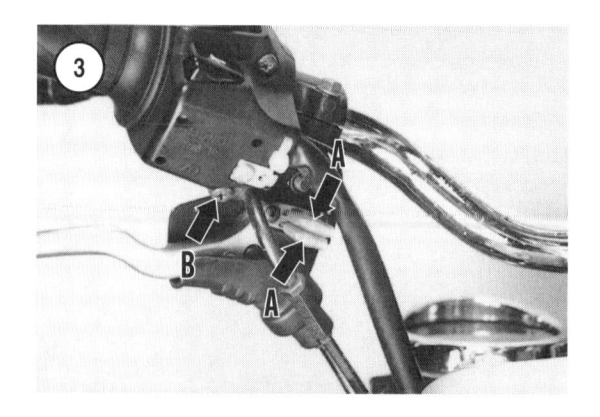

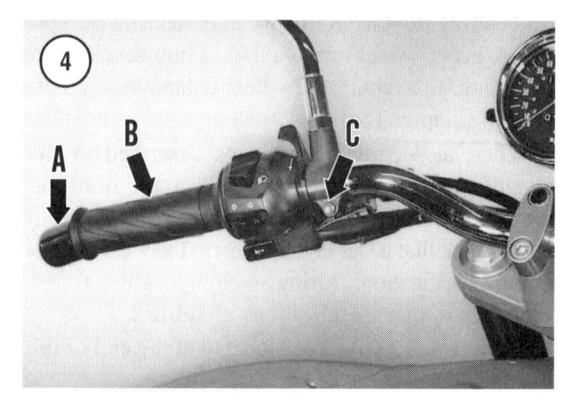

FRONT SUSPENSION AND STEERING

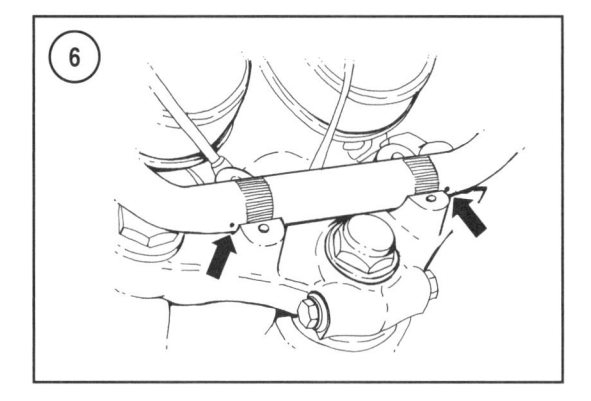

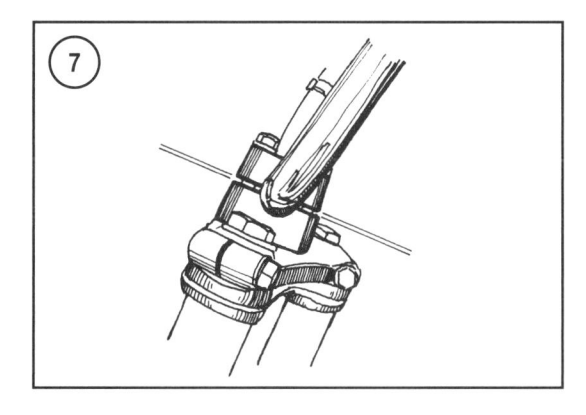

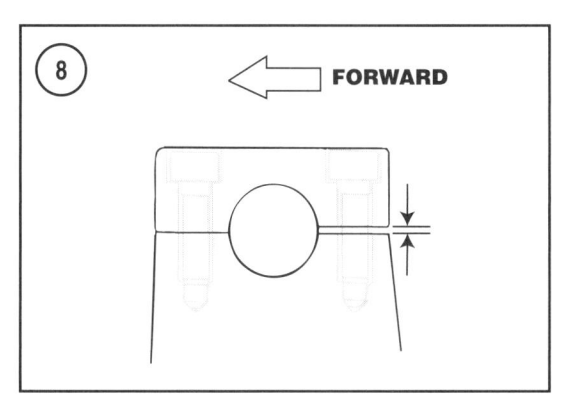

15. Install the handlebar by reversing these steps. Note the following:
   a. Replace the handlebar if it is bent.
   b. Position the handlebar so its punch mark aligns with the mating surface of the lower handlebar holder (**Figure 6**).
   c. On 1995-1999 models, tighten the handlebar clamp bolts so the gap at the front of the handlebar holders equals the gap behind the holders. See **Figure 7**.
   d. On 2000 models, tighten the front handlebar clamp bolt first and then tighten the rear handlebar clamp bolt so the gap between the handlebar holders faces the rear of the motorcycle. See **Figure 8**.
   e. Torque the handlebar clamp bolts and master cylinder clamp bolts to the specification in **Table 2**.
   f. Apply a light coat of multipurpose grease to the right handlebar end before installing the throttle grip.
   g. Install the left handlebar grip as described in this chapter.
   h. Adjust the throttle and clutch cables as described in Chapter Three.

Inspection

Check the handlebar along the entire mounting area for cracks or damage. Replace a bent or damaged handlebar immediately. If the motorcycle is involved in a crash, examine the handlebars, steering stem and front fork carefully.

LEFT HANDLEBAR GRIP REPLACEMENT

NOTE
The right grip is part of the throttle grip assembly and cannot be replaced separately.

1. Remove the screw securing the left balance set (A, **Figure 4**) and remove the parts from the handlebar end.

2. Slide a thin screwdriver between the left grip (B, **Figure 4**) and handlebar. Spray an aerosol parts cleaner into the opening under the grip.

CHAPTER ELEVEN

STEERING STEM

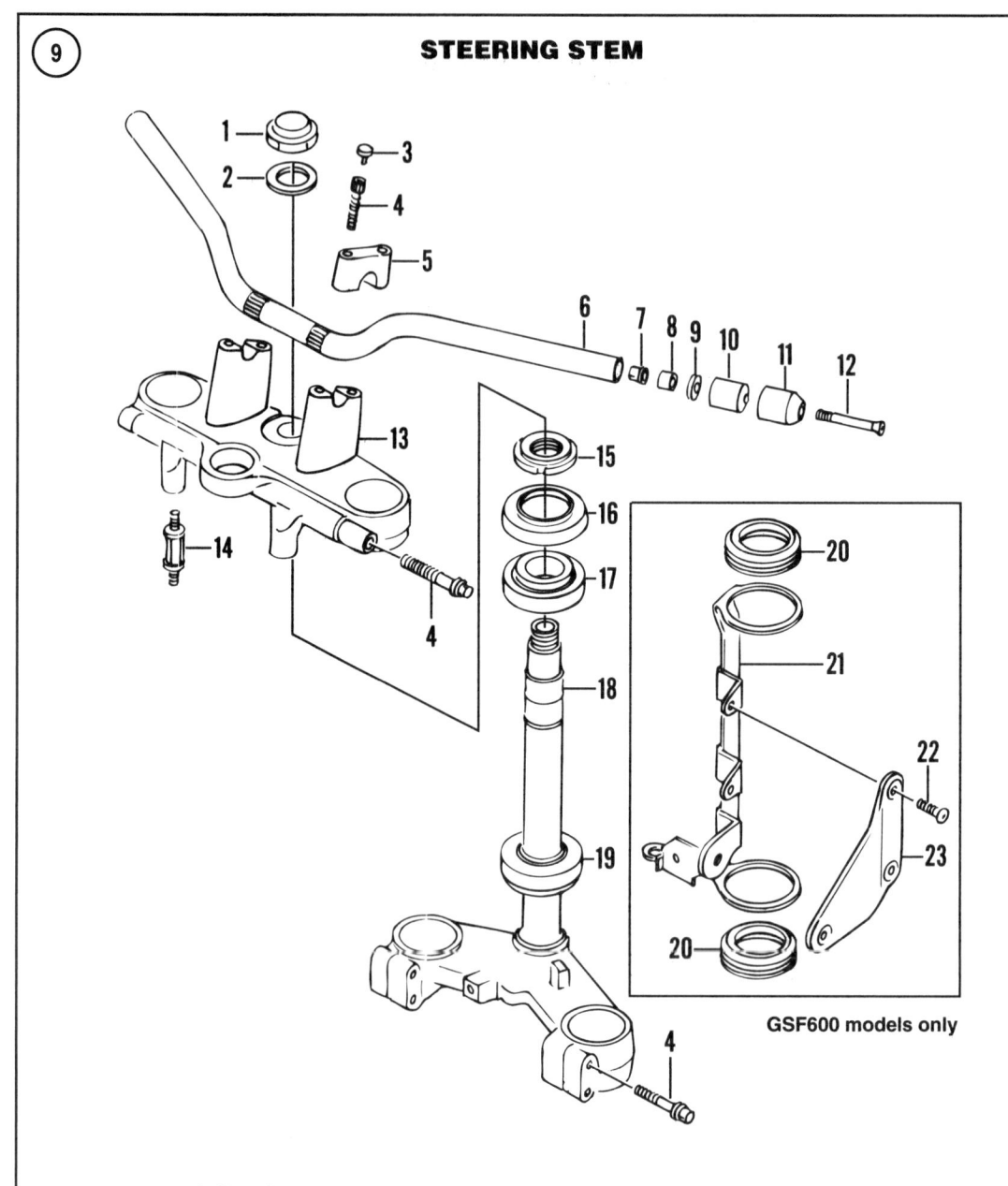

(9)

1. Steering stem head nut
2. Washer
3. Cap
4. Clamp bolt
5. Upper handlebar holder
6. Handlebar
7. Nut
8. Spacer
9. Expander
10. Balancer
11. Handlebar cap
12. Screw
13. Upper fork bridge
14. Stopper
15. Steering stem adjust nut
16. Dust seal
17. Upper bearing
18. Steering stem assembly
19. Lower bearing
20. Spacer
21. Mounting bracket
22. Screw
23. Headlight holder

GSF600 models only

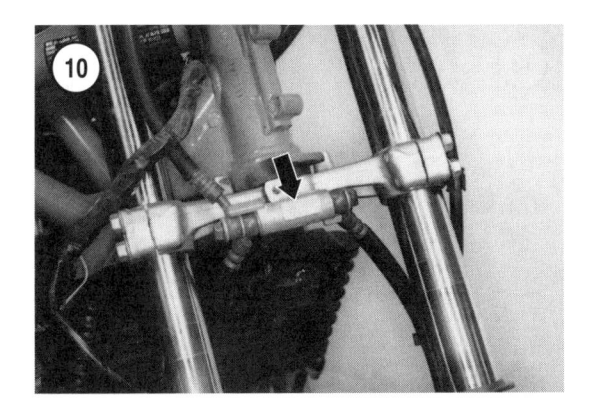

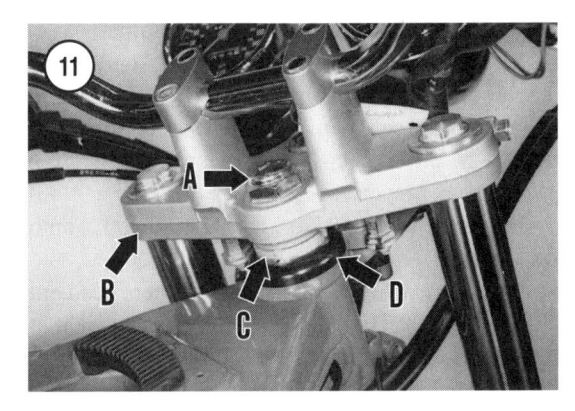

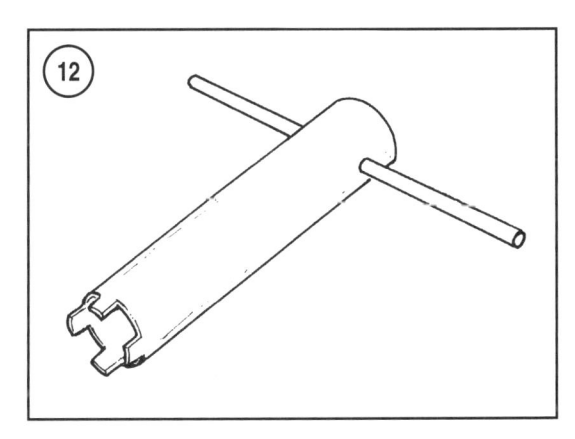

FRONT SUSPENSION AND STEERING

STEERING HEAD AND STEM

Removal

Refer to **Figure 9**.

1. On GSF600S models, remove the front fairing as described in Chapter Fourteen.
2. Remove the front wheel as described in Chapter Ten.
3. Remove the handlebar as described in this chapter.
4. Remove each fork leg as described in this chapter.
5. On GSF600 models, perform the following:
   a. Disconnect the connectors inside the headlight housing and remove the headlight housing.
   b. Remove the turn signals and the headlight housing holders from the mounting bracket.
   c. Remove the mounting brackets.
6. Remove the combination meter and the horn as described in Chapter Nine.
7. Remove the brake hose joint (**Figure 10**) from the lower fork bridge.
8. If still connected, disconnect the ignition switch connector from the wiring harness.
9. Remove the steering stem head nut (A, **Figure 11**) and washer.
10. Remove the upper fork bridge (B, **Figure 11**) and the ignition switch wiring harness.
11. Loosen the steering stem adjust nut (C, **Figure 11**) with a ring nut wrench, a hammer and drift, or fabricate a tool like the one shown in **Figure 12**.

NOTE
Support the weight of the steering stem while removing the adjust nut, or the assembly will drop out of the steering head.

12. Hold onto the steering stem and remove the adjust nut.
13. Gently lower the steering stem assembly out of the frame. Do not worry about catching any loose steel balls. Both bearings are caged with no loose parts.
14. Remove the dust seal (D, **Figure 11**) from the top of the frame.

3. Pull the screwdriver out and quickly twist the grip to break its bond with the handlebar and then slide off the grip.
4. Clean the handlebar of all rubber or sealer residue.
5. Install the new grip following the manufacturer's directions. Apply an adhesive, such as ThreeBond Griplock, between the grip and handlebar. When applying an adhesive, follow the manufacturer's instructions for drying time before operating the motorcycle.

15. Carefully remove the inner race and the upper bearing from the upper bearing race in the steering head (**Figure 13**).

CAUTION
Do not attempt to remove the lower bearing from the steering stem unless the bearing will be replaced. The bearing is pressed onto the steering stem and will be damaged during removal.

16. Inspect the steering stem as described in this chapter.

Installation

Refer to **Figure 9**.
1. Make sure the steering head outer races are clean and properly seated on the steering head.
2. Apply an even, complete coat of Suzuki Super Grease A or equivalent to the steering head outer races, both bearings, the dust seal and the head nut.

NOTE
The fork receptacles in the steering stem are offset and must face toward the front of the motorcycle. This is necessary for proper alignment with the fork receptacles in the upper fork bridge.

3. Install the upper bearing and the inner race into the outer race in the top of the steering head (**Figure 13**).
4. Position the lower fork bridge so its fork receptacles face toward the front of the motorcycle. Carefully slide the steering stem up into the steering head. Take care not to dislodge the upper bearing or race. If this happens, reseat the bearing.
5. Pack the underside of the dust seal with grease. Install the dust seal (D, **Figure 11**) and steering stem adjust nut (C, **Figure 11**) and perform the following:
  a. Tighten the steering stem adjust nut (**Figure 14**) to the torque specification listed in **Table 2**.
  b. Turn the steering stem from side-to-side five or six times to seat the bearings.

NOTE
In step c, the adjustment amount varies from motorcycle to motorcycle. After loosening the adjust nut the 1/4 to 1/2 turn, there must be no play detected in the steering stem.

  c. Loosen the adjust nut 1/4 to 1/2 turn.
6. Once again, turn the steering stem from side-to-side five or six times. The steering stem should move freely with no looseness or stiffness. If necessary, repeat Steps 5 and 6 until the steering stem moves properly.
7. Install the upper fork bridge (B, **Figure 11**) onto the steering stem.
8. Install the washer and the steering stem head nut (A, **Figure 11**). Tighten the head nut finger-tight at this time.

NOTE
Steps 9-13 must be performed in this order to assure proper upper and lower fork bridge-to-fork alignment.

9. Temporarily slide the fork legs into position until they are just above the top surface of the upper fork bridge. Tighten the lower fork bridge clamp bolts securely.
10. Temporarily install the front axle into the fork legs and tighten the axle nut securely.
11. Tighten the lower fork bridge clamp bolts to the specified torque.
12. Tighten the steering stem head nut to specification.
13. Remove the front axle. Loosen the lower fork bridge clamp bolts, and slide the fork legs out from the upper and lower fork bridges.
14. Install the brake hose joint (**Figure 10**) onto the lower fork bridge. Tighten the bolt securely.
15. Install the combination meter as described in Chapter Nine.
16. Install the handlebar assembly as described in this chapter.
17. Install the front fork assembly as described in this chapter.

FRONT SUSPENSION AND STEERING

Steering stem
Adjust nut

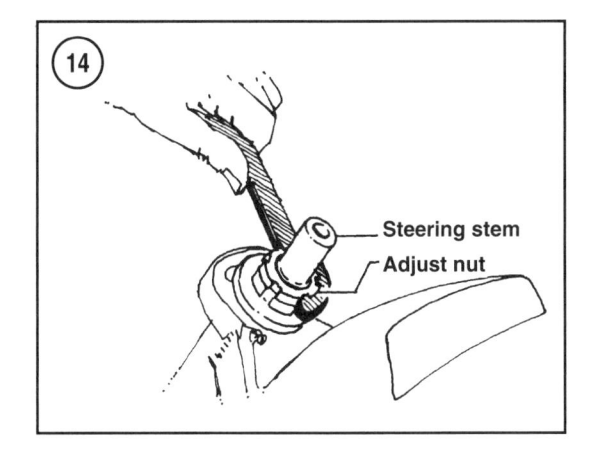

18. Check the movement of the front fork and steering stem assembly. The steering stem must turn freely from side-to-side but without any binding or free play when the fork legs are moved fore and aft.
19. Connect the ignition switch electrical connector to the main wiring harness.
20. Install the combination meter and the horn as described in Chapter Nine.
21. On GSF600 models, perform the following:
    a. Install the turn signals and headlight holders onto the mounting bracket.
    b. Reinstall the headlight housing and reconnect the electrical connectors.
    c. Reinstall the headlight as described in Chapter Nine.
22. On 1995-1999 models, install the fender brace as described in Chapter Fourteen.
23. Install the front fender as described in Chapter Fourteen.
24. Install the front wheel as described in Chapter Ten.
25. On GSF600S models, reinstall the front fairing as described in Chapter Fourteen.

Inspection

1. Clean the upper and lower bearings in a bearing degreaser. Make certain that the bearing degreaser is compatible with the rubber covers on each bearing. Hold onto the bearing so it will not spin and thoroughly dry both bearings with compressed air. Make sure all solvent is removed from the lower bearing still installed on the steering stem.
2. Wipe the old grease from the outer races located in the steering head and then clean the outer races with a rag soaked in solvent. Thoroughly dry the races with a lint-free cloth.
3. Check the steering stem outer races for pitting, galling and corrosion. If any race is worn or damaged, replace the race and bearing as an assembly. Follow the procedure described in this chapter.
4. Check the welds around the steering head for cracks and fractures. If any damage is found, have the frame repaired at a competent frame or welding shop.
5. Check the balls/needles for pitting, scratches or discoloration indicating wear or corrosion. Replace the bearing if any balls/needles are less than perfect.
6. If the bearings are in good condition, pack them thoroughly with Suzuki Super Grease A or an equivalent, good-quality, waterproof bearing grease. To pack the bearings, spread some grease in the palm of your hand and scrape the open side of the bearing across your palm until the bearing is packed completely full of grease. Spin the bearing a few times to determine if there are any open areas; repack if necessary.
7. Thoroughly clean all mounting parts in solvent. Dry them completely.
8. Inspect the steering stem head nut and steering stem adjust nut for wear or damage. Inspect the threads. If necessary, clean them with an appropriate size metric tap or replace the nut(s). If the threads are damaged, inspect the appropriate steering stem thread(s) for damage. If necessary, clean the threads with an appropriate size metric die.
9. Inspect the steering stem head nut washer for damage and replace if necessary. If damaged, check the underside of the steering stem head nut for damage and replace as necessary.
10. Inspect the steering stem and the lower fork bridge for cracks or other damage. Make sure the fork bridge clamping areas are free of burrs and that the bolt holes are in good condition.
11. Inspect the upper fork bridge upper for cracks or other damage. Check both the upper and lower surface of the fork bridge. Make sure the fork bridge clamping areas are free of burrs and that the bolt holes are in good condition.

STEERING HEAD BEARING RACE REPLACEMENT

The upper and lower bearing outer races must not be removed unless they are going to be replaced. These races are pressed into place and are damaged during removal. If removed, replace both the outer race and the bearings at the same time. Never reuse an outer race that has been removed. It is no longer true and will damage the ball bearings if reused.

NOTE
The following procedure describes simple home techniques to remove the bearing races. If removal is difficult, do not chance damage to the motorcycle or new bearing races. Have the task performed by a Suzuki dealership or a qualified specialist.

1. Remove the steering stem as described in this chapter.
2. Insert an aluminum drift into the steering head and carefully tap the lower race out from the steering head (**Figure 15**). Repeat this procedure for the upper race.
3. Chill the new bearing races in a freezer for a few hours to shrink the outer diameter of the race as much as possible.
4. Clean the race seats (**Figure 16**) in the steering head. Check for cracks or other damage.
5. Insert the new race into the steering head with the tapered side facing out (**Figure 17**), and square the race with the race bore (**Figure 18**).

CAUTION
To avoid damage to the races and to the race seats in the steering head, install the races as described below.

6. Assemble a puller tool as shown in **Figure 19**. The block mounted at the bottom of the threaded rod is used as a T-handle to hold the rod stationary when the bearing race is being installed from the opposite end. To make the tool without the handle, the bottom of the rod can be held with two nuts locked together. The hole drilled through the block should be large enough to accept a suitable rod for the T-handle. Two or more *thick* washers are also required. The outer diameter of the washers must be greater than the outer diameter of the bearing races.

CAUTION
When installing the bearing outer races with the threaded rod or similar tool, do not let the rod or tool contact the face of the bearing race. It could damage the race.

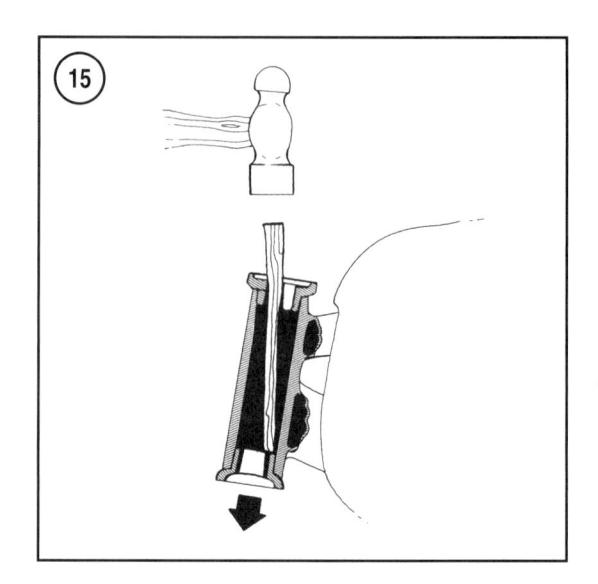

7. To install the upper race, insert the puller through the bottom of the steering head. Seat the lower washer or plate against the steering head.
8. At the top of the steering stem, slide the large washer down and seat it squarely on top of the bearing race. Install the required washers and coupling nut onto the rod.

FRONT SUSPENSION AND STEERING

(18)

(19) BEARING RACE INSTALLATION TOOL

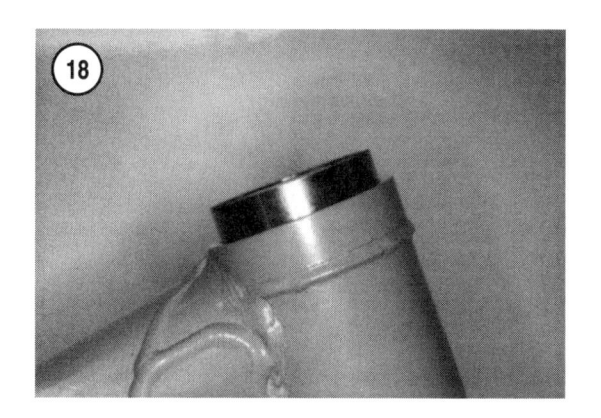

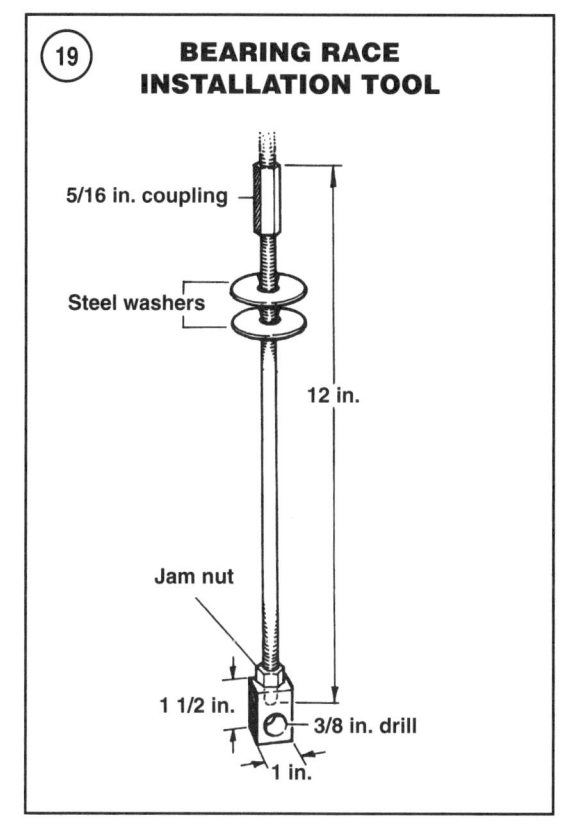

- 5/16 in. coupling
- Steel washers
- 12 in.
- Jam nut
- 1 1/2 in.
- 3/8 in. drill
- 1 in.

(20)

(21)

9. Hand tighten the coupling nut and center the washer on the upper bearing race.

10. Hold the threaded rod to prevent it from turning and tighten the coupling nut with a wrench (**Figure 20**). Continue to tighten the coupling until the race is completely drawn into the steering head. Remove the puller assembly and inspect the bearing race. It should be bottomed in the steering head as shown in **Figure 21**.

11. Turn the special tool over and repeat this procedure for the lower bearing race.

STEERING STEM BEARING REPLACEMENT

Do not remove the steering stem lower bearing and lower seal unless it is going to be replaced. The lower bearing can be difficult to remove. If it cannot be removed as described in this procedure, have a dealership service department replace the bearing and seal.

Never reinstall a lower bearing that has been removed. It is no longer true and will damage the rest of the bearing assembly if reused.

1. Install the steering stem head nut onto the top of the steering stem to protect the threads.

2. Loosen the lower bearing assembly from the shoulder at the base of the steering stem with a chisel as shown in **Figure 22**. Slide the lower bearing and grease seal off the steering stem.

3. Clean the steering stem with solvent and dry it thoroughly.

4. Position the new grease seal with the flange side facing up.

5. Slide a new grease seal and the lower bearing onto the steering stem until it stops on the raised shoulder.

6. Align the lower bearing with the machined shoulder on the steering stem.

7. Slide the Suzuki steering bearing installer (part No. 09941-74910 for 1995-1999 models; part No. 09941-74911 for 2000 models) or a piece of pipe (**Figure 23**) over the steering stem until it seats against the inner portion of the *inner* race of the lower bearing. Drive the lower bearing onto the steering stem until it bottoms.

8. Pack the bearing with Suzuki Super Grease A or an equivalent waterproof wheel bearing grease.

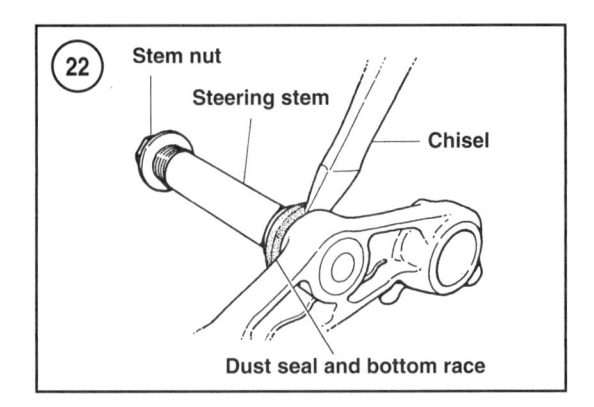

FRONT FORK

Front Fork Service

Before disassembling the fork, drain the front fork oil and refill each fork leg with the proper type and quantity fork oil as described in this chapter. If trouble persists, such as poor damping, a tendency to bottom or top out, or leakage around the oil seals, follow the service procedures in this section.

To simplify fork service and to prevent the mixing of parts, remove, service and install each fork leg individually.

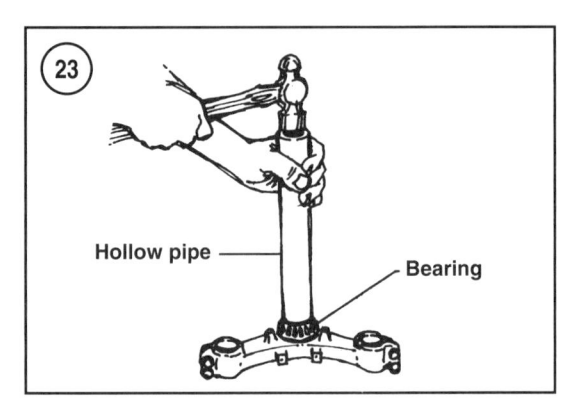

Removal

NOTE
For fork leg removal only, do not perform Step 6. This step is only necessary if the fork leg is going to be disassembled for service.

1. On GSF600S models, remove the front fairing as described in Chapter Fourteen.
2. Remove the front wheel as described in Chapter Ten.
3. Remove the front fender as described in Chapter Fourteen. On 1995-1999 models, remove the front fender brace as described in Chapter Fourteen.
4. Remove the brake hose clamp from the fork leg.
5. Remove the brake caliper as described in Chapter Thirteen. Suspend the caliper from the frame with wire or a bungee cord.

NOTE
The damper rod Allen bolt at the bottom of the fork leg cannot be loosened without a T-handle (part No. 09940-34520) and a Suzuki attachment tool. On 1995-1999 models, attachment tool G (part No. 09940-34592) is required. On 2000 models, attachment tool A (part No. 09940-34531) is needed. Do not disassemble a fork leg unless these tools or their equivalent are available.

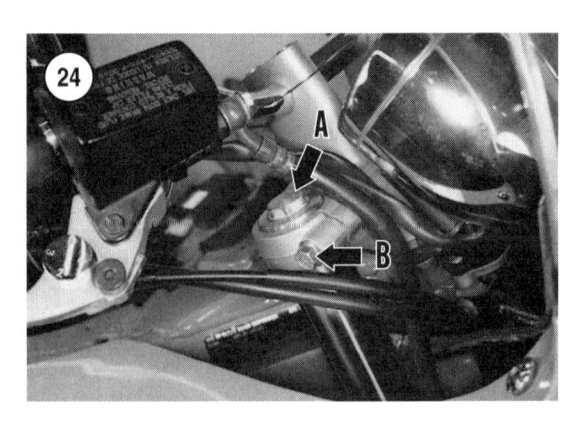

6. If the fork leg is going to be disassembled, loosen the cap bolt (A, **Figure 24**).

7. Loosen the clamp bolt (B, **Figure 24**) on the upper fork bridge.

FRONT SUSPENSION AND STEERING

right to avoid spilling fork oil through the top of the fork tube.

11. If both fork leg assemblies are going to be removed, mark them with an R (right side) and L (left side) so they will be reinstalled on the correct side.

Installation

NOTE
If both fork assemblies are removed, make sure to install the fork assembly on the correct side of the motorcycle. Refer to the marks made during removal (Step 10).

1. Slowly install the fork tube into the lower fork bridge and then the upper fork bridge. On GSF600 models, make sure the fork tube also passes through the mounting bracket (21, **Figure 9**) that sits between the fork bridges.
2. Slide the fork tube assembly into position until the top edge of the fork tube aligns with the top surface of the upper fork bridge (**Figure 26**).
3. Tighten the lower fork bridge clamp bolts (**Figure 25**) to the torque specification listed in **Table 2**.
4. If the fork was disassembled for service, tighten the cap bolt (A, **Figure 24**) to the specified torque.
5. Torque the upper fork bridge clamp bolt (B, **Figure 24**) to the specification.
6. On 1995-1999 models, install the fender brace as described in Chapter Fourteen.
7. Install the front fender as described in Chapter Fourteen.
8. Install the front wheel as described in Chapter Ten.
9. Install the brake caliper as described in Chapter Thirteen.
10. On GSF600S models, install the fairing as described in Chapter Fourteen.

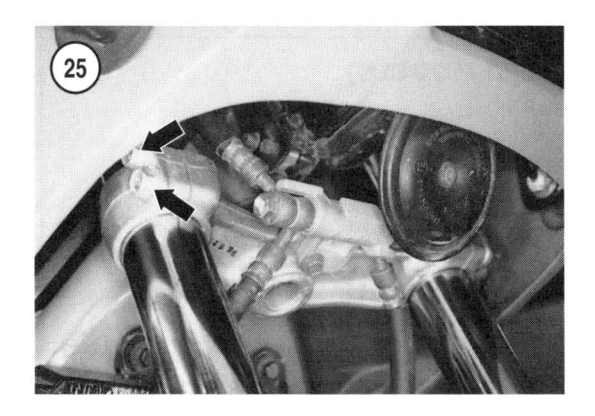

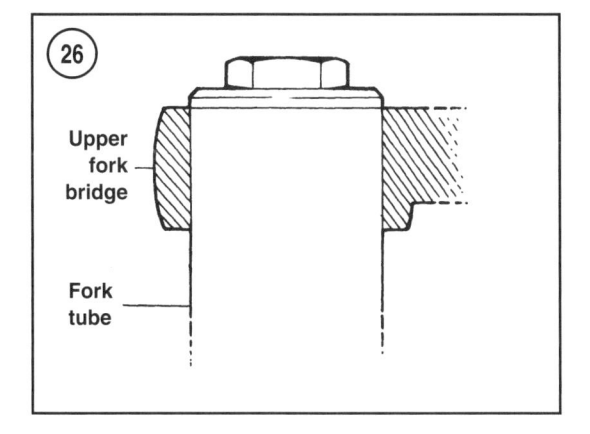

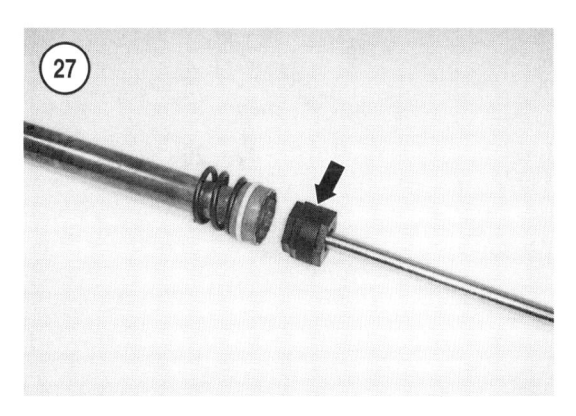

8. Loosen both clamp bolts (**Figure 25**) on the lower fork bridge.
9. Carefully pull the fork assembly from the upper and lower fork bridges. It may be necessary to rotate the fork tube slightly while pulling it down and out. Take the fork assembly to a workbench for service. If the fork is not going to be serviced, wrap it in a towel or blanket to protect the surface from damage.
10. If the Allen and cap bolts were loosened in Step 4, place the fork assembly in a drain pan. Keep it up-

Disassembly

NOTE
*The damper rod Allen bolt at the bottom of the fork leg cannot be loosened or tightened unless the damper rod is held with a T-handle (part No. 09940-34520) and a special Suzuki attachment tool. On 1995-1999 models attachment tool G (part No. 09940-34592) is required. See **Figure 27**. On 2000 models, attachment tool*

FRONT FORK (1995-1999 MODELS)

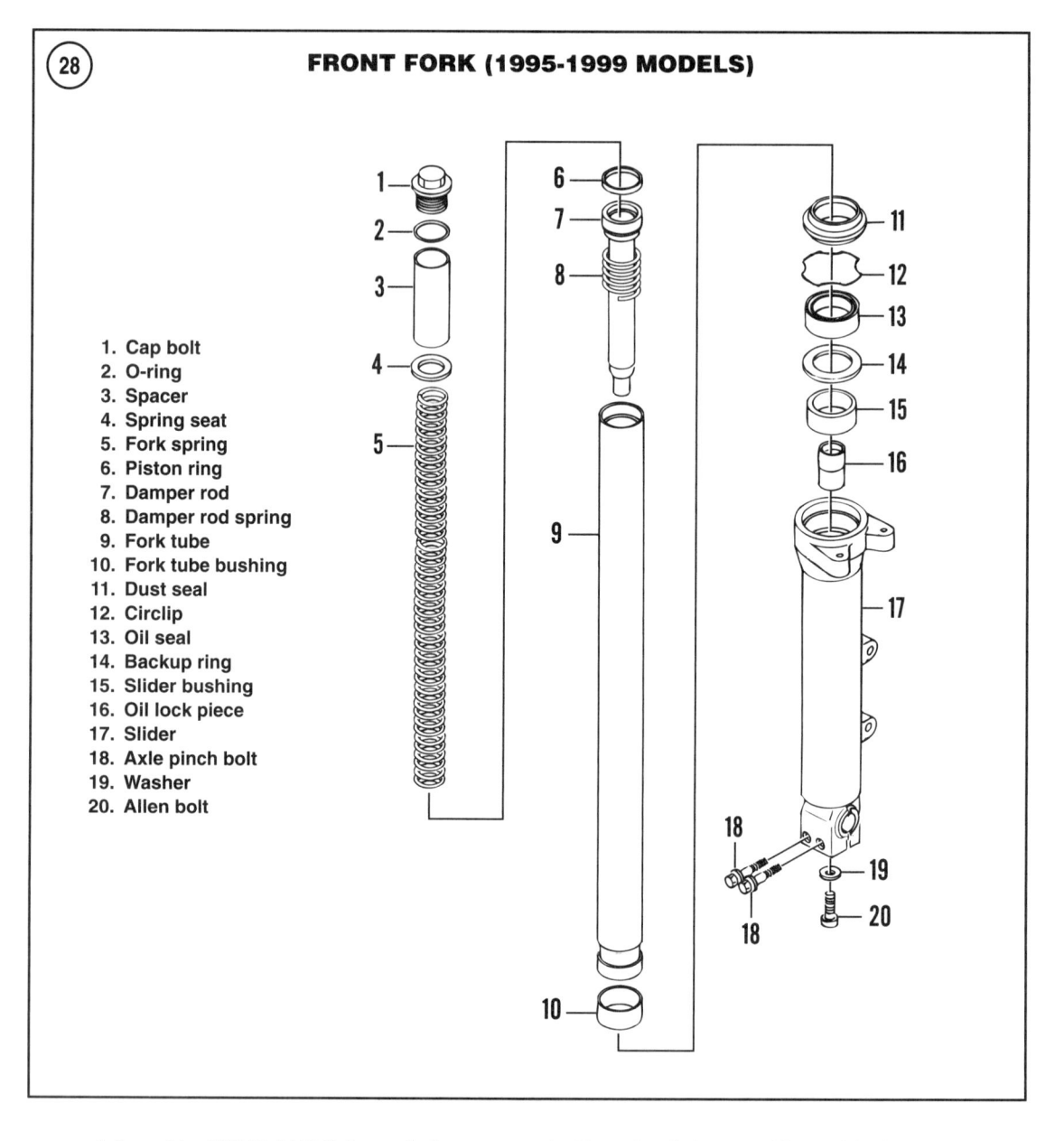

1. Cap bolt
2. O-ring
3. Spacer
4. Spring seat
5. Fork spring
6. Piston ring
7. Damper rod
8. Damper rod spring
9. Fork tube
10. Fork tube bushing
11. Dust seal
12. Circlip
13. Oil seal
14. Backup ring
15. Slider bushing
16. Oil lock piece
17. Slider
18. Axle pinch bolt
19. Washer
20. Allen bolt

A (part No. 09940-34531) is needed. Do not attempt to disassemble a fork leg unless the appropriate attachment tool or its equivalent are available.

Refer to **Figure 28** when servicing the front fork on 1995-1999 models; refer to **Figure 29** for 2000 models.

1. With the fork held upright, completely unscrew and remove the cap bolt (A, **Figure 30**) from the fork tube.
2. Remove the spacer (C, **Figure 30**), spring seat (B, **Figure 30**) and the fork spring.
3. Turn the fork assembly upside down and drain the fork oil into a suitable container. Pump the fork several times by hand to expel most of the remaining oil. Dispose of the fork oil properly.
4. Remove the damper rod Allen bolt and washer by performing the following:

 a. Secure the slider horizontally in a vise with soft jaws.

 b. Insert the T-handle with the appropriate attachment tool into the fork tube until the tool engages the damper rod.

FRONT SUSPENSION AND STEERING

FRONT FORK (2000 MODELS)

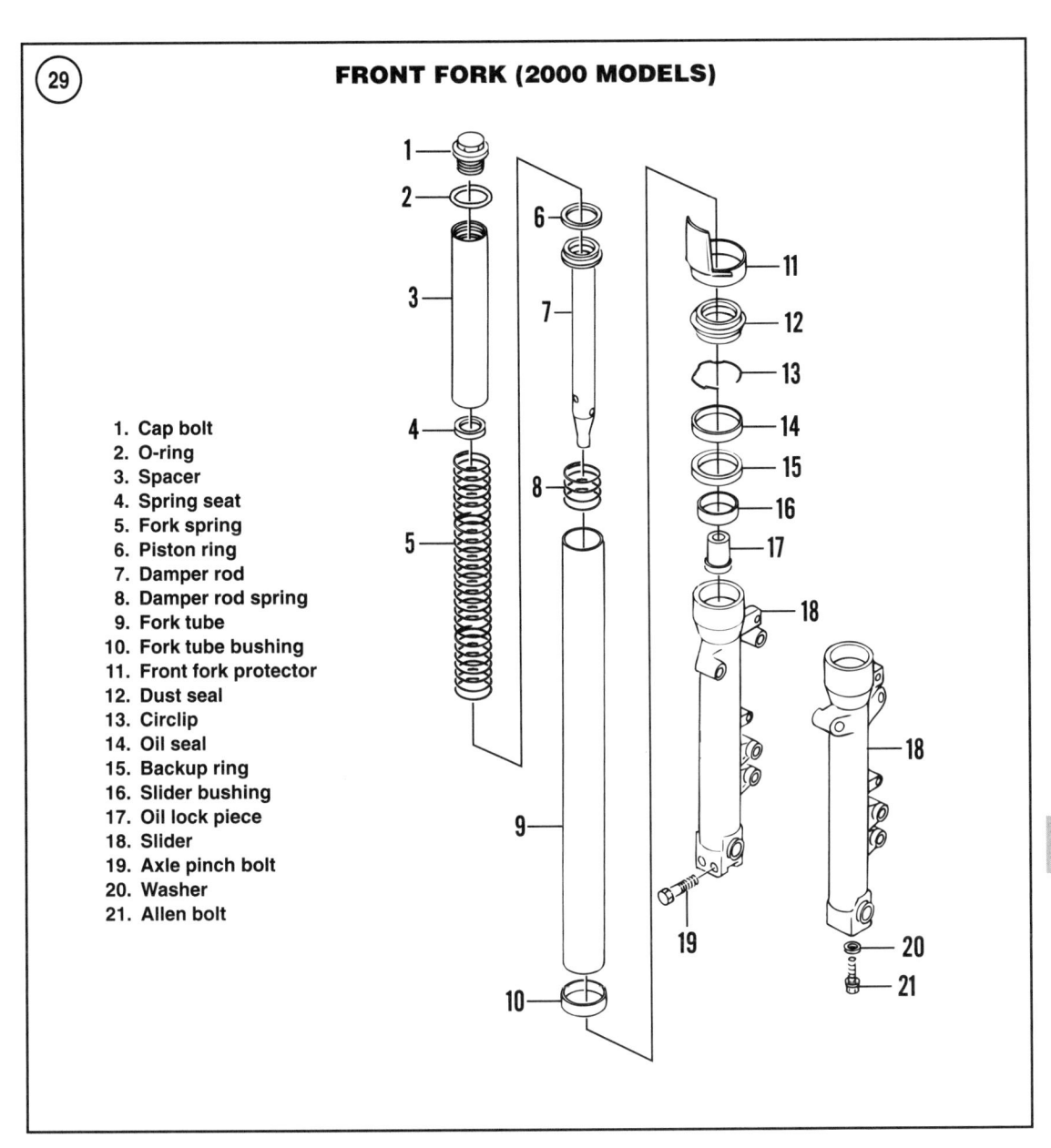

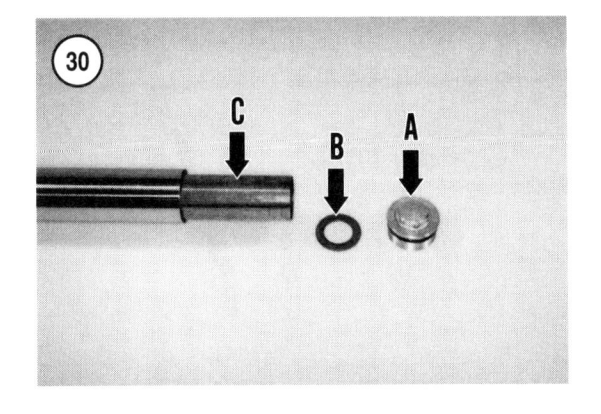

29

1. Cap bolt
2. O-ring
3. Spacer
4. Spring seat
5. Fork spring
6. Piston ring
7. Damper rod
8. Damper rod spring
9. Fork tube
10. Fork tube bushing
11. Front fork protector
12. Dust seal
13. Circlip
14. Oil seal
15. Backup ring
16. Slider bushing
17. Oil lock piece
18. Slider
19. Axle pinch bolt
20. Washer
21. Allen bolt

30

c. Hold the damper rod with the tool and remove the Allen bolt and washer (**Figure 31**) from the bottom of the fork slider.

5. Turn the fork leg upside down and remove the damper rod and rebound spring.

6. Pry the dust seal (A, **Figure 32**) from the slider and move it up the fork tube.

7. Remove the circlip (B, **Figure 32**) from its seat in the slider and move it up the fork tube.

8. On 2000 models, remove the fork protector from the slider.

9. Secure the fork slider horizontally into a vise with soft jaws.

> **NOTE**
> *It may be necessary to slightly heat the area on the slider around the oil seal prior to removal. Heat the area with a rag soaked in hot water. Do not apply a flame directly to the fork slider.*

10. There is an interference fit between the bushing in the fork slider and the bushing on the fork tube. In order to remove the fork tube from the slider, pull hard on the fork tube using quick in-and-out strokes (**Figure 33**) and withdraw the fork tube from the slider. Doing so will also pull the oil seal (A, **Figure 34**), backup ring (B, **Figure 34**) and the slider bushing (C, **Figure 34**) from the slider.

> **NOTE**
> *Do not remove the fork tube bushing (D, **Figure 34**) unless it is going to be replaced. Inspect it as described in this chapter.*

11. Slide the oil seal, backup ring and the slider bushing from the fork tube.

> **NOTE**
> *The oil lock piece is made of plastic and can stick to the bottom of the slider. Do not use a metal dowel when dislodging it from the slider in Step 12.*

12. Remove the oil lock piece. If it sticks to the bottom of the slider, remove it by performing the following:
    a. Insert a wooden dowel down the fork leg.
    b. Press the dowel into the center of the oil lock piece. Make sure the dowel fits snugly in the oil lock piece (**Figure 35**).
    c. Move the dowel from side to side to loosen the oil lock piece from the slider and remove the oil lock piece.
13. Inspect the components as described in this chapter.

Assembly

1. Coat all parts with fresh Suzuki #10, or equivalent, fork oil prior to installation.

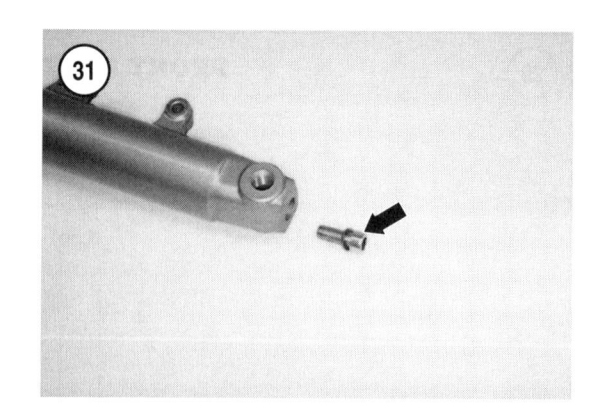

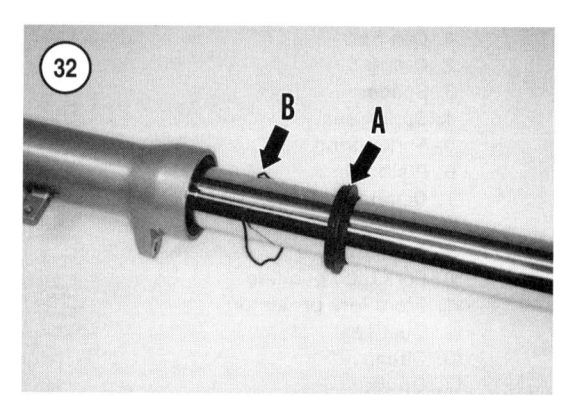

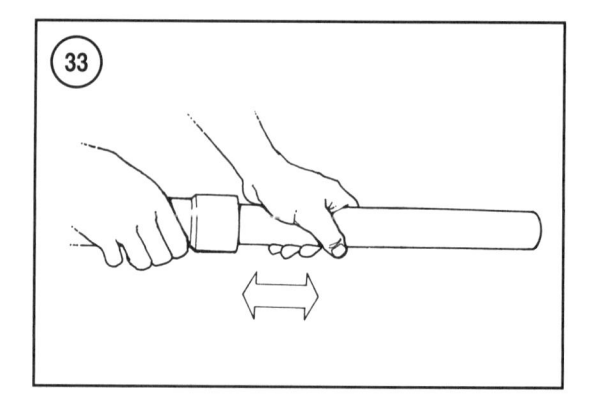

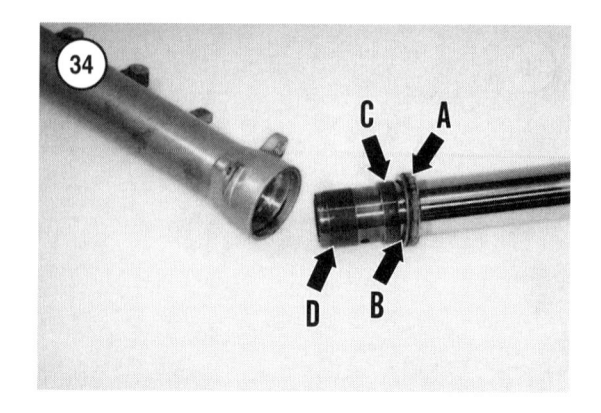

FRONT SUSPENSION AND STEERING   347

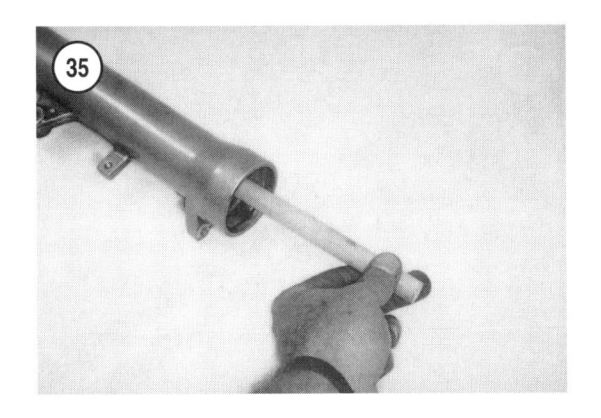

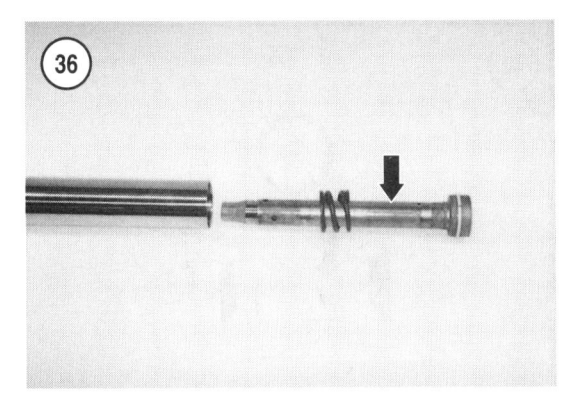

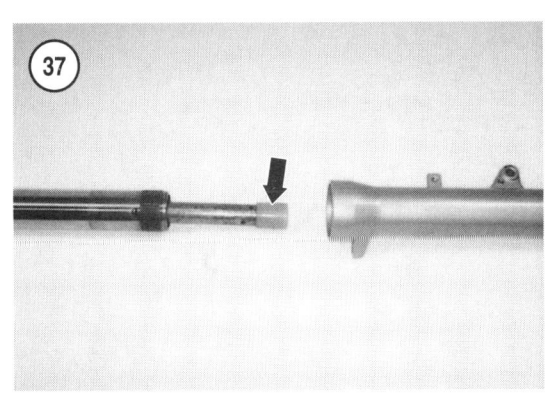

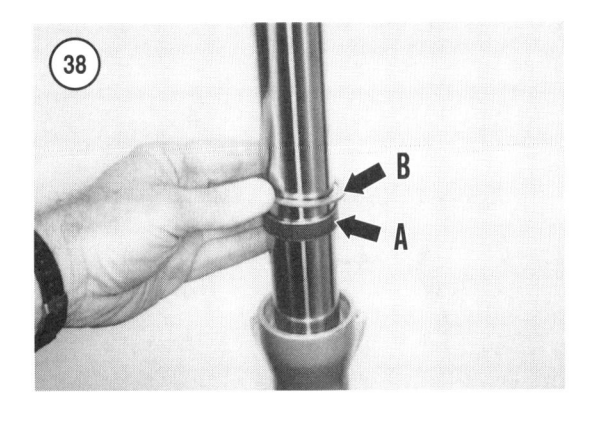

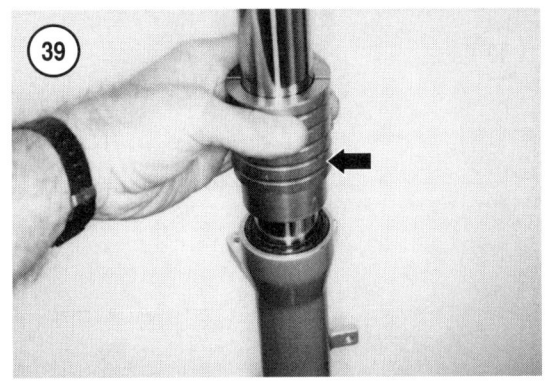

2. If removed, slide the rebound spring onto the damper rod.
3. Insert the damper rod (**Figure 36**) into the fork tube. Slide the damper rod down the tube until the rod emerges from the fork tube end.
4. On 2000 models, check the spring inside the tapered end of the oil lock piece. Make sure the spring is properly seated.
5. Slide the oil lock piece (**Figure 37**) onto the damper rod so the tapered end of the oil lock piece faces the damper rod.
6. Install the fork tube into the slider.
7. Install a *new* washer onto the damper rod Allen bolt. Install the Allen bolt into the end of the slider by performing the following:
   a. Secure the slider horizontally in a vise with soft jaws.
   b. Insert the T-handle with the appropriate attachment tool into the fork tube until the tool engages the damper rod.
   c. Apply ThreeBond Threadlock 1342 to the threads of the Allen bolt. Thread the Allen bolt into the oil lock piece at the bottom of the slider.
   d. Hold the damper rod with the tool and torque the damper rod Allen bolt (**Figure 31**) to the specification in **Table 2**.
8. Secure the fork vertically in a vise with soft jaws.
9. Install the slider bushing and spacer by performing the following:
   a. Slide the slider bushing (A, **Figure 38**) and the backup ring (B, **Figure 38**) down the fork tube.

NOTE
*A fork seal driver (**Figure 39**) can be purchased from a number of aftermarket suppliers. Measure the outside diameter of the fork tube and purchase a driver with the same diameter.*

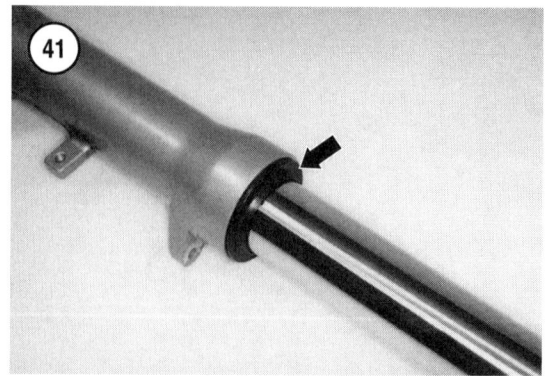

b. Drive the bushing into the slider with a fork seal driver (**Figure 39**).

c. Drive the bushing into the place until it is completely seated in the recess in the slider.

NOTE
To avoid damaging the fork seal and dust seal, place a piece of clinging plastic wrap over the end of the fork tube and coat it thoroughly with fork oil.

10. Install the oil seal by performing the following:

    a. Lubricate the oil seal with fork oil.

    b. Slide the oil seal (**Figure 40**) down the fork tube. Make sure the manufacturer's marks face up.

    c. Drive the seal into the slider with the fork seal driver.

    d. Drive the seal until the circlip groove in the slider is visible above the top of the oil seal.

11. Slide the circlip (B, **Figure 32**) down the fork tube and install it into the slider. Make sure the circlip is completely seated in the circlip groove in the slider.

12. Slide the dust seal (A, **Figure 32**) down the fork tube and seat it in the slider (**Figure 41**).

13. On 2000 models, install the front fork protector. Make sure the tab on the protector engages the notch in the slider.

14. Fill the fork with oil. Set the oil level and complete fork assembly as described in *Fork Oil Adjustment*.

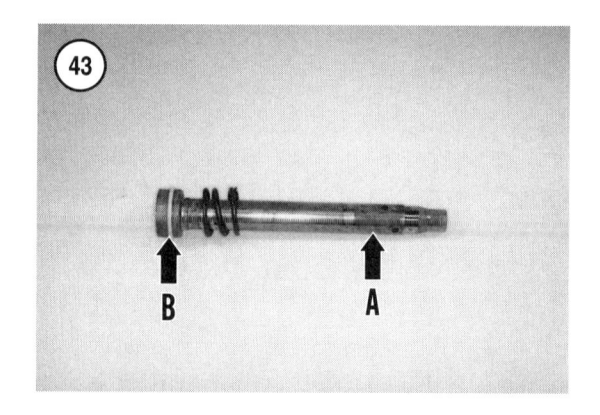

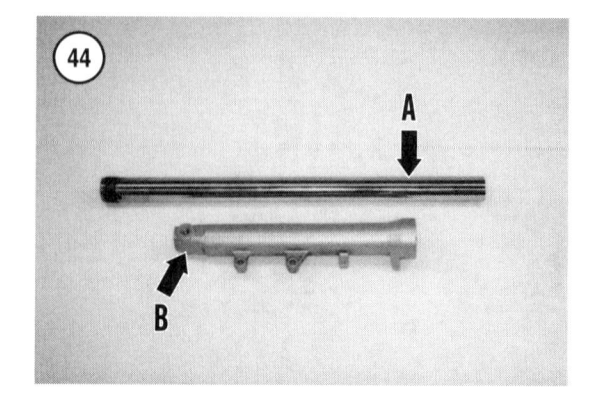

FRONT SUSPENSION AND STEERING 349

45

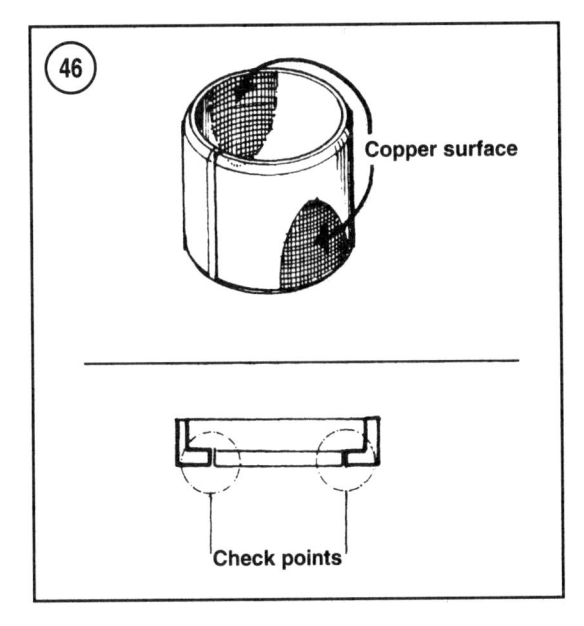

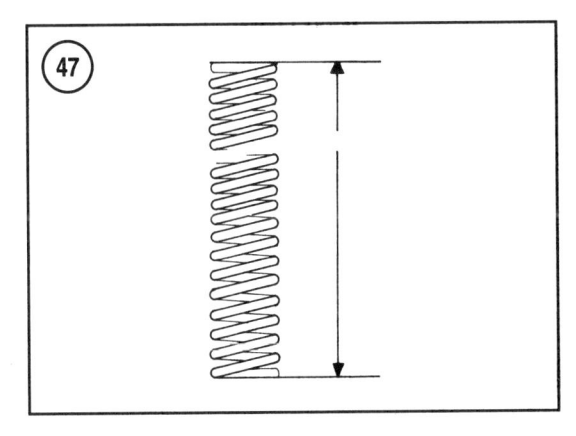

46 Copper surface
Check points

47

Inspection

1. Thoroughly clean all parts in solvent and dry them with compressed air. Check the fork tube for signs of wear or scratches.

2. Check the damper rod for straightness (**Figure 42**). Replace the damper rod if it is worn or if runout equals or exceeds 0.2 mm (0.008 in.).

3. Make sure the oil holes (A, **Figure 43**) in the damper rod are clear. Clean out if necessary.

4. Inspect the damper rod piston ring (B, **Figure 43**) for wear or damage. Replace as necessary.

5. Check the fork tube (A, **Figure 44**) for straightness. If bent or severely scratched, replace it.

6. Inspect the threads in the top of the fork tube for wear or damage. Clean the threads with the appropriate size metric tap if necessary.

7. Check the fork tube for chrome flaking or creasing. This condition will damage oil seals. Replace the fork tube if necessary.

8. Check the slider (B, **Figure 44**) for dents or exterior damage that may cause the fork tube to stick. Replace the slider if necessary.

9. Inspect the inner surfaces (**Figure 45**) of the slider for damage or burrs. Pay particular attention to the circlip groove and the oil seal areas. Clean the slider if necessary.

10. Inspect the brake caliper mounting bosses on the slider for cracks or other damage. Replace the slider if any damaged is noted.

11. Inspect the front axle threads in the slider for damage. If damage is slight, clean out the threads with a metric tap. If damage is severe, replace the slider.

NOTE
Suzuki recommends replacing the bushings whenever a fork leg is disassembled.

12. Inspect the slider bushing (C, **Figure 34**) and fork tube bushing (D, **Figure 34**). If either is scratched or scored, it must be replaced. If the copper base material shows on approximately 3/4 of the total bushing surface (**Figure 46**), too much of the Teflon coating has worn off. Replace the bushing.

13. Inspect the backup ring at the points shown in **Figure 46**.

14. To replace the fork tube bushing, open the bushing slot with a screwdriver and slide the bushing off the fork tube. Lubricate a new bushing with fresh fork oil, open its slot slightly and slide the bushing onto the fork tube slot.

15. Measure the uncompressed length of the fork spring as shown in **Figure 47**. Replace the spring if it has sagged to less than the wear limit specified in **Table 1**.

16. Replace the fork cap O-ring (**Figure 48**) if deformed or damaged.

17. Replace any parts that are worn or damaged. Simply cleaning and reinstalling unserviceable components will not improve front suspension performance.

Fork Oil Adjustment

NOTE
Always adjust fork oil by measuring the fork oil level. Do not rely on the fork oil capacity. Inaccurate setting will result.

1. Secure the fork vertically in a vise with soft jaws.
2. Push the fork tube into the slider until the tube bottoms.
3. Refer to **Table 1** and add the recommended amount of fork oil to the fork assembly.
4. Slowly pump the fork tube up and down several times to distribute the fork oil.
5. After the fork oil settles, compress the fork completely. Use an accurate ruler or the Suzuki fork oil level gauge (part No. 09943-7411) and measure the fork oil level from the top of the fork tube (**Figure 49**). Add or remove oil as necessary until the fork oil level equals the value specified in **Table 1**.
6. Set the fork oil level by performing the following:
    a. After the fork oil settles, compress the fork tube completely.
    b. Use a ruler, the Suzuki oil level gauge (part No. 09943-74111), or equivalent to set the oil level to the value listed in **Table 1**. Refer to **Figure 49**.

NOTE
*An oil level setting device can be fabricated as shown in **Figure 50**. Fill the fork with a few cc more than the required amount of oil. Position the lower edge of the hose clamp against the top edge of the fork tube and draw out the excess oil. Oil is sucked out until the level reaches the small diameter hole. A precise oil level can be achieved with this simple device.*

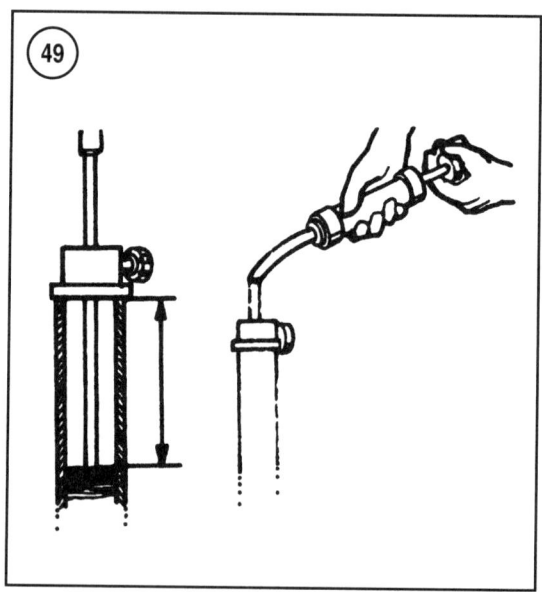

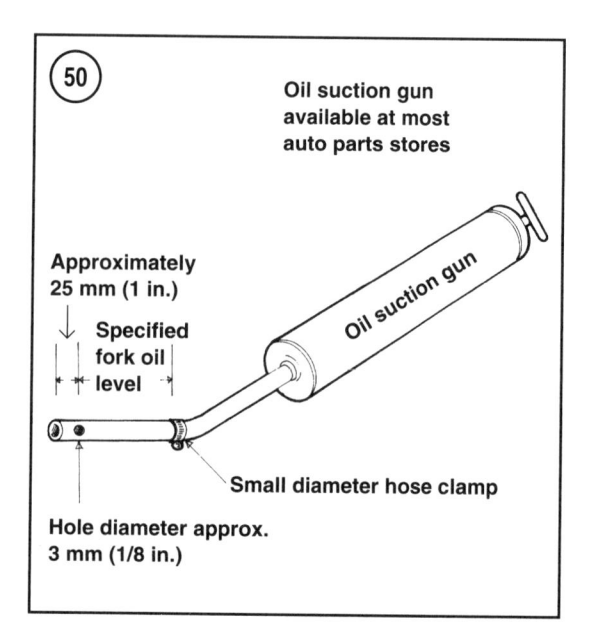

FRONT SUSPENSION AND STEERING

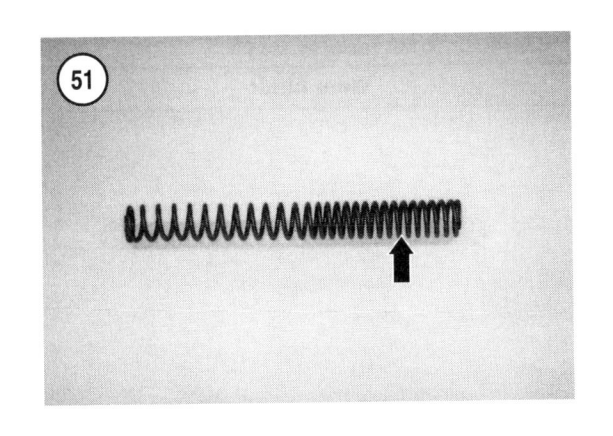

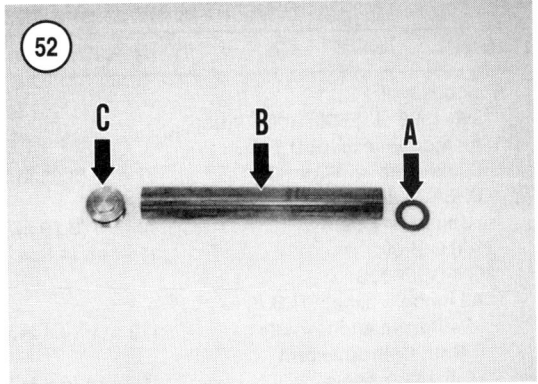

c. Allow the oil to settle completely and recheck the oil level measurement. Adjust the oil level if necessary.

7. Fully extend the fork tube.

8A. On 1995-1999 models, install the fork spring so the end with the closer wound coils (**Figure 51**) is at the top of the fork leg.

8B. On 2000 models, install the fork spring so the end with the closer wound coils (**Figure 51**) is at the bottom of the slider.

9. Install the spring seat (A, **Figure 52**) and the spacer (B, **Figure 52**).

10. Install the fork cap (C, **Figure 52**) while pushing down on the spring. Start the bolt slowly. Do not cross-thread it. Tighten the cap bolt, but do not torque it to specification at this time.

11. Install the fork leg as described in this chapter and tighten the cap bolt to the specified torque listed in **Table 2**.

Table 1 FRONT SUSPENSION SPECIFICATIONS

Item	Specification	Wear Limit
Front fork stroke	130 mm (5.12 in.)	–
Fork spring free length service limit		
1995-1999 models	–	281 mm (11.1 in.)
2000 models		
GSF600	–	358 mm (14.1 in.)
GSF600S	–	356 mm (14.0 in.)
Fork oil viscosity	Suzuki #10 or equivalent fork oil	–
Fork oil capacity (per leg)		
1995-1999 GSF600 models	521 ml (17.6. U.S. oz., 18.3 Imp. oz.)	–
1996-1999 GSF600S models		
All models except U.S.A., California and Canada	521 ml (17.6. U.S. oz., 18.3 Imp. oz.)	–
U.S.A., California and Canada models	522 ml (17.7 U.S. oz., 18.4 Imp. oz.)	–
2000 GSF600 models	508 ml (17.18 US oz., 17.9 Imp. oz.)	
2000 GSF600S models		
U.S.A., California and Canada models	506 ml (17.11 U.S. oz., 17.8 Imp. oz.)	–
All models except U.S.A., California and Canada	510 ml (17.24 U.S. oz., 18.0 Imp. oz.)	–
Fork oil level		–
1995-1999 GSF600 models	97 mm (3.82 in.)	–
1996-1999 GSF600S		

(continued)

Table 1 FRONT SUSPENSION SPECIFICATIONS (continued)

Item	Specification	Wear Limit
Fork oil level		
1996-1999 GSF600S (continued)		
All models except U.S.A., California and Canada	97 mm (3.82 in.)	–
U.S.A., California and Canada models	96 mm (3.78 in.)	–
2000 GSF600	114 mm (4.5 in.)	–
2000 GSF600S		
All models except U.S.A., California and Canada	112 mm (4.4 in.)	–
U.S.A., California and Canada models	116 mm (4.6 in.)	–

Table 2 FRONT SUSPENSION AND STEERING TORQUE SPECIFICATIONS

Item	N•m	in.-lb.	ft.-lb.
Axle	65	–	48
Axle pinch bolt	23	–	17
Caliper mounting bolt			
1995-1999 models	25	–	18
2000 models	39	–	29
Damper rod Allen bolt	30	–	22
Fork cap bolt	23	–	17
Handlebar clamp bolt	23	–	17
Lower fork bridge clamp bolts	23	–	17
Master cylinder clamp bolt	10	88	–
Steering stem adjust nut	45	–	33
Steering stem head nut	65	–	48
Upper fork bridge clamp bolt	23	–	17

CHAPTER TWELVE

REAR SUSPENSION

This chapter contains procedures for the removal, disassembly, lubrication and repair of the rear suspension components. Rear wheel removal, rear hub service, tire changing, tire repair and wheel balancing are covered in Chapter Ten.

The rear suspension on the Bandit features the Suzuki link-type suspension, which consists of the swing arm, a single shock absorber and a shock-lever and tie rod assembly. The pivot joints on all components must be disassembled, inspected and lubricated frequently to provide proper operation of the suspension as well as maximum service life.

The swing arm is supported by a caged roller bearing on each side where the pivot mounts to the frame. The lower end of the shock absorber is connected to the swing arm via the shock linkage.

When inspecting rear suspension components, compare all measurements to the rear suspension specifications listed in **Table 1**. Replace any component that is damaged, worn to the wear limit or out of specification. During assembly, tighten fasteners to the torque specifications listed in **Table 2**. **Table 1** and **Table 2** appear at the end of the chapter.

SHOCK ABSORBER

Removal/Installation

1. Securely support the motorcycle. If a motorcycle stand or jack is not available, use wooden block(s) under the engine to support the motorcycle so the rear wheel is off the ground.

2. Remove the rear wheel as described in Chapter Ten.

3. Remove the muffler as described in Chapter Eight.

4. Remove the lower shock mounting nut (A, **Figure 1**).

5. Remove the lower shock mounting bolt (A, **Figure 2**) and separate the shock absorber from the shock lever.

6. Support the swing arm and remove the lower tie rod nut (B, **Figure 1**).

7. Remove the lower tie rod bolt (B, **Figure 2**) and lower the swing arm to the floor. On 2000 models, do not lose the washer between each tie rod and the shock lever.

8. Remove the upper shock mounting nut (A, **Figure 3**).

9. Remove the upper shock mounting bolt (B, **Figure 3**), lower the shock absorber from the shock bracket in the frame and remove the shock absorber from the hole in the swing arm.

10. Inspect the shock absorber as described in this chapter.

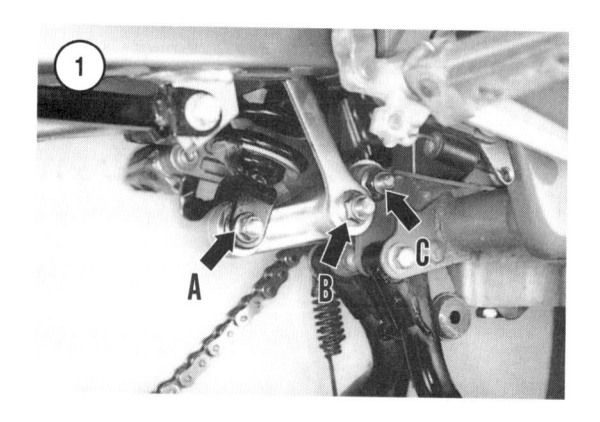

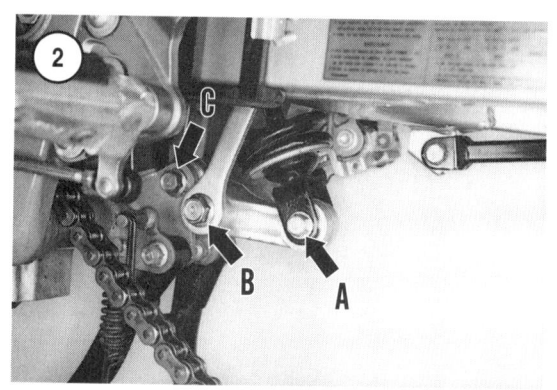

Installation

1. Clean the mounting bolts and nuts in solvent and dry them thoroughly.

2. Apply a light coat of waterproof grease to the shock absorber upper and lower mounts.

3. On 1999-2000 models, position the shock so the index line (A, **Figure 4**) on the lower shock mount faces rearward.

4. Fit the shock absorber through the hole in the swing arm and then lift the shock into place in the frame.

5. Carefully align the upper mounting hole with the shock absorber bracket in the frame.

6. Install the upper shock mounting bolt (B, **Figure 3**) from the left side of the motorcycle and then install the nut (A, **Figure 3**). Finger-tighten the nut at this time.

7. Raise the swing arm and support it so the shock lever is easily accessible.

8. Align the rear mount on the shock lever with the shock absorber lower mount. Install the lower shock mounting bolt (A, **Figure 2**) from the left side and install the nut (A, **Figure 1**). Finger-tighten the nut at this time.

9. Raise or lower the swing arm as necessary to align the tie rods with the center mount on the shock lever. On 2000 models, install a washer between each tie rod and the shock lever.

10. Install the lower tie rod bolt (B, **Figure 2**) from the left side and then install the nut (B, **Figure 1**).

11. Tighten the upper shock mounting nut, the lower shock mounting nut and tie rod nut to their respective torque specifications in **Table 2**.

12. Install the rear wheel as described in Chapter Ten.

13. Install the muffler as described in Chapter Eight.

REAR SUSPENSION

2. Check the spring (A, **Figure 5**) for cracks or other damage.
3. Check the upper (B, **Figure 5**) and lower spring seats (A, **Figure 6**) for cracks or looseness.
4. Inspect the shock absorber upper mount bushing (C, **Figure 5**) for elongation, cracks or other damage.
5. Inspect the shock absorber lower mount (B, **Figure 6**) for elongation, cracks or other damage.
6. If any damage is noted, replace the shock absorber.

SHOCK LEVER ASSEMBLY

Removal

Refer to **Figure 7**.
1. Remove the rear wheel as described in Chapter Ten.
2. Remove the muffler as described in Chapter Eight.
3. Remove the lower shock mounting nut (A, **Figure 1**) and pull out the lower shock mounting bolt (A, **Figure 2**). Separate the shock absorber from the shock lever.
4. Support the swing arm so it will remain up when the lower tie rod bolt is removed.
5. Remove the lower tie rod nut (B, **Figure 1**) and pull the lower tie rod bolt (B, **Figure 2**) from the assembly. Do not lose the washer that sits between each tie rod and the shock lever.
6. Remove the shock lever mounting nut (C, **Figure 1**).
7. Remove the shock lever mounting bolt (C, **Figure 2**) and lower the shock lever from the frame.
8. Inspect the shock lever as described below.
9. Installation is the reverse of removal. Pay attention to the following:
   a. Apply Suzuki Super Grease A or an equivalent waterproof grease to the bearings in the shock lever. Also apply grease to the pivot points on the lower shock mount and on the frame mounting boss.
   b. Make sure the collars are in place on the shock lever and install the three pivot bolts from the left side.
   c. On 2000 models, install a washer between each tie rod and the shock lever.
   d. Install the three mounting nuts finger-tight

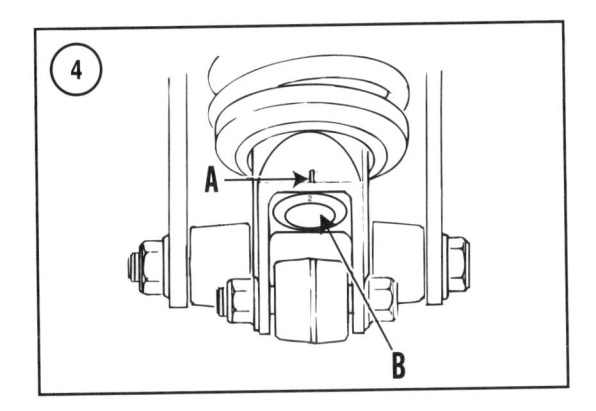

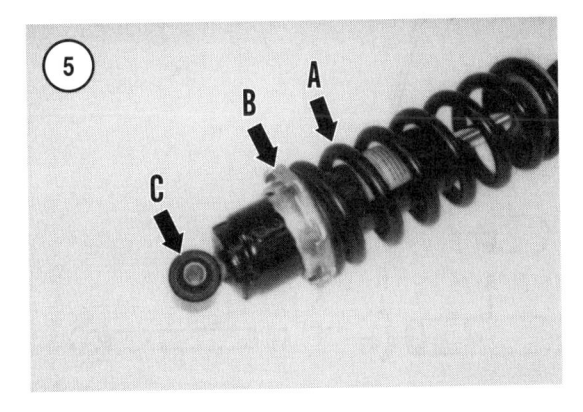

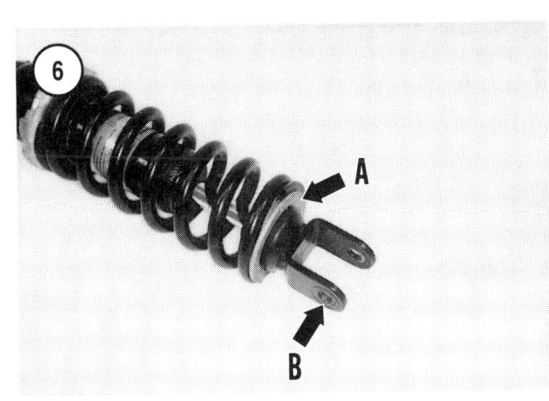

14. Take the motorcycle off the jack or stand and push down on the rear of the motorcycle to make sure the linkage is operating correctly with no binding.

Inspection

Replacement parts are not available for the original equipment shock absorber. If any part of the shock absorber is faulty, replace it.
1. Inspect the shock absorber for oil leaks.

SHOCK LEVER ASSEMBLY

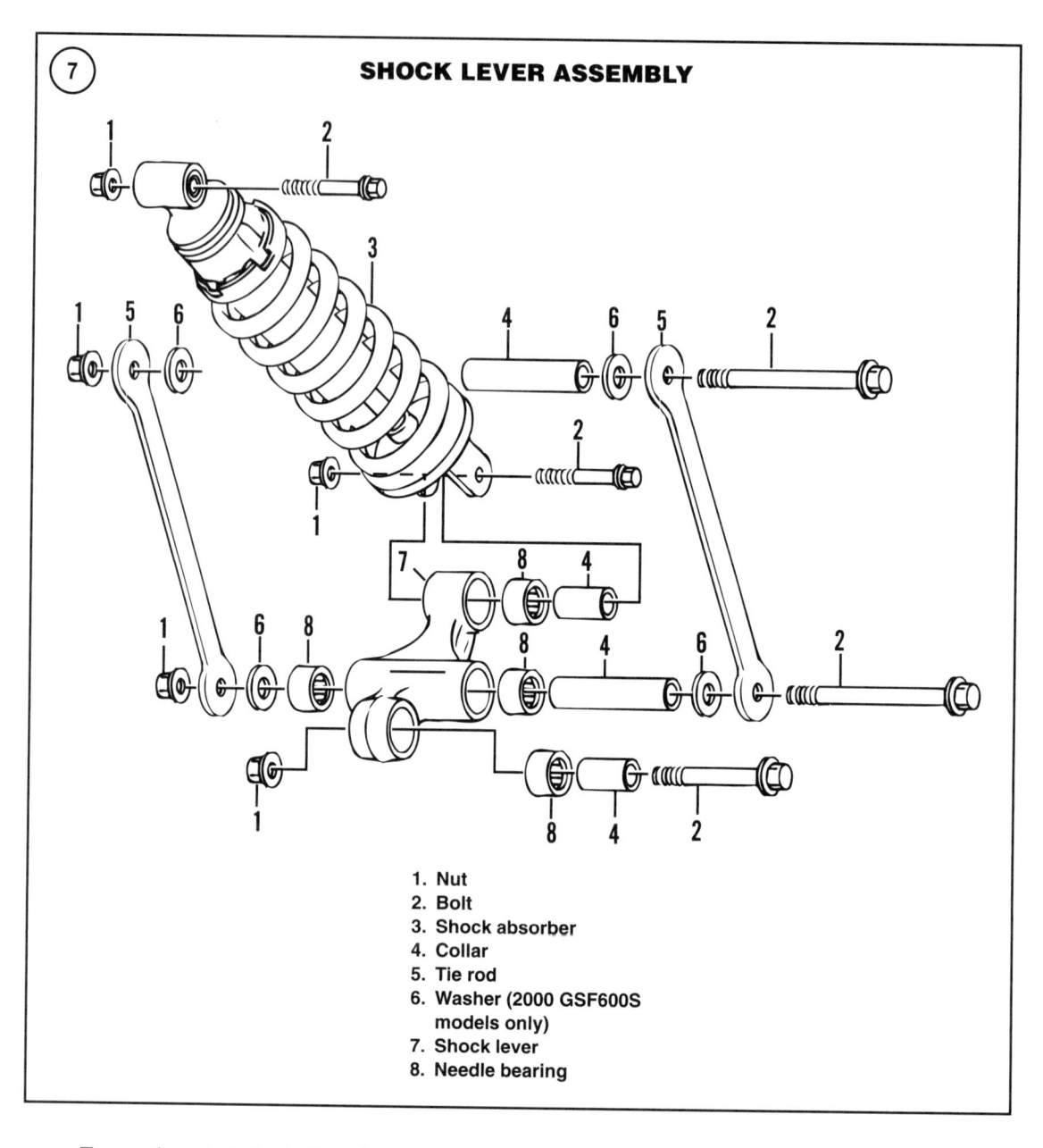

1. Nut
2. Bolt
3. Shock absorber
4. Collar
5. Tie rod
6. Washer (2000 GSF600S models only)
7. Shock lever
8. Needle bearing

e. Torque the nuts to the indicated torque specification (**Table 2**) in the following order: first, torque the lower tie rod mounting nut (B, **Figure 1**), next torque the lower shock mounting nut (A, **Figure 1**) and finally torque the shock lever mounting nut (C, **Figure 1**).

Inspection

1. Inspect the shock lever pivot bearings as follows:

a. Remove the pivot collars (**Figure 8**) from the shock lever.

b. Use a clean lint-free rag and wipe off surface grease from the needle bearings (**Figure 9**) in the shock lever.

c. Turn each bearing by hand. The bearing should turn smoothly without excessive play or noise. Check the rollers for evidence of wear, pitting or rust.

d. Reinstall the pivot collars into the bearings and slowly rotate each pivot collar. Each col-

REAR SUSPENSION

5. Clean the pivot bolts and nuts in solvent. Check the bolts for straightness. If a bolt is bent, it will restrict the movement of the rocker arm.

6. Prior to installing the pivot collars, coat the inner surface of the bearings with Suzuki Super Grease A or an equivalent waterproof bearing grease.

SWING ARM

Swing Arm Bearing Preliminary Inspection

The condition of the swing arm bearings can greatly affect the handling of the motorcycle. Worn bearings will cause wheel hop, pulling to one side under acceleration and pulling to the other side during braking. To check the condition of the swing arm bearings, perform the following procedure.

1. Remove the rear wheel as described in this chapter.
2. Remove the tie rod mounting nut (B, **Figure 1**) and bolt (B, **Figure 2**), and separate the tie rods from the shock lever. The tie rods do not have to be completely removed.

NOTE
On 2000 models, do not lose the washer between each tie rod and the shock lever.

3. The swing arm is now free to move under its own weight.
4. Make sure the swing arm pivot nut (**Figure 10**) on the right side is tight.

NOTE
Have an assistant steady the motorcycle when performing Step 5 and Step 6.

5. Grasp both ends of the swing arm and attempt to move it from side to side in a horizontal arc. If more than a slight amount of movement is felt, the bearings are worn and must be replaced.
6. Grasp both ends of the swing arm and move it up and down. The swing arm should move smoothly with no binding or abnormal noise from the bearings. If there is binding or noise, the bearings are worn and must be replaced.
7. Move the swing arm and the tie rods into position. Install the rear tie rod bolt from the left side. Install the tie rod nut and tighten it to the torque specification listed in **Table 2**.
8. Install the rear wheel as described in this chapter.

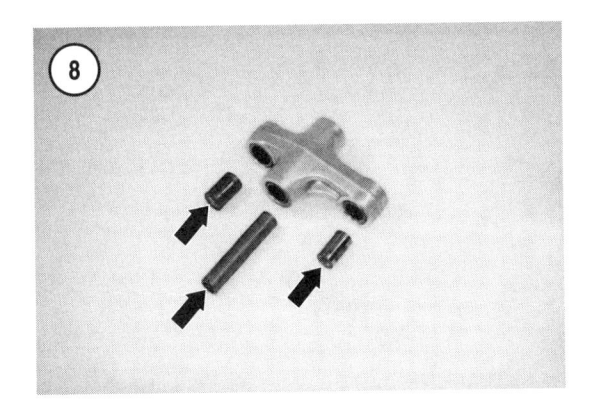

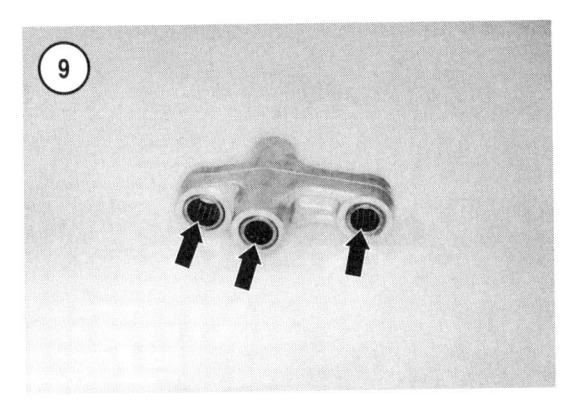

lar must turn smoothly without excessive play or noise.

  e. If the needle bearings must be replaced, refer to *Shock Lever Needle Bearing Replacement* in this chapter.

2. Inspect the pivot collars (**Figure 8**) for wear and damage. Replace each collar as necessary.

3. Inspect the shock lever for cracks or damage. Replace as necessary.

4. If removed, inspect the tie rods for bending, cracks or damage. Replace as necessary.

SWING ARM

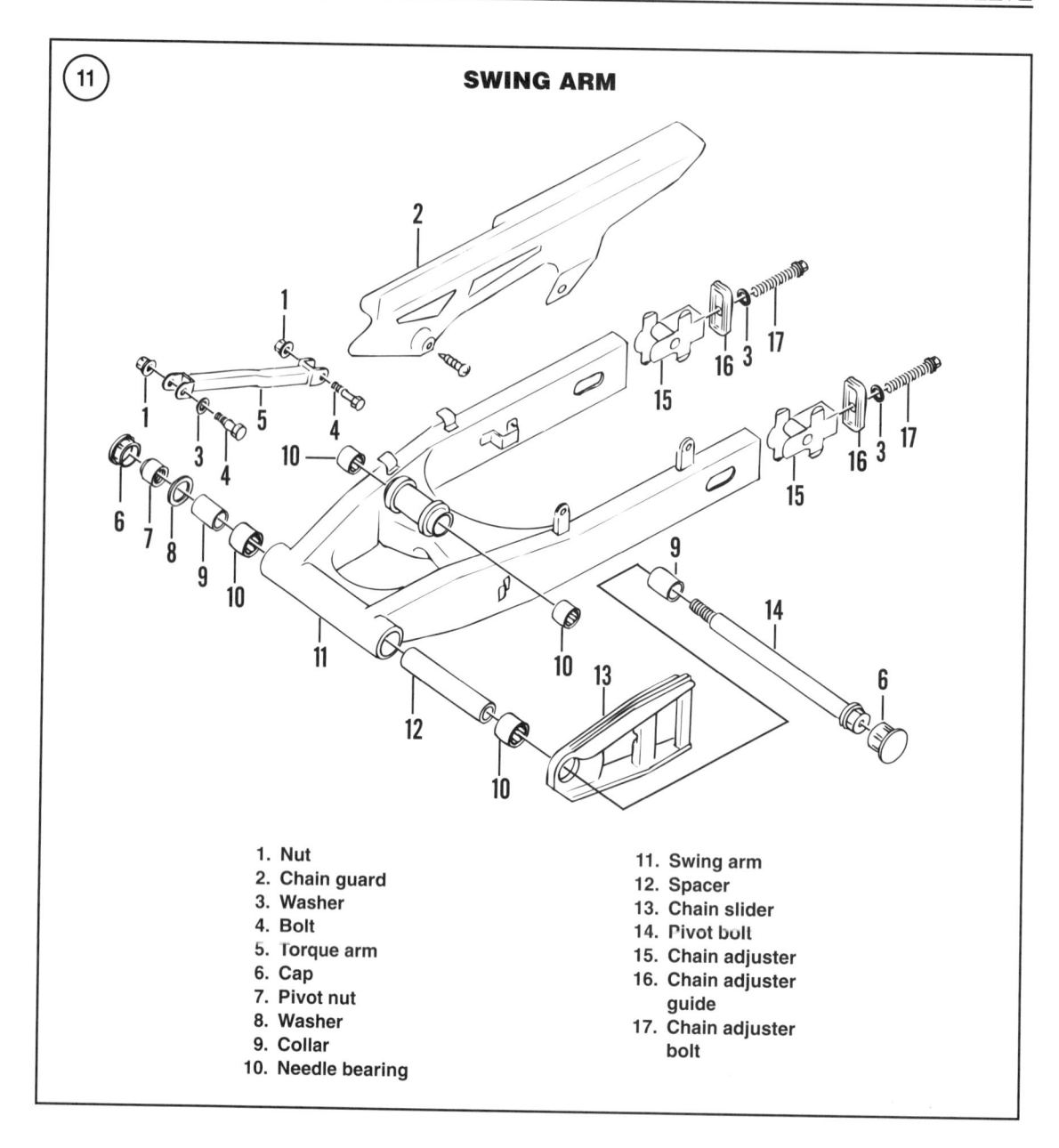

1. Nut
2. Chain guard
3. Washer
4. Bolt
5. Torque arm
6. Cap
7. Pivot nut
8. Washer
9. Collar
10. Needle bearing
11. Swing arm
12. Spacer
13. Chain slider
14. Pivot bolt
15. Chain adjuster
16. Chain adjuster guide
17. Chain adjuster bolt

Removal

Refer to **Figure 11**.

1. Remove the rear wheel as described in Chapter Ten.
2. Remove the muffler as described in Chapter Eight. Wrap a plastic bag around the exhaust pipe to keep contaminants out of the exhaust system.
3. Remove the mounting screws (A, **Figure 12**) and the chain guard (B, **Figure 12**) from the swing arm.
4. Remove the brake hose (A, **Figure 13**) from the rear caliper. Place the loose end of the brake hose in a recloseable plastic bag and close the bag.

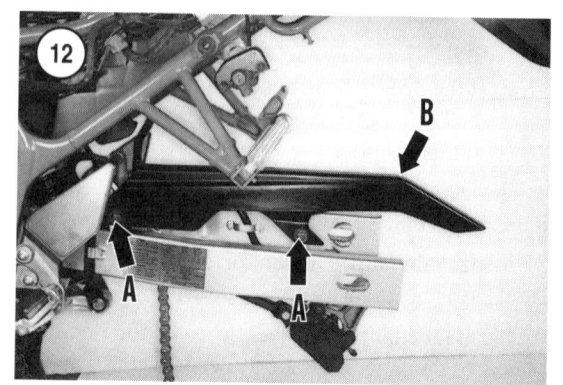

REAR SUSPENSION

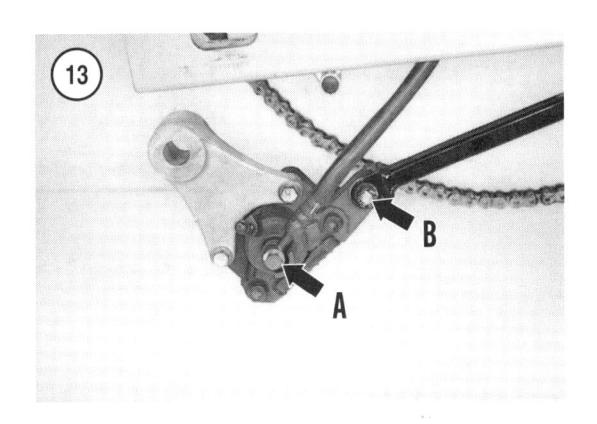

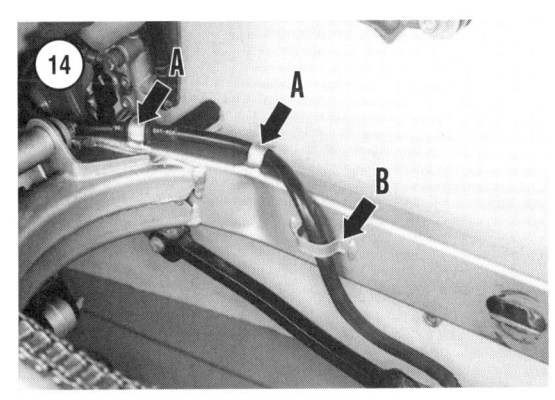

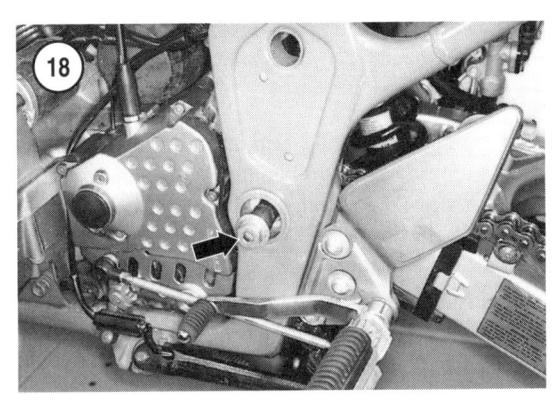

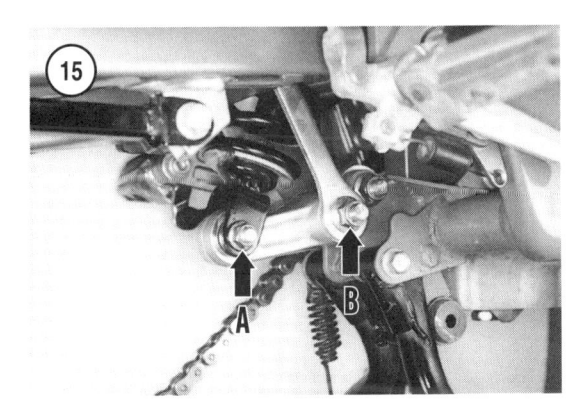

5. Remove the torque arm bolt (B, **Figure 13**) and set the rear brake caliper aside.
6. Unhook the brake hose from the two clamps (A, **Figure 14**) on top of the swing arm.
7. Carefully pull the rear of the brake hose out from the guide (B, **Figure 14**) on the inner surface of the swing arm and remove the brake hose.
8. Remove the lower shock mounting nut (A, **Figure 15**) and the lower shock mounting bolt (A, **Figure 16**).
9. Support the swing arm with a box or wooden blocks.
10. Remove the lower tie rod nut (B, **Figure 15**) and pull the tie rod bolt (B, **Figure 16**) from the left side of the motorcycle. Separate the tie rods from the shock lever. On 2000 models, do not lose the washer between each tie rod and the shock lever.
11. Remove the caps from the swing arm pivot bolt.
12. Remove the pivot nut and washer (**Figure 17**) from the right side.
13. Carefully tap the pivot bolt into the right side of the frame and then pull the bolt (**Figure 18**) from the left side of the frame.
14. Lower the swing arm from the frame and remove it.

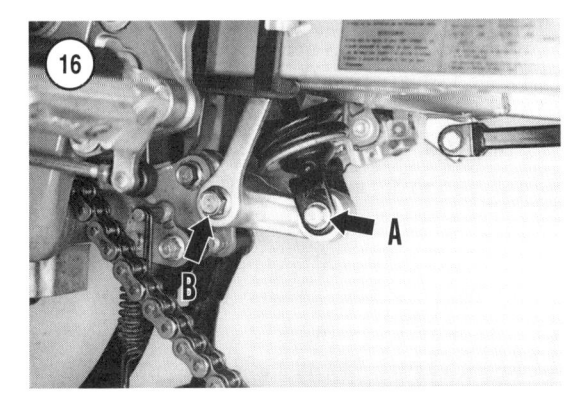

15. If the swing arm bearings are not going to be serviced, place a strip of duct tape over each pivot. This will protect the bearing assemblies and prevent the loss of any small parts.
16. Inspect the swing arm as described in this chapter. Lubricate all bearings as described in this chapter.

Installation

NOTE
Have an assistant available before starting swing arm installation. The swing arm can be installed by one person, but the job is much easier with help.

1. Lubricate the swing arm and shock lever bearings, the pivot bolts and collars with Suzuki Super Grease A or an equivalent waterproof grease prior to installation.
2. Install the chain slider onto the swing arm. Make sure the slider is secured beneath the notch (**Figure 19**) on the side of the swing arm.
3. Secure the rear brake hose above the swing arm mount in the frame so the hose will not be pinched by the swing arm.
4. Insert the left arm of the swing arm between the drive chain runs and set the swing arm in place beneath the frame. Check that the chain properly engages the engine sprocket.
5. Raise the swing arm so the shock absorber passes through the hole in the swing arm and fit the swing arm pivot between the mounts in the frame.
6. From the left side of the motorcycle, install the swing arm pivot bolt (**Figure 18**) through the frame and the swing arm pivot.
7. Install the washer and pivot nut (**Figure 17**) onto the end of the pivot bolt. Torque the swing arm pivot nut to the specification in **Table 2**.
8. Grab the end of each arm, and raise and lower the swing arm. The swing arm should pivot smoothly with no binding or abnormal noise from the bearings.
9. Raise the swing arm until the shock lever sits within the lower shock mount (**Figure 20**).
10. Align the rear mount on the shock lever with the lower shock mount and install the shock mounting bolt (A, **Figure 16**) from the left side. Install and finger-tighten the shock mounting nut (A, **Figure 15**).

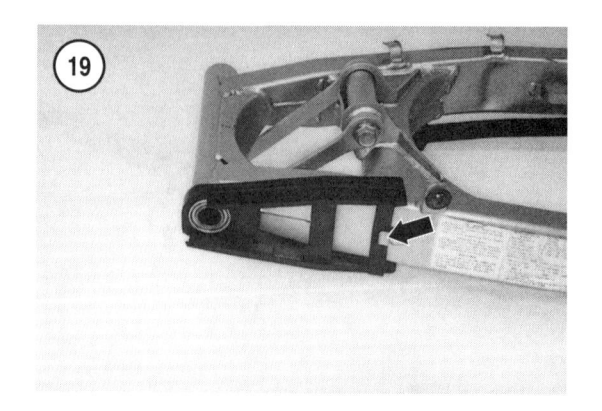

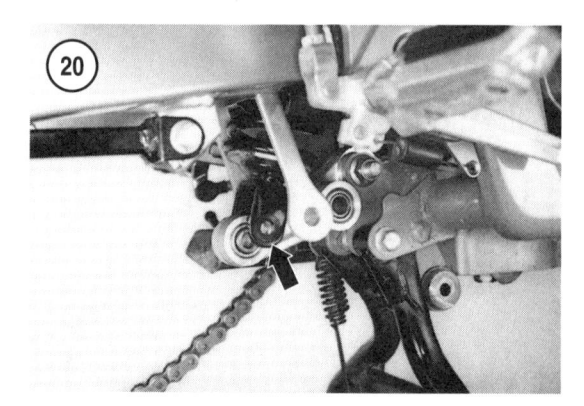

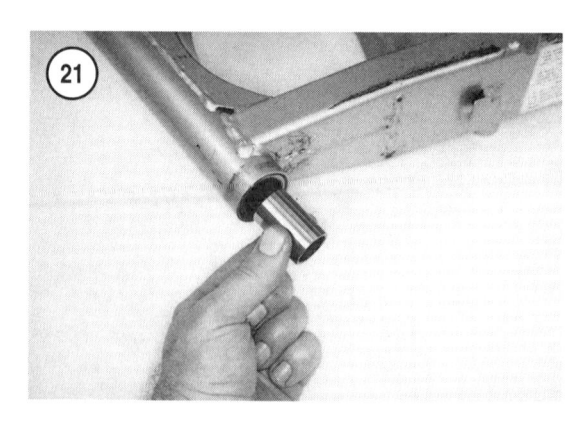

11. Align the tie rods with the center mount on the shock lever and install the tie rod bolt from the left side (B, **Figure 16**). On 2000 models, install a washer between each tie rod and the shock lever.
12. Install the tie rod mounting nut (B, **Figure 15**). Finger-tighten the nut at this time.
13. Torque the nuts to the specification in **Table 2**. Torque the lower tie rod nut (B, **Figure 15**) and then torque the lower shock absorber nut (A, **Figure 15**).
14. Carefully route the brake hose through the guide (B, **Figure 14**) on the inner surface of the

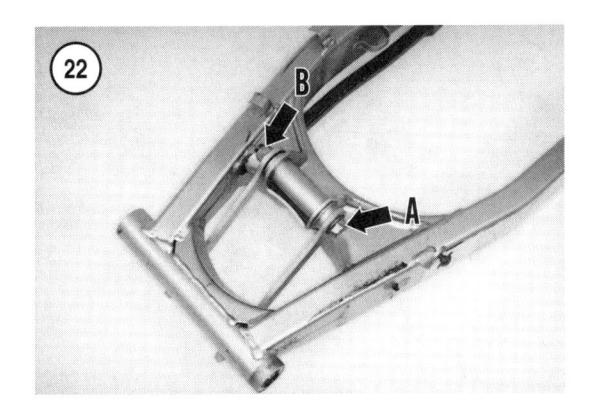

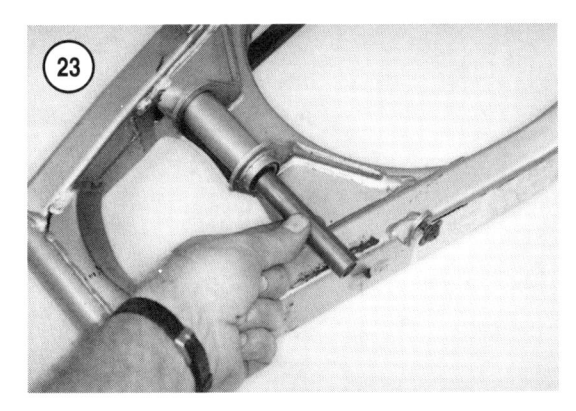

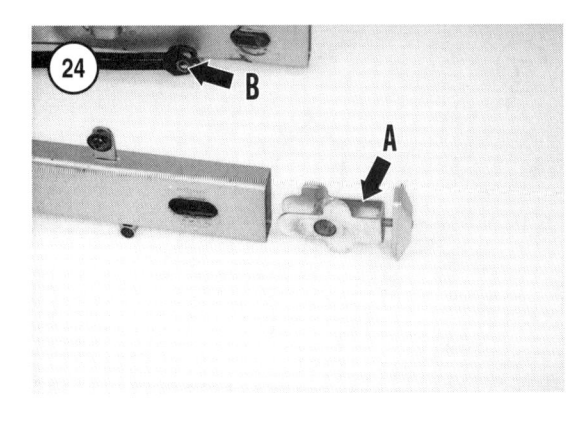

REAR SUSPENSION

17. Install the rear wheel as described in Chapter Ten.
18. Install the muffler as described in Chapter Eight.
19. Adjust the chain as described in Chapter Three.
20. Bleed the brakes as described in Chapter Thirteen.

Disassembly

Refer to **Figure 11**.

1. Remove the swing arm as described in this chapter.
2. Remove the chain slider (**Figure 19**) from the swing arm.
3. Remove the pivot collar (**Figure 21**) from the needle bearing on each side of the swing arm pivot boss.

> *NOTE*
> *The tie rods are symmetrical and can be installed on either side of the shock lever. After prolonged use, they develop a unique wear pattern. Prior to removing the tie rods, mark them with an L (left) or R (right) so they can be reinstalled in their original positions.*

4. Remove the tie rod mounting nut (B, **Figure 22**) and pull the tire rod bolt (A, **Figure 22**) from the mounting boss. Lift the tie rods from the hole in the swing arm. On 2000 models, do not lose the washer between each tie rod and the mounting boss.
5. Remove the pivot collar (**Figure 23**) from the tie rod mounting boss.
6. If necessary, remove each chain adjuster (A, **Figure 24**) and the torque arm (B, **Figure 24**) from the swing arm.
7. Inspect the swing arm as described below in this chapter.

swing arm and secure the brake hose beneath the two clamps (A, **Figure 14**) on top of the swing arm.

15. Install the torque arm and the brake hose onto the rear caliper. Install new sealing washers on either side of the brake hose fitting as described in Chapter Thirteen. Torque the banjo bolt (A, **Figure 13**) and the torque arm nut (B, **Figure 13**) to specification.
16. Install the chain guard (B, **Figure 12**) onto the swing arm. Tighten the mounting screws securely (A, **Figure 12**).

Assembly

1. If removed, install the chain adjusters (A, **Figure 24**) and torque arm (B, **Figure 24**) onto the swing arm. Install the forward torque arm bolt and nut. Torque the nut to the specification in **Table 2**.
2. Lubricate the needle bearings and collars with Suzuki Super Grease A or an equivalent waterproof bearing grease.

3. Install the pivot collar into the tie rod mounting boss (**Figure 23**) on the swing arm. Make sure the ends of the collar are flush with the end of each needle bearing.

4. Install the tie rods onto the swing arm by performing the following:
   a. Refer to the marks made prior to removal and reinstall each tie rod onto its original side (left or right).
   b. Position the tie rods so they point down through the hole in the swing arm.
   c. Align the tie rods with the mounting boss on the swing arm and install the tie rod bolt (A, **Figure 22**) from the left side of the swing arm.
   d. On 2000 models, make sure a washer sits between each tie rod and the pivot boss.
   e. Install the tie rod mounting nut (B, **Figure 22**). Torque the nut to the specification in **Table 2**.

5. Install the collar (**Figure 21**) into the needle bearing on each side of the swing arm pivot boss.

6. Install the chain slider onto the left side of the swing arm. Be sure the slider is secured beneath the tab (**Figure 19**).

7. Install the swing arm assembly as described in this chapter.

Inspection

1. Wash the bolts and collars in solvent and thoroughly dry them.

2. Inspect the pivot collars (**Figure 25**) for wear, scratches or score marks.

3. Check the bolts for straightness. If a bolt is bent it will restrict the movement of the swing arm.

4. Inspect the needle bearings by performing the following:
   a. Use a clean lint-free rag and wipe off surface grease from the pivot area of the needle bearing.
   b. Turn the bearing (A, **Figure 26**) by hand. The bearing should turn smoothly without excessive play or noise. Check the rollers for evidence of wear, pitting or rust.
   c. Insert the collar (**Figure 21**) into the bearings and slowly rotate the collar. The collars must turn smoothly without excessive play or noise.
   d. Repeat this procedure for each bearing in the swing arm pivot boss and in the tie rod mounting boss.

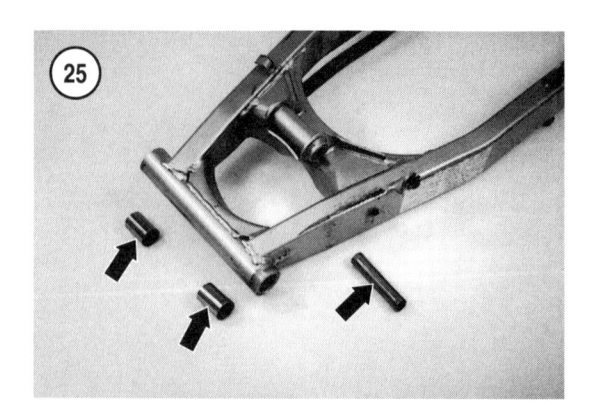

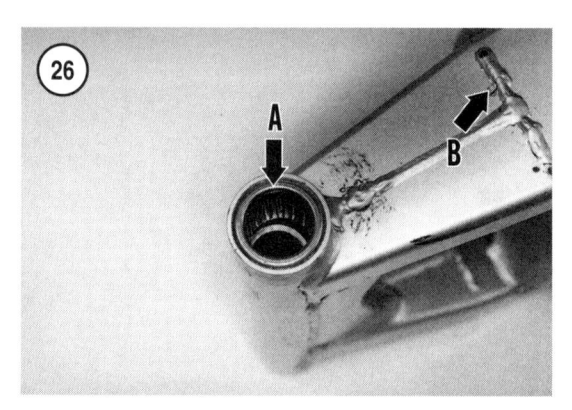

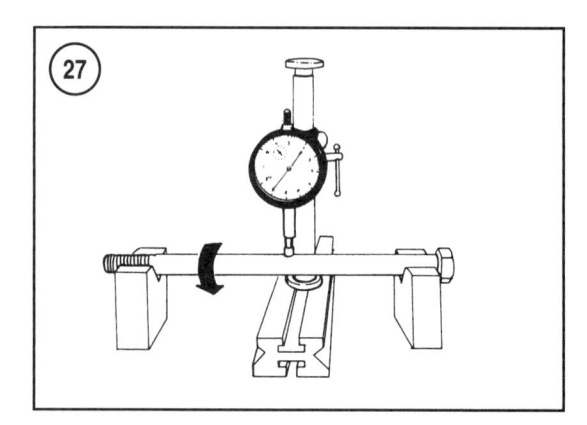

5. Replace any worn or damaged needle bearing as described in this chapter.

6. Check the welds (B, **Figure 26**) on the swing arm for cracks or fractures.

7. Inspect each drive chain adjuster assembly (A, **Figure 24**).

8. Check the pivot bolt for straightness with V-blocks and a dial indicator (**Figure 27**). Replace the pivot bolt if its runout equals or exceeds the wear limit specified in **Table 1**.

9. Inspect the tie rods (**Figure 28**) for wear or damage.

REAR SUSPENSION

Use Suzuki Super Grease A or an equivalent waterproof bearing grease when grease is called for in this procedure.

NOTE
If the needle bearings are replaced, replace the pivot collars at the same time. Always replace these parts as a set.

1. If still installed, remove the pivot collars from the needle bearings.
2. Insert the Suzuki bearing puller (part No. 09923-74510) or an equivalent blind bearing puller through the needle bearing and expand it behind the bearing.
3. Using sharp strokes of the slide hammer, withdraw the needle bearing from the pivot boss.
4. Remove the bearing puller and the bearing.
5. Withdraw the spacer located between the bearings in the swing arm pivot bore.
6. Repeat Steps 2-4 for the bearing on the other side.
7. Thoroughly clean out the inside of the pivot bore with solvent and dry it with compressed air.
8. Apply a light coat of grease to the exterior of the new bearings, the spacer and to the inner circumference of the pivot bore. This will make bearing installation easier.
9. Install the spacer into the pivot bore.

NOTE
Install one needle bearing at a time. Make sure the bearing enters the pivot boss squarely, otherwise the bearing and the pivot boss may be damaged.

10. Position the bearing with the manufacturer's marks facing out.

NOTE
*The bearing can be easily installed using a homemade tool consisting of a piece of threaded rod, two thick washers, two nuts, a socket that matches the outer race diameter, and two wrenches as shown in **Figure 30**.*

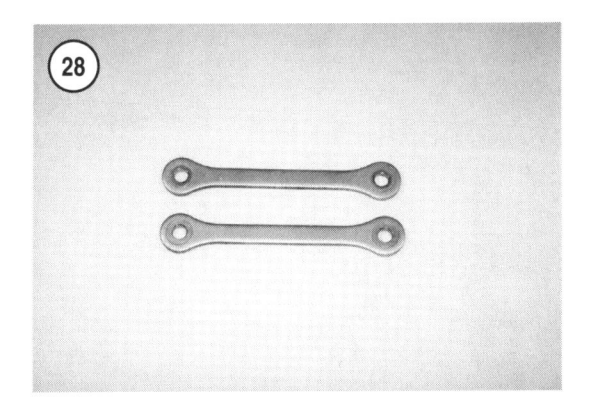

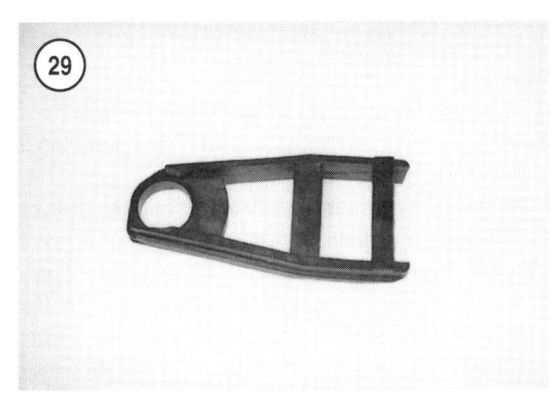

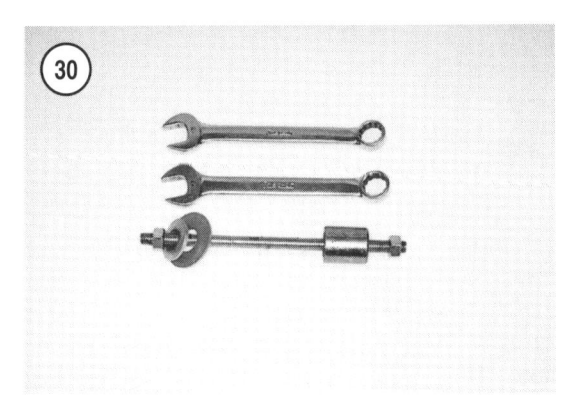

10. Inspect the drive chain slider (**Figure 29**) for wear, cracks or other signs of damage.

BEARING REPLACEMENT

Swing Arm Needle Bearing Replacement

Do not remove the swing arm needle bearings unless they must be replaced. The needle bearings are pressed onto the swing arm. A blind bearing puller is required to remove the needle bearings. The needle bearings can be installed with a homemade tool.

11. Locate and square the new bearing in the pivot bore. Assemble the homemade tool through the

pivot bore so the socket presses against the bearing. See **Figure 31**.

12. Hold the nut adjacent to the socket. Tighten the nut on the opposite side and pull the bearing into the pivot bore until the bearing is flush with the outer surface of the bore (A, **Figure 26**).
13. Disassemble the tool.
14. Reinstall the tool on the opposite side and then repeat Steps 9-13 and install the other bearing.
15. Make sure the bearings are properly seated. Turn each bearing by hand. It should turn smoothly.
16. Lubricate the new bearings with grease.
17. If necessary, replace the bearings in the tie rod pivot boss on the top of the swing arm by repeating this procedure.

Shock Lever Needle Bearing Replacement

Do not remove the shock lever needle bearings unless they must be replaced. The needle bearings are pressed onto the shock lever. A blind bearing puller is required to remove the needle bearings. The needle bearings can be installed with a homemade tool, or socket and hammer.

Use Suzuki Super Grease A or an equivalent waterproof bearing grease when grease is called for in this procedure.

NOTE
If the needle bearings are replaced, replace the pivot collars at the same time. Always replace these parts as a set.

1. If still installed, remove the pivot collars.
2. Insert the Suzuki bearing puller (part No. 09923-73210) or equivalent through the needle bearing and expand it behind the front bearing.
3. Using sharp strokes of the slide hammer, withdraw the needle bearing from the front pivot hole.

NOTE
Three different-sized bearings are used in the shock lever. Mark the bearings front, center and rear as they are removed. The center two bearings are identical.

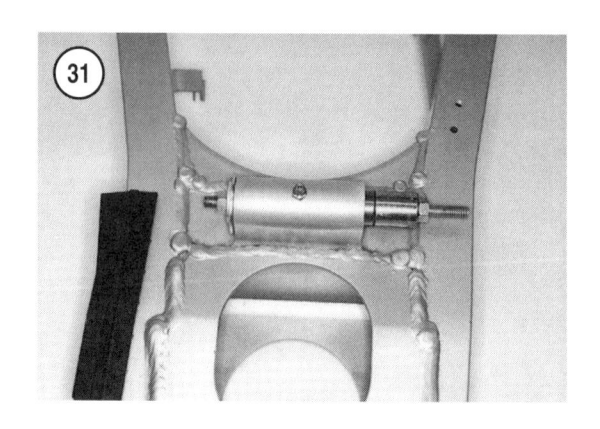

4. Remove the special tool and the bearing.
5. At the center pivot area, repeat Step 2 and Step 3 for the bearing on each side.
6. Repeat Step 2 and Step 3 for the rear bearing.
7. Thoroughly clean out the inside of the pivot bores with solvent. Dry them with compressed air.
8. Apply a light coat of grease to the exterior of the new bearings and to the inner circumference of the pivot bores. This will make bearing installation easier.
9. Locate and square the new bearing in the pivot bore.

NOTE
*Use the homemade tool shown in **Figure 30**, an appropriate size drift or a socket to install the bearings.*

10. Install the bearings with an appropriate size drift or socket that matches the outer race diameter. Tap the bearings into place.
11. Check that the bearing is properly seated in the bore. Turn each bearing by hand. The bearing should turn smoothly.
12. Lubricate the needles of the new bearing with grease.
13. Repeat for the other bearings.
14. Prior to installing the pivot collars, coat the inner surface of the bearings with grease. Install the pivot collars as described in this chapter.

REAR SUSPENSION

Table 1 REAR SUSPENSION SPECIFICATIONS

Item	Specification
Rear wheel travel	
1995	121 mm (4.8 in.)
2000 models	126 mm (5.0 in.)
Swing arm pivot bolt runout wear limit	0.3 mm (0.01 in.)

Table 2 REAR SUSPENSION TORQUE SPECIFICATIONS

Item	N•m	in.-lb.	ft.-lb.
Brake hose banjo bolt (front and rear)	23	–	17
Shock absorber Mounting nut (upper and lower)	50	–	37
Shock lever mounting nut		–	
1995-1999	76	–	56
2000	78	–	58
Swing arm pivot nut	100	–	74
Tie rod nut			
1995-1999			
Lower (tie rod to shock lever mount)	76	–	56
Upper (tie rod to swing arm mount)	76	–	56
2000 models			
Lower (tie rod to shock lever mount)	78	–	58
Upper (tie rod to swing arm mount)	78	–	58
Torque arm bolt/nut	35		26

CHAPTER THIRTEEN

BRAKES

This chapter covers service, repair and replacement procedures for the front and rear brake systems. Brake specifications are located in **Table 1** and **Table 2** at the end of this chapter.

The brake system consists of dual discs up front and a single disc mounted in the rear.

BRAKE SERVICE

The disc brake system transmits hydraulic pressure from the master cylinders to the brake calipers. This pressure is transmitted from the caliper(s) to the brake pads, which grip both sides of the brake disc(s) and slow the motorcycle. As the pads wear, the pistons move out of the caliper bores to automatically compensate for wear. As this occurs the fluid level in the reservoir goes down. This must be compensated for by occasionally adding fluid.

The proper operation of this system depends on a supply of clean brake fluid (DOT 4) and a clean work environment when any service is being performed. Any tiny particle of debris that enters the system can damage the components and cause poor brake performance.

Brake fluid is hygroscopic (easily absorbs moisture) and moisture in the system will reduce brake performance. It is a good idea to purchase brake fluid in small containers and discard any small quantities that remain. Small quantities of fluid will quickly absorb the moisture in the container. Use only fluid clearly marked DOT 4. If possible, use the same brand of fluid. Do not replace the fluid

BRAKES

FRONT **REAR**

(1)

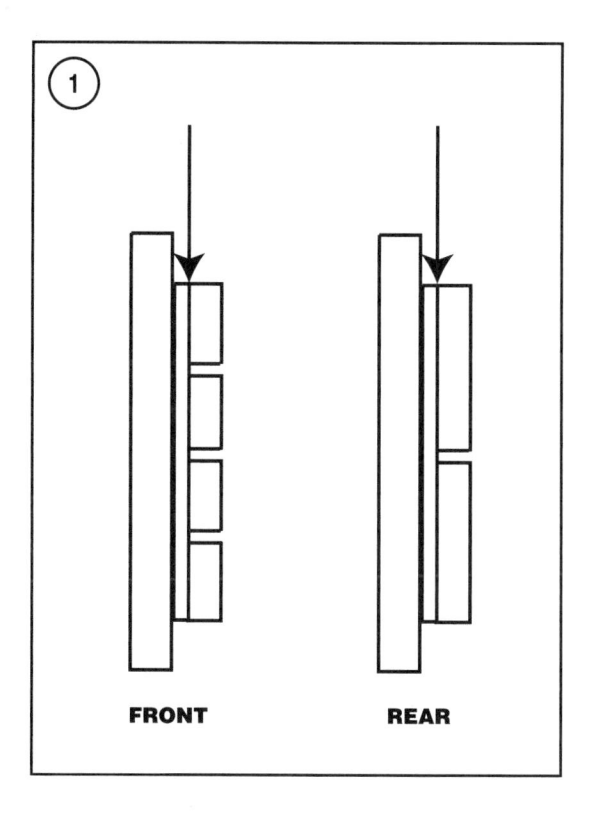

with DOT 5 (silicone) fluid. It is not possible to remove all of the old fluid and DOT 5 is not compatible with other types. Silicone type fluids used in systems for which they were not designed will cause internal seals to swell and deteriorate. Do not reuse drained fluid and discard old fluid properly.

Proper service also includes carefully performed procedures. Do not use any sharp tools inside the master cylinders or calipers or on the pistons. Any damage to these components could cause a loss in the systems ability to maintain hydraulic pressure. If there is any doubt about having the ability to correctly and safely service the brake system, have a profession technician perform the task.

Consider the following when servicing the brake system:

1. The hydraulic components rarely require disassembly. Make sure it is necessary.
2. Keep the reservoir covers in place to prevent the entry of moisture and debris.
3. Clean parts with an aerosol brake cleaner or isopropyl alcohol. Never use petroleum based solvents on internal brake system components. They will cause seals to swell and distort.
4. Do not allow brake fluid to contact plastic, painted or plated parts. It will damage the surface.

5. Dispose of brake fluid properly.
6. If the hydraulic system has been opened (not including the reservoir cover) the system must be bled to remove air from the system. Refer to *Bleeding the System* in this chapter.
7. The manufacturer does not provide wear limit specifications for the caliper and master cylinder assemblies. Use good judgement when inspecting these components or consult a professional technician for advice.

WARNING
Do not add to or replace the brake fluid with Silicone (DOT 5) brake fluid. It is not compatible with the system and may cause brake failure.

WARNING
*Whenever working on the brake system, do **not** inhale brake dust. It may contain asbestos, which can cause lung injury and cancer. Wear a face mask that meets OSHA requirements for trapping asbestos particles and wash hands and forearms thoroughly after completing the work.*

WARNING
NEVER use compressed air to clean any part of the brake system. This releases the harmful brake pad dust. Use an aerosol brake cleaner to clean parts when servicing any component still installed on the motorcycle.

FRONT BRAKE PAD REPLACEMENT

Pad wear depends greatly on riding habits and conditions. Check the pads regularly for wear and replace them when the wear indicator reaches the edge of the brake disc. After removal, examine the pads. If either pad is worn to the wear limit (**Figure 1**), replace the brake pads.

To maintain even brake pressure on the disc, always replace both pads in a caliper at the same time. When replacing the front brake pads, replace both pads in *both front brake calipers* at the same time. If any front brake pad is worn to the wear limit, replace all four front brake pads as a set.

CAUTION
Check the pads more frequently as the pad thickness approaches the wear

limit (**Figure 2**). On some pads, the limit line is very close to the metal backing plate. If pad wear happens to be uneven for some reason, the backing plate could come in contact with the disc and cause damage.

NOTE
The brake hose does not need to be disconnected from the caliper during brake pad replacement. If the hose is removed, the brakes must be bled. Disconnect the hose only when servicing the brake caliper.

1. Read the *Brake Service* information at the beginning of this chapter.
2. Place the motorcycle on the centerstand on level ground.
3. To prevent the front brake lever from being applied, place a spacer between the brake lever and the throttle grip and secure it in place. That way, if the brake lever is inadvertently squeezed, the pistons will not be forced out of the cylinders.
4A. On 1995-1999 models, remove the cap (A, **Figure 3**) from the pad bolt and remove the pad bolt (B, **Figure 3**) from the caliper.
4B. On 2000 models, remove the clip (A, **Figure 4**) from the inboard side of the pad pin and remove the pad pin (B, **Figure 4**) from the caliper.
5. Remove both brake pads from the caliper assembly (**Figure 5**).
6. Clean the pad recess and the end of both sets of pistons with a soft brush. Do not use solvent, a wire brush or any hard tool that would damage the cylinders or pistons.
7. Carefully remove any rust or corrosion from the disc.
8. Thoroughly clean any corrosion or road dirt from the pad bolt or from the pad pin and clip.
9. Check the friction surface of the new pads for any debris or manufacturing residue. If necessary, clean the pads with an aerosol brake cleaner.

NOTE
When installing new pads, make sure the friction compound of the new pad is compatible with the disc material. Remove any roughness from the metal backs of the new pads with a fine-cut file and clean them with aerosol brake cleaner.

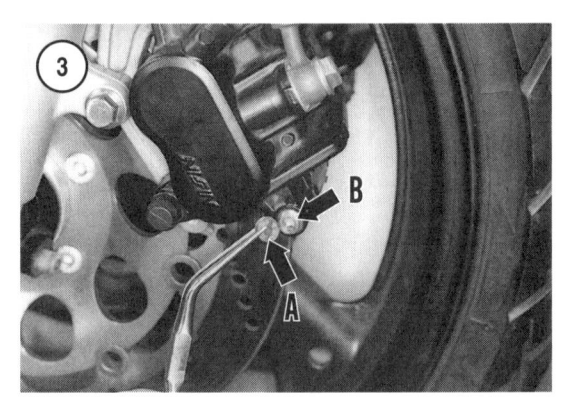

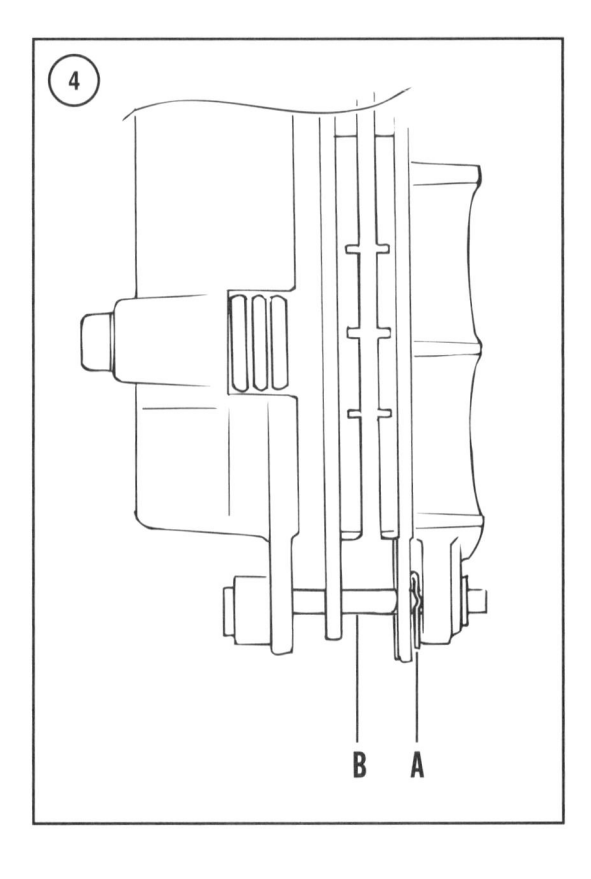

BRAKES

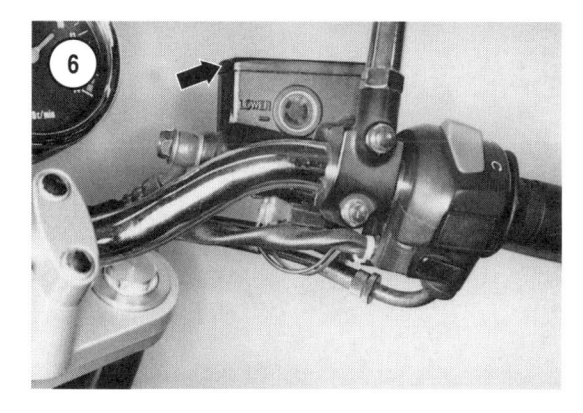

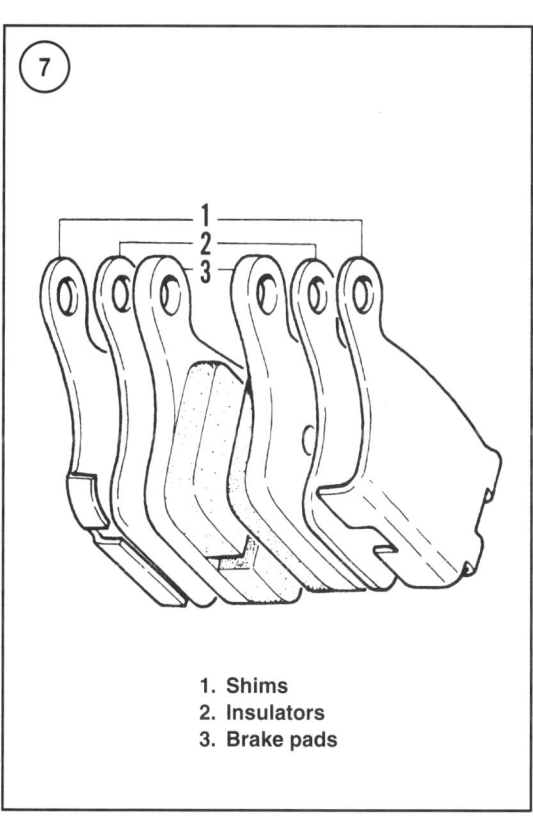

10. Repeat Steps 4-9 and remove the brake pads in the other caliper assembly.

11. When new pads are installed in the calipers, the master cylinder brake fluid level rises as the caliper pistons are repositioned. Perform the following:

   a. Clean all debris from the top of the master cylinder.

   b. Drape a plastic drop cloth over the fairing and other parts beneath the master cylinder to protect them from brake fluid spills.

   c. Remove the top cover (**Figure 6**), diaphragm plate and diaphragm from the master cylinder reservoir.

   d. Temporarily install the old outboard brake pads into the caliper. Seat the pad between the pistons and the brake disc.

   e. Grasp the caliper and brake pad with a large pair of slip-joint pliers and squeeze the piston back into the caliper. Pad the caliper with a shop cloth to prevent scuffing it. Repeat for each side until the pistons are completely in the caliper. Constantly check the reservoir and make sure the fluid does not overflow. Draw out excess fluid if necessary.

   f. The pistons should move freely. If they do not, remove and service the caliper as described in this chapter.

   g. Remove the old brake pads.

   h. Repeat this process for the other caliper.

12A. On 1995-1999 models, install the insulator and shim onto the outside of each pad as shown in **Figure 7**.

12B. On 2000 models, make sure the shim is installed on the back of the inboard pad.

13. Install the pads on either side of the disc. Carefully push them into the caliper until they bottom. Make sure the pads engage the guide in the caliper (**Figure 8**).

14A. On 1995-1999 models, install the pad mounting bolt (**Figure 9**). Make sure the bolt passes through both pads. Tighten the bolt to the torque specification in **Table 2**.

14B. On 2000 models, perform the following:

   a. Install the pad pin (B, **Figure 4**) into the caliper. Make sure the pin passes through both pads and emerges on the inboard side of the caliper.

1. Shims
2. Insulators
3. Brake pads

b. Secure the pin in place with the clip. The clip (A, **Figure 4**) must sit between the inboard pad and the caliper.

15. Remove the spacer from the front brake lever.

16. Pump the front brake lever to reposition the brake pads against the brake disc. Roll the motorcycle back and forth and continue to pump the brake lever as many times as it takes to refill the cylinders in the calipers and correctly locate the brake pads against the disc.

WARNING
Use brake fluid clearly marked DOT 4 from a sealed container. Other types may vaporize and cause brake failure. Always use the same brand of brake fluid. Do not intermix brake fluid brands. Many brands are not compatible. Do not intermix silicone based (DOT 5) brake fluid as it can cause brake component damage, leading to brake system failure.

NOTE
To control the small flow of hydraulic fluid, punch a small hole into the seal of a new container of hydraulic (brake) fluid next to the edge of the pour spout. This will help eliminate fluid spillage, especially while adding fluid to the very small reservoir.

17. Refill the master cylinder reservoir, if necessary, to maintain the correct fluid level. Install the diaphragm and plate. Install the top cover and tighten the screws securely.

WARNING
Do not ride the motorcycle before making sure the brakes are operating correctly with full hydraulic advantage. If necessary, bleed the brake as described in this chapter.

18. Bed the pads in gradually for the first two to three days of riding by using only light pressure as much as possible. Immediate hard application will glaze the new pads and greatly reduce the effectiveness of the brake.

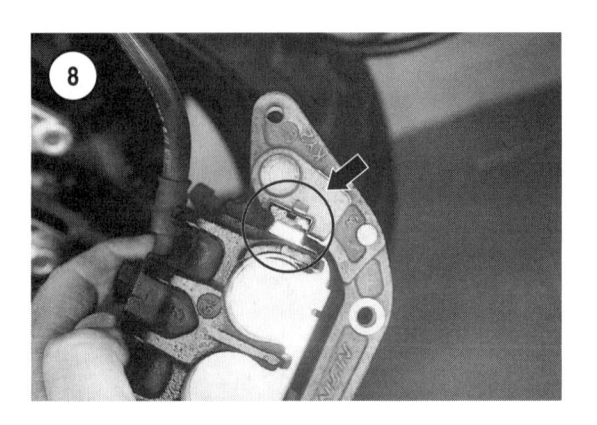

FRONT CALIPER

Removal/Installation

When servicing the front caliper, refer to **Figure 10** for 1995-1999 models. Refer to **Figure 11** for 2000 models.

1. If servicing the left caliper on 1995-1999 models, perform the following:
   a. Remove the bolt (A, **Figure 12**) and remove the speedometer cable guide from the caliper.
   b. Remove the speedometer cable from the speedometer gear and secure the cable out of the way.

CAUTION
Do not spill any brake fluid on the front fork or front wheel. Brake fluid will damage the finish on any plastic, painted or plated surface. Use soapy water to wash off any spilled brake fluid immediately.

2. If the caliper assembly is going to be disassembled for service, perform the following:

BRAKES

FRONT BRAKE CALIPER (1995-1999 MODELS)

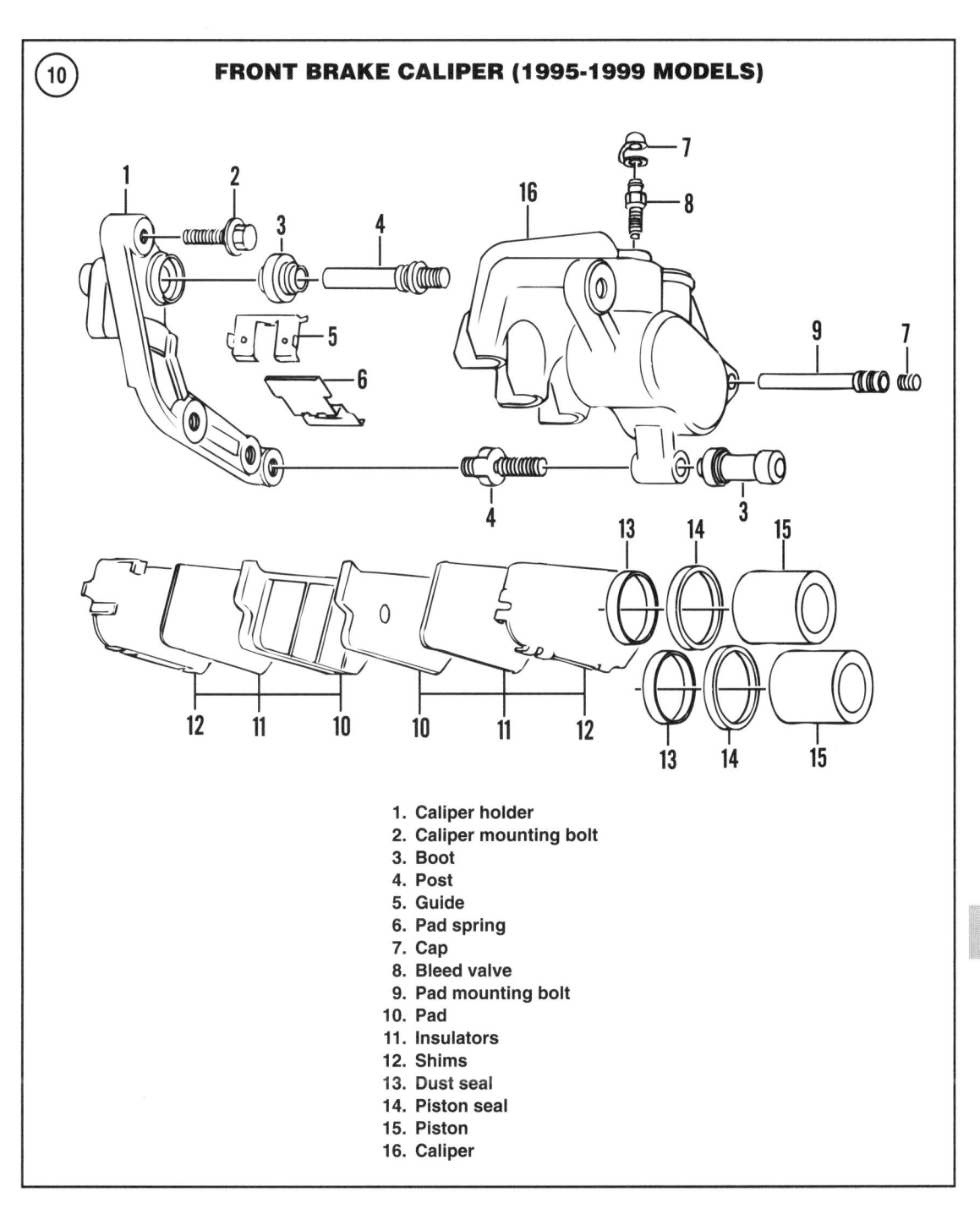

1. Caliper holder
2. Caliper mounting bolt
3. Boot
4. Post
5. Guide
6. Pad spring
7. Cap
8. Bleed valve
9. Pad mounting bolt
10. Pad
11. Insulators
12. Shims
13. Dust seal
14. Piston seal
15. Piston
16. Caliper

a. Remove the brake pads as described in this chapter.

CAUTION
Do not allow the pistons to travel out far enough to come in contact with the brake disc. If this happens, the pistons may scratch or gouge the disc during caliper removal.

NOTE
By performing Step 2b, compressed air may not be necessary for piston removal during caliper disassembly.

CHAPTER THIRTEEN

FRONT BRAKE CALIPER (2000 MODELS)

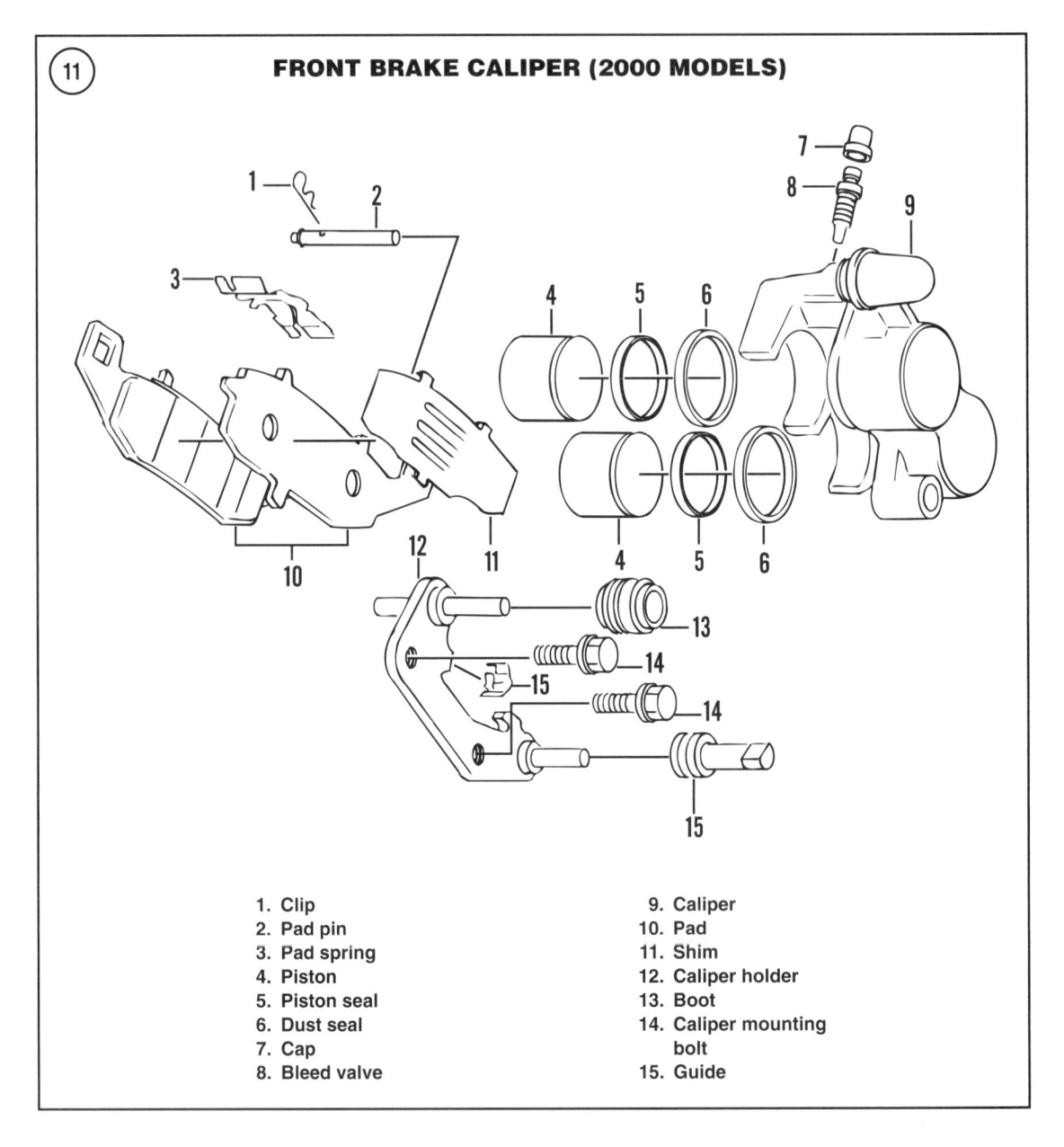

1. Clip
2. Pad pin
3. Pad spring
4. Piston
5. Piston seal
6. Dust seal
7. Cap
8. Bleed valve
9. Caliper
10. Pad
11. Shim
12. Caliper holder
13. Boot
14. Caliper mounting bolt
15. Guide

b. Slowly apply the brake lever to push the pistons part way out of the caliper assembly for ease of removal during caliper service.

c. Remove the banjo bolt (B, **Figure 12**) and sealing washers attaching the brake hose to the caliper assembly.

d. Place the loose end of the brake hose in a recloseable plastic bag to prevent residual brake fluid from dribbling onto the wheel or fork leg.

3. Remove the two caliper mounting bolts (C, **Figure 12**) and lift the brake caliper from the disc.

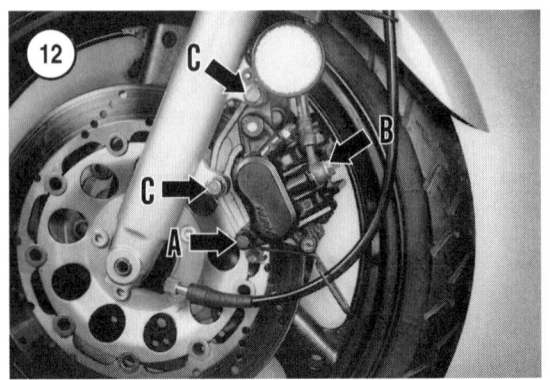

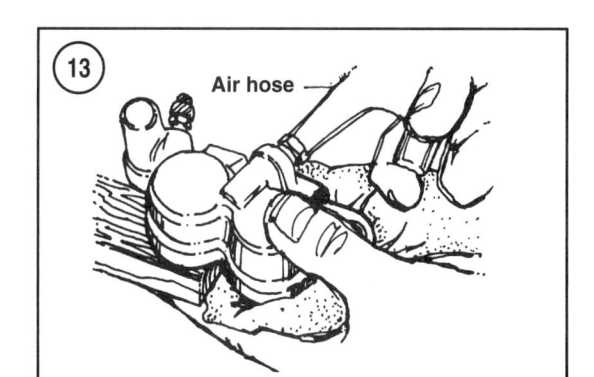

BRAKES

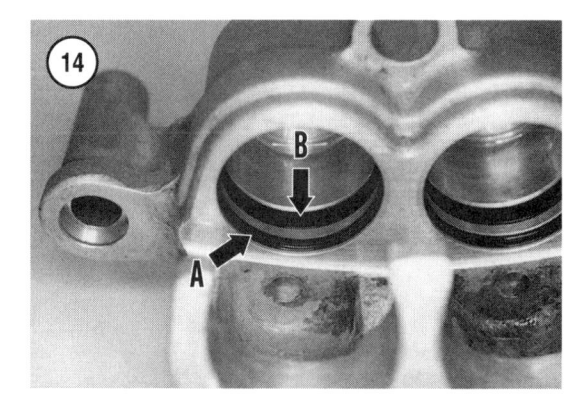

13

Air hose

14

B
A

4. If necessary, disassemble and service the caliper assembly as described in this chapter.

5. Install by reversing these removal steps while noting the following:
   a. Carefully install the caliper assembly onto the disc, being careful not to damage the leading edge of the brake pads.
   b. Install the two caliper mounting bolts (C, **Figure 12**) and secure the brake caliper to the front fork. Torque the caliper mounting bolts to the specification listed in **Table 2**.
   c. On 1995-1999 models, torque the pad mounting bolt to specification.
   d. If removed, install the brake hose onto the caliper. Install a *new* sealing washer on each side of the brake hose fitting(s) and install the banjo bolt (B, **Figure 12**). Tighten the banjo bolt to the specified torque.
   e. Bleed the brakes as described in this chapter.

WARNING
Do not ride the motorcycle before making sure that the brakes are operating properly.

Disassembly

Refer to **Figure 10** for 1995-1999 models and **Figure 11** for 2000 models.
1. Remove the caliper and brake pads as described in this chapter.
2. Remove the caliper holder from the caliper body.
3. Remove the pad spring from the caliper.

NOTE
If the pistons were partially forced out of the caliper body during removal, Steps 4-6 may not be necessary. If the pistons or caliper bores are corroded or very dirty, a small amount of compressed air may be necessary to completely remove the pistons from the bores.

4. Tighten the bleed valve.

WARNING
In the next step, the piston may shoot out of the caliper body with considerable force. Keep hands and fingers out of the way. Wear shop gloves and safety goggles when using compressed air to remove the pistons.

5. Pad the pistons with shop rags or wooden blocks as shown in **Figure 13**. Apply compressed air through the caliper hose joint and force the pistons out of the caliper.
6. If only one piston comes out of the caliper body, perform the following:
   a. Push this piston back into the caliper body and set the caliper body face down on the mat.
   b. Place a flat piece of plastic or a wooden shim over the piston that came out.
   c. Pad the remaining piston and apply compressed air again. The shim will prevent the first piston from coming out too far so that the other piston can be removed.
   d. Remove each piston by hand from its bore.

CAUTION
In the following step, do not use a sharp tool to remove the dust and piston seals from the caliper cylinders. Do not damage the cylinder surface.

7. Use a piece of wood or plastic scraper and carefully push the dust seal (A, **Figure 14**) and the piston seal (B, **Figure 14**) in toward the caliper

cylinder and out of their grooves. Remove the dust and piston seals from both cylinders in each caliper half and discard all seals.

8. If necessary, unscrew and remove the bleed valve assembly.

9. Inspect the caliper assembly as described in this section.

Assembly

NOTE
Never reuse old dust seals or piston seals. Very minor damage or age deterioration can make the seals useless.

1. Soak the new dust and piston seals in fresh DOT 4 brake fluid.
2. Coat the piston bores and pistons with clean DOT 4 brake fluid.
3. Carefully install the *new* piston seals (B, **Figure 14**) into the lower groove in each cylinder. Make sure the seals are properly seated in their respective grooves.
4. Carefully install the *new* dust seals (A, **Figure 14**) into the upper grooves. Make sure all seals are properly seated in their respective grooves.
5. Position the pistons with the open ends facing out and install the pistons into the caliper cylinders. Push the pistons into the bores until they bottom.
6A. On 1995-1999 models, apply Suzuki silicone grease (or equivalent) to the post (**Figure 15**) on the caliper and to the post on the caliper holder (**Figure 16**).
6B. On 2000 models, apply Suzuki silicone grease (or equivalent) to the posts on the caliper holder.
7. Slide the caliper holder (**Figure 17**) into place on the caliper.
8. Install the pad spring (**Figure 18**) into the caliper.
9. If removed, install the bleed valve. Tighten it to the torque specification listed in **Table 2**.
10. On 1995-1999 models, install the pads by performing the following:
    a. If removed, install the insulator and shim onto the outside of each pad as shown in **Figure 7**.
    b. Install the pads into the caliper so the pads engage the guide in the caliper holder as shown in **Figure 8**.
    c. Loosely install the pad bolt. Make sure the bolt passes through both brake pads. The bolt will be torqued to final specification after the caliper has been installed on the fork slider.
11. On 2000 models, perform the following:
    a. If removed, install the shim on the outboard pad.
    b. Position the outboard pad so the shim faces the pistons in the caliper.
    c. Install the outboard pad into the caliper so the pad engages the guide in the caliper holder.
    d. Install the inboard pad into the caliper.
    e. Install the pad pin (B, **Figure 4**). Make sure the pin passes through both brake pads.

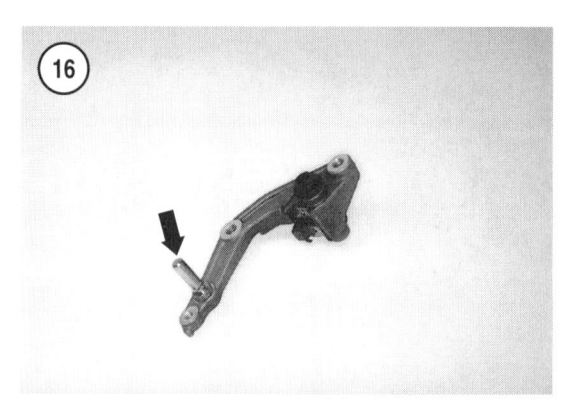

BRAKES

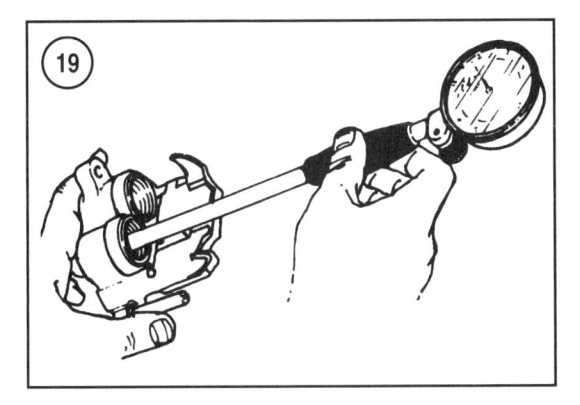

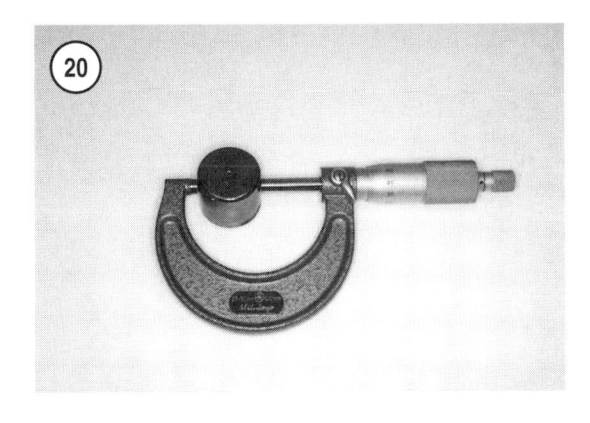

f. Install the clip (A, **Figure 4**) through the pad pin. The clip should sit between the inboard pad and the caliper.
12. Install the caliper as described in this chapter.
13. Bleed the brake as described in this chapter.

Inspection

When inspecting brake components, compare any measurements to the specifications in **Table 1**.

Replace any part that is damaged or out of specification.

1. Clean the caliper body and pistons in fresh DOT 4 brake fluid or isopropyl alcohol. Thoroughly dry the parts with compressed air.
2. Make sure the fluid passageways in the base of the piston bores are clear. Apply compressed air to the openings to make sure they are clear. Clean out the passages, if necessary, with fresh brake fluid.
3. Make sure the fluid passageways in the caliper body halves are clean. Apply compressed air to the openings to make sure they are clear. Clean them with fresh brake fluid, if necessary.
4. Inspect the piston and dust seal grooves in both caliper cylinders for damage. If any groove is damaged or corroded, replace the caliper.
5. Inspect the banjo bolt threaded hole in the caliper body. If worn or damaged, clean the threads with a metric thread tap or replace the caliper assembly.
6. Inspect the bleed valve threaded hole in the caliper body. If worn or damaged, clean the threads with a metric tap or replace the caliper assembly.
7. Inspect the bleed valve. Apply compressed air to the opening and make sure it is clear. Clean out, if necessary, with fresh brake fluid. Install the bleed valve and tighten it to the torque specification listed in **Table 2**.
8. Inspect the pad spring for cracks or other signs of damage.
9. Inspect the caliper body for damage. Check the caliper mounting bolt hole threads for wear or damage. Clean the threads with an appropriate size metric tap or replace the caliper assembly.
10. Inspect the caliper holder for cracks or other signs of damage.
11. Inspect the cylinder walls and pistons for scratches, scoring or other damage.
12. Inspect the boots for tears or other damage. Replace any boot that is damaged or becoming hard.
13. Measure the cylinder bores with a bore gauge (**Figure 19**) or vernier caliper.
14. Measure the outside diameter of the pistons with a micrometer (**Figure 20**) or vernier caliper.

REAR BRAKE PAD REPLACEMENT

Pad wear depends greatly on riding habits and conditions. Regularly check the pads for wear and replace them if the wear indicator reaches the edge of the brake disc. To maintain even brake pressure on the disc, always replace both pads in the caliper at the same time.

NOTE
The brake hose does not have to be disconnected from the caliper during brake pad replacement. Disconnect the hose only when servicing the brake caliper.

1. Read the information listed in *Brake Service* in this chapter.
2. Place the motorcycle on the centerstand on level ground.
3. To prevent the rear brake pedal from being applied, tie the end of the pedal to the frame. That way, if the brake pedal is inadvertently pressed, the pistons will not be forced out of the cylinders.
4. Squeeze the sides of the pad cover and remove the cover (**Figure 21**).
5. Remove the clip (**Figure 22**) and then withdraw the pad pins (**Figure 23**) from the caliper. Remove the springs.
6. Withdraw both brake pads and shims from the caliper assembly.
7. Clean the pad recess and the end of both pistons with a soft brush. Do not use solvent, a wire brush or any hard tool which would damage the cylinders or pistons.
8. Carefully remove any rust or corrosion from the disc.
9. Thoroughly clean any corrosion or debris from the springs, pad pins and clip.
10. Check the friction surface of the new pads for any debris or manufacturing residue. If necessary, clean the pads with an aerosol brake cleaner.
11. When new pads are installed in the calipers, the rear master cylinder brake fluid level will rise as the caliper pistons are repositioned. Remove the hydraulic fluid from the master cylinder reservoir by performing the following:
    a. Remove the rear frame cover as described in Chapter Fifteen.
    b. Clean the top of the master cylinder reservoir of all dirt and debris.
    c. Remove the top cover mounting screws and remove the top cover and diaphragm (**Figure 24**).
    d. Temporarily install an old brake pad into the caliper and seat it against the piston.

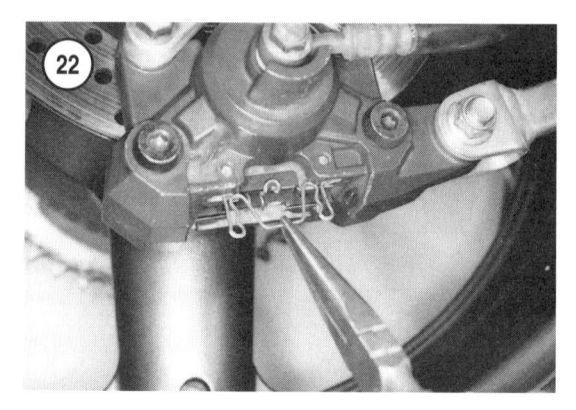

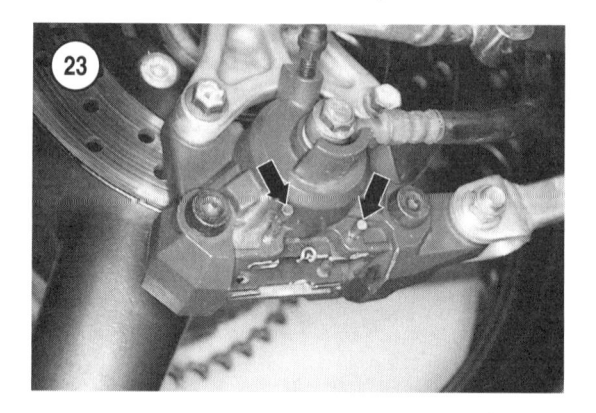

BRAKES

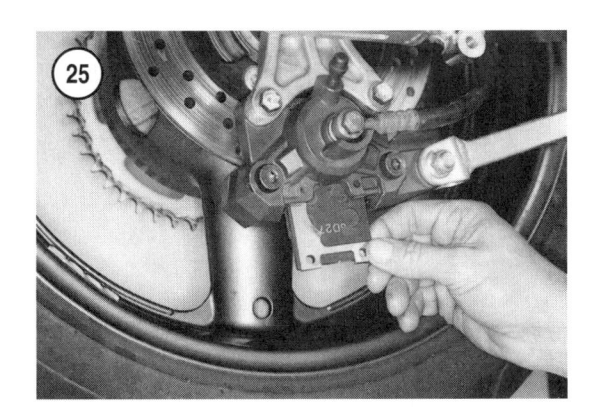

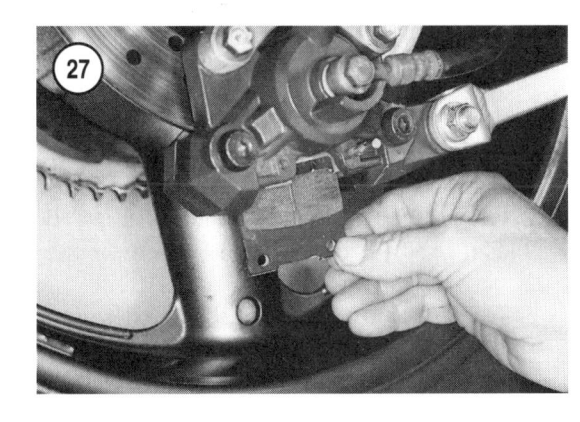

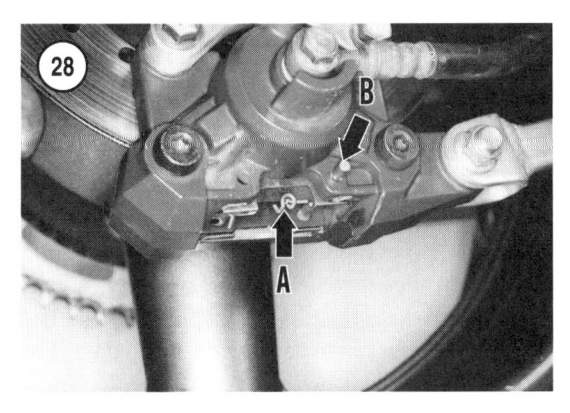

e. Press the pad against the piston and slowly push the caliper piston all the way into the caliper. Constantly check the reservoir to make sure brake fluid does not overflow. Remove fluid, if necessary, to prevent any overflow.

f. The piston should move freely. If it does not, remove and service the caliper as described in this chapter.

g. Remove the old brake pad and repeat this process for the piston on the other side.

12. Install the shims onto the new brake pads so the closed end of the shim faces the rear of the motorcycle as shown in **Figure 25**.

13. Install the outboard brake pad (**Figure 26**) and the inboard pad (**Figure 27**) into the caliper.

14. Install the anti-rattle spring (A, **Figure 28**) into place on both brake pads.

15. Position the front pad pin (B, **Figure 28**) so its clip hole faces down and then insert the front pad pin through the caliper and into both pads. Make sure the pad pin is positioned above the anti-rattle springs in order to hold them in place.

16. Install the rear pad pin through the caliper and into both pads. Make sure the pad pin is positioned above the anti-rattle springs and that the clip hole faces down.

17. Push the pins into the caliper until they bottom.

18. Slide the pin clip fingers (**Figure 22**) through the hole in both pins and push the clip into the caliper until the clip locks onto the pins (**Figure 29**).

19. Install the pad cover (**Figure 21**) and make sure it is locked in place.

20. Untie the rear brake pedal.

21. Pump the rear brake pedal to reposition the brake pads against the brake disc. Roll the motorcycle back and forth and continue to pump the brake pedal as many times as it takes to refill the cylinders

in the caliper and correctly locate the brake pads against the disc.

WARNING
Use brake fluid clearly marked DOT 4 from a sealed container. Other types may vaporize and cause brake failure. Always use the same brand of brake fluid. Do not intermix brands. They may not be compatible. Also do not intermix silicone based (DOT 5) brake fluid. It can cause brake component damage leading to brake system failure.

NOTE
To control the small flow of hydraulic fluid, punch a small hole into the seal of a new container of brake fluid next to the edge of the pour spout. This will help eliminate fluid spills, especially while adding fluid to the very small reservoir.

22. Refill the master cylinder reservoir, if necessary, to maintain the correct fluid level as indicated on the side of the reservoir. Install the diaphragm and the top cover. Install the screws and tighten them securely.

WARNING
Do not ride the motorcycle before making sure the brakes are operating correctly with full hydraulic advantage. If necessary, bleed the brake as described in this chapter.

23. Bed the pads in gradually for the first two to three days of riding by using only light pressure as much as possible. Immediate hard application will glaze the new friction pads and greatly reduce the effectiveness of the brake.

REAR BRAKE CALIPER

Removal/Installation

CAUTION
Do not spill brake fluid on the rear wheel or swing arm. Brake fluid will damage the finish on plastic, painted or plated surfaces. Wash off any spilled brake fluid immediately. Use soapy water and rinse the area completely.

1. If the caliper assembly is going to be disassembled for service, perform the following:

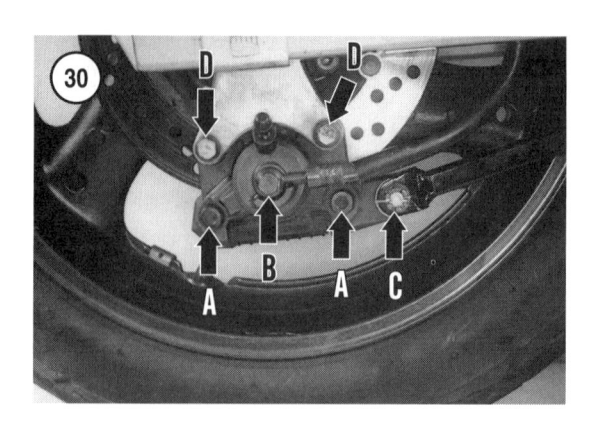

   a. Remove the brake pads as described in this chapter.

   CAUTION
   Do not allow the pistons to travel out far enough to contact the brake disc. If this happens, the pistons may scratch or gouge the disc during caliper removal.

   NOTE
   By performing substep b, compressed air may not be necessary for piston removal during caliper disassembly.

   b. Apply the brake pedal to push the pistons part way out of caliper assembly for ease of removal during caliper service.
   c. Loosen the caliper housing bolts (A, **Figure 30**).
   d. Place a drain pan under the rear caliper and remove the banjo bolt and sealing washers (B, **Figure 30**) securing the brake hose to the caliper assembly.
   e. Place the loose end of the brake hose in a recloseable plastic bag to prevent contamination and brake fluid from dribbling onto the motorcycle.

2. Remove the torque arm nut and bolt (C, **Figure 30**) and separate the torque arm from the caliper.
3. Remove the caliper mounting bolts (D, **Figure 30**) and lower the caliper from the caliper carrier and brake disc.
4. If necessary, disassemble and service the caliper assembly as described in this chapter.
5. Install by reversing these removal steps while noting the following:

   a. Install the caliper assembly onto the disc, being careful not to damage the leading edge of the brake pads.

BRAKES

Figure 31: REAR BRAKE CALIPER

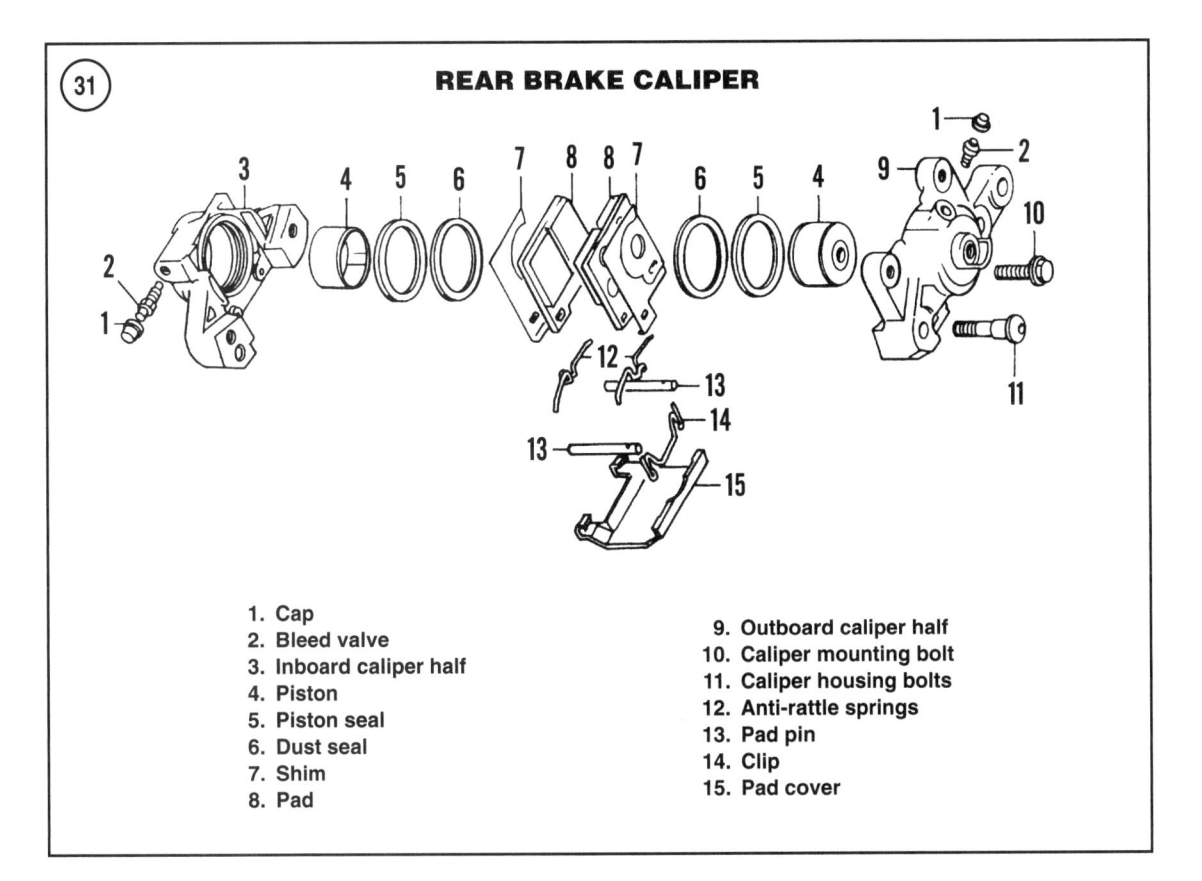

1. Cap
2. Bleed valve
3. Inboard caliper half
4. Piston
5. Piston seal
6. Dust seal
7. Shim
8. Pad
9. Outboard caliper half
10. Caliper mounting bolt
11. Caliper housing bolts
12. Anti-rattle springs
13. Pad pin
14. Clip
15. Pad cover

b. Install the caliper mounting bolts (D, **Figure 30**) and tighten them to the torque specification listed in **Table 2**.

c. Secure the torque arm to the rear caliper. Tighten the torque arm nut (C, **Figure 30**) to the listed torque specification.

d. Install a *new* sealing washer to each side of the brake hose fitting and install the banjo bolt (B, **Figure 30**). Torque the banjo bolt to specification.

e. Torque the rear caliper housing bolts (A, **Figure 30**) to specification.

f. Bleed the brake as described in this chapter.

WARNING
Do not ride the motorcycle before making sure that the brakes are operating properly.

Disassembly

Refer to **Figure 31**.

1. Remove the rear caliper and brake pads as described in this chapter.
2. Remove the two caliper housing bolts (**Figure 32**) loosened during the removal procedure.
3. Separate the caliper body halves. Remove the O-rings (**Figure 33**). Make sure new O-rings are installed every time the caliper is disassembled.

NOTE
If the pistons were partially forced out of the caliper body during removal,

Steps 4-6 may not be necessary. If the pistons or caliper bores are corroded or very dirty, a small amount of compressed air may be necessary to completely remove the pistons from the body bores.

4. Place a piece of soft wood or folded shop cloth over the end of the piston and the caliper body. Turn this assembly over with the piston facing down onto the workbench top.

WARNING
In the next step, the piston may shoot out of the caliper body with considerable force. Keep hands and fingers out of the way. Wear shop gloves and safety goggles when using compressed air to remove the pistons.

5. Apply the air pressure in short spurts to the hydraulic fluid passageway and force the piston out of the caliper bore. Remove the piston from the bore. Repeat for the other caliper body half. Use a service station air hose if an air compressor is not available.

CAUTION
In the following step, do not use a sharp tool to remove the dust and piston seals from the caliper cylinders. Do not damage the cylinder surface.

6. Use a piece of wood or plastic scraper and carefully push the dust seal and the piston seal (**Figure 34**) in toward the caliper cylinder and out of their grooves. Remove the dust and piston seals from the other caliper half. Make sure *new* seals are installed during assembly.

7. If necessary, remove the bleed valve (A, **Figure 35**).

8. Inspect the caliper assembly as described in this section.

Assembly

NOTE
Never reuse old dust seals or piston seals. Very minor damage or age deterioration can make the seals useless.

1. Soak the new dust and piston seals in fresh DOT 4 brake fluid.

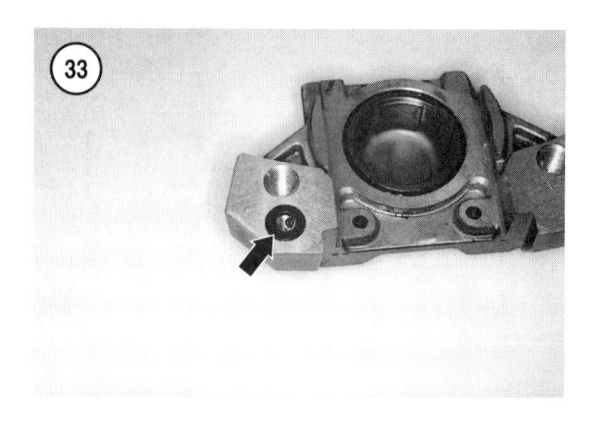

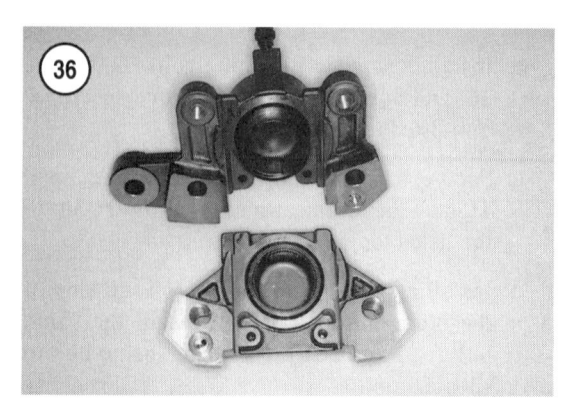

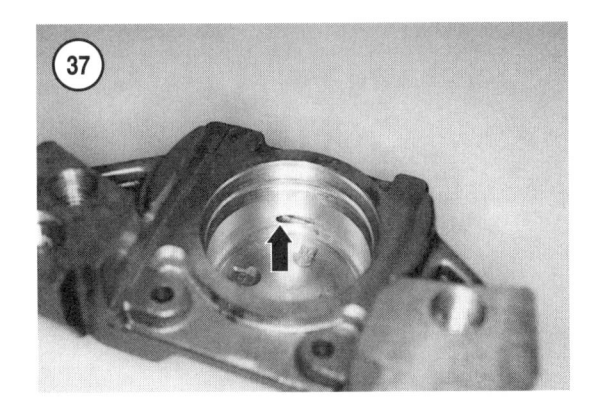

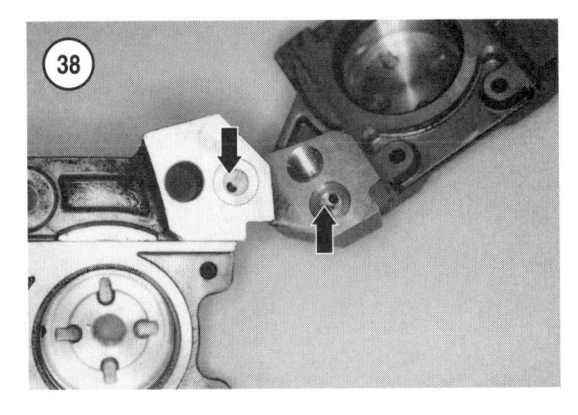

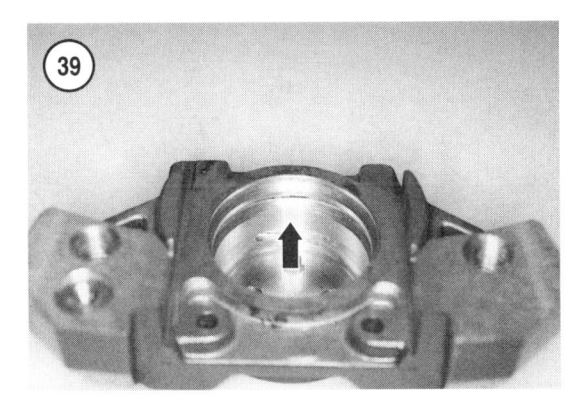

BRAKES

7. Repeat Step 6 for the other caliper body half (**Figure 36**). Make sure both pistons are installed correctly.
8. Coat the *new* O-rings with DOT 4 brake fluid and install the O-ring (**Figure 33**).
9. Make sure the O-ring is still in place and assemble the caliper body halves.
10. Install the two caliper housing bolts (**Figure 32**) and tighten them securely. Torque the bolts to the final specifications after the caliper is installed on the rear caliper bracket.
11. Install the bleed valves and tighten them to the torque specification listed in **Table 2**.
12. Install the caliper and brake pads as described in this chapter.
13. Tighten the two caliper housing bolts (A, **Figure 30**) to the torque specification listed in **Table 2**.
14. Bleed the brake as described in this chapter.

Inspection

Compare all measurements to the specifications in **Table 1**. Replace any part that is damaged or out of specification.

1. Clean both caliper body halves and pistons in fresh DOT 4 brake fluid or isopropyl alcohol. Dry the parts with compressed air.
2. Make sure the fluid passageways (**Figure 37**) in the base of the cylinder bores are clean. Apply compressed air to the openings to make sure they are clear. Clean them with fresh brake fluid if necessary.
3. Make sure the fluid passageways (**Figure 38**) in the caliper body halves are clear. Apply compressed air to the openings to make sure they are clear. Clean them with fresh brake fluid if necessary.
4. Inspect the piston and dust seal grooves (**Figure 39**) in both caliper bodies for damage. If damaged or corroded, replace the caliper assembly.
5. Inspect the banjo bolt threaded hole (B, **Figure 35**) in the outer caliper body. If worn or damaged, dress the threads with a metric tap or replace the caliper assembly.
6. Inspect the bleed valve threaded hole in each caliper body. If worn or damaged, dress the threads with a metric tap or replace the caliper assembly.
7. Inspect the bleed valves. Apply compressed air to the opening in each valve and make sure it is clear. Clean the valves with fresh brake fluid, if necessary. Install the bleed valves into the caliper body

2. Coat the piston bores and pistons with clean DOT 4 brake fluid.
3. Carefully install the *new* piston seal into the lower groove.
4. Carefully install the *new* dust seal into the upper groove. Make sure both seals are properly seated in their respective grooves (**Figure 34**).
5. Repeat Step 3 and Step 4 for the other caliper body half.
6. Position the piston with the open end facing out and install the piston into the caliper cylinder. Push the piston in until it bottoms.

halves. Tighten the valves to the torque specification listed in **Table 2**.

8. Inspect both caliper bodies (**Figure 40**) for damage. Check the threads of the caliper mounting hole for wear or damage. Clean the threads with an appropriate size metric tap or replace the caliper assembly.

9. Inspect the cylinder walls and pistons (**Figure 41**) for scratches, scoring or other damage.

10. Measure the cylinder bores with a bore gauge (**Figure 42**) or vernier caliper.

11. Measure the outside diameter of the pistons with a micrometer (**Figure 43**) or vernier caliper.

FRONT MASTER CYLINDER

Removal

CAUTION
Cover the fuel tank and front fairing with a heavy cloth or plastic tarp to protect them from accidental brake fluid spills. Brake fluid will damage the finish on any plastic, painted or plated surface. Immediately wash any spilled brake fluid from the motorcycle. Use soapy water and rinse the area completely.

Refer to **Figure 44**.

1. Clean all dirt and debris from top of the master cylinder.

2. Remove the top cover (A, **Figure 45**), diaphragm plate and diaphragm from the master cylinder reservoir.

3. Using a shop syringe, draw all of the brake fluid out of the master cylinder reservoir. Temporarily reinstall the diaphragm, plate and cover. Tighten the cover finger tight.

4. Disconnect the brake light switch electrical connectors from the brake switch (B, **Figure 45**).

5. Place a rag beneath the banjo bolt, (C, **Figure 45**) and remove the bolt. Separate the brake hose from the master cylinder. Do not lose the two sealing washers, one from each side of the brake hose fitting.

6. Place the loose end of the brake hose in a recloseable plastic bag to prevent brake fluid from leaking onto the motorcycle. Tie the loose end of the hose to the handlebar.

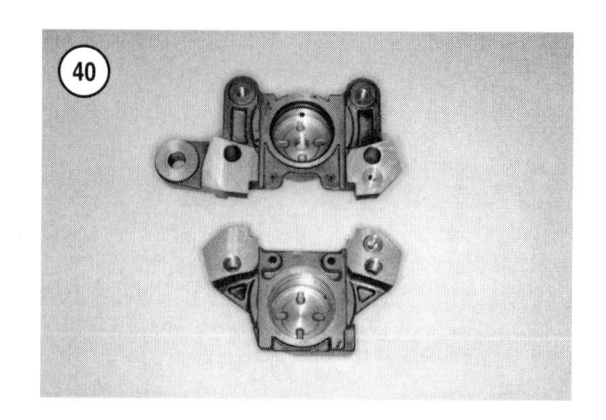

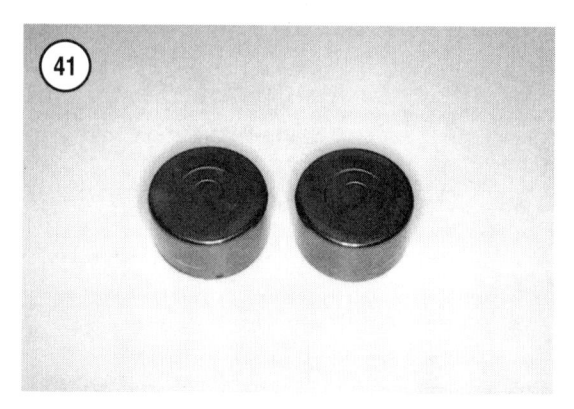

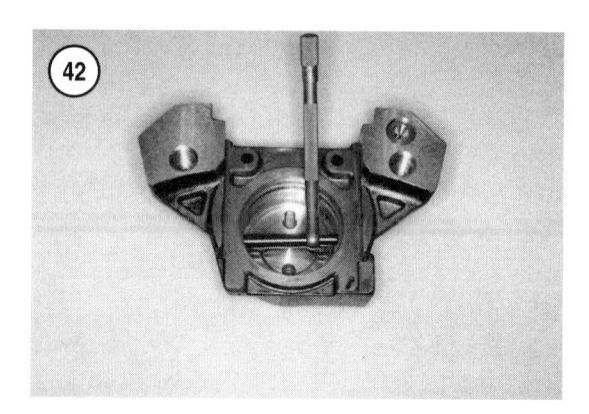

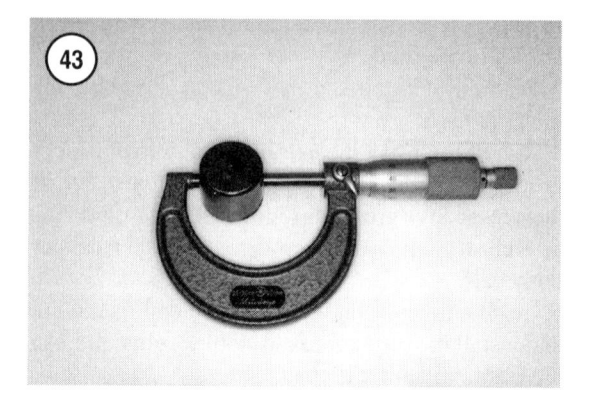

BRAKES

44 **FRONT MASTER CYLINDER**

1. Cover screw
2. Top cover
3. Plate
4. Diaphragm
5. Protector
6. Bolt
7. Clamp
8. Reservoir
9. Boot
10. Piston assembly

45

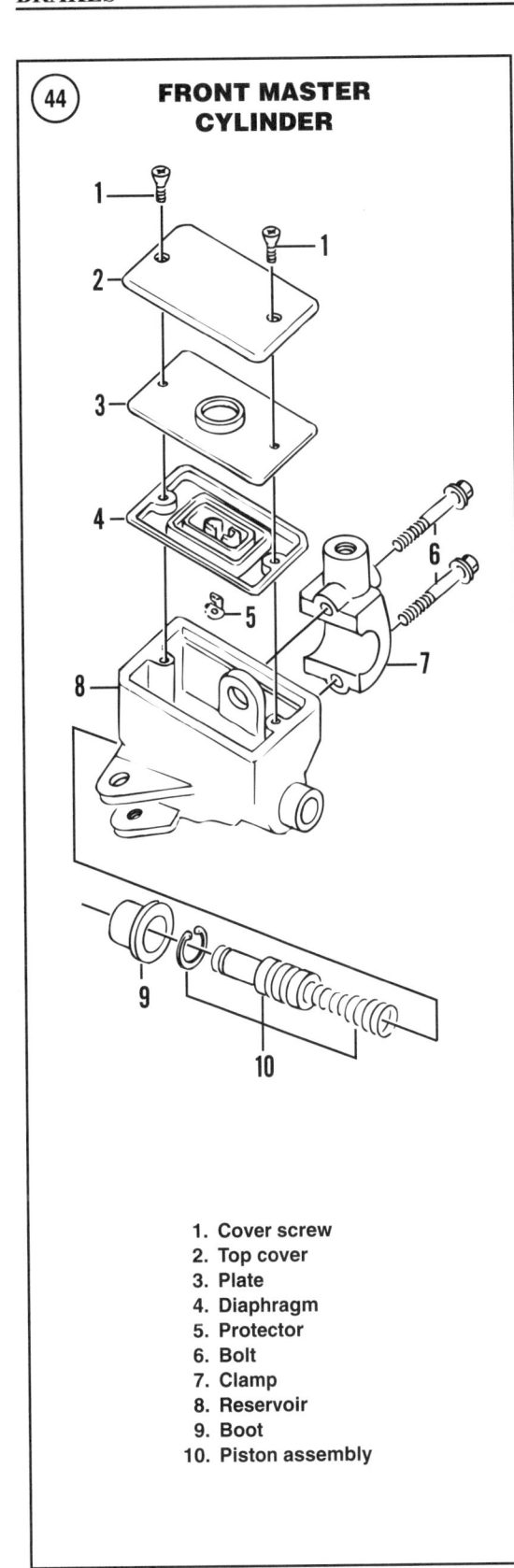

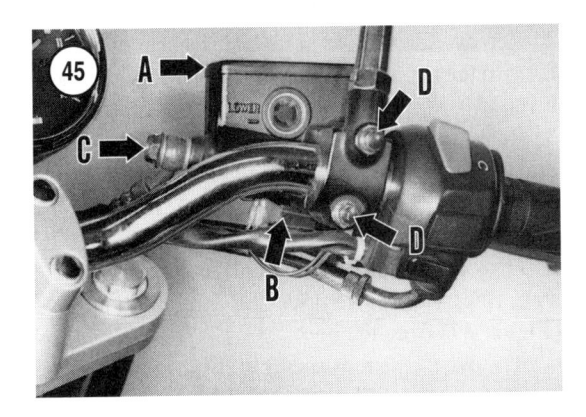

7. Remove the master cylinder clamp bolts (D, **Figure 45**) and the clamp.
8. Remove the master cylinder from the handlebar.
9. Drain any residual brake fluid from the master cylinder and reservoir. Dispose of fluid properly.
10. If the master cylinder is not going to be serviced, place it in a recloseable plastic bag to protect it from contamination.

Installation

1. Position the front master cylinder onto the right handlebar and align the mating surface of the master cylinder with the handlebar punch mark.
2. Position the clamp with the UP mark facing up and install the master cylinder clamp bolts (D, **Figure 45**). Tighten the upper mounting bolt first and then the lower bolt, leaving a gap at the bottom. Tighten the bolts to the torque specification listed in **Table 2**.
3. Install the brake hose onto the master cylinder. Install a *new* sealing washer onto each side of the hose fitting and torque the banjo bolt (C, **Figure 45**) to specification
5. Reconnect the front brake light switch electrical connectors to the brake switch (B, **Figure 45**). Make sure the electrical connectors are locked into place.
6. Refill the master cylinder and reservoir with fresh DOT 4 brake fluid and bleed the brake system as described in this chapter.

Disassembly

1. Remove the master cylinder assembly as described in this chapter.

2. Remove the nut and pivot bolt securing the hand lever to the master cylinder body. Remove the hand lever.
3. Remove the mounting screws and remove the brake switch from the master cylinder assembly.
4. Remove the rubber boot (**Figure 46**) from the cylinder bore on the master cylinder.
5. Press the piston into the cylinder bore and use snap ring pliers to remove the internal snap ring (**Figure 47**) from the bore.
6. Remove the piston assembly (**Figure 48**) and the spring from the cylinder bore.
7. Inspect the components as described in this chapter.

Assembly

Refer to **Figure 44**.
1. Soak the *new* cups and the *new* piston assembly in fresh DOT 4 brake fluid for at least 15 minutes to make them pliable. Coat the inside of the cylinder bore with fresh brake fluid prior to the assembly of parts.
2. If removed, install the primary cup onto the spring and install the secondary cup onto the piston (**Figure 49**). Position the spring with its tapered end (**Figure 48**) facing the piston.

CAUTION
When installing the piston assembly, do not allow the cups to turn inside out. They will be damaged and allow brake fluid leakage within the cylinder bore.

3. Install the spring and piston assembly. Push them into the cylinder until they bottom in the bore.
4. Press the piston assembly into the cylinder and install the snap ring (**Figure 47**). Make sure it is correctly seated in the circlip groove.
5. Slide the rubber boot (**Figure 46**) into place in the cylinder bore.
6. Install the hand lever, pivot bolt and nut. Tighten the bolt and nut securely, Make sure the hand lever operates freely within the master cylinder. There should be no binding.
7. Set the front brake switch in place so the knob on the switch engages the dimple in the lever and then tighten the mounting screw securely.
8. Release the brake lever and make sure the switch plunger moves in and out with no binding.

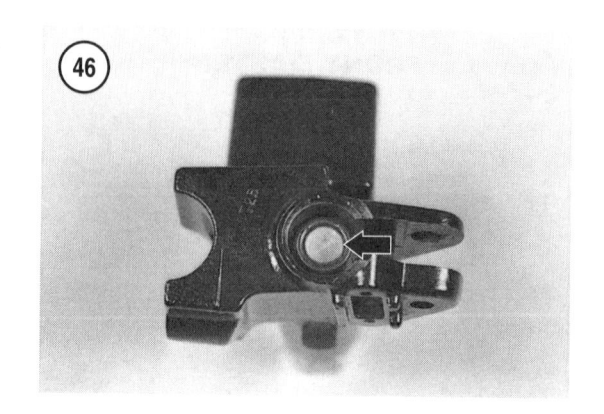

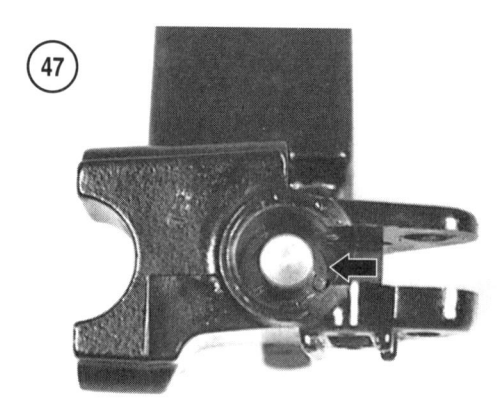

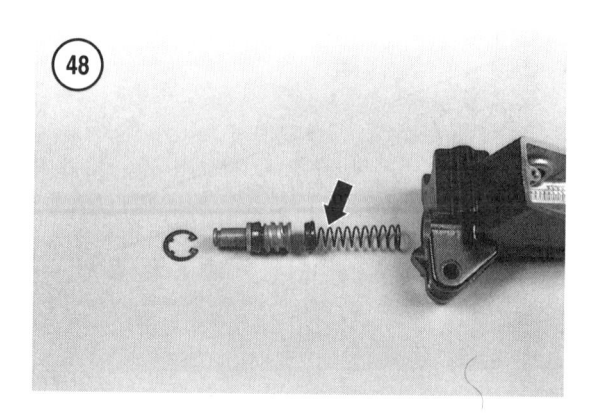

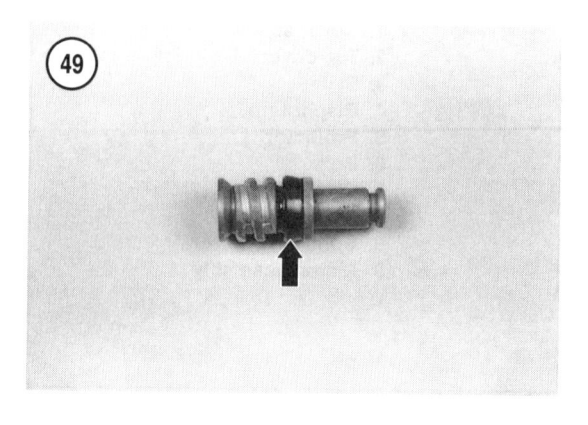

BRAKES

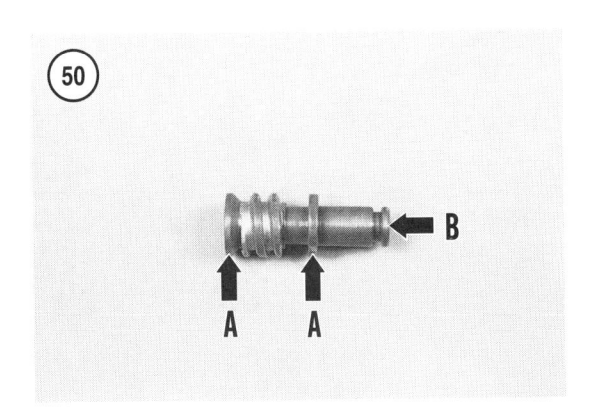

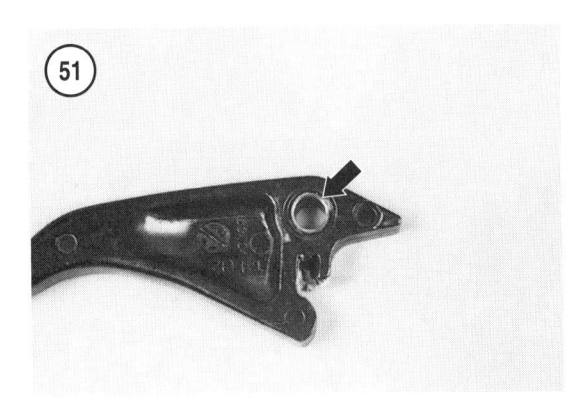

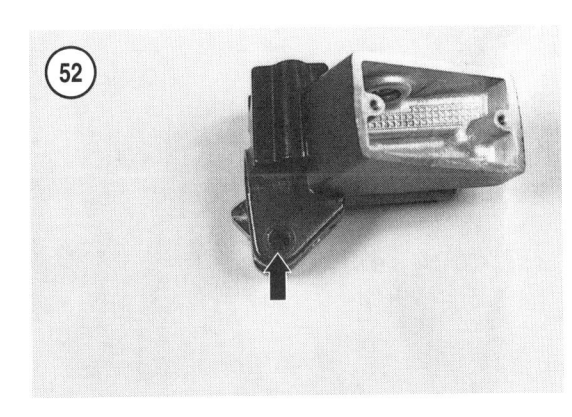

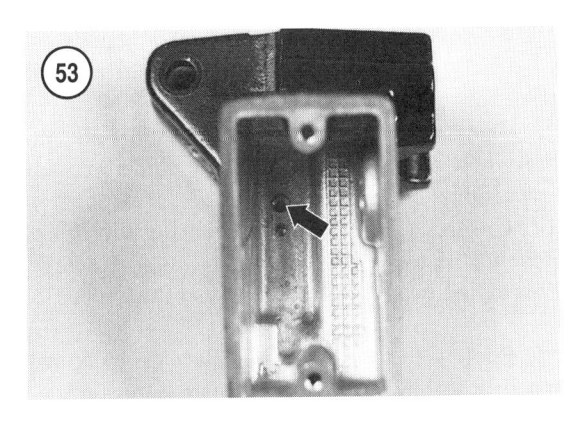

9. Install the master cylinder as described in this chapter.

Inspection

Compare all measurements to the specifications in **Table 1**. Replace any part that is damaged or out of specification.

1. Clean all parts in isopropyl alcohol or fresh DOT 4 brake fluid. Inspect the cylinder bore surface for signs of wear or damage. If less than perfect, replace the master cylinder assembly. The body cannot be replaced separately.
2. Inspect the piston cups (**Figure 49**) for signs of wear and damage. If less than perfect, replace the piston assembly. Individual cups cannot be replaced.
3. Inspect the piston contact surfaces (A, **Figure 50**) for signs of wear or damage. If less than perfect, replace the piston assembly.
4. Check the end of the piston (B, **Figure 50**) for wear caused by the hand lever. If worn, replace the piston assembly.
5. Inspect the pivot hole in the hand lever (**Figure 51**). If worn or elongated, the lever must be replaced.
6. Inspect the pivot lugs on the master cylinder (**Figure 52**) for cracks or other signs of damage.
7. Make sure the fluid passage (**Figure 53**) in the bottom of the reservoir is clear. Clean it if necessary.
8. Inspect the threads in the cylinder bore. If worn or damaged, clean the threads with a metric thread tap or replace the master cylinder assembly.
9. Measure the cylinder bore with a bore gauge (**Figure 54**) or vernier caliper.

10. Measure the outside diameter of the piston with a micrometer (**Figure 55**).

11. Check the top cover (**Figure 56**), diaphragm and diaphragm plate for damage and deterioration; replace as necessary.

12. Inspect the adjuster on the hand lever. If worn or damaged, replace the hand lever as an assembly.

REAR MASTER CYLINDER

Removal

CAUTION
Drape a heavy cloth or plastic tarp over the swing arm and rear wheel to protect them from accidental brake fluid spills. Brake fluid will damage the finish on any plastic, painted or plated surface. Wash any spilled brake fluid off these surfaces immediately. Use soapy water and rinse the area completely.

1. Remove the seat as described in Chapter Fourteen.
2. Remove the rear frame cover as described in Chapter Fourteen.
3. Clean all dirt and debris from the top of the master cylinder reservoir.
4. Remove the top cover mounting screws and remove the top cover (A, **Figure 57**) and diaphragm.
5. Using a shop syringe, draw all of the brake fluid out of the master cylinder reservoir.
6. Attach a hose to the bleed valve on the rear caliper and open the bleed valve.
7. Place the end of the hose over a container and let the brake fluid drain into the container. Slowly apply the rear brake pedal several times to expel most of the brake fluid from the rear hose and the master cylinder. Dispose of this brake fluid properly. Never reuse brake fluid.
8. Remove the hose and close the bleed valve.
9. Remove the reservoir mounting bolt (B, **Figure 57**).
10. Remove the cotter pin (A, **Figure 58**) from the end of the clevis pin and then withdraw the clevis pin (A, **Figure 59**) that secures the master cylinder pushrod to the brake pedal. Do not lose the washer behind the pushrod yoke.
11. Loosen, but do not remove, the banjo bolt (B, **Figure 58**) securing the brake hose to the inboard side of the master cylinder.

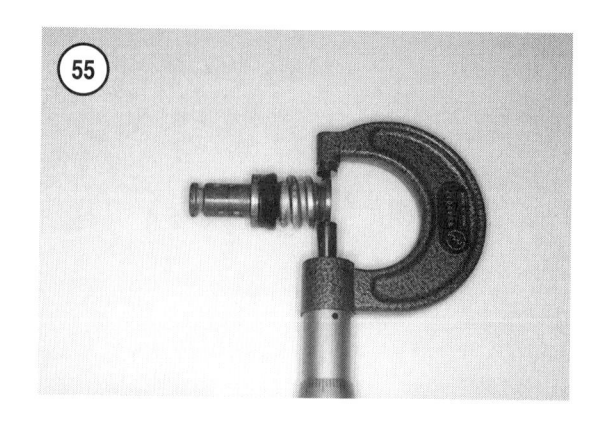

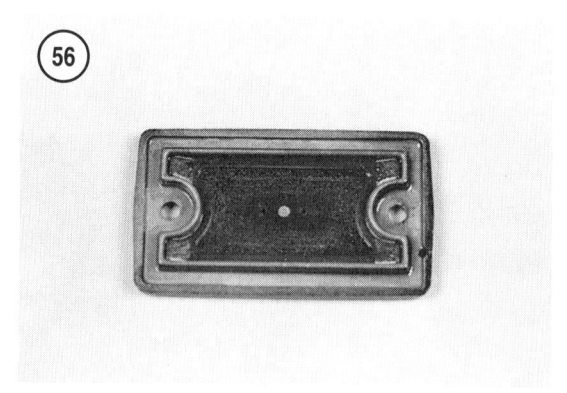

12. Remove the master cylinder mounting bolts (B, **Figure 59**). Move the master cylinder part way out from behind the footpeg bracket.

13. Place several rags under the banjo bolt and brake hose at the top of the master cylinder to catch any residual brake fluid.

14. Unscrew the banjo bolt securing the brake hose to the top of the master cylinder. Remove the sealing washer from each side of the hose fitting.

15. Remove the brake hose and place the loose end in a recloseable plastic bag to keep moisture and de-

BRAKES

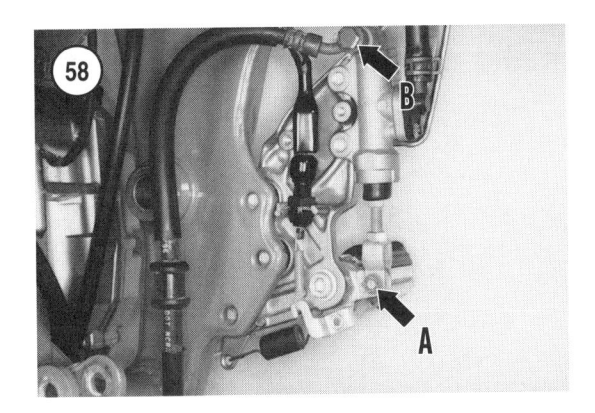

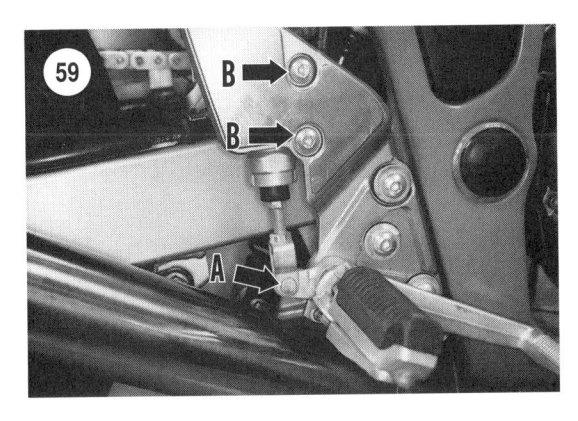

bris out of the system. Tie the loose end of the hose to the frame.

16. Remove the master cylinder and reservoir assembly.

17. If the master cylinder and reservoir will not be serviced, place them in a recloseable plastic bag to protect them from contamination.

18. Wash any spilled brake fluid immediately.

Installation

1. Correctly position the brake hose onto the top of the master cylinder. Place a sealing washer onto each side of the brake hose fitting and install the banjo bolt. Tighten the banjo bolt finger-tight.

2. Install the reservoir up through the rear frame and move the master cylinder into the correct position behind the footpeg bracket. Align the mounting holes and loosely install the master cylinder mounting bolts (B, **Figure 59**).

3. Align the master cylinder pushrod yoke with the brake pedal and install the clevis pin (A, **Figure 59**) through both parts. Slide the washer over the inboard end of the clevis pin. Install a *new* cotter pin (A, **Figure 58**) and bend the ends over completely.

4. Tighten the master cylinder mounting bolts (B, **Figure 59**) securely.

5. Torque the banjo bolt (B, **Figure 58**) to the specification in **Table 2**.

6. Install the mounting bolt (B, **Figure 57**) and secure the reservoir to the frame. Tighten the bolt securely.

7. Fill the reservoir with fresh DOT 4 brake fluid and bleed the rear brake as described in this chapter.

8. Install the rear frame cover and seat as described in Chapter Fifteen.

Disassembly

Refer to **Figure 60**.

1. Remove the rear master cylinder and reservoir assembly as described in this chapter.

2. Release the hose clamp (A, **Figure 61**) and disconnect the hose (B, **Figure 61**) from the fitting on the master cylinder.

3. Remove the connector mounting screw (A, **Figure 62**) and remove the connector (B, **Figure 62**) from the master cylinder. Remove the O-ring (**Figure 63**) from the connector port on the master cylinder. Make sure a *new* O-ring is installed during assembly.

4. Slide the rubber boot (A, **Figure 64**) down the pushrod and out of the way.

5. Using snap ring pliers, remove the internal snap ring (B, **Figure 64**) securing the pushrod assembly in the master cylinder body.

6. Withdraw the pushrod assembly, the piston assembly and spring from the master cylinder body.

7. Pour out any residual brake fluid.

8. If necessary, loosen the master-cylinder-rod locknut (A, **Figure 65**) and then remove the push rod yoke (B, **Figure 65**) and nut from the pushrod.

9. Inspect the master cylinder as described below.

Assembly

Refer to **Figure 60**.

1. Soak the new cups in fresh DOT 4 brake fluid for at least 15 minutes to make them pliable. Install the *new* cups onto the *new* piston assembly.

2. Coat the inside of the cylinder bore with fresh DOT 4 brake fluid prior to the assembly of parts.

CHAPTER THIRTEEN

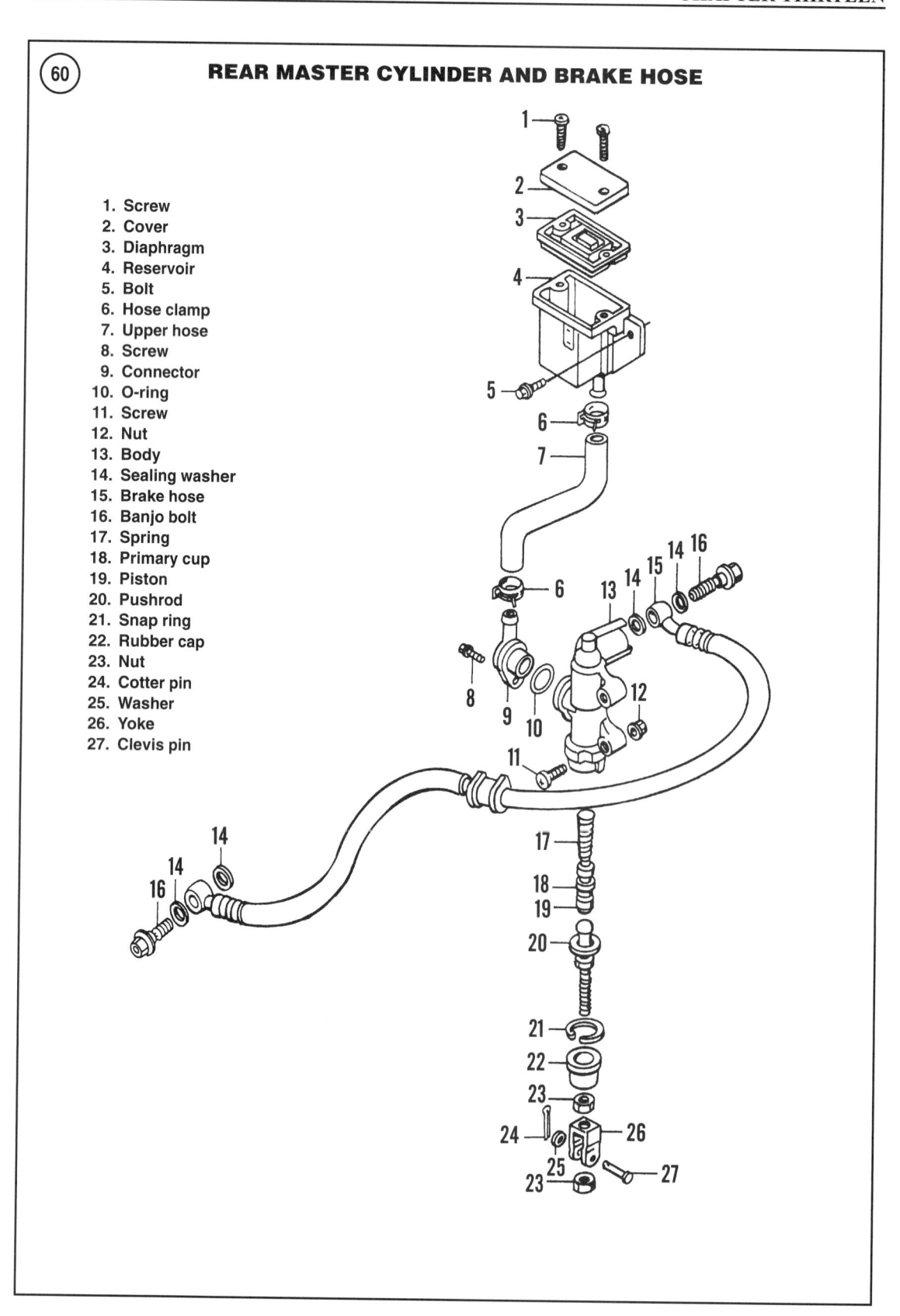

REAR MASTER CYLINDER AND BRAKE HOSE

1. Screw
2. Cover
3. Diaphragm
4. Reservoir
5. Bolt
6. Hose clamp
7. Upper hose
8. Screw
9. Connector
10. O-ring
11. Screw
12. Nut
13. Body
14. Sealing washer
15. Brake hose
16. Banjo bolt
17. Spring
18. Primary cup
19. Piston
20. Pushrod
21. Snap ring
22. Rubber cap
23. Nut
24. Cotter pin
25. Washer
26. Yoke
27. Clevis pin

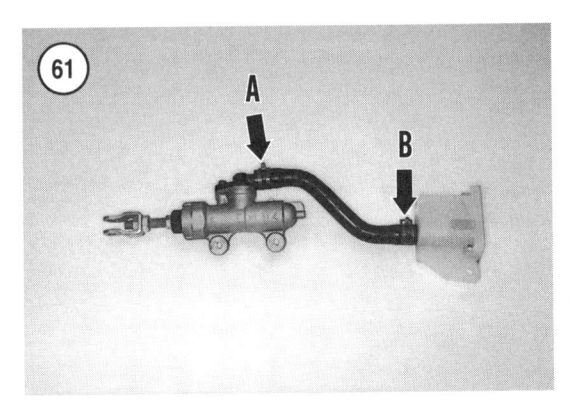

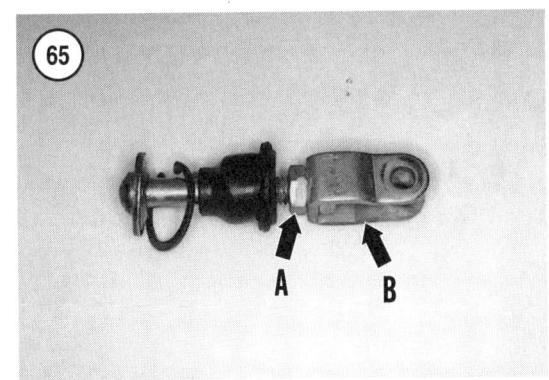

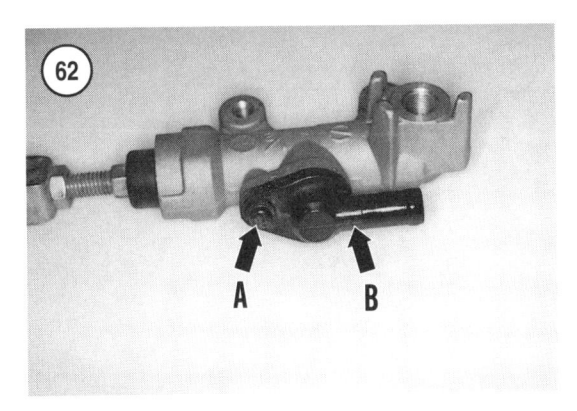

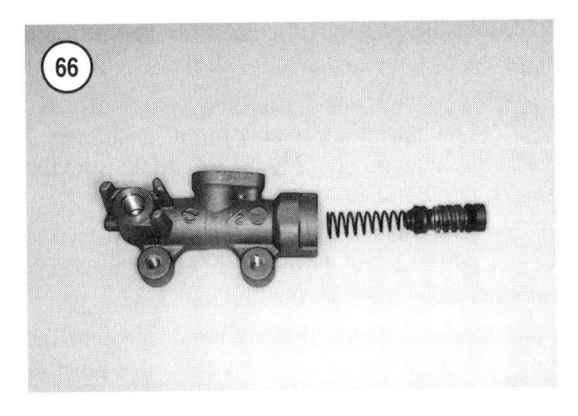

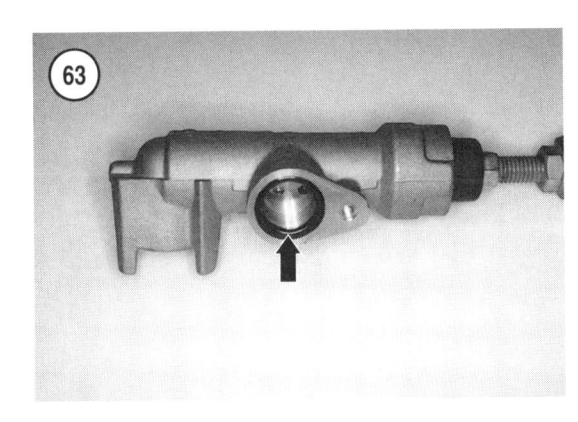

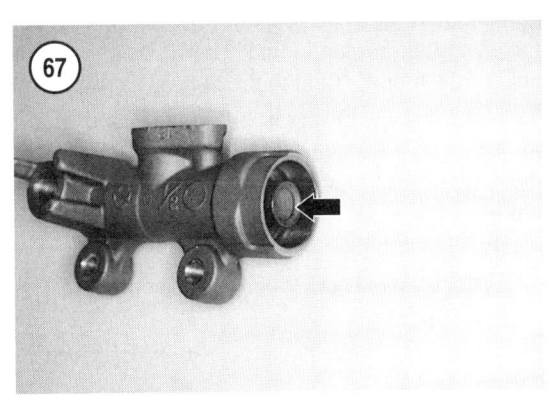

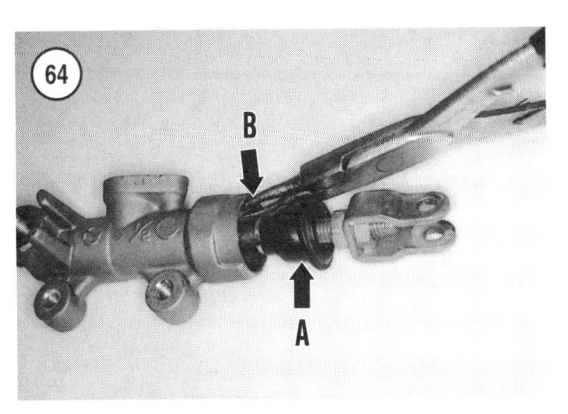

BRAKES

CAUTION
When installing the piston assembly, do not allow the cups to turn inside out. They will be damaged and allow brake fluid leakage within the cylinder bore.

3. Position the spring with the tapered end facing the piston assembly (**Figure 66**). Install the spring and piston assembly into the cylinder together (**Figure 66**). Push the piston assembly all the way in until it bottoms in the cylinder (**Figure 67**).

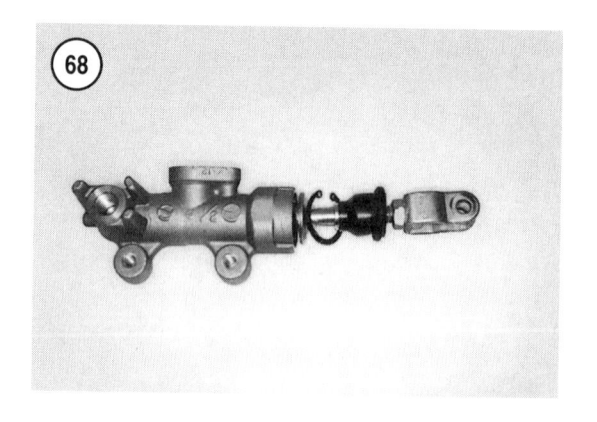

4. Install the pushrod assembly (**Figure 68**) and push the piston cup assembly all the way into the cylinder.

5. Hold the pushrod assembly in this position and install the snap ring (B, **Figure 64**). Make sure the snap ring is correctly seated in the groove.

6. Slide the rubber boot up into the body so it is completely seated in the cylinder (**Figure 69**). This is necessary to keep out dirt and moisture.

7. If removed, install the yoke and nut onto the pushrod. Do not tighten the locknut at this time, as the brake pedal must be adjusted.

8. Install a *new* O-ring (**Figure 63**) into the connector port in the master cylinder body. Apply a light coat of fresh brake fluid to the O-ring.

9. Make sure the O-ring is still in place and install the reservoir hose connector (B, **Figure 62**) onto the master cylinder. Secure the connector in place with the mounting screw (A, **Figure 62**). Tighten the screw securely.

10. Install the master cylinder as described in this chapter.

11. Adjust the brake pedal height as described in Chapter Three.

Inspection

Compare all measurements to the specifications in **Table 1**. Replace any part that is damaged, worn to the wear limit or out of specification.

1. Clean all parts in isopropyl alcohol or fresh DOT 4 hydraulic fluid.

2. Inspect the cylinder bore surface (**Figure 70**). If it is less than perfect, replace the master cylinder assembly. The body cannot be replaced separately.

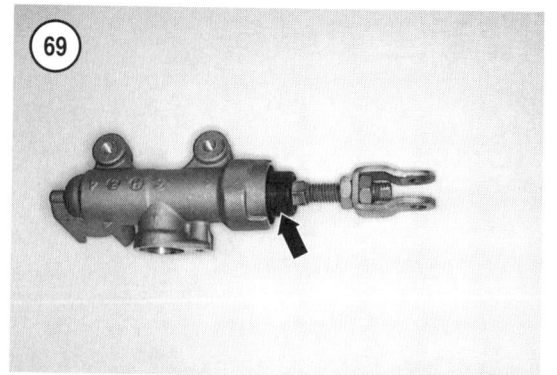

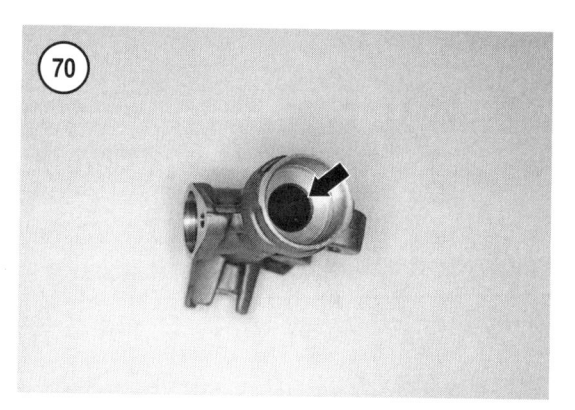

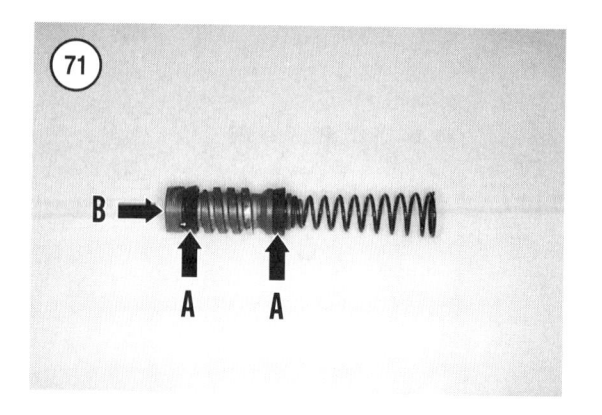

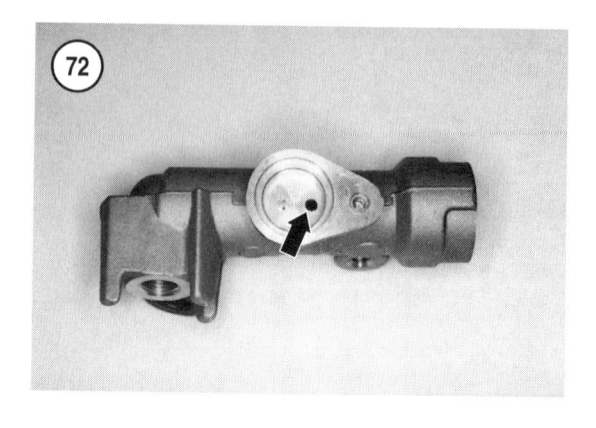

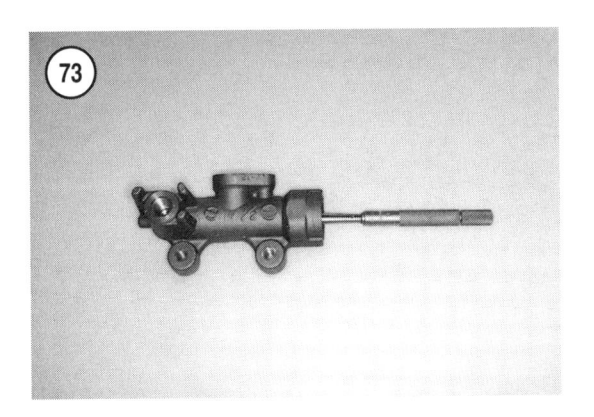

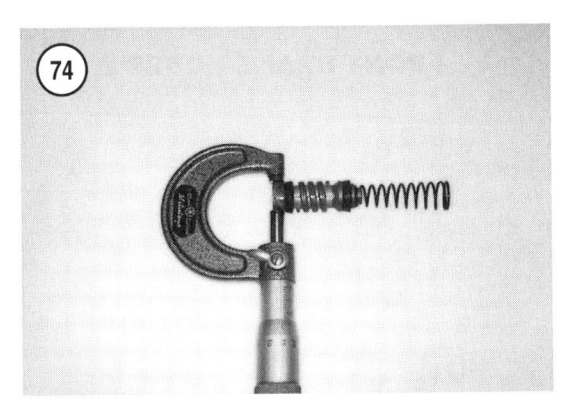

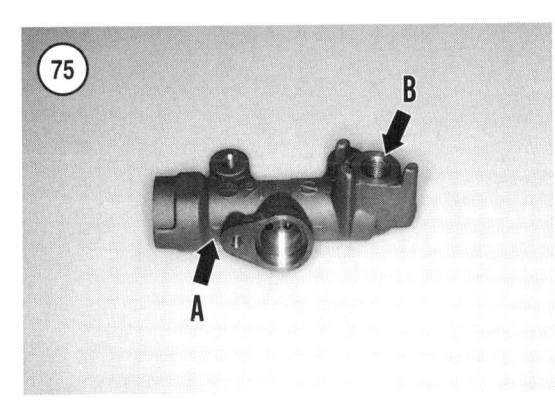

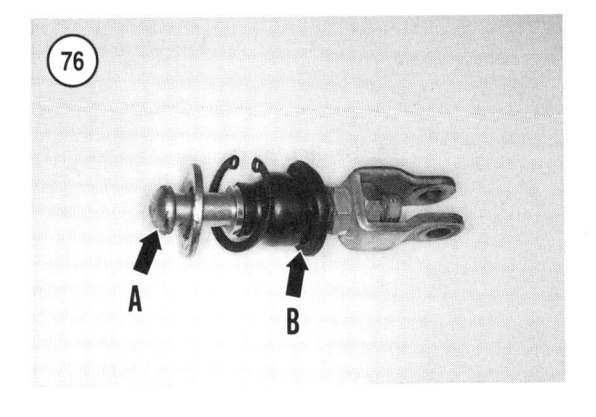

BRAKES

3. Inspect the piston cups (A, **Figure 71**) for signs of wear and damage. If less than perfect, replace the piston assembly. The cups cannot be replaced separately.

4. Check the end of the piston (B, **Figure 71**) for wear caused by the pushrod. If worn, replace the piston assembly.

5. Make sure the fluid passage (**Figure 72**) in the master cylinder body is clear. Clean it if necessary.

6. Measure the cylinder bore with a bore gauge (**Figure 73**) or vernier caliper.

7. Measure the outside diameter of the piston with a micrometer (**Figure 74**).

8. Check the entire master cylinder body (A, **Figure 75**) for wear or damage. If damaged in any way, replace the master cylinder assembly.

9. Inspect the banjo bolt threads in the master cylinder body (B, **Figure 75**). If worn or damaged, clean the threads with a thread tap or replace the master cylinder assembly.

10. Inspect the piston push rod assembly (A, **Figure 76**) for wear or damage. Make sure the rubber boot (B, **Figure 76**) is in good condition. Replace the boot if necessary.

11. Inspect the banjo bolt threads for damage. If damaged, clean the threads with a metric thread die or replace the bolt. Make sure the brake fluid hole is clear. Clean out or replace if necessary.

12. Check the connector for damage.

13. Remove the cover and diaphragm (**Figure 77**) from the reservoir. Check all components for damage and deterioration.

14. Inspect the reservoir and hose (**Figure 78**) or wear or deterioration.

BRAKE HOSE REPLACEMENT

Suzuki recommends replacing all brake hoses every four years or when they show signs of cracking or damage.

Front Brake Hoses

Refer to **Figure 79**.

> *CAUTION*
> *Drape a heavy cloth or plastic tarp over the front fender to protect it from accidental brake fluid spills. Brake fluid will damage the finish on plastic, painted or plated surfaces. Immediately wash spilled brake fluid off the motorcycle. Use soapy water and rinse the area completely.*

1. On models with a front fairing, remove the fairing as described in Chapter Fourteen.
2. Clean all dirt and debris from the top of the master cylinder.
3. Remove the top cover (A, **Figure 80**), diaphragm plate and diaphragm from the master cylinder.

> *NOTE*
> *Place a shop cloth under the banjo bolts and brake hose fittings to catch any spilled brake fluid that might leak out during this procedure.*

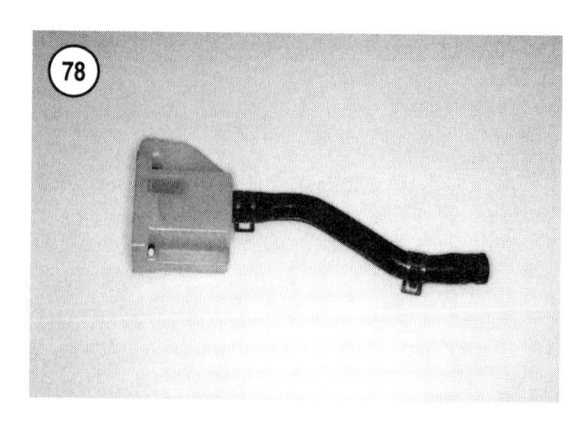

4. Remove the banjo bolt (A, **Figure 81**) and sealing washers securing the brake hose to the left caliper.
5. Place the end of the brake hose over a container and let the brake fluid drain out into the container. Apply the front brake lever several times to force the fluid out of the brake hose. Dispose of this brake fluid properly. Never reuse brake fluid. Place the loose end of the brake hose in a recloseable plastic bag to prevent brake fluid from leaking onto the motorcycle.
6. Remove the retainer bolt (B, **Figure 81**) and release the hose from the retainer securing the brake hose to the fork slider.
7. Repeat Steps 4-6 for the right caliper.
8. Remove the banjo bolt and two sealing washers (A, **Figure 82**) from the left side of the brake hose joint and remove the left lower brake hose.
9. Disconnect the banjo bolt and the three sealing washer (B, **Figure 82**) from the right side of the brake hose joint and remove the right lower fork hose.

FRONT BRAKE HOSES

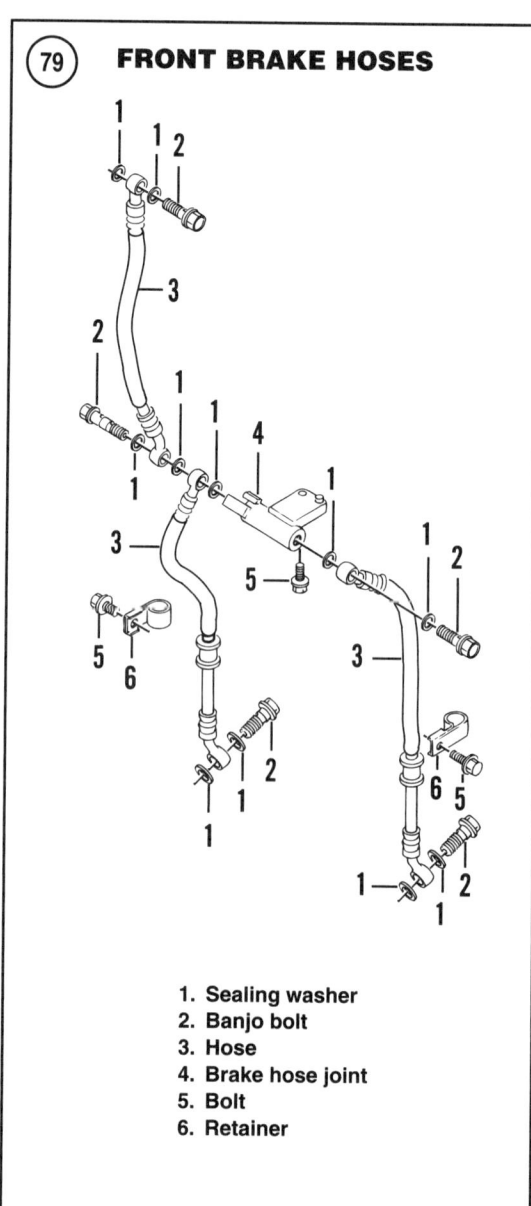

1. Sealing washer
2. Banjo bolt
3. Hose
4. Brake hose joint
5. Bolt
6. Retainer

BRAKES

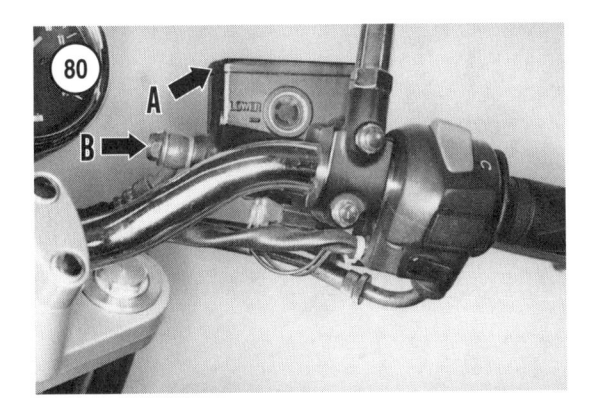

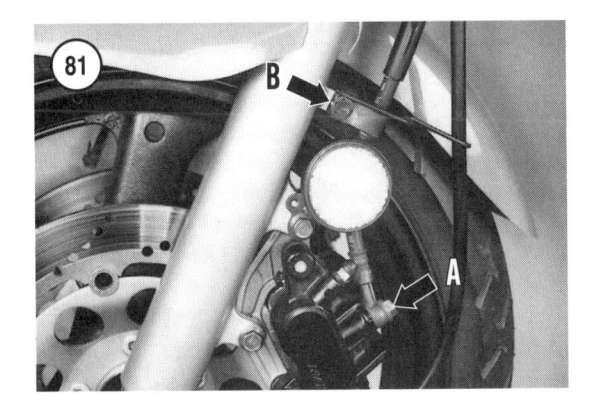

10. Remove the banjo bolt (B, **Figure 80**) and two sealing washers securing the upper brake hose to the master cylinder.
11. Carefully pull the lower end of the upper hose down and out from behind the throttle cables on the right side.
12. Wash off any spilled brake fluid that may have leaked out of the hoses during removal.
13. Install the hoses in the reverse order of removal while noting the following:
    a. Install *new* sealing washers on each side of the hose fittings.
    b. Use three sealing washers when securing the upper brake hose and the right lower brake hoses to the brake hose joint (B, **Figure 82**).
    c. Tighten the banjo bolts to the torque specifications listed in **Table 2**.
    d. Refill the master cylinder reservoir and bleed the front brakes as described in this chapter.

Rear Brake Hose

Refer to **Figure 60**.

> *CAUTION*
> *Cover the surrounding area with a heavy cloth or plastic tarp to protect components from accidental brake fluid spills. Brake fluid will destroy the finish on plastic, painted or plated surfaces. Wash spilled brake fluid off any of these surfaces immediately. Use soapy water and rinse the area completely.*

> *NOTE*
> *The reservoir hose replacement procedure is covered in **Rear Master Cylinder** in this chapter.*

1. Remove the rear frame cover as described in Chapter Fourteen.
2. Perform Steps 1-15 of *Rear Master Cylinder Removal* and disconnect the brake hose from the master cylinder.

> *NOTE*
> *Place a shop cloth under the banjo bolts and brake hose fittings to catch any brake fluid that leaks out in the following steps.*

3. Remove the banjo bolt (**Figure 83**) and sealing washers attaching the brake hose to the rear caliper

assembly. Do not lose the sealing washer from each side of the hose fitting.

NOTE
Figure 84 is shown with the rear wheel removed for clarity. This procedure can be performed with the rear wheel on the motorcycle.

4. Unhook the brake hose from the two clamps (A, **Figure 84**) on top of the swing arm.

5. Carefully pull the rear of the brake hose out from the guide (B, **Figure 84**) on the inner surface of the swing arm and remove the brake hose.

6. Install the hose in the reverse order of removal while noting the following:
   a. Install *new* sealing washers on each side of the brake hose fittings.
   b. Tighten the banjo bolts to the torque specifications listed in **Table 2**.
   c. Make sure the brake hose is correctly installed through the guide (B, **Figure 84**) on the swing arm so that it will not contact the rear wheel.
   d. Refill the master cylinder reservoir and bleed the rear brake system as described in this chapter.

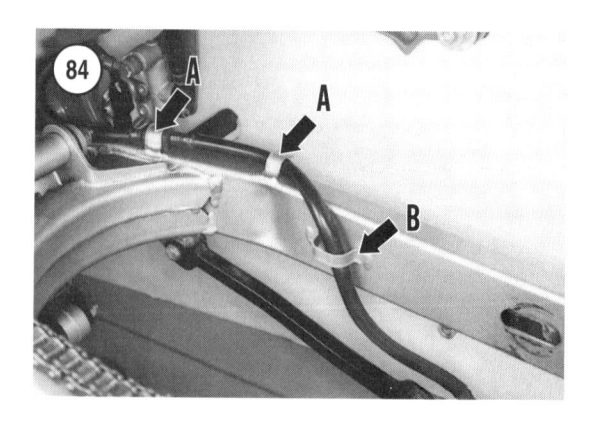

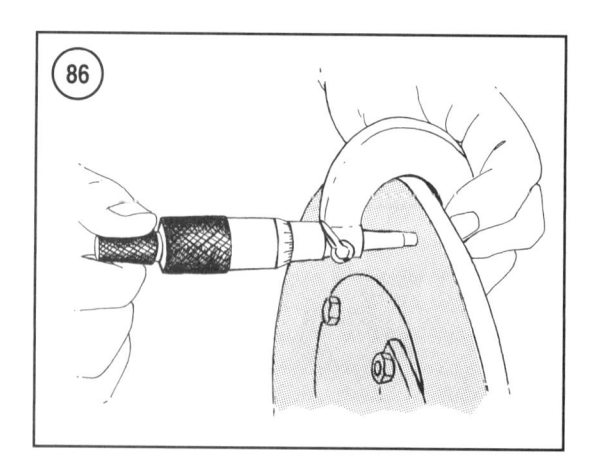

BRAKE DISC

The brake discs are separate from the wheel hubs and can be removed once the wheel is removed from the motorcycle.

Inspection

The brake disc can be inspected while it is installed on the wheel. Small nicks and marks on the disc are not important, but radial scratches deep enough to snag a fingernail reduce braking effectiveness and increase brake pad wear. If these grooves are evident and the brake pads are wearing rapidly, replace the disc.

The specifications for the standard thickness and wear limits are listed in **Table 1**. A minimum (MIN) thickness is also stamped on the disc face (**Figure 85**). If the specification stamped on the disc differs from the wear limit listed in **Table 1**, refer to the specification on the disc during inspection.

Do not have the discs machined to compensate for any warp. The discs are thin and machining only makes them thinner, causing them to warp quite rapidly. If the disc is warped, the brake pads may be dragging on the disc due to a faulty caliper and causing the disc to overheat. Overheating can also be caused when there is unequal pad pressure on the sides of the disc.

NOTE
Disc thickness can be measured with the wheel installed or removed from the motorcycle.

BRAKES

NOTE
When checking the front disc, turn the handlebar all the way to one side and then to the other side.

3. Slowly rotate the wheel and watch the dial indicator. Replace the disc if runout is out of specification.

4. Excessive runout is usually caused by the disc overheat due to unequal pad pressure. Consider the following possibilities and determine the cause before installing a new disc.
   a. The floating caliper is binding on the caliper bracket shafts.
   b. The brake caliper piston seals are worn and allowing the pads to drag on the disc.
   c. The master cylinder relief port is plugged.
   d. The master cylinder primary cup is worn or damaged.

5. Clean any rust or corrosion from the disc and wipe it clean with brake cleaner. Never use an oil-based solvent that may leave an oil residue on the disc.

6. On front brake discs, inspect all fasteners (A, **Figure 88**) between the outer and the inner rings of the disc. If any are loose or damaged, replace the disc.

Removal/Installation

1. Remove the front or rear wheel as described in Chapter Ten.

CAUTION
Set the tire on two wooden blocks. Do not set the wheel down on the disc surface, as it may get scratched or warped.

NOTE
Insert a piece of wood or vinyl tube between the pads in the caliper(s). This way, if the brake lever or pedal is inadvertently applied, the pistons will not be forced out of the cylinders. If this does happen, the caliper will have to be disassembled to reseat the pistons and the system will have to be bled.

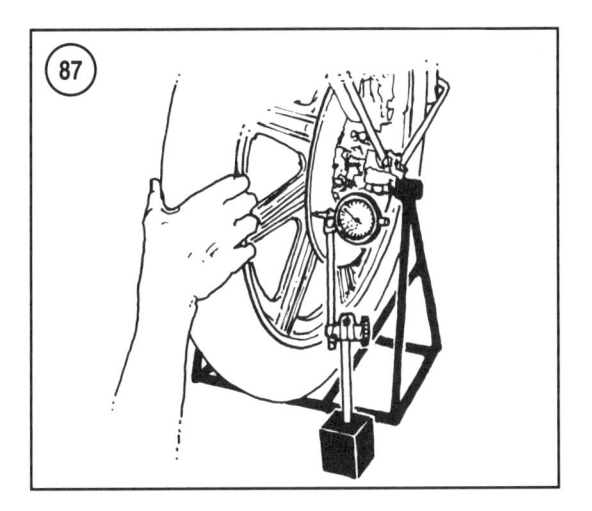

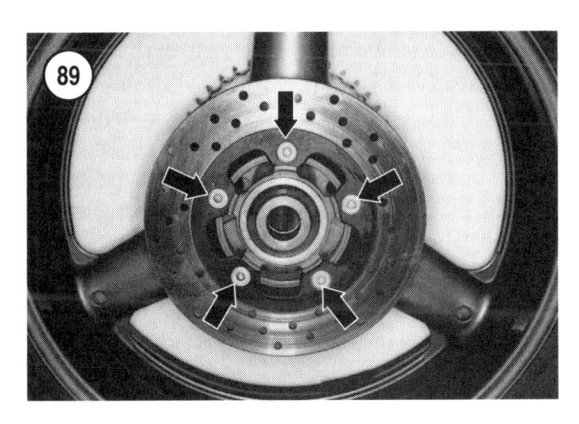

1. Measure the thickness of the disc at several locations around the disc with a vernier caliper or a micrometer (**Figure 86**). The disc must be replaced if the thickness in any area is less than the specification in **Table 1** or the MIN dimension stamped on the disc.

2. Check the disc runout with a dial indicator as shown in **Figure 87**. Make sure the disc mounting bolts are tight prior to running this check.

2. Remove the bolts (**Figure 89**) securing the brake disc to the hub and remove the disc.

3. Install by reversing these removal steps while noting the following:

a. On discs so marked, position the disc so the arrow (B, **Figure 88**) points in the direction of tire rotation.

WARNING
*The disc bolts are made from a harder material than similar bolts used on the motorcycle. When replacing the bolts, always use standard Suzuki brake disc bolts. Never compromise and substitute another type of bolt. They will **not** properly secure the disc to the hub.*

b. Use a small amount of a locking compound such as ThreeBond No. TB1360 on the brake disc bolts prior to installation.
c. Tighten the disc mounting bolts to the torque specification listed in **Table 2**.

BLEEDING THE BRAKES

Bleeding the brakes removes air from the brake system. Air in the brakes increases brake lever or pedal travel and it makes the brakes feel soft or spongy. Under extreme circumstances, it can cause complete loss of brake pressure.

The brakes can be bled manually or with the use of a brake bleeding tool. The manual method is described here. When using a vacuum pump or other brake bleeding tool, follow the instructions that came with the tool. Only use fresh DOT 4 brake fluid when bleeding the brakes. Do not reuse old brake fluid and do not use DOT 5 (silicone based) brake fluid.

Protect the motorcycle from accidental spills by covering the areas beneath the calipers and master cylinders with a tarp. Brake fluid will damage the finish on most surfaces, so immediately clean up any spilled brake fluid. Wash the affected parts with soapy water and completely rinse the area with plenty of clean water.

NOTE
The rear caliper is equipped with two bleed valves, one for each caliper body half. Bleed the inner caliper body half first, and then bleed the outer caliper half.

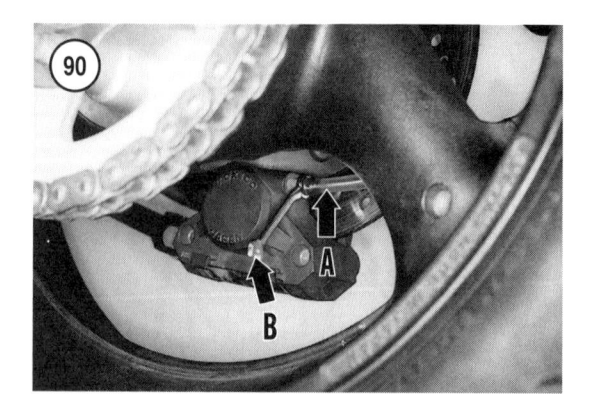

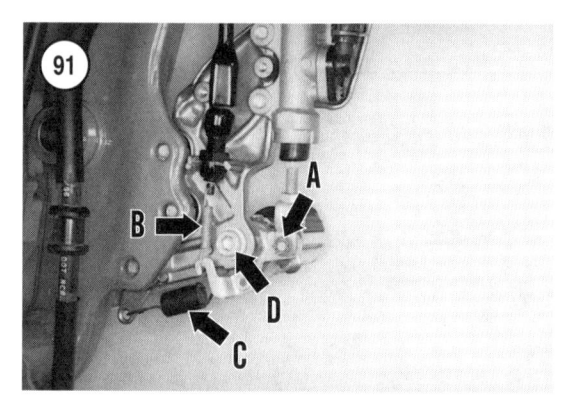

1. Check that all banjo bolts in the system are tight.
2. Remove the dust cap from the bleed valve on the caliper assembly.
3. Connect a length of clear tubing to the bleed valve (A, **Figure 90**). Place the other end of the tube into a clean container. Fill the container with enough fresh brake fluid to keep the end submerged. The tube should be long enough so that its loop can be higher than the bleed valve to prevent air from being drawn into the caliper during bleeding.
4. Clean all dirt or debris from the top of the front or rear master cylinder reservoir. Remove the top cover, diaphragm plate (front reservoir only) and the diaphragm from the reservoir.
5. Add brake fluid to the reservoir until the fluid level is at the upper limit. Loosely install the diaphragm and the cover. Leave them in place during this procedure to prevent the entry of dirt.
6. Pump the brake lever or pedal a few times and then release it.
7. Apply the front brake lever or the rear brake pedal until it stops and hold it in this position.
8. Open the bleed valve with a wrench (B, **Figure 90**). Let the brake lever (or brake pedal) move to the

BRAKES

limit of its travel and then close the bleed valve. Do not release the brake lever (or brake pedal) while the bleed valve is open.

NOTE
As brake fluid enters the system, the level in the reservoir drops. Add brake fluid as necessary to keep the fluid level 10 mm (3/8 in.) below the reservoir top so air will not be drawn into the system.

9. Repeat Steps 6-8 until the brake fluid flowing from the hose is clear and free of air. If the system is difficult to bleed, tap the master cylinder or caliper with a soft mallet.
10. Test the feel of the brake lever or pedal. It should feel firm and offer the same resistance each time it is operated. If the lever or pedal feels soft, air is still trapped in the system. Continue bleeding.
11. When bleeding is complete, disconnect the hose from the bleed valve. Torque the caliper bleed valve to the torque specification in **Table 2**.
12. If necessary, add brake fluid to the master cylinder to correct the fluid level.
13. Install the diaphragm, diaphragm plate (front reservoir only) and top cap. Make sure the cap is secured in place.

WARNING
Do not ride the motorcycle before making sure the brakes are operating

correctly with full hydraulic advantage. If necessary, bleed the brake as described in this chapter.

REAR BRAKE PEDAL

Removal/Lubrication/Installation

NOTE
This procedure is shown with the rear wheel and swing arm removed for photographic clarity. It is not necessary to remove either of these components, but it does allow more working room.

1. Remove the cotter pin (A, **Figure 91**), and remove the washer from the back end of the clevis pin that secures the master cylinder pushrod to the brake pedal.
2. Withdraw the clevis pin (**Figure 92**) and separate the pushrod yoke from the brake pedal.
3. Unhook the rear brake light switch spring (B, **Figure 91**) from the brake pedal.
4. Use vise grip pliers and disconnect the pedal return spring (C, **Figure 91**) from the brake pedal.
5. Remove the footpeg bolt (D, **Figure 91**) from the inboard side of the mounting bracket.
6. Remove the footpeg and rear brake pedal assembly. Do not lose the washer between the brake pedal and the footpeg mounting bracket.
7. Inspect the brake pedal for fractures or damage. Replace it if necessary.
8. Clean the footpeg bolt with solvent and then inspect it for wear or damage. Replace if necessary.
9. Lubricate the footpeg bolt and bushing with waterproof grease.
10. Install the pedal by reversing these removal steps while noting the following:
    a. Tighten the footpeg bolt securely.
    b. Install a new cotter pin and bend the ends over completely.
    c. Adjust the rear brake pedal height as described in Chapter Three.

Tables 1-2 are on the following pages.

Table 1 BRAKE SPECIFICATIONS

Item	Standard mm (in.)	Wear limit mm (in.)
Brake fluid	DOT 4	–
Brake disc runout (front and rear)	–	0.30 (0.012)
Brake disc thickness		
Front	4.3-4.7 (0.169-1.85)	4.0 (0.16)
Rear	4.8-5.2 (0.189-0.205)	4.5 (0.18)
Front master cylinder		
1995-1999 models		
Cylinder bore	14.000-14.043 (0.5512-0.5529)	–
Piston diameter	13.957-13.984 (0.5495-0.5506)	–
2000 models		
Cylinder bore	15.870-15.913 (0.6248-0.6265)	–
Piston diameter	15.827-15.854 (0.6231-0.6242)	–
Front caliper		
Cylinder bore		–
1995-1999 models	25.4000-25.450 (1.0000-1.0020)	–
2000 models	30.230-30.306 (1.1902-1.1931)	–
Piston diameter		
1995-1999 models	25.335-25.368 (0.9974-0.9987)	–
2000 models	30.150-30.200 (1.1870-1.1890)	–
Rear master cylinder		
Cylinder bore	12.700-12.743 (0.5000-0.5017)	–
Piston diameter	12.657-12.684 (0.4983-0.4994)	–
Rear caliper		
Cylinder bore	38.180-38.256 (1.5031-1.5061)	–
Piston diameter	38.098-38.148 (1.4999-1.5019)	–
Brake pedal height		
1995-1999 models	45 (1.8)	
2000 models	50 (2.0)	

Table 2 BRAKE TORQUE SPECIFICATIONS

Item	N•m	in.-lb.	ft.-lb.
Bleed valve (front and rear)	8	71	–
Brake disc bolt (front and rear)	23	–	17
Brake disc mounting	23	–	17
Brake hose banjo bolt (front and rear)	23	–	17
Front caliper mounting bolt			
1995-1999 models	25	–	18
2000 models	39	–	29
Front caliper pad mounting bolt			
1995-1999 models	18	–	13
Front master cylinder clamp bolt	10	88	–
Rear caliper housing bolt			
1995-1999 models	33	–	24
2000 models	30	–	22
Rear caliper mounting bolt	25	–	18
(continued)			

Table 2 BRAKE TORQUE SPECIFICATIONS (continued)

Item	N•m	in.-lb.	ft.-lb.
Rear master cylinder mounting bolt	23	–	17
Rear master cylinder rod locknut	18	–	13
Torque arm bolt/nut	35		26

CHAPTER FOURTEEN

BODY AND FRAME

This chapter contains removal and installation procedures for the body panels and the sidestand.

Whenever removing a body or frame member, reinstall all mounting hardware (such as small brackets, bolts, nuts, rubber bushings and metal collars) onto the removed part so they will not be misplaced. Suzuki makes frequent changes during the model year, so a part and the way it attaches to the frame may differ slightly from the one used in the service procedures in this chapter.

The plastic fairing and frame cover parts are very expensive to replace. After each part is removed from the motorcycle, wrap it in a blanket or clean newsprint, and place it in a cardboard box. Store it in an area where it will not be damaged.

SEAT

Removal/Installation

1. Insert the key into the seat lock on the left side and turn the lock clockwise.
2. Lift up the rear of the seat and pull the seat rearward.
3. To install the seat, slide the seat forward until the tang (A, **Figure 1**) on the seat engages the retainer (B, **Figure 1**) behind the fuel tank.
4. Press the seat down until it locks into place.

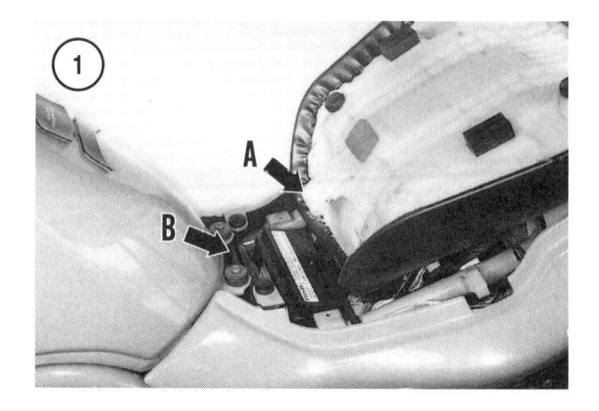

FRONT FENDER AND BRACE (1995-1999 MODELS)

1. Remove the front wheel as described in Chapter Ten.

BODY AND FRAME

CAUTION
Do not turn the fender bolt when removing the fender. The 3 mm threads can be easily stripped.

2. Hold each fender bolt (A, **Figure 2**) and remove its nut and washer from beneath the fender.

3. Remove the fender bolts from the fork brace.

4. Lower the fender from the fork brace and pull the fender from between the fork legs.

5. If necessary, remove the fender brace bolt (B, **Figure 2**) from each fork leg and lift the brace from the fork legs.

6. Installation is the reverse of removal. Pay attention to the following:

a. Install the fender brace so its arrow (**Figure 3**) points forward.
b. Install a washer on the fender side of each fender bolt.
c. Hold each fender bolt and tighten the fender nut.

FRONT FENDER (2000 MODELS)

1. Remove the front wheel as described in Chapter Ten.

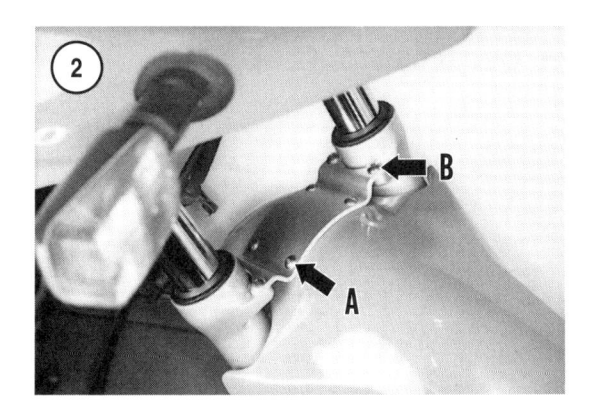

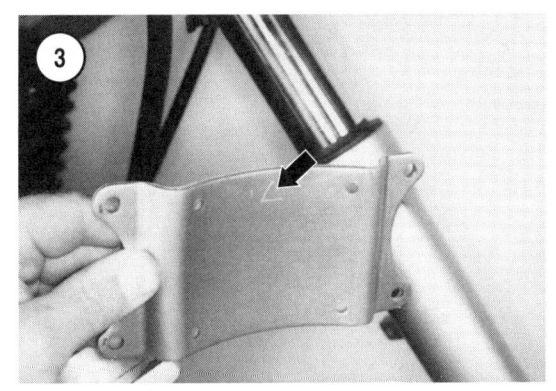

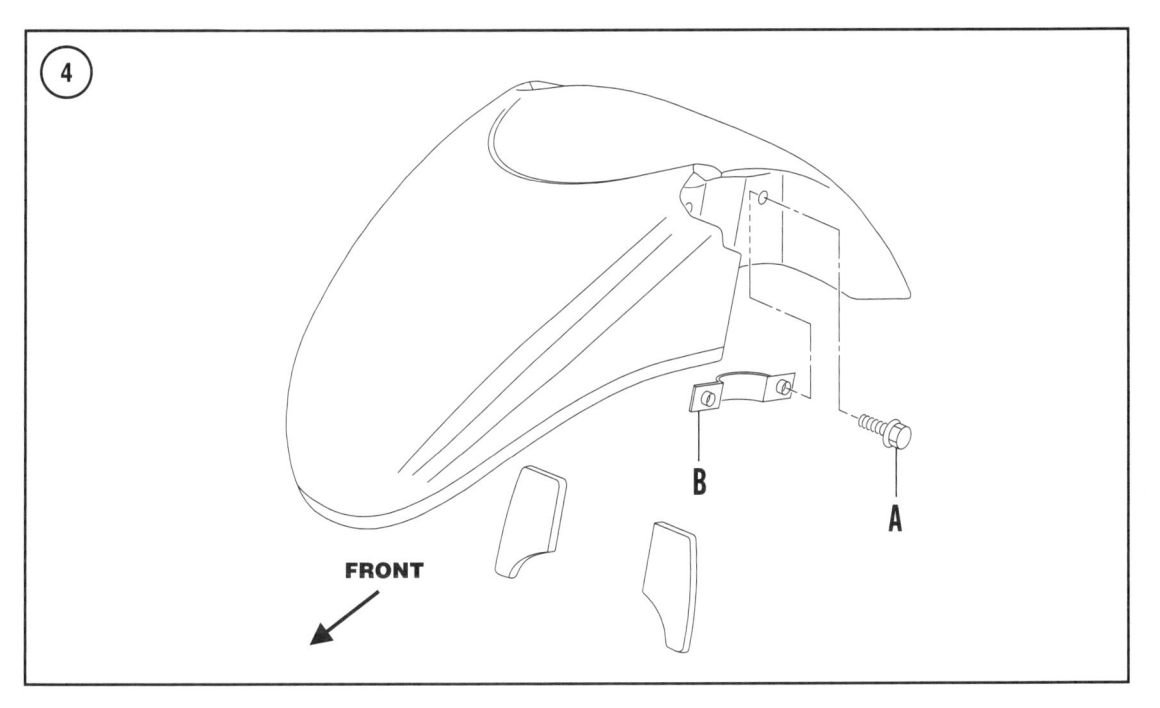

2. On one side, remove the two fender bolts (A, **Figure 4**) and remove the fender plate (B, **Figure 4**) from inside the fender.

FRONT FAIRING (1995-1999 GSF600S MODELS)

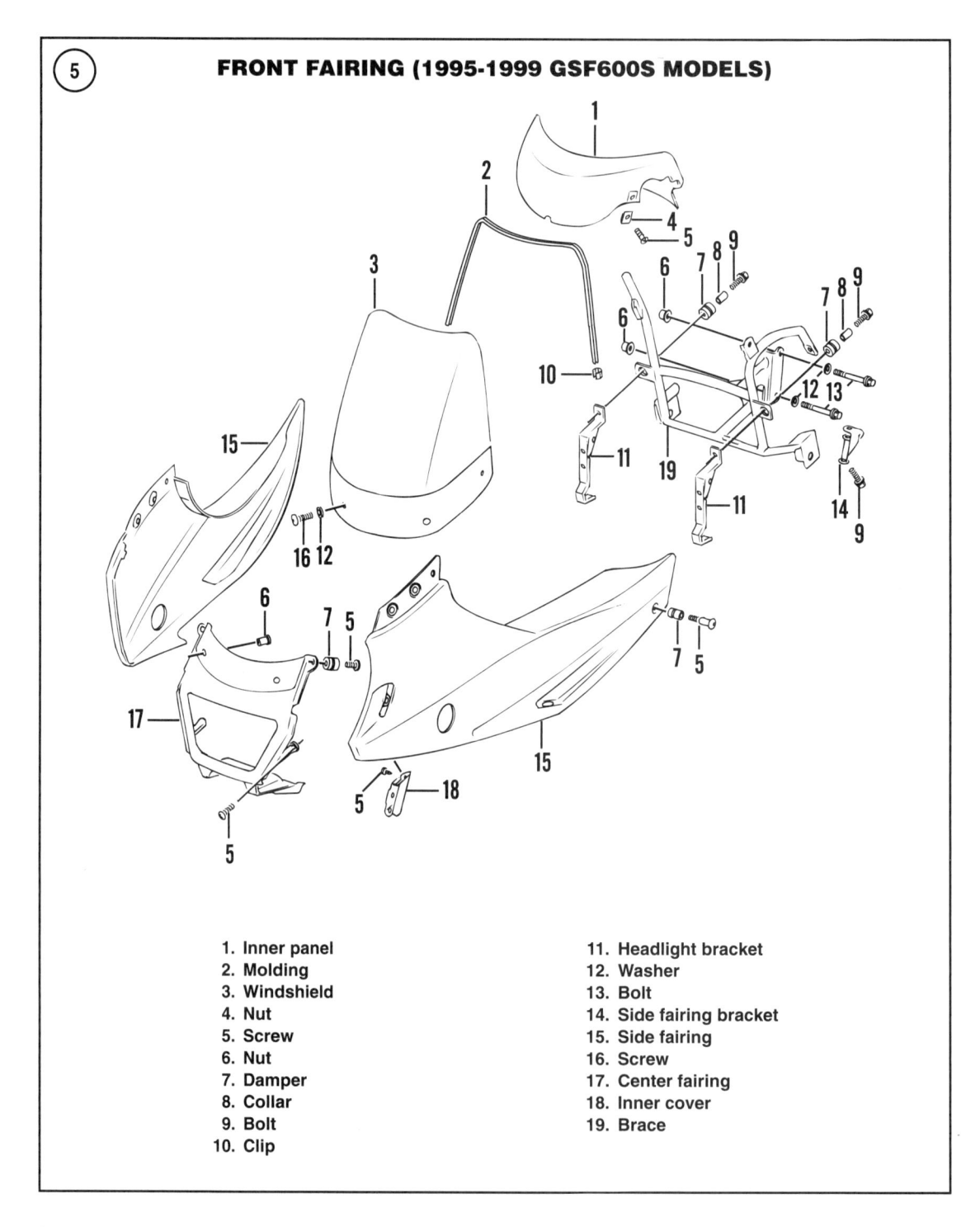

1. Inner panel
2. Molding
3. Windshield
4. Nut
5. Screw
6. Nut
7. Damper
8. Collar
9. Bolt
10. Clip
11. Headlight bracket
12. Washer
13. Bolt
14. Side fairing bracket
15. Side fairing
16. Screw
17. Center fairing
18. Inner cover
19. Brace

3. Repeat Step 2 on the other side.

4. Pull the fender forward and remove it from between the fork legs.

5. Installation is the reverse of removal. Tighten the fender bolts securely.

FAIRING (1995-1999 GSF600S MODELS)

Removal/Installation

Refer to **Figure 5**.

BODY AND FRAME

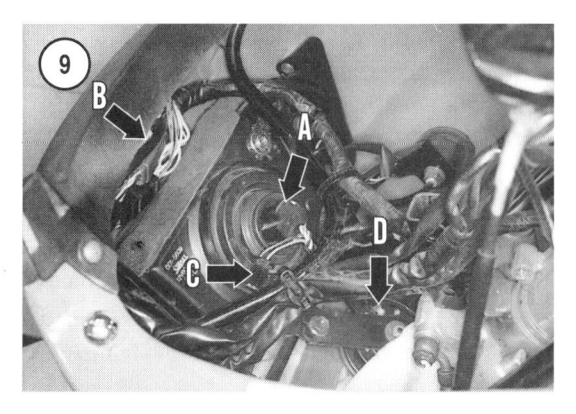

1. Remove the fuel tank as described in Chapter Eight.
2. Remove the windshield by performing the following:
   a. Remove the windshield mounting screws and washers (**Figure 6**).
   b. Lift the windshield from the fairing. Make sure the rubber grommet at each screw position remains in the fairing.
3. Remove the mount (**Figure 7**) from the rear of each side fairing.
4. Drape a thick towel over the front fender.
5. Remove the two fender brace mounting bolts that secure the fender brace to the steering head. The upper bolt is secured with a washer. The lower bolt, however, threads into a weld nut on the brace.
6. Pull the fairing forward enough to gain access to the electrical connectors. See **Figure 8**.
7. Disconnect the plastic ties holding the wiring harness in place.
8. Disconnect the headlight connector (A, **Figure 9**) from the headlight.
9. Disconnect both handlebar switch connectors and the combination meter connector. These sit on top of the headlight (B, **Figure 9**).
10. Disconnect the 2-pin connector (C, **Figure 9**) for each turn signal and remove the spade connectors from the horn (D, **Figure 9**).
11. Carefully remove the fairing from the motorcycle.
12. If necessary, remove the side fairing bracket (**Figure 10**) from each side of the frame.
13. Inspect the fairing as described in this chapter.
14. Installation is the reverse of removal.
15. Once the fairing is installed, turn on the ignition switch and check the operation of the combination meter, lights, each turn signal, horn and all the switches in each handlebar switch.

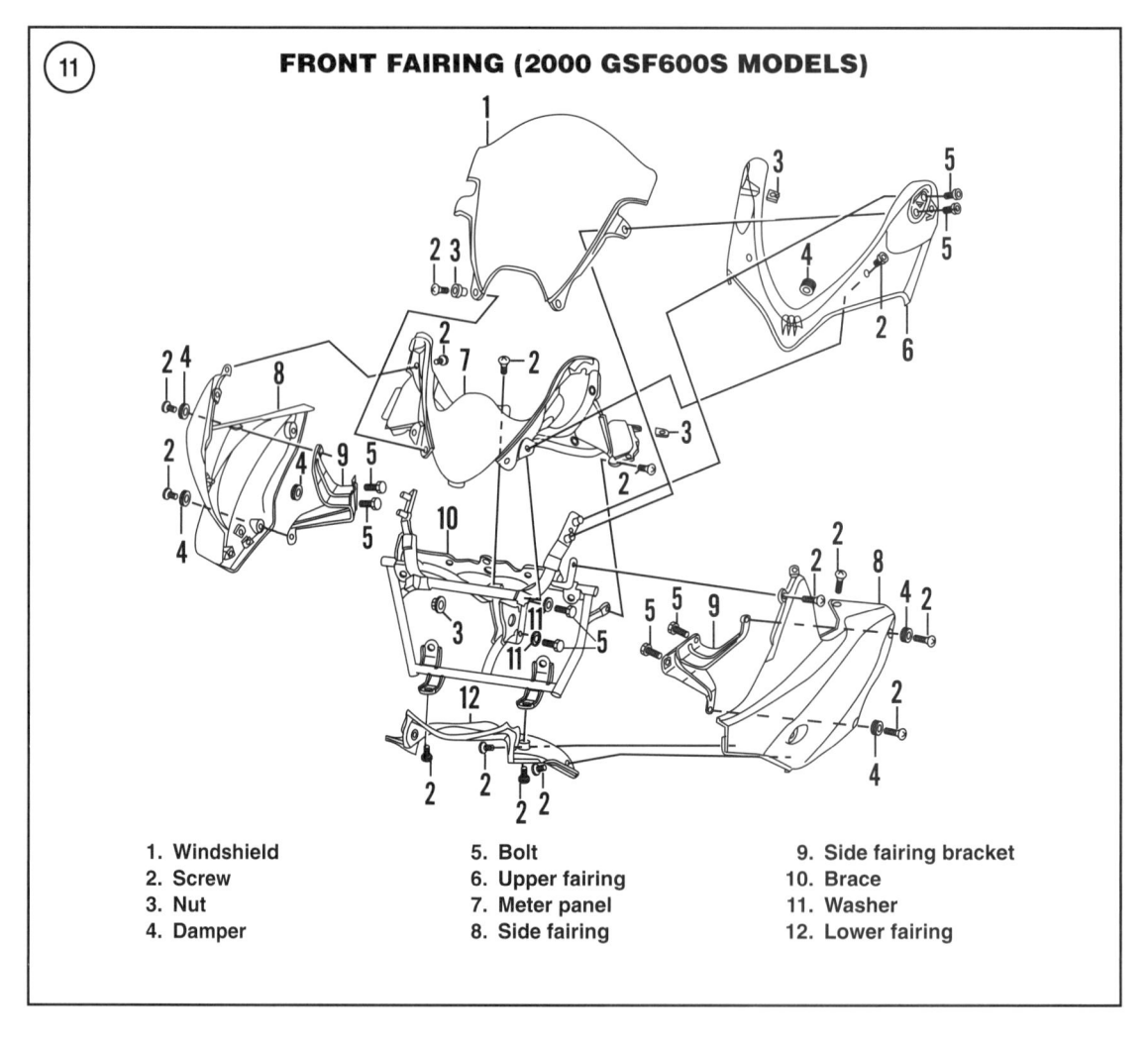

FRONT FAIRING (2000 GSF600S MODELS)

1. Windshield
2. Screw
3. Nut
4. Damper
5. Bolt
6. Upper fairing
7. Meter panel
8. Side fairing
9. Side fairing bracket
10. Brace
11. Washer
12. Lower fairing

FAIRING (2000 GSF600S MODELS)

Removal/Installation

The fairing on 2000 GSF600S models (**Figure 11**) cannot be removed as a complete assembly. Fairing removal, therefore, consists of disassembling the fairing.

1. From behind the fairing, remove the two screws securing the meter panel to each side of the upper fairing.
2. Remove each rear view mirror from the upper fairing.
3. Stand in front of the motorcycle. Remove the upper fairing mounting screws and remove the upper fairing from the motorcycle.
4. Remove the lower fairing mounting screws and remove the lower fairing.
5. Remove one side fairing by performing the following:
   a. Remove each side fairing mounting screw.
   b. Pull the side fairing away from the frame and disconnect the turn signal connector.
   c. Remove the side fairing.
6. Repeat Step 6 for the other side fairing.
7. Remove the two windshield screws from the front of the windshield and remove the windshield.
8. If necessary, remove the meter panel by performing the following:
   a. Remove the headlight and combination meter as described in Chapter Nine.
   b. On models with a position light, disconnect the position light connector.
   c. Remove the mounting screws and remove the meter panel.

BODY AND FRAME

12 **REAR FRAME COVER (1995-1999 MODELS)**

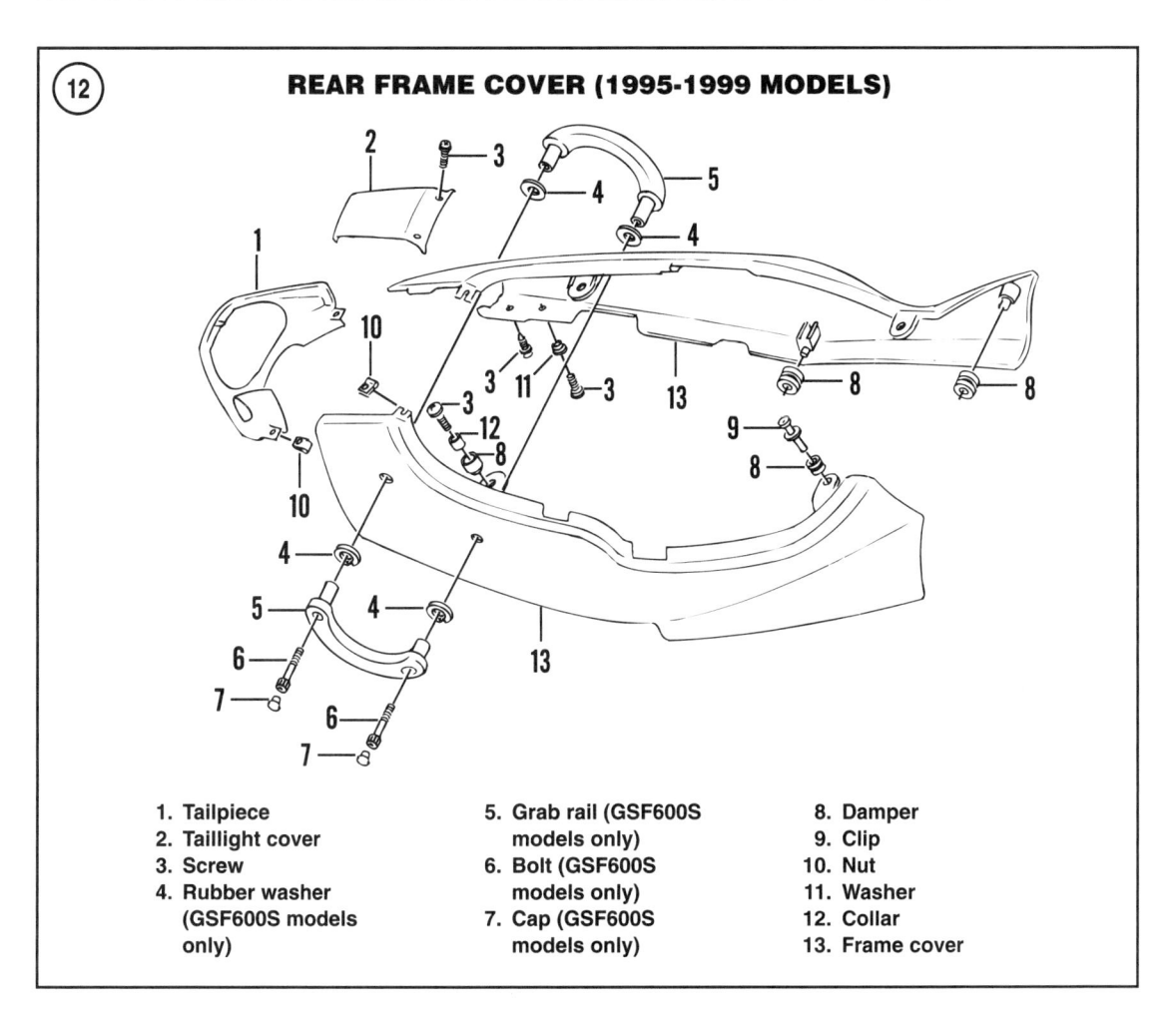

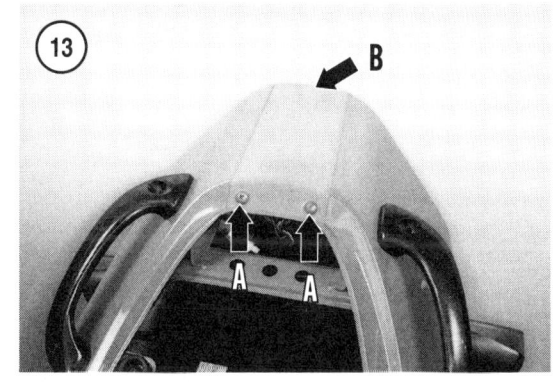

1. Tailpiece
2. Taillight cover
3. Screw
4. Rubber washer (GSF600S models only)
5. Grab rail (GSF600S models only)
6. Bolt (GSF600S models only)
7. Cap (GSF600S models only)
8. Damper
9. Clip
10. Nut
11. Washer
12. Collar
13. Frame cover

9. Inspect the fairing as described below in this chapter.
10. Installation is the reverse of removal.
11. Once the fairing is reinstalled on the motorcycle, check the operation of the turn signals and any other electrical components disconnected during removal.

FAIRING INSPECTION

1. Inspect all components for damage, cracks or fractures. Check each mounting hole for elongation or fractures from overtightening of fasteners.
2. Examine the raised post, on parts so equipped, for damage or cracks.
3. Repair or replace any damaged part.
4. If removed, inspect the mounting bracket for bending or other damage, replace if necessary.

REAR FRAME COVER

Removal/Installation (1995-1999 Models)

Refer to **Figure 12**.

1. Remove the seat as described in this chapter.
2. Remove the mounting screws (A, **Figure 13**) and remove the tail piece (B, **Figure 13**).

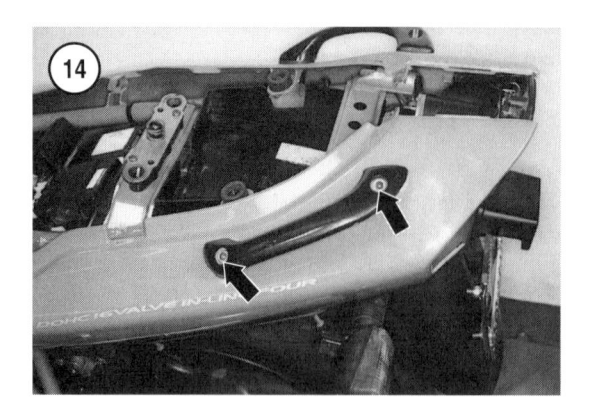

3. On 1996-1999 GSF600S models, remove the grab rail by performing the following:
   a. Remove each cap from the grab rail.
   b. Remove the grab rail mounting bolts (**Figure 14**) and the grab rail.
   c. Do not lose the damper behind each grab rail mount.
   d. Repeat substeps a-c for the other grab rail.
4. Remove the left frame cover by performing the following:
   a. Remove the mounting screws and washers located behind the turn signal (**Figure 15**).
   b. Remove the frame cover mounting screw from the rear mount. Do not lose the damper and collar from this mount.
   c. Remove the clip from the front mount (A, **Figure 16**). Do not lose the damper from this mount.
   d. Pull the post (B, **Figure 16**) at the front of the frame cover from the damper in the frame and remove the frame cover.
   e. Repeat substeps a-d for the right frame cover.
5. Installation is the reverse of removal. Note the following:
   a. Press the post (B, **Figure 16**) on each frame cover into the damper in the frame.

Removal/Installation (2000 Models)

Refer to **Figure 17**.
1. Remove the seat as described in this chapter.
2. Remove the caps from each side of the grab rail.
3. Remove the mounting bolts from each side of the grab rail and the grab rail. Do not lose the damper and collar at each grab rail mount. 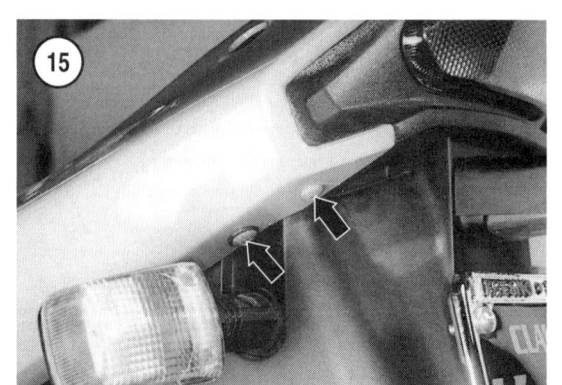 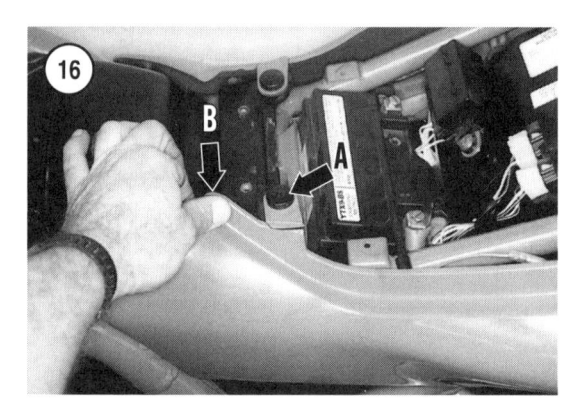
4. Disconnect the taillight/brake light connector from the wiring harness.
5. Remove the mounting screws from beneath the frame cover.
6. Remove the mounting bolts from the mounts on each side of the cover. Do not lose the collar and damper from each mount.
7. Lift the frame cover from the frame.
8. Installation is the reverse of removal.

SIDE COVER (2000 MODELS)

Refer to **Figure 18**.
1. Remove the front and rear mounting screws from the side cover assembly. Do not lose the collar from the rear mount.
2. Gently pull the lower edge of the frame cover until the post is freed from the damper in the frame. Remove the side cover assembly.
3. If necessary, remove the front cover from the rear cover.
4. Installation is the reverse of removal.

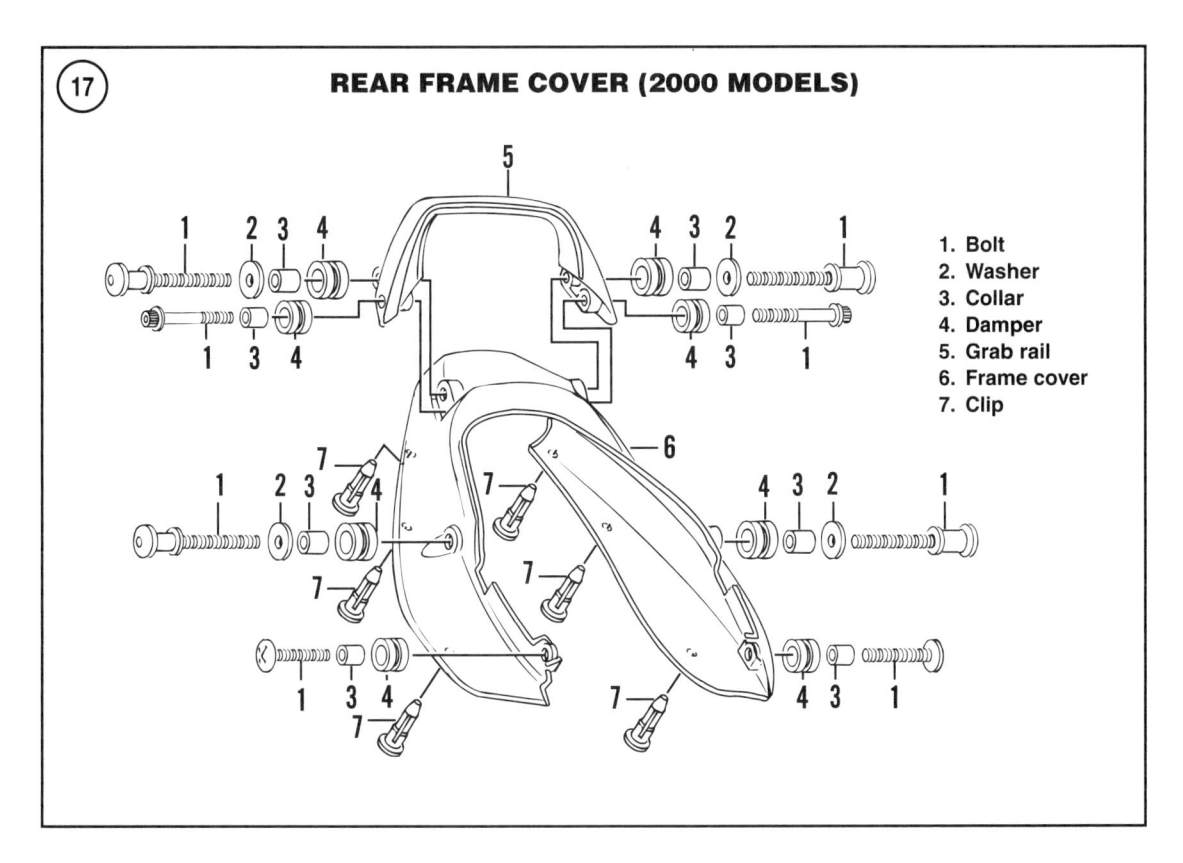

BODY AND FRAME

REAR FRAME COVER (2000 MODELS)

1. Bolt
2. Washer
3. Collar
4. Damper
5. Grab rail
6. Frame cover
7. Clip

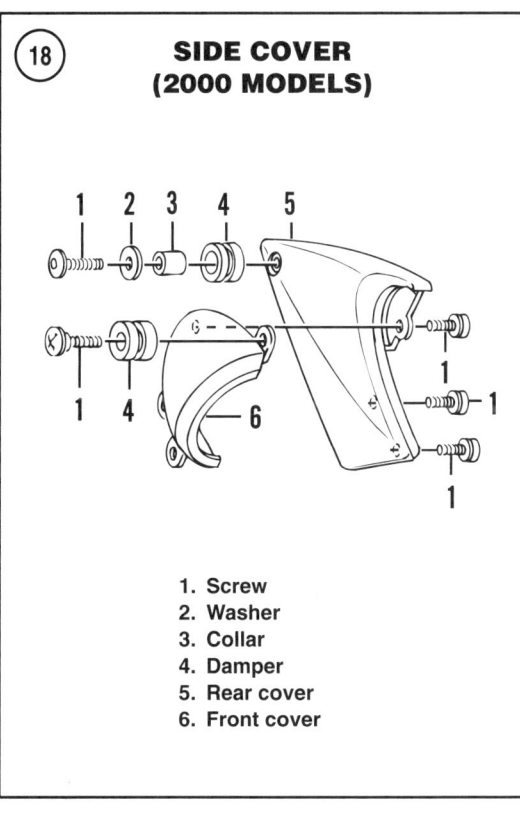

SIDE COVER (2000 MODELS)

1. Screw
2. Washer
3. Collar
4. Damper
5. Rear cover
6. Front cover

a. Make sure the post securely engages the damper in the frame and then reinstall the mounting screws.

b. Make sure the collar is in place in the rear mount.

SIDESTAND

Removal/Installation

1. Securely support the motorcycle in an upright position.

2. Disconnect both springs from the sidestand.

3. Remove the nut (**Figure 19**) from the bolt on the sidestand bracket and remove the sidestand.

4. Installation is the reverse of removal.

   a. Lubricate the pivot and the springs with Suzuki Super Grease A or an equivalent waterproof bearing grease.

   b. Make sure the inner spring sits inside the outer spring and that both springs are connected to the post on the sidestand.

   c. Tighten the nut securely.

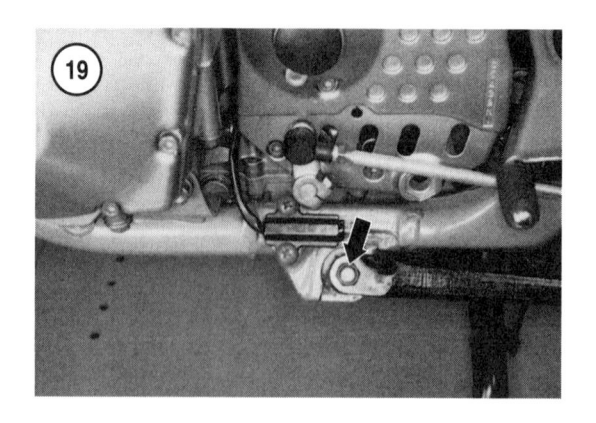

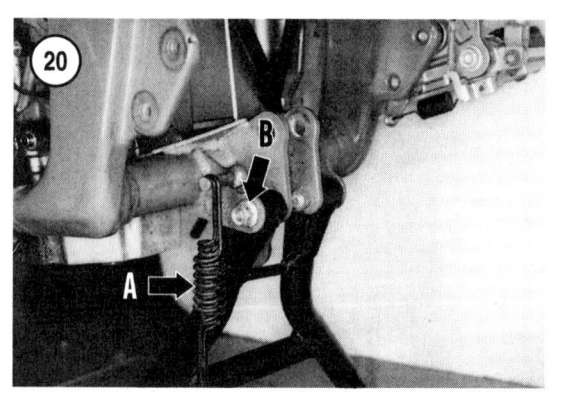

CENTERSTAND (GSF600S MODELS)

Removal/Installation

1. Securely support the motorcycle in an upright position.
2. Disconnect both springs (A, **Figure 20**) from the centerstand.
3. Remove the bolt (B, **Figure 20**) from each side of the centerstand mount and remove the centerstand from the frame. Do not lose the collar that sits inside each centerstand pivot.
4. Installation is the reverse of removal.

   a. Lubricate the pivots, collars, and the springs with Suzuki Super Grease A or an equivalent waterproof bearing grease.

   b. Tighten each bolt securely.

INDEX

A

Air filter
  housing 235-237
Alternator 263-270

B

Basic service methods 23-29
Battery 63-66
  negative terminal 260
  state of charge 100
Bearing race replacement,
  steering head 339-341
Bearing replacement, steering stem 341-342
Bearing, replacement 363-364
Body
  centerstand, GSF600S models 408
  fairing
    1995-1999 GSF600S models 402-403
    2000 GSF600S models 404-405
    inspection 405
  front fender
    2000 models 401-402
    and brace, 1995-1999 models 400-401
  seat 400
  sidestand 407
Brace
  and front fender, 1995-1999 models . . . 400-401
Brakes 59-60
  bleeding 396-397
  disc 394-396
  front
    brake pad replacement 367-370
    caliper 370-375
    master cylinder 382-386
  hose replacement 392-394
  rear
    brake pad replacement 375-378
    brake pedal 397
    caliper 378-382
    master cylinder 386-391
  service 366-367
  specifications 398
  torque specifications 398-399
Break-in 179-180

C

Caliper
  front 370-375
  rear 378-382
Cam chain tensioner 112-113
Cam chain 114
Camshafts 105-112
Carburetor 223-227
  assembly 219-223
  heater
    UK models 228-230
  operation 218-219
  separation 230-232
  service 219
  specifications
    1995 models 254
    1996 models 254-255
    1997 models 255-256
    1998 models 256-257
    1999 models 257
    2000 models 258
Centerstand
  GSF600S models 408

INDEX

Charging system 53, 260-263
Clutch 44-45, 185-192
  cable replacement 192-193
  release mechanism 192
  specifications 193-194
  torque specifications 194
Combination meter 301-305
Connecting rod
  bearing insert selection 183
  insert color, thickness, Part No. 183-184
Connecting rods 176-179
Conversion tables 32-33
Crankcase 158-170
  breather system 241
Crankshaft 170-176
  insert color, Part No., thickness 183
  main bearing insert selection 182
Cylinder
  block 131-134
  head 116-122
  head cover 103-105
  leakdown test 43-44

D

Decimal
  and metric equivalents 32
  place values 16
Drive chain 330
  wheels and tires
    specifications 331
    torque specifications 331-332
Drivetrain noise 45-46

E

Electrical system
  alternator 263-270
  charging system 260-263
  combination meter 301-305
  fundamentals 22-23
  fuses 305-306
  ignition system 270-277
  lighting system 285-291
  main fuse 306
  negative battery terminal 260
  preliminary information 259-260
  relays 299-300
  replacement bulbs 307
  specifications 306-307

  starter
    motor 277-284
    relay 284-285
  starting system 277
  switches 292-299
  torque specifications 308
  troubleshooting 46-48
  wiring diagrams 306
Emission control
  evaporative emission control system,
    California models only 241-243
  PAIR system, 1995-1999 California
    and Switzerland, 2000 models 243-252
  purge control valves and
    charcoal canister 243
Engine
  drive sprocket 196-197
    cover 195-196
  lower end 146-150
    break-in 179-180
    connecting rod bearing
      insert selection 183
    connecting rod insert color,
      thickness, Part No. 183-184
    connecting rods 176-179
    crankcase 158-170
    crankshaft insert color,
      Part No., thickness 183
    crankshaft main bearing
      insert selection 182
    crankshaft 170-176
    oil
      cooler 152-153
      pan, strainer and
        pressure regulator 154-156
      pump 150-152
    servicing the engine in frame 146
    specifications 180-181
    starter clutch and gears 156-158
    thrust bearing selection 183
    torque specifications 181-182
  lubrication 43
  noises 42-43
  performance 41-42
  sprocket torque
    specifications 217
  top end
    cam chain 114
      tensioner 112-113
    camshafts 105-112

INDEX

cylinder
  block 131-134
  head 116-122
  head cover 103-105
  general specifications 142
  piston and piston rings 134-141
  principles 103
  rocker arms 114-116
  service notes 101-103
  specifications 142-144
  torque specifications 144-145
  valves and valve components 122-131
tune-up 86-90
Evaporative emission control system,
  California models only 241-243
Exhaust system 253
External gearshift mechanism 197-200

F

Fairing
  1995-1999 GSF600S models 402-403
  2000 GSF600S models 404-405
  inspection 405
Fasteners 4-6
Fender, front, and brace,
  1995-1999 models 400-401
Float height, adjustment 232-233
Fluids and lubricants,
  recommended 98-99
Frame
  noise 60
  serial numbers 30-31
  rear cover 405-406
  side cover, 2000 models 406-407
Front fender
  2000 models 401-402
  and brace, 1995-1999 models 400-401
Front fork 342-351
Front, wheel 311-314
Fuel
  system 45
  air filter housing 235-237
  carburetor 223-227
    assembly 219-223
    heater, UK models 228-230
    operation 218-219
    separation 230-232
    service 219
  specifications
    1995 models 254
    1996 models 254-255
    1997 models 255-256
    1998 models 256-257
    1999 models 257
    2000 models 258
    test specifications 258
  crankcase breather system 241
  filter 241
  float height adjustment 232-233
  pilot screw 227-228
  starter cable replacement 234-235
  tank 237-239
  throttle cable replacement 233-234
  throttle position sensor,
    2000 models 228
  torque specifications 258
  valve 239-241
Fuses 305-306

G

Gears
  and starter clutch 156-158
Gearshift mechanisms
  engine drive sprocket cover 195-196
  engine drive sprocket 196-197
  external 197-200
  internal 211-216
Gearshift
  specifications 217
General engine specifications 142
General information
  basic service methods 23-29
  conversion tables 32-33
  decimal
    and metric equivalents 32
    place values 16
  electrical system
    fundamentals 22-23
  fasteners 4-6
  frame serial numbers 30-31
  metric tap and drill sizes 35
  serial numbers 4
  shop supplies 6-9
  specifications, general torque 33-34
  storage 29-30
  technical abbreviations 34
  tools
    basic 9-14
    precision measuring 14-22
    special 23

General information (continued)
  vehicle
    dimensions 31
    weight 32
General torque specifications 33-34

H

Handlebar. 333-335
  left grip replacement. 335-337
Handling. 58-59
Hubs
  front and rear 320-325

I

Ignition system 53-55, 270-277
Internal gearshift mechanism 211-216

L

Lighting system 285-291
Lubrication
  periodic 66-71
  recommended lubricants and fluids 98-99

M

Main fuse 306
Maintenance
  and tune-up
    torque specifications 100
    specifications 99
  battery 63-66
    state of charge. 100
  non-scheduled 82-86
  periodic 71-82
  pre-ride check list 61-62
  schedule 62, 96-98
  spark plugs 90-96
  storage 96
  tires
    and wheels 62-63
    specifications 98
Master cylinder
  front 382-386
  rear 386-391
Metric
  and decimal equivalents 32
  tap and drill sizes 35
Motorcycle stand 309-311

N

Negative battery terminal 260

O

Oil
  cooler 152-153
  pan, strainer and
    pressure regulator 154-156
  pump 150-152
  strainer, pan and pressure regulator . . . 154-156
Operating requirements 36-37

P

PAIR system, 1995-1999 California
  and Switzerland, 2000 models 243-252
Pilot screw 227-228
Piston and piston rings 134-141
Pre-ride check list 61-62
Purge control valves and
  charcoal canister 243

R

Rear suspension
  bearing replacement 363-364
  shock
    absorber 353-355
    lever assembly 355-357
  specifications 365
  swing arm 357-363
  torque specifications 365
Rear
  coupling, and rear sprocket 319-320
  sprocket, and rear coupling 319-320
  wheel 314-319
Relays 299-300
Replacement bulbs 307
Rocker arms 114-116

S

Seat 400
Serial numbers 4
Servicing the engine in frame 146
Shock
  absorber 353-355
  lever assembly 355-357
Shop supplies 6-9
Side cover, 2000 models 406-407

INDEX

Sidestand 407
Spark plugs 90-96
Specifications
  battery state of charge 100
  brake 398
    torque 398-399
  carburetor
    1995 models 254
    1996 models 254-255
    1997 models 255-256
    1998 models 256-257
    1999 models 257
    2000 models 258
    test 258
    torque 258
  clutch 193-194
    torque 194
  connecting rod
    bearing insert selection 183
    insert color, thickness, Part No. 183-184
  crankshaft
    insert color, Part No., thickness 183
    main bearing insert selection 182
  electrical system 306-307
    torque 308
  engine, sprocket torque 217
  frame serial numbers 30-31
  front suspension 351-352
    and steering torque 352
  gearshift 217
  general
    engine 142
    torque 33-34
  lower end 180-181
    torque 181-182
  maintenance
    and tune up torque 100
    and tune-up 99
    schedule 96-98
  rear suspension 365
    torque 365
  recommended lubricants and fluids 98-99
  replacement bulbs 307
  thrust bearing selection 183
  tire 98
  top end 142-144
    torque 144-145
  transmission 217
  vehicle
    dimensions 31

    weight 32
  wheels
    tires and drive chain torque 331-332
    tires and drive chain 331
Starter cable, replacement 234-235
Starter clutch and gears 156-158
Starter
  motor 277-284
  relay 284-285
Starting system 56-58, 277
Starting
  difficulties 38-41
  the engine 37-38
Steering
  and front suspension
    torque specifications 352
  handlebar 333-335
  head
    and stem 337-339
    bearing race replacement 339-341
  left handlebar grip replacement 335-337
  stem bearing replacement 341-342
Storage 29-30, 96
Suspension
  front
    and steering torque
      specifications 352
    fork 342-351
    specifications 351-352
  rear
    specifications 365
    torque specifications 365
Swing arm 357-363
Switches 292-299

T

Tap and drill sizes, metric 35
Technical abbreviations 34
Test
  basic procedures 50-52
  cylinder leakdown 43-44
  equipment 48-50
Throttle cable, replacement 233-234
Throttle position sensor,
  2000 models 228
Thrust bearing selection 183
Tire specifications 98
Tires 325-329
  and wheels 62-63
  repairs 329-330

Tires (continued)
wheels
and drive chain
specifications 331
torque specifications 331-332
Tools
basic 9-14
precision measuring 14-22
special 23
Transmission 45, 200-211
specifications 217
Troubleshooting,
brakes 59-60
charging system 53
clutch 44-45
cylinder leakdown test 43-44
drivetrain noise 45-46
electrical 46-48
engine
lubrication 43
noises 42-43
performance 41-42
frame noise 60
fuel system 45
handling 58-59
ignition system 53-55
operating requirements 36-37
starting system 56-58
starting
difficulties 38-41

the engine 37-38
test
basic procedures 50-52
equipment 48-50
transmission 45
Tune-up
and maintenance
specifications 99
torque specifications 100
engine 86-90

V

Valves and valve components 122-131
Vehicle dimensions 31
Vehicle weight 32

W

Wheels 325
front 311-314
front and rear hubs 320-325
rear 314-319
coupling and rear sprocket 319-320
tires
and drive chain
specifications 331
torque specifications 331-332
Wiring diagrams 415-433

WIRING DIAGRAMS

WIRING DIAGRAMS

ALL 1995-1996 GSF600 MODELS, 1996 GSF600S BRAZIL, U.K. AND EUROPE MODELS

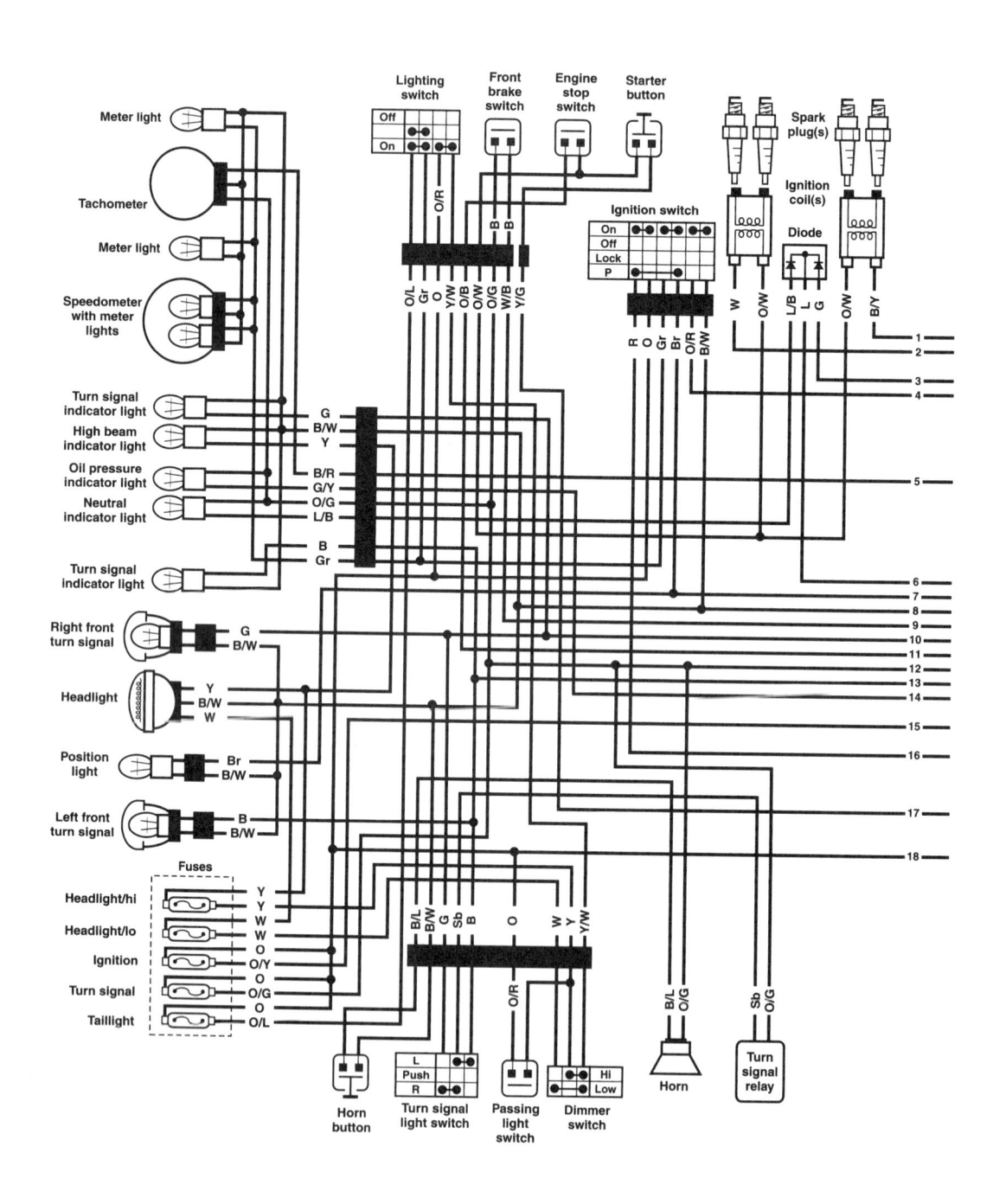

WIRING DIAGRAMS

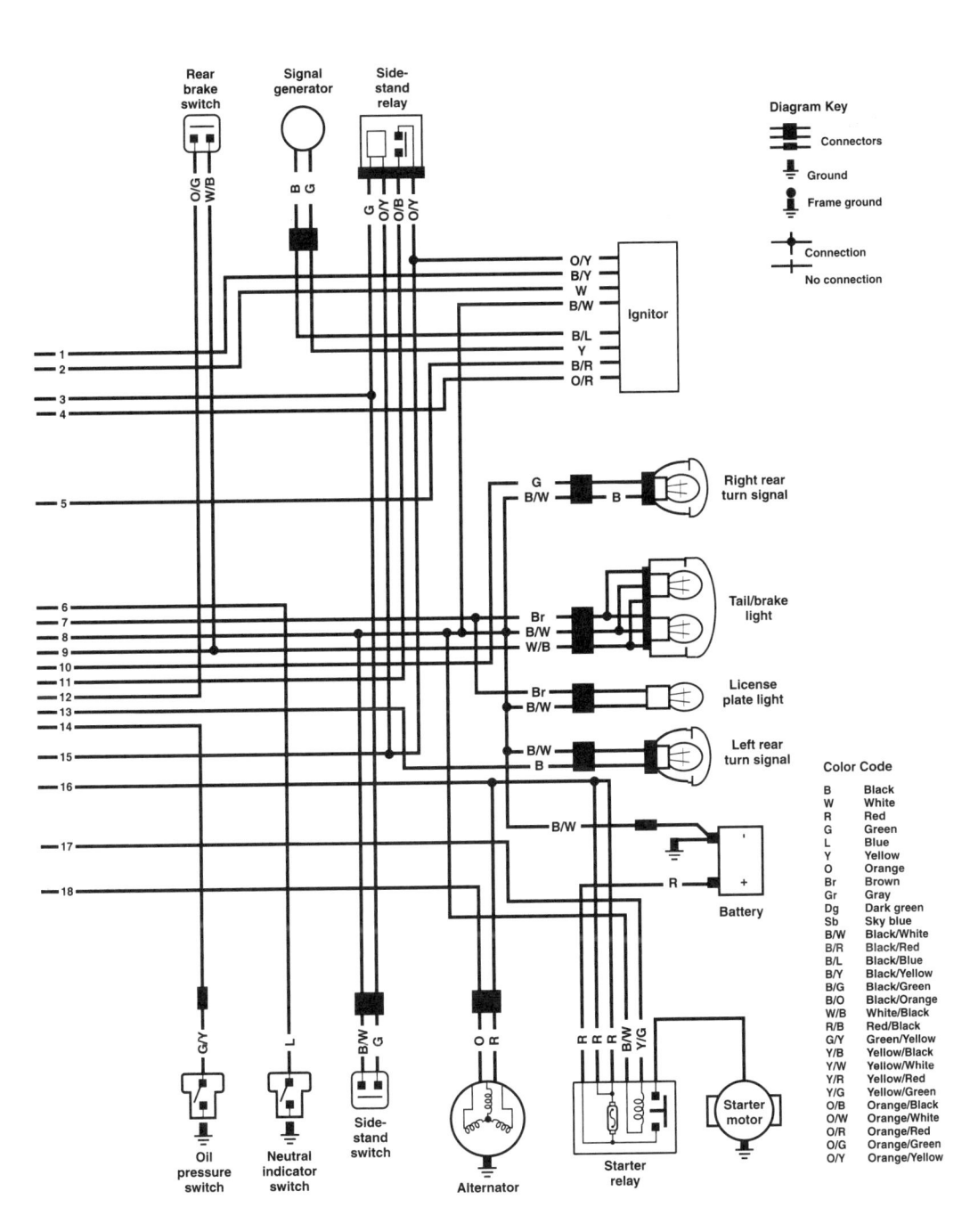

417

1996 GSF600S U.S.A., CALIFORNIA AND CANADA MODELS

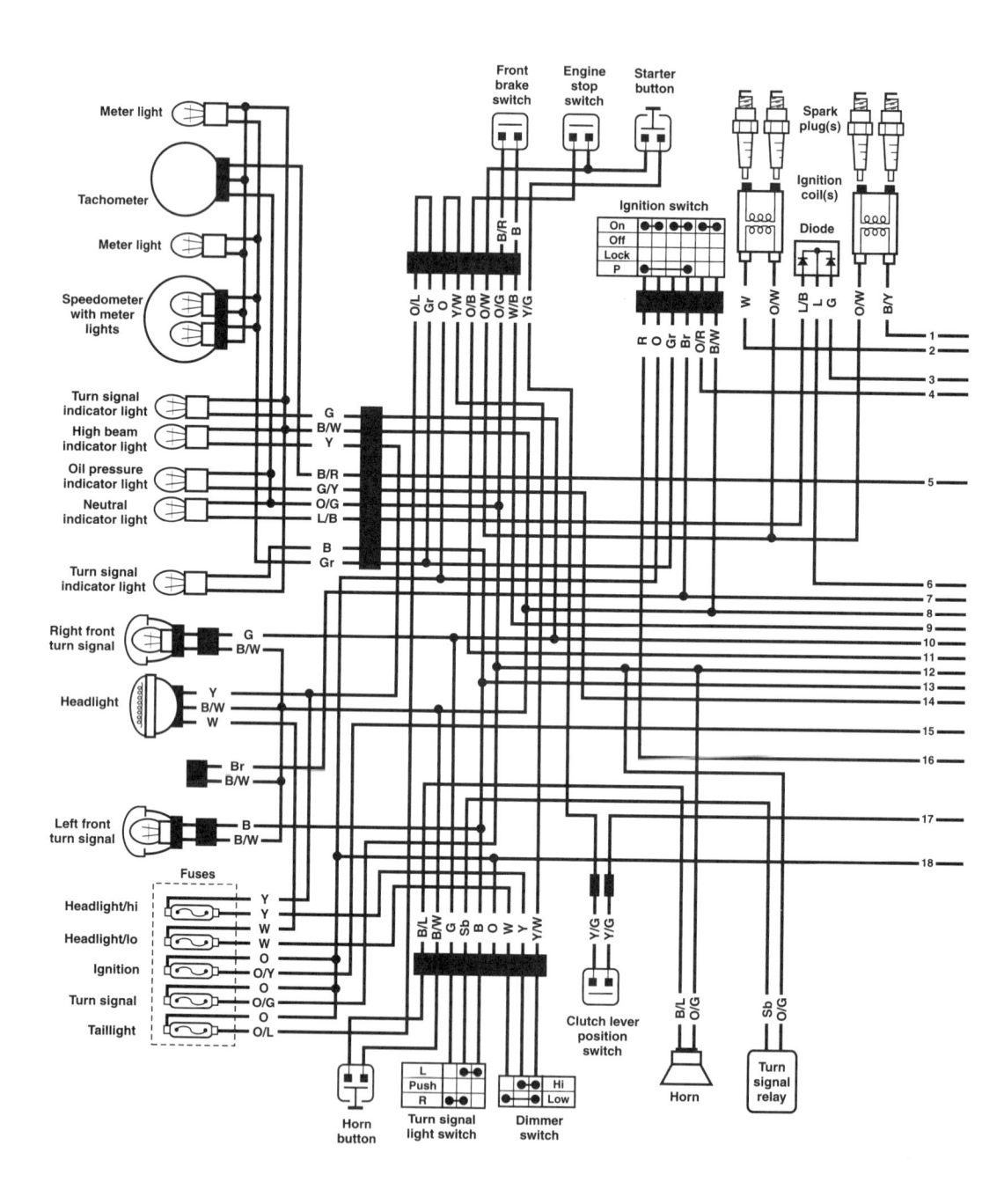

WIRING DIAGRAMS

419

Rear brake switch
- O/G
- W/B

Signal generator
- B
- G

Side-stand relay
- G
- O/Y
- O/B
- O/Y

Ignitor
- O/Y
- B/Y
- W
- B/W
- B/L
- Y
- B/R
- O/R

Right rear turn signal
- G
- B/W — B

Tail/brake light
- Br
- B/W
- W/B

License plate light
- Br
- B/W

Left rear turn signal
- B/W
- B

Battery
- B/W
- R

Oil pressure switch: G/Y

Neutral indicator switch: L

Side-stand switch: B/W, G

Alternator: O, R

Starter relay: R, R, R, B/W, Y/G

Starter motor

Diagram Key
- Connectors
- Ground
- Frame ground
- Connection
- No connection

Color Code
B	Black
W	White
R	Red
G	Green
L	Blue
Y	Yellow
O	Orange
Br	Brown
Gr	Gray
Dg	Dark green
Sb	Sky blue
B/W	Black/White
B/R	Black/Red
B/L	Black/Blue
B/Y	Black/Yellow
B/G	Black/Green
B/O	Black/Orange
W/B	White/Black
R/B	Red/Black
G/Y	Green/Yellow
Y/B	Yellow/Black
Y/W	Yellow/White
Y/R	Yellow/Red
Y/G	Yellow/Green
O/B	Orange/Black
O/W	Orange/White
O/R	Orange/Red
O/G	Orange/Green
O/Y	Orange/Yellow

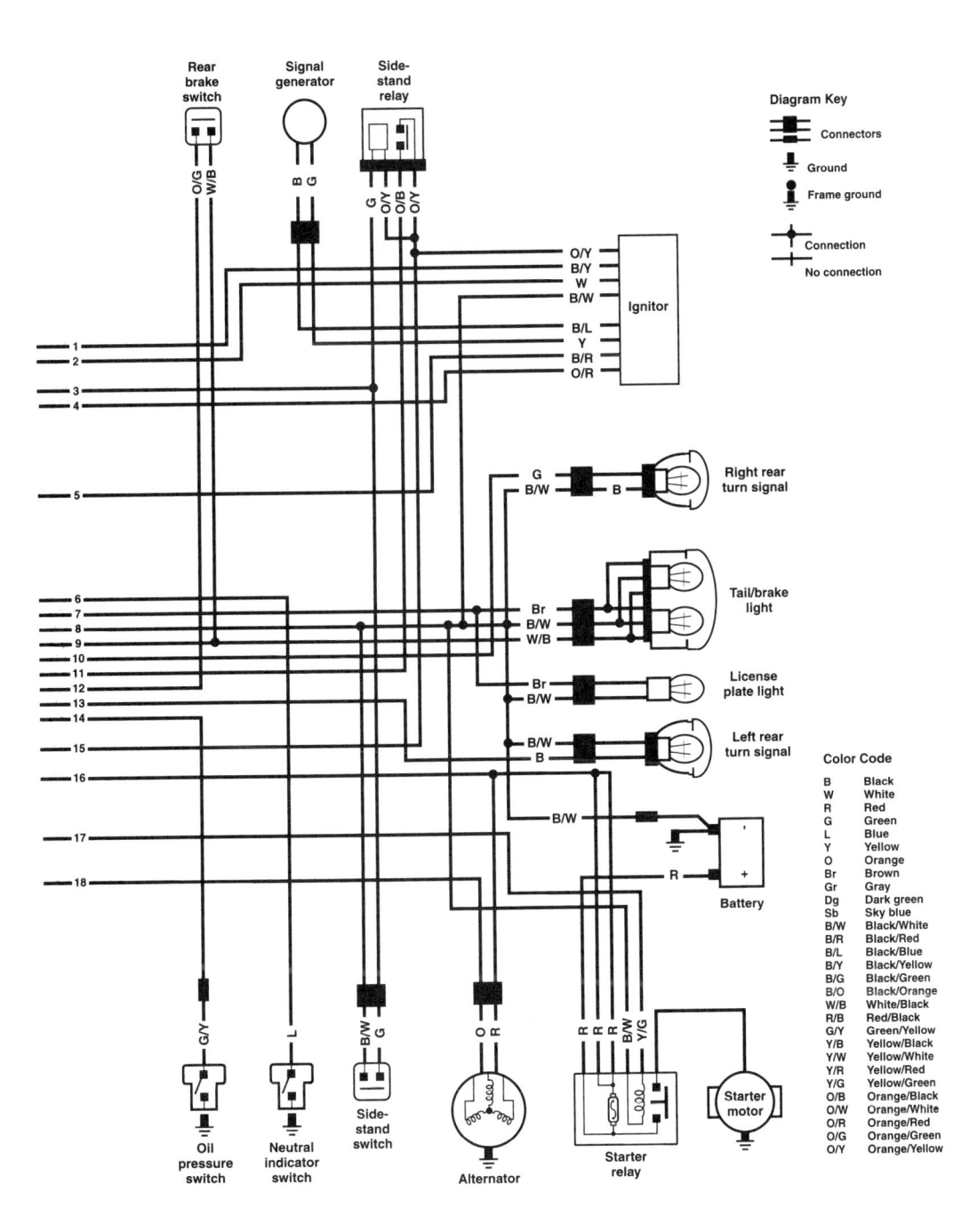

16

1996 GSF600S AUSTRALIA MODELS

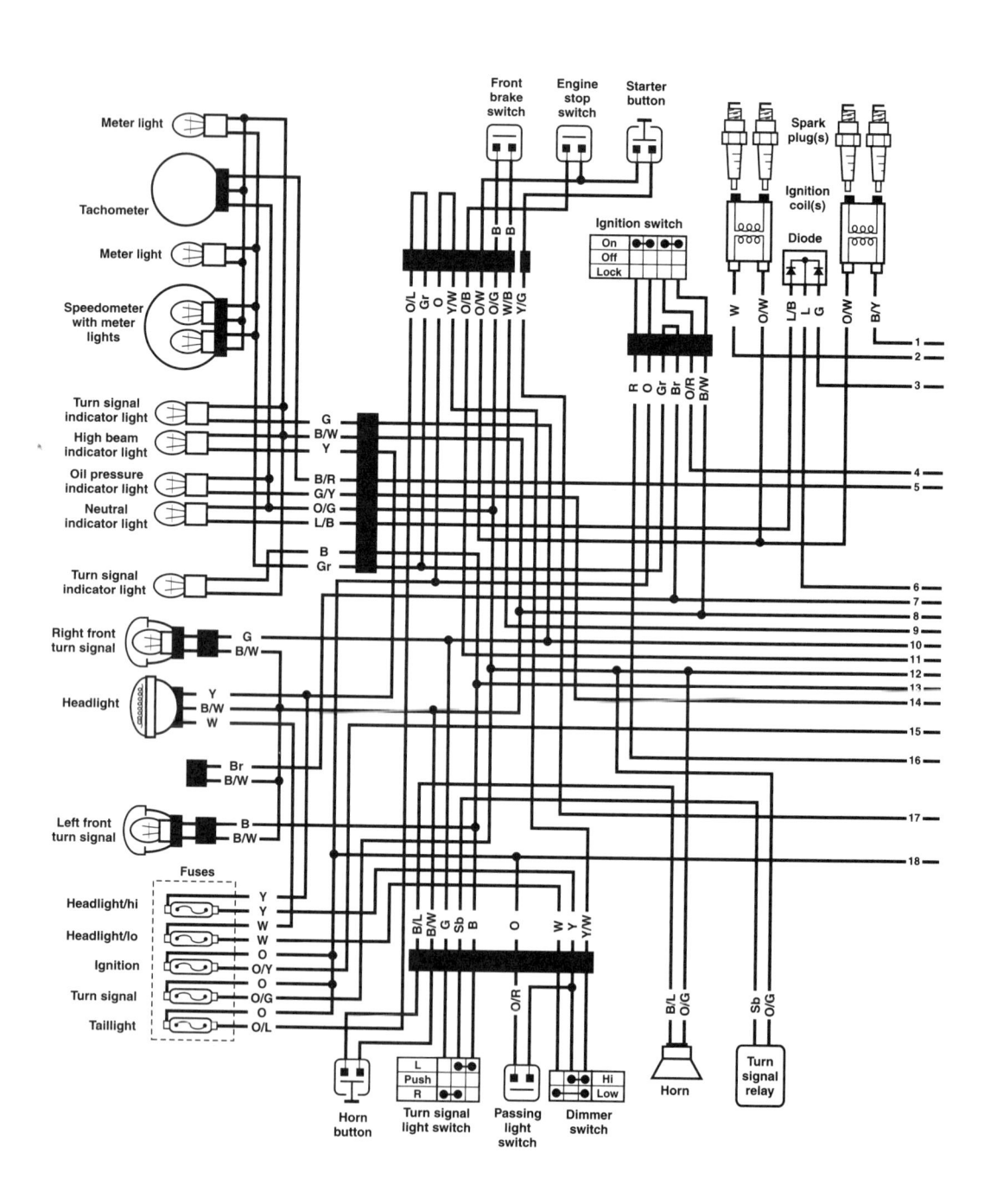

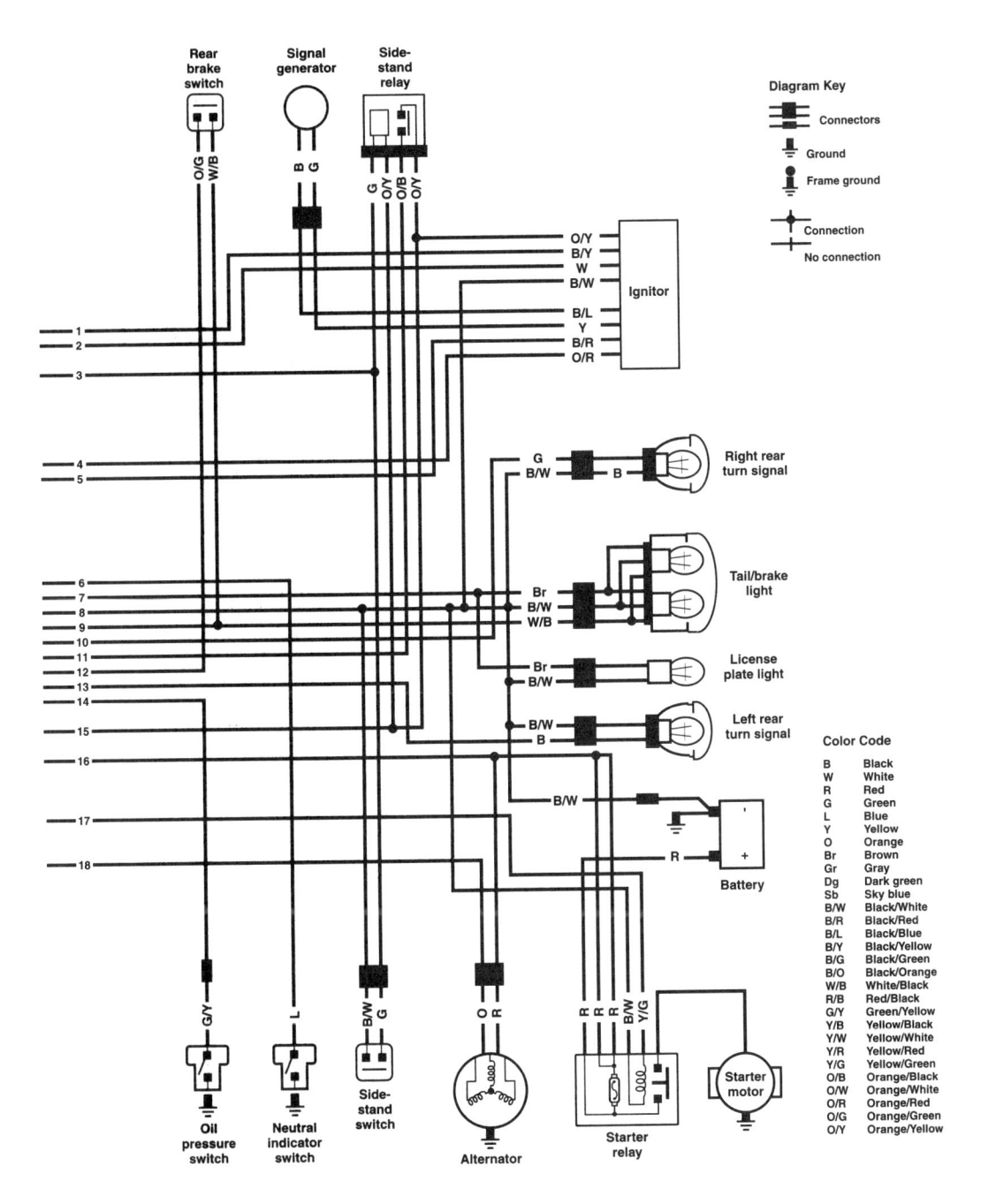

WIRING DIAGRAMS

421

1997-99 GSF600/GSF600S U.S.A., CALIFORNIA AND CANADA MODELS

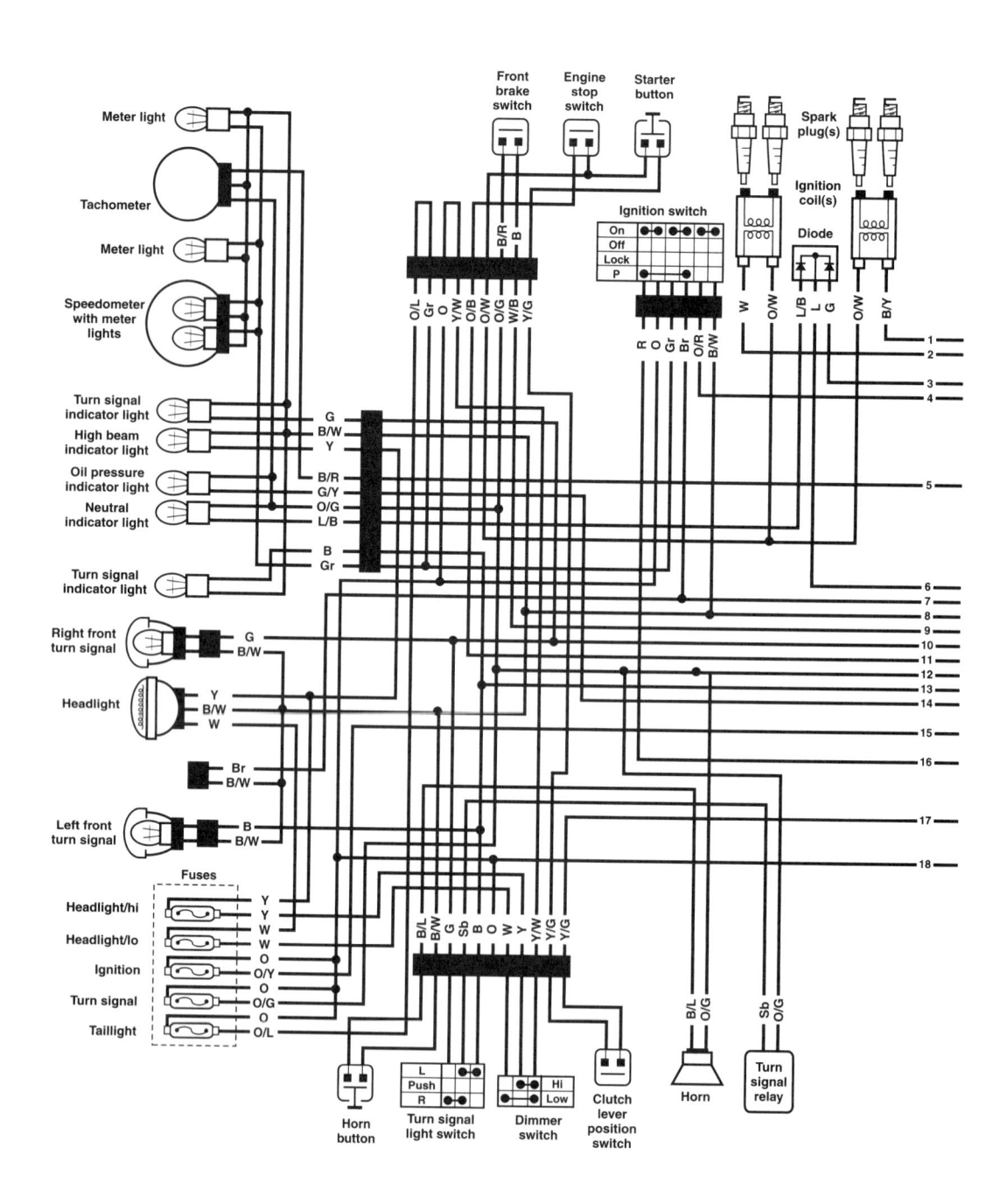

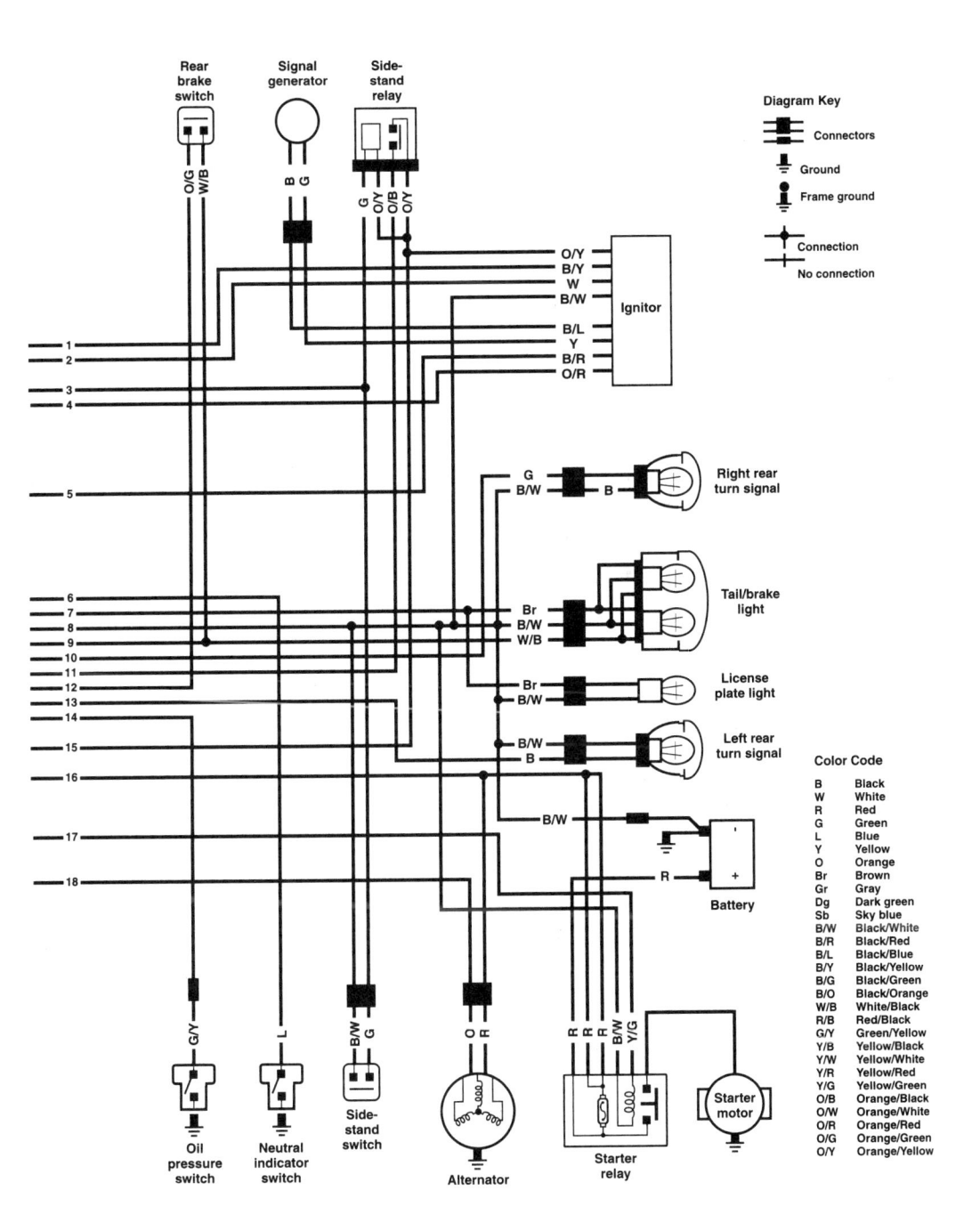

WIRING DIAGRAMS

423

16

1997-99 GSF600/GSF600S AUSTRALIA MODELS

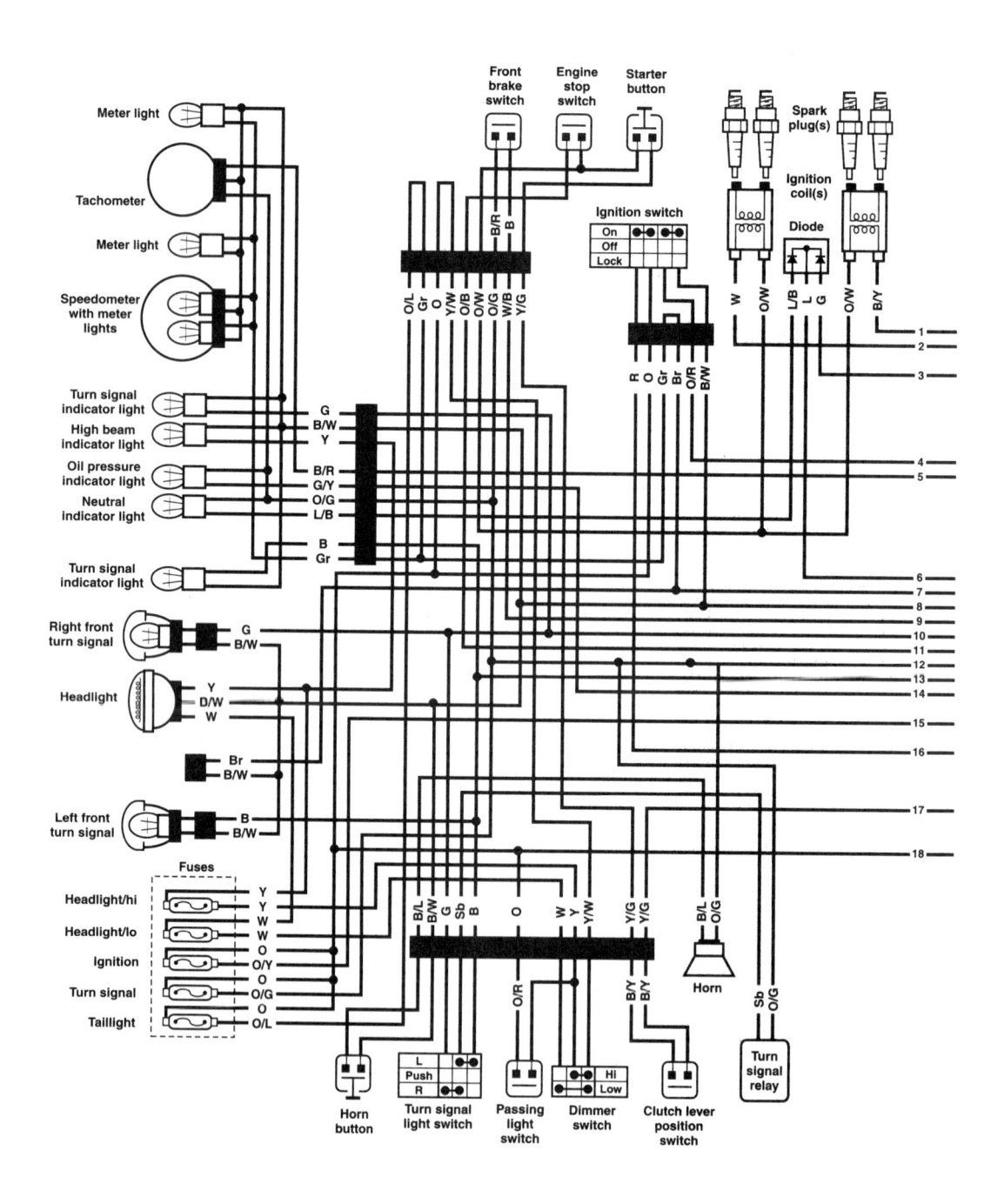

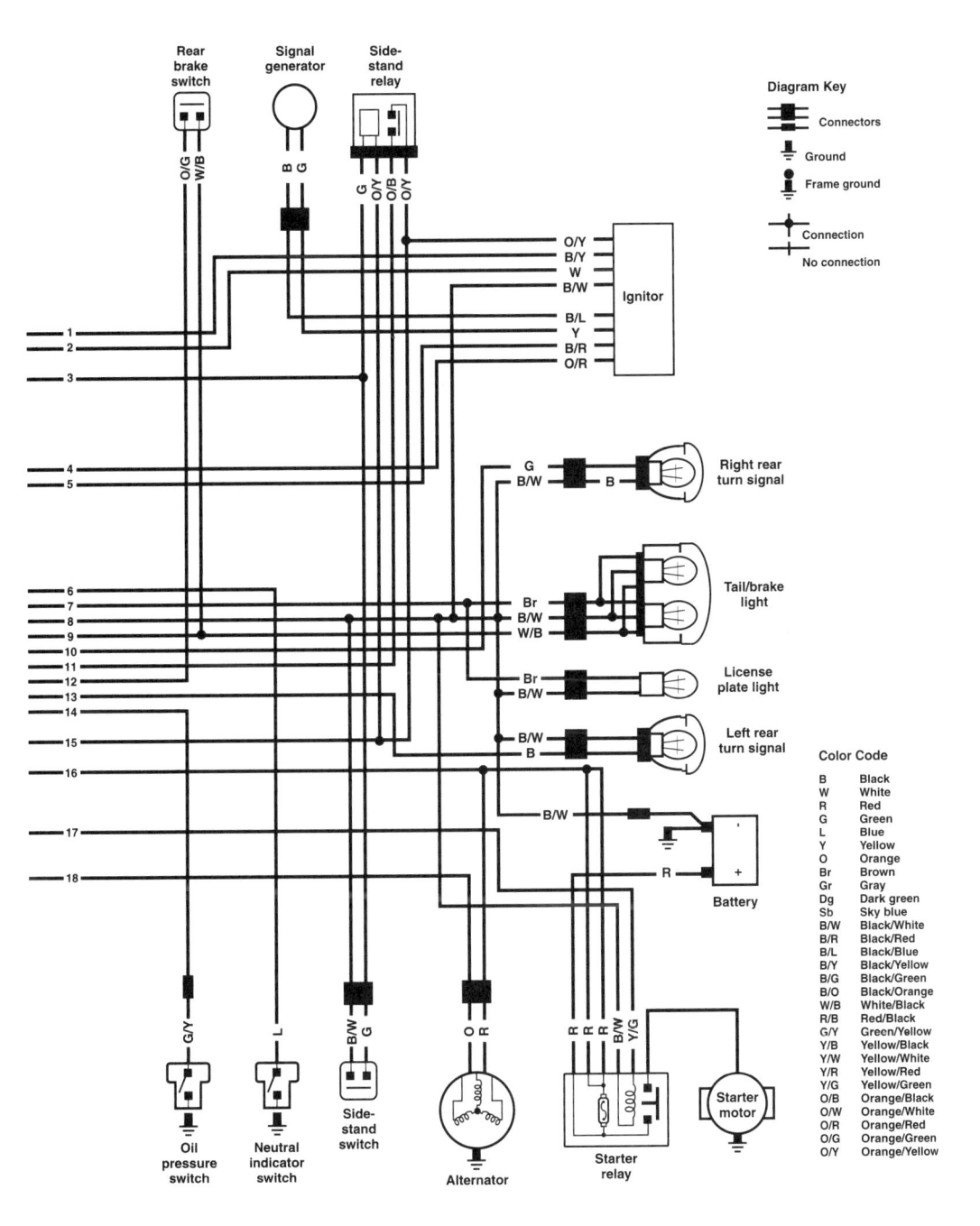

WIRING DIAGRAMS

425

Diagram Key

- Connectors
- Ground
- Frame ground
- Connection
- No connection

Color Code

B	Black
W	White
R	Red
G	Green
L	Blue
Y	Yellow
O	Orange
Br	Brown
Gr	Gray
Dg	Dark green
Sb	Sky blue
B/W	Black/White
B/R	Black/Red
B/L	Black/Blue
B/Y	Black/Yellow
B/G	Black/Green
B/O	Black/Orange
W/B	White/Black
R/B	Red/Black
G/Y	Green/Yellow
Y/B	Yellow/Black
Y/W	Yellow/White
Y/R	Yellow/Red
Y/G	Yellow/Green
O/B	Orange/Black
O/W	Orange/White
O/R	Orange/Red
O/G	Orange/Green
O/Y	Orange/Yellow

Components labeled on diagram: Rear brake switch, Signal generator, Side-stand relay, Ignitor, Right rear turn signal, Tail/brake light, License plate light, Left rear turn signal, Battery, Oil pressure switch, Neutral indicator switch, Side-stand switch, Alternator, Starter relay, Starter motor.

16

1997-1999 GSF600/GSF600S BRAZIL, U.K. AND EUROPEAN MODELS

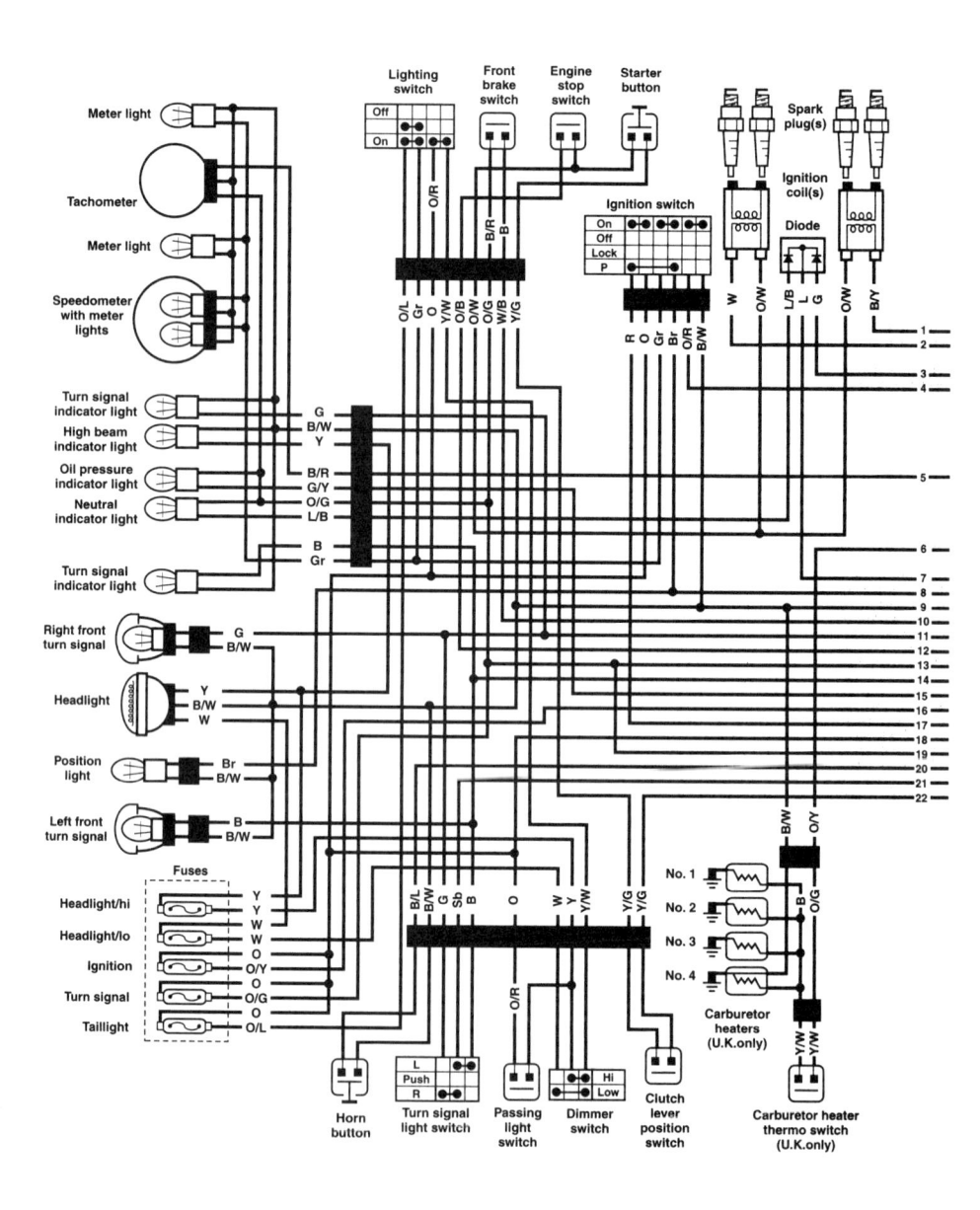

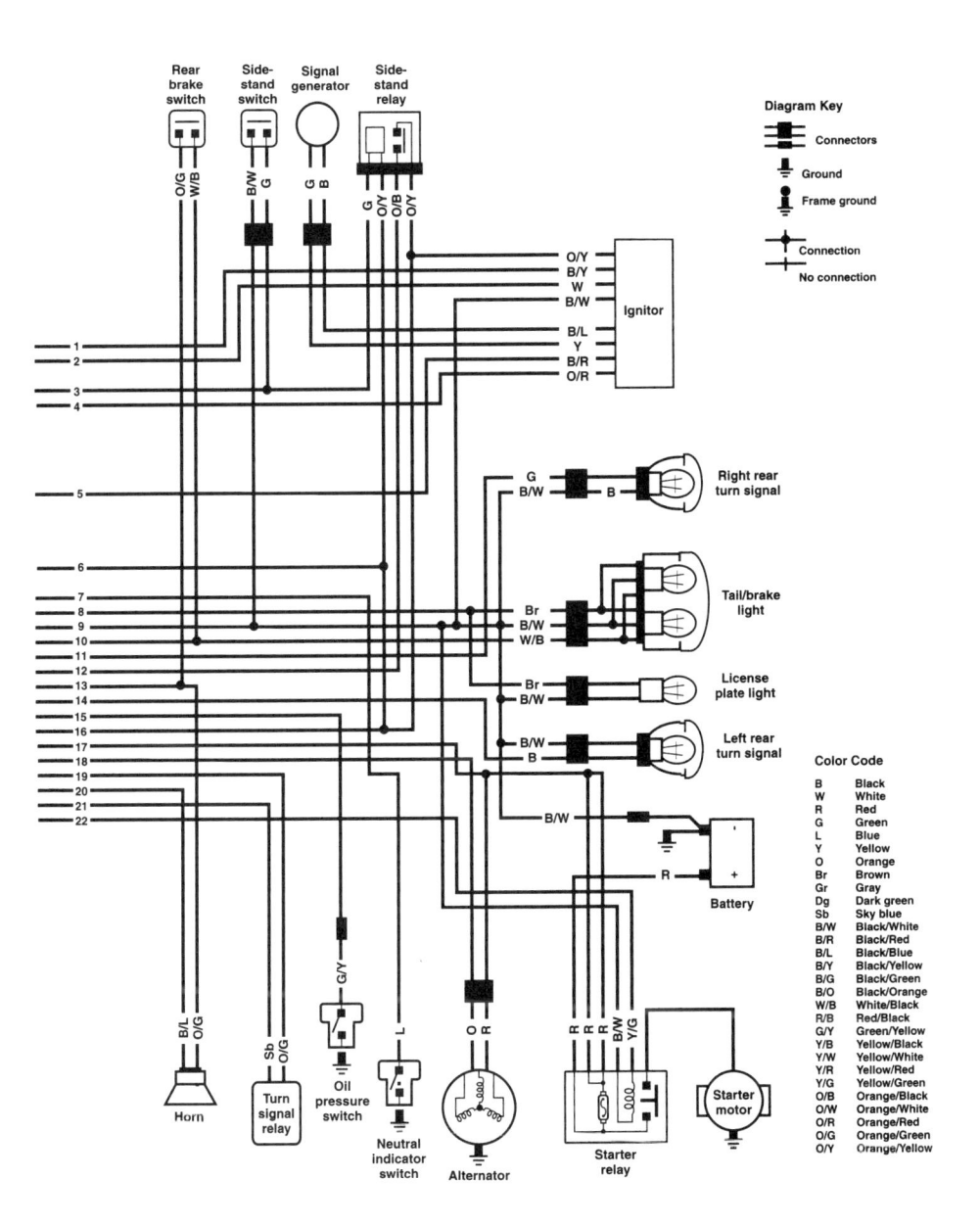

WIRING DIAGRAMS

427

2000 GSF600S U.S.A., CALIFORNIA AND CANADA MODELS

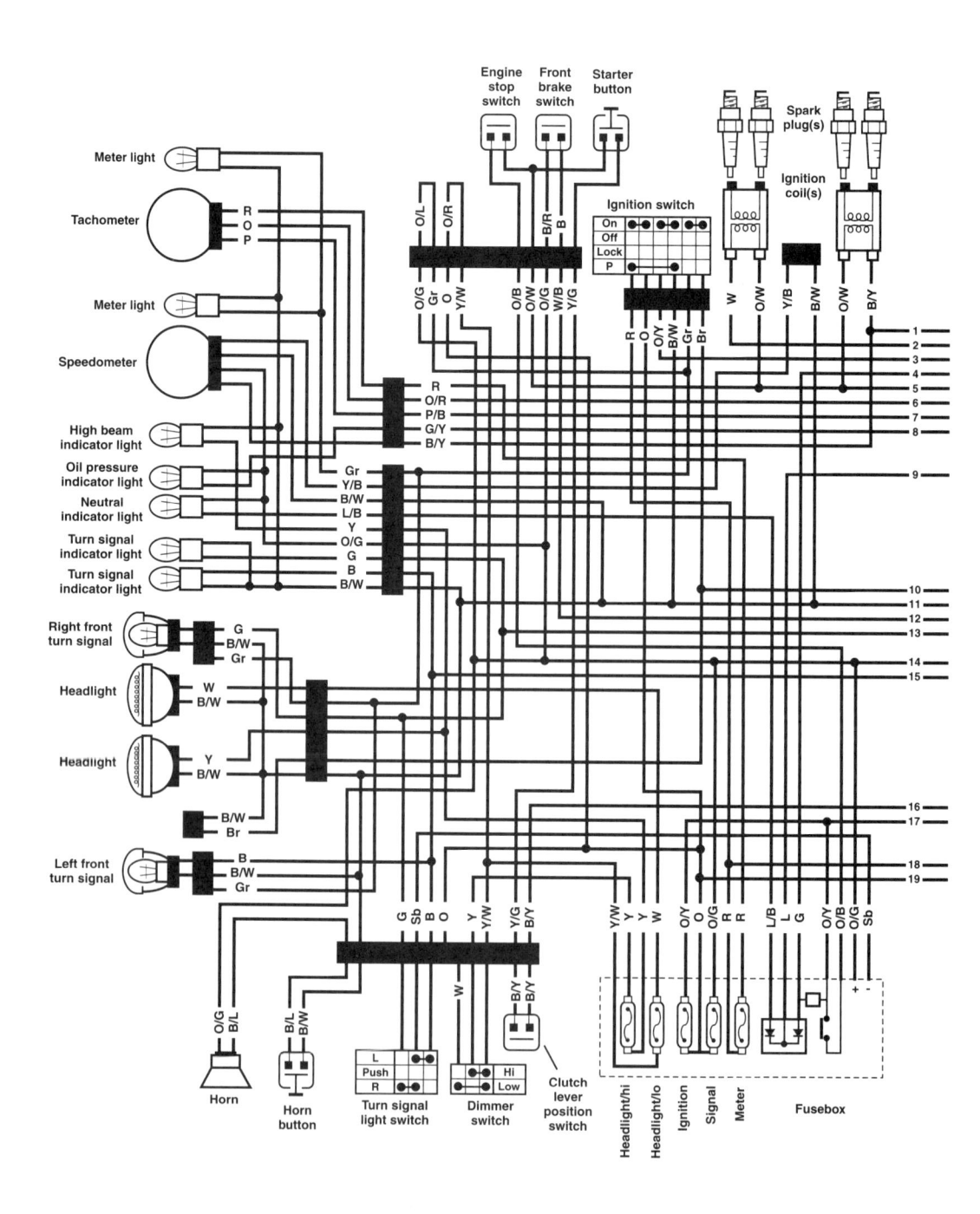

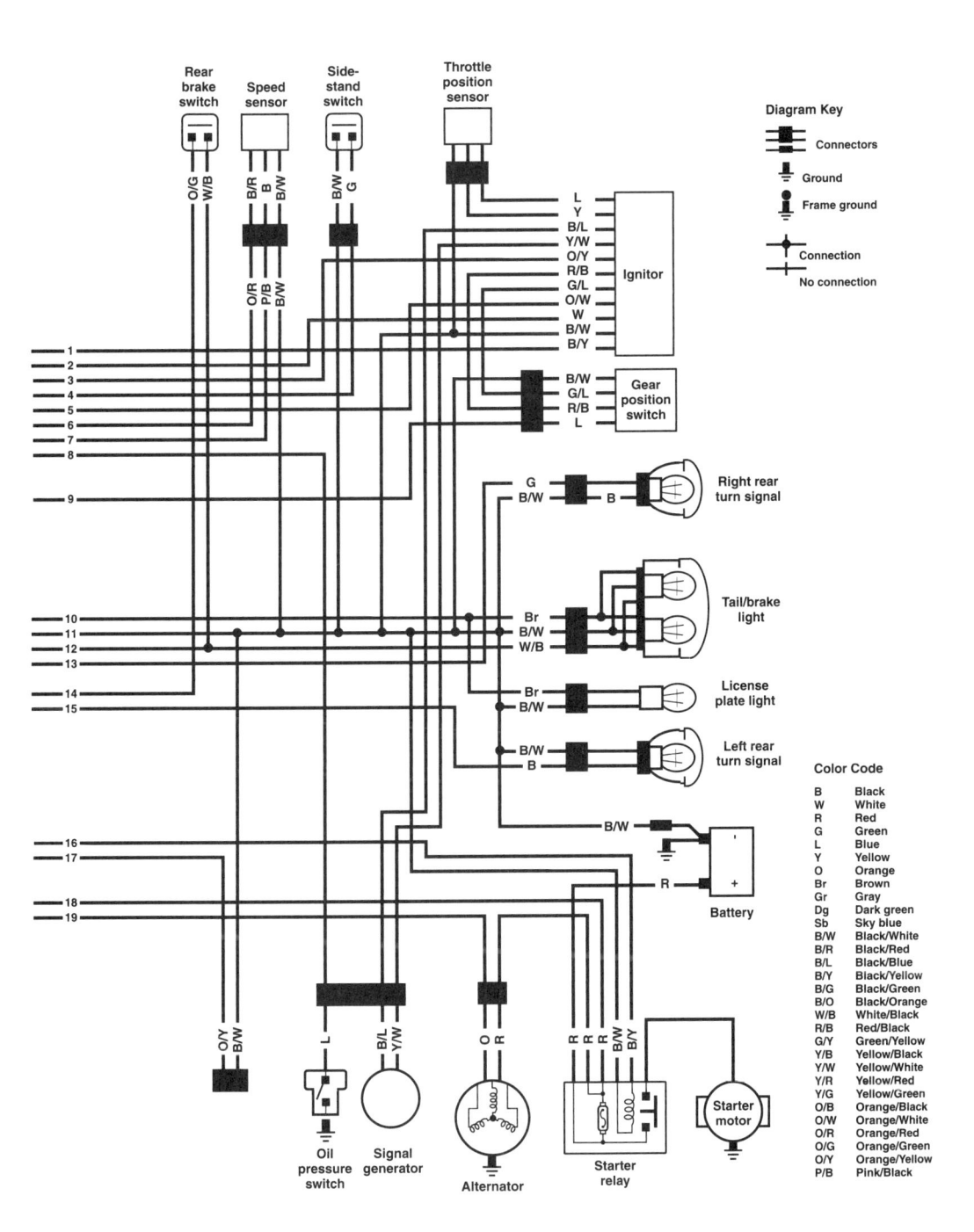

WIRING DIAGRAMS

429

2000 GSF600S AUSTRALIA, U.K. AND EUROPE MODELS

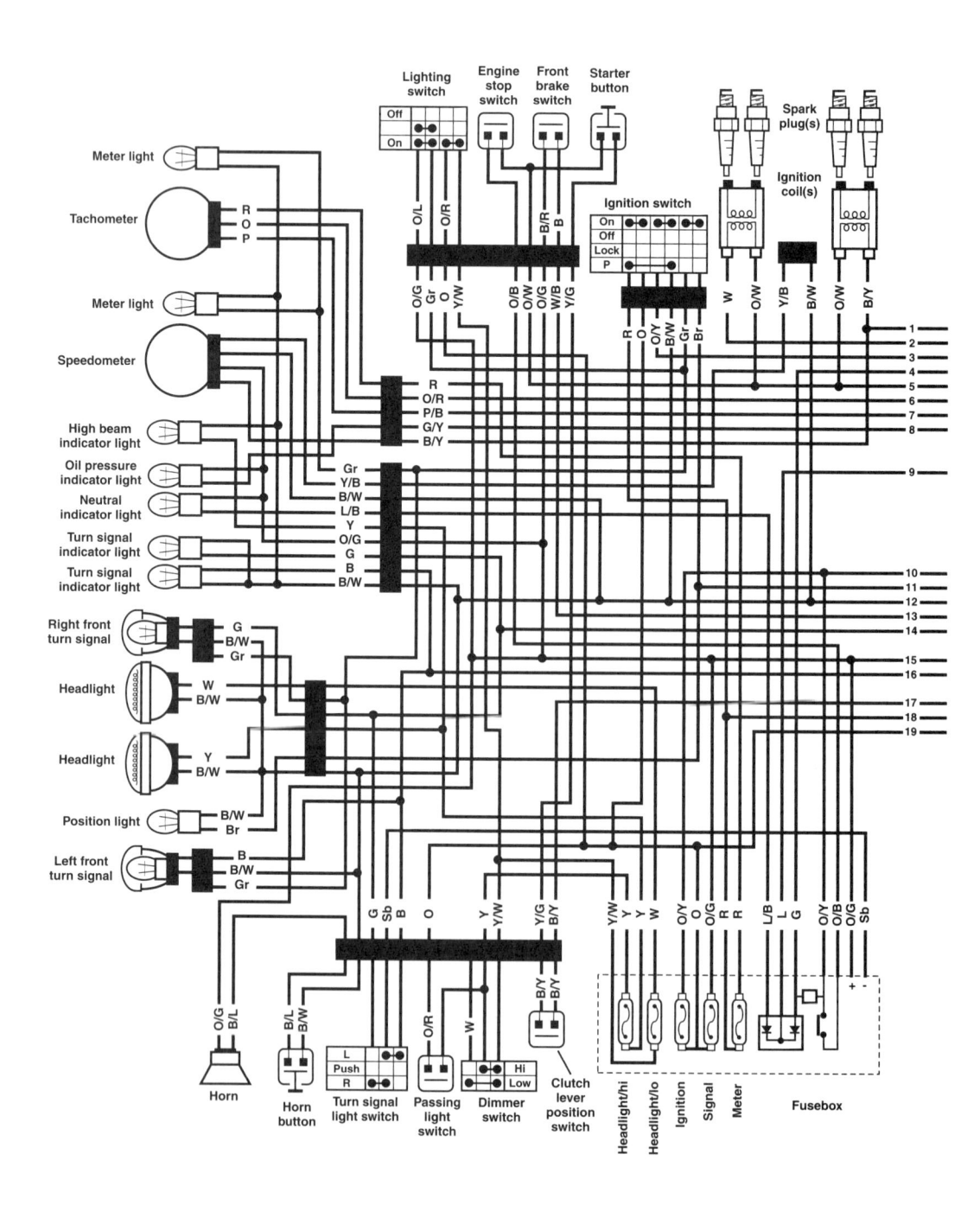

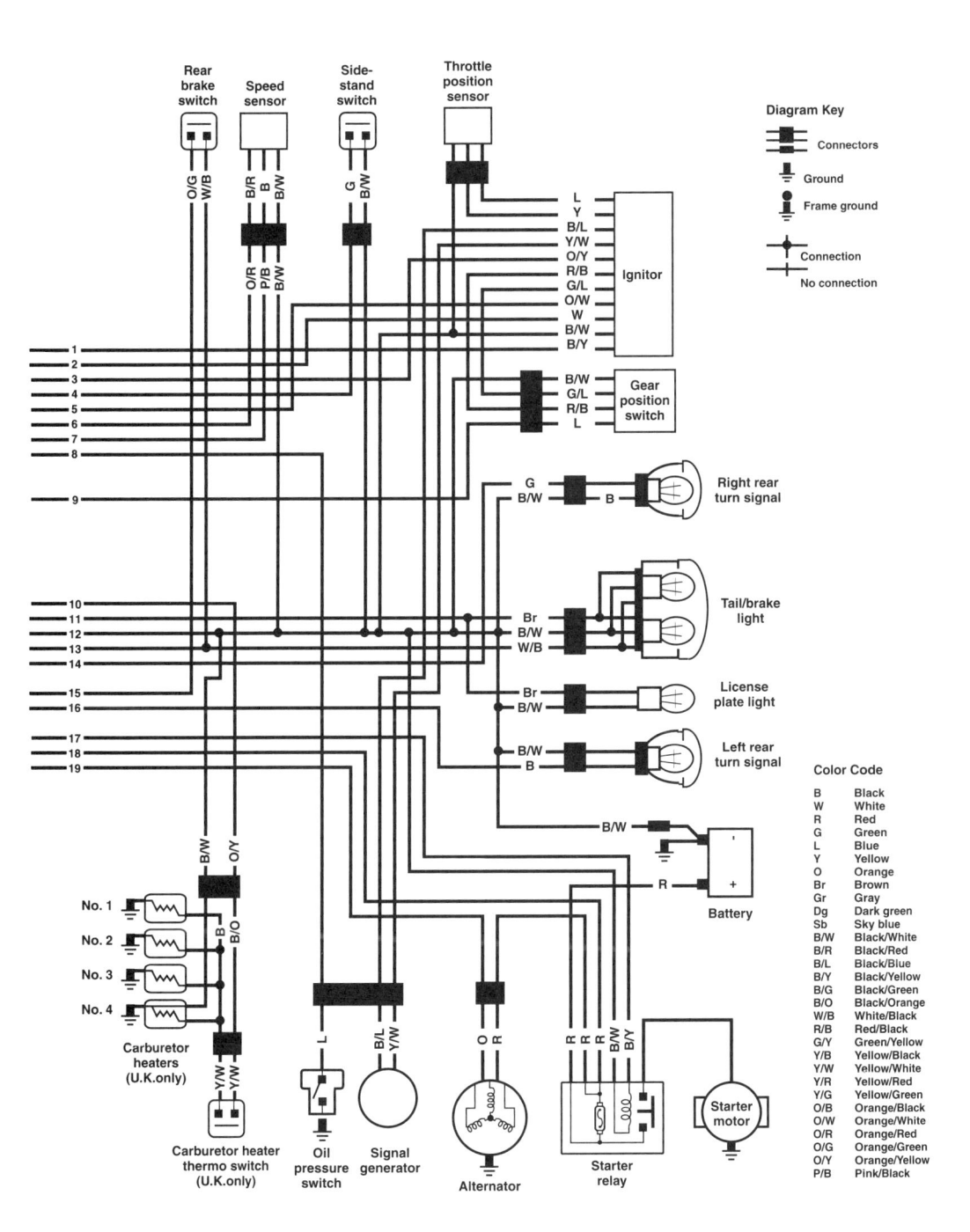

WIRING DIAGRAMS

431

WIRING DIAGRAMS

2000 GSF600 MODELS

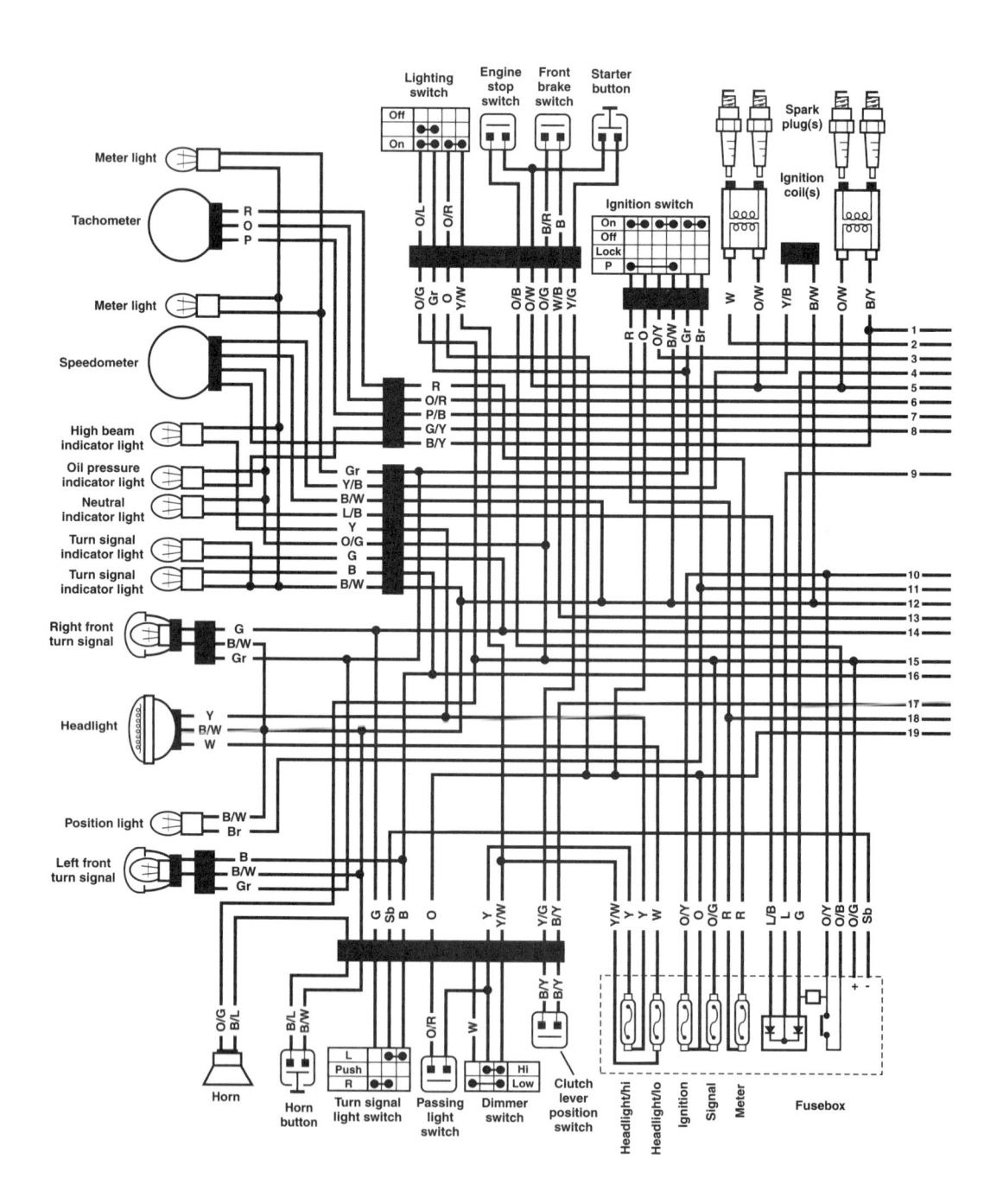

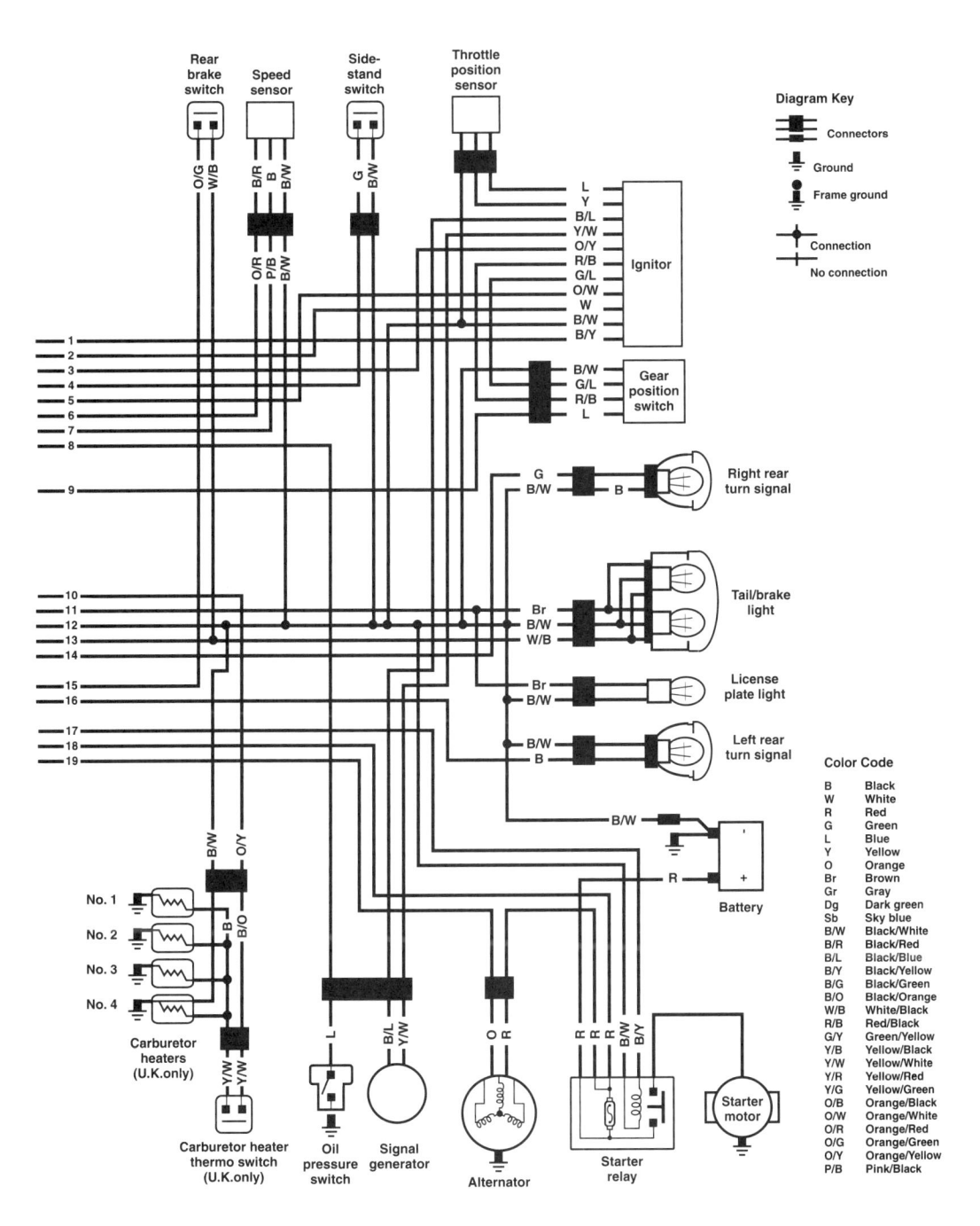

WIRING DIAGRAMS

433

NOTES

NOTES

NOTES

NOTES

MAINTENANCE LOG

Service Performed   **Mileage Reading**

Service Performed					
Oil change (example)	2,836	5,782	8,601		